CHILD MENTAL HEALTH
AND THE LAW

CHILD MENTAL HEALTH AND THE LAW

Barry Nurcombe
David F. Partlett

THE FREE PRESS
A Division of Macmillan, Inc.
NEW YORK

Maxwell Macmillan Canada
TORONTO

Maxwell Macmillan International
NEW YORK   OXFORD   SINGAPORE   SYDNEY

The Free Press
A Division of Macmillan, Inc.
866 Third Avenue, New York, N.Y. 10022

Maxwell Macmillan Canada, Inc.
1200 Eglinton Avenue East
Suite 200
Don Mills, Ontario M3C 3N1

Macmillan, Inc. is part of the Maxwell Communication
Group of Companies.

Printed in the United States of America

printing number
1   2   3   4   5   6   7   8   9   10

Library of Congress Cataloging-in-Publication Data

Nurcombe, Barry
    Child mental health and the law / Barry Nurcombe, David F.
    Partlett.
        p.   cm.
    Includes bibliographical references and index.
    ISBN 0-02-923245-7
    1. Mentally ill children—Legal status, laws, etc.—United States.
2. Mental health laws—United States.   I. Partlett, David F.
II. Title.
KF3828.N87   1994
346.7301'38—dc20
[347.306138]   93-50557
                                                              CIP

TO ALISON AND NAN

CONTENTS

Acknowledgments   ix

1. THE MENTAL HEALTH PROFESSIONS AND
   THE LAW   1
   Introduction   1
   Lawyers, Scientists, and Clinicians   1
   Philosophical Differences   3
   The Challenge of Psychodynamic Psychiatry   5
   The Forensic Setting   5
   Bridging the Gap   9
   The Organization of This Book   10

2. THE LEGAL SYSTEM   12
   The Nature and Purposes of Law   12
   The Sources of the Law   16
   The Legislative Process   24
   The Court System   26
   Judicial Procedings   29
   The Adjudicative Process   30
   Legal Advocacy   37

3. THE RIGHTS OF CHILDREN   39
   Introduction   39
   Legal Definitions of Infancy and Childhood   39
   The Historical Evolution of Children's Rights   42
   Recognition of Children's Rights   44
   Specific Legal Rights of Children   49

4. THE EDUCATIONAL RIGHTS OF
   HANDICAPPED CHILDREN   72
   Background   72
   The Education for All Handicapped Children Act of 1975   75
   The Role of the Mental Health Consultant   84

5. CHILD CUSTODY DISPUTES 87
   Introduction 87
   Marriage and Parental Obligations 87
   The Termination of Marriage 88
   The Determination of Custody 89
   The Effect of Divorce on Children 109
   Legal Proceedings 114
   Clinical Evaluation in Child Custody Disputes 116

6. FORENSIC EVALUATION IN CASES OF
   CHILD MALTREATMENT 132
   Introduction 132
   Child Abuse in the Legal System 132
   Child Protection Services 138
   Court Proceedings 138
   Evidentiary Issues 139
   Disposition 143
   Foster Care 144
   Permanent Planning 146
   Adoption 148
   Physical Abuse 150
   Nonorganic Failure to Thrive 152
   Neglect 153
   Sexual Abuse 154
   Forensic Evaluation in Cases of Alleged Sexual Abuse 167
   Preparing the Child to Give Testimony 180
   Preparing the Report 184

7. PSYCHOLOGICAL TRAUMA AND CIVIL LIABILITY 186
   Legal Principles 186
   Proof of Case 206
   The Forensic Evaluation of Civil Liability Cases 207

8. MALPRACTICE 220
   A Profile of Medical Malpractice 220
   The Doctor–Patient Relationship 224
   Liability to Third Parties 243
   Liability Contexts 243
   Liability for Communication of Information 256
   Liability Under New Health Structures 259
   Reform of the Law 263
   Conclusions 264
   Appendix to Chapter 8 266

9. JUVENILE DELINQUENCY 273
   Legal Principles 273

Definition, Epidemiology, and Prediction 283
The Prediction of Delinquency 288
The Clinical Classification of Delinquency 289
Etiology and Psychopathology 291
Treatment 303
The Forensic Evaluation of Juvenile Offenders 306

10. THE RIGHTS OF INSTITUTIONALIZED CHILDREN 318
Introduction 318
Legal Principles Pertaining to Psychiatric Hospitalization 320
Civil Commitment 322
The Rights of Institutionalized Patients 328
The Rights of Minors in Psychiatric Hospitals 335
The Rights of Juveniles in Correctional Institutions 339
Summary 340

11. THE CHILD MENTAL HEALTH PROFESSIONAL AS
EXPERT WITNESS 342
Introduction 342
The First Contact with the Referring Agent 345
Liability Issues 349
The Evaluation 349
The Report 351
Records 354
The Subpoena 354
The Pretrial Conference 355
Preparing to Give Testimony at a Deposition or Trial 356
The Deposition 357
Testifying in Court 360
Summary 387

Appendix 1. Sample Reports 389
Appendix 2. Landmark Cases 458
Notes 493
Bibliography 547
Table of Cases 593
Index 615

ACKNOWLEDGMENTS

The challenge in preparing this book was that of relating child mental health to criminal, constitutional, juvenile, administrative, and family law and to the rules of evidence and legal procedures. It could not have been accomplished without the efforts of Bill Catlett, Scott Dresser, Patti Kussman, Courtney Stout, and Jason Wright, students at Vanderbilt University Law School. Patti and Jason should be especially acknowledged: Patti was not only a co-explorer of the intricacies of custody law but also an incisive stylistic critic. Jason spent many hours checking citations, ferreting out references, and revising the page proofs.

Craig Iscoe, now Assistant U.S. Attorney, formerly of Vanderbilt University Law School, accepted our invitation to co-author Chapter 10, bringing to the chapter his expertise in civil procedure and his courtroom experience. We thank him for his invaluable contribution.

Renee Hawkins typed the entire manuscript and put up with us as we amended drafts. Hers was a feat of organization and skill effected with aplomb and cheerfulness. She is the most professional and competent of secretaries and deserves our lasting thanks. Alison and Lisa Nurcombe typed the initial drafts of many chapters, and Alison prepared the index.

Vanderbilt University Law School supported us with two summer stipends. Our colleagues and students at the Vanderbilt schools of medicine and law provided the intellectually spirited environment without which this endeavor would not have been completed.

CHAPTER 1

THE MENTAL HEALTH PROFESSIONS AND THE LAW

INTRODUCTION

C linicians dread the arrival of a subpoena. The thought of testifying conjures up images of arcane rules in an alien domain where lawyers badger and witnesses are demeaned. Unfamiliar with the adversary system, clinicians expect the truth will be hostage to warring strategists. How much better, they imagine, if panels of experts could provide the courts with unfettered, impartial, scientifically informed advice.

Lawyers shudder at the prospect of trial by white coat. To them, mental health professionals are "bleeding hearts or hangmen's helpers"[1] who cloak personal prejudice in the vestments of authority. What is the difference between social workers and psychologists, and how are they different from psychiatrists? To which of the numerous "schools" do they belong? Aren't their techniques so "squishy"[2] they can be bent to any point of view? Isn't their jargon designed to confuse? When it comes down to it, aren't they so muddle-headed and unreliable as to be basically irrelevant?

Much of the antagonism between the two fields is due to a mutual ignorance of purposes and techniques. This book addresses barriers between the professions, for when clinicians appreciate the aim of the adversary system and the legal issues with which the courts must grapple, and when, without distortion, they can adapt their techniques and reasoning to the requirements of the law, they will advance interprofessional understanding and strengthen the administration of justice.

Nevertheless, clinicians and lawyers are divided by gulfs that run deeper than mere ignorance. This chapter will analyze the differences between the professions in function, training, and philosophy. It will also debate the limits of mental health expertise, and go on to consider whether the mental health professions have anything of substance to offer the legal process.

LAWYERS, SCIENTISTS, AND CLINICIANS

Put broadly, the purpose of the law is to settle disputes fairly, to punish and deter malfeasors, to compensate the victims of wrongdoing, to keep order, and to promote social policy. In order to fulfill its functions, the law has evolved complex precedents, rules, and procedures (see Chapter 2). Prominent among them is the adversary system, a method of resolving disputes that pits contending parties against one another. Thus, in contrast to a clinician, who seeks compromise and adjustment, and compared with a scientist, who strives to disconfirm his hypotheses, a legal advocate presents a polemic that both favors his own side and impugns the other.* In Anglo-American law, a judge presides over proceedings wherein adversarial parties elicit and test evidence from which the jury will determine the facts, weigh them according to instructions given by the judge, and reach its verdict.

The purpose of science is to discover truths about the relationship between objects, events, and states. Scientists observe natural phenomena with fresh eyes in order to discern scientific puzzles and generate ideas to explain them. They test their hypotheses in a controlled, deductive manner, employing reliable measurement, in a strategic attempt to disprove their pet notions. Good science demands the capacity to entertain alternative hypotheses, a respect for accurate and impartial data gathering, and a frame of mind best characterized by both curiosity and constructive skepticism.[3]

The purpose of clinical work is to diagnose and treat sick, impaired, or troubled people. Psychologists and social workers who eschew "the medical model" prefer such words as "client" over "patient," and "management" over "treatment." Nevertheless, what they do is essentially the same: They attempt to understand the nature of their patients' or clients' problems in order to help them overcome or alleviate distress or impairment. Clinicians are pragmatic: they borrow from basic sciences to facilitate diagnosis or treatment. However, psychiatry, clinical psychology, and clinical social work are not sciences in themselves. When legal cross examiners ask clinicians to concede that psychiatry, psychology, or social work are "not exact sciences," the truthful answer would be that clinical work is not science, though it may draw upon it.

Lawyers and clinicians are alike in identifying with their clients or patients; scientists are (or should be) objective. Lawyers and scientists are akin in their preoccupation with facts; clinicians are absorbed in the personal reality of those they treat. Scientists and clinicians both apply scientific knowledge, but to different ends, the one to advance knowledge, the other to help impaired or troubled people. Lawyers and clinicians are similar in their pragmatism; they borrow information from other fields in order to judge cases, advance their clients' causes, or diagnose and treat their patients. If it works, they are inclined to use it. Indeed, the hunger of clinicians for diagnostic aids and new therapies may sometimes persuade them to endorse techniques that have not been adequately tested. Ironically, the law seeks to monitor professional standards by deferring to professional judgment while at the same time ensuring that accepted measures are not too readily dismissed.

Judges and juries seek to find the facts of the case, just as scientists search for the truth about objects and events. In that, legal fact-finders and scientists differ subtly from the pragmatists—clinicians and attorneys—who are primarily interested in helping their patients and clients. The clinician is more concerned with the patient's real-

---

* Throughout this book, human beings in general are referred to with masculine pronouns simply for ease of expression.

ity than with actuality itself; the legal advocate proposes to marshal the evidence most favorable to his client's case. However, a further distinction is apparent, for judges and juries seek facts in order to settle disputes, whereas scientists gather data in order to discover the laws of the universe. Unlike science, the law makes no pretense of reaching "true" solutions; rather, it aims to resolve disputes fairly and regulate society normatively. In the late nineteenth century, law was viewed as a science in which legal principles were deducted from precedents. However, contemporary schools of thought have undermined the scientific model, to the point that law today cannot be properly understood apart from its implicit social, economic, and philosophical basis.[4]

PHILOSOPHICAL DIFFERENCES
Autonomy and Determinism

The law assumes that, unless it can be proven otherwise, people are competent both to do what they do and to intend the consequences of their actions. We mean what we say, choose to do what we do, and are responsible for what results. Indeed, the driving force of the common law is the idea of individual responsibility. The law in regard to torts, contracts, and criminal offenses turns upon this idea. In its earliest form, tort law protected the physical integrity of the individual, while at the same time ensuring social peace. The new tort of informed consent is founded on the same principle—that is, the autonomy of the individual can be protected only if he knows the full implications of what it is proposed should be done to him. In criminal law, if legal insanity is established, the defendant is held not responsible for an otherwise criminal act.

In contrast, the dominant theories of psychiatry and psychology are deterministic. Geneticists discern the origins of behavior in the genome. Neuropsychiatrists regard it as stemming from neuronal activity induced by disease, trauma, or inherited abnormality. Behaviorists view behavior as systematically related to stimulus and response, reward and punishment. Psychodynamicists explore the unconscious impulses and conflicts imbedded in psychopathology. Family systems theorists describe the intrasystemic roles, boundaries, and relationships that result in disturbed behavior. Mental health clinicians and scientists alike view behavior as determined. Volition, intention, and consciousness—the ingredients of the legally autonomous person—have always been difficult to contain within a scientific framework.

The Forensic Assessment of Scientific Evidence

As indicated above, scientists are often irritated that the courts do not evaluate science in a scientific manner. The law frequently calls upon scientific evidence, but requires it to satisfy the criteria of reliability defined by the law. Probability estimates—the keystone of scientific method—do not resonate in a court of law, for opinion must be marshaled within the framework of the adversary system. One check against the admission of invalid scientific evidence is the requirement that a witness may not testify as an expert unless the court first finds him to be qualified to do so on the basis of his knowledge, skill, experience, training, or education. Depending on the jurisdiction, a court may not permit an expert to testify unless it also finds that the testimony will be about a proposition that has achieved a level of acceptance in the scientific community or that is based on procedures reasonably relied upon by experts in the particular field. The requirements of qualification and scientific acceptability therefore permit the judge to exclude testimony for which there is little or no scientific support.

General Statements and Particular Instances

Scientists deal with group data, seeking generalizations that summarize universal relationships. Clinicians, lawyers, and juries are concerned with particulars. The application of statistical studies to individual cases is regarded as conveying the risk of unjust decisions.[5] Aware of that risk, the Supreme Court in *McCleskey v. Kemp* (1987)[6] found that the death penalty exacted by Georgia did not breach the Constitution, even though it was demonstrated that a statistically disproportionate number of blacks were sentenced to death if they had killed whites.

Often, legal inquiry will relate to motivation and causation. Science may have established explanations that are valid generally but have insufficient power to explain behavior in a particular case. For that, historical and biographical information are usually required.[7]

Rights and Needs

Lawyers advocate for their clients' rights, in a discourse so compelling that the whole fabric of the law may seem to be made of rights. In Anglo-American law, the rights of the individual are prime, for individual freedom undergirds the liberal state.[8] We note, in Chapter 10, the attempt to draw within the discourse of rights the plight of patients in mental health institutions. The same approach is taken with respect to the educational needs of handicapped children (Chapter 4).

Aside from diverting attention from the agenda of clinicians, the pursuit of rights also injects legal considerations into professional decision-making. Individual rights concerning the termination of life support have inspired a complex legal framework that impedes the formerly personalized function of the physician.[9] Lawyers advocating patients' rights clash with clinicians advocating patients' needs in such matters as involuntary commitment to hospital and the refusal of treatment.[10] Powerful constitutional rights may appear to do violence to the most vulnerable of witnesses: the right of the accused to face his accuser in court, for example, collides with the desire to protect a sexually traumatized child from the stress of having to confront her victimizer.[11]

Individual freedom is at the core of our society. Law schools instill it by emphasizing the presumptive right of citizens to be free of state interference. (We discuss the application of those rights to children in Chapter 3.) Law students are taught to be skeptical of government and of other social institutions with disproportionate power, such as corporations and the medical profession. Legal skepticism may be perceived as hostility when the attempt of clinicians to serve patients' needs comes under the scrutiny of the courts. Just as malpractice risk can induce costly defensive medicine,[12] the assertion of rights, it may be argued, interferes with the mission of clinicians. As we shall observe in Chapter 8, recent developments in the law of informed consent undermine medical dominance in decision-making concerning patient welfare, while concerns expressed by the nonmedical members of medical ethics committees have led to other constraints upon traditional professional prerogatives.

Given their traditions and training, it is not likely that the gulf between court and clinic will disappear. However, as we note in this book, the courts are not indifferent to family values and professional roles and do not favor judicial scrutiny in every instance. For example, in the face of vehement criticism, the Supreme Court in *Parham*[13] preferred the medical model of decision-making to judicial review, with regard to the admission of minors to psychiatric hospitals.

THE CHALLENGE OF PSYCHODYNAMIC PSYCHIATRY

The psychoanalytic view of behavior challenges the law. Michael S. Moore has described three areas of difference.[14] The first replaces legal concepts of responsibility and culpability with medical notions of mental health and illness; in this view, "badness" is interpreted as "illness." How then could criminals be accountable? The second challenge to legal precept refers to the psychoanalytic concept of the unconscious. Having no knowledge of this shadow mind, an individual cannot be responsible for its actions. The third challenge is a fractionated variant of the second: causal agency is attributed to subpersonal entities—ego, superego, and id. An individual cannot be held responsible since no one is a single rational agent.

These challenges strike at the vitals of criminal and civil law. Moore proposes that law and psychiatry share a new view of the person,[15] and that the gap in understanding between law and psychiatry calls for a new philosophical basis for forensic psychiatry. Moore recommends that psychiatry and law should both view people as agents "with irreducible causal powers who act for reasons, that is, as autonomous and rational agents."[16] He recognizes that the vocabulary of "intention" is embattled by challenges from genetics, psychiatry, psychology,[17] and neurobiology. However, the conception of the person as a rational and moral agent is a fundamental philosophical issue that society and the law must not jettison.

THE FORENSIC SETTING

The Scientific Status of Developmental Psychology and Psychiatry

Unlike a physical science, psychology has no single paradigm. Admittedly, all scientific paradigms are provisional; however, contemporary developmental psychology is pre-paradigmatic. None of the classical, encompassing theories—psychoanalysis, behaviorism, and genetic epistemology—ever attained predominance. Today, smaller-scale theories (e.g., information processing, social learning, and attachment theory) occupy center stage.

Unsurprisingly, there is no single accepted form of psychotherapy. The polyglot nature of the clinical field undermines its authority, while guild disputes between mental health professions further weaken their claims to expertise. As we shall discuss in Chapter 10, the Supreme Court has been obliged to deal with conflicting briefs from the American Psychological Association and the American Psychiatric Association with regard to the administration of antipsychotic drugs and the hospitalization of juveniles. From a legal standpoint, these internal fissures engender doubt concerning the objectivity of psychiatrists and psychologists alike. Courts have difficulty utilizing a body of scientific knowledge that may have the potential to uncover facts and facilitate justice yet is much disputed. Indeed, the Supreme Court has remarked that psychiatry is "not . . . an exact science, and psychiatrists disagree widely and frequently."[18]

The Legal Response

Despite doubts about the scientific validity of psychology and psychiatry, the law must reach its decisions. Little wonder, therefore, that psychological and psychiatric knowledge and testimony have been used selectively, unevenly, and sometimes obliquely.

Despite the challenge of psychoanalysis, the law has not ceased to ascribe responsibility to individuals. Following Aristotle, the law regards people as agents who intend to do what they do in order to get what they want and not as the victims of fate or chemistry.

Nevertheless, the first challenge—that of replacing legal responsibility and culpability with medical concepts of health and illness—has had a perverse impact. The "medical" view has been impugned from within psychiatry by those who contend that "mental illness" is a myth.[19] This assault is convenient for those advocates, jurists, and legislators who would like to clear the decks of the pesky claims of psychiatry. If mental illness were a myth, the law could judge behavior without taking account of psychiatry or psychology. The doctrines of legal insanity and competency to stand trial (Chapter 9) would evaporate. Furthermore, if mental health clinicians treat no real diseases, they could not be judged by the same standards that apply in medical malpractice cases.[20] Expert mental health evidence would then be useless, for, as Morse says, "because determinations of craziness depend on observations of behavior and social norms, such determinations can be made by laypersons and experts alike. . . . Consequently, the question of who is crazy should be decided by the society's representatives—judges and juries of laypersons."[21]

This strong version of relativism would render vast tracts of scientific knowledge useless to the law; there would be no justification for the courts to prefer psychology to astrology. In our view, however, legal inquiry should favor rationality, informed by an appropriation of social norms and settings. By dint of research and expertise, psychology and psychiatry can inform courts about normal behavior and mental illness, just as internal medicine can provide legitimate information about the diagnosis of lung cancer.[22]

By the 1990s it was evident that radical critics had shaken but failed to destroy the foundation of psychiatry. Nevertheless, the admission of psychiatric and psychological evidence into courts of law has continued to attract vociferous opponents.[23]

The Validity of Mental Health Expertise

Faust and Ziskin (1988) impugn the competence of mental health clinicians to provide expert testimony, contending that their opinions lack sufficient certitude to be admissible. They cite evidence, for example, that clinical reasoning is riddled with error, that psychiatric diagnosis is unreliable, that psychological testing lacks sufficient rigor, that clinical training and experience confer no expertise, and that the diagnostic conclusions of mental health professionals have inadequate relevance to the issues at stake in courts of law. To be sure, scientific uncertainty mitigates the power of mental health testimony. However, the adversary system is designed to expose uncertainty. Scientific uncertainty alone does not degrade the power of all psychological and psychiatric evidence to the level of lay testimony. Such a conclusion would disqualify existing scientific information, replace it with casual "common sense," and exclude new findings capable of shedding light upon the legal issues.[24]

A slightly different argument, like Morse's,[25] is that mental health opinions are nothing more than moral, social, or legal prejudices in scientific camouflage. In other words, the benchmarks of forensic evaluation—normalcy and irrationality—are moral, social, and legal matters properly dealt with by judges, juries, and legislatures.[26]

This argument also goes too far. Undoubtedly, forensic issues are multifaceted. Lawyers understand that the form and structure of the law are strongly imbued with moral and social perspectives, and that psychiatric conclusions should not be determinative.[27] But this is not to say that mental health experts cannot inform the court about human behavior and help it to base its decisions on firmer ground. Laymen are unlikely to have had experience with autism, schizophrenia, or bipolar disorder, for example; they lack the experience or clinical perspective to evaluate the normalcy of particular behavior.

Expansion of the law in accordance with growth in scientific knowledge about the etiology of disease has raised questions about the admission of expert evidence in court. The United States Supreme Court has opted for a liberal admission of such evidence.[28] The capabilities of the jury and the adversary system are adequate, in the Court's opinion, to admit a wide scope of evidence without insistence on its acceptability within the scientific community. The criterion of scientific acceptability, however, remains effective in deciding whether the testimony concerns "scientific knowledge," a status it must achieve for admission. The Court stressed that the rules of evidence are not designed for an "exhaustive search for cosmic understanding but for the particularized resolution of legal disputes." To demand "general acceptability" or "certainty" would straitjacket the judicial inquiry. Mental health professionals have a body of knowledge that is "scientific." Their expert testimony will be admissible to the extent that it allows "the trier of fact to understand the evidence or to determine a fact in issue." The Supreme Court recognizes the contingent character of scientific knowledge. Given this opinion, the Faust and Ziskin attack appears to misunderstand the law of evidence.[29]

This book is testimony to the fact that the courts have not been persuaded by radical criticisms of forensic psychiatry and psychology. However, these criticisms should be a healthy corrective to the ill-founded arrogance of some mental health experts. Even as scientific knowledge accrues, the law will transcend it. Mental health experts should not be permitted to frame operative rules or define the line between guilt or innocence, lest both psychiatry and the law be brought into disrespect.[30] When the dust of debate has settled, it will be seen that the true value of Faust and Ziskin's philippic will have been to put mental health experts on their mettle; for the debate, now encouraged by the Supreme Court, gives cross examiners the ammunition they need to test the validity of an expert witness's methods and conclusions. It also confronts experts with the fragility or frank incompetence of their opinions concerning such legal issues as a defendant's mental state at the time of an offense, or the prediction of future dangerousness; and it spurs them to continue to refine the reliability and validity of their diagnostic techniques. In short, it calls for a radical overhaul of the quality of forensic evaluation.[31]

Ethical Conflicts

If the mental health expert is accepted as having a function in the court, how can a clinician reconcile forensic work with his clinical mission? As we shall see, the liability of clinicians varies according to their function. To be sure, although they may be immune from defamation action when preparing evaluation reports for use by the court, the essential question is whether the forensic context mitigates the ethical imperatives that apply to clinical work.

Lawyers, scientists, and mental health clinicians are bound by ethical codes. Lawyers and clinicians must act in the best interests of their clients and patients. A mental health clinician, for example, must strive to ease the patient's suffering, or at least do no harm. However, the purpose of law courts is not to treat sickness. If anything, the primary moral duty of those who serve the courts is to be faithful to the processes of justice.

When a forensic psychiatrist conducts a legal evaluation, does the ethic of beneficence apply? The uneasy status of forensic psychiatry is reflected in the heated debate on this question. The principles of beneficence and non-maleficence are promoted by some,[32] but this view is inconsistent with the role that forensic psychiatrists must play in the justice system. Although the ultimate decision is for courts and juries, mental health evaluations are the crux of deliberations that could have immense destructive potential. For example, testimony concerning competency to stand trial, dangerousness, mental state at the time of an offense, or the best interests of a child raises serious ethical questions. Clearly, the ethical code fashioned for a therapeutic relationship is inappropriate to forensic work.

One response to this dilemma is for mental health clinicians to shun forensic work on the ground that the potential for harm outweighs the likelihood of doing good— an objection that cannot be restricted to a narrow range of legal situations but must apply to all. A less drastic approach is to establish a separate code of conduct for clinicians engaged in forensic work. Such a code would call for adherence to the truth, a respect for those evaluated, and fidelity to the processes of justice. Though harm may follow to the individual (e.g., one parent may be found less competent than another to care for a child), a more abstract good is served in the furtherance of justice.[33]

A more subtle ethical conflict arises, however, when mental health experts are asked to testify concerning relative matters in categorical terms. Take, for example, a minor's capacity to waive Miranda rights (see Chapter 9). Can a particular adolescent (from thirteen to seventeen years in age, varying from borderline retarded to superior in intelligence, and from emotionally unstable to stable in personality, and under more or less duress) forgo his right to counsel before giving a confession to the police? Strictly speaking, the expert's task is to illuminate these relative matters and leave it to the court to make the categorical decision. However, it is not always possible for experts to recuse themselves in this manner. Indeed, most of the battles between experts that have received such adverse publicity are caused by the requirement of the courts for black-and-white opinions when shades of gray apply.[34]

BRIDGING THE GAP

Lawmakers, judges, and lawyers have always assumed that the law has a psychosocial background. They have also presumed that, by dint of the law, society can be properly ordered. But the burgeoning social sciences have called into question some of the traditional assumptions of lawmakers; today the efficacy of legal rules can be tested by their consequences. While once formality and logic predominated, modern views of jurisprudence favor overt policy-making. Thus, as legislation has multiplied, much of the courts' work is to interpret that enormous body of law.

A strong fillip for judicial policy-making has been the ubiquitous presence of issues related to constitutional law. This book will frequently refer to minors' rights, the source of which is often the U.S. Constitution.[35] Although it was only forty years ago, in *Brown v. Board of Education*[36] that the Supreme Court first accepted a purely social science brief,[37] that controversial decision[38] has led to a revolution in constitutional law. Today the Court deals openly with a plethora of social science data, from free speech (e.g., theories of democracy derived from political science) to equal protection (e.g., sociological evidence of the disparate impact of separate schools). This book will allude to many instances where the courts have dealt with psychological and social issues.

It is unrealistic to suggest that lawmakers should be social scientists. Rather, lawmakers, particularly judges, should be asked to take account of social science. Procedure, judicial independence, tradition, and good sense are available to ensure that the process is effective and fair. Judges and legislators should not be expected to find their way unaided through the labyrinths of neurobiology, neuropsychiatry, or developmental psychopathology. That is the task of expert evidence. However, the law should allow knowledge from these fields to be introduced and weighed whenever relevant. The introduction of this information requires collaboration between the bar and the mental health professions in order to define the qualifications of expert witnesses and establish the criteria for acceptability.[39]

However, psychologists and psychiatrists must understand the purposes and constraints of the law; and they must demonstrate that their information can provide useful insights for fact-finders and decision-makers. Many law schools have encouraged this; the burgeoning specialty of health law, for example, provides a new venue for these perspectives.[40] Mental health experts can directly influence lawmaking by working as consultants to legislators, lobby groups, and government commissions. Information can also be brought before appellate courts by way of *amicus curiae* ("friend of the court") briefs.[41]

THE ORGANIZATION OF THIS BOOK

The next chapter of this book, "The Legal System," discusses the nature and purposes of the law and its sources in the Constitution, legislation, and the common law. In view of their importance to children's mental health law, the First, Fourteenth, and Fifth Amendments are considered at some length. Next, the legislative process, the court system, types of judicial proceeding, and the principles of the adjudicative process are summarized. Finally, the function of the legal advocate is described.

Chapter 3, "The Rights of Children," outlines the history and current status of children's rights with regard to the definition of legal competence, the common law, financial support, access to health care, commercial exploitation, education, and participation in research. The chapter also discusses a number of situations (e.g., drinking, driving, sexual activity) in which minors' freedoms, parental rights, and the obligation of the state may collide.

Chapter 4, "The Educational Rights of Handicapped Children," traces the rapid recent evolution of the law as it applies to handicapped or disabled children, with particular reference to the legal definitions of "handicapped" or "disabled," "free and appropriate education," "related services," and "least restrictive environment." The chapter also describes the function of the mental health clinician as a witness for a child who is petitioning for (or protesting the provision of) special services, or for the school district that is defending its educational plan for the child.

The next six chapters ("Child Custody Disputes," "Forensic Evaluation in Cases of Child Maltreatment," "Psychological Trauma and Civil Liability," "Malpractice," "Juvenile Delinquency," and "The Rights of Institutionalized Children") follow a similar pattern. First, the history of the law in that area is outlined, its current status analyzed, and future trends predicted. In several instances, the law with regard to adults is extensively reviewed, for otherwise its application to children cannot be understood. This is of particular importance in the rapidly growing field of civil liability and malpractice law and with regard to juvenile justice and the rights of institutionalized children. Next, in each of these chapters, relevant scientific research is reviewed. An up-to-date knowledge of basic and applied research will encourage mental health experts to base their opinions, so far as possible, on scientific evidence rather than mere experience; moreover, it will inform lawyers concerning the validity of expert opinions offered on particular subjects. Each chapter ends with a description of the function of the mental expert in the forensic evaluation of such cases, with particular reference to how clinical evaluation, report writing, opinions, and recommendations can be adapted to the elements of the law in accordance with which the court must reach its decision.

The final chapter ("The Child Mental Health Professional as Expert Witness"), written with Craig Iscoe, provides practical recommendations in regard to how an aspiring mental health expert should operate, from the first telephone discussion with an inquiring attorney to the giving of testimony. Special attention is given to the way in which the adversary system influences the behavior of opposing attorneys and to the ethical strategy and tactics of the mental health consultant in court.

Child Mental Health and the Law advocates a synergy among policy-makers, attorneys, judges, developmental psychologists, and mental health clinicians, a synergy that can only occur if there is a concerted interchange and diffusion of ideas in an environment of mutual understanding. This book is dedicated to that end.

CHAPTER 2

THE LEGAL SYSTEM

THE NATURE AND PURPOSES OF LAW
A Functional Definition

There have been many attempts to define the law; it would be inappropriate, in this chapter, to review the intricacies of this continuing debate. Instead, we shall explore the purposes, characteristics, sources, creation, and administration of the law in the American legal system.

American law has been greatly influenced by the positivist school of jurisprudence, which holds that there is a division between law and morality and that the law is primarily a body of rules incorporated in an assemblage of authoritative constitutions, statutes, regulations, case law, and legal conventions.

The law is multifaceted. *Public law* regulates the relations of a citizen to his or her government, and the way that the departments of government relate with each other; whereas *private law* regulates the rights and obligations of citizens vis-à-vis one another. In some circumstances, this distinction becomes blurred. Tort law, for instance, was once regarded as being in the private domain since it dealt with cases in which one person would be legally obliged to remedy a wrong perpetrated upon another. Tort law thus adjusted the rights and obligations of private parties interacting with one another (an adjustment spurred by ideas of corrective justice). Today, however, tort law has evolved into a tool for the reallocation of social resources, much in the way that public law operates. In this sense, contemporary tort law is "public law in private law garb." In contrast, contract law is more purely a private matter, for its rules are designed to facilitate commercial exchange.

The Purposes of Law

Although the law is a body of rules, it is neither static nor immutable. The law changes, sometimes a little behind the times, but change it must, because its purpose is to facilitate interests and protect rights. Consequently, it may at times seem untidy or inconsistent. Oliver Wendell Holmes said: "The law is always approaching, and never reaching, consistency. It is forever adopting new principles from life at one end, and it always retains old ones from history at the other which have not yet been absorbed or sloughed off. It will become entirely consistent only when it ceases to grow."[1]

A wider and more substantive definition of this body of rules, the law, is "an outward expression of the community's sense of right or justice." The law of torts, for example, has greatly changed over the last forty years, as it shifted from the private to the public domain. Tort law was originally generated in medieval times in order to deal with simple accidents. It was subsequently fashioned to cope with the tide of accidents as a result of the Industrial Revolution. It is now employed by the courts to deal with environmental litigation on a massive and complex scale. Another example of change is the periodic reinterpretation of constitutional law in order to accommodate technological or social change. The Supreme Court's recent decisions concerning abortion reflect the consideration of contending pressures as the rights of individuals are balanced against the state's legitimate interest in regulating abortion.[2] Yet another example is the manner in which constitutional law has changed as the individuality ("personhood") of the child has been increasingly recognized.[3]

The law is *authoritative* in that it springs from sources or persons with the authority to prescribe rules. American law, which is within the tradition of the English common law, is largely made up of *case precedents,* the past decisions of courts of law. In recent times, however, legislation has become increasingly important. Whether applied from common law or statute, the law must be interpreted by an authoritative body. For example, if a dispute arises concerning the liability of a psychiatrist for injuries perpetrated on others by a former patient, it will be necessary to determine whether courts with proper jurisdictional authority have established rules for reaching conclusions in similar cases. It will be essential, also, to ascertain whether there are legislative provisions that regulate the liability of psychiatrists in such cases. Furthermore, it will be necessary to interpret case law and statutes, given the particular facts of the case in question.

Courts and legislatures interact. Sometimes, for example, a legislature will override a rule prescribed by a court. Take, for example, the doctrine of informed consent in medical malpractice. By the early 1970s, many courts had abandoned the original rule that customary professional practice should dictate how much a physician must disclose in obtaining a patient's informed consent. The "customary practice" rule was regarded as perpetuating medical paternalism and submerging the fundamental value of the patient's autonomy and right to know.[4] However, many legislatures responded by reaffirming the customary practice standard.[5] Ultimately, it will be for the courts to interpret whether or not the overriding of case precedent by legislation was efficacious. For example, in the Washington case *Helling v. Carey* (1974),[6] ophthalmologists were held to a new standard of care in testing for glaucoma. The Court ruled that an ocular pressure test should have been administered to a plaintiff-patient whose vision later became grossly impaired because corrective steps were not taken. The Washington legislature passed legislation to overrule this decision, but the statute was subsequently interpreted by the court to be ineffectual in changing the *Helling* holding.[7]

It can no longer be asserted, as it once was, that the courts merely declare the law. The common law is not the "brooding omnipresence in the sky" described by Oliver

Wendell Holmes;[8] rather, like legislatures, courts make law. However, they are constrained by complex assumptions about their legitimate role in a democratic society. In creating law, the courts are bound by precedent; thus, their lawmaking is both backward-looking and norm-creating. However, different courts will vary in the degree to which they are constrained by precedent.

Activist courts are more likely to break free of precedent,[9] perhaps because American legislatures have often been perceived as unresponsive to public needs. For example, damage claims for personal injury are subject to a legislative requirement that they be brought within a limited time—the limitation period—after an injury has been sustained. It became apparent that some victims are unaware of the injuries they have sustained, such as the onset of lung disease from asbestos dust. In these cases the victim may be deprived of a legal remedy because the limitation period expired before the disease became manifest. The injustice can be cured by amending legislation to provide that the limitation period will not start until the injury is discovered (or is reasonably discoverable). Many courts, however, have decided not to wait for legislatures to act but to cure the injustice by adding a judicial "gloss" to their interpretation of legislation.[10]

The divide between public and private law is fundamental. Constitutional law is quintessentially public; it defines the limits of power of branches of government, particularly vis-à-vis the citizen. Americans are accustomed to written constitutions, although, as the British example shows, a constitution can operate without a separate document. Public law has its effect at different levels. At its highest, it is embodied in the U.S. Constitution and the state constitutions; it descends to the laws that regulate the rights and obligations of public officials in town councils.

Embedded within public law is the notion of *the rule of law*—that ultimately we are governed by law, not men. All authority is subject to the control of law. However high the offending official, a wronged citizen has a remedy against abuse of power. The framers of the American Constitution deemed the rule of law alone too feeble a protection; therefore, they decided that the powers of the three branches of government—executive, legislative and judicial—should be separated. The separation of powers was designed to check any branch that overreached itself in relation to the others. However, the freedom and liberty of the individual required still greater fortification; accordingly, the first ten Amendments were added to the Constitution in order to protect such individual liberties as the right to be free from arbitrary searches and the seizure of personal property.[11] Moreover, in criminal proceedings, citizens were afforded the right to be accorded due process, to have a public hearing, to be represented by counsel, and to confront and present witnesses.

The ideas of equality contained in the Bill of Rights—the first ten Amendments—were later underscored by the enactment, after the Civil War, of the Thirteenth and Fourteenth Amendments. Under those Amendments, a crucial step was taken: The states were compelled to afford constitutional protection to all citizens. Other amendments have gradually been added. The slow, haphazard accretion of Amendments follows from the purposely unwieldy process required to pass them, which is itself a recognition that the basic law embodied in the Constitution should be alterable only after sober reflection, and not subject to whim or passing fashion.

The criminal law is part of public law. The state lays down rules of conduct, and a person who breaches the rules is subject to criminal sanction. A sanction can be as little as a fine and as drastic as capital punishment. The law imposes protections when personal liberty is at stake. Thus, it is common during the administration of the criminal law for the defendant's constitutional rights to be invoked.

The Characteristics of the Law

ADVERSARIAL AND INQUISITORIAL PROCESSES

The law can be viewed in many ways. In Chapter 1 we compared law with science and clinical work, demonstrating its separate methodology and purpose. In jurisprudence the dominant positivist school conceives of law as the ultimate regulator of society. Positivists view the law as a tool of social engineering. Legislatures and the courts enunciate rules of law to achieve certain ends. But the law is more than an instrument for achieving a certain distribution of things in the world. It is the means of creating and sustaining a political and ethical community. The law both embodies values and creates them. Since the grist of common law is the resolution of actual cases, it is expressed in terms of social experience. Common law courts often describe their task as that of resolving disputes while applying and developing the law. In contrast, the civil law system requires academic exegesis for its declaration and transformation. Civil law is embodied in codes, which are interpreted and applied by the courts with the guidance of authoritative academic commentaries. Codification and legislation are emerging features of American law. In interpreting and applying statutes, on the other hand, the courts establish precedents that may bind or persuade other courts attempting to resolve subsequent disputes.

The common law is *adversarial,* whereas civil law is *inquisitorial.* Ideally, in the common law, the judge rules on legal questions while the jury judges the facts within the framework of the law. As an institution, the jury was originally a body of ordinary men sworn to give a true answer (*veredictum:* verdict) to a question. The local sheriff was commanded by writ issued from the King's Court to gather together twelve truth sayers, unrelated to the parties, in order to come before the court and make inquiries. With the discarding of trial by ordeal in 1215, the jury assumed a more neutral, judgmental role, such as that of the "petty" (petit) or trial jury, which determined the guilt of suspected criminals.

The adversarial process stems from the ancient procedure of trial by battle. Under Henry II, the petty and grand assizes replaced this cumbersome and unjust institution, the last judicial battle being fought around 1485. (The King's Bench was stunned in 1818 when a gauntlet was thrown down in an attempt to initiate a trial by battle.) The remnants of trial by battle can be detected in the formalized contest of a modern trial, the purpose of which is to expose important facts for the court to cogitate, while the champions of trial by battle have evolved into the opposing counsel.

In like manner, common law pleadings were designed to hone disputes, thus enabling evidence to cluster about the legal issues exposed. Wider issues, seemingly important to laymen, may be rendered inapposite by this process, for it requires each side to ransack statutes and case law in order to bolster its case. Each side will then adduce evidence to demonstrate that its case falls within the law that, it asserts, applies.

Thus the courts have two distinct functions: *dispute resolution* and *rule-making*. From a private perspective, trials resolve disputes. From a public viewpoint, trials are a mechanism of collective choice for the interpretation and creation of the laws that regulate society.

THE LAW AS THEATER

Slovenko (1973) compares a trial to a game, not in the sense of pleasurableness, but because it recreates a traumatic event with the aim of resolving it. Through this re-enactment, society seeks to gain mastery over incidents that disturb the peace and to reassert the primacy of its rules. The elaborate, formalized procedures of the court are designed to hold passion at bay in order that reason may prevail. That is why the law usually disfavors self-help remedies, unless they pose little risk of social friction. From another viewpoint, Slovenko and Ball suggest, the courtroom is a dramatic stage upon which good and evil, right and wrong, protagonist and antagonist contend, seeking a verdict that will resolve their conflict. The theater of Law, so to speak, enacts morality plays which uphold the rules of society and demonstrate that no sanction is imposed without due concern for the rights of the individual.[12]

THE SOURCES OF THE LAW

The authoritative sources of the law are case law and statutes. Case law is the substance of the common law. In the United States, state courts decide the common law for each jurisdiction. Federal courts are not common law tribunals; their powers stem from the Constitution. The federal courts possess federal jurisdiction and such additional jurisdiction as Congress bestows.[13] In only limited areas (e.g., admiralty and maritime law), may the federal courts develop a federal common law. In *Erie R. Co. v. Tompkins* (1938),[14] the Supreme Court found that, in cases under the jurisdiction of the federal courts, the court should not develop its own common law; it must conform with the precedents of the state courts, provided those precedents are consistent with constitutional and federal statutory requirements. All law—state or federal, judge-made or statutory—must comply with the requirements of the Constitution. This, if you will, is the basic law.

The states have also enacted constitutions that reflect the federal constitution but sometimes contain provisions that go beyond it. For example, state constitutions commonly provide that its courts are open to all parties making legal claims, while the federal constitution contains no such provision.

We have already seen how constitutional requirements dictate that, except in limited areas, the federal courts cannot develop a separate federal common law. Thus, the common law is fractured into fifty separate bodies. For example, the law applying to negligence, corporations, and criminal offenses is separate and distinct in every state, except that it must comply with the dictates of the federal Constitution. This is not to say that courts blindly strive for diversity. Often universal rules will be adopted because uniformity is desirable. The American Law Institute aims to achieve more uniformity through its restatement projects. In the legislative branch, uniform acts are drafted to encourage consistency, for example the Uniform Putative and Unknown Fathers Act (1988). Uniformity may be sufficiently desirable for Congress to exercise its Constitutional powers and enact laws formerly the province of the states. (See the Federal Parental Kidnapping Prevention Act of 1980.)

Constitutional Law

As we have noted, the Founding Fathers were convinced that the individual citizen was best protected by a government that had several centers of power. Furthermore, the Bill of Rights was regarded as necessary to prevent abuse by the central government. At the outset of the Republic, each state was expected to shield and protect its own citizens. The Civil War would change this, with additions to the Bill of Rights that bind the states. The centerpiece of these additions is the Fourteenth Amendment (discussed later in this chapter).

Mental health clinicians are affected by the Constitution because it profoundly influences the shape of the law. The Supreme Court decision in *DeShaney v. Winnebago County Dept. of Social Services* (1989)[15] provides a good example. In *DeShaney,* the mother of an abused child sued the State of Wisconsin. She alleged that the failure of state welfare officers to protect her child from repeated beatings (at the hands of his father) breached her child's constitutional protection under the Fourteenth Amendment. The Supreme Court rejected her claim on the grounds that, had it been allowed, a significant area of state tort law would have been constitutionalized. In other words, people with a grievance against the state could have brought suit under a deprivation of a constitutional right, thus circumventing state law and undermining states' rights. In contrast, the Supreme Court decision in *Brown v. Board of Education* (1955)[16] shows that state autonomy could be trumped by the constitutional value of racial equality. If a state agency should incarcerate or institutionalize somebody, that person will have a claim under the Fourteenth Amendment should he be denied the equal protection or due process of the law. For example, if the state should place a child in a foster home, it will have an affirmative duty to protect the child, a breach of which could yield a claim under the Fourteenth Amendment.[17]

In *In re Gault* (1967) the Supreme Court upheld an appeal for a writ of habeas corpus issued by the mother of a fifteen-year-old boy. A juvenile court, having adjudged Gault delinquent for making lewd telephone calls, had placed him in an industrial school until he reached the age of twenty-one. The maximum penalty for an adult guilty of such a crime was a few months in jail or a relatively paltry fine. The boy had not been afforded counsel, no witness had appeared against him, no record was made of the proceedings, and he was not informed of his right to remain silent. The Supreme Court did much to elevate the rights of minors when it stated that "neither the Fourteenth Amendment nor the Bill of Rights is for adults alone."[19]

Constitutional adjudication involves legal interpretations in light of the fundamental values found in (or fashioned out of) the Constitution (particularly the Bill of Rights and subsequent Amendments). The principles of value identification tax the analytical ability of legal scholars, but the results are of significant moment for the mental health practitioner. In *Parham v. R.* (1979), for example, Justice Stewart recognized the pervasive impact of the constitution on the professional life of the mental health practitioner when dealing with children. He said: "Issues involving the family and issues concerning mental illness are among the most difficult that courts have to face, involving as they often do serious problems of policy disguised as questions of constitutional law."[19]

THE FIRST AMENDMENT

The text of the First Amendment reads:

Congress shall make no law respecting an establishment of religion or prohibiting the free exercise thereof; or abridging the freedom of speech or of the press; or the right of the people peaceably to assemble, and to petition the Government for a redress of grievances.

The terms of the text are extended to the states under the Fourteenth Amendment.

The freedom of speech and religion embodied in the First Amendment runs deep. At its heart is a distrust of government regulation. Government cannot, for example, compel a show of respect for the flag.[20] It cannot ban symbolic speech that denigrates the flag.[21] Recognizing that public schools may be a medium of indoctrination, the Supreme Court in *Tinker v. Des Moines Independent Community School District*[22] found that the First Amendment safeguarded the academic freedom of students and teachers. The First Amendment has also been deployed in order to protect the status of private schools.[23] However, freedom of speech is abridged if it constitutes "fighting words"[24] or incites others to damage property or business.[25] A pertinent limit on freedom of speech is the protection the Court gives to children in order to guard them from sexual exploitation by pornographers[26] (see Chapter 3).

The First Amendment assures the *free exercise and nonestablishment of religion.* The nonestablishment clause has been interpreted as effecting a separation of church and state. The chief battleground for the application of this clause has been the permissibility of school prayer. In *Wallace v. Jaffree* (1985),[27] a majority of Supreme Court Justices found that Alabama statutes permitting silent prayer or meditation in schools were unconstitutional; similarly, in *Lee v. Weisman* (1992), the Court found that school officials' organization of prayerful invocations and benedictions during graduation ceremonies breached the establishment clause. In these cases, the Justices have emphasized that the putatively coercive nature of a school necessitates close constitutional scrutiny of regulations that trespass upon First Amendment freedoms. In *Lee* it was noted that research in psychology supported the assumption that adolescents are susceptible to peer pressure toward conformity, particularly in matters of social convention.[28]

Wisconsin v. Yoder involved a direct clash between the free exercise clause of the First Amendment and the state's compulsory education statute.[29] In this case, the court exempted Amish children from compulsory school attendance after the eighth grade because it would have gravely interfered with their religion. *Yoder* illustrates how the Court must examine the centrality of any religious tenet allegedly jeopardized by state regulations; otherwise, legitimate authority could be defeated by cheap religious excuse. Even a central religious tenet will bend to a generally applicable or neutral state regulation if, on balance, the state's interest takes precedence over the religious practice. Thus, Oregon was permitted to deny unemployment compensation to employees who were fired because they had used peyote for religious purposes.[30]

THE FOURTEENTH AMENDMENT

Section 1.   All persons born or naturalized in the United States and subject to the jurisdiction thereof, are citizens of the United States and of the State wherein they reside. No State shall make or enforce any law which shall abridge the privileges or immunities of citizens of the United States; nor shall any State deprive any person of life, liberty, or property, without due process of law; nor deny to any person within its jurisdiction the equal protection of the laws.

This amendment prohibits *state action* that deprives "any person of life, liberty, or property, without *due process of law* . . . or [denies] the *equal protection* of the laws." We have already alluded those elements of the amendment that have captured the courts' attention. It should be noted that *the state must have acted;* a private individual, whatever his power, will not be subject to these constitutional requirements. "State action" refers to a state's legislative, executive, or judicial function. Zoning laws segregating black and white would represent state actions.[31] The enforcement by a state court of a racially restrictive covenant would also bespeak state action.[32]

The *due process* requirement of the Fourteenth Amendment is shared with the Fifth Amendment. Its long and checkered history began with the substantive due process jurisprudence employed by the Supreme Court when it struck down legislation interfering with freedom of contract.[33] The same line of decisions was reversed by the Court when it upheld the constitutionality of New Deal legislation.[34] In Chapter 3, we shall explore substantive due process in its modern context. If a right discerned within the Constitution can be described as a *liberty interest,* any state action that interferes with it will be subject to the court's determination of the balance between that right and the demands of organized society. The right to an abortion is the roiled and bloody battlefield of this judicial balancing.[35] Because of the problematical role of the Court in identifying a right, due process has become primarily a procedural safeguard. Government is restricted in its actions when a person's interest in "life," "liberty," and "property" is at stake. A citizen is entitled to a hearing sufficient to protect those interests. The core of procedural due process is the duty to give notice, and the opportunity to be heard in an open forum before a "neutral and detached magistrate."[36] As we shall discuss, due process must be accorded to juveniles in juvenile courts,[37] correctional facilities, and psychiatric institutions (see Chapter 10). It is through the due process clause that the Court has applied the Bill of Rights to the states and has evolved almost all the protections that bind the federal government in the exercise of its powers.

The equal protection clause of the Fourteenth Amendment proscribes invidious discrimination. The Supreme Court thus regards state-sponsored discrimination against certain groups as highly suspect. Reflecting its post–Civil War origins, discrimination has traditionally been on grounds of race. A state may justify discrimination against other groups if it can show that, by doing so, it is rationally promoting a legitimate state purpose. Discrimination on the basis of gender requires a level of justification more demanding than "rational connection," but not the level demanded in the scrutiny of racial matters.[38] As we have noted, constitutional rights attach to children.[39] The state may subject children to discrimination if it can show a "significant" state interest "not present in the case of an adult."[40] However, in *Cary,* the Court held that the state did not have an interest sufficiently significant to ban the sale of contraceptives to minors under sixteen; however, the state's interest may be sufficient to require parental consent for a minor's abortion, provided allowance is made for application to a court for a "bypass" of that requirement.[41]

THE FIFTH AMENDMENT

No person shall be held to answer for a capital or other infamous crime unless on a presentment or indictment of a grand jury, except in cases arising in the land or naval forces, or in the militia, when in actual service, in time of war or public danger; nor shall any person be subject for the same offense to be twice put in jeopardy of life or limb; nor shall be compelled in any criminal case to be a witness against himself, nor be deprived of life, liberty, or property, without due process of law; nor shall private property be taken for public use without just compensation.

The Fifth Amendment has been called the "due process" clause. The Fifth Amendment binds the federal government as the Fourteenth Amendment binds the states. The due process requirement has also been interpreted as incorporating the equal protection (or equality) provision of the Fourteenth Amendment. Both amendments are conflated for the purposes of this discussion.

In its pure form, the due process clause of the Fifth Amendment, together with the Fourteenth Amendment, embodies a fundamental notion in common law: Persons should be accorded the elements of *natural justice.*

The due process clause has a broad reach, overlapping other Bill of Rights protections. In *United States v. Kantor,*[42] the producers of a movie, *Those Young Girls,* were indicted under the federal Child Protection Act. According to this Act, it was unlawful to pay persons under the age of eighteen in exchange for sexually explicit performances, actual or simulated, for the purpose of making films or photographs. The defendants claimed that the Act violated the First and Fifth Amendments. Under the Fifth Amendment, two questions were posed: (1) Can Congress criminalize the employment of an underage performer without requiring proof that the employer knew the performer's actual age? (2) If Congress can criminalize underage employment of this type, should such a severe penalty have been exacted? The court found that neither lack of knowledge of age nor the severity of the penalty was enough to violate the Fifth Amendment, in the context of the activity proscribed. A similar result would have followed, under the Fourteenth Amendment, had the protective legislation been pursuant to state legislation.

Like adults, minors enjoy due process rights, equal protection freedom, and other constitutional safeguards. At the same time, as we have observed, the state (i.e., the Congress or the state legislature) has sufficient legitimate interest to take special measures to protect children, even though the constitutional freedom of others is thereby abridged. However, the state's regulatory power may be trumped by competing fundamental rights, a predicament described by Reppucci *et al.* (1984) as the parent–child–state triad. Much public policy is focused upon the web of interests within these interactions.

Indeed, the place of children in the Constitution is still being debated. As *parens patriae,* the state is allowed greater control over children than would be permitted over adults. Balancing state control is the constitutional right accorded to parents to control the upbringing and conduct of their own children. This is a species of right of the privacy or autonomy right enunciated in the *Yoder* case.[43] The powers of the state as *parens patriae* often clash with the autonomy of the family unit. For example, a parent has a right to give or withhold consent to medical treatment;[44] but this right has been usurped when the life of the child is endangered.[45] In *Parham v. J.R.,* the Supreme Court upheld the rights of parents or legal guardians to commit children to mental health institutions without a formal legal hearing, provided a neutral physician conducts a preadmission inquiry.[46] In contrast, state legislation permitting psychiatric personnel forcibly to medicate involuntarily committed adult psychiatric patients was held to be unconstitutional because it lacked adequate procedural due process protections, such as a hearing or counsel.[47] The balance struck in the parent–child–state triad by the *Parham* decision has been commended by some observers as supporting the family's efforts to provide sustenance to children.[48] Institutionalized minors draw special due process protection.[49] However, *Parham* has been vehemently attacked by others, for the values at issue are confounded by divergent perceptions of mental illness and the mental health system (see Chapter 10). This issue is further considered in Chapter 3.

Conflicts like this highlight the constructive role mental health practitioners can play in shaping the very stuff of constitutional law. Better research will allow clinicians and developmentalists a fuller role in the formation of policy stemming ultimately from the Constitution.

OTHER CONSTITUTIONAL PROTECTIONS

Other Bill of Rights protections are material in the conjunction of mental health, children and the law. The Fourth Amendment provides:

> The right of the people to be secure in their persons, houses, papers and effects, against unreasonable searches and seizures, shall not be violated, and no warrants shall issue but upon probable cause, supported by oath or affirmation, and particularly describing the place to be searched, and the persons or things to be seized.

A warrant may be issued only on *probable cause*—a reasonable suspicion of wrongdoing. The warrant must be issued by an independent judicial officer.[50] This amendment protects person and property from arbitrary search and ensures a zone of personal privacy. Thus, a person may read what he likes in his own home. The home excludes government surveillance and "provide[s] the setting for those intimate activities that the Fourth Amendment is designed to shelter from governmental interference."[51]

Schoolchildren may claim the benefit of the Fourth Amendment. However, the right is more abridged for schoolchildren than for adults. When a high school principal searched the purse of a fourteen-year-old girl suspected of smoking cigarettes and found marijuana, charges were brought against the child. The New Jersey Supreme Court found the search unconstitutional. However, the U.S. Supreme Court overturned the decision. It held that searches by schools need only be reasonable, that no warrant was required, and that there was no need for probable cause.[52]

An invasion of Fourteenth Amendment rights (as with other rights) may permit the person suffering loss to sue for damages.[53] State officials (e.g., state child welfare officers) who deny a person's constitutional rights are liable in a damages suit under §1983 of the Civil Rights Act.[54]

The Sixth Amendment states:

> In all criminal prosecutions. the accused shall enjoy the right to a speedy and public trial, by an impartial jury of the State and district wherein the crime shall have been committed, which districts shall have been previously ascertained by law, and to be informed of the nature and cause of the accusation; to be confronted with the witnesses against him; to have compulsory process for obtaining witnesses in his favor, and to have the assistance of counsel for his defense.

This amendment deals with citizens' trial rights in criminal cases: It requires that the following be accorded to the accused:

1. A speedy public trial.
2. An impartial jury.
3. Information as to the nature and cause of the accusation.
4. The right to confront and cross-examine his or her accusers.
5. The right to secure witnesses in his or her favor by subpoena.
6. The right to counsel.

The right to a public trial applies to criminal, not civil, cases. The court may be closed only in exceptional cases, for example if it is likely that jurors will be prejudiced by rampant public outcry. The issue of the public nature of the trial and the right to confront witnesses is germane to the legitimacy of using videotaped testimony in sexual abuse hearings, a contentious matter considered at greater length in Chapter 6. Generally, the public nature of the trial is bolstered by First Amendment protections that allow publicity of matters within the court. For example, in *Smith v. Daily Mail Pub. Co.,*[55] the Supreme Court held unconstitutional a West Virginia statute prohibiting newspaper identification of a juvenile offender without the juvenile court's permission. The Court found that the state's interest in protecting and rehabilitating juvenile offenders was outweighed by First Amendment press protection. The right to counsel, who may be court-appointed, generally applies only to cases involving substantial jeopardy.

The Eighth Amendment has received attention in relation to the death penalty. In *Prejean v. Blackburn,*[56] an illustrative case involving a minor, a first-degree murder conviction of an eighteen-year-old male of limited mental capacity was upheld. The court noted that, while age is a factor in sentencing, capital punishment for youthful offenders was not cruel and unusual *per se*. According to the Supreme Court, the death penalty does not violate the Eighth Amendment's prohibition against cruel and unusual punishment as long as all possible Fourteenth Amendment safeguards are present, including the opportunity for a defendant to present any mitigating circumstances to a jury before sentencing.[57] The Eighth Amendment states:

> Excessive bail shall not be required, nor excessive fines imposed, nor cruel and unusual punishments inflicted.

Juveniles have no right to bail. However, the right to be free of cruel and unusual punishment has been held to apply to inmates in a juvenile training school who were subjected to solitary confinement and brutal methods of crowd control,[58] a matter discussed in Chapters 3 and 10.

The Eighth Amendment has been held inapplicable to school discipline, although the Fourteenth Amendment requires that a schoolchild be accorded due process. In *Ingraham v. Wright,*[59] the Court determined that the provision by the state for liability on the ground of excessive punishment was sufficient to safeguard against maltreatment. The Court put weight on the detrimental effect of overelaborate procedural safeguards that might exacerbate the eventual punishment by increasing the child's anticipatory anxiety.

Legislation

"Legislation is commonly perceived as legally articulated policy adopted and promulgated by a representative body or by the electorate where the initiative and referendum exist."[60] Direct electoral participation is uncommon; however, in California a segment of the public may require that propositions be placed upon the ballot. More usually, representative bodies such as Congress or the state legislatures enact the statutes that enunciate the law. We shall have occasion to discuss many statutes. State mental health legislation, for example, sets forth the conditions upon which people may be institutionalized on the grounds of mental illness (see Chapter 10). Legislation may be *amended* to keep it up to date, or *repealed* if it is no longer needed. More problematically, legislation may be *repealed by implication*. The court in *County of DuPage v. Harris* stated that "implied repeal" is found in two general situations:

1. Where a subsequent statute covers the whole subject matter of a former one and is intended as a substitute for it; and
2. Where a subsequent statute's provisions are so repugnant to those of the earlier that the two are irreconcilable.[61]

Under the U.S. Constitution a federal statute covering the same field as a state statute will take priority. For example, when an Indiana statute allowing train rides to be exchanged for advertising was in direct conflict with a federal statute requiring payment in money, the Supreme Court held that "[n]o state enactment can be of any avail when the subject . . . has been covered by an act of Congress."[62] Federal regulations on the labeling of tobacco products preempt most state liability rules respecting these products.[63] Any statute, state or federal, that conflicts with the federal Constitution will be unconstitutional and therefore void. A state constitution will have a similar precedence over conflicting state legislation.

An administrative agency may engage in rule-making that is a form of legislation. This is known as *delegated legislation,* because the legislature sets the "adequate standards" for the exercise of delegated power by the agency. If the agency makes rules beyond its power (i.e., *ultra vires*) or not in accordance with stipulated procedures, either as found in the legislation or under the Administrative Procedure Act, the rules are invalid. The rules must also accord with the federal Constitution. In *Bob Jones University v. United States,*[64] for example, the Court reviewed the regulations of the Internal Revenue Service for conformity with the First Amendment's guarantee of freedom of religion; no infraction was found.

Courts interpret legislation in order to determine whether its terms apply to a particular dispute. However, the statute may not be clear, so the Court may have to refer to the history of the legislation in order to discern its intent. In reviewing the history of a statute, the Court will consider committee reports, debates, and bills.

THE LEGISLATIVE PROCESS

It is through the legislative process that policies are transformed into laws. Congress is at the center and may make laws within its constitutional limits. The federal Constitution prescribes and enumerates the heads of legislative power. Within those heads, legislative power is subject to the constitutional constraints surrounding Congress.

State legislatures enact legislation within the bounds of their constitutional authority. The federal Constitution outlines a complicated system whereby power is divided between the state and federal governments. Within each level, the executive has a distinctive place. The roles of the executive and the legislature have changed with the exigencies of the time. Some Presidents, like Harding and Coolidge, have proposed modest legislative programs, while Roosevelt's and Johnson's were extensive.[65] Other Presidents who have proffered far-reaching programs have been frustrated by Congressional inaction.[66]

Congress has significant investigative powers. Through these powers it generates information required for the design of legislation, checks on the effectiveness of the operation of responsible officials, and informs and educates the public. The arm of the Congressional committee that performs this function is the General Accounting Office—a legislative support agency of Congress.[67] Inspectors General have been appointed under legislation to audit the operations of the federal establishment.

The legislative process is represented in Figure 2–1. The standard pattern is *bicameral;* bills may be introduced in either house, but both houses must approve the bill in identical form before it is sent to the President for his signature. Many bills are introduced, but few survive their referral to the appropriate committee. Surviving bills are further honed, once out of committee. Thus few bills become law, and even fewer do so in their original form. The majority of bills are initiated by executive departments, private organizations, or individual citizens. The most important bills tend to be drafted by executive agencies or special interest groups. Often they are sponsored by a committee chairman or a group of influential members of Congress.

The President has assumed an increasingly active role. The chief aspects of his legislative program are announced in the State of the Union address. Thereafter, the President sends to Congress special messages detailing his proposals in particular areas.

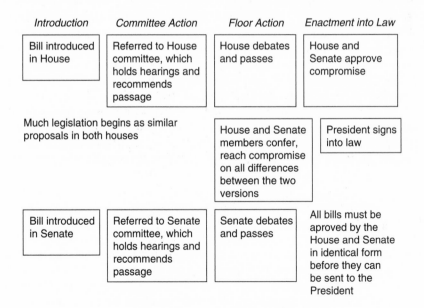

Figure 2–1. How a Bill Becomes Law

Executive agencies draft the bills, and committee chairmen usually introduce them simultaneously as "companion" bills in both chambers.

An example of the passage of a bill is the Health Care Quality Improvement Act. Congressional action was prompted by a 1985 federal jury award of $2.2 million in antitrust damages, on the ground that peer review sanctions were part of a conspiracy to monopolize medical practice.[68] Several national medical and hospital organizations urged that federal antitrust and state law liability threatened good faith peer review and thus undermined the quality of health care. Their pressure was responsible for the eventual legislation. The original bill was introduced in the House of Representatives and the Senate in October 1986 and referred to the Committee on Energy and Commerce. A committee may report (i.e., approve) the bill, possibly after some changes, or choose not to act, which effectively kills it. After hearings and certain changes by its Subcommittee on Health and the Environment, the House Committee reported the amended bill. The Congressional Budget Committee reported the bill's effect on the budget, and it was consolidated with other bills. The consolidated bill was passed by the House and Senate later in October 1986, and President Reagan signed it into law (P.L. 99-660 100 Stat. 3743) on November 14, 1986.

The power of the purse is vested in the Congress. If enacted legislation requires expenditure of moneys, a separate appropriations law must be enacted. Thus, a dichotomy is established between authorization and appropriation.[69] Customarily, appropriations bills originate in the House.

The *omnibus bill* is a feature of modern Congressional legislation. If action is not completed on appropriations bills by the end of the fiscal year, funding is authorized through a *continuing resolution.* In 1986 and 1987, Congress consolidated all the regular appropriation bills into continuing resolutions, the largest spending measures in Congressional history. Congress has employed omnibus legislation to gain strategic advantage over the President. Though the bill may contain material unpalatable to the President, he has no ability to veto only the portion of it he dislikes. Moreover, riders can be incorporated and thus gain passage because they are buried in legislation. An example of important health care legislation found in an omnibus bill is the Consolidated Omnibus Budget Reconciliation Act of 1985 (COBRA), which establishes criteria for the safe transfer between hospitals of critically ill or injured people and women in labor.

The President is the final authority. Under the Constitution (Article 1, Section 7), he has a qualified veto power. A copy of the "enrolled" bill is signed by the Speaker and the presiding officer of the Senate and sent to the President, who has ten days, excluding Sundays, to sign or veto it. If no action is taken, the bill becomes law. If the President vetoes it, Congress may override the veto by a two-thirds vote of the members present in each house.

THE COURT SYSTEM
Federal Courts

The hierarchy of federal courts is illustrated in Figure 2–2.

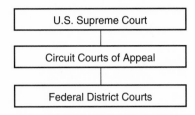

Figure 2–2. The Federal Court System

DISTRICT COURTS

The federal district courts are trial courts that hear cases involving disputes arising under federal law, such as tax evasion, civil rights infringements, claims for entitlements under federal law, crimes perpetrated on federal property, the transportation of illicit drugs, and interstate disputes in which the amount involved exceeds $50,000.

FEDERAL COURTS OF APPEAL

There are eleven regional federal circuit courts, which hear cases on appeal from the federal district courts and from certain administrative agencies.

THE UNITED STATES SUPREME COURT

This is the court of last resort. The Supreme Court reviews decisions involving federal law; it cannot adjudicate state court decisions on state law. It is not a citizen's right to take a case before the Supreme Court; the Court decides which cases it will hear, on the basis of their constitutional significance. Access must be limited, because of the sheer volume of petitions. In 1988 the Court granted review to 147 of the 5,657 cases brought before it and wrote opinions on 156.[70]

Direct appeal is not the usual route to the Court. The only decisions that may be appealed are those made by three court federal judges[71] and Congress has greatly restricted access to them.[72] By 1988 Congress had virtually eliminated mandatory review by the Court.

The most common way to bring a case before the Supreme Court is by *petitioning for a writ of certiorari* (an order to produce a trial record for review). Four votes by Supreme Court Justices are required before the writ can be issued. Approximately 14 percent of petitions for certiorari are accepted.[73] In general, the court chooses to hear cases arising from social policy disputes which involve substantive constitutional questions. For example, in a recent series of cases, the Court has sought to balance the following profound policy issues: (1) the legitimate desire of the state to regulate abortion; (2) the right of women to privacy; (3) the competence of minors to make decisions about their own health; and (4) the right of parents to rear their children without state interference.[74]

State Courts

The structure of the state court system varies from state to state. While almost all colonial state systems were organized like English courts, individual jurisdictions adapted their courts to meet local needs, and state judicial systems have continued to evolve over the years. In the Eastern states, colonial vestiges remain in many systems; in the Western part of the United States, courts tend to be structured in a more streamlined fashion.

Despite different names and organizations, state courts have common features. All have at least three levels: a court of first instance, an appellate-level court, and a court of last resort.

COURTS OF FIRST INSTANCE

A court of first instance is where a case is initially heard. This court may be of limited or general jurisdiction.

A *court of limited jurisdiction* is either a specialized court or one that deals with minor cases. Specialty courts include *probate, traffic,* and *juvenile court.* These courts developed from the county, city, and town courts of the nineteenth century. *Courts of general jurisdiction* evolved from state district courts and are empowered to hear all cases not tried in the courts of limited jurisdiction.

Since very few are appealed, decisions by courts of first instance are particularly important, for they constitute day-to-day law.

APPELLATE COURTS

In the United States, virtually every litigant has the opportunity to appeal a judgment at least once. In some states, appeals are heard by the state's court of last resort. Twenty-three states have *intermediate appellate courts.* Created primarily to reduce the load on the state's supreme court, they are mainly in areas with large urban populations. They may be either a step to the state's court of last resort or the final step in the appeals process. Intermediate appellate courts have various formal names, such as "Superior Court," "Court of Appeals," or "Appellate Division of the Supreme Court."

COURT OF LAST RESORT

This is the final step when a lower state court's decision is appealed. In some states a citizen has the right of appeal to the court; in others, the court has discretion over which suits it will hear. In most states the court of last resort is known as the "Supreme Court." In others, it is called the "Court of Appeals" (Kentucky, Maryland, New

York), the "Supreme Court of Errors" (Connecticut), and the "Supreme Judicial Court" (Massachusetts, Maine).

Although the Constitution does not indicate whether the United States Supreme Court can review state court decisions, in 1816 the Supreme Court affirmed its own power to do so.[75] While a final judgment by the highest state court cannot be directly appealed to the Supreme Court, the Supreme Court can issue a writ of certiorari at its own discretion and review decisions or statutes challenged on constitutional or federal grounds.[76]

JUDICIAL PROCEEDINGS

The three types of judicial proceedings are:

1. Criminal
2. Civil
3. Administrative

Only the first will be described in this section.

Criminal prosecutions involve offenses punishable by execution, imprisonment, or fine. In these actions, the prosecution must prove its case against the accused *beyond a reasonable doubt*. The accused must be afforded full due process—in other words, the right to be informed of the offense for which he is charged; a speedy public trial with judge, jury, and counsel; the right to present witnesses on his own behalf and the right to cross-examine the other side's witnesses. Child mental health clinicians are most likely to be involved in criminal proceedings when a child is the victim of a crime.

After the detention and booking of the accused, the state must show, at an initial hearing, that it has sufficient reason (probable cause) to pursue the case further. *Misdemeanor* charges may be tried forthwith. Those charged with *felonies* are further detained, released on bail, or released on their own recognizance.

At various points, defense counsel may seek to discover the prosecution's case or make a motion to suppress certain elements of the case.

Next, in a *prima facie* hearing before magistrate or judge or an indictment before a grand jury, the prosecution attempts to substantiate that it has a sufficient case against the accused to proceed.

At the arraignment, the accused pleads guilty, not guilty, nolo contendere, or not guilty by reason of insanity. A guilty plea is likely to have been lodged following plea bargaining, as a result of which the accused agrees to plead guilty to a lesser offense than that with which he had originally been charged. Those who plead guilty may be dealt with at the arraignment. Those who plead not guilty, or not guilty by reason of insanity, proceed to trial.

A jury trial begins with the empaneling of a jury. Twelve-person juries are required for felony cases in many states, although six-member juries are increasingly common. Next, in opening statements, prosecution and defense outline their sides of the case. The state then presents the evidence against the accused through material exhibits and the direct examination of witnesses. The defense may challenge the materiality of the evidence presented, object to the direct examination of the prosecuting counsel, and cross-examine the state's witnesses. The defense then presents its case through exhibits, documents, and witnesses. Any of these may be challenged, objected to, or cross-examined by the prosecution. Throughout the trial the judge keeps order and rules on points of procedure, thus ensuring that the rules of evidence are followed.

When the evidence has been presented, the defense may lodge a motion for acquittal. If that is unsuccessful, each side summates its case, the judge instructs the jury as to the law, and the jury retires to consider the verdict (which must usually be unanimous). If the jury cannot agree, a new trial is held. If the accused is found not guilty, he is discharged. If the verdict is guilty, a disposition hearing is scheduled for sentencing. In reaching a conclusion about the appropriate disposition of, or sentence for, the guilty party, the judge will take into account all aspects of the case (e.g., the defendant's past record, presentence reports from probation officers, and reports from mental health clinicians). Sentencing usually involves a fine, probation, imprisonment, or, occasionally, community service.

The state is not permitted to appeal an acquittal. The defendant, however, may appeal a verdict or sentence on the grounds of facts (e.g., insufficient evidence) or legal error (e.g., improperly obtained evidence). Less often, the defendant will lodge a writ of habeas corpus asserting that his detention is illegal on the ground that the trial was improper.

The defendant may be released before serving the full sentence if, at a subsequent dispositional review, his behavior is considered to have been good, or other mitigating circumstances (e.g., advanced age) are held to apply.

The State's Attorney (from the office of the District Attorney or Attorney General) acts as the prosecutor in criminal cases. The Attorney General's Office is empowered to decide whether there is sufficient evidence to pursue a case, to determine the grade of offense with which the accused will be charged, and to plea bargain with the defendant. The accused is represented by a defense attorney, who is privately retained, appointed by the court, or provided by the Public Defender's Office.

The Clerk of the Court collates documents for the judge and schedules the docket of cases. Probation officers prepare presentence reports. Child Welfare caseworkers prepare diagnostic or periodic review reports for the family court.

The other kinds of proceedings (juvenile, civil, and administrative) will be described later (see Chapters 4–9). The rules of evidence, standards of proof, and the expert witness will be discussed next and in Chapter 11.

THE ADJUDICATIVE PROCESS
Evidence

Evidence refers to factual proofs concerning an issue in dispute, presented during a trial for the purpose of inducing belief in the minds of the court or the jury. Evidence may be direct or circumstantial. Direct evidence is "evidence that, if believed, resolves a matter in issue."[77] Circumstantial evidence indicates the resolution of an issue only when combined with other evidence. For example, evidence offered on "battered child syndrome," combined with the fact that a defendant has had exclusive custody of a child and the improbability that the child's injuries could have been accidentally caused, is strong circumstantial evidence of child abuse. Circumstantial evidence may be the basis of a conviction, but only if it forms a complete chain of facts leading to a conclusion that excludes any other "rational hypothesis."[78]

The judge determines whether evidence is admissible. Generally, evidence that is *relevant* is admissible; irrelevant evidence is not.[79] Evidence is considered relevant if it is *material* (i.e., directly related to the issue in question) and has *probative value* (i.e., demonstrates the probability that a fact is more or less true).[80]

A judge may refuse to admit evidence that is relevant if the danger of confusion or prejudice outweighs its probative value.[81] The judge balances the probative value of evidence against the possibility that the evidence would distract the jury from the main issue or arouse its emotions in a prejudicial manner. When a grandfather was accused of molesting a child, the court did not admit evidence of his son's abuse of same child. The court held that the danger of convicting the defendant because of his family rather than his own actions (as a result of a prejudicial impression of "bad family") outweighed the significance of the fact.[82] Another court allowed evidence of the number of times an expert had recently testified in malpractice cases and the amount he was being paid, reasoning that the possibility of inflaming the jury was less than the need to "probe bias, partisanship or financial interest" as a "safeguard against errant expert testimony."[83]

EXPERT WITNESSES

To ensure accurate sources of information, testimony by laymen is limited to personal knowledge from firsthand observation.[84] Inferences, conclusions, and opinions are considered the province of the jury, rather than the witness. The main differences between lay and expert witnesses is that expert testimony may include opinions while lay testimony may not, and expert testimony based on hearsay is admissible in some circumstances.

When the testimony is technically complicated, the judge may choose to allow expert testimony to aid the jury in understanding the evidence or determining a fact in issue.[85] An expert must have knowledge, skill, experience, or training in the area at issue.[86] An expert may have to be a member of a given profession but is not usually required to be a specialist.[87]

Traditionally, experts have been limited to testimony based on firsthand knowledge of the facts. For example, a doctor's testimony on behalf of a man claiming whiplash from an automobile accident was not admitted because the doctor relied for his diagnosis on the man's subjective description of his symptoms rather than physical or radiological examination.[88] Courts that adhere to this rule sometimes allow expert testimony without personal knowledge of the facts if questions are framed hypothetically (see Chapter 11). However, critics of this rule point out that facts presented hypothetically can be incomplete or potentially biasing.[89] Modern rules also allow an expert to testify about facts that become known at the hearing.[90] We discuss the child mental health professional as an expert witness in Chapter 11.

Rules of Evidence

THE OPINION RULE

Laymen's opinions are usually not admissible. Experts may give opinions when their testimony will enhance the jury's understanding of an issue. While usually not permitted to give an opinion as to whether a witness is telling the truth, an expert may be allowed to address credibility in some circumstances. When a man convicted of raping his fourteen-year-old daughter challenged her testimony because she retracted her story at one point, expert testimony was permitted to show that retraction was characteristic of sexually abused children.[91] However, expert testimony that explicitly addresses whether a particular child is telling the truth is rarely allowed, for this is the province of the jury or judge. This type of testimony is generally excluded to avoid putting a "stamp of scientific legitimacy" on a particular witness's testimony.[92]

CHARACTER

Negative testimony concerning a person's character is allowed only when character is a central issue in a case. In a criminal trial, testimony concerning a person's bad character may be introduced only to challenge earlier testimony about that person's good qualities. This type of evidence is usually excluded because it could prejudice the jury; moreover, it would be repugnant to convict someone on the basis of past misdeeds or bad reputation.

Expert testimony concerning psychological profiles cannot be used by the prosecution as a means of attacking character. Testimony that a man accused of child abuse matched the profile of a "battering parent" has been ruled inadmissible. The court noted that the defendant was not required to defend or explain his personality and stated that it was necessary for the defendant to raise the issue before it would be admissible. "We feel this finding is required until further evidence of the scientific accuracy and reliability of syndrome or profile diagnoses can be established."[93] In another case, expert psychological testimony that included an opinion that the defendant had abused his child was barred even though testimony as to the child's credibility was allowed, because, while the expert could testify concerning someone she had examined, the court doubted her ability to "peer into the mind" of a third person and draw a valid conclusion.[94]

THE HEARSAY RULE

"Hearsay" is a statement purportedly made by someone other than the person testifying offered to prove the matter asserted.[95] Statements may include records and behavior, as well as conversation. As a rule, hearsay is not admissible because of possible deficiencies in perception and memory or bias of witnesses.[96] Reliability of the evidence being asserted cannot be tested by cross-examination, by the jury's observations on demeanor of the person asserting it, or by the legal and moral weight of the oath. However, in some jurisdictions, expert medical opinion will be admitted if based on information received from a member of the patient's family. One court allowed a physician to offer testimony based on the history of an infant, reasoning that the mother had no motive to lie when originally providing the history to the physician.[97] Ohio has created a "child hearsay exception," which leaves the question of admissibility of hearsay statements from abused or neglected children to the discretion of the judge.[98]

There are some general exceptions to the hearsay rule. Some examples are excited utterances, and business and public records.[99] An excited utterance must be the result of an exciting event and made under the stress of the moment. When a child less than four years old was injured in a motorcycle accident caused by a dog, her statement to a policeman in the emergency room was considered an excited utterance, and thus an exception to the hearsay rule, despite the presumption that the child's age made her incompetent to testify.[100] In *State v. Wagner*,[101] a three-year-old child used dolls to describe sexual abuse to a police detective six days after the molestation had occurred. The Court found the description to be within the excited utterance exception because the child was still under the stress of the incident. Furthermore, due to his limited verbal ability, he had had no earlier opportunity to communicate.

Physician's records may be admissible because they are considered business records. An ophthalmologist's office records were allowed in a malpractice suit because of their day-to-day nature.[102] However, records may be ruled inadmissible if they contain opinions, and reports prepared for litigation are generally inadmissible because they are not kept in the ordinary course of doing business.

Hearsay will be allowed in evidence if two conditions are met: The witness is unavailable, and there are some indicia of reliability (i.e., matters that bolster the trustworthiness of the statement). When a child is too young to testify, he or she will often be considered "unavailable."[103] Hearsay testimony may be admitted if it is adequately corroborated.

The United States Supreme Court upheld an Idaho ruling that a physician's testimony concerning his interview with a two-year-old victim of sexual abuse was inadmissible. The Idaho court reversed the lower court's verdict because the doctor's (inadmissible) testimony was a significant factor leading to conviction. The court was concerned about the reliability of the child's statements because of the possibility that the physician had asked leading questions that incorporated preconceived ideas about the answers. The Supreme Court commented that, while this particular interview appeared "suggestive," leading questions were not inappropriate in all circumstances. In a five-to-four majority, the Court found that evidence of physical abuse did not necessarily corroborate the victim's identification of the alleged sexual abuser.[104]

PRIVILEGE

Confidentiality is an ethical and legal obligation not to disclose communication by a client or patient. Privilege is the legal rule that protects portions of that communication from disclosure in court. Attorney–client privilege, the earliest privilege recognized at common law, was developed to prevent attorneys from having to disclose in court information communicated to them by their clients in the context of the litigation.[105] Policy balances the need for all available evidence against the quality of legal advice that comes from full disclosure by a client by which the administration of justice is better served. Without full knowledge of the facts, an attorney's advice is of little value. Consequently, most attorney-client communication is privileged, and disclosure cannot be forced. Information that is confidential but outside the purposes of the litigation, on the other hand, may be ordered into evidence.[106]

In contrast with attorney–client communications, no doctor–patient privilege was recognized in common law. Such a privilege was recognized during the nineteenth century, but it was later withdrawn. Usually, therapeutic privilege applies only between a patient and a mental health clinician in a psychotherapeutic situation.[107] It does not exist in all states.[108] Although the purpose of this privilege is to promote effective therapy, it can be overridden. Courts can order disclosure if the evidence is very important.

Originally, exercise of the attorney–client privilege was the prerogative of the attorney. It allowed an attorney to abstain from having to testify against his client and violate his (the attorney's) honor. The privilege now belongs to the client, who can make the decision to waive it. In a similar vein, it is the patient's decision whether to waive therapeutic privilege. For example, a person bringing an action for psychological injury waives therapeutic privilege.

A waiver can be express or implied. An express waiver is given by the person entitled to the privilege. For example, applications or policies for life or health insurance may stipulate waiver of privilege. Filing suit may waive privilege by implication. When a child injured by falling off a truck sued for mental pain and suffering and psychiatric expenses, the appellate court found waiver of that privilege. While recognizing the need to facilitate diagnosis and treatment, the court noted that it was inconsistent for the child to claim damages based on a mental condition and then to withhold vital evidence about it. The appellate court held that the trial court needed to balance the child's need for confidentiality against the defendant's interest in contesting the claim.[109]

Jurisdictions differ in regard to whether psychotherapist–patient privilege extends to children. Oregon's statute ORS 418.775.1 excludes children because of the state's policy of promoting the safety of abused children.[110] California, on the other hand, reads the privilege broadly in order to promote free disclosure, diagnosis, and treatment.[111]

Burden of Proof

Considering that facts relevant to issues in trials are never fully known, the question of the burden of proof often determines the result of litigation. Burden of proof encapsulates two separate matters. The first is the burden of producing evidence pertaining to the particular fact in issue; the second is the burden of persuading the trier of fact that the alleged fact is true.

The burden of production is placed upon the party who pleads the existence of a fact. Certain facts must be established in order to found actions and raise defenses. *A* is injured when he dives into a swimming pool allegedly manufactured by *B*. In bringing suit against *B,* he will have to establish among other facts that *B* made the pool. If he fails to produce this evidence his action will fail on a motion for a directed verdict.

If *A* produces evidence pertaining to these issues, he bears the further burden of persuasion. The evidence must persuade the jury (or judge, if no jury is empaneled) that the essential facts are true (here, that *B* made the pool). Failure to meet the burden of persuasion will result in an adverse verdict for the person upon whom the burden was placed.

The satisfaction or standard required for the burden of persuasion will vary according to the nature of the case. The swimming pool case is one of civil liability, in which the customary formula is "preponderance of the evidence" or "balance of probabilities." Thus, *B* must show, on a preponderance of the evidence, that *A* manufactured the pool. Sometimes, in civil cases, the burden is stated as requiring proof "by clear, strong, and convincing evidence." In criminal cases, the formula of "beyond a reasonable doubt" is employed.

The definition of these standards has taxed judges and confused jurors. The preponderance standard is that which leads a jury to find that a contested fact (*B* is manufacturer of the pool) is more probable than not. Some courts have required that the jury have the element of belief in the truth of the fact. This, however, is too high a standard, for it would approach that of "clear and convincing proof."

A party faced with the burden of "clear and convincing" proof must show that the truth of the contention is "highly probable." In Chapter 10 we note that the grounds for involuntary commitment must be established by clear and convincing evidence.[112] The same standard is often applied in civil rights cases or when evidence can be easily fabricated. The Supreme Court of Virginia requires clear and convincing proof of causation in psychological injuries claims.[113]

It is fear of error that motivates the "beyond reasonable doubt" standard in criminal law.[114] This is the measure of persuasion by which the prosecution must convince the trier of all essential elements of criminal guilt. It is among the essentials of due process required at trial of a juvenile who has been charged with an offense that would constitute a crime if committed by an adult.[115] Unfortunately, judicial attempts to define "reasonable doubt" have not been enlightening.

For affirmative defenses in criminal law, both the burden of production and the burden of persuasion are commonly placed on the defendant. Insanity and self-defense fall into this category. In *Leland v. Oregon,*[116] the Supreme Court held that the defendant could be required to prove his insanity at the time of the alleged crime beyond a reasonable doubt. Nevertheless, outside these affirmative defenses, the burden of persuasion[117] may not be placed upon the defendant. Otherwise, it would violate the constitutional requirement that the prosecution bear the burden of proving guilt beyond a reasonable doubt.[118]

The burden of proof and its operation in tort cases is discussed in Chapter 7.

Judicial Reasoning

In addition to their function in court proceedings, judges play a central role in the development of the law. Judges are either appointed or elected. The Constitution provides for Supreme Court Justices to be nominated by the President and confirmed by the Senate. Their appointment is for life.

In a trial, the judge is the tribunal of law and the jury the tribunal of fact. The judge rules upon issues of law that arise in the course of the court proceedings. For example, the judge decides upon the admissibility of evidence and the qualification of experts. Depending upon the jurisdiction of the court or the election of the parties, the case may be tried solely by a judge, who then becomes the tribunal of both law and fact. In this instance, the judge must weigh the facts and apply the law accordingly. In the usual trial, the jury weighs the evidence, a function that entails, among other things, reviewing the credibility of the witnesses. Once both sides have presented their evidence, the judge may summarize the evidence and instruct the jury on the points of law pertinent to their deliberations. For example, if in a murder trial the accused pleads "not guilty by reason of insanity" the judge will inform the jury of the legal tests for insanity in that jurisdiction.

Much of the judicial process is designed to ensure that the issues at stake during the trial are well focused. The pleadings (today less rigorously regulated than formerly) define the points of law in dispute. Pretrial discovery and interrogatories are designed to ferret out the facts that can be agreed upon, so that what is in dispute can be more efficiently dealt with by the trial court. The court assumes control over these processes; pretrial motions may be necessary to resolve disputes on pleadings and discovery.

These processes not only fashion a case for trial but encourage the parties and their counsel toward compromise and settlement. The vast majority of claims never come to trial but are settled on the relative strengths of the case in the light of the law and the facts.[119]

The judicial institution is designed to insulate the judge from partisan politics, for the hallmark of judicial method is independence. Independence is encouraged not only by tenure and salary arrangements but by the adherence to precedent, which limits individual discretion. Within the discretion remaining, the judge is expected to reach reasoned conclusions, leaving a record which may be reviewed on appeal or examined by other judges or legal commentators.

Case Law and Precedent

In the previous section. we mentioned that judges proceed by reasoned elaboration, deferring to precedent as either binding or influential. A precedent is an earlier authoritative case that is applicable to the facts in the instant case. In a technical sense, it is the *ratio decidendi* (the reasoning that led to the decision) of a case that binds later courts subject to that case. In the course of rendering an opinion, a court may make other statements of law not essential to the decision in that case. Such statements are known as *obiter dicta*. They are not binding (although they may be influential). As a general rule, the decisions of courts higher in the judicial hierarchy dictate the decisions of courts lower in the hierarchy. Referring to Figure 2–2, the decision of the state supreme court will control the decision of any lower court if the facts in both cases are materially the same. If a material fact is different, the earlier decision may be "distinguished," i.e., a rationale turning on the different material fact may be presented for not applying it in the later case.

A noteworthy feature of modern decision-making is the willingness of judges not only to rely on precedents in a formalistic way but also to provide public policy reasons as to why the law should be enunciated in a particular form. For example, the Supreme Court allowed child abuse victims to testify via closed-circuit television despite a defendant's argument that his Sixth Amendment right to confrontation was abridged. The Court noted that the primary purpose of the confrontation clause is "to ensure the reliability of the evidence against a criminal defendant by subjecting it to vigorous testing in the context of an adversary proceeding." Justice O'Connor wrote that the fact-finding purpose of the clause could sometimes be served by hearsay evidence. By insisting on an absolute right to confront, hearsay would be inadmissible. Balancing the truth-inducing function of confronting witnesses against "societal interests in fact-finding," the Court held that the right to face-to-face confrontation was not absolute.[120]

Courts at the apex of the judicial hierarchy—the U.S. Supreme Court and state supreme courts—have the power to overrule prior inconsistent authorities. However, even in an era of judicial creativity, courts remain reluctant to overrule prior authorities. In the *Casey* case,[121] fidelity to precedent, shaped by the legitimacy of the judicial function, dissuaded the United States Supreme Court from overruling *Roe v. Wade*.[122] Citizens had relied upon that law, evolution in legal principle had left it intact, and its factual underpinnings were still valid. More was required than a doctrinal disposition to jettison *Roe v. Wade;* circumstances had not changed sufficiently in respect of the precedent to justify its renunciation.[123]

LEGAL ADVOCACY

Lawyers or attorneys are persons licensed to practice law in a state. They offer advice on legal matters and argue cases in court, where they are referred to as counsel. They will have graduated from a law school whose degree is recognized by the licensing state, and will subsequently have passed the bar examination of that state. The authorities of the bar also assure themselves of the character and reputation of candidates for admission.

The majority of graduates go into the private practice of law, but a significant number are employed by corporations or government. Although the profession does not formally recognize separate specialties, as in medicine, private practitioners often do specialize in such fields as criminal, family, tax, real property, and personal injury laws. Some firms have become highly specialized; for example, in Florida, medical malpractice claims are commonly handled by specialist firms. Mental health clinicians are likely to interact with lawyers whose private practice encompasses criminal, family, juvenile, and tort law. State agencies with authority over family or mental health will include numbers of lawyers. Trial lawyers from the District Attorney's or Public Defender's office will often be involved in prosecutions in which mental health clinicians have a central role.

A lawyer, when consulted by a client, will assess the legal dimensions of the claim. The advisability of pursuing the claim will be decided on its legal merits, its estimated eventual worth, and its economic and human costs. Many negligence claims will not be brought. In a recent Harvard study carried out in New York State it was estimated that sixteen times as many patients suffered an injury from negligence as received compensation from the tort system.[124] The lawyer will often negotiate a contingency fee, which, in malpractice claims, will usually be a quarter to a third of the damages recovered. In other cases, a client may agree to recompense his lawyer on an hourly basis.

Often, legal research is necessary. The attorney will draw together pertinent cases, statutes, and regulations. The traditional method of presenting a case has been by oral argument. In appellate courts the questions are primarily legal, and oral argument has largely been replaced by written arguments called legal briefs. A brief comprises an argument on the basis of the prevailing law. It may contain medical, psychosocial, or sociological material that informs the court about the social policy implication of any legal decision.[125]

A mental health professional may be asked by an attorney to submit an affidavit, a document filed in court wherein the *affiant* expert attests to a fact or facts relevant to a case (e.g., the psychopathology of sexually abused children). Affidavits may require substantiation by testimony in court. If affidavits are taken in evidence, they represent sworn testimony and carry a penalty if consciously misleading.

The attorney has a primary obligation to represent his client. Each side will strive to present the most convincing case based on the applicable law. Presentation necessarily involves an attack on the other side's case by introducing contrary evidence or by cross-examination to impugn the evidence or the credibility of the witnesses for the other side. Scientific evidence will be attacked in this way. Scientists and clinicians will find that their evidence is subjected to a scrutiny that may appear unfair, but which should be understood as part of the adversarial role that attorneys assume when vigorously representing their clients. Although tension is thereby created, lawyers have much in common with other professionals who deal with the frailties of individuals and the imperfections of human institutions. John Updike has said of lawyers: "They, of course, like social workers and clergymen, dwell in that chiaroscuro where our incorrigible selves intertwine with society's fumbling discipline."[126]

CHAPTER 3

THE RIGHTS OF CHILDREN

INTRODUCTION

This chapter discusses the special provisions for children in American law and the way in which contemporary social changes are influencing legal doctrine regarding the authority of children to control their own lives. The sexual revolution, the dangers of illicit drugs, and the recognition of child abuse are but a few of the social pressures that have placed children's rights at the center of the legal stage. In order to reach just decisions in this field, the courts must balance two contending rights. On the one hand is the right of people to control their private lives without unwarranted interference, along with the appreciation that some minors have already begun to work, conduct their own financial and social affairs, and look after their own health. On the other hand, the courts must weigh the constitutional privacy rights of the family, the desirability of upholding the integrity of family life, and the relative inexperience of minors.

The next section of this chapter defines infancy, childhood, minority, emancipation, and the common law rights of minors. The one following outlines the ways in which minors' rights have evolved in a changing society. The way judges reason from the Constitution in arriving at their decisions regarding minors' rights is then summarized. How children's rights expand when the state enacts legislation and creates agencies that protect children is described in the same section. A final section details the particular areas, both public and private, where rights have been defined in accordance with constitutional requirements and legislative demands. Rights are subject to philosophical debate.[1]

LEGAL DEFINITIONS OF INFANCY AND CHILDHOOD

In American law the terms "infant" and "child" have two distinct meanings. The latter refers to parentage (the child as a descendant, issue, or offspring of another person); the former refers to a person who has yet to reach maturity. An infant or child is defined as a minor, a person who has not attained majority and whose majority does

39

not follow from his mental or physical attributes. Like minority, majority is a legal status, a condition specified by law, not a fixed right vested in the individual.

At common law, a minor assumed majority on the day preceding the twenty-first anniversary of birth. Today, the age of majority is a matter for legislative regulation by individual states. Most states have adopted eighteen years, a trend reflected in Article I of the United Nations' proposed Draft Convention on Rights of the Child.

The Age of Legal Competence, the Age of Consent, and the Concept of Emancipation

Upon reaching majority, individuals are legally permitted to enter into binding contracts. In most states the age of majority is eighteen for contractual purposes, marriage, and military service. Until such time, minors remain under the age of legal competence. The age of consent refers to the age when the person, though still a minor by statute, can legally contract marriage or consent to sexual intercourse. Drivers' licenses may be issued at age sixteen, however, and drinking is prohibited until twenty-one.

The common law doctrine of emancipation severs the mutual rights and obligations of the parent–child relationship. The parents' legal right to control their children's earnings and services is thereby terminated, as is their obligation to provide social and financial support. Most emancipated minors have been explicitly or implicitly conceded independence by their parents, so the matter is not at issue. However, if emancipation is legally disputed, its judicial determination is customarily based upon commonsense criteria: the express agreement of the parties; marriage; military service; independent living or employment; independent payment of debts; and ownership of valuable property, such as a motor vehicle. The burden of proof is upon the party who wishes to establish emancipation. Common law emancipation does not affect the youth's legal rights as determined by his or her status as a minor. For example, emancipation does not end the youth's right to disaffirm contracts; nor does it grant permission to drink or vote, convey full responsibility for criminal offenses, or affect any other of his or her legal rights as a minor.

Examples of the Common Law Rights of Minors

In America, common law regarding children's rights recognizes that "the object of the law is to secure (minors) from damaging themselves or their property by their own improvident acts or prevent them from being imposed on by the fraud of others."[2] Children have limited freedom under the law because, as John Stuart Mill said, in contrast to adults, they need to be protected against their own actions, while society, in addition, needs to be protected from their "untutored" behavior. The common law concept of protecting minors from society, society from minors, and minors from themselves indicates that the legal rights of minors will differ from those of adults in several areas:

1. *Property.* Under common law, a minor is capable of acquiring property, but not of managing it. Common law places a minor's property rights in the hands of a guardian until he reaches majority. Although the guardian may manage the use of the property in the minor's estate, he may not diminish its value. Furthermore, the minor has no legal capacity to contract away his property rights. Hence, those who negotiate concerning property owned by minors must exercise care that they deal with the person authorized to act for the minor and that the transaction has no adverse effect on the minor's estate.

Recognizing the vulnerability of children, the common law also protects a minor's property rights in his or her dealings with the public. For example, common law allows one person to acquire title to real property from another through adverse possession. Adverse possession is the open, actual, and intentional possession and use of the property for a statutory period of time by a person other than the person holding legal title. However, when a minor's title is challenged by a person asserting adverse possession, the usual statute of limitations requirement is waived. Either the statute of limitations will not begin to run until the minor reaches majority, or the minor will be allowed a period after majority to contest the adverse possession begun in his infancy.

Any discussion of minors' inheritance rights is beyond the scope of this chapter, except to say that, under the Uniform Parentage Act (1979), if an illegitimate child establishes paternity or maternity, he or she is accorded the same inheritance and support rights as a legitimate child.

2. *Contracts.* Although a minor has no capacity to contract at common law, the state legislature may regulate conditions under which he or she can do so. Contracts entered into by minors are not necessarily void; but they are voidable if the minor elects to disavow them. The minor must give back any goods transferred under the voided contract. Even if the goods are lost or depreciated, the minor still has the right to disavow the contract; however, some courts require the minor to repay any value received under the contract. A child is usually not liable for tortious breach of contract. Certain exceptions to the contractual exemption were recognized at common law, as when minors contract for the purchase of "necessaries" (such items as food, clothing, shelter, medical aid, or minimal education). In *Cidis v. White,*[3] a case with a modern ring about it, the court determined that since contact lenses were a necessary the minor defendant was liable for their reasonable value.

3. *Torts.* A minor may bring a tort action or be liable for a tort to the same degree as an adult; maturity is merely one element in the determination of liability. If the minor is below a specified age (often set at seven years), he or she may be immune from liability. Even when no formal immunity is provided, very young children are regarded as incapable of negligence.[4] The temporal limitations on the lodging of a suit are usually suspended ("tolled") until the child reaches majority.

4. *Crimes.* The presumption is that children are incapable of committing crimes. However, children with sufficient intelligence and moral perception both to distinguish between right and wrong and to comprehend the legal consequences of their acts are subject to criminal law and may be prosecuted under it, unless exempted by statute. On the other hand, the desirability of reclamation and reform usually miti-

gates the punishment appropriate for adults. However, differential treatment for minors is not required if rehabilitation is deemed unlikely. In such cases, the youth may be waived to adult court and tried there (see Chapter 9).

5. *General.* A minor may sue or be sued, but the action must be by or through a "next friend" or guardian *ad litem* (guardian for the purpose of litigation). The function of the guardian *ad litem* is to act on behalf of the minor as would a concerned parent. The guardian may legally represent the minor[5] or appoint legal counsel.[6] Upon institution of litigation, the minor becomes a ward of the court. The court therefore has a duty to protect the minor's interests even if he or she is represented (provided that the rights of any parties to the litigation are not prejudiced thereby). For instance, if minors' attorneys err while representing them, judges must intervene on the children's behalf, provided they do not favor the minors to the disadvantage of the adults. The guardian *ad litem* concept is not without critics; Landsman and Minow distrust the capacity of the adult representatives of children to represent either children's wishes or their best interests.[7]

THE HISTORICAL EVOLUTION OF CHILDREN'S RIGHTS

Scholars divide the historical evolution of children's rights in American law into four distinct periods: before the nineteenth century; 1800–1900; 1900–1967; and 1967 to the present.[8] During the first era, 1600–1800, children were regarded as the property of their parents. This doctrine derived from English common law and reflected the functioning of the family as an agrarian work unit. Thus parents were entitled to the services of their children until they reached majority. If parents were unable to provide for them, children were in effect indentured into the service of other masters.[9] Tender attitudes toward children, however, may be observed as early as the sixteenth century.[10]

Between 1800 and 1900, with increasing industrialization and the growth of urban poverty, the plight of neglected, homeless, and abandoned children influenced legislators to enact benevolent laws, while rehabilitative institutions were established by concerned citizens. In Western societies, children came to be "valued less for their economic contributions than as objects of love and affection."[11] Family courts were established in most states, and the doctrine of *parens patriae* reached its apogee. The legal system first acknowledged "the best interests of the child" in *Chapsky v. Wood.*[12]

Under the doctrine of *parens patriae*, the state has a duty to protect those of its citizens who have a legal disability. Thus, the state is obligated to ensure that every child within its jurisdiction receives proper care, and it will assume parental authority over a minor deprived of parental care, control, and oversight. In *Prince v. Commonwealth of Massachusetts*,[13] the Court stated that "it is in the interest of youth itself, and of the whole community, that children be both safeguarded from abuses and given opportunities for growth into free and independent well-developed men and citizens." But the power of the state is not unlimited and arbitrary; it may be exercised only when the child does not receive due parental care and protection. If the child is abused or exploited, he may be protected by the state, under its police power, in order to safe-guard the health, safety, morals, and general welfare of the public at large. This broad police power enables the state to protect children from abuse or exploitation, no mat-ter what the source. Consequently, the state's duty as *parens patriae* gives it the right to regulate the equity court's jurisdiction over matters affecting minors' rights and welfare; whereas the state's police power empowers the state to protect its children as the youngest members of the general population.

Between 1900 and 1967 family courts eschewed formal adversarial hearings. In-stead, they leaned heavily upon judicial discretion in dealing with orphaned, aban-doned, abused, neglected, wayward, or delinquent children. However, by the 1960s many observers had begun to lose faith in the effectiveness of rehabilitative programs for juvenile delinquents and status offenders, and the family court came under attack. The juvenile court's procedural processes were criticized as arbitrary, unfair, and overdiscretionary. At the same time, communities were outraged by the growth of ju-venile crime thought to have arisen from social-demographic changes beyond the in-fluence of private and public institutions.[14] These two trends have ushered in the contemporary legalistic era. As a result, the state's role as *parens patriae* in civil and criminal proceedings has been reasserted (see Chapter 9).

The year 1967 marked the beginning of the contemporary era—an era during which rights rather than protections have become the legal touchstone.[15] Two Supreme Court cases, *Kent v. United States*[16] and *In re Gault*,[17] acknowledged that the Bill of Rights and due process provision of the Fourteenth Amendment applied to minors as well as adults. In reaching its decisions, the Court balanced (1) the state's paternal duty to pro-tect minors against (2) the rights of minors to individual self-determination and (3) the family's privacy interest in exerting parental authority. On the one hand, the state should acknowledge the individual right of minors to self-determination; on the other hand, as *parens patriae*, the state must protect minors against delinquency and mal-treatment, a protection extended on the basis that the consent of minors is irrelevant and immaterial because they are by law incapable of determining what is in their best interest.

In subsequent cases, the Supreme Court has extended to children legal rights pre-viously thought reserved for adults. In *In re Winship*,[18] the Court held that the state should prove its case beyond a reasonable doubt in juvenile delinquency adjudica-tions concerning criminal conduct. In subsequent holdings, the operation of correc-tional institutions for juvenile delinquents has come under scrutiny in accordance with the Eighth Amendment's proscription of cruel and unusual punishment.[19] A number of juvenile offender statutes have been attacked on the grounds that they were un-constitutionally vague.[20]

In summary, contemporary American law has established a triad of children's rights whereby the interests of child, parent, and state are weighed in order to achieve the best public policy solution. In particular cases, the courts will base their decisions on case law reflecting the current view of the proper balance in the triad. A child may be competent in some spheres of human activity but not in others. For the purposes of the law, minors may be regarded as "adults" or "children." The patchwork thus created has been criticized as not reflecting competence but based rather on social choices about many issues.[21] However, competence has been the fulcrum of legal development and its psychological formulations deserve brief exploration.

RECOGNITION OF CHILDREN'S RIGHTS
Maturation of the Child

Legal capacity assumes the capacity to engage in rational thought and to assume responsibilities. The rules of law reflect changes in social attitudes and scientific evidence about the actual maturation of the child.[22]

Judicial Challenge

In balancing interests within the triad of children's rights, it is often important to determine whether the minor is mature. Minors pronounced mature are accorded greater rights than other minors. However, the idea of maturity has changed markedly.

As society recognizes minors' capacity for self-determination, the courts are placed in a dilemma. The protection of minors may be a basic tenet of American common law, but if minors are no less responsible for their actions than adults, it would follow that they must be prosecuted and punished like adults. Furthermore, laws that grant minors rights equivalent to those of adults erode both parental authority and the state's legitimate protective interest. Thus, a controversy continues as to whether a minor should be subject to the same ultimate punishment as that sanctioned for adults.[23] While it prohibited the execution of persons under sixteen years of age,[24] the Supreme Court has recognized the constitutionality of imposing a death sentence on individuals who commit crimes at that age.[25]

Little wonder that confusion has arisen in the concept of the "mature minor"—one who, though not fully emancipated, is potentially competent to make certain decisions. Although it is established that constitutional rights have been extended to minors, no clear criteria have been articulated concerning how to determine when a particular unemancipated youth is competent to make decisions concerning his or her own life.[26] In recent abortion cases, the Supreme Court has held that the maturity of a minor should be determined case by case.[27] The same *ad hoc* procedure has been criticized as arbitrary and standardless, particularly when minors are sentenced to capital punishment.[28] The concept of constitutional rights for minors begs questions about the current status of the other two elements of the triad of children's rights—the support of family integrity and the protection of minors. In effect, the expansion of children's constitutional rights undermines both parental authority and state paternalism.

Many clamor for increased state involvement. As protectors of minors, the states must enforce the laws safeguarding a growing number of children's rights against a background of meager public resources. Failures of state courts and agencies to deal with reported cases of child abuse and juvenile crime are common journalistic fare.[29]

Children's Rights in Case Law

THE CONSTITUTIONAL TECHNIQUE OF WEIGHING VALUES

The recognition of minors' rights to self-determination appears to have engendered inconsistencies in the treatment of children under the law. Horowitz and Davidson have noted such inconsistencies in Supreme Court rulings concerning the following matters:[30] minors' rights to due process before potential confinement,[31] *Miranda* rights,[32] and contraceptive and abortion rights.[33] In one case, the holding might appear to grant minors rights equal to those of adults, and in another to deny them the same rights.

In defense of the Supreme Court's rulings, an assertion of minors' rights in one case does not necessarily deny the relevance of parental authority or the state protection in subsequent cases. To the contrary, parental authority and state protection will be reviewed and interpreted in the light of the most recent holdings regarding the third element of the triad, the rights of minors. In accordance with the accretions of case law, vectors within the triad change, though slowly. Apparent inconsistencies result when one element of the triad prevails at the expense of the other two.

Constitutional jurisprudence provides the framework for an analysis of these cases. In a particular case, the Court will decide which vector prevails by ascertaining the state's objective in interfering in the private life of the individual or family. Is the right intruded upon fundamental (i.e., protected by the constitution)? If so, is the state's objective in intervening *compelling* or merely *legitimate? If the right infringed upon is found to be fundamental, the state must have a compelling interest for intervening. If the interest is compelling, the means chosen by the state for intervening in the individual's life must be the least intrusive possible.* This mode of analysis, generally called *strict scrutiny,* when applied by the Supreme Court is so exacting that it has been regarded as "strict" in theory but "fatal" in fact.[34]

If the individual's right is deemed not to be fundamental, the state must still have a legitimate or rational (though not necessarily compelling) objective for intruding. *The state's intrusion must then be rationally related to the legitimate objective.* In recent years a third level of scrutiny has evolved whereby state intrusions (e.g., discrimination on the basis of gender) are scrutinized by an intermediate standard less demanding than "compelling interest" but more stringent than "rational basis."

EXAMPLES OF THE RATIONALE USED IN "CHILDREN'S RIGHTS" HOLDINGS

The Supreme Court's rulings may appear inconsistent when two apparently similar statutes generate opposite holdings, one being held constitutional and the other unconstitutional. On closer examination, however, it can be seen that the Court's decisions have either reinforced or further elaborated prior rulings.

Take, for example, *In re Gault* and *Parham v. J.R.* (see note 31 above). The first case supports the need for juveniles to have an adversary hearing before incarceration; the second case does not. In *Gault,* a juvenile court, without adversarial hearing, had incarcerated a fifteen-year-old boy for six years after he had allegedly made an obscene telephone call. The state was held to have infringed upon the juvenile's fundamental liberty interest when it placed him in a detention home on criminal charges. The Court found that, under the Constitution, the liberty interest of a minor demanded the same protection as that of an adult. Thus, the Court applied strict scrutiny in determining that the procedures of the state's Juvenile Court did not meet the due process requirements of the Fourteenth Amendment.

Whereas *Gault* was a criminal proceeding requiring no parental consent, *Parham* concerned juveniles admitted to a state mental institution upon the request of their parents or guardians. In *Parham,* the foster parents had initiated the admission of their foster son to the mental institution following a medical determination that his mental condition warranted admission to the hospital. (J.R. had been removed from his natural parents at the age of three and had been placed in seven different foster homes.) It was common ground that the juvenile enjoyed due process rights under the Fourteenth Amendment; however, in contrast to *Gault,* the juvenile's admission was voluntary, in the sense that the boy's foster parents sought out and consented to the child's treatment. Accordingly, in *Parham,* the issue was to determine whether hospitalization, consented to by parents or those *in loco parentis,* was equivalent to incarceration, as in *Gault.* The Court held that to regard hospitalization as incarceration would ignore the parental role; in most circumstances, parents can be trusted to act in the interests of their children. Provided there was some check against abuse, hospitalization could be treated as consensual. The Court determined that the medical evaluation conducted prior to admission was an efficient check against abuse; to require a full hearing might both undermine the state's interest in the proper care of mentally ill minors and interfere with family privacy. The dynamics of the triad are quite different in the two cases. The presumption, in *Parham,* that parents make decisions in the best interests of their children was not relevant to *Gault.* That is not to say that the presumption or the impact of hospitalization relied upon and characterized by the *Parham* court is well founded (see Chapter 10).

Although the Supreme Court has clearly enunciated that constitutional rights apply equally to adults and children, the parental role complicates the application of those rights. The firm rule of full constitutional rights was applied in *Fare v. Michael C.*[35] In this case, a juvenile being questioned by police requested but was denied access to his probation officer. The court held that the minor's request to consult his probation officer was not necessarily an invocation of his Fifth Amendment rights under *Miranda,* because a request for someone whom the accused merely trusts is not tantamount to asking for a lawyer. On the other hand, had the juvenile asked for a lawyer, the police would have been constitutionally obliged to cease questioning him. Nothing in this case diminishes the firm rule: The minority of an accused person does not of itself disentitle him to *Miranda* protections.

Fare also addresses the question of when a person entitled to *Miranda* protections may voluntarily waive them. In the case of a juvenile, it was held, the determining factors are the juvenile's age and experience combined with the care with which interrogating officers have ensured that the juvenile understood the implications of waiving his or her rights. In one case, a request for a parent was held equivalent to a request for legal counsel;[36] however, other courts have reached opposite conclusions.[37]

Contrary to some opinion, Supreme Court holdings on minors' contraceptive and abortion rights have not been inconsistent. They too exemplify the firm rule, although the debate in these cases is indicative of the dilemma in which the Court finds itself when it attempts to legislate morality.[38]

In *Planned Parenthood of Southeastern Pennsylvania v. Casey,*[39] the Supreme Court drew on the contraception decisions in *Griswold v. Connecticut, Eisenstadt v. Baird,* and *Carey v. Population Services International*[40] to support the underlying rationale in *Roe v. Wade* and the conclusion that a Pennsylvania abortion statute was in the main constitutional. The statute, which imposed informed consent requirements, a twenty-four hour waiting period, and a reporting and record-keeping provision, was in respect of those provisions consistent with the law as reinterpreted stemming from *Roe.* In other words, statutory provisions did not impose an undue burden on the right of unemancipated women under the age of eighteen to obtain an abortion. The parental consent requirement allowed the minor to apply to a court in order to waive parental consent (judicial bypass) upon a determination that she was mature enough to give informed consent and had in fact given such consent, or that an abortion would be in her best interests. In contrast, a provision requiring spousal consent was struck down. The prevalence of spousal abuse, the changing understanding of the family, and the greater impact of regulation on the liberty of the mother compared with that of the father led the court to reject the spousal consent provision, for it posed an undue burden on the rights of the woman.

SUMMARY

The Supreme Court has consistently upheld the rights of minors to self-determination with regard to procreation. These and other "children's cases" actually fall within traditional categories the Court is called upon to interpret: Fourteenth Amendment rights, First Amendment rights, Equal Protection, protection under the Eighth Amendment, and statutory interpretation. Furthermore, some cases involve issues (such as abortion and the death penalty) that have long plagued the Court, regardless of the client group.[41]

The Constitution does not define the concept of "mature minor." Maturity is merely one factor to be weighed when the Court must balance the vectors within the triad of children's rights. *The child enjoys full constitutional rights except insofar as his or her autonomy is limited by the legitimate interests of the family and the protective obligations of the state.*

THE IMPLICATION OF RIGHTS FROM STATUTES

Our age has been described as one of statutes.[42] To a much greater extent than was formerly the case, the law derives from the statutes of Congress and state legislatures. Many statutes accord rights to children and regulate their treatment. Such statutes may provide for intervention by public officials or rely upon the enforcement machinery of the criminal law, but sometimes such enforcement proves feckless. In those circumstances, avenues to bring an action for damages may be available for a child injured by lack of compliance with a statute.

The child may be able to sue in three situations:

1. He may sue under the Civil Rights Act §1983.[43] To do so he must point to his deprivation, by a person acting on behalf of a state, of a right secured by the Constitution or laws of the United States:

> Every person who, under color of any statute, ordinance, regulation, custom, or usage, of any State or Territory or the District of Columbia, subjects, or causes to be subjected, any citizen of the United States or any other person within the jurisdiction thereof to the deprivation of any rights, privileges or immunities secured by the Constitution and laws, shall be liable to the party injured in an action at law, suit in equity, or other proper proceeding for redress.

2. He may sue on constitutional grounds if a federal official or agency deprives him of a constitutional right. Section 1983 is not available because no "state" official or agency has acted.
3. He may sue if a state or federal statute implies a cause of action in favor of a child.

Exemplifying the first category is the recent case of *Wilder v. Virginia Hospital Association*[44] discussed below (under "Access to Health Care"). In *Wilder,* the United States Supreme Court found that provisions under the Medicaid legislation mandating reasonable access to facilities of adequate quality were enforceable in a private right of action against the state. Building on *Wilder,* the plaintiff foster children in *Suter v. Artist M* argued that private rights may be fashioned from the Adoption Assistance and Child Welfare Act of 1980, which was enacted by Congress as an amendment to the Social Security Act.[45] This Act, aimed at deemphasizing foster care and encouraging permanent placement,[46] provided for the systematic monitoring of foster home children. The legislation required that states must make "reasonable efforts" to obviate the removal of children from their homes or to enable those who have been removed to be reunified with their families.[47] The Supreme Court,[48] upholding an appeal from the Seventh Circuit Court of Appeals,[49] found that no private right of action could be fashioned from the terms of the legislation. In contrast to *Wilder,* the requirement of "reasonable efforts" was designed to impose only a generalized duty on the state to be enforced by the Secretary of Health and Human Services, not a specific duty that could be the subject of a private right of action.

Will other provisions of this legislation or different child welfare legislation be interpreted to bestow private rights of action? The answer will turn on whether the provisions clearly prescribe an operational duty and need a private right to make them effective. The law after these two cases is unclear. It is likely that considerable litigation will ensue in an attempt to define the scope of protection derived from similarly worded statutes. Congress may act to bestow an express right of action, a course taken by the House of Representatives in reaction to the *Suter* case.[50]

State child welfare legislation may also be a source of children's rights, as in the third item in the list above. State legislation prescribes duties, obligations, and standards intended to promote the welfare of minors. The enforcement of these provisions is often left to the state's child welfare department or to its attorney general (through criminal law proceedings). The courts appear increasingly willing to allow minors who have been injured by persons or state agencies that *owe obligations* under the legislation to bring an action in tort for the statutory breach. Such a procedure is commonly called an "implied right of action." Actions based on *implied rights* are rooted in the theory that, in enacting the legislation, the legislature intended to bestow upon the minor the right to bring a civil action against the state, in addition to any other enforcement mechanism found in the legislation. In *Burnette v. Wahl,*[51] a number of children sued their mothers for emotional and psychological injury as a consequence of abandonment. The Oregon legislature had previously enacted a criminal penalty for intentional abandonment of a child under fifteen years of age. The majority of the state's Supreme Court, for reasons having to do with the incompatibility of tort actions in the mother–child relationship, found that no private right to sue had been established. A broader interpretation of such statutes would support a private right to sue if such a right furthered the purpose of the legislation. However, the *Burnette* court realistically recognized the action as a creature of judicial policy-making and eschewed the "implied right" rationale. The *Burnette* court's approach does not require a dubious assumption of legislative intent.

Federal statutes may also give rise to a private right of action, but because there is no federal common law, that right is directly a creation of Congress. Accordingly, the question of whether a right may be implied turns entirely on the question of whether Congress intended to provide such a private right of action. The court is unable to take the forthright approach of the *Burnette* court. In respect of federal statutes, the courts presume that the full panoply of remedies are available unless otherwise indicated. But this determination is most uncertain and has excited criticism of the Supreme Court. In *Franklin v. Gwinnett County Public Schools,*[52] the Supreme Court found that the plaintiff, a high school student who had been subjected to sexual harassment by a teacher contrary to Title IX,[53] had a good cause of action against the school district.

SPECIFIC LEGAL RIGHTS OF CHILDREN
Parental Financial Support

Regardless of the sex or legitimacy of the child, parents are obligated to support their children until they are eighteen years of age (twenty-one in some states). Parental obligations are terminated when the child is emancipated or when parental rights have been legally severed. Parental obligations may continue beyond the age of majority if so stipulated in the terms of a legal separation between parents. (See Chapter 4.)

Public Support

Binding themselves to comply with federal regulations, all states accept federal matching funds in order to provide income support to poor families (AFDC). In 1981, 11.1 million individuals received AFDC benefits. Eligibility criteria are complex, but essentially refer to needy children who have been deprived of adequate parental support. Since eligibility requirements vary from state to state, different standards determine what constitutes bona fide income and acceptable expenses. Moss found that an Alaskan family of three received a combined annual support of $10,244, whereas the same family in Mississippi would receive $3,540.[54]

Medicaid payments are tied to the needs and resources of the state's AFDC. If children are disabled and qualify for the Supplemental Security Income (SSI) Program and its benefits, they automatically qualify for Medicaid. The criteria for a child to qualify for SSI are significantly different from (and more restrictive than) those required for an adult. Thus, although the mechanism is there to provide impoverished minors with needed assistance, onerous eligibility requirements often exclude the very children the program is designed to help.[55]

Access to Health Care

Poverty severely curtails access to health care.[56] As powerless persons within a powerless segment of society, poor children are especially susceptible.[57]

Laws Against Exploitation

CHILD LABOR

Since the eighteenth century, state and federal governments have enacted laws that regulate child labor. In general, children under sixteen years of age may not be employed in hazardous work or in circumstances that interfere with their schooling. In most states, employers must obtain a work permit to employ youths between fourteen and eighteen years of age, and the hours of employment are restricted. Currently, there is a struggle between employers (e.g., fast food purveyors) who want to liberalize these somewhat outdated laws, and labor unions who fear that adult workers will be displaced.

CHILD ABUSE

In *DeShaney v. Winnebago County Department of Social Services,*[58] the Supreme Court ruled that, although children have no substantive right to due process protection from abuses at the hands of private actors, under limited circumstances where the state acts to exercise sufficient control over children, it and officers acting on its behalf have an obligation to protect children from such abuse. Any enforcement of the state's interest, however, must fully account for parents' constitutional rights. It should be pointed out that Justice Blackmun's dissent in *DeShaney* faulted the *sang-froid* of the majority in regard to its strict interpretation of the law; children were thereby denied the affirmative right to government aid to protect them against private violence at the hands of an abusive parent.[59] Other commentators have since urged the courts to interpret and forge the rules of law more sympathetically, arguing that compassion should empower jurists with an appreciation of the human situations affected by the law.[60] Numbers of cases have established liability for removal of children.[61] Furthermore, the *DeShaney* decision, which required the state to assume responsibility over the child, may suggest to social workers that the safer legal course is to leave an endangered child in the home rather than remove him. However, it is unlikely that such arguments will be accepted by the majority of the present Supreme Court.

In *Baltimore City Department of Social Services v. Bouknight*,[62] the Supreme Court found that an order for a mother to present her child for the evaluation of suspected child abuse did not violate her Fifth Amendment rights regarding self-incrimination, since she was custodian of the child pursuant to a court order. In the absence of parental rights and in the presence of a welfare system that exercises dominion over children, a constitutional right will arise. Thus, in *LaShawn A. v. Dixon*,[63] the Court found that the statutes and policies which form the child welfare system may create constitutionally protected liberty and property interests. Accordingly, the Court held that the District of Columbia must exercise professional judgment in its operation of the child welfare system in order adequately to protect the interests of children in its custody.

SEXUAL EXPLOITATION

During the past fifteen years, legislators have become aware of a thriving international traffic in pornography involving children. Child pornography ("kiddie porn") is sold commercially or distributed informally among groups of pedophiles. Sometimes the children themselves are passed around. Earlier laws concerning the distribution of obscene materials failed to deal with those who produced the films. In 1978 the Protection of Children Against Sexual Exploitation Act (1977)[64] was signed into law. This law provides criminal sanctions against those who produce films or photographic materials which depict explicit sexual activity among minors. Parents or guardians can also be prosecuted if they allow their charges to be exploited in this manner.

The Anti-Child Pornography Act of 1990[65] amends the 1977–78 federal child pornography law. To knowingly view or possess materials depicting sexually explicit conduct involving minors is now a federal offense punishable by up to ten years' imprisonment. Thus, the entire distribution chain for child pornography has been criminalized, from producer to distributor to ultimate viewer. In *New York v. Ferber*,[66] the Court upheld state legislation prohibiting the distribution of material depicting sexual performances by persons under sixteen years of age, finding that child pornography is not entitled to First Amendment protection. In *Osborne v. Ohio*,[67] the Supreme

Court upheld a statute making private possession of child pornography a criminal offense, despite Osborne's claim that the law infringed on his First Amendment rights.

Some defendants have claimed that they were mistaken about the minor's age. This defense has been disallowed when the pornographer intended to conduct a sexual performance.[68] Although mistake as to the minor's age does not constitute a defense of constitutional dimensions,[69] the relative significance of the accused's guilty or innocent intent (*mens rea*) and mistake of fact has generally been left to the discretion of the state.[70] Nevertheless, the severity of potential sentence under federal law (ten years' imprisonment and a fine of $100,000)[71] may indicate that the *mens rea* of the defendant should be taken into account in order adequately to protect his or her First Amendment rights.[72]

PROSTITUTION

Many states have laws that proscribe child prostitution and specify penalties for those who promote the prostitution of minors of either sex.[73] As with the prosecution of child pornographers, the prosecution of pimps and panderers is problematic. Pornography and prostitution are entangled in a common sequence of events: Having run away from home in order to avoid incest or abuse, the juvenile is picked up by a pimp or pedophile who procures the child for prostitution or pornography. The child may become so dependent on, or afraid of, the panderer that he or she will decline to testify against him.

The Rights of Adolescents

In most respects, minors enjoy the constitutional protections afforded to adults. In certain matters, however, the state has a rational and reasonable basis to withhold from minors the rights and privileges it accords to adults.

MARRIAGE

Eighteen years is the minimum age at which people can marry without parental consent, except in Mississippi (twenty-one), Nebraska, and Wyoming (both nineteen). The minimum age with parental consent varies from fourteen to sixteen years. In some states, a court may approve the marriage of a pregnant minor without parental consent.

DRIVING

The usual minimum age for obtaining a driver's license is sixteen. Many states give restricted licenses to minors as young as fourteen years if they can show special need (to go to school, for example) or if they are employed on the family farm.[74] Unless the minor is emancipated, parents may be liable for their minor child's negligent driving.

CURFEWS AND THE FREEDOM OF MOVEMENT AND ASSEMBLY

Curfew laws are usually local ordinances that bar minors from public places during specified hours. They may, for example, bar any minor unaccompanied by a responsible adult from being on the street or in a public place after a certain time in the evening. The constitutionality of these laws is problematical. Some courts have struck down curfews, while others have found that they pass constitutional muster.

Curfew laws must be precise about the class of minors affected and the hours of the curfew. In *Naprstek v. Norwich,*[75] the court found a curfew statute "void for vagueness" because it failed to designate the hour at which the curfew should end. Even well-drawn' statutes will be held unconstitutional if their terms are so broad that they affect people other than those they aim to protect or conceive to be the cause of specified mischief. In *Waters v. Barry,*[76] a Washington, D.C., curfew was designed to combat drug-dealing and related crime. Despite its imperative purpose, the statute was not upheld because, in the terms in which it was written, it would have trampled on First Amendment and equal protection rights. General curfew laws involving minors appear to suffer from a fundamental constitutional infirmity.

As shopping centers have become meeting places for youth, some proprietors have attempted to discourage gatherings that disrupt commerce. Since shopping centers are private areas, proprietors do not face the array of constitutional constraints that are invoked when local governments seek to regulate public places.[77] However, minors have the right to sue in tort if proprietors should overzealously eject or confine them against their will.

Schoepflin defines the central issue as the individual's right of access to a public area versus the private property rights of the shopping center owner.[78] Several earlier cases found shopping centers to be equivalent to business districts, hence public places, to which right of access was protected by the Constitution.[79] However, in *Hudgens v. NLRB,*[80] the Supreme Court ruled that a shopping center is not the functional equivalent of a municipality and that an individual could not be protected from restriction by a private entity.[81] The Constitution protects freedom of expression from infringement by the government, not private actors.

Opinion is split as to whether the state should be able to protect public assembly within shopping centers. State Supreme Courts in California, Massachusetts, and Washington have held that their constitutions protect such activities. On the other hand, Oregon, Connecticut, Michigan, New York, North Carolina, Pennsylvania, and Wisconsin have held that their constitutions do not protect expressive rights on private property. In *Pruneyard Shopping Center v. Robins,*[82] the U.S. Supreme Court upheld a California constitutional provision that allowed students to distribute pamphlets in the concourses of malls. The Court ruled that minors could reasonably exercise free speech in a privately owned shopping center provided that doing so did not usurp the mall owner's property or violate his First Amendment rights.

Some statutes and local ordinances proscribe the admission of minors to pool halls, dance halls, bowling alleys, or videogame arcades. These regulations aim to reduce delinquency and truancy or to prevent psychological impairment. Activity in these places does not implicate central First Amendment values but only the social right of association. Any restriction, therefore, must merely be rationally related to a legiti- mate governmental end. Such regulations have usually been challenged on the basis that they represent an unreasonable restriction of commercial activity. In *Dallas v. Stanglin*,[83] the Supreme Court found that a city ordinance restricting minors between fourteen and eighteen years old from admission to dance halls was reasonable in light of the city's interest in protecting young minors from the corrupting influence of older minors or adults. In contrast, in *Aladdin's Castle v. City of Mesquite*,[84] a videogame arcade prevailed on the basis that the local ordinance's age restriction was not ratio- nally related to its stated purpose of preventing truancy and the use of narcotics.

ALCOHOL AND TOBACCO

The sale of alcohol and tobacco to minors is forbidden in all states, and the posses- sion of alcohol is a delinquent offense in some. After a trend toward lowering the drinking age, all states have recently elevated it to twenty-one in an attempt to curb drunken driving. The elevation of the drinking age was encouraged when federal law reduced federal funding for surface transportation unless the state's drinking age were twenty-one years,[85] a step recommended by President Reagan's Commission on Drunken Driving (1984).

ACCESS TO PORNOGRAPHY

State child pornography statutes are potentially at odds over First Amendment rights. If the purpose of a statute is to control what citizens read, it is objectionable under the First Amendment. In *Stanley v. Georgia*,[86] the Supreme Court invalidated laws that prohibited the private possession of obscene material. On the other hand, if a statute is aimed to protect the victims of child pornography or destroy the exploitative mar- ket, it could be construed as rationally related to a legitimate state interest and thus constitutional.

Nineteen states have enacted statutes making the private possession of child pornography a criminal offense.[87] The validity of such statutes has been challenged on the basis that they infringe First Amendment rights.[88] The Ohio statute prohibited persons from possessing or viewing material depicting a nude minor, unless the ma- terials had a bona fide "proper purpose" or the parents had consented to their child's depiction in the materials. Writing for the majority, Justice White found it "evident beyond the need for elaboration" that the state's compelling interest in the well- being of minors outweighed the accused's right to receive information in his own home. The state's obligation to protect victims of child pornography was also considered compelling. In contrast, the interest asserted in *Stanley* of preventing the "poisoning" of an adult's mind was not regarded as compelling.[89] The Ohio law also promoted the destruction of pornography that could haunt child victims in the future and be used by pedophiles as a tool of seduction.

The Court appreciated that, in order to avoid being struck down, the statute must be narrowly construed. "Nudity" was accordingly given a narrow meaning ("lewd exhibition or involving a graphic focus on the genitals"). In sum, the Supreme Court will demand carefully drawn statutes that focus on the legitimate purpose of protecting child victims. A general assertion of immorality will not pass constitutional muster. Law enforcement is difficult, and the government may use undercover agents. However, the agents may not implant in the mind of an innocent person the disposition to commit an offense.[90]

Most states prohibit the sale of pornography to minors. In *Ginsberg v. New York,* a New York State law prohibited the sale to minors of "prurient" materials lacking "redeeming social merit," despite the fact that the materials were not legally obscene for adults. Even though scientific evidence for such a connection was lacking, the Court determined that there was a link between pornography and the corruption of moral values, particularly in the case of minors. The Court found, further, that the state's legitimate interest in the moral values of its minors was rationally related to prohibiting the sale of pornography to them, "since obscenity is not a protected expression"; thus, the sale of pornography could be suppressed without challenging the protection accorded free speech.[91] The test for obscenity enunciated in *Pope v. Illinois*[92] does not refer to whether an ordinary member of the community would find literary, artistic, political, or scientific value in the material, but whether a "reasonable person" would find such value in the material. The question of whether a minor might be considered a "reasonable person" for purposes of judging the value of arguably obscene materials was recently raised in *American Booksellers v. Webb.*[93] In this case, the Court found that a Georgia statute which prohibited distribution or display of material "harmful to minors" should be judged by the standard of a "reasonable minor." If "any reasonable minor" could find serious value in the material, it could not be regulated as "harmful to minors."

In addition to direct purchase, minors today have access to pornography through such media as broadcasting and telephone services ("dial-a-porn"). The problem of pornography in broadcast messages was addressed in *F.C.C. v. Pacifica Foundation.*[94] In this case, the Court upheld as constitutional the Federal Communication Commission's (FCC) banning of the afternoon radio broadcast of a profane monologue. The Court noted that a radio broadcast is received without notice of content and readily accessible to all minors. Unlike broadcast messages, "dial-a-porn" services require the listener to initiate the communication. In 1983 Congress amended Section 223(b)(1)(A) of the Communications Act of 1934, criminalizing both indecent and obscene interstate telephone calls to minors. In a subsequent series of cases involving regulations under the section restricting "dial-a-porn" services, the Supreme Court held that obscene speech was not protected by the Constitution; thus, such services could be banned by the FCC. However, the Court also held that indecent telephone messages could not be totally banned in the interest of preventing minors from listening to them; to do so would also violate adults' First Amendment rights to have access to such material.[95] Any restriction must provide the least restrictive means of protecting minors. In subsequent litigation, the Court found that the FCC had not given sufficient consideration to the use of blocking device systems.[96] Later FCC regulations were approved in *"Carlin III"*[97] and *Sable Communications of California v. F.C.C.*[98] The Court of Appeals in *Dial Information Services v. Thornburgh,*[99] however, found that "voluntary blocking" would not adequately shield minors from dial-a-porn. Signaling a view protective of minors and restrictive in terms of First Amendment interests, the Court underscored testimony concerning the psychologically damaging effects on children of even minimal exposure to indecent messages. Voluntary blocking could not prevent such exposure.

SEXUAL ACTIVITY

Do minors have a constitutional right to indulge in voluntary sexual activity? Does the state have the right to limit minors' sexual activity in order to avert illegitimate pregnancy and check the spread of disease?

Such questions are not readily answered. To the extent that adults have a right to engage in consensual sexual activity, minors enjoy that right except that restrictions can be made in recognition of their need for special protection. For any law to pass constitutional muster, there must be a rational nexus between the restriction and the state's legitimate end in protecting the minor. Justice Brennan has said that the "power of the State to control the conduct of children reaches beyond the scope of its authority over adults" and involves a "broader authority to protect the physical, mental, and moral well-being of its youth than of its adults."[100]

Although at common law it was twelve years, the *age of consent* for sexual intercourse is now sixteen in many states. Statutory rape laws originally penalized men, but recently a number of states have amended them to apply to both sexes. However, in *Michael M. v. Superior Court of Sonoma County,*[101] the Supreme Court upheld a California statutory rape law that discriminated against men by punishing them for having sexual intercourse with females under eighteen to whom they were not married. In upholding the statute, the Court supported the state's rationale of limiting illegitimate pregnancy. The Court pointed out, furthermore, that the burden of such pregnancies falls more heavily on women; hence, the discriminative criminal penalty incurred by men roughly equalizes the deterrence of unwanted pregnancy.

Statutory rape laws override the possibility that a minor might make an informed choice. These laws impose arbitrary age limits on sexual activity in order to protect minors from those who would take advantage of them. Thus, what would otherwise be a consenting intimate sexual relationship between two individuals becomes illegal. The tension between the state's paternal role and the minor's liberty interest in sexual self-determination has not been directly addressed by the courts. In *Michael M.,* the Supreme Court Justices, both majority and dissenters, affirmed that the state has a legitimate interest in prohibiting sexual intercourse among teenagers. In *Fleisher v. City of Signal Hill*,[102] the Court found that, even though the right to privacy protects an individual from unjustified government intrusion into highly personal or intimate relationships, it does not protect all sexual conduct; nor does it extend the privacy right to unmarried individuals except in regard to contraception and abortion. Thus, the Court ruled that the Constitution does not grant privacy protection to the perpetrators of illegal acts such as statutory rape.

Educational Rights

COMPULSORY ATTENDANCE

Although there is no constitutional right to an education, all states have enacted education laws which empower the state to provide, fund, and regulate the education of its citizens. They do so by distributing federal moneys to the local school districts and by empowering municipalities to levy taxes to support schooling.

Compulsory attendance laws have been held by the Federal Fifth Circuit Court of Appeals as triggering a special custodial relationship that attracts the protection of the Fourteenth Amendment.[103] On the other hand, the Third Circuit Court of Appeals has denied that a special relationship applies.[104] Accordingly, the rights of students claiming that school officials have not protected them from violence or sexual molestation will vary until the Supreme Court clarifies the matter.

State education laws bestow a right and an obligation to attend school up to a statutory age; but the state may not require attendance at a *public* school.[105] In *Wisconsin v. Yoder*,[106] the Supreme Court considered the competing claims of the state and the Amish. Wisconsin required school attendance to the age of sixteen years; the Amish contended that this requirement violated their religious beliefs. The Court decided in favor of the Amish, holding that the state's legitimate interest in universal education did not outweigh the fundamental right to religious freedom and the traditional right of parents to rear their own children (particularly as the Amish, in effect, provided agricultural training for their children).

In *Plyler v. Doe*,[107] the Court ruled that a state is obligated under the equal protection clause of the Fourteenth Amendment to apply state education laws equally to any person within its jurisdiction. Consequently, the Court required Texas school districts to educate the children of unregistered aliens despite the strain on local schools caused by the influx of illegal immigrants. The Court found that discrimination against the children of illegal aliens was not the most rational means of furthering the state's substantive interest in reserving its limited resources for the education of lawful residents.

DISCIPLINE IN PUBLIC SCHOOLS

School authorities have a range of penalties that may be imposed upon recalcitrant pupils, up to and including corporal punishment, suspension, transfer, and expulsion. In most places these penalties have statutory support, although several states expressly forbid corporal punishment. In *Ingraham v. Wright,*[108] however, the use of corporal punishment withstood a challenge based on violation of the student's rights under the Eighth (cruel and unusual punishment) and Fourteenth (due process) Amendments. The Court affirmed the legitimacy of paddling children as a means of maintaining discipline in public schools, holding that the availability of tort action and criminal penalties served as sufficient check against unreasonable punishment.[109] If discipline is applied within reasonable and recognized limits, a child subjected to it will have no claim in tort for damages. Nevertheless, the custodian of the child, whether teacher, minder, or bus driver, must exhibit discretion in administering discipline, or else liability will follow from the use of excessive force.[110]

Depending on the severity of the penalty being considered, pupils accused of infractions must be provided with due process protections. In *Goss v. Lopez,*[111] the Supreme Court ruled that the suspension of a student for less than ten days did not require full due process considerations. However, the pupil must be given notice of the charges and their basis and a chance to answer them. Prior to transfer or expulsion, the student's due process rights must be protected in a formal hearing.

The rights to religious liberty, free expression, and assembly are at times at loggerheads with school discipline. In *West Virginia State Board of Education v. Barnette*[112] the Supreme Court held that, if such actions violated individual religious beliefs, the school could not compel children to salute the flag or take the pledge of allegiance. Most courts have upheld students' rights to wear long hair, beards, and mustaches, provided they are not safety hazards, but school dress codes have generally been supported.

The Supreme Court has confirmed minors' First Amendment rights, but only within the confines of "legitimate pedagogical concerns."[113] The case of *Tinker v. Des Moines Independent School District*[114] concerned the right of students to wear black armbands to school as a protest against the Vietnam War. The Supreme Court upheld the right of students to express their views provided school activities were not thereby disrupted. However, in *Hazelwood School District v. Kuhlmeier,*[115] the Supreme Court delimited minors' First Amendment rights by upholding the right of school authorities to remove material concerning pregnancy and divorce from a newspaper produced in a journalism class. The right of censorship is conditioned on the school's acting to maintain its neutrality in matters of political controversy and to regulate school publications in accordance with the youth of the audience and the lack of opportunity for third parties to respond.

In a recent case, *Planned Parenthood of Southern Nevada v. Clark County School District,*[116] the Ninth Circuit Court of Appeals applied *Kuhlmeier*. In this case, school educators declined advertisements for Planned Parenthood in student newspapers, yearbooks, and athletic programs. The Court found that the school board's action did not infringe students' First Amendment rights, since these publications were not an open or public forum of opinion. The Ninth Circuit gave school officials substantial deference in concluding that the content of school publications could be regulated so as to maintain neutrality on controversial issues. The guidelines under which the Clark County School District rejected the advertisements were considered viewpoint neutral, and the content was regarded as controversial. The trend, Minow suggests, is to "restrict student expression as part of the educational and social mission of the schools."[117]

CURRICULA

School boards have the right to administer curricula in such a manner as to convey the values of the community. However, students' First Amendment rights could be construed as allowing them free access to nonprurient information. To what degree, therefore, is a school board exercising legitimate authority in refusing to purchase a particular book or in removing the book from a school library? In *Board of Education, Island Trees Union Free School District No. 26 v. Pico,*[118] the Court held that school boards may not remove books from school libraries if their intent is to deny students access to ideas, unless the books were "pervasively vulgar" or "not educationally suitable." O'Neil argues that a student's right to receive information warrants protection through a judicial review of school board decisions;[119] conversely, Diamond recommends that the courts show greater deference to school boards.[120]

The First Amendment prohibition against governmental establishment of religion, as reinforced by the Fourteenth Amendment, prohibits publicly funded schools from promoting or suppressing a particular religious viewpoint,[121] as embodied for example in school prayer.[122] Hence, the courts have upheld a school's refusal to allow student prayer meetings[123] and have found it unconstitutional for a school to allow voluntary student prayer meetings outside regular school hours on public school property, or to arrange prayerlike invocations and benedictions at graduation ceremonies.[124] A school was restrained by the court when a religious group operating in buses parked outside school premises was promoted by school officials.[125]

FOURTH AMENDMENT RIGHTS

The Supreme Court has established standards for searches and seizures in schools.[126] The "reasonable suspicion" test as set forth in *New Jersey v. T.L.O.* requires that the search be justified at its inception and "reasonably related in scope to the circumstances which justified the search in the first place." Thus, in *T.J. v. State,*[127] the state was not allowed to introduce as evidence in a delinquency hearing cocaine discovered incidentally to a search for a knife. In *Commonwealth v. Carey,*[128] applying *T.L.O.,* the Court found a search to be reasonable after fellow students had informed police that the accused possessed a gun. With regard to seizures of the person, the standard in *U.S. v. Mendenhall*[129] established that a person is "seized" only if a reasonable person would believe he was not free to go. Restraining a person's liberty through a mere show of authority does not constitute seizure. Thus, in *California v. Hodari*[130] the Supreme Court allowed into evidence the crack cocaine jettisoned by a youth who was being chased, on the ground that the officer's pursuit of the fleeing youth, unaccompanied by any use of physical force, did not constitute seizure.

SCHOOL RECORDS

The Family Educational Rights and Privacy Act of 1974 (FERPA) affords families the right to inspect all school records, to have them explained, and to challenge and correct them, if appropriate. Furthermore, before the school may disclose the records to third parties, parental permission is required.

FOURTEENTH AMENDMENT RIGHTS: RACIAL AND SEXUAL DISCRIMINATION

In its momentous *Brown v. Board of Education*[131] decision, the Supreme Court held that racially segregated schools, being inherently unequal and deleterious, violated the Fourteenth Amendment (equal protection under the laws). The progeny of this decision are discussed in Chapter 4, on special education.

The equal protection clause of the Fourteenth Amendment proscribes one-sex public schools.[132] Sexually segregated public schools have been found to violate the Fourteenth Amendment.[133] Intention to discriminate must be shown.[134]

SEXUAL HARASSMENT AND PHYSICAL ABUSE

When a school receives federal funding it is subject to Title IX of the Civil Rights Act (Education Amendment of 1972), which proscribes gender-based discrimination and sexual harassment. A breach of these provisions will permit a student to sue in damages an offending school district.[135] In the absence of a breach of this Act, the Courts are divided on whether the student and school relationship is sufficient to provide an action under §1983 for failure to protect students from physical and sexual abuse at school. In one case the Third Circuit Court of Appeals held that students who were physically, sexually, and verbally abused over a five-month period had no §1983 action.[136] However, in a later case the Fifth Circuit Court of Appeals held that the failure of a school superintendent and principal to protect a fourteen-year-old student from sexual molestation visited upon her by a teacher was actionable under §1983 as a deprivation of her constitutional rights under the Fourteenth Amendment.[137]

RIGHT TO SUE IN TORT: NEGLIGENCE IN EDUCATION

If, due to the negligence of school staff, a child suffers injury while in school, he may have cause to sue for damages. Action by an injured pupil may be available against the school board (or other responsible authority) for failure to establish and maintain safe conditions at school. An action is also available where teachers overreach the bounds of discipline and batter, assault, or falsely imprison students.[138] More problematical, however, is a suit for failure adequately to educate a child (an action that has become feasible because state law in many instances has stripped school authorities of immunity from tort liability).[139] The three types of cases in this regard are related to the following issues:

1. Inadequate instruction in basic skills
2. Negligent evaluation and inappropriate class placement
3. Negligent education of the student causing loss to a third party

Under the first category, the courts have generally resisted finding a duty of care in the school board that would lead to liability (for definition of "duty of care," see Chapters 7 and 8). The courts have usually reasoned that educational performance is a matter of complex judgment concerning which the courts have little expertise. Moreover, the courts have been reluctant to open the floodgates to actions filed by disgruntled students and parents.[140]

The second group of cases is usually treated similarly, although claims based on negligent evaluation or placement are not so amorphous as in the first category. The court may review a particular educational decision and decide, on the basis of expert evidence, whether it conformed to the established professional standard. *Hoffman v. Board of Education of the City of New York*[141] is a foundational case. In *Hoffman*, the plaintiff's intellectual abilities were evaluated when he entered kindergarten. The examining psychologist for the school district determined that the child should be placed in special classes for the mentally handicapped. A speech impediment, however, raised some uncertainty. The psychologist recommended that the plaintiff be reassessed within two years. The recommendation was not heeded. It was only after twelve years, when he entered a training facility for retarded youths, that the plaintiff was finally retested and found not to be intellectually handicapped. The Court of Appeals of New York reversed a $750,000 jury verdict, finding that the claim had to be rejected because the negligence related to the school board's discretion. To have allowed the action would have opened school boards to attack for many educational procedures. Other cases have similarly rejected liability for psychological misdiagnosis leading to improper placement of pupils.[142] In another case, however, when the plaintiff was confined to a state school operated along hospital lines, the Court labeled the negligence, "medical malpractice" and found liability.[143] The examining doctor in this case had failed to assess the plaintiff's intelligence after he had been found to be deaf. There is a tissue-thin distinction between this case and those that rejected liability. In our view, liability should adhere if a court is able to judge the reasonableness of the decision. If the decision is one that relates to educational policy, the competing concerns are for the school board to determine and should not be second-guessed by a court. Educational authorities should be able to exercise legitimate authority without fear of judicial interference. The limit is reached, however, if the decision is purely mechanical, without the exercise of discretion.

The Education of the Handicapped Act[144] provides federal funds for the encouragement of special education. In accepting funding a state undertakes to identify and evaluate children who might need special programs. A breach of these provisions could provide an additional avenue of redress for children under a theory of *per se negligence* (see Chapter 4) or an *implied right of action*, described above. However, litigants have relied on other legislation to ground rights to education. For example, the parents of homeless children have filed suit against the District of Columbia for violation of the McKinney Homeless Assistance Act,[145] alleging failure to consider the best interests of the children, to provide transport, to coordinate social services and public education, and to assure access to public education.[146]

Access to Health Care

THE NATURE OF HEALTH CARE

Parents have the obligation to provide their children with adequate medical care; otherwise, the state may intervene. Respect for parental autonomy rights, however, makes the courts loath to interfere; before the state will step in, the child must face serious harm from the want of medical care.[147]

As with education, the public tends to view health care as an obligation that should be assumed by the state. It is well established, however, that citizens have no constitutionally based right to health care. The President's Commission for the Study of Ethical Problems in Medicare and Biomedical and Behavioral Research (1983) could articulate no legal right; however, it concluded that society "has a moral obligation to ensure that everyone has access to adequate care without being subject to excessive burdens."[148] Nevertheless, once the state assumes an obligation such as health care, it must not discriminate in constitutionally impermissible ways. For example, it would be unconstitutional for the state to exclude women, children, or a particular ethnic or racial group from Medicaid benefits. Children are subject to special treatment in the provision of health care. In one respect, they are afforded fewer rights than adults; in another, the succor of the state is preferentially extended to them. Since children lack the legal capacity to consent to medical procedures, parents or guardians act on their behalf. Courts may grant emancipated minors the right to consent. Emancipated minors, then, are accorded confidentiality not given to all minors.[149] The larger issue concerns the circumstances in which the state may override the wishes of a parent or guardian. Insofar as constitutional law implicates health care, the question immediately arises whether children enjoy commensurate rights or whether their minority permits the state to modify their rights.

Where the parents are unable to give consent, the question arises as to the judgment to be applied in deciding whether the child should undergo the medical procedure. The choice, as elsewhere, is between *substituted judgment* and the *best interest* standard. Under substituted judgment the surrogate decision-maker—the guardian—is expected to reach as accurately as possible the decision that the patient would have reached. The decision-maker would thus look to prior declarations and the value system of the patient. By stating the analysis in this way it is clear that the doctrine cannot apply to nonemancipated or "immature" minors. The standard to be used, then, is that of the best interests of the minor.[150] The guardian must determine whether medical treatment would be in the minor's best interests.

In respect of some medical procedures, the courts will not defer to the parents' consent or the guardian's determination of best interests, but will insist, rather, upon a thorough judicial review. This is the case where the question arises of whether the minor should undergo surgical sterilization. The right here is fundamental and goes beyond the "health and welfare of the individual" to the "well being of our society."[151]

The following section briefly spells out some of the public measures taken to overcome barriers to health care caused by poverty or impecuniosity. The remainder of the sections in this chapter deal with the legal incapacity of the child and the potential tension that arises between the child's interests and the parents' rights. Here the child is denied access not because of financial status but rather because of legal incapacity.

ACCESS TO PUBLIC HEALTH CARE

Despite sources of support through AFDC, SSI, Medicaid, Title V Maternal and Health Care Block Grant Programs, and Title X Family Planning Programs, inability to pay remains the most common obstacle to adequate health care.

Hospitals may provide uncompensated care at emergency rooms or outpatient clinics. Indeed, hospitals were once obliged to do so under the federal regulations imposed on them if they had been the recipients of Hill–Burton funds. At present, twenty-two states require hospitals to render emergency medical care regardless of ability to pay.[152] This requirement is bolstered by the Federal Emergency Care Act (1986), known as COBRA.[153] COBRA requires hospitals with emergency departments to examine and treat any person who has an emergency medical condition or who is in active labor; the condition must be stabilized before transfer to another facility.[154]

These measures afford limited access to children in an emergency, but of greater significance are provisions under Medicaid. Medicaid is a federal program designed to provide medical services to the poor, in accordance with Title XIX of the Social Security Act. Although the state has no constitutional obligation to provide it, equal access to health care has a strong moral and political appeal, and disadvantaged children have a special need. Through the Health Care Financing Administration of the Department of Health and Human Services, the federal government reimburses the state for 50–80 percent of the cost of medical services. Reimbursement rates are determined by the states and must be reasonable and adequate to meet the costs of efficiently operated facilities. The state must also assure the federal government that people have reasonable access to facilities of adequate quality.[155] All recipients of AFDC must be given Medicaid. Thus, over 60 percent of the nation's Medicaid recipients are covered under the category of Aid for Families with Dependent Children. The states are free to choose whether or not they wish to provide Medicaid services to needy children under twenty-one who do not qualify as "dependent" under AFDC regulations (e.g., certain children in psychiatric hospitals). The states may also fund services to medically needy children whose family incomes are above the stipulated poverty line but whose parents would be beggared by medical bills.

In 1986 the federal law was amended to require states to provide Medicaid for all poor children under five years of age, whatever their family situation,[156] and the states are allowed to expand eligibility for children. The Family Support Act of 1988 further extends Medicaid eligibility. Since 1990 the states must make Medicaid available to two-parent families when one parent with a work history is now unemployed. All families seeking Medicaid are subject to means testing.

Many problems are involved in affording access to health care. Advocates of children's rights propose solutions that may improve the quality of life for poor children. However, the debate is broader than can be encompassed by a narrow focus on constitutional rights. A person may have the right to an abortion, for example, yet the state has no legal obligation to pay for it.[157] In this chapter, we have eschewed any attempt to deal with the wider issues of public policy.

ABORTION

We have already briefly discussed Supreme Court decisions on abortion and contraception in the course of explaining the Court's application of consistent constitutional principles. The foundational precedent on minors' abortion rights is *Planned Parenthood of Central Missouri v. Danforth.*[158] In *Danforth,* the Court held that, like adults, minors mature enough to have become pregnant have the right to privacy in abortion matters, and that this right outweighs a parent's desire to block the child's decision. Thus, parental consent is not an absolute requirement prior to abortion. The Court indicated that, regardless of age or maturity, not every minor is competent to give effective consent to abortion; but it offered no guidelines as to when a minor might be regarded as competent, nor did it rule on whether parental notification was required.

In *Planned Parenthood v. Casey* (1992), the Supreme Court, while refusing to overrule *Roe v. Wade,* found that the State, in exercise of its legitimate interest in protecting life or potential life throughout pregnancy, may enact regulations consistent with a woman's constitutionally protected liberty interest. Such regulations are constitutional provided that they do not impose an "undue burden" on the woman's right. Before viability of the fetus, the state may regulate abortion only to the extent that the woman is not deprived of the ultimate choice. The Supreme Court observed that "regulations which do no more than create a structural mechanism by which the State, or the parent or guardian of a minor, may express profound respect for the life of the unborn are permitted, if they are not a substantial obstacle to the woman's exercise of the right to choose."[159] In this case the court, while striking down a spousal notification requirement, upheld the state requirement for parental or guardian consent provided there is an adequate judicial bypass procedure.[160] The *Casey* decision invests considerable power in the federal courts that review state abortion legislation. Federal courts must now interpret the vague "undue burden" test in determining the constitutionality of proliferating abortion statutes.

Currently, thirty-five states have legislation requiring some degree of parental involvement in minors' abortion decisions.[161] The effectiveness of judicial bypass is enhanced by legislation requiring the appointment of a guardian *ad litem* to represent the minor in the judicial hearing. As protector of the minor's interests, under the arrangement, the guardian *ad litem* would be obliged to seek the bypass.[162] The by-pass procedure must be a confidential and expeditious alternative to parental notification.[163]

CONTRACEPTION

The Supreme Court has found that the use of contraceptives raises issues of the same constitutional kind as abortion. The issues relate to a "woman's liberty because they involve personal decisions concerning not only the meaning of procreation but also human responsibility and respect for it."[164] In *Carey v. Population Services International*,[165] the Supreme Court held unconstitutional a New York statute prohibiting the sale of contraceptives to minors under sixteen years of age. The Court ruled that state restrictions on the privacy rights of minors are valid only if they serve a significant state interest that is not relevant for adults. The state's interest in opposing the sexual activity of minors was not considered sufficient to override their privacy interest. Thus, in *Carey*, the Court extended to minors as well as adults the right to privacy in connection with decisions affecting procreation. It has been held that the distribution of contraceptives to minors without parental notification does not interfere with the constitutional rights of parents. The states may require parental notification, however.[166] The issue of whether statutes requiring parental consent to contraception are constitutional is as yet unresolved.[167]

Unforeseen responsibilities may come with the procreative right. The right to procreate presupposes the capacity to appreciate the ramifications of reproductive choices.[168] Many consider that, if the minor lacks this capacity, the authority to make decisions regarding her procreative rights should remain with the parent;[169] for, once the decision to procreate is made, the rights of another human are involved. The result is a potential conflict between the mother's right to control her own body and the interests of the fetus. Once the fetus reaches viability—the point in development when extrauterine existence can be sustained—the mother may lose her right to body autonomy if the potential child's well-being is threatened.[170]

REFUSAL OF MEDICAL TREATMENT

Parental Refusal

At common law, any medical attention to a minor requires parental consent. In the absence of consent, even though the child suffers no ill consequences, the practitioner will be liable for an action in battery.[171] However, a physician may intervene without consent in an emergency (i.e., a threat to life or limb). Similarly, even in the face of parental refusal to consent, a physician may render emergency care. Many state legislatures have regulated these matters; it is wise to refer to local legislation on the question.

When parents refuse necessary medical treatment (for example, on religious grounds), a physician may file *medical neglect* charges. He or she may then seek an expeditious judicial hearing on whether medical treatment can be authorized despite parental objection. All appropriate courts and Child Welfare departments have emergency services that facilitate such determinations. These cases reflect the irreconcilable nature of the values involved. In general, if the child's life is in danger, the court will always intervene, even against parental religious objections, but only to the extent necessary to allow treatment to be provided.[172] Nevertheless, the courts are reluctant to intervene unless the child's life is threatened, even in circumstances involving serious medical conditions.[173] It is wise to refer to local legislation on the question. In Alabama, for example, a doctor may operate without consent if an attempt to secure consent results in delay that would increase the risk to health, mental health, or life.[174] When emergency care has been rendered, the child's parents have been held responsible for payment for medical services.[175]

In a recent case, *Newmark v. Williams*,[176] a three-year-old child of Christian Scientist parents faced death from Burkitt's lymphoma. The physician prescribed a radical form of chemotherapy with a 40 percent chance of success, but the parents refused to authorize the treatment. The trial court awarded temporary custody to the Delaware Division of Child Protective Services so that it could authorize chemotherapy. The central issue in *Newmark* was whether the child was neglected when his parents refused to comply with the medical recommendations. In an attempt to provide guidelines, the Court proposed that the linchpin in these cases should be *the balance between the risks of the procedure and its potential success*. In this case, chemotherapy was likely to be highly invasive and painful, with serious side effects (including death), and a relatively low chance of success. However, in other cases where medical treatment was essential for the preservation of life, the best interests of the child have overridden parental religious objections.[177]

The courts have intervened in some cases even though the condition was short of life-threatening. They have done so when the condition was regarded as likely to ruin the child's emotional and social life and provided the medical procedure was not dangerous.[178] A different problem arises when a physician considers that parents' choice of treatment is adverse to the health of the child. If parents insist on actions that are likely to be detrimental to the health of the child, the privacy of family life must give way to the responsibility of the state to act in the best interests of the child. Thus in *Custody of a Minor*,[179] parents were restrained from administering to their leukemic child a concoction composed of laetrile, large doses of vitamins A and C, enzyme enemas, and folic acid. The court found that the parental choice of treatment was not only ineffective but also poisonous.

How far should the state intrude in order to sustain the life of defective neonates? Physician surveys indicate a willingness, in accordance with parental wishes, to withhold treatment from defective children who need surgery.[180] Such decisions require a prediction of the quality of the infant's life, the well-being of the remainder of the family, and the social cost of caring for these children.

The celebrated *Baby Doe* case puts the debate into relief.[181] Infant Doe was born with Down's syndrome, esophageal atresia and tracheo-esophageal fistula. In consultation with their physicians, Baby Doe's parents decided to withhold surgery, nutrition, and fluid support. The case had begun to run the gamut of the Indiana courts, when infant Doe died. Usually such decisions reach litigation only on the rare occasions when the surgeon disagrees with the parents. However, on the instigation of President Reagan, the Secretary of the Department of Health and Human Services notified hospitals receiving federal funds that the Rehabilitation Act of 1973 forbade the withholding of medical care from handicapped patients. Reporting measures were adopted. After these measures were struck down by the federal court, Congress passed legislation proscribing the withholding of nutrition, hydration, and medical care from handicapped infants, unless the infant were irreversibly comatose or dying and treatment would merely prolong dying or be otherwise futile and inhumane. The conservative attack on the withholding of treatment switched from an interpretation of the Rehabilitation Act of 1973 to an enactment of new statutory authority dealing directly with lifesaving treatment for infants, an approach premised on the prevention of child abuse and neglect.

Refusal by Competent Minors

All courts regard emancipated minors as competent to make health care decisions. Some recognize the right of unemancipated minors in this regard, provided that the medical procedure is uncomplicated and likely to be beneficial; it would be impractical to get parental consent; and the minor has the maturity to give informed consent. The IJA/ABA Standards advise that, in conditions of chemical dependency, venereal disease, pregnancy, contraception (other than sterilization), and psychiatric crisis, the prior consent of parents need not be obtained. Nevertheless, before medical care is provided to a minor, the clinician should attempt to notify the parents, provided that the minor gives the clinician permission to do so. If the minor refuses consent, parents should be contacted only if the procedure could seriously affect the minor's health. The medical justification for breaching the minor's confidence should be noted in the file. While the courts may grant emancipated minors the right to consent to confidential health care, if there is no source of payment, access is effectively denied.[182]

The requirement of consent in respect to children has been thought to rest upon the right of the parents "whose liability for support and maintenance of (the) child may be greatly increased by an unfavorable result,"[183] an argument that harks back to an earlier era. In consideration of the revolution in children's constitutional rights, the proper basis should be the capacity of the minor to understand the nature of the medical procedure. Weithorn has reviewed psychological research into the competency of minors.[184]

LEGAL ACKNOWLEDGMENT OF THE PSYCHOLOGICAL DETERMINATION OF MATURITY

The concept of the "mature minor" has been widely discussed.[185] Because few appellate cases define "maturity," the concept remains vague and must be judged case by case. States differ in the guidelines offered to physicians concerning parental disclosure and consent, and there is much confusion in the field.[186] Some states define the "mature minor" statutorily, but the concept applies only to those at least fifteen years of age. Furthermore, maturity will be defined differently according to the issue at stake; it is likely to be struck differently for the drinking of alcohol than for consent to medical treatment.

The courts emphasize their role as interpreters of the findings of fact in determining the capacity of minors.[187] When maturity affects the issue before them, the courts have attempted to delineate the criteria they used in determining maturity. Rather than reinforce the authority of courts to make such determinations, such rulings expand the criteria that the law finds pertinent. In *Kent v. United States,* an appendix to the opinion sets forth the criteria to be applied by Juvenile Court judges in waiving jurisdiction over minors.[188] The maturity of the juvenile is to be determined by home life, environmental situation, emotional attitude, and pattern of living. The importance of such criteria in an adversarial hearing creates a need for expert professional clinical assessment of a minor's capacity. Whenever possible, the court defers to others the weighing of such criteria in determining mental competency and recognizes the special place of the mental health professional. In *Addington v. Texas,* the court announced: "The determination of whether [a person] is mentally ill turns on the meaning of the facts which must be interpreted by expert psychiatrists and psychologists."[189] In relation to admission and treatment decisions in hospitals, the Supreme Court has adopted a medical review model of decision-making as fulfilling the due process rights of minors (see Chapter 10).

In the landmark case *Parham v. J.R.,* the Court put faith in medical review rather than in legal hearings prior to the committal of a minor for mental health treatment. The court conceded that medical error could occur; nevertheless, comparing the expertise of judges and physicians, the Court affirmed that a medical evaluation would be superior to a legal hearing.[190] Thus, in regard to the committal of minors, the courts have disavowed their prerogative to determine maturity and have affirmed the need for qualified professional opinion.

THE CLINICAL ASSESSMENT OF A MINOR'S COMPETENCE TO CONSENT TO MEDICAL TREATMENT

Freedom and autonomy are relative matters. Younger children, and some older children, do not perceive themselves as having rights or freedom of choice. Even if the law extended freedom of choice to such children, it is unlikely that they would demand or exercise it. There is a need for more research. Both artificial and real-life situations should be used to explore the capacity of minors to exercise free choice.

According to the *Restatement (Second) of Torts* (1979), "If a person consenting is a child or one of deficient mental capacity, consent may still be effective if he is capable of appreciating the nature, extent and probable consequences of the conduct consented to." The terms "competence," "capacity," "maturity," "voluntariness," and "mature minor" represent the virtually synonymous issues at stake in a formal clinical assessment.

A test of competency in treatment situations involves the following factors:

1. Evidence of having made a choice
2. Evidence that the option chosen has reasonable potential outcome
3. Actual understanding of the issues
4. Choice based on "rational" reasons
5. Ability to understand[191]

A number of commentators contend that children fourteen and older possess cognitive ability comparable to adults with regard to their capacity to consent to medical treatment.[192] Weithorn recommends that, unless demonstrated otherwise, minors should be considered competent if they are fourteen years of age or older.[193] She suggests that preadolescents between ten and thirteen require case-by-case definition.

Here is a more detailed set of guidelines:

1. At fourteen years of age, minors should be presumed competent to give informed consent to medical treatment, unless, during the course of informing them of their options, it becomes apparent (a) that they lack the requisite capacity to understand the issues involved; (b) that they lack the capacity for independent choice; (c) that they have been coerced or persuaded by others; or (d) that they are too emotionally disturbed to make a rational choice. If any of these four conditions is suspected, the clinician should evaluate the child's competence formally.
2. Between ten and fourteen years of age, minors should be evaluated for competency on a case-by-case basis.
3. Regardless of age, children should be involved in treatment decisions and kept informed of the progress of treatment.

In a formal competence evaluation the following factors should be assessed:

1. *Knowledge.* Does the patient have factual knowledge of (a) the nature of the disease; (b) the components of the treatment; (c) the rationale for the treatment; and (d) the prognosis of the disease, treated and untreated, in terms of probability of outcome within a specified time?

2. *Educability.* If the patient does not have the requisite understanding to make a choice, is he or she educable? If the subject's knowledge is inadequate, the clinician should attempt to correct it or recommend the education or counseling required in order to enable the subject to make a reasonable decision.

3. *Cognitive capacity.* After being given the requisite information, does the patient have the capacity (a) to consider all options; (b) to consider the pros and cons of each option; (c) to state the risks and benefits of the chosen option; and (d) to state the possible consequences of the option chosen?

It would be desirable to test this question first by using hypothetical dilemmas, then the real-life dilemma in question.[194] If the child does not appear to have the cognitive capacity, this should be checked by formal intelligence testing.

4. *Capacity for self-determination.* Is the patient free of coercion (e.g., by threat), undue persuasion (e.g., by misinformation), or inducement (e.g., by hope of reward)?

To what degree does the child appreciate that he or she is in control of his or her own life? Is he or she inclined to exercise personal choice? This matter is related to socioeconomic class and ethnic differences. A clinical impression could be checked by means of the Locus of Control test.[195]

5. *Emotional freedom.* Does the patient exhibit psychiatric illness or impairment which could impede self-determination generally (e.g., thought disorder, dysphoria, anxiety) or specifically (e.g., suicidal ideation, unresolved conflict, or guilt)? Does the patient have the capacity to make the choice in question without undue stress? Would the child's capacity be so diminished by the very stress of making the choice that he or she could not exercise his or her potential cognitive capacity to appreciate all options and weigh the advantages and disadvantages of each option?

If the patient lacks the emotional freedom or ego strength to make the choice, is it likely that, following treatment, freedom or strength could be enhanced, and competence restored? If so, how long do you estimate this would take?

Participation as a Research Subject

During the 1970s, in view of the burgeoning of research on human subjects, the federal government established the National Commission for the Protection of Human Subjects of Biomedical and Behavioral Research. In its final recommendations, the commission recommended the establishment of Institutional Review Boards (IRBs) at each research center. The purpose of an IRB is to assure that proposed research studies are scientifically sound, that human beings are to be used as subjects only after appropriate animal studies have been completed, that subjects' privacy is respected, that risks are minimized, that the proposed benefits of the research outweigh the risks, and that subjects are selected in an equitable manner.

The commission recommended that, if the above conditions are met, it is ethically permissible to do research on children, provided parental permission and the consent or assent of children seven years of age or older have been obtained. The commission found that biomedical and behavioral research involving children is important for the health and well-being of all children and can be conducted in an ethical manner. Refusal by a child of seven years or older should be overridden only if the parents' consent and the research holds out the possibility of direct benefit otherwise unavailable. In that case, if the IRB determines that parental permission alone is an inadequate protection, it should appoint an independent advocate for the child. If the proposed research involves more than minimal risk, a child's objection should be binding.

These recommendations were accepted and incorporated into the regulations of the Department of Health, Education and Welfare.[196] These regulations charged the IRBs with ensuring that proper consent or assent was obtained and required that both parents give consent if the research involved some risk but no direct benefit. In summary, the commission's recommendations and current federal regulations allow minors to participate as research subjects, while protecting them from involuntary nontherapeutic or unreasonably risky research investigations. However, no independent right to elect or refuse to be a research participant is accorded to them.

Note the following recommendations:

1. The informed consent of a parent, or legal guardian, is required in all instances, unless the child is emancipated.
2. Informed consent should be obtained from children at least twelve years of age, in all instances, but only after parental consent is obtained. This provision may be overridden only if the child can be shown to be incompetent.
3. Assent should be sought from all children between seven and twelve years of age, if the parent or legal guardian has consented. *Assent* is thus distinguished from *consent*.
4. Consent or assent should not be based on coercion, inducement, or hope of reward.
5. Informed consent requires full disclosure of the nature of the proposed research, its purpose, risks, and direct benefits, the compensation provided for any unintended effects of the study, and the provisions made to protect the child. This information should be discussed by a knowledgeable person with the parents and child, and provided in readily understood written form.

The subject of informed consent is discussed at greater length in Chapter 8, on malpractice.[198]

CHAPTER 4

THE EDUCATIONAL RIGHTS OF HANDICAPPED CHILDREN

BACKGROUND
Early Case Law and Legislation

The first organized efforts to educate the mentally retarded began around 1848 when residential centers were established for the dual purpose of sheltering inmates from the general public and preparing them to contribute to society. About 1900, public school systems began to form special education classes or "opportunity" classes.[1] The avowed intent of these embyronic developments was dissonant with realty; education and training aimed to assimilate the handicapped into society,[2] whereas segregation and isolation was their lot. Programs referred to as "classes for idiots and the feebleminded" served no purpose other than to keep the disabled apart from the "normal" school populace,[3] as was consistent with their pariah status.[4] The rejection of the needs of the handicapped reached its zenith in the early 1900s, as a thriving eugenics movement, case law, and legislation promoted the elimination of handicapped people from society.

In 1912 the American Breeders Association recommended that all feebleminded women be sterilized and all feebleminded men castrated. Alternatively, euthanasia was suggested as a means of reducing their number.[5] By 1936, twenty states had passed sterilization statutes.[6] In *Buck v. Bell* (1926), the Supreme Court upheld Virginia's compulsory sterilization law, with the ringing endorsement of Oliver Wendell Holmes:

> It is better for all the world, if instead of waiting to execute degenerate offspring for crime, or to let them starve for their imbecility, society can prevent those who are manifestly unfit from continuing their kind. . . .Three generations of imbeciles are enough.[7]

Educational policy relating to handicapped children reflected the same sentiments. The disabled were either completely excluded from public school systems or placed in segregated classes where they received little attention. In *Watson v. City of Cambridge* (1893), the Supreme Court of Massachusetts upheld the expulsion of a handicapped pupil on the grounds that he was "too weak-minded to derive profit from instruction."[8] In *Beattie v. Board of Education of City of Antigo,* a Wisconsin Court ruled that "the right of a child . . . to attend public schools of the state cannot be insisted upon when its presence therein is harmful to the best interests of the school."[9] The exclusion of handicapped children from "regular" classes was generally based on the grounds of their inability to benefit from traditional instruction[10] and their detrimental impact on "normal" students.[11] At the same time, exclusion resulted from financial constraints at the state and local levels, reinforced by state and local laws that authorized schools to exclude children without consultation with their parents.[12] As a result, millions of handicapped children "were either totally excluded from schools or were sitting idly in regular classrooms awaiting the time when they were old enough to 'drop out.' "[13]

Changes in the Educational Approach Toward the Disabled

The Supreme Court's decision in *Brown v. Board of Education* (1954) was a milestone in the movement to improve the education of handicapped children. The court, interpreting the Fourteenth Amendment, stated that education is a "right which must be made available to all on equal terms."[14] Racially segregated schools were held unconstitutional on the ground that they were inherently unequal, and thus detrimental to minority children.[15]

Bearing the imprimatur of the Supreme Court, the *Brown* decision served as a foundation for those seeking greater educational opportunity for children with disabilities. The profound activism of the time reached beyond the rights of minorities and women to the handicapped. Advocacy groups such as the National Association for Retarded Children (NARC) and the Council for Exceptional Children (CEC) lobbied to change popular conceptions of the handicapped and procured the passage of new legislation to benefit the disabled.[16] Throughout the 1960s and early 1970s Congress took steps to provide funding and encourage the development of programs to this end.[17]

Perhaps the most important of these early legislative acts was the passage of Section 504 of the Rehabilitation Act of 1973. Section 504 of the Act states:

No otherwise qualified handicapped individual in the United States . . . shall, solely by reason of her or his handicap, be excluded from the participation in, be denied the benefits of, or be subjected to discrimination under any program or activity receiving Federal financial assistance . . .[18]

An accretion of later regulations and amendments have elaborated the application of Section 504 to federally funded programs. With respect to education, all handicapped children must receive a "free and appropriate" education in the "least restrictive setting."[19]

Section 504 of the Rehabilitation Act was a response to two landmark court decisions in the early 1970s: *Pennsylvania Ass'n. for Retarded Children v. Pennsylvania* and *Mills v. Board of Education.*[20]

PARC was a class action suit brought against the State of Pennsylvania on behalf of all mentally retarded persons who had been excluded from receiving a public education.[21] Pennsylvania law had imposed no obligation on the state to educate children certified as "uneducable and untrainable."[22] State law had also allowed that those children who had not achieved a mental age of five years could be indefinitely excluded from public school.[23] Based on these statutes, 70,000 to 80,000 of Pennsylvania's 116,000 retarded children between the age of five and twenty-one were denied access to any public education, while only 46,000 retarded children were enrolled in public schools.[24]

The district court held that the state had violated the plaintiff's Fourteenth Amendment equal protection rights in that it provided public education to other children while denying mentally retarded children a similar opportunity.[25] Of critical importance was the court's acceptance of the proposition that handicapped children can benefit from an education. This decision obligated the State of Pennsylvania to provide mentally retarded children with access to a free public education.[26] In addition, an elaborate procedural scheme was created to provide parents due notice and the opportunity for a hearing if any change in the child's education were proposed.

One year after the *PARC* decision, *Mills v. Board of Education* was handed down. This class action suit challenged the constitutionality of excluding from the public schools both mentally retarded children and those labeled as having behavioral and emotional disorders.[27] The *Mills* court, as in *PARC*, held that all children had a right to a "free and suitable" public education regardless of the degree of their disability.[28] Exclusion could not be justified on the ground of insufficient funds. The court stated:

> If sufficient funds are not available to finance all of the services and programs that are needed and desirable in the system then the available funds must be expended equitably in such a manner that no child is entirely excluded from a publicly supported education consistent with his needs and ability to benefit therefrom.[29]

Mills also provided an extensive procedural mechanism to guarantee the due process rights of children and parents when educational decisions were made.[30]

Mills sent an alarm through school district boards across the country. How far could shrinking resources be spread? How extensive and elaborate must special education be? Given the limited potential of many children, are not elaborate programs wasteful? These questions persist to the present day.

PARC and *Mills* signaled that Congress must take further action if a public education was to be assured for all handicapped children; for, although Section 504 of the Rehabilitation Act had established the right of handicapped children to a free public education, progress was slow. In 1975, over one-half of the nation's eight million handicapped children were described as receiving an inadequate education, while more than one million were completely excluded from the public school system.[31]

Congress responded by enacting the Education for All Handicapped Children Act of 1975.[32]

THE EDUCATION FOR ALL HANDICAPPED CHILDREN ACT OF 1975
Legislative History and Goals

The Education for All Handicapped Children Act (EAHCA) was designed to ensure that

> . . . all handicapped children have available to them . . . a free appropriate public education which emphasizes special education and related services designed to meet their unique needs, to assure that the rights of handicapped children and their parents or guardians are protected, to assist states and localities to provide for the education of all handicapped children, and to assess and assure the effectiveness of efforts to educate handicapped children.[33]

While Section 504 of the Rehabilitation Act had established the principle that handicapped children should receive a "free and appropriate" education, the EAHCA provided federal moneys in order to spur the states to develop educational programs for the handicapped.[34] In 1988 the Supreme Court discussed the EAHCA in the case of *Honig v. Doe.*

> [The Act is more than] a simple funding statute [and instead] confers upon disabled students an enforceable substantive right to public education in participating States, . . . and conditions federal financial assistance upon States' compliance with substantive and procedural goals of the Act.[35]

Thus the statute goes beyond the mere provision of funding. In blending civil rights with funding, it sets a precedent that has been described as a model for disability policy-makers in times of budgetary strictures.[37]

As in *PARC* and *Mills,* Congress placed emphasis on procedural requirements for school boards. Under the EAHCA, procedural safeguards were viewed as the best means of "translating the legal rights of children into meaningful educational placements and programs."[38] The need for individual assessment at the local level was thus accommodated.[39] The primacy of the state's responsibilities was entrenched.[40] Broad substantive standards were eschewed.[41] Substantive terms like "appropriate education," "least restrictive environment," "special education," and "handicapped children" were left vague in order to allow leeway for interpretation during the child's evaluation.[42]

Procedural Aspects of the EAHCA

Under the Education for All Handicapped Children Act, each handicapped child is evaluated by a local committee. The committee is to be made up of a representative of the local educational agency qualified in special education, the child's teacher, the child's parents or guardian, and, "whenever appropriate," the child.[43]

The inclusion of the child's parents in the process promoted the child's best interests over the former authority of the school board.[44] One policy-maker stated: "We intended to strengthen the hands of parents. . . . It was a way of . . . involving parents in the process. . . . It's a way of enforcing what should be delivered to kids."[45] Thus, a "committee" is established to evaluate each handicapped child and to define the term "appropriate education" according to the needs of the individual child. Pursuant to Section 1401(a)(20) of the Act, the Individual Educational Plan (IEP) must contain the following elements:

1. A statement of the present levels of educational performance of such child
2. A statement of annual goals, including short-term instructional objectives
3. A statement of the specific educational services to be provided to such child, and the extent to which such child will be able to participate in regular educational programs . . .
4. The projected date for initiation and anticipated duration of such services
5. Appropriate objective criteria and evaluation procedures and schedules for determining, on at least an annual basis, whether instructional objectives are being achieved[46]

The IEP is the "cornerstone" of the EAHCA.[47] It requires school districts to evaluate each child and make a determination regarding how the child's needs can be met throughout the child's education. The plan thus developed must be reviewed at least annually and revised whenever appropriate.[48]

Parents may challenge the committee's findings in the IEP.[49] They may review all documents related to their child's education.[50] When the IEP is initiated, or when its alteration is proposed, the school board must give the parents notice. Parents who have a complaint with "any matter relating to the identification, evaluation, or educational placement" of their child have extensive review alternatives.[51] The educational plan is first reviewed in an impartial administrative hearing. If disagreement still exists, the parents may appeal to the state educational agency for further review.[52] If these administrative routes are exhausted or deemed incapable of providing relief within a reasonable time, review may be sought in the federal courts.[53] Parents are entitled to "appropriate relief" but not to monetary damages. The relief is prospective in the form of affording access to services denied or to compensatory education.[54]

The procedural protections for parents and children are bolstered by the parents' entitlement to "be accompanied and advised by counsel."[55] In order to encourage legal representation, Congress enacted the Handicapped Children's Protection Act (HCPA) in 1986,[56] providing, among other things, for the award of attorneys' fees to the prevailing party under EHA administrative proceedings.[57] Access to representation is "one step toward making the procedural rights of Public Law 94-142 work for everyone."[58] The parents have prevailed, and are entitled to attorney fees, if the legal relationship between the school district and the child is changed and the resolution fosters the purposes of the law. A settlement reached prior to the hearing will suffice.[59] The total or partial reversal of a consistent refusal to supply services will meet the standard of "changed relationship" and "furtherance of purpose." The purposes of the HCPA are fostered by the child's receipt of "appropriate special services necessary to education that the child had not received prior to the request for the due process hearing."[60] Fees must be reasonable and based on prevailing rates for the type and quality of services.[61] Parents are increasingly represented by attorneys.[62] In a survey of New York State hearing officers, attorney representation was found to improve the efficacy of the hearing process and its fairness as perceived by parents.[63]

In order to protect the best interests of the handicapped child, Congress placed a "stay put" provision in the Act, providing that "during the pendency of any proceedings . . . unless the State or local educational agency and the parents or guardian otherwise agree, the child shall remain in the then current educational placement."[64] The purpose of the "stay put" is to give the child stability during protracted proceedings.

Substantive and Definitional Aspects of the EAHCA

The vague substantive terms of the EAHCA are subject to interpretation by the local school board, from which is tailored an educational plan for the individual needs of the handicapped child. The act defers to local school boards for two reasons. In the first place, the diversity of disabilities under the act militates against universal standards.[65] Second, the formulation of substantive educational standards has traditionally been within the domain of state and local governments.[66]

The EAHCA contains a multitude of terms subject to crucial interpretation. The most important (and most disputed) terms are "handicapped" or "disabled,"[67] "free and appropriate public education" ("FAPE"),[68] "related services,"[69] and "least restrictive environment."[70]

"HANDICAPPED" OR "DISABLED"

The term "handicapped" or "disabled" refers to those children with

> . . . mental retardation, hearing impairments including deafness, speech or language impairments, visual impairments including blindness, serious emotional disturbance, orthopedic impairments, autism, traumatic brain injury, other health impairments, or specific learning disabilities.[71]

This definition is often at issue when parents consider their child has been wrongfully characterized as "disabled."[72] The terms utilized for the definition—"mental retardation," "seriously emotionally disturbed,"[73] and "specific learning disabilities"—are both undefined and extremely broad. Such indeterminacy extends the scope for dispute if the label "disabled" is abhorrent to the child or parent.[74] Unfortunately, case law is often confused and unhelpful. Mental health professionals should familiarize themselves with the regulations in their respective states and with the local interpretation of the key terms.

"FREE AND APPROPRIATE EDUCATION" OR "FAPE"

Once a child is characterized as "disabled" under the Act, the school district has an obligation to provide the child with a "free and appropriate" education (FAPE). Implementation of this requirement has followed the bulk of EAHCA litigation and involves the most basic dispute: How will the child be educated? The vague and nonfunctional definition of "free and appropriate education" in the EAHCA is as follows:

> . . . special education and related services that—(A) have been provided at public expense, under public supervision and direction, and without charge, (B) meet the standards of the State educational agency, (C) include an appropriate preschool, elementary, or secondary school education in the State involved, and (D) are provided in conformity with the individualized education program . . .[75]

In 1982, in the case of *Board of Education v. Rowley,* the Supreme Court examined the meaning of "free and appropriate" education (FAPE).[76] The district court had defined "free and appropriate education" as "an opportunity to achieve full potential commensurate with the opportunity provided to other children."[77] The "commensurate opportunity" test was designed to provide a substantive standard for application in the subsequent judicial review of educational plans established by local school boards.[78] However, the district court's attempt to articulate a reviewable standard and to check the discretion of the school districts was overruled by the Supreme Court.[79] The Supreme Court held that reviewing courts are not free to "substitute their own notions of sound educational policy for those of the school authorities which they review." The Court further stated that a child receives a "free and appropriate public education" when the school provides "personalized instruction with sufficient support services to permit the child to benefit educationally from that instruction."[80]

The Supreme Court decision in *Rowley* was confirmed in a number of later decisions,[81] and eased the way for states to meet the "free and appropriate education" standard. The states had to follow the statutory procedures and provide a child with a program sufficient to confer "some educational benefit" or to enable the child to achieve a "reasonable degree of self-sufficiency." However, they were not obliged to strive to actualize the child's full potential.[82] The relaxed standard must conform to the basic premises of the legislation, hence an IEP does not conform to the FAPE standard if it is premised on the condition that the child be medicated without the parents' permission.[83]

The *Rowley* decision has been expanded upon in recent years.[84] In *Polk v. Central Susquehanna,* the Third Circuit Court of Appeals stated that *Rowley* was an "avowedly narrow opinion" designed to ensure a "basic floor of opportunity."[85] Relying upon the language in *Rowley* itself, as well as on the legislative history of the EAHCA, the court in *Polk* concluded that the "educational benefit" conferred by the state must be more than minimal.[86] In *Polk* and an earlier case, *Board of Education v. Diamond,* the state was obliged to improve upon services that were being provided.[87] Recent opinions have sustained this activist strain and have moved beyond the deference to school authorities characterizing *Rowley*. Accordingly, while *Rowley* does not require a school to provide the "best education that money can buy," the educational plan must provide the means of achieving "satisfactory or meaningful progress" toward the child's unique educational goals.[88]

In implementing the FAPE requirement, the states may impose standards that exceed the requirements of the EAHCA. Prior to 1982, in Iowa, for example, legislative policy was

> . . . to provide and to require school districts to make provisions, as an integral part of public education, for special education opportunities sufficient to meet the needs and maximize the capabilities of children requiring special education.[89]

This was interpreted as requiring a parity of education opportunities between handicapped and nonhandicapped children.[90] The legislature recognized that the parity interpretation would demand a heavy commitment of state funds, and therefore amended the legislation to bring it into conformity with the less exacting FAPE standard. Other states have acted similarly, whereas still others have allowed the more onerous parity standard to remain.[91]

Free appropriate public education requires the education of emotionally handicapped children in "hospitals and institutions" where necessary. For example, after their son's expulsion from school because of his behavior, parents asked the school system to evaluate their son for psychiatric disturbance. Their request was denied. The parents hospitalized their son and brought an action against the school system in order to recover costs of hospitalization. Rejecting the defense that the son had been hospitalized for noneducational, medical reasons, the court held that the parents were entitled to the hospitalization costs.[92]

"RELATED SERVICES"

Another term that has been subject to dispute is "related services." The EAHCA requires that "disabled" children receive the "related services" necessary to help them benefit from their educational program.[93] The act states that

> . . . "related services" means transportation, and such developmental, corrective, and other supportive services (including speech pathology and audiology, psychological services, physical and occupational therapy, recreation, including therapeutic recreation, social work services, counseling services, including rehabilitation counseling, and medical services except that such medical services shall be for diagnostic and evaluation purposes only) as may be required to assist a child with a disability to benefit from special education . . .[94]

The expense of raising handicapped children is often heavy; parents will sometimes seek to obtain state assistance by arguing, for example, that medical procedures should be characterized as a "related service."[95] In *Irving Independent School District v. Tatro,* the Supreme Court addressed the issue of whether a school must provide clean, intermittent catheterization as a "related service" to a child with spina bifada.[96] The court stated that "only those services necessary to aid a handicapped child to benefit from a special education must be provided, regardless of how easily a school nurse or layperson could furnish them."[97] Because catheterization was necessary to allow the child to derive "benefit from her education," it was deemed a "related service." Without catheterization, the child would have been unable to attend school.[98] The court rejected the argument that, since catheterization was not a diagnostic or evaluative medical service, it was excluded from the act. The definition of "medical services" was confined to those services provided by a hospital or licensed physician. Because catheterization could be performed by the school nurse, it was not a "medical service" but rather a "supportive service" and covered under the act.[99]

"LEAST RESTRICTIVE ENVIRONMENT"

The EAHCA requires that schools educate handicapped children in the "least restrictive environment." The act requires states to ensure that

> . . . to the maximum extent appropriate, handicapped children . . . are educated with children who are not handicapped, and that special classes, separate schooling, or other removal of handicapped children from the regular educational environment occurs only when the nature or severity of the handicap is such that education in regular classes with the use of supplementary aids and services cannot be achieved satisfactorily.[100]

"Mainstreaming" is based on the logic that integrated classrooms will alter social attitudes toward the handicapped and facilitate their adjustment to society.[101] Despite the EAHCA, the attempt to "mainstream" handicapped children has been largely unsuccessful.[102] It was estimated that in 1987, 74 percent of all "disabled children" were being educated in pull-out or separate programs.[103] In schools that offer strong administrative support to parents, teachers, and children, mainstreaming is more successful.[104] Junior high school teachers were found to be the most resistant, particularly in the absence of adequate support.[105] One critic has stated that "professional practices and incentives tend to emphasize pull-outs, self-contained classes, or completely segregated institutional settings rather than the delivery of programs and services to children placed in integrated classrooms."[106]

The Supreme Court has not announced a test regarding the EAHCA "mainstreaming" or "least restrictive environment" provision; however, several Circuit Courts have spoken.[107] The Fifth Circuit in *Daniel R.R. v. State Board of Education* (1989), and the Eleventh Circuit in *Greer v. Rome City School District* (1991) applied a two-part analysis to determine whether a school district was making proper efforts to "mainstream" disabled children.[108]

The first part of this test asks whether "education in the regular classroom, with the use of supplemental aids and services, can be achieved satisfactorily." Thus, before and during the IEP process, and before the decision not to "mainstream" is made, school boards must consider whether the child can be satisfactorily educated in a regular classroom.[109] The court in *Greer* stated that, in making this decision, school boards should consider (1) the comparative benefits of "mainstreaming" versus separating the child; (2) the effect of the child on the education of other children in the classroom; and (3) the costs of the supplemental aids and services necessary to accommodate the "mainstreamed" child.[110]

If the school intends to remove the child and place him in a pull-out classroom, the second part of the *Daniel R.R.–Greer* test is applied. Has the school mainstreamed the child to the maximum extent appropriate?[111] The force of *Daniel R.R.* and *Greer* goes to the school board's decision making: it must closely consider and justify its decisions on "mainstreaming". The criteria in these tests oppose the persistent practice of placing children with difficult behavior in special classes.[112]

These procedural requirements will draw support from a recently promoted doctrine known as the Regular Educational Initiative (REI). The REI is based on the philosophy that, since the United States is characterized by multicultural diversity, normal children are better educated with others who are widely divergent in ability. However, educational pluralism has costs in terms of teacher and student stress. In practice, physically, sensorily, and emotionally handicapped children tend to be mixed with the nonhandicapped in classrooms taught by staff without special training. The handicapped child may be marooned in a stressful environment. Support services may bolster the REI, but little research has been done on its impact, costs, limits, and effectiveness or into the nature of those necessary support services.[113] The REI may lead, it is feared, to a dismantling of special education without providing adequate alternative.[114]

Amendments to the EAHCA

A variety of amendments have been made since the original passage of the Education for All Handicapped Children Act. In 1986 Congress enacted Public Law 99-457, "The Education of the Handicapped Act Amendments," and in 1991 enacted Public Law 102-119 entitling the act, the Individuals with Disabilities Education Act (IDEA). These amendments extended the legislation to handicapped and developmentally delayed children below six years of age.[115] Prior to this change, the act covered only children between the ages of six and twenty-one.

Title I of the 1986 Amendments implements a system of early intervention for infants and toddlers from birth to two years of age with cognitive, physical, language, speech, psychosocial or self-help skill development problems. Early screening, identification and evaluation are provided together with health services to enable the infant or toddler to benefit from early intervention. If it seeks to receive federal funding, the state must provide early intervention services, including:

1. Family training and counseling
2. Home visits and special instruction

3. Occupational and physical therapy
4. Speech pathology and audiology
5. Psychological services
6. Diagnostic and evaluative medical services[116]

The state is also required to establish an Individualized Family Service Plan (IFSP). Building upon the IEP concept, the IFSP requires a statement of the natural environments in which services are provided. It includes the following, as amended by the 1991 act,[117] emphasizing the central role of parents in designing and implementing services.

In assessment and program development, each infant or toddler with a disability and his or her family shall receive:

1. A multidisciplinary assessment of the strengths and needs of the infant or toddler, and the identification of services appropriate to meet such needs
2. A family-directed assessment of the resources, priorities, and concerns of the family and the identification of the supports and services necessary to enhance the family's capacity to meet the developmental needs of their infant or toddler with a disability
3. A written individualized family service plan developed by a multidisciplinary team including the parent or guardian as required by subsection (d) of this section[118]

The written plan must comply with detailed statutory requirements in containing:

1. A statement of the infant's or toddler's present levels of physical development, cognitive development, communication development, social or emotional development, and adaptive development, based on acceptable objective criteria
2. A statement of the family's resources, priorities, and concerns relating to enhancing the development of the family's infant or toddler with a disability
3. A statement of the major outcomes expected to be achieved for the infant or toddler and the family, and the criteria, procedures, and timelines used to determine the degree to which progress toward achieving the outcomes is being made and whether modifications or revisions of the outcomes or services are necessary
4. A statement of specific early intervention services necessary to meet the unique needs of the infant or toddler, and the family, including the frequency, intensity, and the method of delivering services
5. A statement of the natural environments in which early intervention services shall appropriately be provided
6. The projected dates for initiation of services and the anticipated duration of services
7. The name of the case manager (referred to as the "service coordinator") from the profession most immediately relevant to the infant's or toddler's or family's needs (or who is otherwise qualified to carry out all applicable responsibilities under this

part), who will be responsible for the implementation of the plan and coordination with other agencies and persons

8. The steps to be taken supporting the transition of the toddler with a disability to services provided under the Act to the extent such services are considered appropriate

The 1991 amendments require that the contents of the IFSP be explained fully to parents or guardians and that they give informed consent to the intervention services described in the plan.

Title II of the 1986 Amendments provides funding for handicapped children three to five years of age. Title III of the Amendments deals with discretionary programs for deaf-blind children.[119] This section also discusses secondary and postsecondary education for handicapped individuals as well as grants for research, demonstrations, and personal training.[120]

In 1990, the EAHCA was further amended and retitled "The Individuals With Disabilities Education Act" (IDEA). The term "handicapped children" has been replaced throughout the act with the term "children with disabilities."[121] In addition, a variety of definitional changes were made. Traumatic brain injuries and autism have been added to the list of disabilities, and "mainstreaming" has been prioritized as a goal of the Act.[122] The 1991 Amendments were designed to facilitate the development of a comprehensive "seamless" system of services for children from birth to five years of age inclusive, who are "experiencing developmental delays" in one or more of the following areas—physical development, cognitive development, communication development, social and emotional development, or adaptive development—and thus need special education and related services.[123] It was reasoned that children experiencing developmental delays do not fall precisely under the established categories. Recognition of this category as a "disability" would avoid procrustean diagnosis. IFSPs may be used for children aged three to five, inclusive, instead of IEPs. The amendments also continue the tradition of procedural safeguards. Section 17 clarifies that the parent or guardian has the right to written notice of, and written consent to, the exchange of information among agencies. Early intervention may be declined without jeopardizing other services.[124]

Summary

The EAHCA was enacted with idealism. Unfortunately, the federal funds provided by the act were insufficient to make it work. School systems, out of necessity, sought to provide services as inexpensively as possible, sometimes simply seeking to exclude certain children from services altogether. Nevertheless, the overall impact of the EAHCA has been positive, for services are now more readily available to families and to their disabled children, while judicial intervention protects the interests of the disadvantaged.

THE ROLE OF THE MENTAL HEALTH CONSULTANT

The mental health clinician becomes involved in EAHCA hearings in one of two circumstances: as a witness for the child, or as a witness for the school district.

The first involves a request for an expert witness on behalf of a student whose parents are seeking an IEP, now an IFSP (or an alteration of an existing IEP or IFSP). Commonly, the parents will be seeking special mental health services such as placement in a day hospital or residential program. In these circumstances, the task of the clinician is to provide a comprehensive evaluation, to discuss the treatment alternatives (analyzing their relative desirability, feasibility, and costs), and to render an opinion concerning the preferable alternative. The clinician should have a close knowledge of the local regulations derived from the legislation in order to render an opinion that can be interpreted or applied by the hearing officer.

The evaluation involves a review of school, medical, and mental health records, along with any other documents that could shed light on the child's biopsychosocial adjustment, strengths, and weaknesses. Parents and child will be interviewed for history-taking and mental status examination. Testing will be performed, as required, in order to assess intellectual, neurocognitive, speech and language, and psychoeducational functioning, together with personality and psychological adjustment. The evaluation converges upon the following questions:

1. Does the child suffer from a psychological disorder?
2. If so, what is its nature? How severe is it? Does it impede learning? And if it does, for how long has it done so?

Does it involve at least one of the following?

3. An inability to build or sustain personal relationships (e.g., as in autism, schizoid or schizotypal personality, or avoidant personality)?
4. Inappropriate behavior or feelings (e.g., as in attention deficit disorder, schizophrenia, bipolar disorder, obsessive-compulsive disorder, dissociative disorder, organic brain disorder, or tic disorder)?
5. Pervasive depression (e.g., as in depressive disorder)?
6. Physical symptoms or fears associated with school problems (e.g., as in psychological factors affecting physical condition, somatoform disorder, or separation anxiety disorder)?

Finally,

7. Can "social maladjustment" be excluded?

The meaning of "social maladjustment" can be twisted in many directions. It is usually interpreted as "conduct disorder" (i.e., long-standing delinquent or antisocial behavior) or behavior that is predominantly the result of family dysfunction. When cross-examined in a due process hearing, clinicians should expect challenges wielding "social maladjustment" as a blunt weapon.

The serious emotional disturbance most likely to impress hearing officers is characterized as follows: It is severe in intensity and of at least twelve months' duration; there is evidence that the disturbance seriously impedes learning, in that the student's achievement is markedly below expectation; the disturbance seriously disrupts social relationships or is characterized by depression, physical symptoms, or fear. Furthermore, the condition must be distinguishable from conduct disorder or a transient reaction to family dysfunction or psychosocial stress.

If the clinician can substantiate the diagnosis of "seriously emotionally disturbed" ("behaviorally disordered"), "related services" must be recommended. What are the alternative treatment services that could help the student benefit from the IEP? What are their advantages, disadvantages, relative expense, and feasibility? Which would be preferred, and where could it be implemented?

The evaluation, opinion, and recommendations should be incorporated in a report, organized under the following headings.

1. Circumstances of Referral
2. Purpose of Evaluation
3. Informed Consent
4. Sources of Data
   a. School records
   b. Previous evaluations
   c. Interviews
   d. Psychological testing
5. Review of Documents and Records
6. Summary of Interviews
7. Psychological Test Results
8. Discussion
9. Opinion
10. Recommendations for Related Services
11. Appendixes

This is the only type of forensic report in which jargon is *de rigueur*. Whenever possible use the terminology adopted in the local version of the EAHCA. In composing the report, the clinician should be careful to exclude confidential material of a sensitive nature, a particular problem when a treating clinician is subsequently asked to prepare a report and testify. In that circumstance, it is usually preferable to refer the case elsewhere for evaluation. If it is necessary to discuss privileged information (e.g., parental mental illness), the clinician must seek permission of those who would be affected by such a disclosure and who have the right to keep such matters confidential. Generally, however, the focus of the report should be kept upon the child. If the child's emotional disturbance can be construed as a reaction to family dysfunction ("social maladjustment"), the complainant will probably not prevail.

The second situation in which a mental health clinician may become involved is when, as a consultant to a school system, he or she is asked to evaluate a case in which a parent claims that related mental health services are required. Sometimes the consultant is asked to critique another clinician's report on this matter.

Recalling that many of these matters are hard-fought, the clinician can expect to be called as a witness at a due process hearing. During this hearing, he or she will be qualified, examined directly, and cross-examined. Due process hearings are conducted in adversary fashion. Complainant and respondent present evidence through documents and witnesses, each attacking the other side's case in cross-examination.

CHAPTER 5

CHILD CUSTODY DISPUTES

INTRODUCTION

Divorce is a serious social problem with a high risk of emotional disturbance in both parents and children. In most industrial countries, the incidence of divorce is high and rising. In 1985 there were 1.19 million divorces in the United States, affecting 1.1 million children.[1] In 1980, 23 percent of all children under eighteen years of age (17 percent of white and 60 percent of black children) were living with single or foster parents. At least one marriage in three will end in divorce, and one-half of all divorces will occur within six years of marriage. Remarriages have a 50 percent chance of breaking up.

In 1982, more than six million single-parent families were headed by women, a 70 percent rise since 1970. Between 1970 and 1980, the absolute number of single-parent families headed by fathers dropped from about 700,000 (11 percent) to 600,000 (9 percent).[2] Of all divorced women raising children singlehandedly, only 30 percent get any financial child support from their former husbands. This is usually quite modest, and often irregular. In 1980 a single mother raising two children had a median income of $8,500, in contrast to a married couple with two children, who had a median income of $23,000.

MARRIAGE AND PARENTAL OBLIGATIONS

The term "marriage" refers to the act of becoming married, to the wedding ceremony, and to the state of being married. Legally, it refers to a contract between a man and a woman that formalizes their union and binds them together until parted by death or divorce. Incumbent on people who marry are legal obligations to each other, to the community, and to the children who spring from the union.

The freedom to marry is a basic constitutional right[3] not to be infringed upon (e.g., by antimiscegenation laws), except that the state may prohibit plural marriages,[4] homosexual marriages,[5] and marriages between closely related kin.

In most states the wedding ceremony need follow no specified procedure, as long as it is properly witnessed and recorded. Common law marriage is also a contractual legal union, despite the lack of a formal ceremony. Nonmarital cohabitation, a common practice today, may affect the division of property when the union is dissolved.[6]

The state may not infringe upon a married couple's right to use contraceptives[7] or to obtain surgical sterilization,[8] or, for that matter, upon most aspects of their procreational sexual lives. In *Roe v. Wade* (1973), the Supreme Court held that, in the first trimester of pregnancy, a woman's privacy right is paramount and the state may not intervene to prevent abortion. However, in the second and third trimesters, the state has a compelling interest in the health of the mother and the fetus, and the right to regulate abortion. While adhering to *Roe v. Wade,* the Supreme Court has rejected this trichotomy and replaced it with a more generalized criterion that the state may not place an undue burden on the woman's exercise of her privacy rights.[9] The extension of these contentious rights is discussed in Chapter 3. The role of the state in reproductive decisions continues to be hotly debated.

The state regulates relatively few aspects of the marital relationship; however, courts are authorized to intervene in the parent–child relationship in order to protect children from neglect or abuse. For example, a court may order medical treatment for a child over his parents' religious objections.[10]

Parents are obligated to support their children until the age of eighteen (twenty-one in some states), regardless of the sex or legitimacy of the child. This obligation ends when the child is emancipated or if parental rights have been legally severed. The obligation may continue beyond the age of majority if so stipulated in the terms of a legal separation between parents[11] or if required by statute.[12]

A novel aspect of the issue of parental obligations is defining who is a parent. Technological advances have created options unheard of just a few years ago. In surrogate parenting, for example, a woman contracts to bear a child, usually following artificial insemination, and to deliver the child to the sperm donor and his infertile wife. Another form of surrogate parenting involves the implantation of an embryo in the uterus of a surrogate mother who agrees to carry the fetus to term and then deliver the child to the persons with whom she has contracted. If the legal definition of "parent" is expanded to include a surrogate mother, new legal relationships will be created and family litigation will multiply (see later in this chapter).

THE TERMINATION OF MARRIAGE

Marriage is legally terminated by annulment or divorce. The relatively uncommon procedure of annulment is based on a condition operating at the time of the marriage (e.g., impotence or insanity) which invalidated the marriage from the outset. Most terminated marriages are ended by divorce, often preceded by legal separation.

Until recently, the grounds for divorce were adultery, physical or mental cruelty, habitual drunkenness, desertion, and conviction for a felony. If one party could prove the other to be at fault, the guilty party might then be subject to penalties (e.g., loss of child custody or the payment of legal costs). The party sued for divorce might attempt to reverse the charges, aiming to prove his or her spouse to be at fault or to block divorce by disproving the spouse's allegations of impropriety. During the past two decades, however, most states have adopted a "no-fault" divorce policy, although some retain the traditional grounds for divorce as well. "No-fault" divorce usually requires evidence that the marriage is "irretrievably broken." The mere consent of the parties is generally unacceptable.

In the hope of curbing overprecipitate divorce, many states require a period of waiting between the filing of a divorce action and the hearing of the case. In some states conciliation counseling can be ordered by the court and provided, if necessary, at public expense. If reconciliation has not been achieved, divorce may be preceded by mediation in order to help the couple decide upon child custody and the division of property. If mediation is unsuccessful, the couple can go to judicial arbitration or a full adversary hearing.

Alimony and child support may be awarded to the economically weaker spouse, usually the wife, if she is prevented from working by the demands of child care. In some states, a husband regarded as "at fault" may be penalized, although this practice is declining. Alimony usually ends if the former spouse remarries. The problem of defaulting on child support payments has received recent attention resulting in the enactment of the Child Support Recovery Act of 1992.[13] This creates an offence of willful failure to pay past due child support obligations to a child residing in another state.

The Uniform Parentage Act (UPA) suggests the following guidelines for determination of the amount of, and period for, child support:

1. The needs of the child
2. The standard of living and circumstances of the parents
3. The relative financial means of the parents
4. The earning ability of the parents
5. The need and capacity of the child for education, including higher education
6. The age of the child
7. The financial resources and earning ability of the child
8. The responsibility of the parents for the support of others
9. The value of services contributed by the custodial parent

THE DETERMINATION OF CUSTODY

In most divorces, custody is not disputed. In 80–90 percent of contested cases, child custody is awarded to the mother and visitation to the father. Custody litigation usually arises later. *Custody proceedings* occur when the dispute is between biological parents. When a nonparent (e.g., a grandparent) challenges a biological parent for custody, the term *guardianship proceedings* is applied. In the initial custody proceeding, the court usually looks only to the child's best interests and does not require either parent to prove the other unfit. In a guardianship proceeding, on the other hand, there is a presumption in favor of the biological parent, which the nonparent must overcome by proving the parent unfit. Sometimes one parent will attempt to prove the other unfit in order to defeat a prior custody award.

Two major policy changes in awarding custody have occurred within the English and American legal systems. The first is the shift in focus from parental rights to children's interests. The second is the trend away from custody determinations based on parental sex. In order to understand the modern criteria according to which judges award custody in contested cases, it is helpful to review the historical evolution of child custody litigation. In the end, however, the law of child custody continues to evolve upon an unstable policy foundation.[14]

Legal Doctrines

PATERNAL PREFERENCE

In common law, it was the father's responsibility to care for his offspring. They, in turn, were the father's property and, along with all marital property, reverted to him after divorce. Paternal preference originated in Roman jurisprudence and was seen as an expression of natural and divine law. It was not until the reign of Henry VIII that the Court of Wards and Liveries began to view custody as encompassing the protection of children as well as the transfer of property.[15] The father's right was considered superior to the mother's because he bore the primary responsibility of supporting and maintaining the child.[16]

The presumption favoring the father began to break down in the nineteenth century. In one famous case, *Shelley v. Westbrooke,*[17] Percy Bysshe Shelley was unable to prevail over his deceased wife's parents in a dispute concerning the custody of his children, because of his "irreligious and immoral" behavior. The poet was a professed atheist, and the court expressed horror that he would educate his children according to his "blasphemous" beliefs.

American courts followed the paternal preference rule, but less strictly than the English courts. In *Brenneman v. Hildebrandt,*[18] when an abusive father seeking custody invoked the common law's paternal preference, the court found for the mother, reasoning that in "cases of this nature the best interests of the children is the primary object to obtain. All else being equal, the father's rights are superior."

MATERNAL PREFERENCE AND THE TENDER YEARS DOCTRINE

In the nineteenth century the presumption of *maternal preference* was first articulated. According to this, the *tender years doctrine,* the mother was the more appropriate parent to raise the children, unless she was proved "unfit" (see below). The doctrine of maternal preference had a practical basis: Unless a wet nurse could be obtained, a weaned infant might not survive the primitive techniques of artificial feeding available before the 1920s.

The doctrine survived well into this century. In the 1970s, thirty-one states explicitly preferred to give custody to the mother in the absence of other factors.[19] The presumption in favor of the mother "[springs from the truth] well known by all men, [that] no other love is quite so tender, no other solicitude quite so deep, and no other devotion quite so enduring as that of a mother" for a child,[20] and illustrates the reverence with which the depth of a mother's love for her child was regarded.[21]

In America, the tender years doctrine was first articulated in *Helms v. Franciscus* ("While the father is the rightful and legal guardian of his minor children, it would violate the laws of nature to snatch an infant from an affectionate mother and place it in the coarse hands of the father.")[22] and in *Miner v. Miner*.[23] The upper age of tenderness varied from five years in some states to thirteen in others. In England, the tradition of paternal preference was stronger, and the tender years doctrine was not codified until 1839, in Justice Talford's Act,[24] which allowed the Chancery Courts to award custody to the mother if the children were under seven years of age. This doctrine modified the presumption of paternal preference by postulating that the mother should be the preferred caregiver, particularly when the child was young.

Preference based on parental sex has been challenged on the basis that it violates Fourteenth Amendment equal protection rights. It was ruled unconstitutional by state courts in Alabama, Illinois, New York, and Utah[25] because, with the blurring of sharply divided family roles,[26] the sex of the parent does not necessarily determine which is the better caretaker, and maternal preference discriminates against fathers. West Virginia and Oklahoma, on the other hand, found the presumption in favor of the mother constitutional because, in fact, mothers customarily provide the majority of child care.[27] Though never decided in federal court, the Oklahoma decision was called into doubt by a later state court decision.[28] West Virginia has subsequently abandoned maternal preference in favor of awarding custody to the primary caregiver, regardless of sex.[29]

Most legislatures have abolished maternal preference and the tender years presumption in favor of "best interests of the child" criteria. By 1990 only Tennessee allowed parental sex to be considered when awarding custody, and then only when a child is of tender years.[30] In the Tennessee practice guide *Divorce, Alimony and Child Custody,* because of the dubious constitutionality of the presumption, attorneys for the mother are advised to rely on expert testimony rather than the tender years presumption if the child is over thirty months old.[31]

THE BEST INTERESTS OF THE CHILD

The *"best interests" doctrine* arose after the latter part of the last century.[32] In recent years, most states have codified the criteria to be considered in deciding what is in a child's best interests. In 1974 the Uniform Marriage and Divorce Act (UMDA) was approved by the American Bar Association. Adopted wholly or in modified form by most states, the UMDA contains a section concerning the best interests criteria which represents a distillation of contemporary thinking on this matter. The relevant section (402) is as follows:

The court shall determine custody in accordance with the best interests of the child. The court shall consider all relevant factors including:

1. The wishes of the child's parent or parents as to his custody
2. The wishes of the child as to his custodian
3. The interaction and interrelationship of the child with his parent, his siblings, and any other person who may significantly affect the child's best interests
4. The child's adjustment to his home, school, and community
5. The mental and physical health of all individuals involved

The relevant section (722.23) of the Michigan Child Custody Act (1970) defines the "best interests" criteria in more detail:

a. The love, affection, and other emotional ties existing between the parties involved and the child
b. The capacity and disposition of the parties involved to give the child love, affection, and guidance and continuation of the educating and raising of the child in its religion or creed, if any
c. The capacity and disposition of the parties involved to provide the child with food, clothing, medical care or other remedial care recognized and permitted under the laws of this state in place of medical care, and other material needs
d. The length of time the child has lived in a stable, satisfactory environment, and the desirability of maintaining continuity
e. The permanence, as a family unit, of the existing or proposed custodial home or homes
f. The moral fitness of the parties involved
g. The mental and physical health of the parties involved
h. The home, school, and community record of the child
i. The reasonable preference of the child, if the court deems the child to be of sufficient age to express preference
j. The willingness and ability of each of the parents to facilitate and encourage a close and continuing parent–child relationship between the child and the other parent
k. Any other factor considered by the court to be relevant to a particular child custody dispute

The judge has broad discretion in applying the above criteria. Given the fact that the mother has often been made primary custodian in the initial order, or that she has become *de facto* the primary custodian, the desirability of preserving continuity of care typically puts the burden on the father to prove maternal unfitness or to substantiate some other compelling interest that would override the argument for continuity.

Generally, it is assumed that it is in a child's best interests to be placed in the custody of a biological parent. Under the "best interests" doctrine, however, if a child's welfare conflicts with the parent's rights, the child's interests will be given the greater weight.[33] When, without allowing testimony by the child or the child's psychologist, a trial court reinstated and expanded visitation by a father who had been accused of sexually abusing his three-and-a-half-year-old daughter, the appellate court reversed the decision, because the trial court had focused on the father's interest rather than the child's. While there was some concern that the accusations might be false, the court noted that "the extreme harm caused by child sexual abuse requires the court to subordinate all matters and, if necessary, to place a parent's interests second to the best interests of the child," and required all future visitation be in the presence of a court-approved monitor until a full hearing could be concluded.[34]

PREFERENCE FOR THE PRIMARY CARETAKER

When both parents are equally fit, an increasingly popular way for judges to determine the best interests of a child of tender years is to look to which parent was the child's *primary caretaker* immediately prior to, or at the time of, the custody hearing. The primary caretaker can be determined by examining which parent usually performs the following functions:

1. Preparation and planning of meals
2. Bathing, grooming, and dressing the child
3. Buying, cleaning, and caring for the child's clothes
4. Providing medical care
5. Arranging for social activities
6. Arranging babysitting and/or daycare
7. Putting the child to bed and waking him or her
8. Disciplining the child
9. Providing religious, cultural, and social education
10. Teaching basic skills[35]

In some states, preference is given to the primary caretaker; in other states that is no more than one important factor. In West Virginia, it is a legal presumption. Whether preference or presumption, in order to defeat a custody award to the primary caretaker, the petitioner must demonstrate him or her to be unfit. To be considered fit, the primary caregiver must provide adequate and appropriate child care and refrain from immoral behavior in the child's presence.

Although the primary caretaker premise is worded neutrally, it is usually the mother who provides most of the care for young children and receives custody in jurisdictions that follow this rule.[36] Theoretically, parental sex is not a factor; parental affection, motivation, health, and competence are accorded due weight. However, in reality, if the mother has been named custodian in the initial order, it is difficult for the father to overcome the continuity-of-care argument or, for that matter, to countervail any residual "tender years" bias on the judge's part.

INDETERMINACY: THE PROBLEM WITH THE "BEST INTERESTS" CRITERIA

Has the "best interests" principle resulted in better custody decisions than awards based on maternal presumption, or has there been merely an exchange of one set of problems for another?

The chief criticism of the best interests doctrine is its indeterminacy: the difficulty of determining the probable or even possible outcome of placing the child with one parent or the other when neither is clearly unfit. In order to determine the appropriate custody arrangement, a judge must have adequate information to predict the effect of granting custody to either parent, and must be able to weigh the value of the respective outcomes. However, there is no universally acknowledged method for prediction.[37] Even if the outcomes were knowable, there is no clear consensus as to which values are clearly superior.[38] Little, if any, statutory guidance is afforded to judges in choosing among such influences as intellectual stimulation, spiritual and religious training, and so on. While in other circumstances parents can usually speak to the child's interests, in a custody dispute it is unrealistic to expect unbiased opinions. Placing the burden of the decision on the child puts him or her in the uncomfortable position of straining the relationship with the other parent.[39]

One byproduct of abandoning earlier presumptions in favor of vaguer discretionary, "best interests" criteria is that litigation has been encouraged. A drawn-out custody dispute is not in the best interests of the child; it causes pain, anxiety, and strain in parent–child relationships.[40] The parent with temporary custody has an incentive to prolong litigation because it increases his or her chances of being awarded custody as the primary caretaker. The parent with greater financial resources also has reason to do so, for he or she can hang on and wear the other down.[41] Despite the formal standard, some courts continue to favor mothers,[42] while others view working mothers as having a diminished role and conclude equality in parental responsibility.[43]

As an alternative to the "best interests" criteria, a return to maternal preference has been recommended. It is suggested that fewer custody contests would result, thus averting trauma to many children.[44] Another proposal is to allow the divorcing couple to negotiate custody, with judicial intervention only if the parties are unable to settle the matter themselves.[45] This proposal is premised on the fact that, since parents have more information about the child than a judge does, they can make a more informed decision. However, at present there seems to be no trend away from the gender-neutral, highly discretionary, best interests criteria. Mnookin suggests that the child's best interests be realized in the situation in which he or she will have the most future options.[46]

The practical result of the "best interests" standard is that custody determinations are inconsistent from state to state and from judge to judge. Lowery asked judges to rank order the factors they considered the most important in making custody awards. The most significant factors cited were in the following order:

1. Parental mental instability
2. The parent's sense of responsibility for the child
3. Kinship ties
4. Parental moral character
5. The capacity to provide stability
6. The parent's affection for the child
7. The desirability of keeping siblings together
8. The capacity to provide access to schools
9. The child's tender years
10. Parental physical health[47]

Of particular interest are the high ranking given to "mental instability" and the reappearance of the "tender years" presumption, despite the qualifications that currently surround these issues. Wyer, Gaylord, and Grove point out that such presumptions as the "tender years" doctrine simplify (and regularize) custody determination. [48] Without presumptions, the judge must proceed case by case, weighing the facts presented in court—a situation of extreme uncertainty. Small wonder, then, that some judges tend to revert to presumptive guidelines, particularly if they coincide with personal biases.

Lowery's 1981 study suggests that judges weigh parental character and competence more highly than the child's wishes or the desirability of maintaining continuity in the child's life. Alarmingly, the study also suggests that mental health experts' recommendations are perceived as separate from the dominant factor, parental competence, and accorded low weight.

Types of Custody

The custodial parent or parents have the right to make all decisions about the child's "care, control, education, health and religion."[49] As a rule, unless the custody decree specifically confers a right of consultation on a noncustodial parent, the custodial parent alone chooses the child's schools, religious training, and residence.[50]

The states have based their preference for sole custody or joint custody on the "best interest" doctrine; however, they have reached quite different conclusions. For example, some statutes create a rebuttable presumption that joint custody is in a child's best interests, provided the parents agree.[51] If parental agreement is not addressed in a statute favoring joint custody, some courts have held that it is a prerequisite to joint custody,[52] while others have held that it is necessary only for the child to have a strong relationship with both parents, and that there be no requirement for the parents to have an amicable relationship, as long as the potential for cooperation exists.[53] Other states prefer sole custody and find a presumption against joint custody because "such orders are usually unworkable."[54]

JOINT CUSTODY

Joint custody is roughly synonymous with "shared parenting," "coparenting," "concurrent custody," "cocustody," and "joint managing conservators." "Split custody" or "divided custody" refers to the division of physical custody between the parents.

Berman and Kirsh (1982) describe joint custody as comprising two elements: *legal custody* and *physical custody*. Legal custody refers to the parent who has the authority to make decisions about the child's welfare; in joint custody, decisions are shared between the parents. Physical custody refers to the parent with whom the child will reside; in joint custody, physical custody may be alternated between those having legal custody or may remain primarily with one of the legal custodians.

The alternation of physical custody between parents when both sought custody was surprisingly common at the turn of the century.[55] When examined in light of the child's best interests, the practice declined. The division of physical custody between parents is currently avoided because of a child's need for continuity in order to ensure emotional well-being and development.[56] In contrast, joint legal custody with sole physical custody is looked on favorably in many jurisdictions.[57]

Joint custody appears to be most successful when parents and children want it and are committed to making it work; when the parental homes are in reasonable proximity so that the children's usual routine is not disrupted; when the parents respect each other and are able to communicate about the children without letting extraneous matters intrude; when the parents have similar values concerning childrearing; and when the parents' work hours make joint custody practicable.[58]

Davidson and Gerlach (1984) describe four kinds of joint custody statute:

1. The statute leaves it to the judge's discretion to award joint custody. Without guidelines, the discretion allowed may be quite broad.[59]
2. The parents must agree before the judge will award joint custody. This form of statute may coerce some parents into agreeing to joint custody for fear of having the other party designated a "friendly parent" (and thus awarded sole custody).[60]
3. Joint custody can be awarded on the application of only one party. Thus, joint custody may be forced upon an unwilling parent.[61]
4. Joint custody is presumed to be in the best interests of the child, but other options will also be considered. In this circumstance, judges may feel constrained to force joint custody upon parents who do not want it.[62]

Joint custody appeals to the casual observer as the resolution that is least disruptive to children and parents.[63] Research, however, does not allow such a facile conclusion.

Early research studies concerned highly selected middle-class families who had chosen joint custody and were committed to making it work. Nunan (1980), Welsh (1982), Travisano (1982), and Luepnitz (1982) found no difference in overall adjustment between children in joint custody when compared with matched controls in single-parent custody. Abarbanel (1979) and Steinman (1981) found that parents were generally satisfied with joint custody but that some children were stressed by the disruption involved in moving between parental homes, and that, by adolescence, children were likely to want a primary residence. Studies by Cowan (1982) and Wolchik, Braver, and Sandler (1985) found no significant advantage for joint custody in terms of psychological symptomatology in the children; and Cowan found an increase in children's symptomatology when there was conflict between parents, whatever the form of custody.

Grief (1979) found that joint custody promoted greater paternal involvement in child care, whereas Ahrons (1983) noted that this was not invariably the case; and Bowman's (1983) study suggests that, whereas joint custody is more satisfactory for fathers, it is not necessarily so for mothers. Rothberg's (1983) survey of parents who had opted for joint custody found them generally favorably disposed toward it: Mothers appreciated the additional time available to pursue their lives, while fathers enjoyed the sense of continuity. Irving, Benjamin, and Trocme (1984) found that parental satisfaction with joint custody was mitigated if this custodial arrangement was forced upon them by the court, especially if there had been marked conflict between them prior to separation.

The issue of parental conflict has been addressed in several studies. Ilfeld, Ilfeld, and Alexander (1982) found significantly less relitigation after joint custody than after single-parent custody; however, when joint custody had been forced on unwilling parents, the relitigation rate was no different from that associated with single-parent custody. Ilfeld and associates interpreted the relitigation rate as an index of parental conflict. Irving, Benjamin, and Trocme (1984), however, question the validity of this index, and Phear and associates (1984) found no reduction of relitigation following joint custody awards, many of which were forced on parents who had originally applied for single-parent custody.

In summary, joint custody appears to be appropriate in certain circumstances but not in others. For those parents who choose it and are committed to making it work, it can be a satisfying alternative; however, there is no evidence that it is superior for children; indeed, some children are stressed by the changes of domicile involved. There is growing evidence that judicially coerced joint custody is not satisfactory, particularly if there is persisting conflict between the parents. This factor overrides the custodial arrangement itself as a predictor of poor outcome. Felner and Terre (1987) conclude that there is no support for the contention that there should be a rebuttable legal presumption that joint custody is in the best interests of children. Furthermore, a proportion of fathers seek custody as a strategic ploy in order to break down maternal settlement demands; it would be a mistake to lock such parents into a joint custodial arrangement.

SOLE CUSTODY AND VISITATION

The prevalent custody award is that of sole custody to one parent, with visitation allowed to the other. Often, courts will award "reasonable" visitation and leave the parents to arrange the details. However, if the parties cannot agree, the court will decide the details for them. Courts assume that visitation is in the best interests of the child because a relationship with both parents is encouraged, acknowledging the noncustodial parent's interest in continuing contact with the child.[64] Thus, the courts lean toward liberal visitation unless there is good evidence that contact with the noncustodial parent would be deleterious. Visitation will rarely be denied without a finding that the child would be physically or psychologically endangered.[65]

If a child could be harmed by exposure to the noncustodial parent, visitation may be restricted in some fashion or supervised. In rare cases it may be terminated. Visitation restrictions sometimes limit access for the new sexual partner of the noncustodial parent. For example, a lesbian mother was allowed visitation with her children only when her lover, who had attempted to turn the children against their father, was absent.[66] While one father persisted in living in a common-law relationship that was thought to be causing emotional problems for his seven-year old son, overnight visits were suspended.[67] Visitation restrictions may also apply to certain activities; an openly homosexual father was forbidden to take his twelve-year-old son to gay activist social gatherings.[68]

Allegations of sexual abuse can have significant effects on visitation privileges. The court may order supervised visitation until the accused parent is exonerated.[69] Evidence of sexual abuse may result in termination of visitation.[70] When children have been physically abused in the past, the court may require supervision by a third party as a condition of visitation.[71] Criminality, substance abuse, and mental illness commonly bar visitation.

A father serving a thirty-year prison term for attempting to murder his wife and son petitioned the court to allow visitation. Although incarceration alone was not regarded an adequate reason to bar visitation, the circumstances of the case led the court to suspend visitation indefinitely, while allowing contact by telephone and mail.[72] Threats to abduct the child or refusal to return the child after visits are likely to interfere with visitation. In *Mittwede v. Mittwede,* when the father refused to return the child following a visit, the court suspended visitation in order to enforce a previous custody order.[73]

Failure to exercise prior visitation rights is generally not regarded as an adequate reason to block visitation, nor is failure to pay child support or the child's stated preference. When a woman sought to terminate her ex-husband's visitation and parental rights in order to allow her current husband to adopt the child, she argued that the child's father had not visited their child for ten years and had never paid any financial support for the child. The court refused to allow the adoption or to prevent the natural father from resuming visitation (reasoning that the interests of the child would not be endangered), and upheld the father's right of access to his child. The court further noted that a preference expressed by a child who did not know his father should be given slight consideration because a "choice based on emotions inspired by one parent is no choice at all."[74]

THE LEAST DETRIMENTAL ALTERNATIVE

In *Beyond the Best Interests of the Child,* Goldstein, Freud, and Solnit (1973) articulated a controversial approach to custody determination. Basing their conclusions on the young child's different perception of time from that of adults (making it problematic for the child to delay solutions) and on the desirability of maintaining continuity between caregiver and child, they advanced the concept of the *psychological parent,* that is, the particular adult with whom the child has the closest reciprocal relationship. Given the desirability of preserving continuity of care with the psychological parent, of settling custody disputes quickly, and of preventing future legal interference with primary parent–child relationships, Goldstein, Freud, and Solnit recommended that sole custody be awarded to one parent, that the sole custodian should determine all visitation, and that the noncustodial parent should have no legal right to visit the child. This recommendation was designated *the least detrimental alternative.*

The doctrine of least detrimental alternative has been criticized on both scientific and legal grounds. In preparing their argument, the authors relied heavily on research into the impairment of institutionalized infants deprived of maternal care and the effect upon older children of disruptions in maternal care. Their conclusions are arguably more pertinent to permanency planning for neglected infants than to custody determination for older children. Furthermore, older children usually have more than one psychological parent; there is increasing evidence of the deleterious results of excluding noncustodial parents, usually fathers, from contact with their children.[76]

From a judicial standpoint, Goldstein, Freud and Solnit have raised several contentious issues. The least detrimental alternative arrangement effectively terminates the parental constitutional rights of the noncustodial parent. The custodial parent would be in a position to use visitation to manipulate or punish the other party. Custody battles and parental kidnapping would probably be exacerbated. Furthermore, the courts are unlikely to abrogate their authority to regulate custody, for the termination of marriage does not end a parent–child relationship.[76]

PARENTAL PREFERENCE

Scott (1992) criticizes the best interests standard as diluting the importance of prior parental roles. Instead, she argues that past parental roles should be the basis of future custody after divorce. The judicial focus, she suggests, should be to approximate the predivorce patterns of responsibility. Such an arrangement would be less disruptive to the child. Furthermore, it would offer stability in reflecting true preferences and avoid the defects of the best interests standard by mitigating the adversarial nature of custody disputes. However, Scott's recommendation carries the danger that in anticipation of later custody battles, a parent planning divorce could manipulate his or her predivorce involvement in parenting. In other words, the recommendation provides scope for manipulative behavior on the part of parents to the detriment of children. Nevertheless, in comparison with other models, Scott's may lead to less wasteful and destructive posturing, especially if the courts carefully note potential anticipatory behavior changes by parents.

Another important stream of criteria—feminist legal theory—is likely to have an impact of the shape of child custody law. However, the feminist literature is inconsistent and likely to remain riven by ideological differences concerning the role of women in childrearing and their place in society.[77] Some feminists assert that the law should strongly support mothers' claims, whereas others see the law's bias as blocking the way to desirable change in gender roles. This schism reflects the gulf between "sameness" feminists, who seek equality on all levels, and "difference" feminists, who stress women's unique characteristics, needs, and experience.[78]

Factors Influencing Custody Decisions

MORAL UNFITNESS

In the past, adultery, unconventional life-styles, and other irregularities were regarded as sufficient evidence of moral unfitness to preclude custody. In *Graves v. Wooden,* a mother who had had an affair during her first marriage was denied custody of her daughter, despite her subsequent marriage and the apparent lack of adverse effect on the child. The court found a "not inconsiderable risk that the child might tread the same primrose path, seek the same fleshpots, and indulge the same lusts" as the mother. The child's academic excellence was without merit unless "crowned by the inculcation of high ideals, the development of good character, and the preservation of decency, morality and virtue."[79] A year earlier, eight children of a polygamous couple in Utah were removed from their parents' custody because the parents exposed the children to "an immoral environment."[80]

In contrast, the contemporary emphasis on the child's best interests seeks to eliminate moralistic decisions; aberrations of parental conduct are supposed to be taken into account only insofar as they affect the parent's relationship with the child. When a mother engaged in "swinging" and advertised for partners in *Screw* magazine, the court allowed her to retain custody of her six- and nine-year-old children because her activities did not "involve or affect" her children.[81] However, if a parent engages in sexual activity or takes drugs in the presence of the child, custody will be awarded to the other parent.[82]

PARENTAL MENTAL ILLNESS OR IMPAIRMENT

Parental mental disorder or impairment (that is, psychosis, severe personality disorder, substance abuse, or mental retardation) is not necessarily a bar to custody. It must be established that the disorder or impairment is current and that it disrupts childrearing to the extent of causing neglect or potential physical harm.[83]

A mother on a methadone maintenance program was allowed to retain custody of her child. The court found she was the child's psychological parent and able to function normally on methadone, even though she was not attempting to detoxify herself.[84] On the other hand, if it appears that a parent's mental condition is damaging to the child and unlikely to improve, he or she will not be awarded custody. In *In the In-*

terest of Bachelor, a child was removed from the custody of a mother who was mentally retarded and psychologically disturbed. Based on the testimony of expert witnesses, the court concluded it was improbable that either parent would ever meet "minimal standards of parental fitness."[85]

RACE AND RELIGION

In *Palmore v. Sidoti,* the Supreme Court held that race cannot be considered in awarding custody.[86] The Court reversed an initial decision granting a Caucasian father custody because his Caucasian ex-wife had married a black man. The sole reason given by the trial court for changing custody was the effect of community racial prejudice on the child. The Supreme Court held that to affirm a custody award based on prejudice would effectively be condoning it.

Because of the constitutional guarantee of freedom of religion, courts are reluctant to base a custody decision exclusively on a parent's religion or to restrict a parent's religious practices. Custody decisions based solely on a court's preference for the religious training in one parent's home over a lack of religion in the other's are unconstitutional, because the First Amendment recognizes the right to believe or disbelieve.[87] Courts may consider religion as one factor when determining custody.[88] However, judicial consideration of religion must be concerned only with its effect on the child; a judge may not evaluate the merits of one religion against another.[89] If a custodial parent's religious beliefs preclude medical care or endanger the child in some other way, the courts have either changed custody or conditioned it on allowing medical care. When a custodial mother who was a devout Jehovah's Witness disregarded earlier court orders and indicated she would not allow her children to receive blood transfusions, the court transferred custody to the children's father because of the threat to the children's life and health.[90] However, if the custodial parent seems willing to abide by court orders, custody is usually not disturbed. For example, a mother's adherence to the tenets of Christian Science was not sufficient to deny her custody, as long as she allowed monthly medical examinations of the child and permitted necessary medical and surgical care.[91] The fact that a custodial mother attended the Freewill Holiness Pentecostal Church, in which poisonous snakes were sometimes handled during services, did not result in a change of custody to the father, since the mother had not handled the snakes herself, and the child had not been exposed to the risk of being bitten.[92]

Occasionally, disputes arise when one parent refuses to honor an agreement that a child be raised in a particular faith. Courts may order compliance with the agreement's terms, particularly in joint custody states, where both parents have the legal right to decide the child's religion.[93] Agreements have also been enforced because, under the terms of the initial custody agreement, the custodial parent had promised to raise a child according to a particular faith.[94] Other courts have refused to require compliance with agreements, recognizing the prerogative of the custodial parent to make decisions about the child's religious upbringing.[95]

THE CHILD'S PREFERENCE

In most states, following the UMDA, "the wishes of the child as to his custodian" should be considered as one factor (though not necessarily the determining factor) in custody awards. The judge is given the discretion to accord the child's preference as much weight as he deems fit. Usually, the weight will "vary according to the age, intelligence and maturity of the child as well as the reasons given for the preference."[96] When examining the child's reasons for the preference, the judge will usually look to whether those reasons are rational rather than capricious or the result of indoctrination.[97]

In some states the child's preference is to be considered only one factor in determining custody; in others the child's wishes are controlling. The consideration that a child's preference should be only one factor reflects a concern that it is not in a child's best interests to place the entire decision on him.[98] In practice, however, the wishes of an adolescent carry great weight, unless they are patently unreasonable. In some states, rather than treat the child's wishes as a factor, children of a certain age (usually ten to fourteen or older) have the legal right to choose, provided the selected parent is fit and proper. At the extreme, some courts have severed the legal bond between parent and child at the behest of the child.[99] Generally, a child's opinion may not be completely discounted. Several appellate decisions have reversed earlier decisions that failed to take the child's wishes into account.[100] Children's views concerning custody arrangements and proposed changes in custody must also be ascertained in some jurisdictions.[101]

SIBLINGS

The courts are very reluctant to separate siblings. Usually siblings will not be parted unless there is a strong showing that separation of the children will somehow be in their best interests. Recognizing the trauma that accompanies divorce, courts attempt to avoid further disruption of the family[102] by fostering the "full benefit of companionship and affection" that comes from continuing to live with siblings.[103] This policy has some empirical support.[104]

THE MODIFICATION OF CUSTODY ORDERS:
SUBSTANTIAL CHANGE OF CIRCUMSTANCES

The UMDA stipulates that custody awards should not be modified for two years. However, there is no fixed standard for determining when changes in parental circumstances justify a change in custody; it is largely a matter of judicial discretion. Generally, the parent challenging the original award must prove that there has been a *substantial change in circumstances* since the original award and that *the change would favorably affect the child's welfare*. For example, a custodial mother who had undergone a transsexual change from female to male was allowed to retain custody of his children. The court found that, while parental sex change was a substantial alteration in circumstance, the mere fact of the change had no adverse effect on the quality of the children's lives.[105]

Either custody or visitation may be challenged under the changed circumstances doctrine. The custodial parent might, for example, allege that the child is psychologically harmed by visitation because the noncustodial parent neglects or abuses the child or is otherwise unfit. Visitation may be terminated, for instance, if a child returns from visits bearing visible signs of physical or sexual abuse.[106] Noncustodial parents may make the same allegations.

The doctrine of "changed circumstances" has been criticized as allowing too much judicial discretion. The usual practice when a noncustodial parent's financial condition changes is to adjust the support due rather than to change custody.[107]

RELOCATION

The mobility of professional men and women is such that quite frequently a custodial parent will wish to relocate in order to pursue a career elsewhere or to accompany a new spouse who has been transferred. Does relocation represent such a change of circumstances and such a block to visitation that a custodial arrangement could be altered? Generally not. Many custody decrees contain a clause enjoining the custodial parent from leaving the home state. However, restrictions of the right to move may be unenforceable, given the constitutionally protected right to travel. Another factor that comes into play is the right of the custodial parent to select the child's residence. There are various approaches to balancing the custodial parent's freedom of movement and custodial rights against the rights of the noncustodial parent. Some courts require a hearing before permitting the move, in order to determine whether the move is in the best interests of the child and parent.[108] Other courts find that visitation rights convey no restriction on the movement of custodial parents.[109]

Current Controversies

"SURROGATE" MOTHERS

"Surrogate parenting" is a contractual arrangement in which a fertile woman agrees to bear a child for a married couple and surrender the child to them for adoption. The woman may either be artificially inseminated by the husband (a "genetic" surrogate mother) or carry a fertilized embryo to term for the couple (a "gestational" surrogate mother). Generally, a surrogacy agreement is arranged through a third party, who, for a fee, matches the couple with a surrogate mother, arranges for necessary medical procedures such as genetic testing and artificial insemination or implantation, and provides a form contract. The provisions of the contract typically include the schedule of payment to the surrogate mother and address such contingencies as stillbirth, miscarriage, and birth defects. Surrogacy contracts include a clause in which the surrogate mother agrees to terminate her parental rights and allow adoption. When the surrogacy contract is for insemination, the parties to the contract are the genetic mother, her husband, and the biological father. In order to avoid violation of laws prohibiting "baby selling," the biological father's (infertile) wife is generally not a party to the contract.[110]

By statute, artificial insemination creates a parent–child relationship between the child and the mother's husband.[111] Generally, the identity of sperm donors is confidential and there is no contact between donor and recipient. However, anonymity is impossible in a surrogacy agreement. Litigation arises when the surrogate mother does not wish to surrender the child according to the terms of the agreement. Since surrogacy agreements are a relatively recent method for circumventing infertility, the matter has been addressed by relatively few state legislatures. States have taken different approaches to surrogacy agreements, ranging from prohibition (e.g., totally banned in Arizona and Utah;[112] commercial contracts banned in Kentucky, Louisiana, and Nebraska) to allowing the contracts (e.g., Arkansas and West Virginia).[113] Washington and Michigan award custody based on the best interests of the child.[114] In the absence of a statute, it has been left to the courts to determine whether to allow these agreements.

When the issue is breach of a surrogacy contract by the biological surrogate mother, courts may or may not honor the agreement. In the *Baby M* case, Mary Beth Whitehead refused to surrender the child to the Sterns and sought custody. The New Jersey Supreme court held the surrogacy contract invalid, because it violated state laws against paying money for adoption and selling children. The court reasoned that no adoption could take place unless state procedures for termination of parental rights had been followed. Furthermore, it held that a surrogacy contract was not an acceptable substitute for statutory procedural requirements.[115] The court gave the Sterns custody of the baby, reasoning that this arrangement was in the child's best interests, but declined to terminate Mrs. Whitehead's parental rights because she had not been found unfit. The case was remanded to the trial court in order to consider visitation.

Until the issue was addressed by the state legislature, Kentucky courts did not prohibit surrogacy agreements.[116] When the Kentucky Attorney General wanted to revoke the charter of Surrogate Parenting Associates, Inc. on the ground that the company's business violated Kentucky laws forbidding baby-selling, the court considered the surrogate agreement to be similar to any other adoption arrangement. Since Kentucky law allows a mother five days after the birth of a child to change her mind about adoption, the court concluded that women who were parties to surrogacy contracts had the same option. The court refused to enforce the contract if the surrogate mother changed her mind within the statutory period.[117] The court also noted that it was up to the legislature, not the courts, to ban surrogacy agreements. In 1988 the Kentucky State Legislature prohibited surrogacy contracts that involved payment.[118]

The parental rights of a gestational surrogate mother are less clear than those of a genetic mother. In *Anna J. v. Mark C.,* Johnson had given birth to a child following embryonic implantation. The genetic mother and Johnson, the birth mother, each brought actions for declaration that she was the "natural mother." The California trial court, confirmed on appeal, refused to recognize Johnson's parental status because she and the child had no genetic link.[119] Critics of this decision refer to the repugnant practice of using poor women as "host" mothers for wealthy people. However, the decision is consistent with those establishing paternal support obligations based on genetic testing.[120] The court called for legislative action to resolve the dilemma.[121]

Lawyers and medical professionals who arrange surrogate parent contracts owe a duty of care to the surrogate mother to take reasonable measures to prevent harm to her arising from the impregnation or subsequent pregnancy. Such a duty was found in a case where the surrogate mother and her husband were infected with cytomegalovirus (CMV), the source of which was alleged to have been the donor's semen.[122] The court determined that the defendant lawyer and physicians owed a heightened duty of protection because of the profit-generating surrogacy business. Fulfillment of this duty may require testing of the semen and advice to the parties about the perils of surrogacy. The court was encouraged to impose a high standard of care because of the public policy displayed in statutes seeking to protect vulnerable parties. Although not directly addressed, the court's reasoning would also extend a duty to the child. This duty may be far-reaching. Could the arranger of a surrogate contract be liable for placing a child into an abusive home?

ALLEGATIONS OF SEXUAL ABUSE

In 1985 more than 1,900,000 complaints of child abuse and neglect were reported to state and local welfare authorities. Although, in most cases, children's allegations of sexual abuse are genuine, it is estimated that 4–10 percent of the allegations of sexual abuse are fabricated.[123] Custody litigation has increased since automatic maternal preference has been abolished, and accusations of sexual abuse are more frequently made during custody disputes. Such accusations represent a potent method of speeding litigation and cutting off contact between the alleged abuser and the child.[124]

The accusation may be made during the custody dispute or afterward, when the custodial parent, usually the mother, seeks to block visitation. In a number of instances it has become evident that the child has been indoctrinated by a parent to make the dramatic accusation. Once made, the allegation is difficult to dispose of; indeed, the noncustodial parent may never completely clear himself of suspicion, and even if he does so, it is likely that six to twelve months will have passed with little or no visitation. The courts, recognizing the problem, have insisted upon evidence to support allegations of abuse; mere hearsay statements of the child will not suffice and should not stand in the way of return of the child after visitation to the custodial parent.[125]

Benedek and Schetky note the following pattern in false accusations: (1) The charge is initiated by the parent, not the child; (2) the allegation arises after, not before, the marital separation; (3) the child's play and drawing themes are not consistent with the allegation; and (4) the child's observed relationship with the allegedly abusive parent is not consistent with sexual abuse.[126]

The clinician should seek to understand why the false accusation has arisen (e.g., parental vindictiveness, a deliberate attempt to wrest custody from a hated ex-spouse, or a parental delusional system). The clinical evaluation of cases of alleged sexual abuse is described in Chapter 6.

GRANDPARENTS' RIGHTS

At common law, grandparents had no legal right to any access to grandchildren; all contact was subject to the parent's approval.[127] However, as the emphasis has shifted from parents' rights to children's interests, grandparents have received increased recognition. Disputes between a grandparent and a parent involving custody or visitation may be resolved in favor of the grandparents if contact with the grandparents is deemed to be in a child's best interests.

When a grandparent challenges a parent for custody of a child, the child's natural parents are presumed to have a superior claim; the nonparent has the burden of proving the natural parent unfit in order to prevail.[128] However, if a child has been living with grandparents for a substantial period of time, a court will often find it is in the child's best interests to remain with them. For example, when a mother sued for custody of her thirteen-year-old daughter who had been living with her grandparents for eleven years, the court refused to allow the mother to regain custody because she had had little contact with the child and had not previously contributed to her support.[129] When a child has lived with grandparents for a number of years, the burden of proving unfitness will often shift to the parent seeking to regain custody.[130] In the same manner, a grandparent's guardianship may be terminated without notice or hearing where the child has lived with foster parents for ten years with minimal contact with the grandparents.[131]

Grandparents may be awarded visitation in some circumstances. While a grandparent has no legal right *per se* to visit grandchildren, courts have the discretion to award visitation and may do so if it is in the child's best interests.[132] However, courts are unlikely to order visitation over a parent's objections.[133] An award of visitation to grandparents is unlikely if the grandparent would have the opportunity to see the child during visitation with the noncustodial parent.[134]

Some jurisdictions have statutes allowing grandparents to seek visitation. A paternal grandmother has been granted rights where the child's parents had never married and the father had provided no support and maintained little contact, to establish a meaningful relationship with the child.[135] There have been mixed results when a child has been adopted by another family. When a child is adopted by a stepparent following divorce or death of a parent, courts may order visitation in order to sustain the relationship between the child and grandparents.[136] Other courts may deny visitation because adoption severs all ties between the child and the parent relinquishing custody. Courts have reasoned that, since the parent no longer has a legal relationship with the child, neither does the family of that parent.[137]

PARENTAL KIDNAPPING TO REGAIN CUSTODY

Parental kidnapping and failure to return the child after visitation have become serious problems. The child-snatcher, usually a noncustodial father, typically has little appreciation of the deleterious effect of traumatic separation on young children.[138] Often the child is removed as a pawn in a persisting war between the parents.[139]

Estimates of the number of children kidnapped in this way each year range from 25,000 to 100,000.[140] Before 1968, there was a strong incentive for a parent dissatisfied with a custody decree to snatch a child and relitigate the issue in a more receptive state. Although the "Full Faith and Credit" clause of the Constitution[141] requires states to honor each other's rulings, custody decrees are not considered final judgments, since states retain the right to modify custody decrees under the doctrine of changed circumstances. Therefore, a second state could modify the first state's decree without violating the Full Faith and Credit clause.[142]

In 1968 the National Conference of Commissioners on Uniform State Laws adopted the Uniform Child Custody Jurisdiction Act (UCCJA).[143] The UCCJA provided that the state making the original custody determination should generally continue to retain jurisdiction over the child, and stated that the mere presence of a (kidnapped) child was not, by itself, enough to give a different state the authority to alter a custody award. However, adoption of the act was voluntary, and only thirty-two states adopted some variation of it.[144]

In 1980 Congress passed the Parental Kidnapping Prevention Act (PKPA).[145] The PKPA, which represents an attempt by the Federal Government to control the problem, has the following features:

1. Each state must extend "full faith and credit" to other states and not modify custody determinations made in other states if the original decree was made in accordance with the act. A state court must defer to a sister state, and not institute a custody action if custody litigation is pending in the sister state.
2. The PKPA expands the use of the Federal Parent Locator Service (FPLS). The states may enter into an agreement with the federal government to tap the information in the FPLS in order to track offending parents.
3. The PKPA applies the Fugitive Felon Act to parental kidnapping cases. The Federal Bureau of Investigation is thereby empowered to arrest the offender and turn him over to state authorities to await extradition. It should be noted that parental kidnapping is specifically exempted from the federal kidnapping statute.
4. All states but one have passed parental kidnapping felony laws which aim to deter and punish offenders and to facilitate the child's return to the home state.

The PKPA operates in concert with the UCCJA. The UCCJA allows cooperation between the courts of the different states, regulates the jurisdiction of these cases, and requires the states to recognize and enforce custody determinations already made in sister states. The parents of abducted children also have access to the FBI computer files on missing children in the National Crime Information Center. Furthermore, parents of abducted children have the option of bringing suit on their behalf if the children have sustained psychological injury as the result of the abduction.

HOMOSEXUAL PARENTS

The question of parental moral unfitness due to homosexuality is likely to be raised in three kinds of situations. A custodial parent may attempt to block visitation on the ground that the noncustodial parent is homosexual; one parent may attempt to wrest custody from another on this ground; or the initial custody determination may be affected by the consideration that one parent is homosexual.

Homosexuality is a factor in the totality of circumstances in awarding custody. Its consideration neither discriminates on the basis of sexual orientation nor interferes with freedom of association.[146]

Undoubtedly some judges are affected by personal bias in this matter. Homosexuals are popularly thought to be psychologically disturbed, prone to pedophilia, inclined to distort their children's gender role identification, and likely to expose their charges to an immoral life-style.[147] Reflecting this view, courts have imposed restrictions on visitation when a parent exposes a child to homosexual social activities, prohibiting the child's attendance at gay churches, activist events, and social gatherings.[148] Moreover, a homosexual's children are thought to be vulnerable to social stigmatization, and the detrimental effect of societal disapproval has been deemed sufficient justification to award custody to the nonhomosexual parent.[149] One court simply assumed that awarding custody to the nonhomosexual parent is in the best interests of the child.[150] However, stereotyping of this kind is counterbalanced by contemporary trends to assess, case by case, whether parental eccentricities preclude adequate child care.

A number of states have expressly excluded from consideration in custody determinations conduct that does not directly affect the child.[151] Direct homosexuality is sometimes considered exempt under this criterion; as long as passionate or sexual behavior does not occur in the child's presence, homosexuality alone will not be considered a bar to visitation or custody.[156] When a thirteen-year-old boy's school and behavioral problems improved after he went to live with his father, who was homosexual, the court upheld a modification to the original custody agreement transferring custody to the father. The court extensively reviewed research on the subject of homosexual parents and concluded that homosexuality *per se* did not render a parent unfit for custody. Following the precept of looking to the child's best interests, the court found the child's circumstances were demonstrably better with his father.[153] Nonetheless, the prejudice against homosexual parents is still strong; Tennessee, for example, has never awarded custody to a homosexual parent.[154]

Much of the debate concerns women who are raising children while living in a lesbian relationship.[155] Hutchens and Kirkpatrick (1985) and Patterson (1992) have reviewed the literature on this matter. Virtually all of it deals with lesbian mothers. Bell and Weinberg (1978) found no greater prevalence of psychological maladjustment among homosexual men and women than among heterosexuals. Several studies have addressed the question of psychosexual development among the children of lesbian mothers.[156] Homosexual women appear to be similar to heterosexuals in their values and childrearing styles. Among their children, no evidence of gender role disorientation has been detected; however, there has been insufficient research into the adolescent and young adult adjustment of these children. Two clinical studies refer to shock and confusion in adolescents when parental homosexuality is revealed.[157]

In summary, there is insufficient information concerning homosexual fathers. The patchy information concerning lesbian mothers does not indicate deviant childrearing or distortion of gender role identity in their children. Homosexuality *per se* does not appear to preclude competent mothering; consequently, each case should be assessed on its merits.

THE EFFECT OF DIVORCE ON CHILDREN
Longitudinal Studies

Research evidence concerning the effect on children of homosexual parents, paternal custody, and joint custody has already been discussed. The effect of sole custody on child development remains to be considered. The major longitudinal studies in this field are the California study (Wallerstein and Kelly, 1975, 1976, 1980a, 1980b; Kelly and Wallerstein, 1976; Wallerstein, 1983; Wallerstein and Blakeslee, 1989), the Virginia study (Hetherington, Cox, and Cox, 1976, 1978a, 1978b, 1979, 1981; Hetherington, 1979, 1984, 1989; Hetherington, Stanley-Hagen, and Anderson, 1989; Hetherington & Clingempeel, 1992), and studies by Johnston and Campbell (1989), Buchanan, Maccoby, and Dornbusch (1991); Block, Block, and Gjerde (1988); Furstenberg, Morgan, and Allison (1987); Guidubaldi (1988); Glenn and Kramer (1987), and Billingham, Sauer, and Pillion (1989).

The California study concerned 131 children, three to eighteen years of age, from sixty white middle-class families, who were followed for five years after marital separation. The families were recruited through an offer of counseling and were thus essentially a clinical sample. Attrition was low. No control group was observed. All assessments were clinical and relatively unstandardized.

At the time of separation, the rupture in the family was universally disturbing. Few divorces were mutual; few children experienced relief; many were unaware that separation was pending; and only a minority were given an adequate explanation for the breakup. In the first year, parents often became irritable, aggressive, depressed, or even suicidal, and external support was frequently unavailable because of the remoteness of extended families. Commonly, marked changes in family relationships ensued; the noncustodial parent might become more or less involved than before, yet most children experienced a need to maintain contact with the absent parent.

All children experienced fear, anger, guilt, helplessness, a sense of loss, and divided loyalties. Preschool children tended to regress and express fear of abandonment. Children five to eight years of age grieved the loss, felt rejected, and fantasized reconciliation. In about half the cases, school performance deteriorated. At nine to twelve years, children characteristically exhibited anger, grief, and loneliness, split their parents into "good" and "bad" parties, and blamed the "bad" one. About half had problems with school performance. Adolescents became anxious and concerned for their own marital futures.

Five years after the separation, about one-third of the children were in good psychological health. Good outcome was associated with the following: a stabilized family life; a continuing relationship with both parents; the severance of a relationship with an abusive parent; and the reduction of friction between parents. About 40 percent of the children were still clinically disturbed. Poor outcome was associated with

the feelings of having been rejected by either parent; lack of interest by the noncustodial parent; chronic depression, embitterment, or ill health in the custodial mother;
and the continuation of friction between the parents.

Wallerstein (1983) hypothesized that, if the emotional crisis is to be resolved, the
following coping tasks must be completed:

1. Acknowledging the marital disruption
2. Regaining a sense of direction and resuming customary activities
3. Dealing with feelings of loss and rejection
4. Forgiving the parents
5. Accepting the finality of divorce
6. Resolving fear of adult relationships

Ten years after the divorce, of the older group (now 19–29 years of age), a significant number had traumatic memories or amnesia for the earlier trauma. Some young
women who had appeared well-adjusted during adolescence had become anxious concerning love, intimacy, commitment, and betrayal. Some young men pursued a "counterphobic" life-style involving transient sex. Fifteen years subsequently, it has become
apparent that events during the third decade of life (e.g., psychotherapy or establishing a different relationship with the father) can have a significant impact on adjustment. Although boys had more apparent difficulties during the first ten years, girls
began to show more problems during early adulthood, as evidenced by multiple relationships, early marriage, and early divorce.

The Virginia study followed seventy-two white middle-class children, four to five
years of age, along with a matched control group, for six years after divorce. Standardized assessments were used. There was considerable attrition in the sample. If
the parents agreed about childrearing and there was little conflict between them, frequent paternal contact was associated with better mother–child relationships. If conflict continued, or if the father was emotionally immature, frequent paternal visitation
was disruptive to the child. No other relationship outside the home had such potential for good or ill as that with the father. Sex differences were noted among the children's responses. Emotional disturbance tended to disappear among girls after two
years (though it might reappear in adolescence). In contrast, many boys remained disturbed at two years, exhibiting oppositional, aggressive behavior. Boys appeared to
be exposed to more stress, inconsistency, and rejection by mothers. Many families
deteriorated economically after divorce, and the mother's working sometimes resulted
in a chaotic life-style. If the mother remained hostile to the father, the boy's gender
role identity might be disturbed.

At six-year follow-up, when the children were ten years of age, sample attrition
dictated the addition of new subjects, thirty sons and thirty daughters in each of three
groups: remarried mother–stepfather; non-remarried mother custody; and nondivorced. Mother–son relationships in the nonmarried families and parent–child relationships in the remarried families tended to be problematic. In the first two years
after remarriage, mother–daughter relations were likely to deteriorate, whereas
mother–son relations often stabilized. Stepfathers appeared to relate better to their

stepsons than to their stepdaughters. Several adaptive cluster types were defined among the children, for example: (1) insecure, aggressive, impulsive, and withdrawn; (2) self-sufficient, energetic, and popular, but manipulative and opportunistic; (3) warm, compassionate, and sharing (mostly girls).

In a recent, allied study, Hetherington and Clingempeel (1992) have reported the results of research into the effect upon children of parental remarriage. Cohorts of nondivorced, divorced, and remarried families were studied, at an average of four, seventeen, and twenty-six months after remarriage. It was apparent that remarriage was particularly disruptive and that there was little improvement in the resulting disturbance during the first two years of follow-up. Stepchildren were hostile toward their stepfathers, who often withdrew from limit-setting and discipline. Adolescent daughters often became oppositional toward their mothers. Nevertheless, authoritative parenting was associated with better outcome. The especially disruptive effect of parental remarriage on daughters, and the failure of remarried families to readjust within two years, represent the most challenging findings of this study.

The Johnston and Campbell (1989) study concerned a four-year follow-up of one hundred children of parents who were disputing custody. Seventy percent of the children were exposed to verbal and physical abuse between their parents. Younger children tended to become inhibited and "frozen," particularly at times of transition from home to home. Older children often became embroiled in the parental struggles. Many children blamed themselves for the conflict. After two years, aggression, depression, and manipulative behavior were evident, especially among boys. Other children had learned, like chameleons, to "merge" with either parent. Four years after the parental separation, children in court-ordered joint custody were significantly more disturbed than those in single-parent custody. Mother–daughter relationships, particularly, had deteriorated in court-ordered shared custody arrangements. Many girls tended to develop seductive, manipulative relationships with their fathers and hostility toward their mothers. Court-ordered shared custody was regarded as deleterious. The Stanford study (Buchanan, Maccoby, and Dornbusch, 1991) also found that dual residence was harmful to adolescents, who often felt trapped between warring parents.

The National Survey of Children (Furstenberg, Morgan, and Allison, 1987) examined the long-term effect of divorce on several thousand children, comparing them with controls from intact families. As expected, children of divorced families were worse off in regard to school performance, problem behavior, and subjective distress. Younger children appeared more disturbed than older, but sex had no effect. Another finding from this study was the widespread abandonment of children by their fathers.

In the National Study of Children in the Schools (Guidubaldi, 1988), children from divorced families were compared with intact-family classroom controls four and six years after parental separation. Children from divorced families demonstrated poorer school performance, more psychological symptoms, and less popularity. Boys exhibited more adverse effects than girls. Glenn and Kramer (1987), in national cross-sectional studies, have found an intergenerational effect in that the children of divorce are more likely as adults to be involved in divorce themselves. Women seem to be affected more than men, as adults, after having experienced parental divorce: They marry earlier but appear to be less committed to their marriages. Billingham, Sauer, and Pillion (1989) found that college women who had experienced parental divorce were likely to have more sexual partners yet to be less permissive in their attitudes to sex.

Cross-sectional Studies

Aside from the above longitudinal studies, a large number of cross-sectional studies have examined the relationship between children's psychological adjustment after divorce and different personal and environmental variables. Reviews of these studies have been provided by Wolchik and Karoly (1988); Rohman, Sales, and Low (1987); Felner and Terre (1987); Levitin (1979); Shinn (1978); and Emery (1988).

Felner and Terre (1987) describe divorce as a "marker event" in a prolonged period of change leading up to and following the divorce itself. The antecedents and repercussions of this transitional event interact with the child's coping ability and the family's resources in such a way as to determine outcome. In numerous studies, children after divorce have been found to be prone to behavior problems. It appears to be the conditions associated with the divorce (rather than the divorce itself) that lead to psychological disturbance. The following factors have received particular attention:

1. The child's developmental level
2. The child's sex
3. Environmental instability
4. Impoverishment
5. Parental mental health
6. Interparental relations
7. Parent–child relations

DEVELOPMENTAL LEVEL

Although earlier studies suggested that the younger the child, the worse the outcome,[158] recent research has not borne this out.[159] It appears that age affects the pattern rather than the severity, of the disorder. A number of studies have examined the different ways in which preschoolers, latency-age children, and adolescents make sense of their parents' divorces and try to understand their own part in the breakup of the family.[160] Whereas a preschooler responds egocentrically, ascribing the reason for the departure of a parent to his or her own "badness," preadolescents appreciate that parents seek divorce when they no longer care for each other, although they often think that the adults could have "tried harder."

SEX

Several studies have pointed to greater disturbance in boys, following divorce,[161] possibly as a result of vicious-circle interactions between stressed, coercive mothers and their oppositional sons. However, two recent studies have failed to find sex-related differences.[162] This question requires further elucidation.

ENVIRONMENTAL INSTABILITY

Following marital separation, it can be difficult or impossible for the custodial parent to continue familiar household routines.[163] Economic stress, for example, may require the parent to work for the first time or for longer hours, thus putting pressure on the children to contribute more to the maintenance of the household than some are prepared or able to do.

IMPOVERISHMENT

Many families descend below the poverty line following divorce, a problem aggravated if child support payments are in arrears. The average income of a single woman with two children is about one-third that of a married couple with two children. This problem affects mother-headed families only[164] and appears to be correlated with child maladjustment.[165] It is unclear whether the effect of economic deterioration is mediated by a direct loss of resources or through environmental change (such as change of residence), or else through stressed family relationships.

PARENTAL MALADJUSTMENT

Hetherington, Cox, and Cox (1978a) and Patterson (1976) have demonstrated a connection between maternal stress and child maladjustment. This kind of vicious cycle appears to be particularly likely if the mother did not seek the divorce.[166] Interparental conflict, parental stress, and coercive parent–child relationships act in concert.[167]

INTERPARENTAL CONFLICT

Many studies have demonstrated an association between continued interparental conflict after divorce and maladjustment of the child.[168]

PARENT–CHILD DISTURBANCE

Hetherington, Cox, and Cox (1978, 1979a) and Rutter (1981) have demonstrated that the child tends to become emotionally disturbed by ineffective mothering after divorce and that good parent–child relationships are protective. A number of studies have drawn attention to the protective value of nonconflictual contact between noncustodial father and child.[169] Felner and Terre (1987) suggest that the correlation between paternal contact and adjustment is not a simple causation but, rather, is secondary to the fact that nonconflictual contact reflects a generally favorable family situation. On the other hand, it may be better for a child to have no contact with a noncustodial parent than to experience forced contact in an atmosphere of conflict and tension.[170]

Summary

Two major longitudinal investigations and numerous cross-sectional studies have demonstrated a significant prevalence of maladjustment in children after divorce. Maladjustment tends to persist in about 40 percent of children five years after the divorce.

Children of different ages construe the meaning of divorce differently. Younger children tend to blame themselves or one or the other of the parents for the divorce. However, earlier studies indicating that younger children and boys are at increased risk have not been confirmed. It is evident that environmental instability, economic stress, maternal stress, interparental conflict, and conflictual parent–child relationships all interact in such a manner as to convey an increased risk of maladjustment.

Despite an increasing number of appropriately controlled studies that use standardized assessments, most research has focused on middle-class families, and its generalizability is uncertain. Clinicians who make firm predictions about outcome do so without scientific evidence.

LEGAL PROCEEDINGS

Custody litigation is a form of civil proceeding in which the parties involved in a divorce action contend for the possession of children or in which, following an initial custody award, one party seeks to reverse or modify an existing award.

The proceedings begin with a *petition for legal separation* or, less often, with a *petition for custody* without the filing of divorce proceedings. Some states will not award custody in the absence of a divorce. In a divorce action, one party files a complaint alleging grounds for divorce, such as irreconcilable differences that have caused irrevocable breakdown of the marriage. The other party files an answer to the complaint, conceding, or seeking to rebut, the allegations therein. Most divorces are not contested, all issues (e.g., property, support, custody) having been settled before the court appearance.

In a contested case, each side will make pretrial motions. For example, one side may seek to discover the scope of the adversary case through interrogatories (written questions to be answered in writing), through depositions (recorded cross-examinations of potential witnesses, especially experts), by requesting the production of documents, or by requiring the parties to submit themselves for physical or mental examination. The attorney who requests the deposition of an expert witness or the examination of a party must convince the judge that the information in the interrogatories is insufficient and that the issue is material to the case. The conduct of depositions is discussed further in Chapter 11. Commonly, the parties will reach a settlement before the trial, which then becomes nominal. In some jurisdictions, the court has the authority to appoint its own expert investigator, who may be cross-examined by both parties. Because a judge may not delegate his or her authority to decide custody, an investigator's report is considered strictly advisory.

In a contested case, temporary arrangements for custody and child support may be made at a preliminary hearing or hearings. Eventually, following a hearing on the merits of the case before a family court judge, a judgment will be made pending entry of a final *decree nisi*. The standard of proof required for deciding which form of custody is superior is a preponderance of the evidence. Custody decrees can be appealed. There is no time limit on future complaints based on changed circumstances.

In reaching the final determination, a judge will find the facts of the case from the interrogatories, the pleadings of the adversarial attorneys, evidence given in court, the reports and testimony of mental health experts, documents and reports from medical and social service agencies, and interviews conducted in chambers with the children whose custody is being contested. The final custody award will incorporate determinations of the following questions:

1. Joint or sole parental custody?
2. In joint legal custody, what are the arrangements for physical custody (e.g., alternating, split, primarily with one parent)?
3. In sole parental custody, which parent will be custodial, and what are the visitation rights of the noncustodial parent?
4. What child support payments will be required of the noncustodial parent or of one of the joint custodians?
5. What visitation rights will other interested parties (e.g., grandparents) be afforded?

Occasionally the court may appoint someone (not necessarily an attorney) to represent the child during custody litigation. The child's representative is the guardian *ad litem*. Although it is the parents, not the child, who are the parties to the divorce and custody proceedings, it is within the judge's discretion to appoint a guardian *ad litem* in order to protect the child's best interests. For example, in an extremely bitter and hostile custody dispute, the judge may conclude that neither side is able to act in the interests of the child.[171]

The court should make clear the role the guardian *ad litem* is expected to play. Generally, the child's attorney will be expected to act either as an advocate for the child's wishes (the typical attorney–client relationship) or to express an independent opinion as to what best serves the child's interests and welfare under the circumstances.[172] In the *Baby M* case, a guardian *ad litem* was appointed to represent the infant in the center of that custody dispute. The court considered that the guardian's proper role was to protect the child's interests and found the guardian's recommendation to be substantial when deciding to award custody to the biological father.[173]

CLINICAL EVALUATION IN CHILD CUSTODY DISPUTES
Circumstances of Referral

A clinician is most likely to be asked to evaluate the family members involved in a child custody dispute (1) prior to the hearing on the merits of the case; (2) following the custody award, when the noncustodial parent, claiming substantially changed circumstances, wants to reverse or modify an existing custody arrangement; (3) when the custodial parent wants to block or modify visitation by the noncustodial parent; or (4) when one parent wants to change an existing joint-custody award to sole custody.

Frequently the attorney for one parent will request an evaluation of his or her client and the child. As will be described in the next section, there are very few circumstances in which a unilateral evaluation is either useful or ethical. Unless all sides of the dispute can be evaluated impartially, it will be impossible to elicit comparative information. The clinician should advise the attorney to petition the court for a clinical evaluation. If the judge agrees, and the clinician is acceptable to both sides, he or she can then function as *amicus curiae* ("friend of the court") relatively untainted by the presumption of partisanship.

The chief purpose for which it is legitimate to evaluate one parent only is to determine whether that parent is competent to care for a particular child (e.g., when parental mental or physical illness is an issue). Occasionally a child must be examined with reference to a sexual abuse allegation, and the allegedly offending parent is unavailable or unwilling to be interviewed. Obviously, the clinician who examines only one parent is in no position to comment upon the *relative* fitness of that parent or of other parties, unless there is a strong presumption of sexual abuse by the other parent.

Criticisms of Clinicians' Evaluations in Child Custody Disputes

A common criticism, pervasive in the legal community, would have it that psychiatry and psychology are such inexact sciences that practitioners can draw no conclusions sufficiently valid to assist the court in child custody disputes.[174] This question is discussed more fully in Chapters 1 and 11. It is commonly linked with the paradoxical concern that, despite their alleged lack of genuine expertise, the credentials and authority of a mental health clinician might carry the day in court. In actuality, there is some evidence that expert opinions concerning child custody are not highly valued by judges.[175]

More specifically, lawyers often criticize clinicians for failing to conduct adequate examinations. For example, only one parent may be interviewed, stepparents and other significant adults may have been overlooked, the child may not have been assessed, and the interaction between the child and significant adults may not have been observed. Some clinicians base their opinions on separate interviews with the parents and a cursory, nondirective interaction with the child. Others derive their conclusions from psychological tests that are neither reliable nor valid in general, nor relevant to the specific issues involved in custody cases. Finally, some clinicians fail to review available documentation that contains useful information from professionals with no special axe to grind (e.g., pediatricians, teachers).

Clinicians give the impression of bias or gullibility when, without checking, they swallow the hearsay provided by one parent. This is particularly problematic if that parent is, or has been, in treatment with the clinician or is paying the bill for the forensic evaluation.

Sometimes the clinician does not appreciate that the judge must determine custody according to statutory criteria. In some circumstances it is evident that recommendations (e.g., maternal preference) are based on personal bias rather than scientific evidence. In other cases the clinician seems to believe that the finding of mental illness in a parent is dispositive, whereas precedent, and often statute, clearly dictates that mental illness bars custody only to the extent that it disrupts child care.

Other criticisms concern clinicians' reports, particularly of obfuscating jargon (see Chapter 11), the intermixture of observation and inference, the failure to derive conclusions clearly from observations, and inconsistency between conclusions and recommendations. As one judge said, "It's not your conclusions that interest me—it's the thoroughness of your observations and the logic behind your reasoning."

Weithorn and Grisso (1987) and Weithorn (1987) have provided useful discussions of the ethical and practical principles of child custody evaluation. The following two subsections have been influenced by them.

Ethical Principles

1. *Since the ultimate purpose of the evaluation is to aid the court to determine the best interests of the child, the clinician should aim to be employed by the court or by the guardian* ad litem. If a parent seeks a unilateral evaluation, the futility of such a procedure should be explained and the parent advised to seek a court-ordered evaluation. Unilateral evaluations are inevitably biased and are likely to be disregarded, particularly if the clinician bases a recommendation concerning custodial preference upon uncorroborated hearsay.

2. *The clinician should function as an expert, not an advocate or an adversary.* An advocate espouses a cause and promotes it. An adversary is an advocate who defends a cause against attack or who attacks the opposing side in a dispute. During litigation, a legal advocate operates polemically, presenting the best side of the home case, while striving to reveal the flaws in the other side's argument. In contrast, an expert's task is to evaluate the case, prepare a report, and (if required) give testimony in such a manner as to throw light upon the particular legal issues at stake.

In child custody disputes, the danger of becoming partisan is very great. Many clinicians have been exposed to marital breakup in either their own or their parents' marriages. Even those who have not personally experienced divorce are likely to hold strong opinions on matters related to child custody. Such personal views must be curbed by a knowledge of the legal constraints in such cases and by an awareness that parents, attorneys, and even judges will at times press the clinician to choose sides.

3. *The expert should strive to become aware of his or her biases and to hold them in check.* For example, the clinician may note (or be told) that he or she inclines sympathetically toward abandoned wives, leans in the direction of husbands deprived of their children, views ex-wives as grasping, or perceives ex-husbands as chiselers. To some extent, joint evaluation can be used as a reciprocal check on this problem.

4. *As far as possible, the expert should base his or her opinion on the scientific evidence and not go beyond it.* Given this proviso, the clinician can rarely predict long-term outcome with the certainty required for legal deliberation. It may be appropriate, for example, to refer to a risk of lasting psychological damage following the rupture of a parent–child bond, but it would not be legitimate to predict the degree of risk. On the other hand, the clinician may be able to predict immediate distress in a child with a high degree of certitude, a matter that ought not to be ignored, denied, or trivialized.

As with most legal situations, the resolution of a child custody dispute will fundamentally alter the future life of at least one person. Expert opinion proffered with certitude derived not from empirical research but rather from preconception (disguised, perhaps, as "clinical experience") may sometimes sway the court. Whether it does so or not, it adds fuel to the arguments of those who would deny the validity of clinical expertise in forensic matters.

5. *Before the evaluation. informed consent should be obtained from all parties involved.* The parents, stepparents, and other adults involved should know that the content of interviews, psychological tests, and reviews of documents will be presented in the evaluation report and in expert testimony, with the purpose of throwing light upon what would be in the child's best interests. The person responsible for payment should be informed about the clinician's approximate fee and hourly rate, and the estimated time required to review the documents, to interview the people involved, to conduct testing, and to prepare the report. The fee for giving testimony should also be discussed. If it is evident during evaluation that the costs are exceeding the estimate, the clinician should inform the person responsible for the bill as soon as possible, justifying the need for further expense and asking permission to proceed.

6. *The clinician should not evaluate those he or she has treated and should not treat those who have been evaluated.* Otherwise, untenable "double-agency" situations are created, wherein the clinician is responsible to the court for an honest evaluation and to the patient or family to maintain confidentiality. The patient may have discussed matters during therapy that he or she would not have revealed were it known they were to be exposed in a custody evaluation report. The clinician should be aware that the degree to which such material is privileged varies from jurisdiction to jurisdiction. Furthermore, if the clinician proposes to treat a family member after the evaluation or the hearing, it may be made to appear during cross-examination that he or she hopes to profit from his or her own recommendations.

7. *The expert should avoid conclusory or dispositive statements.* It is for the judge to determine parental fitness, to rule upon which parent should be preferred for sole custody, and to decide whether joint custody is the best resolution. The clinician should studiously avoid invading the province of the court. As stated before, the task

is to provide expert information, which, taken along with other information and considerations, may help the judge in determining custody.

This principle can be difficult to honor. Parents, attorneys, and even judges may ask the clinician to offer an opinion as to parental preference. However, it is relatively uncommon to find that one parent is clearly (and irremediably) incompetent; usually both parents are more or less fit to care for the child. In that circumstance, it is preferable for the clinician to enumerate, evenhandedly, the favorable and unfavorable features of each parent, and for the judge to decide what weight to place upon each factor.

Procedural Principles

1. *Child custody evaluation should be oriented toward the legal standards for "the best interests of the child."* These criteria vary somewhat from state to state, being dependent on case law precedent in Rhode Island, for example, and enunciated in detail in Michigan. The clinician should therefore become familiar with the local criteria and specifically address them in the evaluation report.

Essentially these criteria relate to:

1. The wishes of the parents and the child
2. The quality of the relationship between the child and the parents, and any other significant people (e.g., relatives, stepparents, siblings)
3. The child's current adjustment to home, school, and community
4. The mental and physical health of the people involved in item 2

Some statutes (e.g., Michigan's) add the following criteria:

5. The capacity and disposition of the parties to provide basic physical and medical care
6. The desirability of maintaining continuity in home, school, and relationships
7. The capacity and disposition of the competing parties to give love, affection, and guidance; to continue education; and to raise the child in its religion or creed
8. The potential permanence of the existing or proposed custodial home
9. The willingness and ability of the competing parties to facilitate and encourage a close and continuing parent–child relationship between the child and the other parent
10. The moral fitness of the competing parties

The mental health clinician is qualified to throw light upon all criteria with the exception of the last (moral fitness). The above factors may be reordered as follows:

1. The child's preference
2. The relative quality of the current relationship between the competing parties and other significant people

3. The relative physical and mental health of all parties
4. The relative capacity and desire of the competing parties to provide for the child's needs
5. The child's current adjustment and developmental needs
6. The desirability and possibility of maintaining continuity in the child's attachments, residence, schooling, friendships, and religious upbringing
7. The relative permanence of the relationship between the adults in the proposed homes, and the likelihood that the adults will stay in the same area

In Grisso's (1986) terms, the clinician should attempt to evaluate the *congruence* between (a) the child's developmental and special needs, and (b) the relative competence of the parents to provide for those needs. Each of the issues (1 through 7) will be discussed later, from a clinical point of view.

2. *All relevant people should be assessed* (a) *separately,* (b) *in company with the child,* and (c) *in such combinations as are appropriate to understanding the congruence between the child's needs and the capacity of the prospective environments to meet those needs.* For example, a stepparent can be interviewed alone, with his or her spouse, and in company with the child or children whose custody is disputed.

3. Allowance should be made for the fact that a formal interview in an office may not elicit behavior that reliably represents the natural behavior of the person or persons being assessed. *If it is suspected that the person is confused, hampered by anxiety, dissembling, or otherwise behaving unnaturally, the clinician should consider observing him or her in the home environment.*

4. *The clinician should seek convergent validity by assessing the criterial issues from different points of view.* For example, the child's adjustment at school could be assessed from school progress reports, a structured questionnaire completed by the child's teacher, interviews with the child and parents, and psychoeducational testing.

5. *Conclusions should flow from the information gathered, and recommendations should be based on conclusions.* The evaluator should seek to keep inferences separate from observations, to base conclusions on observations and inferences, and to ensure that recommendations are consistent with conclusions.

The Congruence Between the Child's Needs and Parental Caregiving Capacity

In essence, the purpose of child custody evaluation is to determine the relative congruence between the caregiving capacity of the parents and the general and special needs of the child.[176]

A child's needs may be classified as: (1) basic physical needs, (2) socioemotional needs, (3) cognitive needs, (4) communicative needs, (5) educational needs, and (6) moral and spiritual needs.

BASIC PHYSICAL NEEDS

All children have basic requirements for nutrition, shelter, clothing, hygienic sur-roundings, protection from trauma, and adequate health care. As children reach ado-lescence, they can minister increasingly to their own needs.

SOCIOEMOTIONAL NEEDS

All children have the following socioemotional needs:

1. To experience affection, attachment, trust, and a sense of belonging to a family
2. To have reasonable stability and continuity in their physical and social environ-ments
3. To express emotion effectively and to understand the feelings of others
4. To develop a sense of autonomy and self-awareness while exercising control over emotion and physical functioning
5. To develop a sense of independence, initiative, self-respect, and identity
6. To develop interpersonal skills, make and sustain friendships, and find satisfac-tion in group relationships

COGNITIVE AND COMMUNICATIVE NEEDS

The following cognitive and communicative needs are universal:

1. For parental attention and contingent stimulation
2. To develop self-care and survival skills
3. To develop the capacity for problem-solving and planning
4. To develop clear, flexible communicative skills

EDUCATIONAL NEEDS

A child's educational needs include appropriate schooling consistent with the child's abilities; prevocational skills; and access to recreation, sport, and artistic or creative opportunities.

MORAL AND SPIRITUAL NEEDS

All children need a set of ideals, aspirations, values, and spiritual beliefs consistent with the subculture in which they are reared and functional in the wider society.

SPECIAL NEEDS

Children with special impairments, disorders, talents, or skills will need special care in order to treat, protect, compensate for, or remedy their problems and to enhance their assets.

Although the above needs vary as to age of onset and evolve as the child grows older, all remain in effect until maturity. In order that the needs may be met, those responsible for the child's care need the following attributes:

1. Sufficient *understanding* to appreciate that the child has general and special needs, which evolve with age; or, if they lack such understanding, the capacity to benefit from education in this regard
2. Sufficient *affection* for the child to desire to provide for his or her general and special needs
3. Sufficient *physical capacity* to cope with the general and special demands of child care
4. Sufficient *time, opportunity,* and *financial* capacity to minister to the child's needs (For example, a solo custodian father who works very long hours may have the finances but not the time to provide adequate health care for a child with cystic fibrosis, unless someone else can supplement the father's time.)
5. Sufficient *emotional freedom* to recognize and meet the child's needs; that is, to be sufficiently free of emotional stress, preoccupations, anxiety, depression, other pathological affects, disorganization of thinking, confusion, or emotional dyscontrol to be able to register, interpret, and appropriately respond to the child's needs
6. Sufficient *child-rearing skills* and *character* to provide the child with adequate *modeling* and *guidance* in regard to self-care, survival skills, self-discipline, problem-solving, planning, communication, social skills, special talents, and moral and spiritual values

The Mode of Evaluation

The four types of forensic evaluation in child custody are solo, solo assisted, team, and joint.

SOLO EVALUATION

Benedek and Benedek (1980), Trunnell (1976), Gardner (1982), Woody (1977), Weithorn and Grisso (1987), and Derdeyn (1975) have discussed the technique of solo evaluation. In a solo evaluation, the clinician works alone to assess all relevant issues and to integrate them in the evaluation report. Most evaluators work in this way or in the solo assisted mode. Solo evaluations have the virtue of relative simplicity and standardization, at least in experienced hands, but they suffer from a relative failure to correct for bias and the inability of a single clinician to address all aspects of biopsychosocial functioning.

SOLO ASSISTED EVALUATION

In a solo assisted evaluation, the clinician asks a second clinician, usually from a different discipline, to conduct a particular assessment that is beyond the solo clinician's expertise. For example, a psychiatrist might ask a psychologist to assess a child's current academic performance, compare it with his or her school functioning prior to an event, and determine whether there has been a deterioration in performance. A psychologist might ask a psychiatrist to review the psychiatric records of a parent who has had a mental illness treated and to assess the parent's current level of adjustment with a view to predicting the likelihood of future deterioration. A mental health clinician might ask a neurologist to assess the current physical functioning of a child with organic brain disease, with a view to determining the child's special needs.

Aside from its extension of the inevitably limited expertise of a solo clinician, the solo assisted mode can be adapted in such a manner as to correct for one form of bias. In most cases the primary evaluator will read many documents, hence there is a distinct possibility that biasing preconceptions will arise. A current mental status examination, for example, could be influenced if the clinician had previously read a detailed psychiatric case history. Some clinicians attempt to control for this kind of distortion by conducting interviews before reviewing documents, but such a procedure is clumsy and imperfect. However, bias can be limited if the sole clinician requests a specific and limited consultation. (For example, a psychologist might ask a psychiatrist, "Does this woman show evidence of psychosis at the present time? If so, is the psychosis being adequately treated, and is it of such a degree or nature that childrearing could be affected?") Clearly, the solo clinician must studiously avoid conveying his or her own opinion to the consultant. Ultimately, however, the solo clinician must integrate the consultant's assessment into the final evaluation report.

TEAM EVALUATION

Everett (1983), Jackson *et al.* (1980), and Weiner, Simons, and Cavanaugh (1985) have described the technique of team evaluation. Weiner, Simons and Cavanaugh, for example, advocate a team composed of psychiatrist, a social worker or psychologist, and a lawyer. Assessments are divided in such a manner as to avoid redundancy, yet to afford each team member contact with each of the *dramatis personae*. Discrepancies between different assessments are ironed out in team conferences. Home visits are standard if the child is younger than ten years of age. Conferences may be held with the parents in order to sensitize them to the child's needs. The ultimate report is released at a conference with the attorneys in the case. Weiner, Simons, and Cavanaugh claim that 90 percent of their cases subsequently settle out of court. Team evaluations have the advantage of comprehensiveness and internal reliability checks; however, they are cumbersome and expensive.

JOINT EVALUATION

Langelier and Nurcombe (1983) have described joint evaluation, a variant of the team approach. Joint evaluation involves a psychiatrist and a psychologist, one of whom operates as a *primary evaluator* and the other as *secondary*. The primary evaluator contacts the referring attorneys and parents in order to arrange the schedule of interviews, reviews the documents, and poses specific questions to the secondary evaluator. Each evaluator reaches separate conclusions, and the two discuss them at an evaluation conference, where discrepancies are noted and, if possible, resolved. The primary evaluator appends the secondary evaluator's report to, and incorporates its findings within, the final evaluation report.

The joint approach has the virtue of comprehensiveness and complementation of expertise, as well as the potential for improved control of bias. However, like all team approaches, it makes special demands upon team members, is more cumbersome than solo evaluations, and is, perhaps, more expensive.

A Recommended Schedule of Contacts

In view of the way in which most clinicians work, the schedule to be described will be pertinent to the solo or solo-assisted evaluator. However, with a little modification the following schedule can be adapted to team or joint evaluations.

CONTACT WITH ATTORNEYS

The clinician discusses the terms of the evaluation with the attorneys involved: the need for impartial bilateral evaluation (preferably requested by the court); the scope of the evaluation; the probable number of interviews; the probable time required to review documents and prepare the report; and the range of cost (e.g., in terms of hours required and hourly fee). The clinician will also discuss the manner of payment (e.g., by retainer, with balance to be paid on issuance of report). The clinician's fee for expert testimony will also be discussed (e.g., on a half-day and a full-day basis). A written contract will be prepared with regard to expected performance and fees, which the attorneys and parents are asked to sign.

The attorneys should be asked to provide copies of all relevant legal documents (e.g., interrogatories) and to obtain (e.g., from hospitals, private mental health clinicians, physicians, and schools) all records that could contribute to the evaluation. The attorneys can then prepare their clients for the forthcoming evaluation and obtain consent for release of documents.

JOINT INTERVIEW WITH PARENTS

The clinician should contact both parents personally and arrange a joint interview in order to ascertain that they have been properly prepared by their attorneys and to set up the schedule for individual and joint interviews, home visits, and psychological testing. The parents should give informed consent to the evaluation, aware that the evaluation is not therapeutic in purpose and that what they say is not privileged but may be included in the final report.

STANDARDIZED ASSESSMENTS

Each parent is asked to complete the following standard questionnaires:

1. A sociodemographic description and child developmental history
2. A Child Behavior Checklist (CBCL-P) (Achenbach and Edelbrock, 1983)
3. A Minnesota Multiphasic Personality Inventory (MMPI)

If the question of parental physical abusiveness is raised, each parent can be asked to complete as well

4. An Adult–Adolescent Parenting Inventory (Bavolek, 1984; Grisso, 1986)

The Adult–Adolescent Parenting Inventory assesses parental predisposition toward child abuse in terms of four subscales: inappropriate expectations, lack of empathy, belief in physical punishment, and parent–child role reversal. Normative tables are available, reliability is acceptable, and predictive validity studies are promising (though incomplete). However, the range of parental characteristics assessed is narrow; this instrument does not provide a complete description of parental competence. In fact, no existing psychological test does so.[177]

The above four instruments can be completed by each parent under the supervision of a trained secretary.

One parent is also asked to request that the child's teacher complete

5. A Child Behavior Checklist—Teacher Version (Achenbach and Edelbrock, 1983)

INTERVIEWS, TESTS, AND CONSULTATIONS

1. Each parent should be interviewed with regard to his or her early development; marital history; current domestic and occupational circumstances; perception of the child's adjustment at home, school, and socially; and the child's physical health. The parents' motivation for seeking custody should be explored. The parents' knowledge of childrearing, awareness of the child's special needs, psychological adjustment, and physical capacity to care for the child should be explored (with particular reference to parental mental illness, antisocial personality, other personality disorder, alcohol or substance abuse, chronic physical disease or impairment, or intellectual level). Each interview should last an hour to ninety minutes. Two to three interviews are usually required.

2. At least once, and preferably twice, each child in the family should be separately interviewed. Each interview should be of one hour's duration. The clinician should attempt to elicit information concerning the child's adjustment at home, at school, and with peers; the child's special needs; and the child's custodial preference. Kinetic Family Drawings can be helpful if they directly depict the child's perception of those he regards as belonging to his intimate family. Ziskin and Faust (1988b) review the generally negative findings concerning validity of human figure drawings; it is for this reason that their use should be restricted to the enhancement of communication in interview and, sometimes, to the direct depiction of events (e.g., abuse) or circumstances (e.g., the child's conception of his or her immediate family).

3. If required, psychological testing of the children or parents can be undertaken in order to assess intelligence, neuropsychological status or psychoeducational performance. Projective personality testing is not recommended; its level of reliability and validity is insufficient for forensic reports and testimony.[178] If other special investigations (e.g., neurological evaluation) are required, they can be ordered at this time. The clinician should convey to the consultant the essential background information and pose a specific question or questions. (One to two interviews, each one to-three hours long.)

4. If two or more children are involved, all should be interviewed as a family group in order to assess their relationship and cohesion. (One interview, one hour to ninety minutes).

5. Each of the parents should be interviewed in interaction with the child or children. The quality of attachment between parent and preschool child can be gauged by asking the parent to step outside the room, briefly, and then having the parent return. The child's (and the parent's) behavior can be observed as the parent leaves, during parental absence, and after reunion.

The capacity of the parent to communicate with the child can be observed by asking him or her (1) to explain a proverb, (2) to plan an outing, and (3) to help the child complete a jigsaw puzzle.

The following questions can be addressed during an observation of the interaction between parent and child: How close are the parent and child, affectively? Is the parent responsive to the child's needs? Does the parent communicate clearly with the child? Is the parent able to engage in mutually enjoyable activity congruent with the child's developmental level? Can the child tolerate brief separation from the parent?

6. If other adults are involved as stepparents or parental consorts, the quality of their interaction with the child should be assessed.

7. In some cases other informants (e.g., foster parents, grandparents, or teachers) have potentially helpful information and should be interviewed. Beware, however, of the informant who volunteers information but does not want the parent or parents to know.

8. If there is a discrepancy between the parents, or between a parent's account and other sources of information, the clinician should discuss it at a separate interview with the parent or parents in an attempt to correct or clarify it. The clinician should consider the relative credibility of all those who have provided information.

HOME VISITS

Home visits are required for children under ten years of age and, in special circumstances, for older children. The following questions can be addressed with regard to the relative quality of the proposed custodial residence or residences:

1. Is the surrounding neighborhood conducive to adequate childrearing, and in reasonable proximity to suitable schools?
2. Is the home clean and satisfactorily organized?
3. Is there sufficient space in the home and outside for the child or children?
4. Does the child have suitable clothes, toys, play equipment, and room for the storage of personal belongings?
5. If the child is physically impaired, has the house been modified, or could it be modified, to meet his or her special needs?
6. How do the adult or adults in the home interact with the child?
7. In the case of blended families, how well does the child fit in with the children of the other adult's family? Are they of roughly equivalent developmental level?
8. What are the functional, emotional, and nurturant roles of the different members of the family? What are the family's rules, routines, problem-solving techniques, methods of limit-setting, values, and religious principles? How congruent are these with the child's previous experience?
9. Does the family seeking custody have the interest and capacity to foster the child's special talents?

INTERVIEW WITH BOTH PARENTS

In interviewing the parents together, the clinician should address the following questions:

1. Have the parents dealt with their mutual anger, come to terms with their residual affection, and resolved their sense of loss? Are they in step in this regard?
2. Is it likely that one or both parents will enmesh the child in unresolved interpersonal conflict? For example, is one parent likely to derogate the other in front of the child or enlist the child in spying on the other?
3. Has the noncustodial parent been consistently involved with the child, as evidenced by regular visitation, birthday remembrances, regular telephoning, and provision of child support?
4. If joint custody is proposed, what is the capacity of the parents to separate their personal feelings from their need to collaborate concerning the child? Has one of them or have both of them been coerced or indoctrinated to accept joint custody? Are they aware that joint custody requires close communication, geographical proximity, and commitment? Are they prepared to remain in communication and proximity, and to commit themselves to joint custody?

FURTHER DOCUMENTATION OR INFORMATION

Finally, the clinician should decide whether further documentation, interviews, tests, or other information is required, and obtain it, after proper consent has been given.

The Child Custody Evaluation Report

An example of the format of a child custody evaluation report is provided in the Appendix. In this section, a sequence of headings is recommended for the evaluation report, together with the content under each heading.

CIRCUMSTANCES OF REFERRAL

Who referred the family? At what stage in the legal proceedings is the evaluation required? When is the hearing on the merits of the case scheduled to occur?

PRESENT FAMILY SITUATION

What are the names, ages and occupations of all family members? When did the parents separate? Where are they living? Has either parent remarried, or is either parent living with another person? Does that person have a family of his or her own? With whom do the children currently live? What are the visitation arrangements? Are the present custodial and visitation arrangements informal or pursuant to temporary judicial order or *decree nisi?*

PURPOSE OF EVALUATION

What has the court asked the clinician to evaluate? For example, the clinician may be asked to throw light upon (1) which parent should be preferred as custodian, given the child's developmental needs and special requirements; and (2) what visitation rights would be in the child's best interests.

SOURCES OF DATA

1. *Documents reviewed.* Cite each document reviewed with title, signature, and date (e.g., "Psychiatric report to Ms. Jane Doe, caseworker, Rhode Island Department of Child Welfare, signed John Smith, M.D., 11/12/85").
2. *Interviews.* List each interview and home visit with date and duration (e.g., "Interview with Mrs. Jane Doe and Mr. John Doe, 11/12/85 (1½ hours)").

3. *Standardized assessments.* List the standardized assessments, psychological testing, special investigations, and consultations completed, with names and dates (e.g., "Child Behavior Checklist completed by mother, 11/12/88'').

REVIEW OF DOCUMENTS

Summarize the content of each document relevant to the case.

CONTENT OF INTERVIEWS AND HOME VISITS

Briefly describe each person interviewed and assess his or her cooperativeness and apparent reliability. If he or she is thought to be unreliable, cite your reasons for this opinion. Summarize the content of the interview, using direct quotes when relevant.

Special reference should be made to each parent's family background, educational and occupational history, marital history, perceived reason for separation, awareness of the child's general and special needs, experience of child care, and daily schedule, along with history of physical, psychiatric, or personality problems; antisocial behavior; substance abuse; physical abuse; or sexual abuse. The parent's preferred custodial arrangement and visitation should be reported. A summary of pertinent parental mental status features is required.

The child's developmental history should be summarized. If there is reason to consider that the child might be disturbed, a history of the disturbance should be taken from both parents.

The child's affect, capacity to relate, capacity to tolerate separation, and spontaneous behavior should be noted. Is the child of the expected developmental level in verbal communication, social relationships, and intelligence? Do the child's kinetic family drawings directly depict matters of relevance to the case?

Describe the quality of the relationship between the child and all those with whom you have observed him or her interacting, with particular reference to affection, closeness of attachment, capacity to tolerate brief separation, and the adults' capacity for engaging and instructing the child, setting necessary limits, and providing appropriate reinforcement.

Summaries of interviews with other pertinent people should be provided, stating in each case the purpose of the interview.

SPECIAL INVESTIGATIONS AND CONSULTATIONS

If psychological testing or other investigations have been undertaken, cite the specific question posed to the professional who conducted the procedure and list the procedures undertaken, naming the professional who conducted or interpreted them. Summarize the findings of each investigation or consultant, and append each original report to your evaluation report.

DISCUSSION

Orient your discussion to the criteria for the best interests of the child, namely:

1. The relative strength of the *attachment and affection* between the competing parties and the child
2. The relative capacity and disposition of both parties to provide for the child's *basic physical needs*
3. The relative capacity and disposition of both parties to give the child affection, guidance, and education, and to provide for the child's *socioemotional, cognitive, communicative, educational, moral, and spiritual needs*
4. The desirability of maintaining *continuity* and stability in the child's family relationships, school, and peer contacts
5. The relative *permanence* of the proposed custodial residences
6. The *relationship* between the child and *stepparents, blended families,* etc.
7. The *mental and physical health* of the competing parties
8. The *home, school, and social adjustment* of the child
9. The *child's preference*
10. Any other factors

As each of these issues is discussed, the evaluator should cite the documents, interviews, tests, and so forth upon which the discussion is based. For example:

> Extensive documentation from X Hospital and Y Mental Health Center indicates that Mrs. Doe has suffered from recurrent Bipolar Affective Disorder of Mixed Type. This severe mental illness began when Mrs. Doe was eighteen years of age, and has been characterized by. . . . However, recent evaluations provided by Mrs. Doe's psychiatrist indicate that Mrs. Doe is currently well adjusted, aside from an intermittent irritability which is probably secondary to the stress of the current legal proceedings.

CONCLUSIONS AND RECOMMENDATIONS

Summarize the discussion succinctly, for example:

> There is a strong reciprocal bond of affection and attachment between [the child] and both parents. Both parents have the capacity to provide for [the child's] physical, socioemotional, cognitive, communicative, educational, moral, and spiritual needs. Mrs. Doe is more experienced in basic physical care; but Mr. Doe has the ability and motivation to improve his skills in this regard.
> Given [the child's] age, his disrupted early environment, his current learning disability, and his close peer relationships at school, he is likely to be further disturbed by removal from his current school and social environment.

If one parent is incompetent (e.g., as a consequence of active mental illness, substance abuse, or an intransigent lack of appreciation of an impaired child's special needs), the clinician should say so. In most cases, however, neither parent will be clearly unfit. In that circumstance, the clinician should state that there is no scientific basis to prefer one parent to the other, list each parent's pros and cons, and leave the determination to the judge. Recommendations about visitation should also be proffered, if appropriate.

If treatment of the child is required, recommend the kind of treatment that would be appropriate and advise the court concerning the probable duration and cost of treatment. Assess the relative capacity and willingness of the parents to enter into a treatment alliance.

APPENDIXES

Append to your report the reports of all psychological tests or other special investigations that provide information relevant to the case.

CHAPTER 6

FORENSIC EVALUATION IN CASES OF CHILD MALTREATMENT

INTRODUCTION

This chapter deals with the recognition and psychopathology of child maltreatment, the law with regard to abuse and neglect, and the forensic evaluation of cases of this type. Since mental health clinicians are most likely to be involved in cases related to sexual abuse, physical abuse and neglect will be discussed in less detail than sexual maltreatment. The discussion of forensic evaluation will also focus on sexual abuse and will center on children, although adult victims of childhood sexual abuse have begun to employ the courts to obtain redress.[1]

Newberger and Bourne (1978) have described how the problem of child maltreatment—having fallen into the province of medicine and law enforcement—tends to be conceptualized in pediatric, psychiatric, or legal terms. Drawing on Bronfenbrenner (1979), Belsky (1980) proposes an alternative, *ecological* viewpoint according to which child abuse is regarded as the result of disequilibrium in five domains:

1. In the *child* (e.g., temperamental irritability)
2. In the *parents' ontogenetic development* (e.g., when parents were exposed as children to maltreatment)
3. In the *microsystem* (e.g., pathogenic parent–child interaction)
4. In the *exosystem* (e.g., parental substance abuse)
5. In the *macrosystem* (e.g., widespread unemployment)

Belsky's integrative proposal should be kept in mind as this chapter is read.

CHILD ABUSE IN THE LEGAL SYSTEM
Legal Doctrines

The state assumes its authority to interfere in private family life in accordance with two legal doctrines: *parens patriae* and the best interests of the child.

132

Parens patriae, an ancient doctrine derived from English chancery law, empowers the state to protect the interests of the mentally handicapped, the mentally ill, and minors. In *Prince v. Massachusetts,* the Supreme Court applied this doctrine when it upheld the right of the state to prevent children from distributing religious newspapers in contravention of state labor laws, despite the fact that those laws infringed on the liberty and religious freedom of their Jehovah's Witness parents.[2]

The conception known as the best interests of the child emerged in the nineteenth century in the context of child custody disputes (see Chapter 5). This doctrine indicates that, when the interests of parents, relatives, state, and children collide, the court should be guided in its decision by what would be to the children's immediate and ultimate benefit.

Notwithstanding those two doctrines, the rights of parents are constitutionally protected by the Fourteenth Amendment. Thus, the court may not step in to remove a child from a humble home merely because a more privileged family might be thought to offer greater advantages; rather, it must be shown that the child is *at serious risk of substantial physical or psychological harm.* The state's grounds for investigating allegations and assuming custody were greatly influenced by the recognition of "the battered child syndrome"[3] and an appreciation of the prevalence of sexual abuse. Over the last two decades the reported incidence of all forms of child abuse has increased markedly. In excess of 2 million cases were reported in 1987.[4] About 10 percent of these children are severely mistreated; more than 1,200 die each year.[5] At the same time, child welfare authorities became aware of the psychological damage caused by foster care drift and of the need for permanency planning. Clinicians invited to consult in such cases should be aware that the court has the onerous task of balancing the rights of parents against the prospect of damage to the child if there is further maltreatment by the family and the effect on the child of a protracted stay in the limbo of foster care.

Defining Child Abuse

Child abuse is prohibited by statute in all fifty states. The federal Child Abuse Prevention and Treatment Act defines child abuse as "the physical or mental injury, sexual abuse, negligent treatment or maltreatment of a child under the age of 18 by a person who is responsible for the child's welfare."[6]

State laws tend to list the categories of what constitutes child abuse. For example, under the relevant section of New Jersey's child abuse law a parent or guardian abuses the child where he or she:

1. Inflicts, or allows another to inflict, injury on the child by nonaccidental means that causes or creates a serious risk of serious harm or death
2. Creates or allows a risk of serious physical injury to the child
3. Commits or allows sexual abuse on the child
4. Fails to provide adequate food, clothing, medical care, shelter, or supervision for the child

5. Uses excessive corporal punishment or physical restraint on the child
6. Has abandoned the child[7]

Courts must interpret child abuse statutes in the context of modifying custody or visitation, terminating parental rights, or trying criminal cases. The evidence reviewed by a court may include accounts from witnesses, case workers, or the child himself. Medical diagnoses and expert psychological testimony are frequently included in such hearings.

Physical Abuse

All states mandate the reporting of children with suspected nonaccidental injuries; in most jurisdictions statutes proscribe the deliberate infliction of bodily injury by a parent or caretaker. The law recognizes the right of parents to discipline their children. However, the states vary in their definitions of the bounds of reasonable authority. The problem is to distinguish reasonable chastisement from willful abuse.

When evaluating physical abuse, the court will consider the nature and severity of the child's injuries, and the span of time over which they occurred.[8] In addition to testimony about specific abusive acts, courts routinely admit the medical diagnosis of "battered child syndrome" as evidence of physical abuse. Evidence concerning the "battered child syndrome" refers to the recognition of successive injuries unlikely to have been caused by accidental means. The syndrome must be authenticated by an expert, such as a pediatrician or psychologist.[9]

Judicial and statutory concerns about child abuse look to the potential for future abuse as well as past maltreatment. In *People v. Hernandez* (1980), two parents imprisoned a child in a filthy closet for eight years. Although they had not struck her, the parents were convicted of child abuse. The court interpreted the statute prohibiting "act[ing] under circumstances . . . likely to produce great bodily harm or death" to apply to the child's living conditions and noted that severe injuries are not a prerequisite to conviction.[10]

The failure to prevent another person from abusing a child can in itself be child abuse. When a mother claimed she was unable to prevent her husband from beating her three-year-old son because her husband threatened her if she objected, the court was not persuaded.[11] For most criminal offenses, the defendant's intent is an element of the offense, and if a defendant can successfully negate that aspect of a crime, he or she will be found not guilty. However, in cases of child abuse, society's interest in preventing cruelty to children is so compelling that an abuser's mental state is beside the point. Therefore, the court reasoned, it is irrelevant whether an abuser acts intentionally, negligently, or under compulsion.

Abandonment and Neglect

Willfully negligent or abandoning parents fail to provide for a child's basic physical and emotional needs (e.g., for adequate food, clothing, housing, and affection). In many states, willful abandonment is grounds for termination of parental rights; however, economic stringency alone should prompt financial assistance rather than an action for neglect. In actuality, most termination actions are based upon neglect, parental incapacity, and a serious risk of imminent harm.

In some cases status offenders (see Chapter 9) are taken into state custody following a neglect petition, on the grounds that their parents cannot control them or protect them from moral or physical danger.

Sexual Abuse

Sexual abuse is most likely to result in the removal of a child from the home when one parent has been the instigator and the other is unable or unwilling to protect the victim. Sexual abuse also occurs in the form of exploitation by pedophilic sex rings or for ritualistic purposes. The psychopathology of intrafamilial sex abuse and ritual abuse will be discussed later in this chapter.

Without medical evidence, sexual abuse is difficult to substantiate. Child victims being notoriously fragile witnesses, false retractions are all too common. Agency attorneys and prosecutors may be reluctant to file petitions or prosecute unless there is a corroborating witness. The use of psychotherapy to prepare the child witness psychologically and the introduction of videotapes and innovative techniques in order to mitigate courtroom trauma will be discussed later in this chapter.

Emotional Abuse

Emotional abuse refers to the infliction of psychological harm on a dependent child by a parent or caretaker who, by overt attitude, word, and deed, persistently exhibits severe rejection, contempt, or dislike. However, complaints of emotional abuse are so difficult to prove that they are seldom the sole grounds for a petition to assume custody; they are usually added to a broader complaint of maltreatment or neglect. Expert testimony is usually required to substantiate the psychological harm caused by the alleged emotional abuse.

Educational and Medical Neglect

This kind of neglect can vary in its associations. As a consequence of extreme incapacity, some parents are unable or unwilling to ensure that their child goes to school or receives medical care; others, moved by sincere religious convictions, oppose formal schooling or conventional medical care.

Failure to enroll a child in school, the refusal of prescribed remedial services, the tolerance of truancy, or collusion with a child's school refusal may be dealt with either through a truancy petition or under statutes that refer to parents' failing to provide proper care or contributing to the delinquency of a minor. On the other hand, several decisions[12] have supported the right of parents to place children in schools that provide adequate educational programs consonant with their religion. Indeed, in *Wisconsin v. Yoder,* the Supreme Court upheld the right of the Amish to withdraw their children from formal schooling at the age of sixteen in order to provide religious and agricultural training.[13]

The withholding of necessary medical care is generally considered child abuse. Conflicts arise when parental religious beliefs preclude medical care and First Amendment religious freedom rights are raised. In *Prince v. Massachusetts,* the Supreme Court distinguished between parental religious beliefs and practices, saying that "parents may be free to become martyrs themselves. But it does not follow they are free, in identical circumstances, to make martyrs of their children before they have reached the age of full and legal discretion when they can make that choice for themselves." However, the Court limited the exercise of state authority to those situations in which a child is actually endangered.[14]

Some states have created limited statutory exemptions from child welfare laws for members of religious denominations who believe in the virtue of prayer in place of medical treatment. An example is Section 852 of the Oklahoma Statutes Title 21, which allows parents to prescribe faith healing for "minor or trivial complaints" in lieu of medical help. Parental use of faith healing as a form of treatment may not be the sole basis for declaring a child neglected or endangered, "provided that medical care shall be provided where permanent physical damage could result to such child."[15] However, if a child is severely injured or dies when parents fail to provide medical care because of religious beliefs, the parents will be criminally liable. For example, the parents whose four-year-old child died of meningitis following attempted faith healing were convicted of voluntary manslaughter and child endangerment.[16]

Recently, neonates who test positive for drugs have been removed from their mothers on the ground of neglect. Under common law, a fetus was not considered a person. As a result, unless the local child welfare law specifically refers to fetuses, it must be shown that harm or danger occurred or is risked after the child's birth for the child abuse law to apply. The courts have reasoned that persistent parental drug abuse indicates that a child will be at risk in the future. When an infant was born addicted to heroin, the court upheld the grandparents' request for custody, because addicts tend to "nod off," need to get a "fix," and "engage in criminal activities to support their habits."[17] In *Matter of Stefanel Tyesha C.,* the court found cocaine in a newborn's system to be an "actual impairment" because of the "detrimental effects" suffered by addicted infants.[18]

Reporting Requirements

Whether civil or criminal, a child abuse case begins when a report is filed with the appropriate agency. All states have child welfare agencies to which reports can be made. Almost half the states also allow reports to be made to police, to an appropriate court, or to the district attorney.[19] The report is investigated by a social worker, usually within one or two days after it is filed. If the allegation of abuse is deemed to have some basis, the child will be removed from parental custody, or, in the case of a noncustodial parent, visitation will be suspended. A hearing is held almost immediately in order to determine whether the accused should be prosecuted, whether the child should be returned to the parents, or whether change in custody should be sought.[20] Charges of abuse can be prosecuted either civilly or criminally. Neglect charges are generally prosecuted as civil cases in a juvenile or domestic court.

Uniformity among the states has resulted from the funding requirements under the national Child Abuse Prevention and Treatment Act.[21] In order to qualify for funding under the act, a state's child abuse reporting law must (1) specify the purpose of the reporting law; (2) define abuse, neglect, and the classes of persons covered by the act; (3) state the requirements for mandated reporting and the criteria and authority for protective custody; (4) describe the responsibility and composition of child protection teams; (5) establish central child abuse registries and records; (6) appoint guardians *ad litem;* (7) authorize the medical examination of children at risk; and (8) abridge privileged communications of a certain type. All state reporting laws require reporting by persons who, in their professional capacity, come into contact with children (e.g., physicians, mental health clinicians, dentists, nurses, child care workers, or police).[22] Some states have extended the duty to report to anyone who suspects child abuse.[23] Minors up to the age of sixteen or eighteen are protected by reporting laws in all states, and in some states mentally or physically handicapped people are included. Parents, guardians, and others responsible for the child's care are bound by the act.

Failure to report child abuse may result in criminal penalties specified by statute. Professionals are rarely prosecuted successfully on these grounds.[24] Prosecution has occurred, however, as evidenced by the misdemeanor charges against an elementary school teacher who failed to report suspected physical and sexual abuse after students' parents had complained about another teacher's actions.[25] The courts are divided as to whether a child who has been adjudged abused is justified in bringing a civil action against the person who failed to report the abuse. Some courts have reasoned that, by enacting child abuse laws with criminal penalties, the legislature did not intend to create additional civil liability.[26] Other courts have allowed a child to pursue a civil remedy for failure to report, over and above any criminal sanction the state may impose.[27]

Most state reporting statutes grant immunity from civil and criminal actions to any person making a report, so long as the report is made in good faith.[28] Thus a physician making a report that is not later substantiated cannot be sued for defamation.[29] In *Dominguez v. Kelly,* a man was charged with aggravated sexual assault to which the child's mother later confessed. The man sued the physician who reported the abuse for malicious prosecution. The court held that the physician was protected by statutory immunity.[30] However, statutory immunity is limited to any civil or criminal liability that may arise from the act of reporting. A mother who reported that her boyfriend had abused her child was not immunized from prosecution for her own abuse of the same child.[31]

The privilege between physician and patient and between husband and wife is a statutory creation, the purpose of which is to protect the confidential nature of each relationship. However, when child abuse is at issue, reporting laws sharply curtail or eliminate privilege. In *State v. R.H.,* the court narrowly confined the abrogation of psychologist–patient privilege to child protection proceedings, while allowing it to remain in criminal child abuse cases.[32] The court based its decision on the balance of (1) the interest of a criminal defendant in avoiding self-incrimination against (2) the obligation of the state to protect children. Other courts have found there is no privilege when child abuse is criminally prosecuted.[33]

In addition to liability for failing to report, a physician who negligently fails to diagnose abuse can be liable for malpractice. In *Landeros v. Flood,* an eleven-month-old child was brought to a hospital with multiple injuries. The attending doctor examined the child superficially but failed to discern that she had been physically abused. As a result, her condition was not reported to state authorities and she was returned to her abusive parents. Physical abuse was correctly diagnosed two months later. The court found the physician's error to have been negligent, since other physicians in similar circumstances should have had the skill to recognize the signs of maltreatment.[34]

CHILD PROTECTION SERVICES

Typically, child protection services involve a reporting "hotline" and agencies that collaborate with the courts by investigating complaints, taking emergency custody when appropriate, and helping parents remedy defects. By this means, they seek early reunification. If this proves unfeasible, they petition to terminate parental rights and arrange permanent placement.

Child abuse teams are typically composed of social workers, pediatricians, nurses, mental health clinicians, law enforcement officers, and attorneys. A legal representative for the child is most likely to be appointed when termination is sought. Mental health clinicians are most likely to be involved when the child needs treatment or when parental competence is in question.

Records of complaints, investigations, and services provided are entered in central registries. Thus, statistical data are generated, and peripatetic families can be located. Highly confidential material of this type may be released only to agencies investigating complaints, to clinicians providing authorized treatment, to the court, or to the child's attorney or guardian *ad litem.* Some states expunge records if investigators or the court find the complaint unfounded.

COURT PROCEEDINGS

If, after a preliminary investigation, reports of child abuse appear to have some basis, a hearing will be held. Child abuse and child neglect are both civil and criminal offenses. The hearing may be a civil one, in which the court will determine whether or not to remove the child from the custody of the alleged abuser, modify visitation, or, in extreme circumstances, terminate parental rights entirely.

Alternatively or additionally, the accused abuser may be prosecuted for criminal child abuse. Maltreating parents can be charged with homicide, battery, rape, or cruelty. In most states the child protection agency will notify the local law enforcement authority, and a prosecutor will decide whether or not to institute criminal proceedings. Criminal proceedings require a more exacting standard of proof ("beyond a reasonable doubt" rather than "clear and convincing evidence") and are much less expedient than civil actions. Because criminal proceedings carry the most severe sanctions, the rules governing those proceedings include safeguards to protect the rights of the accused. As a result, testimony by victims and experts may be considerably more restricted than it would be in civil proceedings. In contrast to criminal actions, which are generally reserved for the most heinous and incorrigible cases, civil actions are more conducive to therapy and reunification. Furthermore, civil proceedings are generally undertaken in juvenile courts, which have jurisdiction over the whole family and have a much greater variety of dispositional options.

Protective custody is sought when the child has been abandoned or if there would be a serious risk of harm should the child remain in the care of the parents or guardians. Police may be authorized to remove endangered children immediately, or hospitals permitted to detain them.

A detention hearing is usually held within forty-eight hours after the child has been removed from the home. At this hearing the court will determine whether to return the child to the parents or whether to prosecute the abuse allegations. If abuse allegations are to be pursued, the court will also decide where to place the child until the adjudication hearings. A civil protection order (CPO) may be sought as an alternative to removal of the child. This course of action is most often pursued in cases involving spouse abuse or intrafamilial sexual abuse, provided the nonoffending parent is supportive to the child and concurs with the purpose of the order. In such circumstances, the order will put the alleged perpetrator out of the house.

If allegations of abuse are not deemed unfounded, a hearing on the merits will be held. A civil proceeding to adjudicate abuse or neglect charges will be held in a juvenile court. In this type of hearing, the state must prove, by clear and convincing evidence, that it should assert jurisdiction over the child on the ground that the parents or guardians have so abused or neglected the child that he or she would be endangered. A criminal proceeding may also be held before or after the civil proceeding.

Civil and criminal proceedings differ profoundly. The object of a juvenile court proceeding is to protect the child and to arrange the best living situation for him. The purpose of a criminal proceeding is to determine whether the accused is guilty and, if so, to punish him. In contrast to a criminal trial, juvenile court proceedings afford parents no constitutional right to a jury, although state law may allow it;[35] nor does the Constitution afford parents the right to court-appointed counsel.[36] Aside from these differences, similar rules govern civil and criminal proceedings. In some instances, however, the rules have been modified in order to protect the child victim.

EVIDENTIARY ISSUES

The Child as Witness

When physical abuse has occurred, a physician can often testify to the fact of abuse, based on his or her observation of physical injury. Testimony by the child may not be necessary if someone else can identify who perpetrated the abuse or if the circumstances indicate that the only person who could have abused the child was the accused. Compared to physical abuse, the charge of sexual abuse can be more difficult to substantiate from physical examination; consequently, the child's testimony may be required in order to resolve the issue.

If a child's testimony is to be of any value, he or she must be *competent,* in other words, able to observe, remember, and recount an event, and aware of the obligation to tell the truth.[37] At common law, children were presumed to be incompetent to testify (as were atheists, felons, spouses, mentally incompetent persons, and the parties themselves). The parties were incompetent because they were not independent in respect of the matters in issue. The legal view of competency has changed: All witnesses are presumed competent.[38] Some states presume children's competency only after a certain age, while others extend the presumption to all children.[39] Even in those jurisdictions where competency is assumed, the judge has the authority to test a child's capacity to testify. The test may take the form of questions by the judge at trial or an evaluation by an expert before the trial. A child witness found incompetent will not be permitted to testify. The judicial notion of competency may be informed by an inadequate concept of childhood and thus the needs and abilities of children not properly appreciated.[40]

In most states the juvenile court is empowered to appoint an attorney or lay guardian *ad litem* in order to protect the child's interests throughout the legal proceedings. The child's counsel or guardian reviews the investigation of the case, prepares the child to cope with the stress of appearing in court, represents the child in court proceedings, and contributes to dispositional planning. However, attorneys can be placed in an ethical dilemma: Whereas a guardian *ad litem* represents the *best interests* of the child, an attorney is expected to represent the client's *expressed interest,* provided he or she is capable of considered judgment. Some states resolve this potential ethical conflict by empowering the judge to appoint both an attorney for the child and a guardian *ad litem,* when the expressed interests of the child collide with his or her best interests.

Hearsay

The "Hearsay Rule" forbids a witness from offering in evidence a statement made by a third person in order to prove the truth of a matter asserted (see Chapter 2). Under this definition, a person to whom a child reported sexual abuse would be prevented from repeating the child's statement as proof that the child had been abused. The purpose of this rule is to reinforce the reliability of testimony and guarantee the accused's constitutional right to confront and cross-examine witnesses against him. However, because a child may be incompetent to testify, a number of exceptions to the hearsay rule have been established.

Some states have created a special exception for child victims in which a child's statement can be offered in evidence by another person if there is independent support that the statement is true.[41] A child's report of abuse may also fall into the "excited utterance" exception, according to which a hearsay statement can be admitted if the victim made the statement in the stress following a disturbing event.[42] Finally, a child's statement may be offered in evidence by a physician under an exception concerning statements elicited for the purpose of diagnosis or treatment.[43]

In *White v. Illinois* the Supreme Court found that the "spontaneous declaration" and "medical examination" exceptions to the hearsay rule satisfied the constitutional law requirements of the Sixth Amendment's confrontation clause (see below). Statements made by a four-year-old girl immediately after a sexual assault and later repeated to a physician were admitted in evidence to prove that the accused had sexually assaulted the girl. Statements uttered in such circumstances provide "substantial guarantees of this trustworthiness."[44] The Constitution does not require that the utterer of the statement testify in court or be unavailable to so testify. Nor is it necessary to establish that the admission of hearsay evidence, rather than direct testimony, is necessary to protect the physical and psychological well-being of the violated child.[45] The necessity requirement is confined to those contexts where in-court testimony is given in a way avoiding confrontation, such as by closed-circuit television.

The fact that a child is too young to give coherent testimony does not alone justify circumventing the hearsay rule. A court will examine the circumstances surrounding the utterance of the statement to ensure that it possesses "substantial guarantees of trustworthiness." In *Idaho v. Wright* (1990), a two-and-one-half-year-old girl was questioned by a physician while he examined her for signs of sexual abuse. The court held that the physician's testimony about his conversation with the child could not be admitted because it lacked "particularized guarantees of trustworthiness";[46] it did not fall within firmly rooted exceptions to the hearsay rule. The court was concerned that the child's statements to the physician were not spontaneous and that her identification of her father as the perpetrator of her injuries was, rather, a response to the physician's leading questions. The court also pointed out that physical evidence of abuse "sheds no light on the reliability of the child's allegations regarding the identity of the abuser."[47]

The Expert Witness

A child may be an inadequate witness. When physical abuse is alleged, the child is often simply too young to testify. However, there may be substantial physical evidence of abuse about which a physician can testify. As a result, expert testimony about the "battered child syndrome" can be used to show that a child's injuries were inflicted over a period of time, intentionally rather than accidentally. In such circumstances, the victim's testimony is not needed.[48]

Since there may be little or no physical evidence of sexual abuse, the child's testimony can be critical. Standing alone, however, the child's testimony may be unconvincing. His or her account may be confused, inconsistent, or even recanted. Because most judges or jury members are unfamiliar with the behavior of abused children, a mental health clinician can be asked to testify to (1) the psychological health and prognosis of the victim; (2) the likelihood that the child's pattern of symptoms and impairment is caused by maltreatment; (3) apparently inconsistent present behavior with future psychological damage;[49] (4) parental competence; and (5) the kind of treatment likely to help the child or enable the parents to remedy defects in their capacity to provide care.

Expert testimony about the typical behavior of abused children is admitted in order to help the trier of fact (the jury) assess the credibility of a child witness.[50] Mason (1991) examined 122 appellate court decisions, civil and criminal, finding that most courts admit testimony regarding the characteristics of sexually abused children, particularly on rebuttal, even when applied to a particular child. The judge will usually instruct the jury that the expert's testimony should be regarded as information concerning the behavior of sexually abused children in general and not as evidence that sexual abuse has indeed occurred. These courts eschew the labeling of particular behavior (for example, "child sex abuse accommodation syndrome"), but will allow a list of descriptors with no title.

Testimony about whether a particular child is telling the truth will not be permitted, since that is the function of the jury. In *People v. Beckley,* the court did allow an expert to testify concerning behavior that suggests that abuse has occurred, finding that this testimony was acceptable because it was in response to questions asked by the defense rather than the prosecution. The court examined some of the concerns that have led to limiting testimony about whether a particular child is telling the truth; for example, the fact that an expert is usually seeking to help and protect children, and thus not unbiased, and the danger that the jury will rely on "the only seemingly objective source" in its "awesome dilemma of whom to believe."[51] Expert testimony about a particular child's veracity has also been prohibited on the ground that it conveys a misleading aura of "scientific legitimacy."[52]

While testimony that a witness is telling the truth will not be permitted, an expert may express the opinion that a child has been sexually abused. In *In re Cheryl H.*, the court reasoned that a psychological diagnosis of sexual abuse is equivalent to a medical diagnosis of "battered child syndrome."[53]

When a mental health clinician after examining an entire family has concluded that the allegedly abusive parent fits the profile of an abuser, testimony to that effect will rarely, if ever, be allowed, because of its potential prejudice to the defendant.[54] In a criminal trial, the aim is to decide whether the accused committed the specific act or acts alleged, not to determine what type of person he or she is.

In juvenile court proceedings, on the other hand, an expert may be permitted to testify to his or her observations about the accused abuser. This type of testimony is considerably less limited in a civil hearing, because punishment is not the purpose of the proceeding.

The Right to Confrontation

The Sixth Amendment confers upon the accused the right to confront and cross-examine a witness against him. However, recognizing the potential trauma of such a confrontation, a number of states have passed laws that provide alternative means for children to testify, such as closed-circuit television or videotaped interviews. The conflict between the necessity of insuring a fair trial and the desirability of protecting child witnesses has raised questions of whether these child testimony statutes are constitutional.

In *Coy v. Iowa,* the Supreme Court held that placement of a screen between the defendant and the two thirteen-year-old girls he was accused of raping violated the Sixth Amendment, because the right to confront witnesses included the right to face those testifying against him. However, the Court held that the right to confrontation is not absolute, and that some exceptions to that right may exist. In order for an exception to be appropriate, it must be based on "individualized findings that these particular witnesses needed special protection."[55]

In *Maryland v. Craig,* the Court approved one exception: It allowed the conviction of a woman for sexual assault to stand after a six-year-old child testified via closed-circuit television. The Court reasoned that the purpose of the confrontation clause was to ensure that the "evidence admitted against an accused is reliable and subject to the rigorous adversarial testing that is the norm of Anglo-American criminal proceedings."[56] While stating a preference for face-to-face confrontation, the Court found that the "state's interest in the physical and psychological well-being of child abuse victims" would at times outweigh the accused's right to face-to-face confrontation.[57] It stressed the need for a case-by-case finding that trauma could result, thus disallowing statutes that permit all child witnesses to testify outside the court.

Where evidence of sexual assault is properly admitted under exceptions to the hearsay rule, the confrontation clause does not require repetition of that evidence in court in the presence of the accused.[58] The indicia of reliability are fulfilled by the strictures of the exceptions to the hearsay rule. Testimony in court, however, does not carry that reliability unless tested in the usual way by confrontation. These rules have not escaped criticism. Dziech and Schudson (1992) argue that the rules ill serve the victim in reaching the truth of abuse accusations. They support developments including (1) abolition of minor competency requirements; (2) admission of minor out-of-court statements; (3) video-taping and closed-circuit television for testimony; and (4) admission of expert testimony. Broadly, they urge that courts ought to be more sensitive to the needs and nature of children.[59]

DISPOSITION

The following dispositional options are available to the juvenile court: (1) to dismiss the case and return the child to the family; (2) to return the child home but order further diagnostic or therapeutic intervention; (3) to commit the child to the custody of the state but order home-based services with periodic reports to the court; (4) to commit the child to state custody and order foster care or institutional placement with reunification planning; and (5) to commit the child to state custody and plan to terminate residual parental rights as soon as possible. Summary termination of parental rights requires a separate adjudicatory hearing.

In most cases parents stipulate (i.e., formally agree) to the recommended state plan, and the judge ratifies the agreement. However, if parents contest the allegation of maltreatment or the dispositional ruling, an adversary hearing will ensue. Dispositional orders can be reviewed and changed at later hearings, for example if the parents are unwilling to cooperate in reunification plans.

When criminal charges are likely to arise out of a dependency hearing, an accused parent faces a difficult choice: either cooperate with court-appointed mental health workers or refuse to disclose anything that could be used against him in a criminal trial. The Fifth Amendment guarantees that no one will be forced to testify against himself in a criminal trial. However, statements made in therapy can be incriminating. Moreover, therapist–patient privilege has been suspended by most states when a criminal child abuse charge has been filed.[60] The problems inherent in this situation are exacerbated when a family court orders therapy as part of a family reunification plan. Sensitive to the conflict between the Fifth Amendment rights of the accused and the need to facilitate family reconciliation, one California court has held that statements made in therapy cannot be used in a criminal prosecution.[61] The court reasoned that only in this way could both the privilege against self-incrimination and the family's best interests be protected; however, prosecutors would be allowed to use statements made in therapy with the purpose of contradicting the defendant's testimony in a criminal proceeding. This holding is the exception; the majority of states grant no immunity.

Attempts to reschedule dependency hearings may not be successful if their purpose is to avoid admissions that could be used at a later criminal trial. For example, in *Matter of Vance A,* a mother of two children scalded her infant child to death and severely burned her six-year-old son. Dependency hearings were instituted in order to remove the surviving child permanently from his mother's custody, and criminal charges were filed against her for the death of her youngest son. The mother requested that the dependency hearings be postponed until the conclusion of the criminal trial, because some of her testimony in the civil trial could be incriminating at the criminal trial. While recognizing the accused's difficult position, the court found the interests of the child to be more persuasive. The important public policy of finding the child a permanent residence with "care by relatives or others who can give him a sense of lasting love, nurture and security" outweighed the injustice of forcing the mother to choose between remaining silent during the civil child abuse hearing and giving testimony that might incriminate her in the subject criminal trial.[62]

FOSTER CARE
Residual Parental Rights

Juvenile court statutes empower the state to assume custody, to place a child in foster care, and to provide food, shelter, medical care, education, discipline, and control. In some states, guardianship and custody may be split, the parents retaining the right to make major life decisions on behalf of the child (e.g., concerning extraordinary medical care). In some instances the court may retain the right to order a particular medical treatment or school placement. In all jurisdictions, even though the state has assumed custody, parents retain *residual rights* (e.g., to visit the child and to consent to adoption, marriage, or entrance into the armed services). Although there is considerable variation in the definition and extent of residual parental rights, the state may not arrogate these remaining rights without petitioning to terminate them. Nationally 340,000 children are in foster care, with 39 percent remaining two years or more in temporary placements.[63]

Foster Parents' Authority

Foster parents' authority is delegated from the authority of the state agency. The agency makes the major decisions, and the foster parent carries them out. This delegation of authority is specified in statute, agency regulation, foster care contract, or dispositional order. The state has the duty to supervise foster care and may be liable for the wrongful actions of foster parents.[64]

Many states impose licensing standards on foster homes and, to varying degrees, allow foster parents the right to appeal against agency decisions. The general trend is to delegate more authority to foster parents and to regard them as members of the child protection team. Foster parents, for example, have been trained to provide specialized care for emotionally disturbed children. In *Smith v. Organization of Foster Families for Equality and Reform,* the Supreme Court considered whether foster parents have a liberty interest entitling them to due process when the agency proposes to remove foster children from their care.[65] Although no conclusion was reached on this matter, most lower courts, since *Smith,* have held that foster parents do not have a liberty interest.

Foster Children's Rights

Following the initial disposition order, regular hearings may be scheduled in order to monitor the child's progress and the implementation of reunification plans. At these hearings the child is represented by counsel or guardian *ad litem.*

The State must certify and supervise foster homes. Foster children are entitled to adequate food, shelter, medical care, education, and vocational training. As previously discussed, the state owes the duty to protect foster children from maltreatment and to report suspected maltreatment to the relevant law enforcement agency. Reunification services or permanent planning are also increasingly regarded as rights. The state, through its agencies, must also take reasonable steps to avoid placing dangerous foster children in homes where they may cause injury.[66]

Foster children's rights derive from state juvenile codes, statutes, and regulations; from federal foster care law;[67] from the Social Security Act;[68] and from the Education for All Handicapped Children Act.[69]

PERMANENT PLANNING

Principles

Permanent planning embodies the following principles:

1. A child should not be unnecessarily removed from his or her home.
2. Reunification should be effected as soon as possible after the parents have remedied the problems that occasioned the removal of the child in the first place.
3. The ties between child and parents should be sustained while the child is in foster care.
4. The child should not be left to drift in foster care. If reunification efforts fail or are deemed inappropriate, adoption or permanent foster care should be arranged within a reasonable time.

These principles are based upon the consideration that all children require stable, continuous attachment to autonomous parents or parent surrogates who are committed to their welfare.

The Adoption Assistance and Child Welfare Act of 1980 (AACWA) provides fiscal incentives that encourage the states to reform child welfare practices.[70] It requires the establishment of statewide services to prevent removal, promote reunification, and plan for permanent placement. Those services must be reviewed every six months. Within eighteen months of the initial foster placement, a judicial hearing is required in order to determine whether the child should be returned home, adopted, or placed in permanent alternative care. It is required that fair hearings be provided for complainants who consider that they have not received adequate, prompt service. Unfortunately, the wait for permanent homes is painfully slow, exacerbating emotional, behavioral, and academic problems.[71] For too many, delinquency is the outcome.[72]

The Case Plan

Child welfare agencies aim to prevent foster care drift by involving parents in their own case plans. A reunification case plan informs parents what it is they must remedy in order for the child to be restored to them, the tasks and activities that they and the agency must perform in order to resolve the problem, and the timetable for the provision of services and achievement of goals. The case plan is negotiated between parents and agency and mutually agreed upon by them. The agency monitors and documents progress toward the goals of the plan for presentation at court hearings. If the parents are unwilling to follow the plan or unable to remedy the problem within a reasonable time, the state may petition to terminate parental rights. Any plan should stipulate conditions necessary and adequate for parental rights to be reestablished. A failure to notify parents of these conditions has been held to be a violation of parents' due process rights.[73]

Criteria for Termination

The termination of parental rights results in the extinction of all residual parental rights, the complete severance of all contact between parents and child, and the release of the child for adoption or alternative permanent placement. The chief criteria for termination are as follows:

1. Extreme abuse or neglect
2. Abandonment
3. Parental incapacity
4. Failure to remedy defects in parental capacity
5. Irretrievable breakdown in the parent–child relationship

Mental health clinicians can contribute useful information to the Court on all these issues.

EXTREME ABUSE OR NEGLECT

Termination may be effected forthwith if the child has been subjected to such egregious maltreatment that the court could not countenance exposing the child to the risk of future harm. Termination may also be ordered if a parent deliberately exposes a child to abuse or fails to prevent a child from being abused, for example by prostituting the child or supplying him or her to pornographers. In most cases, however, even if the maltreatment has been severe, attempts at reunification are required.

ABANDONMENT

If the parents have abandoned the child and there are no mitigating circumstances, the time necessary for termination may be shortened. The case for termination is strengthened if the parents state that they have no interest in the child; fail to communicate with the child by regular telephone calls, letters or birthday cards; fail to contribute financially to the child's support despite ability to do so; or fail to cooperate in the reunification plan.[74]

PARENTAL INCAPACITY

Parental incapacity is most likely to be raised when parents suffer from severe mental illness, personality disorder, mental retardation, physical handicap, alcoholism, or drug addiction. In such cases the expert witness will be required to testify to parental incapacity and to advise concerning the unlikelihood that the incapacity will improve or respond in a reasonable time to treatment or education, or to testify that reunification would be detrimental to the child's best interests.[75]

STAGNANCY OR FAILURE TO REMEDY

If the parents are unwilling or unable to remedy specified problems within the time stipulated in the reunification plan, termination will be necessary. The court will require good case planning, diligent implementation, and adequate documentation by the agency in order to substantiate stagnation in the reunification plan.

IRRETRIEVABLE BREAKDOWN IN FAMILY RELATIONSHIPS

The child may exhibit hatred or fear of the parents. However, deterioration in the child's tie to the parent is seldom the sole criterion for termination. Sometimes the child's feelings for the parent have become attenuated by parental imprisonment; usually, however, additional factors must be introduced to support termination, for example, that the parent had previously maltreated the child or failed to communicate with him or her.

Termination Proceedings

The severing of residual rights is a dismal measure, properly circumscribed by formal and exacting standards. A termination hearing is a separate proceeding, adversary in nature when contested, and activated by an agency's petition or motion.

In most but not all states the child is represented. In *Lassiter v. Department of Social Services,* the Supreme Court ruled that indigent parents did not have automatic right to counsel but that their need for representation should be considered case by case, in accordance with the complexity of the matter or the potential liability of the parents to criminal prosecution.[76] In *Santosky v. Kramer,* the Supreme Court held that, in view of the poignancy of the action contemplated, the state must prove the case for termination to a clear and convincing degree.[77] Termination must be shown to be in the child's best interests and convincingly based upon at least one of the five criteria already described (extreme abuse or neglect, abandonment, incapacity, stagnation and failure to remedy, or irretrievable breakdown in the parent–child relationship).

In many cases, unless there are unalterable barriers, the aim is to place the child in a closed adoption. However, the following alternatives may be entertained: open adoption (in which the natural parents retain the right to communicate with the child), long-term foster care, or the awarding of legal guardianship or custody to a third person.

ADOPTION

Principles

Adoption is the legal process whereby the ties, rights, and obligations concerning a child are transferred from natural parents to adoptive parents. American adoption reaches back to Roman law in conceptions that a finalized adoption incorporates the adoptee as a full member of the new family, and the adoptee's ties with the biological parents are severed completely.[78] Regulated by statute in all states, adoption is initiated by a petition that is usually filed by the adoptive parents. Unless their rights have been terminated, formal consent must be obtained from the natural parents, from children over a certain age (usually ten to fourteen years), and from the legal custodian, if any. Adoptive parents are located by a state agency or a private agency, or informally. The agency may provide the court with a nonbinding report concerning the desirability of the proposed adoption.

Adoption Proceedings

Although adoption hearings are usually informal, if the natural parent withholds consent they can be adversarial. If the parent or custodian contests adoption, the state must prove that it is in the child's best interests. Essentially, it must be shown that the parents are unable to provide adequate care and that the child would be without a permanent home unless adopted. The states vary concerning the standard of proof required; it is not clear whether the holding in *Santosky v. Kramer* concerning termination applies to adoption proceedings.[79] However, when a child over ten to fourteen years of age refuses to consent, adoption is absolutely barred.

A number of Supreme Court decisions have defined the rights of unmarried fathers.[80] Unmarried fathers who have lived with and supported their children have a full right to contest adoption; those who have never lived with or supported the children do not.

In some states parents have the right to revoke consent, provided they do so within a specified period of time. In other states parents may be required to show that their revocation of consent for adoption is in the child's best interests. Under narrow circumstances, parents may successfully challenge final adoption decrees, for example, if they have not received due notice or if their consent to adoption was a consequence of duress or fraud. Relatives of the child have sometimes been successful in having an adoption annulled on the grounds of lack of notice.

Adoptive parents can abrogate adoption only if it can be shown to have been fraudulent and (usually) that abrogation is in the child's best interest.

Adoption records are kept sealed and may be opened only by court order, for example if vital genetic information is required. In recent years, pressure from adoptee organizations[81] supported by theoretical work advocating "open adoption"[82] has induced some states to relax this prohibition. Thus, some degree of contact between biological and adoptive parents is considered desirable, and adoptees may obtain information about their adoption. It is likely that more states will follow this emerging trend.[83] Litigation has also pried open adoption files where adoptive parents have complained that agencies have misrepresented the background and psychological makeup of the adoptee.[84]

Independent adoptions occur when a parent directly places a child with a third person. In order to prevent the growth of a black market in babies, the states have imposed regulations on private adoptions, for example by limiting legal fees or requiring agency approval.

Children whose special physical, emotional, or educational needs make them difficult to place may be eligible for subsidy under the AACWA.[85] The states generally prefer that adopting parents be couples of childbearing age, and of the same religion and race as the natural parents. Divergence from these guidelines may be allowed if the child has exceptional needs that require specialized placement.

PHYSICAL ABUSE

Recognition

Physical abuse occurs when an adult, usually a parent or guardian, inflicts physical injury on a minor or dependent person. In the United States, the incidence of physical abuse has been estimated at about 250,000 a year, of which 70 percent are new cases. The mortality is approximately 2,000 annually. Possibly 10 percent of all infant emergency cases are associated with physical abuse.[86]

Physical abuse is usually first suspected by physicians, caseworkers, teachers, day care providers, or others who have close contact with children. Schmitt (1987) has described the following characteristics:

1. The parents have inexplicably delayed seeking help.
2. The history given by the parents is implausible or incompatible with the physical findings.
3. The child has a history of, or evidence of, repeated suspicious injuries (e.g., multiple bruises, burns. or fractures).
4, The parents have sought help for their child from different hospitals or emergency facilities.
5. The parents blame a third party (e.g., a sibling) or claim the child has injured himself (e.g., by falling out of a highchair).
6. The parent projects unrealistic expectations onto the child. (One abusive mother, for example, described her six-month-old son as "cunning" because he waited until she changed him before he soiled his diapers; another woman described her infant daughter as "ungrateful" for the care she had been given.)
7. There is a prior history of abuse.
8. The child accuses a caretaker of physical abuse.

Injuries that suggest the possibility of maltreatment have the following characteristics:

1. A pattern of bruising or laceration suggesting punishment (i.e., on the head, face, buttocks, lower back, inner thighs, or genitals)
2. Burns or scalds (particularly lesions suggesting cigarette or contact burns of different ages)
3. Subdural hematoma (with or without fracture)

4. Abdominal trauma (e.g., ruptured liver, spleen, or bowel)
5. Ocular injuries (e.g., retinal hemorrhages or detachment)
6. Mouth injuries
7. Radiologic signs of multiple bone or epiphyseal fractures of different ages, or fracture-dislocations of shoulders, elbows, or hips consistent with the application of a twisting stress

The physician must differentiate physical abuse from blood dyscrasia, bone disease, and accidental injury. Parental physical abuse must be distinguished from injury perpetrated by another child.

Psychopathology

Physical abuse is preponderantly associated with families of lower socioeconomic status, although this observation is undoubtedly affected to some degree by reporting bias. Large family size, unemployment, social isolation, lack of social support, and high intrafamilial stress have all been described in abusive families.[87] Spinetta and Rigler (1972) suggest that such environmental factors are contributory rather than casual. Martin's (1981) observation that abused children are more likely than other children to have been premature has been questioned by Leventhal (1981).

Early studies suggested that the physically abusive parent had herself experienced abusive parenting, as a result of which pathological role reversal occurred and the parent irrationally projected her own needs and frustrations upon the child.[88] Recent empirical studies have found that, compared to controls, abusive mothers have the following characteristics: low intelligence; stressed by environmental forces such as poverty and spouse abuse; isolated; low in self-esteem; negative, harsh, punitive, and prone to deny the complexity of childrearing; subject to chronic mental and physical illness; and liable to have had unplanned pregnancies.[89] Little is known about abusive fathers.

Controlled observations of the interaction between abusive mothers and their children have yielded the following features: less positive, less verbal, more negative interactions; less interaction of any sort; less reciprocity and proximity; avoidance of eye contact; less infant responsiveness; and more infant distress after reunion.[90] The common factor may be a defect in maternal empathy,[91] a problem highly likely to become intergenerational.

Clinical studies of abused children have revealed an increased prevalence of mental retardation, neurological abnormality, and language delay,[92] together with apathy, lack of capacity for pleasure, social withdrawal and violent behavior.[93] The abused infant has been described as prone to depression, irritable crying, feeding problems, social and motor delay, "frozen watchfulness," and a lack of appropriate response to separation.[94] Controlled empirical studies of abused children have found impaired or delayed social development, aggressiveness, violent fantasy, poor impulse control, mistrust, anhedonia, depression, and self-destructiveness.[95]

Green (1985) proposes the following casual sequence in physical abuse: an *abuse-prone parent* in an *unsupportive, stressful environment* interacts with a *difficult child.* The parent having been reared in a punitive, insensitive environment herself, grows to envision human relationships as withholding, victimizing, and unjust; to view herself as hateful; and to have severe defects in the capacity to empathize with other people. She develops the defenses of *projection* (e.g., she tends to see others as hostile when she herself is angered), *displacement* (e.g., when frustrated by her husband she takes it out on the child), and *role reversal* (e.g., she expects her child to be sensitive and to minister to her needs and, if he does not do so, she perceives him as withholding, ungrateful, and rejecting). The failure of the child to meet her pathologically exaggerated needs further aggravates her self-depreciation. Self-hatred, in turn, is projected upon the child, who becomes scapegoated. Thus, the parent repeatedly reenacts yet fails to master her own childhood traumata. The chronically abused child develops *traumatic anxiety* (manifest in the older child as insomnia, nightmares, explosive rage, repetitive traumatic play, and fear of or preoccupation with experiences that resemble previous traumatic situations), *pathological object relations* (with fear of closeness and social withdrawal, or overdependency and undiscriminating familiarity, yet with an inability to sustain relationships), *primitive defenses* (denial, dissociation, projection, and displacement), *impaired impulse control* (explosive rage, unreflectiveness, and tendency to run away when stressed), a *depreciated self-concept, self-destructiveness* (e.g., risk-taking or accident-proneness), *learning problems,* and, in some cases, *impairment of the central nervous system.*

Outcome

If the parents receive no treatment, the risk of subsequent abuse is very great. Cohn (1979) found that one-third of maltreating families (one-half if the original abuse had been severe) abused their children again within twelve months.

There are few prospective studies of abused children. However, circumstantial evidence suggests that children who have been exposed to grossly insensitive, drastically punitive, highly unpredictable parenting are likely to become unempathic, harsh, explosive adults whose unfulfilled needs are projected upon those who depend upon them. This matter is discussed further in a later section of this chapter concerning posttraumatic stress syndromes.

NONORGANIC FAILURE TO THRIVE

Recognition

Nonorganic failure to thrive (NOFT) is diagnosed when an infant's weight is below the third percentile and all organic causes have been excluded. In practice, pediatricians are alert for infant growth curves that decline below the normal. Estimations of the proportion of NOFT infants among all who fail to thrive vary from 15 percent[96] to 50 percent.[97]

Causation

Is NOFT the result of a primary deficiency in food intake, or is the starvation secondary to psychological factors akin to infant depression? It is currently believed that the caloric deficiency and growth failure in NOFT are secondary to disturbed mother–infant interaction and that the apathy so characteristic of these infants is of psychological, not nutritional, origin.[98] NOFT can thus be regarded as a reactive attachment disorder.[99] Of all infants who fail to thrive yet manifest no physical disease, one group gains weight after hospitalization and another does not. Kotelchuk (1980) sounds a warning that not all the potential organic causes of failure to thrive may yet have been discovered.

Psychopathology

The mothers of NOFT children have been described as prone to personality disorder.[100] Evans, Reinhart, and Succop (1972) referred to "depressed" and "chaotic" subtypes. O'Callaghan and Hull (1978); Togut, Allen, and Lelchuck (1969); and Hess, Hess, and Hard (1977) detected depression, low verbal intelligence, and poor impulse control. On the other hand, Newberger and colleagues (1977), Kotelchuk (1980), and Pollitt, Weisel, and Chan (1975), could find no increased prevalence of psychiatric disorder among these women. The description of fathers is even more unclear, varying from supportive to ineffectual or negative.[101] The range in these findings suggest etiological heterogeneity, methodological variance, or both. As is the case in physical abuse, the parents of NOFT children are likely to be of low SES and to be living relatively unsupported, isolated lives, in severely stressful conditions.[102]

On the other hand, the clinical observation of NOFT infants has consistently yielded the following characteristics: hypotonia, inactivity, apathy, social aloofness, lack of exploratory play, insomnia, nocturnal vigilance, and rumination. In the older child, clinicians have described voracious appetite, increased thirst, the scavenging and hoarding of food, indiscriminate attachments, attention-seeking, low frustration tolerance, and aggressiveness.[103] Observation of parent–child interaction in NOFT has revealed social distance,[104] insecure attachment,[105] and a relative absence of verbal separation protest.[106]

NEGLECT

Neglect occurs when caregivers fail to provide adequately for a child's physical, safety, emotional, medical, or educational needs.[107] A legal rather than a medical term, neglect is associated with parental incompetence, rejection, or abandonment. Characteristically involved with and inseparable from other forms of maltreatment (including NOFT), neglect is more prevalent than physical abuse.[108]

Neglect has been associated with poverty, overcrowding, domestic discord, parental intellectual inadequacy, parental physical illness, and parental drug and alcohol abuse.[109] It is said to be more prevalent among children already affected by mental retardation, physical handicap, or temperamental sluggishness.[110] Fewer positive interactions have been observed in neglectful mother–child pairs than in physically abusive and normal controls.[111]

Munchausen syndrome by proxy is a special variant of medical neglect. In this relatively uncommon (though increasingly recognized) syndrome, a mother falsifies a child's illness by deliberately inducing physical symptoms and signs or by presenting symptoms that require intensive medical investigation or treatment.[112] Hematuria, hemoptysis, blood in the stools, apneic episodes, rashes, seizures, and repeated infections are among the factitious conditions that have been reported. The following features should arouse suspicion:

1. The child has repeated, inexplicable illnesses with symptom patterns unlike any known disease.
2. Clinical or special investigations are inconsistent with the claimed illness (e.g. normal electroencephalography despite multiple seizures) or reveal their factitious origin (e.g., avian blood corpuscles in human urine).
3. The illness is unresponsive to treatment (e.g., seizures persist despite adequate anticonvulsant therapy).
4. Symptoms disappear when the mother is away from the child, only to reappear when she returns.
5. The mother is highly attentive to, yet oddly unconcerned about, the child.
6. The mother is fascinated by medical and nursing procedures.

The psychopathology of this condition is unclear, because few parents have been treated. However, it is possible that some mothers are attempting to recreate a vivid childhood hospitalization experience in which they received highly gratifying medical or nursing attention. An alternative speculation would have the mother vicariously reenacting through the child her own childhood medical trauma.

SEXUAL ABUSE
Definition

Sexual abuse involves the sexual molestation of a minor by an older person. Other legal terms, which have been used interchangeably, are *sexual misuse, sexual exploitation, sexual maltreatment, carnal knowledge, carnal abuse,* and *deviate sexual abuse.* By virtue of their immaturity, children cannot ethically or legally give valid consent to sexual activities that violate the norms of family life. However, variations in sociocultural standards and in the legal age of consent, together with the diversity of human behavior itself, ensure that there are so many forms and degrees of sexual abuse that it defies precise definition.

The dimensions of sexual abuse are as follows:

1. Whether the abuse occurred within the family (intrafamilial) or between the child and an outsider (extrafamilial)

2. In the case of intrafamilial sex abuse, the kinship relationship between the victim and the perpetrator (e.g., parent, sibling, stepparent, uncle or aunt, grandparent)
3. In the case of extrafamilial abuse, the familiarity of the perpetrator to the victim (i.e., well known or unknown)
4. The sexes of the perpetrator and the victim
5. The ages of the perpetrator and the victim, and the relative age discrepancy between them
6. The frequency with which the abuse took place (i.e., only once or more than once)
7. The duration of time over which the abuse took place (e.g., on only one occasion or over several years)
8. The intent of the perpetrator (e.g., to stimulate the victim sexually or to produce pornography)
9. Whether coercion or threats were involved
10. Whether the victim was an ostensibly voluntary participant
11. The nature of the sexual activity (e.g., touching, fondling, oral contact, digital penetration, or penile penetration, involving the victim's body, breasts, mouth, or anogenital region)
12. Whether the sexual abuse was physically traumatic to the victim

Moreover, there are consequential distinctions:

13. Whether the victim suffered psychiatric disorder or personality distortion following the abuse, or whether a preexisting disorder was aggravated
14. Whether the abuse was disclosed or kept secret
15. The response of those to whom the abuse was disclosed (e.g., no response, rejection, denial, panic, acceptance, protection)
16. Whether legal action ensued after disclosure
17. Whether the family remained intact after the disclosure, wholly or in part
18. Whether the victim had to be placed outside the home

All the issues listed will be considered in this section.

Prevalence

The legal age of consent to sexual intercourse varies from eleven to seventeen years in different parts of the United States. The criminality of the act turns on whether the perpetrator was an adult or a child (under eighteen).

Research into the prevalence of sexual abuse has been reviewed by Haugaard and Reppucci (1988). The reliability and comparability of different studies are affected by differences in dates of collection, definitions of sexual abuse, population sampling, and rates of participation, as well as by variations in the way data were elicited. It is unclear, for example, whether victims are more honest about sexual abuse if they are interviewed directly or by questionnaire.

Kinsey *et al.* (1953) interviewed 4,441 white female volunteers concerning whether, during childhood, they had had a sexual encounter with a male at least five years older than themselves. The rate of affirmative responses was 24 percent overall but dropped to 9.2 percent when physical contact was specified. Based on a statistically representative sample of 2,153 men and women, and using a questionnaire, a Canadian survey revealed that 28 percent of women and 10 percent of men had had unwelcome childhood sexual experiences, but that 40 percent of those experiences had been with people of the same age, and only 50 percent had involved physical contact.[113] Russell (1988) analyzed interview data from 930 San Francisco women. She found that 54 percent had had a sexually abusive experience before the age of eighteen, but the figure fell to 38 percent if physical contact was specified. Smaller-scale studies of more limited population samples have yielded figures for physical-contact sexual abuse in females ranging from about 7 to 50 percent.[114] Such wide differences are probably related to sample and methodological variance. Large-scale surveys suggest that girls are more frequently abused than boys, that fondling is the most frequent activity involved, that the perpetrator is more likely to be known to the victim than to be a stranger, and, if strangers are involved, they are most likely to be exhibitionists. Overall, the rates for family member perpetration have varied from about 20 to 40 percent. The average age of victims ranges from nine to eleven. Single occurrences are by far the most common; repeated experiences are usually intrafamilial. Males are overwhelmingly the commoner perpetrators against both sexes. Female perpetrators abuse boys more often than they abuse girls.

A higher incidence of intrafamilial sexual abuse has been found among female and male prostitutes,[115] runaway children,[116] abusive and neglectful mothers,[117] child molesters,[118] incest offenders,[119] psychiatric patients who suffer from dissociative disorder,[120] and adolescent females with borderline personality disorder.[121]

Recognition

Sgroi, Porter, and Blick (1982) recommend that sexual abuse be suspected whenever a child or adolescent manifests the following:

1. Overcompliance
2. Aggressiveness
3. Pseudomaturity
4. Hinting about sexual behavior
5. Inappropriate sexual play with toys or peers
6. Frequent indiscreet masturbation
7. Sexually precocious knowledge
8. Poor peer relationships
9. Lack of trust
10. Arriving early to school and leaving late
11. Non-participation in school activities
12. Inability to concentrate

13. Sudden drop in school performance
14. Exaggerated fear of males
15. Seductive behavior toward males
16. Running away from home
17. Sleep disturbance
18. Regressiveness
19. Depression
20. Suicidality

In short, various combinations of overcompliance, pseudomaturity, sexual precocity, inappropriate sexual behavior, low self-esteem, lack of trust, emotional problems (depression, suicidality, regressiveness, sleep disturbance, fears), somatic complaints, and conduct problems (running away, aggressiveness) should raise a suspicion of sexual abuse. Physicians should consider the possibility of sexual abuse when children or adolescents manifest extragenital signs of physical abuse, blood in the stools, sexually transmitted diseases, frequent urinary tract infections, urogenital or ano-rectal foreign bodies, ano-genital trauma, or pregnancy.

Sgroi, Blick, and Porter (1982) have described how abuse perpetrated by a family member or familiar figure typically progresses gradually. Physical force is rarely used. In the engagement phase, the perpetrator waits for opportunities to be alone with the child and offers blandishments or inducements to the victim in order to engage in what is represented as "fun." Sexual interaction proceeds from nudity and exposure to fondling, kissing, oral-genital contact, genital-genital rubbing, digital penetration, and penile penetration of the anus or vagina. After the sexual interaction, the perpetrator enjoins secrecy upon the child, often on pain of reprisal. Disclosure occurs incidentally (e.g., following pediatric examination for injury, sexually transmitted disease, or pregnancy) or deliberately, typically to a parent, sibling, friend, or teacher. The disclosure may be denied or ignored by the mother (or others), or it may lead to investigation with or without legal intervention. Following disclosure, the family may attempt to suppress the child's accusation, and the child may be induced to retract it. Long delays between engagement and disclosure are common. False retractions are probably more common than false allegations.

The Consequences of Sexual Abuse

The consequences of sexual abuse may be divided into immediate effects, intermediate effects, and long-term consequences.

IMMEDIATE EFFECTS

Children abused on one occasion, usually by a stranger, are likely to exhibit emotional reactions ranging in intensity from mild adjustment disorder to severe posttraumatic stress disorder (rape crisis trauma). Sleep disturbance, anxiety, fear, somatic complaints, and regressive behavior are common.[122] The affective numbing, autonomic hyperarousal, psychological reenactment, and reentry fear characteristic of posttraumatic stress disorder may evolve from a nonspecific adjustment disturbance, particularly if the acute crisis is mishandled (e.g., when the parent denies the problem, refuses to discuss it, or blames the child).

INTERMEDIATE EFFECTS

Information about the intermediate consequences of sexual abuse has been derived from clinical studies (which suffer from lack of control and sample skew) and from empirical studies (which lack the detail and richness of clinical reports). Nevertheless, by putting the two together, a reasonably consistent picture emerges.

Clinical studies have been reported by Byrne and Valdiserri (1982), Fischer (1983), Gelinas (1983), Summit (1983), Sturkie (1983), Giarretto (1981), Adams-Tucker (1982), DeYoung (1984), and Rogers and Terry (1984). These studies report a high prevalence of the following symptoms: *low self-esteem, guilt* (arising, for example, from a distorted sense of responsibility, disruption of the home following disclosure, or the disapprobation of the family), *anxiety, a sense of powerlessness, depression* (associated, for example, with loss of the family or a sense of having been deprived of a normal childhood), *anger* (commonly directed more at the nonprotecting parent than toward the perpetrator), *sexually provocative behavior, inappropriate sexual play, sexual identity confusion* (particularly among boys), *lack of trust, social withdrawal, aggression, disruptiveness, antisocial behavior, self-mutilation, suicidal ideation,* and *suicide attempts.*

Empirical studies have been conducted by Gagnon (1965), Tsai, Feldman-Summers, and Edgar (1979), Fritz, Stoll, and Wagner (1981), Bess and Janssen (1982), Orr and Downes (1985), Gomes-Schwartz, Horowitz, and Sauzier (1985), Gold (1986), and Edwall and Hoffman (1988). Gagnon found that females who had experienced repeated abuse were more likely than those who had had a single experience to become involved in homosexual peer play. Tsai and coauthors compared women who had been molested as children and were seeking therapy with women molested as children but now well adjusted, and both with a group of women who had never been molested. The first group had a higher incidence of sexual promiscuity and frigidity. Bess and Janssen found a high incidence of sexual dysfunction in abused psychiatric patients; however, Fritz and colleagues did not. Gold found a much higher incidence of psychopathology and poor self-esteem when adult women who had been abused were compared with those who had not. The Gomez-Schwarz team found abused children to be midway between a clinical and a normal population in the severity of their psychiatric symptomatology. However, Orr and Downes and Fritz found little evidence supporting a significantly increased incidence of psychopathology in abused subjects. Indeed, both Finkelhor (1979) and Haugaard (1987) found a higher incidence in sexually abused subjects of the following effects: alcohol and stimulant abuse, psychiatric hospitalization, suicidality, perceived parental rejection, status offenses, and out-of-home placement.

LONG-TERM CONSEQUENCES

Clinical studies have indicated a number of serious long-term consequences in women who were abused as children, for example: sexual dysfunction, depression, suicide, substance abuse, chronically low self-esteem, guilt, multiple personality disorder, other psychoneuroses, and a passive personality leading to victimization by others or a failure to protect offspring from sexual abuse.[123]

The long-term consequences of sexual abuse have been reviewed by Gelinas (1983), Briere (1984), and Asher (1988), and investigated in controlled studies by Meiselman (1978), Tsai, Feldman-Summers, and Edgar (1979), Herman (1981), and Edwall and Hoffmann (1988). Although Herman found no relationship between sexual abuse and later sexual dysfunction, Tsai and colleagues found that sexually abused women seeking psychotherapy were more likely to complain of sexual dysfunction than both abused women not in therapy and a normal control group. Meiselman found more sexual problems in women who had been abused. Briere found that suicide attempts were more common in sexually abused women, but Herman did not find a significant difference in suicidality between abused women and controls (actually, both groups had a high incidence of depression and suicide). Both Briere and Herman found that sexually abused women were disproportionately likely to be victimized by violent spouses.

Factors Influencing the Effects of Sexual Abuse

The following factors might conceivably be associated with the effects of sexual abuse: the psychological adjustment of the child before the trauma; the age and sex of the victim; the age, sex, familiarity, and kinship relationship of the perpetrator; the duration and coerciveness of, and the sexual activity involved in, the offense; whether or not it was disclosed; and the events that transpired after the abuse (particularly the reactions of the family and the legal proceedings that ensued)—in other words, the characteristics of the child, the abusive experience, and subsequent events. Unfortunately, research in this field is either clinical or, if empirical, of a correlational nature only; it does not allow causative conclusions to be drawn.

THE CHARACTERISTICS OF THE CHILD

1. *Age*. It is not clear whether, or in which direction, age affects outcome. Meiselman (1978), Courtois (1979), MacVicar (1979), and Gomes-Schwartz. Horowitz, and Sauzier (1985) found that younger victims were more severely affected. Adams-Tucker (1982) and Sedney and Brooks (1984) found adolescents to be more vulnerable. Others could discover no significant differences between younger and older victims.[124]

2. *Sex*. It is not clear which sex is more at risk of a disturbed outcome.

3. *Predisposition*. MacVicar (1979) and Ruch and Chandler (1982) found that children with prior emotional disturbance were more likely to be adversely affected

by sexual abuse. Conte and Schuerman (1987) found that disturbed family relationships were associated with more serious effects.

THE ABUSIVE EXPERIENCE

1. *The perpetrator.* Ruch and Chandler (1982) found that children who had experienced incest were more disturbed than those who were molested by nonfamilial perpetrators; however Finkelhor (1979), Russell (1984), and Tsai, Feldman-Summers, and Edgar (1979) could not confirm this. Adams-Tucker's (1982) and Russell's (1983) studies suggest that paternal incest is the most damaging form of intrafamilial abuse, whereas the Tufts New England Medical study (1984) implicated stepfathers. Finkelhor (1979), Fromuth (1986), and Russell (1986) suggest that the age discrepancy between victim and perpetrator is a factor in adverse outcome.

2. *The sexual act.* Russell (1984), Tsai, Feldman-Summers, and Edgar (1979) and Bagley and Ramsey (1985) found that vaginal intercourse was more likely to have the most severe effect. Finkelhor (1979) could not confirm this expected relationship.

3. *Coerciveness.* Fromuth (1986), Finkelhor (1979), and Russell (1984) found that the degree of force involved in the abuse correlated with the severity of the victim's trauma.

4. *Duration.* Friedrich, Urquiza and Beilke (1986), Russell (1984), and Tsai, Feldman-Summers, and Edgar (1979) found that the longer the abuse lasted, the more severe the effect. However, other studies have found no significant relationship.[125]

SUBSEQUENT EVENTS

1. *Disclosure.* Bagley and Ramsey (1985) and Finkelhor (1979) found no association between disclosure and outcome; whereas the Tufts New England Medical Center study (1984) found that disclosure was associated with more severe symptomatology.

2. *Parental reaction.* Schultz (1973), Adams-Tucker (1982), Anderson, Bach, and Griffith (1981), and Rogers and Terry (1984) found that adverse parental reactions aggravated the trauma. Although Conte and Schuerman (1987) found that a supportive environment ameliorated trauma, the Tufts New England Medical Center study (1984) did not. The Tufts study found that removal from the home was associated with more serious trauma.

3. *Legal proceedings.* Runyan and co-authors (1987) found that victims waiting to testify manifested more symptoms than those who were not expected to appear in court, and that symptomatology decreased after testifying. Goodman and associates (1992) compared a group of sexually abused children who testified with a matched control group who did not. Those who testified were more disturbed than those who did not, particularly if they had had to testify on several occasions, had no maternal support, or were not corroborated. Younger, more severely abused children were most affected.

SUMMARY

Some cautious conclusions can be drawn. Incest is more traumatic than extrafamilial abuse, particularly when fathers or stepfathers are involved. Coercive abuse involving vaginal penetration is more traumatic. Adverse parental reaction and out-of-home placement aggravate the trauma of abuse. Children who are already disturbed or those from disturbed homes may be more vulnerable to sexual abuse. The duration of the abuse is probably significant. The effects of the victim's age and sex and of disclosure, are not clear. Legal proceedings can aggravate emotional disturbance, particularly if the child's testimony is not corroborated by her family or if repeated testimony is required.

Family Dynamics in Incest

As reviewed by Haugaard and Reppuci (1988), research into family functioning can be classified as follows:

1. Psychopathology in family members
2. Family chaos
3. Family systems pathology
4. Coercive patriarchy

INDIVIDUAL PSYCHOPATHOLOGY

1. *Fathers.* Severe psychopathology (e.g., schizophrenia) explains few cases of sexual abuse; most perpetrators exhibit no diagnosable psychiatric disorder. Abel *et al.* (1981) found some perpetrators of incest to have an erectile profile on penile plethysmography similar to that of pedophiles, but, Quinsey, Chaplin, and Carrigan (1979) failed to confirm this finding. It is possible that pedophilic incest offenders represent a subset of the entire group.[126] Kaufmann, Peck, and Tagiuri (1954), Cavallin (1966), and Virkkunen (1974) have found a 33–73 percent prevalence of alcoholism in incestuous fathers. Weinberg (1955), Meiselman (1978), and Herman (1981) describe tyrannical, domineering, and paranoid traits in incest offenders. Low SES and unemployment also seem to be prevalent.[127] Weinberg (1955) and Finkelhor (1979) have reported an association with social isolation, particularly in rural areas. Gebhard and associates (1965), Groth and Burgess (1979), and Langevin and co-authors (1983) found an association between paternal incest and a childhood characterized by deprivation, physical abuse, and sexual maltreatment.

2. *Mothers.* The mothers of sexual abuse victims have been described as physically absent,[128] depressed,[129] passive-dependent,[130] sexually frigid,[131] and themselves the victims of rejection, emotional deprivation, and abuse.[132]

SOCIAL TRANSITION

Bagley (1969) and Will (1983) refer to incest occurring during periods of stressful social transition such as immigration. These periods are associated with a dissolution of external controls, rules, and boundaries, and consequent sexual activity between nuclear and extended family members.

FAMILY SYSTEMS PATHOLOGY

In its most strongly stated form, the family systems theory of sexual abuse conceives of incest as buttressing a fragile family against collapse. Lustig and colleagues (1966) and Machotka, Pittman, and Flomenhaft (1967) depict the mother as withdrawing from sexual interaction with the father and consciously or unconsciously allowing her daughter to assume the maternal role. Incestuous families have been described as secretive, authoritarian, and socially isolated.[133] Within the family, privacy is disregarded, and violations of social convention denied, rationalized, and hidden. The father becomes dependent upon the daughter for emotional as well as sexual gratification and opposes her socialization, particularly when she seeks to have a boyfriend. He imposes his will upon the family by intimidation, physical force, humiliation, or divisive manipulation.[134]

COERCIVE PATRIARCHY

As a corrective to theories that implicate the mother as playing a role, feminists view incest as a product of traditional patriarchal society.[135] According to the feminist view, men raised with conventional values consider they have a right to sexual satisfaction and feel justified in turning to their daughters when their wives are unavailable.[136] Feminists have been particularly critical of "the psychoanalytic legacy," as a result of which, it is thought, children who disclose incest are often regarded as fantasists or liars.[137] Furthermore, therapy that focuses on the mother's putatively collusive role in incestuous family relationships is regarded as erroneous and unjust; it is considered more likely that patriarchally oppressed women are dominated by their husbands and afraid of reprisal or loss of economic support if incest is disclosed.[138]

SUMMARY

Sexual abuse is so varied that no single explanation could suffice. The patriarchal theory is applicable to many situations, but not to all. The concept that incest is a pathological means of preventing family disintegration remains useful, in some circumstances at least. Individual psychopathology may also be important in some cases, especially when paternal alcoholism or pedophilia can be diagnosed. Different interpretations have very different implications for treatment. For example, conjoint family therapy is most applicable to families in which covertly collusive psychopathology is evident; it would not be suitable in families in which paternal sociopathy predominates.

The Psychopathology of Sexual Abuse

It is not difficult to understand the traumatic effect of sexual assault by a coercive stranger: inescapable threat to life or limb is a key factor in posttraumatic stress disorder. But why is intrafamilial incest damaging? Incestuous parents are not necessarily overtly coercive. In fact, they may use trickery, blandishments, or gifts to achieve their ends. The answer to the question is likely to emerge from the varied and complex interactions among how the victim perceives sexual activity that violates the conventions of family life, how the victim perceives his or her role in the sexual abuse, and how the family and society relate to the victim.

Haugaard and Reppucci (1988) have classified and reviewed current theories concerning the consequences of sexual abuse under the following headings:

1. Premature sexual stimulation
2. Deviant learning
3. Accommodation
4. Traumagenic dynamics
5. Posttraumatic stress disorder

PREMATURE SEXUAL STIMULATION

Lewis and Sarrell (1969) and Sugar (1983) have hypothesized that children cannot assimilate erotic stimulation imposed upon them by a family member. They cannot do so because they have immature ego-defenses and because the normal resolution of oedipal conflicts is impeded when a parent actualizes what should normally remain fantasy.

DEVIANT LEARNING

A "commonsense" social learning approach accounts for the child abuse victim's precocious sexual behavior in terms of classical and instrumental conditioning. Proneness to subsequent victimization or perpetration is explained in terms of social learning.[139] However, neither psychoanalytic nor learning theory can account for the richness, extent, and variation of psychopathology in incest victims.

THE CHILD SEXUAL ABUSE ACCOMMODATION SYNDROME

Summit (1983) has postulated a sequence of events to explain the delay between the onset and disclosure of sexual abuse, as well as the way victims often falsely retract their allegations. The key to Summit's theory is the secrecy enjoined upon the victim. For example, the perpetrator may threaten to harm the child if she gives him away, or the child may come to fear the destruction of her family. In such a dilemma, the child must accommodate to the abuse. She does so by blaming herself for the abuse or by assuming responsibility for satisfying the perpetrator, either of which may be reinforced by the nonabusive parent. Clearly, Summit's theory applies to incestuous families, not to extrafamilial sexual assault.

TRAUMAGENIC DYNAMICS

Finkelhor and Browne (1985 and 1988) have proposed a tetradic model of "traumagenic dynamics." According to this theory, the phenomenology of abuse is related to four interacting factors, which form a configuration uniquely associated with sexual maltreatment. Each factor represents a set of attitudes to the self and others which entrain predictable sets of behavior. Different emphases among the four factors can be explained by variations in the abusive experience and in the personalities of victims. The four factors are (1) traumatic sexualization, (2) a sense of betrayal, (3) powerlessness, and (4) stigmatization.

1. *Traumatic sexualization* results from premature erotization and the reinforcement by the perpetrator of precocious sexual behavior. Thus, the child may willingly participate in sexual activity—at least to begin with—and solicit sex from peers or adults outside the family.
2. *A sense of betrayal* arises from the child's gradual or sudden realization that he or she has been duped or forced by a trusted adult into shameful behavior. As a consequence, the child may be left with a permanent mistrust of the motives of others.
3. *Sense of powerlessness.* The sexually abused child is likely to feel trapped by the authority or coerciveness of the perpetrator or by the fear of disclosure. Thereafter, she may assume the role of a victim and fail to defend herself against others who oppress her. Alternatively, the male victim may turn the tables and victimize others.
4. *Stigmatization.* The family, society, and legal proceedings may treat the child as deviant, and the child may come to see herself as inherently "bad" or "damaged goods," irreversibly different from others.

POSTTRAUMATIC STRESS DISORDER AND BORDERLINE PERSONALITY

Horowitz (1976), Gelinas (1983), Burgess and Holmstrom (1979), and Goodwin (1985) associate the immediate effects of sexual abuse with posttraumatic stress disorder; Briere (1984) relates the long-term consequences to borderline personality disorder.

As defined in the *Diagnostic and Statistical Manual of Mental Disorders* (*DSM III-R*), posttraumatic stress disorder, an aftermath of exceptional stress, involves psychological reenactment (e.g., in auditory or visual hallucinations of sexual abuse, nightmares of abuse, the compulsion to submit to or victimize others, or intrusive memories of abuse during normal sexual intercourse), persistent avoidance of stimuli associated with abuse (e.g., amnesia for the abusive event or events, dissociative tendencies, avoidance of the perpetrator), psychic numbing (e.g., feelings of estrangement or detachment, restricted affect), and hyperarousal (e.g., insomnia, irritability, poor concentration, persistent anxiety, startle responses).

The connection between sexual abuse and borderline personality disorder is more of a long shot. However, a number of workers[140] have found such an association. An even stronger link to dissociative disorder (especially multiple personality) has also been described.[141]

SUMMARY

Premature sexual stimulation and deviant learning theories are too general to be particularly heuristic, whereas the child sexual accommodation syndrome and the traumagenic dynamics theory, though rich enough to explain many incest phenomena, have not yet been validated empirically. The hypothesis of a link between sexual abuse and posttraumatic stress disorder, borderline personality, and dissociative disorder is likely to be fruitful.

Other Forms of Sexual Abuse

INCEST BETWEEN SIBLINGS

Sexual activity between siblings is probably more prevalent than incest between parents and children.[142] Conceivably, sibling incest is less disruptive to the family, since parent–child molestation more frequently comes to official attention. To the extent that there is an age discrepancy between the siblings and coercive genital penetration is involved, sibling incest is likely to be traumatic. Friedman (1988) has described families in which sibling incest is a response to deprivation of parental attention.

FATHER–SON INCEST

Langsley, Schwartz, and Fairbairn (1968), Berry (1975), Dixon, Arnold, and Calestro (1978), and Mrazek (1981) have described this relatively rarely reported form of abuse. No clear picture emerges. Paternal psychopathology, authoritarianism, and family chaos appear to apply in some cases.

MOTHER–CHILD INCEST

Mother–son incest is rare, and mother–daughter incest even rarer. Maternal psychopathology and alcoholism have been described in these circumstances.[143] Some of these mothers may themselves have been victims of sexual or physical abuse[144] and subjected to loneliness and emotional neediness.[145] Green (1988) suggests that the true prevalence of maternal incest is obscured by social convention.

STEPFATHERS

Finkelhor (1979) and DeYoung (1982) have reported that stepfathers are disproportionately more likely to be involved in incest, possibly because they are not inhibited by kinship ties and because some blended families are disorganized.

GRANDFATHERS

Grandparental incest has been described by Goodwin, Cormier, and Owen (1983) and Tsai and Wagner (1979). Apparently, abusive grandfathers have often previously been sexually involved with their daughters as well as with their grandchildren and other children. There is a possibility that some of these men are true pedophiles.[146]

PORNOGRAPHY

Child pornography is a lucrative international industry into which some children are sold or enticed.[147] Many sexually exploited children come from abusive or neglectful homes, but some may be recruited from corrupt day care establishments. Burgess, Groth, and McCausland (1981) and Lanning and Burgess (1984) have described posttraumatic stress disorder, repetition-compulsion, identification with the abuser, and gender-identity disturbance in these children.

RITUAL SEXUAL ABUSE

In recent years, a flurry of news media reports,[148] together with large-scale sexual abuse investigations,[149] have suggested that satanistic cells are terrorizing and molesting children in perverted religious ceremonies. A significant proportion of patients with multiple personality describe themselves as adult survivors of satanistic abuse.[150] The recognition and phenomenology of this still dubious situation are described by Gould (1988) and Nurcombe and Unutzer (1991). Ritually abused children have been described as exhibiting the physical findings and psychological disturbance characteristic of sexual abuse, along with preoccupations concerning occult ritual and symbols, and as speaking of having witnessed animal or human sacrifice, of having been forced to drink body fluids, and of having been molested by adults dressed in costumes (e.g., of Disney or *Sesame Street* characters).

MALE VICTIMS

Most of the focus of this section has been on girls involved in father–daughter incest. Much less has been written concerning boys, despite the fact that incidence rates of 2.5–5 percent have been reported in surveys of adult males.[151]

A study by the American Humane Association (1981) suggests that, compared with girls, boys are more likely to be abused outside the home, to be younger, and to come from physically abusive, impoverished homes with single parents. Reinhart (1987) found that the perpetrator was male in 96 percent of cases. Francis (1987) has related intrafamilial father–son incest to paternal alcohol abuse and multiple incestuous relationships involving children of both sexes.

FORENSIC EVALUATION IN CASES OF ALLEGED SEXUAL ABUSE
Circumstances and Reasons for Referral

A mental health clinician is most likely to be asked for a forensic evaluation by an attorney or administrator from a child protection agency or, if the case is a criminal one, by the office of the State's Attorney. The clinician may also be retained by the defense (in a criminal case), or by a parent's attorney (in a civil case) in order to review evaluations conducted on behalf of the prosecution or agency, and to complete an independent evaluation. Although the attorney or official may not be explicit, the questions to be addressed are usually one or more of the following:

1. Is the child competent to be a witness?
2. Is the child's account of the events credible?
3. Were the investigative tactics used by the (agency, prosecution) legitimate?
4. Is the child emotionally disturbed?
5. If so, is the pattern of disturbance consistent with sexual abuse?
6. Is the child so traumatized or vulnerable that he or she would be damaged by giving testimony?
7. If so, would treatment help to prepare the child for court?
8. What treatment is required for the child, the parents, and the family?
9. Should the child remain with, or be returned to, one or both parents?
10. If the child is in foster care, should one or both parents be allowed visitation?

The clinician must often help the referring attorney to decide which of these questions apply. It is crucial to define them, for they orient the evaluation and organize the subsequent report.

Documentation

The referring agent should be asked to provide copies of videotapes and transcripts of investigative interviews, agency reports, mental health reports, pediatric examinations, judicial decisions, and any other documents relevant to the case.

The clinician should closely examine transcripts and videotapes of the investigative process. Did the examiner put the child at ease? Were the questions asked of the child couched in a form appropriate for a child of that age or level of maturity? Did the examiner make excessive use of leading questions? Were the examiner's questions suggestive, persuasive, or coercive? Did the examiner introduce anatomically explicit dolls too early in the interview, or employ them in an excessively suggestive manner?

The Pediatric Examination

A comprehensive pediatric examination, as described by Finkel (1988), involves the following procedures: collection of secretions, saliva, or semen from the child's skin, mucosal surfaces, or clothing; examination of the child for extragenital trauma (e.g., of the lips, tongue, teeth, pharynx, or skin); examination of the female or male genitalia, anus, and rectum (with unaided eye and with colposcope) for signs of recent or past trauma; observation of sphincter tone and reflexes; examination for pregnancy; and, if indicated, throat, rectal, and vaginal cultures for sexually transmitted diseases.

Since sexual abuse allegations are rarely corroborated by witnesses, the pediatric examination is of great importance. However, sexual abuse can be validated in only about 50 percent of cases examined;[152] in fact, normal genitalia or nonspecific abnormalities have been described in 39 percent of victims even though the offender had confessed to vaginal penetration.[153] Apparently, the absence of specific findings does not invalidate penetration, let alone nonpenetrative assault. Conversely, some of the cardinal signs of sexual penetration (scarring of the hymen and posterior fourchette, friability of the posterior fourchette, synechiae from the hymeneal ring to the vagina, attenuation of the hymen, and increase in the diameter of the vaginal introitus) have been found with equal frequency in girls who have genital complaints (such as vaginitis, vulvitis, or dysuria) but are not known to have been abused.[154] Brayden and colleagues (1990) found that experienced examiners were more likely than physicians of intermediate or little experience to agree with an acknowledged expert. In fact, pediatricians have only recently become aware of the normal range of variation in hymeneal and anal morphology.[155]

Evaluating the Child

The evaluation of the child involves questions of competency, credibility, biopsychosocial functioning, and the need for treatment or preparation for court.

COMPETENCY

As previously described, a child's competence to testify is determined according to four criteria:

1. Did the child have the capacity to register the event or events accurately?
2. Can the child accurately recall and recount the event or events in question?
3. Can the child distinguish falsehood from truth, fantasy from reality?
4. Does the child appreciate his or her duty to speak the truth?

Competency thus devolves upon the child's capacity and willingness to register and recall emotionally traumatic events and to recount them truthfully in an exacting courtroom situation.

Children are often regarded by judges and jurors as having less compunction against dishonesty than adults and as being relatively suggestible, confused, prone to fantasy, and inaccurate in their memory of events.[156] What is the evidence on these questions?

The normal development of memory and research into the memory, suggestibility, and susceptibility of children has been reviewed with regard to courtroom testimony by Nurcombe (1986) and Goodman and Helgeson (1988). Short-term memory has low capacity and short duration; long-term memory is a more permanent record of past events. The durability of memory depends upon its transfer from short-term to long-term, and its consolidation, retention, and retrieval. Memories can be classified as semantic or episodic. Semantic memory involves the storage and utilization of symbols, words, rules, and concepts. It is enhanced, during development, by the acquisition of mature mnemonic strategies (meta-cognition). Episodic memory, on the other hand, refers to the registration, storage, and retrieval of temporo-spatial events. Memory is enhanced by experience, since new information is assimilated to the child's existing preconceptions of the world. Sexual abuse testimony involves the prior registration and current recall of emotionally charged episodic memory by children whose capacity to understand the meaning of the experience is related to the maturity of their preconceptions about it. Children's preconceptions can change as the months pass between disclosure and courtroom appearance and are open to modification by caretakers, psychotherapists, and others. This may be evident, for example, when a child describes an event using such sophisticated terms or ideas that the question of coaching arises.

The child of four to six years of age is better able to locate events spatially than to order them temporally; the concept of historical time, sequence, and measurement is not usually acquired until the age of ten or later. Although a younger witness will have trouble dating events, he or she may be able to relate them to season, birthday, or Christmas. The younger child also has difficulty with drawing inferences from observations. Compared with adults, children are more egocentric, more concrete, and less relative in their moral judgment,[157] but there is no evidence that they are more dishonest.[158]

It is usual for adults and children to forget details of an event and to incorporate erroneous modifications afterward, which may be recounted with conviction. Events are more likely to be remembered accurately if they are protracted[159] or repeated,[160] when they involve a familiar person,[161] and when central actions rather than peripheral details are concerned.[162]

Dawson (1981) has found that both adults and children can be biased by leading questions. Dale, Loftus, and Rathbon (1978) found preschool children more likely than older children to give incorrect affirmative responses when asked misleading questions. Cohen and Harnick (1980) found younger children more likely than older subjects to accept false suggestions, whereas preadolescents and young adults were roughly equivalent in suggestibility and recall of detail. On the other hand, Duncan, Whitney, and Kunen (1982) found first-graders to be less suggestible than older children, and Marin and colleagues (1979) concluded that preschoolers were no more likely than older subjects to be misled by false suggestions and no less accurate in prompted recall and capacity to identify photographs (although they were inferior in free recall). Hoving, Hamm, and Galvin (1969) found that younger children were less susceptible than older children to peer pressure, but Allen and Newtson (1972) failed to confirm this. Clearly, no firm conclusions can be drawn about age-related suggestibility.

The question of the suggestibility of child witnesses has been directly pursued in recent years by Goodman and her colleagues.[163] Using a pleasurable event (games) and an unpleasurable event (inoculation by a nurse) as stimuli, Goodman, Aman, and Hirschman (1987), found that no four-year-old children accepted misleading questions (e.g., whether the doctor had removed their clothes or kissed them), and that only one-third of three-year-old children acceded to the false suggestions. The question of children's lying will be discussed later in this chapter.

Most laboratory research has dealt with neutral or impersonal memories. It is unclear whether an emotionally charged event such as a sexual assault will be remembered more or less accurately than an emotionally neutral event. Although global traumatic amnesia has been reported in adults,[164] Terr (1985) found no evidence for amnesia in children over four years of age who had been involved in a group kidnapping. Some younger children did not retain memory for the traumatic event—perhaps because they had no symbolic preconceptions with which to accommodate it, perhaps because it was repressed. Terr also noted that traumatized children were more likely to distort time relationships. Goodman, Hepps, and Reed (1986) found that three-to-seven-year-old children were more likely to remember the central details of a frightening event (having blood drawn in a hospital), whereas a comparable group exposed to a nonfrightening event remembered more peripheral details.

Brainerd and Ornstein (1991) describe testimony as a combination of incidental and deliberate memory, both spontaneous and prompted, concerning personally experienced, highly salient events. Recent research on memory suggests that storage failure is more important that retrieval failure, that both kinds of forgetting decline with maturity, and that the fading of storage can be impeded by later questioning. Unfortunately, suggestive questioning can also implant false memories. Zaragoza (1991) has reviewed research concerning the effect of misinformation on young children's ability to remember the original details of an experience. This research has yielded inconsistent findings; there is no unequivocal support for the contention that younger children are especially susceptible to misinformation. Lindberg (1991) asserts that age has a different effect depending upon whether the memory called upon is peripheral or central, whether encoding or storage is affected, and whether elementary details or sophisticated inferences are involved.

Peters (1991) has reported a series of experiments involving the effect of stress and arousal on child witnesses. He concludes that stress does not facilitate the eyewitness accuracy of children. Indeed, in some circumstances, high arousal can impair children's memory and render them more susceptible to misleading information presented after the event.

Goodman and Clarke-Stewart (1991) have summarized the research of their own groups on eyewitness recall. They found that participant subjects were more resistant to suggestion than bystanders, but that both groups were resistant to false suggestions. They did not find that long delay was more likely to be associated with false reports. In one ingenious experiment (Clarke-Stewart, Thompson, and Lepore, 1989), children aged five to six years observed a confederate posing as a janitor who cleaned a room. In one script, the "janitor" cleaned and arranged toys, and in the other he played with them in a rough, suggestive manner. Subsequently a confederate posing as the janitor's "boss" entered the playroom and either questioned the children in a neutral manner or did so in a suggestive, incriminating way. Children exposed neither to leading suggestions nor to persuasive interrogation gave limited but accurate responses in a subsequent interrogation. Leading suggestions by the "boss" significantly affected the accuracy of about two-thirds of the subjects, and false information implanted during the subsequent interrogation carried over into a second interrogation. Biased interrogation had an especially strong effect upon the children's interpretation of what the "janitor" had done (viz. "cleaning" versus "playing"), but less effect upon their memory of factual details. A significant minority of the children, also, were susceptible to a plea by the "janitor" to keep his activities "secret" in the face of subsequent interrogation; the susceptible children were more likely to be socially immature, anxious, and psychologically maladjusted. This experiment has clear implications for coercive clinical questioning. Children do not often invent facts, but a significant proportion can be induced by persuasive or coercive questioning to change their interpretation of an event.

Ornstein (1991) recommends that clinical interviewing be standardized in cases of suspected abuse and that the number of interviewers be minimized. Content-based criteria analysis (Steller, 1989; Raskin and Esplin, 1991) represents one attempt to address this problem.

Davies (1991) argues that there is little evidence for a pervasive trait of suggestibility in children. The tendency to comply with the suggestions or implications of another person is strongly situational. However, it is inherently difficult to reproduce experimentally the stress, expectations, long delays, and repeated interrogations that typically affect the victims of intrafamilial abuse.

All of these studies have relevance to allegations and testimony concerning child sexual abuse. Defense attorneys will attempt to impugn the veracity or reliability of young witnesses by asking misleading questions or posing questions that require the witness to make inferences, date events, or think in relative terms. Parents or therapists may inadvertently shape a child's memory by modifying its conceptual template.

Caught in the legal crossfire and confronted by the perpetrator, the child must recall and convincingly recount upsetting and embarrassing events.

The clinician who evaluates competency will test the child's recent and remote memory for events other than the alleged abuse, assess the child's verbal capacity, and test the child's ability to distinguish false statements from true. Psychological testing for general intelligence, verbal capacity, and memory can be helpful in borderline cases. The child's capacity to testify concerning emotionally laden events and to cope with questions concerning alternative explanations for those events will be tested as his or her account of the experience is explored. A child who freezes or becomes disorganized by shame or anxiety as a result of gentle probing during a clinical interview is not likely to be able to cope with direct examination in open court, let alone a challenging cross-examination. The questions of emotional competency, and whether mental health treatment is required in order to prepare the child to be a witness, are further addressed later in this chapter.

CREDIBILITY

Although in one instance[165] a mental health clinician was allowed to testify concerning the credibility of a child, case law does not support the expertise of clinicians in this area.[166] Credibility is a conclusory issue properly left for the judge or jury to determine. Nevertheless, prosecutors, agency administrators, and defense attorneys commonly seek help in this regard. A forensic report that analyzes the credibility of a child's allegation can be most helpful in the early stages before a trial or hearing. It can help the prosecution or the agency decide whether to go further with the case, and it can aid the defense to find weak spots in the other side's argument.

Quinn (1988) has provided a helpful review of the development of morality and the capacity to lie. In general, children under six years of age lack the ability to concoct or sustain a complex fabrication. Rationales for analyzing credibility may be found in Nurcombe (1986), Quinn (1988), Green and Schetky (1988), Raskin and Steller (1989), and Steller (1989). Probably the great majority of allegations concerning sexual abuse are true. False allegations are most likely to arise in three situations: as a result of parental indoctrination of the child in a context of disputation concerning custody or visitation; as a result of deliberate deception by an adolescent who is seeking to harm someone or to escape adversity; or in a context of emotional contagion engendered by a psychological witch-hunt and aggravated by inept or anxiety-provoking investigative techniques.

In order to determine which, if any, of the alternatives apply, the following sequence of possibilities must be considered:

1. The child lacks the mental capacity to give a reliable account of the event (i.e., the child is *incompetent*).
2. The child is truthful but has *misinterpreted* or has been induced to misinterpret an innocent event.
3. The child is truthful but *deluded*.

4. The child is *fabricating* the allegation.
5. The child is *confabulating* the allegation.
6. The child has been advertently or inadvertently *indoctrinated* by another party.
7. The child has been influenced by *emotional contagion* to allege sexual abuse.

If these situations can be excluded, the clinician can next analyze the data elicited in order to determine whether the child is (1) truthful and credible; (2) possibly truthful but not credible; (3) possibly untruthful but credible; or (4) neither truthful nor credible. Credibility, it should be remembered, is a relative matter: Honest testimony may be incredible for a number of reasons, whereas some liars are very convincing.

EXCLUDING THE DIAGNOSTIC ALTERNATIVES

1. *Incompetence.* The clinical determination of competence has already been discussed. If the child is incompetent, credibility is moot.

2. *Misinterpretation.* Children or parents sometimes misinterpret innocent events. For example, a hypervigilant mother becomes convinced that her ex-spouse's behavior while bathing the child, or when appearing nude before the child, represents sexual molestation. Complicated situations can occur in "modern" families which encourage nudity and overstimulate the child, and activate sexual fantasy. Green and Schetky (1988) advise that, in such situations, the parent–child relationship is usually positive, and the child exhibits no signs of emotional disturbance, apart from sexual overstimulation.

3. *Delusion.* Delusional accusations occur in two situations. In the first, a delusional custodian, usually a mother, has paranoid ideas about sexual abuse and persuades a young child, in a form of *folie à deux,* that the noncustodial parent or someone else sexually abused him or her. In the second situation, a delusional adolescent develops the false idea that he or she has been molested. Disorganized thinking and other psychotic symptoms in the custodian or the adolescent are the discriminating signs.

4. *Confabulation.* Some older children or adolescents who have histrionic, narcissistic, or borderline personalities and a tendency to tell imaginative stories or distort the truth make false accusations which they appear to believe. Sometimes, caught up in the *emotional contagion* of an investigative witch-hunt, they yearn for the limelight. To complicate matters further, the child may actually have been sexually abused but be transposing the allegation from the true culprit to somebody else.

5. *Fabrication.* Confabulation and fabrication are coterminous. The fabricator is typically an unscrupulous preadolescent or adolescent with an avoidant or malicious motive for deception. For example, he or she is attempting to extort money or favors from the accused, desires to take revenge against the accused, seeks to get rid of a troublesome father or stepfather, or hopes to create a reason to get out of an undesired foster home. The earmark of fabrication is its conscious motivation. As with confabulation, the fabricator is all the more convincing if he or she transfers the allegation from the true culprit to an innocent third party.

6. *Inadvertent indoctrination.* When an investigator or clinician employs coercive or suggestive interview techniques (such as the premature introduction into the interview of anatomically explicit dolls), he or she may so distort the child's memory that it is impossible to sift truth from dross. It has been suggested that inadvertent indoctrination by investigators muddied the waters in The Manhattan Beach and Jordan, Minnesota cases. Another more subtle form of indoctrination is educative in nature: psychotherapists or parents may unwittingly indoctrinate a child by supplying terms (e.g., "penis," "vagina") and concepts (e.g., "rape") that were not originally in the child's lexicon or conceptual repertoire.

Investigative indoctrination can be detected from audiotapes, videotapes, or transcripts of interviews. Educative indoctrination can be recognized from the precocious terminology and phraseology used by the child (keeping in mind that some families teach their children the technical words for genital organs and body functions).

7. *Deliberate indoctrination.* This tactic is most likely to be employed when a custodial parent, usually a mother, seeks to halt visitation. She induces the child to bring a false accusation against the noncustodial parent, often on pain of abandonment or withdrawal of love. This devious stratagem is very effective legally: Accused parties can seldom prove the accusation untrue unless the child recants. Green and Schetky (1988) describe the following as suggestive of false indoctrination: The accusation emerges all at once; it is presented first by the mother rather than by the child; the child appears to be prompted or cued by the mother; and the child accuses the father when the mother is present but is comfortable when alone with the father.

8. *Emotional contagion.* It is possible that, in the course of a highly public investigation with "witch-hunting" overtones, parental panic, peer pressure, and biased interviewing can influence suggestible children to allege sexual abuse.

Next, we shall consider the analysis of data to support or not support the hypothesis that the accusation is valid.

VALIDATING THE ALLEGATION

In order to validate the allegation, the clinician should consider three groups of factors: symptom validity, content validity, and contextual validity.

Symptom Validity

The assessment of biopsychosocial functioning is described in a later section of this chapter. Does the child exhibit symptoms and signs consistent with sexual abuse? It should be noted that a diagnosis of acute posttraumatic stress disorder or the finding of personality distortions such as those that match Finkelhor and Browne's (1988) dynamic tetrad are supportive but not probative; on the other hand, the absence of psychopathology does not disprove abuse.

Content Validity

Statement analysis originated in Germany[167] and has been applied to children by Steller.[168] The following content features can be analyzed:

1. *Realism.* The story should make sense; that is, it should not violate the laws of nature. A typical story of intrafamilial abuse, for example, involves a gradual progression of molestation from touching to fondling and genital penetration.

2. *Consistency.* The different elements of the child's story should be consistent at the one telling and at different times. The story should also be consistent with external evidence (e.g., the pediatric examination), if there is any.

3. *Lack of organization.* A valid story is not likely to be disclosed in a structured, chronologically organized manner, but piecemeal; for example, the allegation emerges over several interviews rather than all at once.

4. *Richness of detail.* Valid statements have many details concerning place, time of day, environment, persons involved, clothing, conversations, and actions. Unexpected complications (e.g., somebody walking into the room) may be described.

5. *Peculiarity of content.* Truthful children often provide superfluous detail or misunderstand accurately reported details. Older children may spontaneously refer to their own mental state during the abusive experience. Idiosyncratic details concerning the perpetrator's dress, appearance, actions or sexual behavior enhance credibility.

6. *Hesitancy.* The truthful witness may make spontaneous corrections, admit gaps of memory, deprecate herself, anticipate that others will have doubts about her story, or even pardon the perpetrator. Tentative retractions are often followed by reconfirmations.

7. *Appropriateness of affect.* The truthful child's affect is appropriate to the content of the story. Thus, anxiety, fear, shame, or anger are validating affects. Composure is not. However, it should be remembered that some traumatized subjects dissociate affect, in which case they will appear frozen, numb, or entranced. The abused child is likely to be anxious, avoidant, or seductive in the presence of the accused.

8. *Appropriateness of language.* The language and conceptual understanding involved in the child's story should be appropriate to the child's developmental level. Remember, however, that some families have taught their children to use technical anatomical terms.

9. *Resistance to suggestion.* The credible child resists suggestion. To the extent that the child's responses reflect a following of the interviewer's lead, credibility is reduced.

Contextual Validity

The context of the disclosure and the nature and manner of the questioning ought not to have tended to persuade or coerce the child; nor should the story or elements of the story have been suggested by leading the witness excessively, by offering inducements to the child for telling the story, or by threatening consequences if he or she doesn't tell "the truth." The story should not have been the product of excessively lengthy interviews or an excessive number of separate interviews, or elicited by too many interviewers. The interview or interviews should have been generally adequate. That is, it or they should have proceeded from relationship-building to the question at stake and from general to specific, and the interviewer should have been comprehensive in his or her technique.

Conversely, the child who is fabricating an allegation is less likely to exhibit symptomatology consistent with sexual abuse. His or her statement may not make sense (e.g., one poorly indoctrinated four-year-old described her grandfather as tapping her upon the genitals with a hammer upon which white oatmeal had been spilt, then placing her head upside down upon his own head and repeatedly jumping up and down). The story may waver in its details at different times or within the one interview. An invalid story is likely to be proffered *in toto,* but it lacks detail concerning the environment, conversations, clothing, actions, and unexpected complications. No idiosyncratic, misunderstood, or superfluous details are described; and the witness makes no spontaneous corrections, has no gaps of memory, and delivers her account in a composed or hostile manner. Adult terms (e.g., "intercourse") or turns of phrase (e.g., "When he withdrew. . .") may be noted. Finally, the child may be prone to concur with false, misleading questions.

Steller (1989) notes that in practice the rate of false allegations is so low that it would be difficult for an evaluator using the techniques to beat the base-rate. Field studies suggest that the technique may be better at confirming valid allegations than at detecting falsity (in other words, the technique may have greater sensitivity than specificity in validating true allegations).

BIOPSYCHOSOCIAL FUNCTIONING, PROGNOSIS, AND NEED FOR TREATMENT

Physical health and psychosocial adjustment are evaluated by conventional means. The pediatric examination will extend beyond an examination for trauma to address physical development, nutritional status, and systemic functioning. Past medical history is ascertained, and any relevant documents are obtained (e.g., of hospitalization or emergency room attendance).

Psychosocial functioning is evaluated from the history provided by caretakers, from interviews and mental status examinations of the child, and from psychological testing and psychoeducational assessment. Child Behavior Checklists[169] can be obtained from parents, other caretakers, teachers, and (in the case of adolescents) from the subject. They provide a baseline measure of social competence and psychopathology (for which evaluations may be required at a later date); moreover, inconsistencies or discrepancies between observers can be very informative. The forensic clinician should also obtain records of previous educational assessments, psychiatric hospitalizations, and mental health evaluations or treatment. Evidence of change in behavior or decline in school performance following the date of the alleged abuse could be informative.

From the biopsychosocial data, the forensic clinician addresses the following questions:

1. What is the current level of the child's physical health and psychosocial and educational functioning?
2. Is there evidence for a psychiatric disorder?
3. If so, is the pattern of the disorder consistent with sexual abuse?
4. Are the child's level of biopsychosocial functioning, pattern of psychopathology, or psychosocial, language, or educational defects consistent with neglect or other forms of abuse?
5. If the child is emotionally disturbed, would he or she be competent to testify, or would the child be damaged by further legal procedures?
6. What is the child's prognosis, with or without treatment?
7. What treatment or preparation would be required in order to enable the child to testify?

INTERVIEW TECHNIQUE

Sexual abuse evaluations should be undertaken only by seasoned clinicians who are aware of their biases. Horner, Guyer, and Kalter (1993) have drawn attention to an extreme unreliability among clinicians who evaluated a test case of alleged abuse. The recent influx into the field of inexperienced and narrowly trained sex abuse investigators is a matter for concern. This arena is not suitable, on the one hand, for ideologically motivated crusaders or, on the other, for theoretically inspired invalidators who regard all allegations as products of oedipal fantasy.

The technique of interviewing children who have allegedly been sexually abused has been described by Jones and McQuiston (1985), Sgroi, Porter, and Blick (1982), Schetky (1988), Haugaard and Reppucci (1988), Spencer and Nicholson (1988), and Walker (1988). The clinician should be aware that a sexual abuse evaluation may yield no confirmatory evidence, despite strong suspicion that the abuse did, in fact, occur. Such frustrations notwithstanding, it is essential to proceed with due caution rather than to muddy the waters by leading the child with suggestive or coercive questions or by undertaking repeated interviews in the face of denial. For these reasons, the following guidelines are suggested:

1. Try to avoid documentary bias by leaving the review of documents until after you have interviewed the child.
2. Interview the child alone, if possible, away from any adult who might conceivably influence the child.
3. Try to restrict the total number of investigative interviews to no more than four, and preferably three.
4. Do not attempt to elicit information from the child concerning the alleged abuse until some measure of rapport and trust have been built.
5. Be flexible. Adapt your interview style to the child's developmental level.

6. Start with neutral topics, and move later to emotionally laden issues. When eliciting information about the alleged abuse, start with open-ended questions and
   delay using leading questions or suggestive techniques (e.g., anatomically explicit dolls).
7. Nevertheless, in the general sequence of the interaction, and in the use of diagnostic aids such as drawing and doll play, try to standardize your technique.
8. If the child describes an abusive incident or incidents, try to ascertain the following: the identity of the perpetrator; the details, duration, frequency, and dating of the abuse; whether inducements, coercion, threats or force were involved;
   the emotional response of the child to the experience; the child's perception of
   his or her relationship with the perpetrator and nonoffending parent or parents;
   and the child's expectation regarding the impact of disclosure on the family.
   Young children who cannot enumerate or date events can often refer to the time
   of day (morning, afternoon, nighttime) or to general dates (Christmas, birthday,
   seasons).
9. If possible, videotape or audiotape the interview.
10. Remember that, although the overwhelming majority of all allegations are valid,
    each evaluation is a new one. Furthermore, the proportion of deluded, confabu-
    lated, fabricated, and indoctrinated allegations, though generally small, is prob-
    ably much higher in the mental health context.

DIAGNOSTIC AIDS

The use of anatomically explicit dolls in sexual abuse evaluations has been criticized
in the courts as unacceptably suggestive.[170] The question has been raised whether
nonabused children can be provoked by the dolls to exhibit sexual play. Several researchers have discussed this question.[171] No conclusions can be drawn at this point.
It is recommended that the dolls be used later in the interview in order to check the
child's knowledge of and terms for different body parts and to help the child illustrate
the account of events that has already been elicited in words.

The validity of drawings of sexual abuse incidents[172] is also unclear. Nonabused
children seldom spontaneously draw genitalia on human figures;[173] what is unclear,
however, is whether the depiction of genitalia necessarily indicates sexual abuse. It
is recommended that drawings be interpreted cautiously, in the context of the rest of
the data.

Hypnotherapy has been employed to help patients recall, and to treat the effects
of, sexual abuse. The admissibility of this evidence is debated and uncertain.[174]

Evaluating the Nonoffending Parent

The forensic clinician evaluates the nonoffending parent in order to elucidate the following questions:

1. Physical health, psychological functioning, social competence, educational attainment, occupational history, and social resources. Is there any evidence of psychiatric disorder, personality disorder, substance abuse, or intellectual retardation?
2. Early development, history of physical or sexual abuse, marital history, current sexual functioning. Is there a history of spouse abuse, substance abuse, or marital discord?
3. What is the parent's attitude to the alleged abuse (e.g., anger, remorse, denial)?
4. Is the parent sensitive to the child's needs (or unempathic, unconcerned, rejecting, or blaming)?
5. What are the parent's attitudes to childrearing? Bavolek's (1984) Adult-Adolescent Parenting Inventory is a useful aid in this regard.
6. Would the parent be willing and able to participate in a treatment plan?

Psychological testing using the MMPI, MCMI, and Adult-Adolescent Parenting Inventory is recommended.

Evaluating the Alleged Offender

In many cases, defense attorneys will advise their clients not to submit to an examination. However, if the accused does agree, the following questions can be addressed:

1. Does the accused admit to the offense? If so, does his or her account of the offense match the child's? How does the accused account for the abuse? For example, does he blame the child or his spouse? If physical evidence of sexual abuse has been found, how does the alleged perpetrator account for it?
2. Physical health, psychological adjustment, social competence, educational and occupational attainment. Evidence of psychiatric disorder, substance abuse, personality disorder, or mental retardation. History of antisocial behavior, criminality, and past legal involvement.
3. Early development and environment, history of physical or sexual abuse, marital and sexual history, past history of physical abuse of spouse or children, past history of sexual molestation, current sexual functioning.
4. What is the alleged perpetrator's attitude toward the child's allegation (e.g., denial, blame, rejection, remorse)?
5. Willingness and ability to participate in a treatment program.

Comprehensive evaluations of the male sex offender are described by Becker and Kaplan (1988), Groth (1982), Wolf, Conte, and Engel-Meinig (1988), and McGovern and Peters (1988).

Psychological testing of the cooperative parent is advisable. The MMPI, MCMI, and Adult-Adolescent Parenting Inventory are recommended.

Observing the Relationship Between the Child and the Parents

If it would not be excessively traumatic to the child, it can be very helpful to observe him or her together with the perpetrator and the nonoffending parent. The abused child may exhibit avoidance, fear, or seductiveness toward the abusive parent, and cling to the nonoffending parent. An abused child has difficulty confronting the perpetrator; in contrast, indoctrinated children may readily repeat the accusation, while looking to the indoctrinator for cues or approval.[175]

PREPARING THE CHILD TO GIVE TESTIMONY
Therapy

By disclosing sexual abuse, the child sets in train a series of potentially traumatic events that can lead to the prosecution and incarceration of the offender, and to her own ostracism by the family. Subsequently, the child may have to adapt to a foster family and testify against the perpetrator, typically a father or stepfather whose predicament she has caused and whose enmity she fears.

Court hearings may be delayed and protracted. The child must be prepared to speak the truth while confronted by the perpetrator and cross-examined by an attorney who impugns her testimony as false or unreliable. Ultimately, she may have to cope with the acquittal of the perpetrator on the grounds that she is a liar, a fantasist, or a fool. Even a well-adjusted child would experience stress in such circumstances. A child already suffering from characterological vulnerability or psychiatric disorder is likely to testify unconvincingly or to falsely retract her original allegations.

A child with posttraumatic stress disorder may be so unstable or vulnerable that legal proceedings are contraindicated. Regrettably, it is sometimes necessary to advise the authorities that treatment is likely to be protracted and that one cannot predict if and when the victim will be able to testify. Given several months, however, many disturbed children can be sufficiently improved by therapy to enable them to appear in court.

Goodman and colleagues (1992) have conducted a detailed examination of the effect of testifying in court upon 130 child sexual assault victims, divided into 55 who testified and 75 matched controls, followed three and seven months after giving testimony, and after the prosecution had ended. At seven months, those who had testified were significantly more emotionally disturbed than those who had not, particularly if they had testified more than once, if there was no corroboration of the allegation, if they had no maternal support, or if they were fearful of the defendant. However, after the prosecution had ended the adverse effect of giving testimony abated. The Goodman team recommend better preparation of witnesses for court appearances and changes in the legal system to help children become more effective, less traumatized witnesses.

Remember, however, that forensic evaluation and psychotherapy are poor bedfellows. The forensic expert must be as impartial as possible, whereas the therapist cannot avoid being biased by identification with the patient. Furthermore, the court expert cannot adhere to the standards of confidentiality that are essential to a therapeutic relationship.

TREATMENT FOR SEXUALLY ABUSED CHILDREN

Walker and Bolkovatz (1988) and Porter, Blick, and Sgroi (1982) have described the principles of psychotherapy with sexually abused children. Play therapy provides an opportunity for the child to reexperience traumatic memories, to assimilate the associated affects, and to gain perspective on the experience. The child is thus aided to control fear, rage, and shame; to gain mastery over trauma; and to learn new methods of coping. Fear and lack of trust are countered in the context of a corrective emotional relationship with an adult who does not betray intimacies, and the child is supported in fighting back against those who oppressed her, reversing shame and stigma, and regaining control over her body, her mind. and her life. Mountain and coauthors (1984) identify the following treatment foci:

1. *Fear and lack of trust.* Children fear erotic arousal, the consequences of forbidden sex games, the potential damage to their bodies, the retaliation of the perpetrator, and the rejection of their families. The child may refuse to discuss the trauma until a therapeutic relationship has developed. The preliminary period may be rapid, or it may take months. Some children never achieve sufficient trust to allow psychotherapy to proceed.

2. *Traumatic anxiety.* Play therapy or psychotherapy allow the trauma to be reworked symbolically. The child's tendency to dissociate affect can be observed, clarified, and countered. The aim is desensitization and mastery.

3. *Shame and self-blame* are universal, though initially dealt with, often, by repression, denial, dissociation, manipulativeness, or pseudomaturity. Sexual acting-out may also emanate from sexual guilt, the stigmatized adolescent in effect throwing her vandalized body away. Her sense of being "damaged goods" may be literal, the child feeling that her insides have been injured and that she will never be able to marry or have children. The therapist can reassure the child that, even though she was hurt, her body has healed (assuming, of course, that the examination has not revealed infection or pregnancy). The importance of a thorough pediatric examination cannot be overemphasized in this regard.

4. *Anger.* Though prone to regressive rage, victims are usually cowed by the aggression of others, withdrawing into tears or tantrum. Doll play can help the child to express, assimilate, and control anger. Often, surprisingly, girls are more angry toward their mothers than their fathers. They may feel pity for, or even absolve, their fathers ("Men can't help themselves."), repressing their resentment toward the perpetrator.

5. *Depression* is ubiquitous. An abused child is often depressed prior to disclosure, exhibiting sadness, poor school performance, somatic complaints, and depressive acting-out. After disclosure, if she is separated from her family or the family

rejects her, the problem will be compounded. Children often speak also of their sadness at being robbed of their childhood.

6. *The sense of betrayal* may be associated with pathological narcissism, an inflated sense of being special. Subsequently, suicidality may follow the failure or severance of special relationships.

7. *Lack of assertiveness.* One of the cornerstones of therapy involves encouragement of the child to stand up for her rights. She must learn that she has the right to determine what will be done to her body and what she wants her life to be.

8. *Superficiality.* The omnipotent or histrionic child uses emotion manipulatively, in order to control others. As trust is gained, more authentic emotions of fear, powerlessness, rage, and grief are revealed.

9. *Pseudoindependence and the blurring or reversal of roles.* The child who initially behaves like a self-sufficient, nurturant, or seductive adult will regress before she improves. To the eroticized child, the therapist may explain that sex feels good but is meant for grownups, and that some kinds of touching are affectionate and good, whereas others are for adults. Books are available concerning "good" and "bad" touching. The child who feels guilty because she was erotically aroused may need to understand that the arousal was normal and that she was not to blame for it. The omnipotent child who always needs to win at games can be allowed to do so until later in therapy, when the underlying fear of powerlessness can be interpreted.

The therapist may need to point out repeatedly that a young child cannot be responsible for what has happened and that the fault lies with the perpetrator. The therapist's calm, nonjudgmental approach is important in this regard. As with all therapy, the key is calm acceptance, concern, empathy, communication, authenticity, and patience. None of this is possible unless the therapist is in touch with his or her own feelings about sexuality.

The strategy of therapy is as follows:

1. Establish a corrective emotional relationship.
2. Provide the child with the opportunity to reenact in play the traumatic experience.
3. Facilitate and interpret the child's expression of fear, shame, rage, and betrayal.
4. Alleviate the child's guilt.
5. Suggest and rehearse alternative methods of coping and mastery.

PSYCHOTHERAPY FOR SEXUALLY ABUSED ADOLESCENTS

The principles of treatment are essentially no different for adolescents. The cornerstone of therapy is a trusting relationship, something the adolescent patient is initially likely to test. After trust has been established, the adolescent is encouraged to recover or uncover traumatic memories and to express and assimilate their associated affects. The therapist helps the patient clarify feelings and gain perspective on her feelings in regard to the perpetrator, the nonoffending parent, peers, sexuality, and the legal process. The aim is not so much catharsis as cognitive appraisal and mastery.

GROUP THERAPY

Many older children and adolescents are helped by the peer interaction within a sexual abuse group. Open group membership enables veteran members to help newcomers by sharing experiences, feelings, and coping techniques. The group leader can introduce educational material in order to correct sexual misconceptions. Group therapy can address such issues as the ventilation of anger, shame, and fear; the development of social skills; and preparation for court. Role-playing can be particularly helpful. Optimum benefit from group therapy is said to take from one to two years.[176]

SEVERE PSYCHIATRIC DISORDER

This is not the place to describe the complex and problematic treatment of severe posttraumatic stress disorder, borderline personality, or dissociative disorder. Many of these patients are admitted to hospital, usually as adolescents, for intensive multimodal therapy. Individual psychotherapy, sexual abuse groups, cognitive behavioral therapy (to promote assertiveness and social skills), judicious pharmacologic treatment (e.g., for depression, aggression, anxiety, or hallucinosis), and parental or family therapy are implemented in a protective, structured setting, to be followed by day treatment or outpatient therapy.

THE PARENT

The child with a supportive parent is greatly helped. Failing that, a foster parent can be a vital ally in therapy and in preparing the child for court. The parent needs information about the dynamics of sexual abuse trauma, the need to counteract shame and guilt, and the importance of reexperiencing and mastering trauma rather than suppressing or dissociating it.

Preparing the Child for Court

The following guidelines can be applied when preparing a child victim to give testimony:

1. Do not rehearse the questions the child may be asked—you may be accused of "coaching" the witness.
2. Convey to the child that the process is impersonal: The defendant's attorney must test the truth of her statements so that the jury can make the right decision. Unfortunately, impersonality will be difficult or impossible for the immature child to grasp.
3. Carefully explain the function of the courtroom personnel: the judge, the jury, the attorneys for the prosecution and defense, and the people in the court.

4. Take the child to the courtroom and explain where the judge, jury, attorneys, defendants, and spectators will sit. Let the child sit in the witness chair. Show the child where you and the mother or foster mother will sit.
5. Make sure the child meets the prosecuting attorney. The attorney can explain the process of examination: the direct-, cross-, redirect-, recross-examinations and the nature and purpose of objections. The child should be assured that she is expected to recount only what she can remember as truthfully as possible; she is not expected to know the answer to every question.

Without adequate planning, giving testimony can be very stressful for children,[177] though not always so.[178] Indeed, testimony can bring a kind of finality and can empower the child to redress a wrong.[179]

PREPARING THE REPORT

Examples of sexual abuse reports are provided in Appendix 1, Cases 4(a), 4(b), 5, and 6. The following format is recommended:

   I. CIRCUMSTANCES OF REFERRAL
      Who referred the case? Who is involved? What are the legal circumstances?
  II. PURPOSE OF EVALUATION
      List the issues to be addressed. See the section on "Forensic Evaluation" in this chapter for the alternatives.
 III. INFORMED CONSENT
      Describe the way in which informed consent was obtained from the adults involved.
 IV. SOURCES OF DATA
      A. DOCUMENTS
         List all documents reviewed with title, signature, and date.
      B. INTERVIEWS
         List all interviews conducted by name of interviewee, date, and duration of interview.
      C. PSYCHOLOGICAL TESTS
         List all tests conducted by name of test, tester, testee, and date.
  V. REVIEW OF DOCUMENTS
      Review those aspects of each document that bear upon the issues of the case.
 VI. INTERVIEWS
      Summarize each interview. Quote verbatim excerpts from the interview to illustrate your points. Append transcripts of significant parts of the interview, when it is appropriate to do so.
VII. PSYCHOLOGICAL TEST RESULTS
      Summarize the results of all tests.
VIII. DISCUSSION
      Discuss your reasoning in the case by addressing each of the issues listed in II, "Purpose of Evaluation," drawing points pro and con each issue from all the

sources of data available. A list of possible issues and the sources of data follows:

1. Competence (interview with child; psychological testing)
2. Credibility (interview with child; audiotapes, videotapes, or transcripts of previous interviews; pediatric examinations)
3. Legitimacy of previous interview techniques (audiotapes; videotapes; transcripts)
4. Pattern of emotional disturbance, if present (interviews with parents, caretakers, child; previous records; interviews with the child; psychological testing)
5. Likelihood of harm from legal process (see 4).
6. Treatment of child and family (see 4)
7. Removal, return, visitation (see 4)

IX. SUMMARY

Summarize those opinions concerning the issues in the case that you can proffer with reasonable certainty. State which, if any, of the issues cannot be answered with reasonable certainty.

X. APPENDIXES

A. Psychological test reports
B. Transcripts of interviews, diagrams, drawings, etc.
C. Your curriculum vitae

CHAPTER 7

PSYCHOLOGICAL TRAUMA AND CIVIL LIABILITY

LEGAL PRINCIPLES

Under the rubric of tort law, more and more civil actions are being brought on behalf of children who claim to have sustained psychological injury. Liability suits that require child mental health evaluation run the gamut from motor vehicle accidents, attacks by domestic animals, and accidents in private, industrial, or public places to injuries caused by clinical malpractice, faulty commercial services, or defective industrial products. In effect, the referring attorney asks the forensic clinician whether the child has suffered mental injury, impairment, or distress as a result of a particular event. The clinician assists the attorney for the plaintiff or the defendant by testifying as an expert witness at trial, by evaluating the child in preparation of a civil suit, or by analyzing for flaws the forensic evaluation prepared by another mental health clinician. In order to act in any of these capacities, it is essential that the clinician appreciate the rudiments of tort law. The implications of tort law for clinical practice will be discussed in detail in the next chapter, which deals with malpractice.

An Overview of the Law of Torts

DEFINITION

Under tort law, individuals may bring suit against persons whose wrongful actions have injured them. A tort is a *civil wrong,* other than a breach of contract, for which the law provides a remedy.[1] In liability for breach of contract the parties have entered into a voluntary, consensual relationship, and the terms of the contract set the limits of their liability. In contrast, tort law imposes liability with boundaries that are determined by the law.

The law of torts is concerned with allocating losses that arise out of human activities. Its primary purpose is to compensate injured parties for losses suffered from the wrongdoing of others and to deter such wrongdoing. It is based on the presumption that individuals are responsible for the consequences of their actions. The same notion of responsibility is the source of another basis for tort liability—the correction of a wrong. Torts encompass myriad wrongs, ranging from simple, direct interferences with the person such as assault or battery to the invasion of an intangible interest, such as an individual's reputation. The usual remedy for a tort is monetary damages, although in some circumstances a court may grant an injunction to prevent a wrong from continuing or occurring.

TYPES OF TORTS

Tort law is divided into three categories according to the nature of the defendant's conduct: (1) intentional torts, (2) negligent torts, and (3) strict liability torts.

Intentional torts encompass conduct intended to cause harm. One party must be shown to have acted with the purpose of invading another's protected interest, or to have acted with knowledge that such an invasion would occur with substantial certainty.[2] For example, if a teacher who punishes a child physically injures the child, he will have committed the intentional tort of battery.

Negligent torts are characterized by careless conduct that entails an unreasonable risk of harm. For example, a driver will be liable in negligence if he drives erratically and, in consequence, injures a pedestrian.

Strict liability torts involve liability imposed irrespective of the fault of the person causing the injury. For example, if an industrial product that has caused injury is adjudicated unreasonably dangerous or defective, the manufacturer will be found liable.

TYPES OF DAMAGES IN TORT LAW

Although the primary purpose of tort law is to compensate the victim for wrong, damages are not solely compensatory in nature. There are three types of damages: nominal, compensatory, and punitive. *Nominal damages* are awarded to vindicate a legal right the violation of which has not resulted in compensable harm. Nominal damages are restricted to intentional torts actionable as a result of invasion of a protected interest, such as bodily integrity (see p. 190 below). *Compensatory damages* are designed to compensate a victim for an actual loss. The purpose of compensatory damages is to restore the victim to the position he occupied before the tort, insofar as money can do so. The gist of an action for negligence is damage: No action will be possible if the wrongdoer's negligence resulted in no identifiable injury. *Punitive damages* are awarded when the wrongdoing is intentional and deliberate, outrageous, or malicious. The aim of punitive damages is to deter wrongdoing by the defendant or others. In purpose, it resembles a penalty in criminal law.

THE FUNCTION OF THE MENTAL HEALTH CLINICIAN

The mental health clinician can be of invaluable help to the attorney for the defendant or the plaintiff in any of three stages of preparation for court. First, the clinician can help the attorney decide if there is evidence to show whether the basic requirements (the *prima facie* case) for a particular tort have been satisfied (e.g., whether the normal standard of care has been breached, or whether there is a causal link between a putatively wrongful act and an injury). Second, the clinician can help to identify and develop support for the defenses a defendant might raise in order to avoid liability (e.g., concerning informed consent in a malpractice case, the exculpatory nature of insane delusions in an intentional tort claim, or the extent to which a plaintiff has contributed to his own injury). Last, the clinician can identify evidence to prove the extent and type of damage at issue in the case (e.g., medical expenses, pain and suffering, loss of enjoyment of life, or punitive damages), the presence or absence of preexisting disorder, and the degree to which extraneous factors aggravate or perpetuate the plaintiff's psychological condition.

Intentional Torts

THE NATURE OF INTENT

The requirement that an act be intentional has posed legal problems. In most cases, the plaintiff will seek to show that the defendant acted with the purpose of invading the plaintiff's interest (*purpose intent*).[3] However, the requirement of intention will be satisfied if the defendant knew with substantial certainty that the tortious result would follow (*knowledge intent*). *Garratt v. Dailey*[4] illustrates the principle. In this case, a five-year-old child had pulled a chair away from the spot where the plaintiff was about to sit. The court found that, even though the evidence might not establish that the boy had acted with the purpose of causing the plaintiff to hit the ground, he had acted intentionally if he had known, with substantial certainty, that the plaintiff would have attempted to sit down where the chair had been.[5] *The emphasis in tort law is on whether the defendant intended to perform an action that invaded another person's particular interest, and not upon whether he intended to cause harm.*

Intent is distinguished from the *motive* or *reason* for the act. For example, nurse *A* may intend to lay hands upon patient *B* in order to get *B* to a hospital. If *B* did not consent to the touching, *A*'s action would be tortious in spite of the fact that his motive was to help *B*. Unconsented treatment is actionable even though it may be beneficial.

Intent may be *transferred*. For example, a man throws a stick at a group of boys on a roof with the intent of striking a particular child. The stick-thrower will be liable for battery if the missile misses its target but strikes another boy.[6] If *A* swings a golf club near *B* with the purpose not of hitting *B* but rather putting him in fear, *A* would be liable for *battery* if the head of the club came off and hit *B*. By transferring intent, the courts attempt to deter wrongful conduct.

The nature of intention is exemplified by the way civil courts treat mental illness. Even though a person's insane state renders him unable to appreciate that an act is wrong, he may nevertheless be liable under tort law. *A person is liable provided he is capable of entertaining—and did entertain—intention to perform the act in question.* The tort is proved (unless effective defenses can be presented), if in acting upon that intent, the defendant can be shown to have invaded the plaintiff's particular interest. Good reasons sustain the social policy of holding insane defendants liable for their actions: Injured parties can be compensated, and the caretakers of the insane will be encouraged to protect third parties.[7] Moreover, the courts have voiced concern about the falsification of insanity in order to avoid liability. In exceptional circumstances, however, mental illness can deprive a defendant of the capacity to form intent. For example, a frenzied patient may not be aware he could strike others, and defendants claiming to have been possessed by external forces have been held not liable. Nevertheless, if the defendant was aware that he is susceptible to such a delusion, he might be held liable because he negligently put himself in a situation that endangered others.[8]

The defendant's intentional act must be the cause of actual harm to the plaintiff, or the precipitant of an uninterrupted chain of events leading to injury. ("Cause" is more thoroughly discussed in the section on negligence later in this chapter.) However, in some cases the court will award a nominal sum even though the plaintiff cannot show that he suffered injury or material harm. In other cases, the circumstances of the intentional conduct may have been so blatantly outrageous that the court is persuaded to award substantial damages for mental distress, even though there was little or no injury or material harm. In this sense, the doctrine of intentional tort protects an individual's *dignity*.

SCOPE OF LIABILITY

One consequence of classifying a tort as intentional rather than negligent is that the scope of the defendant's liability is greatly extended. A defendant who merely acts negligently will generally be held liable only for *foreseeable consequences*. A defendant who has committed an intentional tort, in contrast, will be liable for consequences not reasonably predictable at the time of the act. For example, *A* intentionally strikes *B* on the head, merely intending to chastise him, and *B*, slightly injured, is taken to a hospital where he is accidentally poisoned. *A* will be liable for *B*'s resulting death, not just the minor injury.[9]

TYPES OF INTENTIONAL TORT

Among the most common intentional torts are assault, battery, trespass to land, intentional infliction of emotional distress, invasion of privacy, false imprisonment, defamation, and breach of confidence. Defamation, false imprisonment, and breach of confidence will be discussed in Chapter 9. Invasion of privacy will also be discussed in the context of the potential liability of the mental health clinician.

The different kinds of intentional tort protect different interests. Assault protects an individual's right to be free from violent threat; battery his bodily integrity; trespass to land, his right to exclude others from his property; false imprisonment, his freedom of movement; defamation, his reputation; and breach of confidence, his right to have private information kept within a relationship. Intentional torts recognize the value of personal dignity. In battery, though little or no bodily harm results, the plaintiff may have been exposed to hurtful indignities; thus, if the elements of the tort are proved, the court may award substantial damages. For example, a person subjected to racial epithets in the presence of friends and associates may have an action in battery if he can show that the defendant offensively touched him, albeit merely incidentally.[10]

Battery refers to *intentional, harmful or offensive active contact with another person.* A defendant is liable not only for contacts that do actual harm but also for contacts that are merely offensive or insulting. An unwanted kiss, for example, could be battery. However, the law accepts some give and take. Contacts that are within the bounds of ordinary social intercourse do not constitute battery. Acceptability, of course, will vary according to place and time.[11]

Assault is *an intentional action that causes someone to feel apprehension with regard to his safety.* The apprehension must be reasonable, given the nature and acuity of the threat, and must result from the fear of imminent physical contact, coupled with an apparent present ability to effectuate the threat.[12] In contrast to battery, assault requires no actual contact. For example, a nurse, while threatening to force a patient into a hospital, advances menacingly upon her. The nurse has committed assault, not battery. If the nurse then proceeds to lay hands on the patient, battery will have been committed in addition to assault. Usually assault precedes battery, but battery alone may be constituted in some cases (e.g., *A* hits *B* while *B* sleeps).

Intentional infliction of emotional distress protects the individual's psychic tranquility. Originally it was not recognized, for the historic range of protected interests involved only bodily integrity, land, personal property, and freedom of movement. Additional rights have been only slowly recognized. At first, aware of the difficulty of proving and assessing the severity of emotional distress, the courts refused to award damages unless the distress were accompanied by physical symptoms.[13] Today most courts do not require actual physical consequences; however, physical symptoms (e.g., vomiting or insomnia) will strengthen claims based on the intentional infliction of emotional distress.[14] The usual formulation of the tort requires the plaintiff to prove four elements:

1. The defendant's conduct was intentional or reckless.
2. The conduct was extreme and outrageous.
3. There is a causal connection between the conduct and the emotional distress.
4. The emotional distress suffered by the plaintiff is severe.[15]

Mere insult, indignity, or annoyance are generally insufficient to constitute this tort, unless there have been aggravating factors. The unwarranted intrusion into the plaintiff's interest must be calculated as likely to cause severe emotional distress to anyone of ordinary sensibilities.[16] Moreover, the act must be perpetrated for the purpose of causing emotional distress, or at least with reckless disregard of the high probability that distress could occur. For example, attackers who beat a man while his daughter watched from a hiding place were held not liable to the distressed daughter since they did not know she was there.[17] But had defendant known of the plaintiff's presence and the relationship to the man being beaten and the plaintiff had suffered emotional distress as a result, she would have had a good action against the defendant. The element upon which this tort turns is *outrageousness,* the violation of all civilized standards. In one case, the defendant, knowing the plaintiff's phobia of rats, baked a loaf of bread for him containing a gory rat.[18] In another case, a workplace supervisor incessantly mimicked the plaintiff's stutter; however, since it occurred in the rough-hewn surroundings of a motor vehicle assembly plant, the mockery was not regarded as sufficiently outrageous to warrant liability.[19]

With the breakdown of the immunities that once prevented suits between family members, it is now possible for spouses to sue one another and for children to sue their parents. In one case, a wife was allowed to sue her husband for the intentional infliction of emotional distress after the husband had egregiously flaunted his extramarital affairs.[20] Some commentators have expressed reservations about these actions, particularly in view of contemporary "no-fault" divorce legislation, which aims to rid marital dissolution of acrimony.[21]

By the same principle, a child may sue a parent or parents for intentional infliction of emotional distress. Given the emotional impact of divorce on children, a parent whose egregious conduct causes marital breakdown could face a suit. Desertion or neglect alone are not sufficient; nonetheless, children who have been physically or sexually abused may bring actions in assault, battery, or the intentional infliction of emotional distress.

A special case of liability arises if dead bodies are dismembered, mutilated, or interfered with in such a way as to cause emotional distress to relatives of the deceased. When the mother of a drowned three-year-old expressly refused a hospital permission to extract his eyes, the distressed mother had a good action against the medical examiner who had nevertheless removed them.[22] Since the deceased may bring no action, the action for emotional distress vested in those who cared for the deceased provides an impetus to avoid such wrongful conduct.

Invasion of privacy has been developed by the courts in order to protect an individual's right to privacy. This tort is usually divided into three separate categories:

1. *Appropriation:* a taking by the defendant for his own benefit of the plaintiff's name or likeness
2. *Unreasonable intrusion:* a highly offensive intrusion upon the seclusion of another
3. *Public disclosure of private facts:* highly objectionable publication of private information

We shall discuss this tort in the next chapter. At this juncture, we shall merely point out that, like the tort of intentional infliction of emotional distress, it protects a similar psychic interest and is likewise narrowly circumscribed. The courts are concerned to weigh against the third category the public interest of free speech. Thus, they have found that the publication of a rape victim's identity, lawfully obtained, is not actionable even when such publication is prohibited by state law.[23]

The private facts must be "highly offensive." In *Chambon v. Celender,* a reporter approached the mother of an alleged incest victim. He promised that her remarks would be "off the record" and that they would not be used in a story about her husband. He also persuaded her to consent to a photograph, on the agreement that it would be a silhouette. The full story and a recognizable photograph were published. The mother failed in her privacy claim. The court found that this material would not be highly offensive to the reasonable person. Furthermore, the matter, being of legitimate public concern, was protected under the First Amendment.[24] The plaintiff might have been successful had she brought an action for breach of confidence.[25]

DAMAGES

Under intentional tort, the court may award nominal damages—typically a token sum of one dollar—in order to vindicate a legal right. The availability of nominal damages is important when, for example, a plaintiff has established that a defendant frequently trespassed on his land. Although the trespass has caused the plaintiff landowner no material damage, he will be vitally interested in asserting his right to possession of the land, for failure to take action may result in the trespasser's acquiring the right to enter and cross the land by "prescription" (i.e., by uncontested usage). Sometimes nominal damages are awarded in order to indicate that, although the plaintiff has formally proved his case, the claim deserves only a derisory recognition. When one person has committed beneficial battery upon another, it is likely that the damages will be paltry unless the battery invaded the plaintiff's dignity or autonomy. An example of beneficial surgery yielding very substantial damages is the following: a surgeon authorized to perform a cesarean section tied the patient's fallopian tubes because there were fibroid growths on the wall of the uterus. The procedure might have been construed as beneficial, yet the court awarded substantial damages, for the decision to undergo sterilization should be the patient's. In effect, the surgeon's action had invaded the patient's decision-making autonomy.[26]

Punitive damages are awarded when the defendant's wrongdoing is both intentional and in contumelious disregard for the plaintiff's rights. Punitive damages are imposed over and above compensation for the plaintiff's injuries and are awarded in order to punish the defendant and to deter further wrongdoing by the defendant or others. In one case the defendants lent money to their employee, the plaintiff, to pay for dental work, including a dental bridge. The plaintiff quit, enraging the defendants, who, as security for the loan, attempted to remove his dental bridge forcibly. The plaintiff was awarded punitive damages for the defendants' outrageous conduct. In another case the defendant psychiatrist over four years administered between 140 and 171 sodium pentathol interviews, from which the plaintiff received little feedback, became addicted, and suffered posttraumatic stress disorder. Punitive damages are much criticized on the ground that their arbitrariness stems from the jury's sense of outrage against the defendant. Moreover, punitive damages, though tantamount to criminal fines, are awarded without the procedural safeguards of a criminal proceeding (i.e., proof of guilt beyond a reasonable doubt, together with statutory limits). Notwithstanding those objections, the United States Supreme Court has specifically rejected a claim that punitive damages are a denial of due process, although it held that the jury should have guidelines by which to exercise discretion.[28]

The law of damages is composed mainly of rules concerning the award of compensatory damages. In order to arrive at a figure that will restore the plaintiff to his original position, the courts will assess both economic and noneconomic losses. Under economic losses they will take evidence on the plaintiff's loss of earning capacity, and his hospital and medical costs. Under noneconomic losses the courts will take evidence on pain and suffering and loss of the enjoyment of life. Compensatory damages are discussed further in the section on negligence.

DEFENSES AGAINST TORT ACTIONS

Defenses in tort law can be grouped into two categories: (1) The defendant is immune from liability as a matter of *legal privilege,* and (2) the plaintiff *consented* to the invasion of his interest.

Privilege will immunize a defendant from liability in circumstances where ordinarily his conduct would be tortuous. Privilege attaches to actions that "further an interest of such social importance that it is entitled to protection."[29] For example, a defendant is privileged to use reasonable force in order to defend himself when threatened with harmful or offensive bodily contact or tortious confinement or imprisonment. This privilege is called *self-defense.* Within confined circumstances, a person may also enjoy privilege in protecting the life or limb of another. The law is less willing to extend this privilege if the interest that the defendant is seeking to protect is a property matter. In self-defense cases, a clinician may be called upon to indicate the range of normal response in the face of a threat.

The status of the defendant, for example, if it is a government body or charity, may bestow an immunity. This is discussed later.

If a fully informed plaintiff has consented to an intentional interference with his person, the defendant will not be liable for that interference. Intentional torts have at their core the lack of consent. Most courts have held that, as part of his case, the plaintiff must prove that he did not consent to the act of which he complains.

A plaintiff's consent can be express or implied by the plaintiff's conduct, by prevailing custom, or by the circumstances of an event. Unstated mental reservations do not negate consent: If it reasonably appeared to the defendant that the plaintiff gave consent, consent was implied regardless of what the plaintiff was privately thinking. The court will take all the circumstances into account in deciding whether the plaintiff implied consent. A person who queues with others awaiting a vaccination, who knows the purpose of the procedure, and who offers her arm implies consent to vaccination even if she indicates that it is unnecessary. The court takes into account the difficulty of obtaining express consent. When a benefit is bestowed, the court may be inclined to decide that consent can be reasonably implied.[31] In contrast, if the procedure is very risky, takes place in an inherently coercive environment, or bestows no benefit, it may be unreasonable to assume that consent is given. For example, a patient cannot give informed consent to an experimental procedure if he fears that refusal would compromise the rest of his treatment (Capron, 1974).

Children and intoxicated or unconscious adults lack the capacity to give consent. Express consent will be ineffective as a defense if the defendant knew or should have known that the plaintiff was not competent to give consent. However, when immediate action must be taken to save life or guard health, and the person in difficulties gives no indication he would otherwise not consent, and if a reasonable person would consent in the circumstances, the actor may intervene with impunity. For example, if a physician reasonably ascertains that an unconscious plaintiff's foot must be amputated in order to save his life, the plaintiff's consent will be implied, because the surgery is vital and urgent.[32]

Consent must be given on the basis of full *disclosure*. Accordingly, if a physician fails to inform a patient of the material risks involved in an operation or procedure, he may be liable in battery. The failure to inform must either deprive the plaintiff of an understanding of the nature of the procedure or misrepresent it. Failure to inform less extreme than this may be regarded as negligent on the basis that the physician has breached a standard of care that obligates him to disclose material risks. Battery actions are reserved for egregious cases in which the dignity or autonomy of the patient is at stake.

Consent may be given for a minor by his parent or legal guardian. Considerable problems arise when a parent refuses consent for medical procedures, a matter dilated upon in Chapter 3.

Negligence

A cause of action for negligence arises from *conduct that both falls below the standard established by law and creates an unreasonable risk of harm.*[33] The standard by which conduct is measured is that of the reasonably prudent and careful person under the same or similar circumstances.[34] Unlike an intentional tort, the tort of negligence does not turn on the defendant's intention. Rather, the essence of the action is whether the plaintiff suffered harm due to the defendant's unreasonably careless conduct directed toward him. Culpability does not turn on a state of mind but rather depends on a failure to measure up to an expected standard of behavior.[35]

THE COMPONENTS OF THE TORT OF NEGLIGENCE

In order to be awarded compensation for harm caused by a defendant's negligence, the plaintiff must prove the following four elements:

1. The defendant owed a *duty of care* to the plaintiff. In other words, the defendant had a legal duty to avoid exposing the plaintiff to unreasonable risks.

2. The defendant failed to conform to a required *standard of conduct* and thus *breached his duty of care*.
3. There was a sufficiently close *causal connection* between the defendant's wrong-doing and the plaintiff's resulting injury.
4. The plaintiff suffered *actual loss* or *damage*.

1. *Duty of care*. If *A* acts to cause *B* personal injury, *A* will usually have owed a duty of care to *B*. It is necessary for *B* to show that, as a reasonable person, *A* should have foreseen that by acting he would cause injury to *B* (or to persons in *B*'s position). Unless the injury results from a bizarre concatenation of events, it is usually reasonably foreseeable that an injury will follow a negligent act.[36]

The essential function of the duty requirement is to limit the range of the defendant's liability. A duty is not owed to everyone. A relationship entailing *reasonable foreseeability* must be established between *A* and *B*. Take the following example. A railway worker employed by *A* negligently jostles passenger *B*, causing him to drop an apparently innocuous package containing fireworks. The package explodes upon hitting the tracks. At the other end of the platform, *C* is hit by a set of scales toppled by the percussion of the explosion. The court may reason that *A* owed a duty to all those who would foreseeably be injured by the negligent jostling, but that *C* was outside the foreseeable range.[37]

Duty of care is a question of law, not fact. Thus, it is within the province of the judge, and the judge, not the jury, will determine the extent of liability. When asked to allow recovery for omissions rather than acts, and for damages beyond physical injury, most courts will decide the issue by reference to the duty of care.

Usually, negligence law imposes no obligation that people should affirmatively guard others from harm. If *B* is injured by *C*'s negligence, *A* will not be liable for failing to prevent the harm. *A* will owe a duty to *B*, however, if he has established a special relationship with *C* denoted by control over *C*'s activities. Thus *A*, as mother of *C*, will owe *B* a duty of care if *C* falls within the range of persons who might foreseeably be injured by *A*'s failure to supervise her child.[38] The parents of a twenty-seven-year-old schizophrenic man were found liable when the man fatally shot a neighbor. The parents were aware that their son had not taken his medication regularly and that his condition had not improved after his release from hospital. Regardless of this, they had left their son home alone and with access to a gun.[39] A mental health clinician has a special relationship with a patient, which imposes a duty to warn third parties who might be injured by the patient's declared conduct.[40] School counselors have a special relationship with students that obligates them to warn parents of suicidal statements made by students and reported to them.[41] More active steps to prevent suicide are not required, particularly if the suicidal person is an adult.[42] However, if the threatened harm has to do with no more than mental or emotional distress, the courts are hesitant to impose a duty to take active steps.

Case law concerning mental suffering can be divided into four categories: (1) mental suffering resulting from a physical impact with physical consequences; (2) mental suffering with physical consequences but no impact; (3) mental suffering which, although it resulted from impact, has no physical consequences; and (4) mental suffering without either physical impact or physical consequence.

In the first type of case (suffering following impact with physical consequences), the defendant is generally liable not only for the physical consequences but also for the emotional and mental suffering flowing from the impact.

The second category (suffering with physical consequences but no impact) encompasses cases in which the defendant's act does not result in immediate physical impact but does cause the plaintiff physical consequences. Most modern courts allow recovery in these cases. Issues arise when the plaintiff fears not for himself but for another; for example, when a parent is distressed by seeing his child killed. Some courts hold that the plaintiff may recover only if the parent plaintiff was in the *zone of danger* created by the defendant. For example, a mother who had given birth in a hospital saw a nurse drop her baby on the floor and heard the infant's skull crack. The plaintiff mother sued for severe emotional distress, but the court denied the cause of action because the mother was not in the zone of danger.[43]

Other courts, especially in recent years, have abandoned the "zone-of-danger" requirement. The landmark case occurred in California. In *Dillon v. Legg,* a young girl was hit by defendant's automobile while her mother and sister were present.[44] The court reasoned that it was arbitrary and unfair to let the sister, who was in the zone of danger, recover damages but to deny redress to the mother, who was not. Rather, the court held, the plaintiff's recovery should depend on the following: (1) whether the plaintiff was near the accident; (2) whether the plaintiff actually witnessed the accident; and (3) whether the plaintiff was related to the victim. Connecticut, Hawaii, Iowa, Massachusetts, Michigan, New Jersey, Rhode Island, and Texas have followed *Dillon v. Legg.*[45]

In cases that fall under the third category (impact, suffering, but no physical consequences), courts typically allow recovery for mental suffering flowing naturally from the physical impact. Suffering includes fright at the time of injury, pain and suffering associated with the injury, anxiety about possible repetition, and humiliation from disfigurement.[46] The third category of mental suffering applies to cases of improper sexual contact; for example, a treating psychologist was held liable when he engaged in sexual intercourse with a patient "under the guise of therapy," causing her "fear, shame, humiliation, and guilt," as a result of which she was forced to undergo further intensive psychotherapy.[47] A nursing home was found liable when its housekeeper raped the plaintiff patient, who experienced crying spells, nightmares, and flashbacks and was diagnosed as suffering from posttraumatic stress disorder.[48] In such cases, attorneys may seek the aid of an expert to establish the nature and severity of the plaintiff's mental suffering. Though the courts have only vaguely defined the meaning of "emotional distress," it is clearly more than an evanescent upset. As one court put it, "the plaintiff need not allege or prove any physical impact, physical injury, or physical manifestation of emotional distress." What must be proved is "severe emotional distress, constituted by emotional or mental disorder, such as, for example neurosis, psychosis, chronic depression, phobia, or any other type of severe and disabling emotional or mental condition which may be generally recognized and diagnosed by professionals trained to do so."[49]

In the fourth type of case (suffering without either impact or physical consequences), courts have traditionally allowed no recovery at all, primarily for fear that the floodgates will open to fraudulent claims.[50]

Whenever mental suffering claims have been allowed, the courts have insisted that the plaintiff be a person of ordinary phlegm. The plaintiff must establish that a normal person would have suffered emotional distress if exposed to the defendant's negligence. A person who suffered emotional distress because he is exceptionally sensitive may not recover. However, if the plaintiff can show that a normal person would have suffered emotional harm, he may recover for the full extent of his injuries, even if he himself is highly vulnerable.

Why have the courts been slow to find a duty of care for emotional distress alone? In the first place, they have feared fraudulent claims. Second, they have been concerned that liability for an act of negligence could range so broadly and impose such a crushing burden that human enterprise would be paralyzed. The problem of fraudulent claims has been alleviated by improvements in medical and psychiatric diagnosis, but the specter of opened floodgates remains a substantial barrier to extending liability. As a result of a single accident, such as an airplane disaster, many people knowing victims or watching television may suffer emotional distress. Is liability to extend to all of them? To date, the furthest that the American courts have taken liability is the ruling in *Dillon v. Legg*. Indeed, the stringency of the criteria established in that case has been debated.[51]

A miscellaneous group of emotional distress cases may be described. In one, a physician was found liable to the husband of a patient for having negligently misdiagnosed the patient as having syphilis.[52] The patient's husband—the plaintiff—blamed the wife for having possibly infected him, as a result of which the marriage broke up. In other cases, courts have allowed recovery for negligent mishandling of corpses (e.g., poor embalming, misplacement, or dismemberment).[53] A hospital was held to owe a duty to parents who had requested that their brain-dead son's body be decoupled from a respirator. The hospital's failure to comply reasonably resulted in liability for infliction of emotional distress.[54] The courts in these cases have found liability in order to deter defendants from committing negligent acts when in the absence of liability this class of wrongdoers would be systematically undeterred. In such cases, there is no concern about opening the floodgates.[55]

If the negligence had been directed at the plaintiff, or if a special relationship had existed between defendant and plaintiff, the courts will find a duty of care. In *Marlene F. v. Affiliated Psychiatric Medical Clinic, Inc.,* two boys were molested by a therapist at a time when both children and their mothers were receiving treatment from him.[56] The California Supreme Court upheld a cause of action against the therapist on the ground that the mothers had suffered severe emotional distress. The court ruled that the therapist had a duty of care to the mothers, because they were involved in the family therapy. Contrast, however, *Schwarz v. Regents of University of California,* in which the same court rejected a father's claim for emotional distress as a result of the negligent psychiatric treatment of his child.[57] The father was not involved in treatment; thus, the negligence was not directed toward him.[58]

Another category of case bearing the same deterrence rationale is associated with cancerphobia. In these cases, some courts have allowed recovery on the basis of a fear of contracting cancer and other diseases. Epidemiological and statistical advances have made it possible to predict increased likelihood for cancer following exposure to certain substances (e.g., asbestos or agent orange.) In *Hagerty v. L&L Marine Services,* a seaman was soaked with toxic chemicals. The court allowed recovery "for serious mental distress arising from fear of developing cancer where [the] fear is reasonable and causally related to the defendant's negligence."[59] In another case, an obstetrician's negligence exposed the plaintiff to risk of bowel obstruction. The patient's awareness of the risk was held admissible as the ground for emotional distress, over and above her claim based on the increased risk itself.[60] A similar rationale was used in *Johnson v. West Virginia University Hospitals.* A police officer employed by an independent company worked on the security staff at the hospital. He was called to help with a combative patient. Although the staff knew the patient was HIV positive, it failed to warn the officer. The patient bit himself and then bit the officer, introducing blood into the wound. The officer did not develop AIDS but did suffer posttraumatic stress disorder. His wife and children shunned him, his wife refused to have sexual relations with him, and his fellow workers avoided him. The court found that exposure to the disease was sufficient to base emotional distress damages.[61] Not all claims have been successful.[62] Some courts have been receptive, however,[63] recognizing that, if such actions are not pursued, people exposed to toxic substances or physicians' or hospitals' negligence will be undercompensated, and careless manufacturers, physicians, and hospitals will be left underdeterred.[64]

The duty of care must be owed to a *person*. That requirement poses problems if the negligent act results in injury to a fetus. The common law did not recognize a fetus as a person until it was born alive.[65] The courts have readily found that a duty exists if the fetus is injured and, in consequence, born with disabilities, but the legal problem is more challenging if injury causes stillbirth. In that case, the mother may bring an action against the wrongdoer for her injury and emotional distress. However, the courts are divided on whether the parents could bring an action for wrongful death.[66]

Mental health clinicians are likely to become involved in newly recognized actions concerning breaches of the standard of care in regard to conception and birth.[67] Take the following examples.

Case 1. Dr. *A* fails to diagnose that her patient *B* has contracted german measles during the first trimester of pregnancy. *B* gives birth to *C,* who suffers from congenital rubella. Dr. *A* has not caused injury through her negligence; however, she has failed to advised *B* of the consequences of continuing the pregnancy and giving birth to a child. About twenty state courts have awarded damages to *B* and her husband, an action known as *wrongful birth.*[68] Damages have been awarded for emotional distress associated with the birth of the child. The costs of rearing and looking after the child have been rejected, although extraordinary medical costs have been allowed.[69]

Some courts have held that *C* has an action for *wrongful life.*[70] In order to establish the legitimacy of this action, the courts had to overcome a philosophical conundrum: They had to accept that no life would have been preferable to *C*'s defective life, for due care on Dr. *A*'s part would have meant no life for *C*. When the courts have recognized this action, they have usually restricted damages to extraordinary medical expenses necessitated by the child's disability, although in some cases they have allowed recovery for pain and suffering.[71]

Case 2. Dr. *A* performs a negligently ineffective sterilization operation on *B*. In consequence, *B* gives birth to a child. Formerly the courts did not recognize birth as an injury. Recently, a growing number of courts have recognized the action of *wrongful pregnancy.*[72] Damages for wrongful pregnancy include the costs and expenses surrounding the pregnancy and birth, and compensation for emotional distress. The costs of rearing the child are usually excluded.

2. *Breach of duty.* The question of whether a defendant breached the duty of care is factual. An often-disputed issue in litigation, it turns on whether the defendant's conduct fell below the standard of the ordinary reasonable person in the circumstances. The judge instructs the jury to weigh a number of factors in coming to its conclusion. In the most general fashion, a cost-benefit calculus can be applied to the defendant's conduct. The issue will then depend on whether the cost of taking precautions to avoid the accident outweighed the magnitude of the loss and the probability of its occurring.[73] For example, it is not negligent to drive a car over 20 miles per hour, even though such speeds increase the risk of injury and death. The reason for finding no negligence is that the socioeconomic cost of driving so slowly would be inordinate.

In setting standards of care, the law attempts to promote social coordination. People must regulate their conduct in the anticipation that it could effect other reasonable people. Hence, a person does not have to take precautions against the presence of other people who are highly susceptible to injury. Indeed, the latter are usually in a better position to take precautions on their own behalf. Nevertheless, if one person has knowledge of another's susceptibility to injury, he must take reasonable precautions to avoid injuring him. For example, if a person knows, or should know, that blind people often cross a particular road, he must take reasonable precautions. At the same time, a blind person must take steps to warn others of his handicap.[74]

Mental or physical infirmity may make it impossible for a defendant to comply with the standard of the ordinary reasonable person, but the courts are grudging in allowing such exculpation. Fault may be found in the failure to take steps against psychological or physical breakdown where others will be endangered. A pedophile, for example, was found negligent because he failed to seek professional help for his disorder and did not avoid situations in which he was alone with the plaintiff boys.[75]

A well-recognized exception to the objective standard of the reasonable person applies to children. Children are usually held to a standard that would be expected of a reasonably careful child of the same age, intelligence, and maturity.[76] This forgiving standard of care may apply despite a statutory provision setting forth safety measures noncompliance with which would constitute negligence.[77] However, if a child engages in activities generally thought of as adult or dangerous, he will be held to an adult standard of care.[78]

Professionals hold out special skills and must attain a standard of care commensurate with that of the ordinary competent professional. No allowance is made for tyros or for veterans who have lost their capacity to keep abreast of developments. Expert evidence is required to inform the court of the applicable standard of care (see Chapter 8).

3. *Causation.* The plaintiff must prove that the defendant caused the injury of which he complains. Moreover, the defendant's wrongful conduct must have been the *proximate* cause of the injury.

The first stage of the inquiry is whether cause can be established as a matter of fact—*causation in fact.* The second stage is to ask whether the wrongful act was *legally* or *proximately* caused by the wrongful conduct.

Causation in fact turns on whether the wrongful conduct was the *but-for* cause of the injury; that is, whether the injury would not have occurred had there been no wrongful conduct. If the plaintiff would have suffered the injury in any event, the wrongful action cannot be construed as the cause. The courts eschew the philosophical conundrums that arise under the concept of causation, since they are concerned with ascribing responsibility. Therefore, even though the "but-for" test is failed in some cases, the courts will allow recovery. For example, if A's house is destroyed by fire, he may discover that the fire had two sources—the negligent acts of B and C. If the two fires set by B and C joined to destroy A's house, A will face a dilemma. If the separate fires would have been sufficient to destroy his house, A must fail under the "but-for" test: He cannot show that but for B's negligent act, his house would not have been destroyed; and he cannot show that but for C's negligent act his house would not have been destroyed. To deny recovery, however, would fail to deter wrongdoers like B and C; furthermore, it would deprive A of just compensation for the wrongful conduct of others. In this situation, the courts finesse the "but-for" test by asking whether the defendant's actions have been a "substantial cause."[79]

Causation requires positive proof. It is not sufficient merely to show that the plaintiff's condition occurred at the same time as the wrongful conduct. The plaintiff has the initial burden of proving that other causes are less likely than the defendant's wrongful conduct to have caused his injury. In the case of disease, with its complex or uncertain etiology, it is often difficult to sustain this standard of proof. In some cases the courts may relax the rigor of the positive proof rule in order to afford recovery against wrongdoers.[80] In a similar way, the courts may moderate the rule if the plaintiff who has been injured by a wrongful action cannot prove which individuals in a defined group were responsible.[81] In one case, a plaintiff suffered paralysis and atrophy of the shoulder after an appendectomy. The court found that this sort of injury would not ordinarily occur without negligence.[82] Because he was unconscious, however, the plaintiff could not show which professional in the surgical team caused the injury. The court decided that each member of the surgical team should be liable unless he could show he was not responsible.[83]

The modern phenomenon of mass tort litigation has multiplied the problems of proof and has called for innovation. In the well-known diethystilbestrol (DES) litigation, plaintiffs had suffered cervical cancer due to their mothers' ingestion of DES antenatally. DES had been marketed for twenty-four years and distributed by about three hundred companies. The lapse of the time from drug ingestion to disease contraction and the generic nature of the drug made it impossible for plaintiffs to identify the particular company that had supplied the drug. Nevertheless, the courts supplanted the usual requirement of proof and sheeted home liability to the manufacturers.[84]

A single wrongful act could be the "but-for" cause of many injuries. The law is concerned that the burdens of liability would be excessive unless some consequences could be described as too remote. This, the second element in causation, is *proximate cause,* an arcane branch of the law of torts with which even judges have had difficulty. To simplify matters, liability is limited by compelling the plaintiff to prove that the damage was *proximate.* Thus, the courts will require either that the defendant should have *reasonably foreseen* the possibility of the damage, or the damage be the *direct result* of the wrongful act. Whichever formal test is adopted, the court is essentially asking whether the defendant should be liable for the injuries complained of. In doing so, it must balance the costs of taking measures against the accident causing the injury versus the benefits of avoiding injury.

A well-established exception to the reasonable foreseeability rule is the principle that a defendant must "take the plaintiff as he finds him." In other words, if a plaintiff's preexisting condition is aggravated as a consequence of the defendant's action, the defendant may be liable for additional consequences, even if they were unforeseeable. This rule is illustrated by the hypothetical example of the man with the "eggshell skull." If a defendant inflicts a minor impact on this man's head, either negligently *or* intentionally, and the man dies as a result, the defendant will be liable. The "eggshell skull" principle has been extended to mental conditions. For example, a man with paranoid schizophrenia was in a car accident caused by the defendant's negligence. The plaintiff suffered only minor physical injuries, but the injuries caused him to believe that he was no longer capable of pursuing a body-building regimen that had formerly enabled him to feel he had control over his life. As a result of quitting body-building, the plaintiff's psychosis worsened and he became completely disabled. The court held the defendant liable for the aggravation of the plaintiff's preexisting illness, stating that, even though the plaintiff's mental condition might have eventually worsened without the accident, the accident had hastened the plaintiff's deterioration.[85]

One injury will sometimes result from a number of different causes. The task of the court then is to determine whether all or only some of these causes are legal or proximate. The law may immunize some wrongdoers from liability if acts or events intervene between the negligence and the injury. For example, drug manufacturer *A* distributes a prescription drug which synergizes with alcohol and is accompanied by an express warning to that effect. Physician *B* prescribes the drug for patient *C* without warning *C* of the danger. *C* subsequently drinks alcohol, drives, collides with a telephone pole, and is injured. *B* will be liable, because he negligently failed to warn the patient. Drug company *A*, on the other hand, will be absolved from liability, since *B*'s negligence intervened. This, the *learned intermediary rule*, allows the courts to shift responsibility onto the party who is in a better position to take precautions against an accident.[86]

As a general rule an intervening cause will insulate the original wrongdoer from liability if the cause is a bizarre, unexpected natural event or a malicious intentional act of a third party. However, if the intentional act was something that should reasonably have been expected, albeit intentional and malicious, the original wrongdoer will remain liable. In *Haselhorst v. State*, the plaintiffs discovered that their children had been sexually assaulted by a foster child placed with them by the Nebraska Department of Social Services.[87] The court found for the plaintiffs, who had suffered emotional distress, on the basis of the agency's negligence in placing the child in a family with young children. The state argued that the proximate cause of the plaintiffs' emotional distress was the intentional and malicious act of the foster child or of those who had caused his propensity to sexually abuse children. The court rejected the argument, concluding that the state agency's duty was to protect foster families from this kind of danger.[88]

Proof of causation can be a stumbling block in medical malpractice, a matter covered in Chapter 8. We shall foreshadow two issues. The first emerges in informed consent. The plaintiff must show that, if properly informed, he would have chosen not to proceed with the treatment that caused his injury. The courts are divided on which of two tests should apply. The usual test is subjective: Would the plaintiff have decided otherwise had he possessed all the information? However, in hindsight, the plaintiff will naturally believe he would have refused the treatment. The other test is objective: Would a reasonable person have desisted had he known? This test allows the court to substitute an *objective standard* for that of the plaintiff.

The second malpractice issue to do with proof of causation arises in cases alleging negligent diagnosis. If Dr. *A* misdiagnosis *B*'s lung cancer, Dr. *A* will not be liable for *B*'s death unless *B* can show, on the balance of probabilities, that but for the negligent misdiagnosis he would not have died. If evidence shows that his chances of surviving were reduced by 40 percent, *B* will fail the "but-for" test, since it is not more probable than not that *B* would have lived. Nevertheless, some courts, as we shall see, will award damages for the *lost chance* of surviving.

4. *Damages.* Compensatory damages are at the heart of negligence actions. Damages are awarded as a lump sum for past and future losses flowing from the injury. Once bestowed, the damage award satisfies all claims and releases the defendant from further liability.

The assessment of damages is approached by inviting evidence of the plaintiff's damages under established categories. *Special damages* are awarded for pecuniary or economic losses that can be calculated precisely, although attorneys will argue about the proper calculation. Special damages include compensation for any medical expenses, loss of earnings, and property damage that have been caused by the defendant's tortuous conduct.

General damages are awarded in order to compensate the plaintiff for economic and noneconomic losses that cannot be calculated precisely; for example, past and future physical pain, past and future mental distress, suffering and humiliation, loss of future earning capacity, and future medical expenses. Since general damages are difficult to calculate, expert witnesses may be called upon to testify to their extent. For example, actuaries can testify as to life expectancy, and mental health clinicians can give expert evidence concerning past and future mental suffering and the expense of treatment.

In one case, a child was severely burned when her home was consumed by fire.[89] The jury awarded her $2 million in damages. Part of the award was for physical and mental pain and suffering: The child had endured repeated medical procedures and operations and had sustained painful scarring and ankylosis of the extremities. The appeals court referred to testimony concerning the "horrible mental and emotional trauma caused to this child [occurring] at an age which medical experts maintain is crucial to a child's entire psyche and personality foundation." Experts testified that the child suffered from emotional illness and retarded psychological development. In respect of future pain and suffering, the court held that the jury's award was not excessive, given that the child's scarring would continue to cause pain and limit motion in her upper extremities, and that she would incur risks to her health and well-being, while stresses at each phase of life would tax her "debilitated and delicate mental and emotional capacity." The court also noted that the child would be deprived of a normal social and family life and subject to "rejection, stares and tactless inquiries from children and adults." Substantial awards of pain and suffering may be justified if the court is persuaded that the victim was affected by an awareness of immediate and impending death, as in an airplane crash,[90] as well as (more commonly) distress at the knowledge that an injury has shortened one's life.[91]

The mental anguish aspect of pain and suffering is sometimes separately recognized as *loss of enjoyment of life* or *loss of the amenities of life*. Psychiatric evidence is frequently required to inform the jury about the impact of the injury on a plaintiff who is unable to engage in life's activities. On the other hand, damages received by the plaintiff may allow some compensatory pleasurable activity that will reduce damages for loss of enjoyment of life. The recognition of loss of enjoyment as separate from pain and suffering may support an award for nonpecuniary damages, even though the plaintiff is unconscious and insensible to pain as a result of the accident.[92]

Awards for pain and suffering have been criticized as arbitrary and are often exhausted in paying the attorney's contingent fee. As noted in Chapter 8, reforms have been implemented in some states in order to restrict the damages that can be awarded.

The only person with standing to sue is the person physically injured by the defendant's tortious conduct. Exceptions are recognized, however, if a relationship exists between the physically injured person and the plaintiff. For example, physical injury to a spouse, child, or parent may give rise to an action for *loss of consortium:* the loss of care, comfort, society, companionship, and (between spouses) sexual relations. While spouses have usually been successful in loss of consortium actions following injury to their partners, courts have been more reluctant to allow such actions by a parent for an injured child or by a child for an injured parent. Between parent and child, consortium encompasses care, comfort, society, companionship, and guidance.[93] Until 1980, actions by children for loss of parental consortium were simply not recognized.[94] The recognition of a child's cause of action for loss of parental consortium[95] has garnered considerable support from legal commentators.[96] A number of influential courts in the last decade have supported the action.[97] Several courts have declared it "inappropriate" and "anomalous" that a child could recover damages for the death of a parent yet have no recourse when a parent has been rendered permanently comatose.[98] Although money cannot replace the consortium of the lost parent, separate recovery by the child guarantees that the money will be used for that child's benefit and not by the surviving parent for other purposes.[99] For example, a live-in housekeeper or caretaker could be hired, in order to provide both domestic services and a measure of guidance and companionship, or the recovery might pay for necessary psychiatric treatment.[100] Claims for loss of parental consortium are typically limited to minor or handicapped children[101] and are usually combined with the injured parent's underlying claim against the tortfeasor.[102]

DEFENSES

1. *Immunities.* An immunity is a defense allowed to an entire class of persons on the grounds of their relationship with the potential plaintiff, the nature of their occupation, or their status as a governmental or charitable entity.[103] One type of immunity is *familial*—between husband and wife or parent and child. As of 1989, spousal immunity had been abolished by forty states. Immunity between parents and children has been abolished by about a third of the states, predominantly in regard to automobile accident suits, as a consequence of the policy of shifting losses from victims to the deep pockets of liability insurers and the absence, in such claims, of family disruption.[104] Even when a state has not totally abolished parental immunity, it will have a number of exceptions,[105] such as when the child has been legally emancipated,[106] when the defendant is a stepparent or guardian, when the tort is intentional, or when the child plaintiff is suing one parent for the wrongful death of the other.[107] In one case, an illegitimate daughter brought an action against her father's estate for shock, mental anguish, and nervous and physical injuries. She had seen her father shoot the side of her mother's face away and two days later blow off his own head. The court had no hesitation in finding that the daughter had a good cause of action since no relationship was at stake and the injuries resulted from cruel and inhumane treatment.[108]

2. *Contributory negligence.* The contributory negligence defense seeks to bar all recovery to a plaintiff who failed to take reasonable care for his own safety and whose negligence was the proximate cause of his own injury. This defense shifts the loss completely to the plaintiff, even when the plaintiff's failure to act reasonably has been much less significant than the defendant's failure to act reasonably. Contributory negligence is not available as a defense against the claims of intentional torts, willful and

wanton torts, strict liability, or negligence based on a statutory violation. Where the duty is to protect another from harming himself, conduct of that kind will not be regarded as contributory negligence, since the very purpose of the duty would be defeated.[109]

3. *Comparative negligence.* Comparative negligence rejects the "all or nothing" approach of contributory negligence and aims to divide liability between plaintiff and defendant according to the relative fault of each party. As of 1991, only eight states (Alabama, Arizona, Delaware, Kentucky, Maryland, Missouri, North Carolina, and Virginia) had failed to adopt the comparative negligence doctrine.[110] However, it is important to distinguish between *pure comparative negligence* and *fifty-percent comparative negligence.* Pure comparative negligence allows the plaintiff to recover even if his wrongdoing is greater than the defendant's. The fifty-percent approach, in contrast, allows the plaintiff to recover only if his negligence is less than or equal to the defendant's wrongdoing. Only a minority of states have adopted pure comparative negligence; most have opted for fifty-percent comparative negligence.[111]

4. *Assumption of risk.* A plaintiff assumes the risk of certain harm if he voluntarily consents to take his chances that harm will occur. At one time, much like contributory negligence, this defense was a complete bar to recovery. Under the comparative negligence system, however, many courts have held that the assumption of risk defense is not absolute, but to be taken into account in the apportionment of harm.[112]

The assumption of risk can be either *explicit* or *implied.* If explicit, the defense is usually allowed, unless it violates public policy. The courts have consistently found, for example, that providers of health care should not be allowed to contract explicitly out of liability.[113] They take a different view if the services of goods are not vital and consumers have a real choice.[114] Assumption of risk may be implied if the plaintiff had knowledge of the risk and voluntarily consented to bear that risk himself. For example, a defendant dangerously explodes fireworks in a public street, and the plaintiff, watching at close range, is injured by a stray rocket. The plaintiff has assumed the risk and cannot recover if the defendant can show that the plaintiff was aware of the risk.[115] In both explicit and implicit assumption of risk, the courts will make allowance for children who are acknowledged to be unable to take precautions in their own safety to the degree of an ordinary reasonable adult. Rather, the standard adopted is that of the *ordinary reasonable child* of the same age, intelligence, and experience.[116]

5. *Strict liability.* Under the doctrine of *strict liability,* damages are imposed regardless of intent or negligence. Strict liability is most commonly associated with *product liability* cases in which a plaintiff sues a manufacturer or distributor because a defective product has caused injury. The product is defective if it is improperly manufactured, damaged in distribution to the consumer, or so badly designed as to be inherently hazardous. Strict liability may also apply when a defendant has violated certain statutes or if he was engaged in exceptionally dangerous activity (e.g., blasting with explosives or using poisonous gases).

The rationale behind strict liability is that, even though the damaging service or product serves a useful purpose, victims must be compensated. Furthermore, strict liability is thought to spur distributors, operatives, and manufacturers to make their operations and products as safe as possible, while spreading liability costs through insurance and the asking price of their services or goods.[117]

PROOF OF CASE

Chapter 2 provided a brief introduction to civil procedure and evidence in court, including burdens of proof. We shall not revisit those issues except insofar as they pertain to tort actions.

An attorney will gauge the viability of his client's claim by evaluating whether the evidence is sufficient to prove the elements of the action. In a negligence action, the plaintiff has the burden of proving three issues, on a preponderance of evidence: (1) that the defendant owed the plaintiff a duty of care; (2) that the defendant breached the duty of care; and (3) that the breach caused the alleged injury. The defendant, on the other hand, has the burden of establishing the defenses of contributory negligence and voluntary assumption of risk.

The plaintiff will promote his case by adducing evidence from documents and the questioning of witnesses under oath. The defendant may cross-examine. Following the *plaintiff's case in chief,* the defendant may file a *motion for a directed verdict,* based on the premise that the plaintiff's evidence, even in its best light, fails to establish the necessary elements of his action. The evidence for causation, for example, must establish the element by positive proof (for example, through expert evidence) beyond mere speculation.[118] If the judge should deny the defendant's motion, thus allowing the plaintiff's *prima facie* case, the defendant will present his evidence. The defense will attempt to rebut the plaintiff's *prima facie* case and to establish any defenses that the defendant has pleaded. At the end of all the evidence, and before the judge instructs the jury, either party may move for a *directed verdict.* In entertaining this motion, the judge will scrutinize the entire evidence to decide whether or not there is only one reasonable outcome, and will rule accordingly. For example, the judge may determine that no reasonable jury could decide for the defendant, and direct the verdict accordingly. If this motion is rejected, lawyers will make their closing arguments and the judge will instruct (or charge) the jury on the law. The jury will deliberate and return a verdict. The winner will move for a judgment on the verdict and the disappointed litigant may move for judgment notwithstanding the verdict (j.n.o.v.) or for a new trial. A motion j.n.o.v. is akin to a motion for a directed verdict but has the advantage that, if granted and subsequently overruled on appeal, the necessity of a new trial is obviated. Because defective instructions are a common source of appeals, judges adhere closely to established sets of jury instructions that, while prolix, are designed to minimize error.

Clinicians familiar with the law will have heard of the doctrine of *res ipsa loquitur.* Though surrounded by much arcane learning, the doctrine fundamentally describes how a plaintiff may prove his case on the basis of circumstantial evidence. If *B* is hit by a bag of flour as he walks along the sidewalk and can show that the bag fell from *A*'s premise, *B* may argue, without further evidence, that the bag's descent bespeaks negligence on *A*'s part. *B* must show that bags do not usually fall in the absence of negligence, and that *A* was in control of the storage and safekeeping of the bags.

In tort cases, plaintiffs often have difficulty obtaining evidence of the circumstances surrounding the accident and are unable to prove their case on the balance of probabilities. *Res ipsa loquitur* allows them to establish a *prima facie* case on the basis that, in the ordinary affairs of mankind, events such as that causing the injury do not occur unless there has been negligence. Having established a *prima facie* case, the plaintiff puts the onus on the defendant to present evidence in rebuttal. For example, *A* will attempt to show that he took all reasonable steps to prevent bags from falling on passers-by. Such evidence would be sufficient to rebut the inference of negligence.

The courts are reluctant to apply *res ipsa loquitur* in medical malpractice actions. Arguably, juries cannot apply common sense to conclude whether medical actions bespeak negligence; they simply do not have the expert knowledge required to do so. For example, in *Farber v. Olkon,* the Court found that *res ipsa* could not apply where both the plaintiff's femur bones were fractured during electric shock treatment;[119] the consequences of this treatment were in the realm of expert evidence and could not be judged by the jury without the evidence.[120] Pragmatically, the courts' reluctance stems from concern that juries are sympathetic to plaintiffs and, given the opportunity, will favor recovery.[121] This would promote malpractice litigation and increase the burdens imposed thereby. However, the courts have recognized exceptions to the presumption against the use of *res ipsa* if the medical misadventure has been flagrant, as when foreign objects are left in a patient's body after an operation.[122]

THE FORENSIC EVALUATION OF CIVIL LIABILITY CASES
The Legal Questions

The clinician is usually contacted by the claimant's advocate. Given the details of the particular case, the clinician may be asked to help the attorney shape the claimant's interrogatories and answer the defendant's. The attorney will need information about the way any preexisting condition would have been manifested. This will enable him to ask the defendant if he knew that the claimant reacted in certain ways. The attorney may want to mount an argument that, as a reasonable person, the defendant should have been aware that the claimant was unusually susceptible to injury (in other words, that the consequences of *A*'s actions were reasonably foreseeable).

The defendant's interrogatories will attempt to establish the basis of a good defense. For example, the defense may argue that the basis of the plaintiff's psychiatric symptoms is a preexisting condition not known to the defendant. He will further want to assert that a normal person would have suffered no psychological ill consequence. In anticipation of these legal issues, the plaintiff's attorney may ask the clinician his opinion on the following:

1. Does the child suffer from psychiatric disorder, psychosocial impairment, or educational disability? If so:
2. How severe is the disorder, impairment, or disability?

3. How does it manifest itself?
4. Are the history and clinical features of the disorder, impairment, or disability consistent with its having been caused by the event in question?
5. What are the implications of the disorder, impairment, or disability for the claimant's future development?
6. Is the disorder, impairment, or disability amenable to treatment? If so, what treatment, for how long, and at what cost?
7. What degree of disorder would have resulted if an "ordinary child" of the same developmental level had been exposed to the same trauma?

Documents

Alternatively, the forensic clinician may be asked by the defendant's attorney to review another clinician's report in order to detect errors or flaws in the evaluation, conclusions, or recommendations.

Whether retained by plaintiff or by defendant, the clinician should ask the attorney to forward all witness reports, police reports, and other documents relevant to the allegedly causative event, and all available medical, mental health, or educational records concerning the patient's physical health, psychosocial adjustment, or educational performance before and after the event in question. The attorney should also brief the clinician with regard to current national and local legal thinking in similar cases by sending copies of legal reviews, precedent cases, or sections from local statutes concerning the legal issues at stake.

The clinician should indicate to the attorney that the evaluation will require up to three to four interviews with the child, psychological testing of the child, two interviews with the parents, psychological testing of the parents, a review of documents, and the preparation of a report. In some cases it may also be necessary to interview witnesses of the event, people who knew the child well prior to the event in question, and people who saw the child immediately after the event.

The child should not be evaluated until more than six months have elapsed since the accident. If less time has passed it will not be possible to distinguish adjustment reactions from more serious disorders.

The Clinical Questions

The essential questions, in all cases, are as follows:

1. *Diagnosis.* Does the child suffer from psychiatric disorder, psychosocial impairment, or educational disability?
2. *Severity.* How severe is the disorder, impairment, or disability?
3. *Pattern.* What is the pattern of the disorder, impairment or disability? Is the pattern consistent with one that could be the result of trauma? Specially, does it satisfy diagnostic criteria for any of the following disorders?

- Posttraumatic stress disorder
- Adjustment disorder
- Uncomplicated bereavement
- Anxiety disorder
- Somatoform disorder
- Malingering
- Impulse control disorder
- Psychosis
- Academic skills disorder

4. *Causation*. Was the hypothetically traumatic event actually traumatic? If so, was the trauma directly related to the current disorder, impairment, or disability? If the trauma was directly related to the current disorder, impairment, or disability, was it the sole, the major, a contributory, or a minor precipitating factor? Did the family experience other traumatic events which, it could be argued, were alternative explanations for the child's current disorder? What degree of disorder would have resulted if an "ordinary child" of the same developmental level had been exposed to the same trauma?

5. *Preexisting condition*. What was the level of the child's functioning before the hypothetically traumatic event? Was there evidence of disorder, impairment, or disability in psychological adjustment, social competence, or educational performance?

6. *Aggravation*. If the child already had a disorder, impairment, or disability prior to the trauma, was it aggravated by the hypothetical trauma? Was the trauma the sole, the major, a contributory, or a minor aggravant?

7. *Perpetuation*. Has the child's current disorder, impairment, or disability been aggravated by parental distress or shaped or exaggerated by parental indoctrination? Keep in mind that the stress involved in litigation itself can aggravate and perpetuate a child's symptoms.

8. *Prognosis*. What are the implications of the disorder or impairment for the future? Is it likely to affect later psychological, social, sexual, educational, or occupational adjustment?

9. *Recommendations*. Would the disorder, impairment or disability be amenable to treatment? What kind of treatment, for how long, and at what estimated cost?

Each of these questions will be discussed after the clinical procedures required to elucidate them are described.

Evaluation Procedures

The following interviews and tests will be required in most cases:

1. Interview the parents to gather historical information about the circumstances of the event; the history of the child's current adjustment at home, in school, and with

peers; and the history of the child's previous contact with mental health professionals (two interviews, each of 60–90 minutes).

2. The parents should complete a Child Behavior Checklist (CBCL-P)[123] and a Child Information Form (see Appendix) concerning the child, and each parent should complete a Minnesota Multiphasic Personality Inventory, MMPI, concerning his or her own mental health, and in order to provide data concerning the child's current adjustment, family background, early development, past medical and psychiatric history, and school performance, and concerning parental mental health. The parents should also complete inventories of life events experienced by the family (1) in the year prior to the hypothetical trauma, and (2) since the trauma. The questionnaire designed by Coddington (1972) is a useful aid in this regard. This information can be elicited in your office with secretarial supervision, for example when the parents are waiting while the child is being interviewed.

3. A further interview (or interviews) with the parents is required in order to explore the personalities of the parents, the marital adjustment, and the quality of the parent–child relationship, particularly in regard to whether the parents have knowingly or inadvertently exaggerated or aggravated the child's disorder (ninety minutes to three hours).

4. Interview the child in order to gather information concerning the hypothetical trauma and the child's reaction to it. Explore current adjustment to school, with peers, and at home with parents and siblings. If the differentiation of the pattern of the disorder is unclear, conduct a structured interview with the child, or with the parent if the child is too young to be reliable. The Diagnostic Interview for Children and Adolescents, DICA,[124] is recommended for this purpose, since its reliability and validity have been corroborated. (Two or three interviews, each of 60–90 minutes.)

5. Psychiatrists may need to refer children for psychological evaluation if there is a suspicion of learning difficulty or neuropsychological impairment. The psychologist should analyze previous psychological or psychoeducational test results (particularly those obtained prior to the hypothetical trauma) in the light of current testing, in order to detect evidence for a deterioration in performance. Psychological testing may also be helpful in the corroboration (or disconfirmation) of particular questions concerning current adjustment (e.g., the presence of depression). In order to avoid biasing the psychologist, the referring psychiatrist should scrupulously avoid conveying his or her own impressions and conclusions. Only essential background information should be forwarded and specific questions asked, for example:

This ten-year-old boy witnessed his father being killed in an automobile accident twelve months ago [date]. Given these data [e.g., school progress and psychological or psychoeducational testing reports] obtained prior to the accident, is there any evidence of a current deterioration in academic performance? Does he currently suffer from a learning disability? Does he suffer from psychiatric disorder or social impairment? If so, of what type? For example, does he suffer from clinically significant depression or anxiety?

The psychologist's report should address only those questions posed in the referral (one or two testing sessions, each of two hours' duration). The psychologist should avoid the use of tests whose reliability and validity are low or uncertain. In general, testimony based upon projective testing is not adequate for forensic purposes; an informed cross-examining attorney will have a field day dismantling it. The issue of psychiatrist–psychologist collaboration in forensic evaluation will be discussed further in Chapter 11.

6. In some cases it may be necessary to interview people who witnessed the event in question and saw the child immediately after the event. The forensic clinician may wish to interview other people (preferably unrelated observers such as teachers) who, prior to the event, knew the child well and who knew the child now. Sometimes telephone contact is sufficient, but a personal interview is required if the information is of crucial importance. The Child Behavior Checklist—Teachers' Version (CBCL-T)[125] is a helpful adjunct to parent interviews. It should be noted, however, that a child may behave one way at school and one way at home. In school, depression, anxiety, and sleep disturbance are less likely to be observed than inattention, disruptiveness, and poor performance.

7. A further interview with the parents or the child may be necessary in order to check details and clarify inconsistencies in the data elicited.

Elucidating the Clinical Questions

THE TRAUMA

Did the hypothetical trauma actually traumatize the child? The answer to this question may be self-evident if the event was extreme (e.g., rape or the witnessing of a parent's death). The impact of the alleged trauma is corroborated if the child's symptomology incorporates elements of the traumatic event in the form of repetitive dreams, intrusive memories, "flashbacks," reenactive play, or marked psychophysical arousal when exposed to reminders of the event.

THE PRESENCE, SEVERITY, AND PATTERN OF THE DISORDER, IMPAIRMENT, OR DISABILITY

Evidence for a current disorder or impairment is derived from interviews with the parents, child, teachers, and other observers, and corroborated by the results of the CBCL-P and CBCL-T questionnaires, independent school progress reports, information from other relevant educational, mental health, or pediatric clinicians, and the results of psychological testing.

The severity of the disorder is gauged from the number and intensity of symptoms and the degree of social and academic impairment. To be more precise, severity can be attested by the behavior problem and social competence scores on the CBCL-P and CBCL-T, the printouts from which provide a ready comparison with both age-based and sex-based percentile norms, and with the probability that the patient's level of symptomatology is within the clinical range.

The pattern of the disorder is derived from clinical interviews with the parents and child, supported if necessary by a structured diagnostic interview (preferably with the child) and by the CBCL profile pattern.

Which disorder patterns are most likely after, and most consistent with, a hypothetically traumatic event? The most likely, and least serious, outcome of trauma is an *adjustment disorder,* that is, a temporary reaction to a stressor. The essence of this disorder is its time-limited nature. According to *DSM*-III-R (1987), if adjustment disorder is to be diagnosed, the child's symptomatology or impairment must have become evident within three months after the onset of the stressor and have persisted no longer than six months. Adjustment disorders are likely to be colored by anxiety, depression, conduct disturbance, physical complaints, social withdrawal, or academic inhibition. The last may foreshadow what evolves into a more persistent learning problem. It is possible that the other forms of adjustment reaction will evolve, in some cases, into a more serious disorder (e.g., a somatoform, mood, or anxiety disorder).

It is useful to distinguish *uncomplicated bereavement* from adjustment disorder. Children involved in motor vehicle accidents may have lost a parent or parents. One month after bereavement, most children experience depressive mood, while poor school performance and bedwetting are also common.[129] Children are likely to exhibit sadness, irritability, aggressiveness, dependent behavior, academic inhibition, insomnia, restless sleep, and change in appetite. In some cases, unresolved grief evolves into more persistent mood, anxiety, or conduct disorder. Persistent depressive disorders appear to be more common among adolescent boys who have lost fathers.[127] Persistent academic problems may also follow bereavement.

If the child's symptoms have persisted longer than six months, the diagnoses of adjustment disorder and uncomplicated bereavement are superseded.

If symptoms have been present for longer than one month, the diagnosis of *posttraumatic stress disorder* is made on the basis of the following features:

1. The patient has experienced an *extraordinarily distressing event* (e.g., a threat to life, or harm to or loss of an attachment figure, or the serious threat of harm to, or of loss of, an attachment figure).

2. The patient complains of *reenactments* or *reliving* of the traumatic event in the form of recurrent, involuntary recollections of intrusive nature, dreams, "flashbacks," and emotional distress at exposure to events that resemble or symbolize the trauma. Children are prone to be involved in repetitive traumatic play without apparent resolution of the trauma.

3. *Psychological anesthesia and avoidance* are evident in a conscious avoidance of recollections and reminders of the event, amnesia for part of the event, diminished interest in normal activities, feelings of detachment and estrangement, restricted affect, and the ominous sense of a foreshortened future. In cases involving repeated trauma, particularly physical or sexual abuse, more dramatic or chronic dissociative symptoms are encountered.

4. *Increased arousal* is experience as insomnia, irritability, outbursts of anger, poor concentration, hypervigilance, exaggerated startle response, and an exaggerated autonomic response to reminders of the original trauma.

Posttraumatic stress reactions in children and adolescents have been studied in the aftermath of natural disasters, such as a winter storm, the shelling of a kibbutz, damburst, and brushfire;[128] and after such personal events as dog bite, burns, familicide, child snatching, child abuse, and kidnapping.[129]

The most detailed study is that by Terr, who has followed the child victims of a 1976 kidnapping that took place in Chowchilla, California.[130] In this widely publicized event, twenty-five schoolchildren aged from five to fourteen were abducted at gunpoint from a school bus, transferred to two blackened-out vans, driven around for eleven hours, and finally transferred to a truck-trailer, which was buried underground. The children eventually escaped when two of the victims dug them out. Terr's study is particularly useful because of its detailed, clinically sophisticated nature and because it deals with emotional trauma untrammeled by the effects of physical injury or bereavement.

Four years after the experience, the Chowchilla victims remembered the anxiety they felt during the event, tended to feel ashamed of their helplessness, and suffered from a variety of fears. Although suppression, denial, and repression of memories were encountered, in most cases the event was remembered clearly, sometimes with associated metaphorical expression, visualization, displacement of affect, and autonomic arousal. Memories of misperceptions were noted along with distortions in the duration or sequence of events. Some children evinced a belief in omens and the sense of a foreshortened future. Reenactive phenomena were prominent and included posttraumatic dreams, repetitious play, and physical restaging of the abduction.

Terr noted that children from multiproblem or isolated families seemed to have more symptoms. This observation is consistent with a study by McFarlane (1987), who found that mothers' reactions to a natural disaster (a brushfire) predicted posttraumatic phenomena better than whether the children were directly exposed to the disaster.

Terr (1983) concluded that brief therapy provided within thirteen months after the event apparently had little effect upon the progress of the posttraumatic symptoms. Compared with adults, children were less likely to manifest amnesia, psychological "numbing," "flashbacks," or decline in performance (i.e., at school); on the other hand, they were more likely to exhibit repetitive play and reenactment and to experience time skew and the sense of a foreshortened future.

Anxiety disorders are a common aftermath of severe stress. They generally represent a complex interplay between premorbid predisposition, traumatic precipitation, and perpetuation by parental anxiety.

A seven-year-old boy, the only child of a middle-aged couple, was playing on the front lawn of the family home. At the same time, his mother was speaking on the telephone with a nurse in the hospital to which, the day before, her husband had been admitted for acute myocardial infraction.

A large dog belonging to a neighbor entered the yard and attacked the child from one side, knocking him to the ground. The mother heard her son's cries for help, put down the telephone, and ran to the front of the house where she saw the growling dog standing guard over the prone body of the child, who was bleeding from wounds on the calf, arm, and forehead. With the aid of a passerby, she drove the dog from the yard. The victim was not severely injured; however, a deep puncture in his calf became infected, necessitating antibiotic medication.

Immediately after the attack the child was weepy, frightened, insomniac, and clingy. Within one month, he began to exhibit night terrors, once or twice each week, during which he would wake up screaming, "No! . . . No! . . ." He had no memory of these terrors the next day. He was afraid to pass the house in which the dog had lived and became apprehensive whenever he saw a dog approaching. Prior to the attack he was known to be behind his age group in reading and mathematics; however, his concentration and school performance deteriorated further after the accident. At the time of referral for forensic evaluation, his symptoms had persisted for more than twelve months.

His mother had suffered two grievous blows almost simultaneously. Her son was traumatized and her husband had been rendered a chronic cardiac invalid, in need of her constant support. Previously a somewhat dependent woman, she became anxious and exhausted: antidepressant medication was prescribed by her family practitioner. Feeling acutely responsible for her son's injury, she would lie down beside him at night to comfort him before he went to sleep. His restless sleep, fears, and school problems filled her with apprehension for the future.

Many cases, like this one, represent incomplete forms of posttraumatic stress disorder, with complex environmental interplay. Patterns that admix anxiety, phobia, depression, aggressiveness, and performance inhibition are commonly associated with parental perpetuating factors. It is possible that the full pattern of posttraumatic stress disorder will appear only if the victim has been in mortal fear for a significant period of time. Case report 8 in the appendix illustrates the forensic evaluation of a case of this type.

The most common form of *somatoform disorder* is represented by those cases in which a symptom originally of physical origin, such as pain or impairment of sensory or motor functioning, is prolonged or exaggerated for unconscious psychological reasons. Somatoform psychopathology is commonly rooted in a fear of returning to school. The complex entanglement of physical symptoms, desire for redress, chronic resentment, and litigation stress, characteristic of adult "compensation neurosis," is unusual in children. Somatoform symptoms may be confused with *malingering,* particularly by nonmedical observers. However, a child under the age of twelve is unlikely to be able to sustain a bogus symptom pattern convincingly; even adolescents will have difficulty in doing so.

In distinguishing physical from somatoform disorder, it is important to remember that psychological stress can accentuate or apparently precipitate physical symptoms, that symptoms of physical origin may be presented in an exaggerated or emotionally demanding manner by emotionally labile patients, that the physical symptoms sometimes diminish when the patient is asleep or not being observed, that *belle indifference* is neither universal nor pathognomic in in hysteria, and that physical symptoms do not always follow anatomic or physiologic boundaries.[131] No single feature clinches or excludes somatoform disorder; the clinician must be prepared to elicit, weigh, and summate the entire pattern of positive and negative features. The most difficult diagnostic tasks are encountered when a patient with histrionic personality reacts dramatically to symptoms of basically physical origin, and when there is a perpetuating interplay between parent and child.

Explosive, aggressive behavior has been described as a consequence of physical abuse,[132] and irritability is a recognized component of the post traumatic stress syndrome (*DSM* III-R, 1987). It is possible that an *impulse control disorder* of *intermittent explosive* type could be a sequel of trauma. This disorder is characterized in *DSM*-III-R by discrete episodes of assaultiveness or destructiveness out of proportion to the triggering stress, in the absence of intoxication, psychosis, personality disorder, or conduct disorder. The validity of this diagnostic category is unclear, and no research has clearly associated it with discrete traumatic events. It is likely, however, that the aggressive component of a preexistent behavior or personality disorder (e.g., oppositional deficit disorder, major depressive disorder, conduct disorder, or borderline personality disorder) could be aggravated following trauma. As previously discussed, the determination of the extent to which a long-standing disorder has been aggravated by trauma can be quite difficult; indeed, it is virtually impossible in the absence of objective data elicited before the trauma.

Can psychosis be precipitated by psychological trauma? *DSM*-III-R contains a category, *brief reactive psychosis,* that refers to an episode of brief duration (more than a few hours and less than a month). It follows marked stress and is characterized by emotional turmoil, incoherent thinking, disorganized behavior, and, sometimes, delusions and hallucinations.

A sixteen-year-old youth who had not previously exhibited emotional instability or behavior disorder was taken on a camping trip by a close adult male friend of the family. One night, after both men had consumed a considerable amount of beer, the friend made an explicit homosexual advance to the youth, who repelled him and angrily demanded to be driven home next day. The subsequent twenty-four hours were remembered only vaguely by the youth, as though devoid of emotional content. He recalls going fishing with his friends and wondering whether they were making sly allusions to homosexuality. He also remembers how, on another occasion, he saw two people looking in his direction and laughing.

Unable to tell his parents about the incident because they were entertaining guests, he took his father's rifle, loaded it, put it to his head, and pulled the trigger. The gunblast blew away his nose and most of his maxilla and mandible.

After he recovered from emergency surgery, he required numerous reconstructive operations. He adjusted to his facial disfigurement remarkably well, exhibiting no psychotic symptoms. His parents decided to bring suit against the family friend.

In the following case, an adolescent's psychological disturbance was significantly clouded by numerous psychological problems both before and after the alleged trauma.

A sixteen-year-old boy was the older of two siblings. Shortly before the forensic evaluation, his parents had separated, and his father was charged with embezzlement of funds from the law practice of which he had been a senior partner.

The trauma was alleged to have occurred on a number of occasions when the patient was fourteen to fifteen years of age. A married man who lived next door to the patient's family was accustomed to going on camping trips with the patient and the patient's father. During one of these trips, reportedly, the neighbor seduced the patient, masturbating him to orgasm, and on several subsequent occasions he had homosexual contact with the patient in a garage attached to the patient's house.

Diagnosis was complicated by preexisting psychiatric disorder. Prior to the homosexual experiences, since early primary school, the patient had exhibited a behavior disorder involving hyperactivity, attention deficit, learning problems, and oppositional behavior. Moreover, at the time of the hypothetical trauma he was aware of the deterioration in his parents' marriage; had begun to drink alcohol, smoke marijuana, and take illicit drugs (especially LSD and quaaludes); and had become defiant, rebellious, and disruptive at home and in school.

Ten months before the forensic evaluation, he was admitted to a psychiatric hospital in acute emotional turmoil. Affectively labile, cognitively incoherent, and fearful of attack by delusional pursuers, he complained of auditory hallucinations and exhibited marked flight of ideas and pressure of speech. Initially he was thought to have a drug-induced psychosis, but his thought disorder did not clear quickly. The diagnoses of schizophreniform disorder and bipolar disorder were entertained. Two months after admission, still emotionally labile, explosive, incongruent, and hallucinated, he said that he could hear the neighbor speaking insinuatingly to him and revealed the story of the homosexual seduction. In therapy he was able to discuss his fear of becoming a homosexual. Gradually the psychosis subsided, leaving a resentful youth, by now far behind in school, with borderline personality features.

Clinically, the chief problem was to sort out the contributions of preexisting psychiatric disorder, learning disability, family stress, substance abuse, and homoseuxal seduction to his acute psychosis and residual personality problems. The most that could be said was that the seduction was emotionally traumatic for him, that the trauma was a contributory factor to the acute psychosis, and that the acute psychosis, in turn, had aggravated his preexistent learning problems and vulnerable personality. Ultimately the case was settled out of court.

The final diagnosis in this case was uncertain. The duration of the psychotic episode rules out brief reactive psychosis and is not consistent with substance-induced hallucinosis. However, there is evidence that, in vulnerable (Cluster B) personalities, sexual coercion can precipitate a dissociative hallucinosis.[133]

Can schizophreniform, schizophrenic, or bipolar disorder be precipitated by emotional trauma? Clinical experience suggests it can. Indeed, acuteness and reactivity are regarded as favorable prognostic indicators in schizophrenia. However, it is unclear whether stress causes disorder, whether the behavioral precursors of the disorder expose the individual to increased stress, or whether there is a third causative factor underlying both disorder and exposure to stress.[134] Nevertheless, there is some evidence from controlled studies of an association between stress and neurosis, suicide, depression, and schizophrenia.[135]

It is conceivable that a preexisting academic skills disorder could be aggravated by psychological trauma. Could psychic trauma be the primary cause of a learning disability? It seems unlikely, but Terr (1983) has suggested a possible association between learning inhibition and posttraumatic psychopathology. This question needs further study.

PREEXISTING CONDITION

As discussed earlier in this chapter, the law takes its victims as it finds them, applying the so-called eggshell skull principle. The aggravation of preexistent disorder is as compensable as the precipitation of a new disorder.

The claimant's former psychological adjustment and academic performance can be ascertained from mental health or educational evaluations completed prior to the hypothetical trauma. School progress reports may also contain allusions to behavior and adjustment. If such reports are not obtainable, or if the information they provide is equivocal, the clinician should attempt to interview an unbiased informant, such as a teacher, who has known the child both before and since the trauma.

The clinician will also be required to address the question of whether a normal child of the same developmental age would have suffered psychological damage as a result of the allegedly traumatic event. Recall that the child's action will fail unless this element can be proved.

PRECIPITATION, AGGRAVATION, AND CAUSATION

If there is evidence for psychological disturbance, the clinician will be asked to address the question of its cause. The question of causation has already been discussed in regard to the patterns of disorder consistent with a traumatic etiology.

How does the child remember the event? Is it recalled in detail, or are there significant gaps, errors, or skewing of time perspective? While older children and adolescents are generally quite capable of describing events, children under seven may need toys or drawings to help them tell the story. Did the child feel in danger of dying? If so, for how long did the child feel so vulnerable? Did the victim feel there was anything he or she could do in self-defense or escape, or was the feeling one of helplessness?

The clinician should examine the duration of time between the alleged trauma and the onset or exacerbation of symptoms. The shorter the duration, the more convincing the causation. It should be pointed out, however, that emotional trauma may leave many victims emotionally benumbed, for a time, before symptoms emerge.

Have other stresses affected the family before or since the hypothetical trauma? As mentioned before, the results of the Coddington Life Change Questionnaire could be helpful in this regard. If other stresses have operated, could any or some of them be plausible explanations for the current disorder?

Was the hypothetical trauma the sole precipitant, a major contributing precipitant, or a minor contributing precipitant of the claimant's current disorder, impairment, or disability? On the other hand, was it noncontributory? If there is evidence of a preexisting disorder, was the hypothetical trauma the sole aggravant, a major contributing aggravant, or a minor aggravant of the patient's current disorder? Recall that the law requires the wrongful act to be the "but for" cause of the psychological condition.

PERPETUATION

Analyze the interaction between parents and child in order to explore the possibility that the parents have aggravated or caused the child's symptomatology. Is there evidence for parental mental disorder from the history, examination, and the MMPI? If so, could this have been the cause of, or a major perpetuating factor in, the current problem? Is there evidence for parental involvement that has caused the child to become hypochondriacally preoccupied with symptoms? Is there any evidence that a parent has deliberately indoctrinated the child to present bogus symptoms? Is it possible that the stress of investigation or litigation has precipitated, aggravated, or perpetuated the child's disturbance? Recall that the defendant will attempt to prove that the plaintiff has failed to take reasonable steps to reduce the psychological impact of the accident. To the extent that the plaintiff was able to alleviate his injuries but failed to do so, damages will be diminished.

PROGNOSIS

Given the nature, severity, and duration of the disorder, what are its implications for future adjustment? In most instances, unless a clearly irremediable deficit is present, it will not be possible to predict the future "with reasonable medical certainty." Thus, the clinician will be able to speak only of a range of possibilities.

RECOMMENDED TREATMENT

If the child has a psychosocial disorder, impairment, or disability stemming from or aggravated by the injury, what treatment would you recommend, in what setting should it take place (institution or home), by whom should it be implemented, how long do you predict it would take, and what would you estimate the range of cost would be?

The Forensic Report in Civil Liability Cases

The report of the evaluation can be organized under the following headings:

I. CIRCUMSTANCES OF REFERRAL
Who referred the child? Summarize briefly the circumstances from which the suit was originated.

II. REASON FOR REFERRAL
List the questions posed by the attorney.

III. INFORMED CONSENT
Summarize the information conveyed to the people evaluated in order to ensure that they collaborated voluntarily and knowingly in the evaluation.

IV. DOCUMENTS REVIEWED
List all the important documents to which you had access, with appropriate dates and signatories.

V. REVIEW OF DOCUMENTS
Summarize the contents of relevant documents.

VI. INTERVIEWS CONDUCTED
List all interviews, giving dates and durations.

VII. INTERVIEWS
Describe the significant content of all interviews.

VIII. PSYCHOLOGICAL TESTING
If psychological testing has been performed at your request, list the questions put to the psychologist, summarize the results, and append the full psychological evaluation report to your report.

IX. DISCUSSION
Organize your discussion of the findings around the clinical questions described on pp. 207–209.

X. CONCLUSIONS AND RECOMMENDATIONS
Answer the questions posed by the attorney, indicating when you can do so "with reasonable medical certainty" and when you cannot. What is the prognosis of the disorder, if one is present? Finally, provide recommendations concerning the type, probable duration, and probable cost of the therapy or remedial education required to restore the patient to health or to make good any educational deficit.

XI. APPENDIX
Append the psychological test report and other relevant documents.

CHAPTER 8

MALPRACTICE

A PROFILE OF MEDICAL MALPRACTICE

Two waves of liability have hit the medical profession.[1] In the mid-1970s the number of claims mounted and damages awards grew exponentially, precipitating a crisis in the cost and availability of liability insurance.[2] Again, in the mid-1980s, the profession felt the impact of a rising number of claims and an exacerbation of damage payouts. In consequence, medical malpractice law was catapulted from relative obscurity to the forefront of social and political debate. Total expenditures on liability insurance increased from about $60 million in 1960 to more than $7 billion in 1988.[3] Accusatory fingers were pointed at a legal system driven by rapacious lawyers, at insurance companies intent on gouging physicians, and at physicians and hospitals for shoddy professional work. More recently, sober research has begun to delve into the nature of medical malpractice and to suggest reforms.[4]

The impact of legal liability is measured by the interplay between two factors: claim frequency and claim severity. Claim frequency is defined by the number of tort claims per 100 physicians. These have risen from about 1:100 physicians in 1960 to a high of 17:100 in the mid-1980s.[5] It has been estimated that about one physician in twenty-five is sued every year. Claim severity is ascertained by the average compensation awarded by juries or agreed to in settlements. Figure 8–1 shows the increase in severity. Insurance premiums paid by physicians reflect the increases in both claim frequency and severity (see Figure 8–2). Table 8–1 presents median premiums. Premiums can be risk-rated according to specialty. In Figure 8–3 median and mean premiums are set forth for some specialties, including psychiatry. As is well known, certain areas of the country are prone to high insurance rates (see Table 8–2).

Medical malpractice claims produce higher awards than other forms of liability but are relatively more difficult to win, as illustrated in Table 8–3.

Psychiatrists have avoided the worst of medical malpractice litigation. The following factors, however, indicate that their relative tranquility may soon be disturbed:

1. The courts have shown a willingness to accord greater protection for psychic injury, thus acquainting attorneys and judges with psychiatric illness and practice.
2. The courts have begun to address the relational and fiduciary nature of the clinician–patient relationship as a basis for liability.

Figure 8–1. Severity

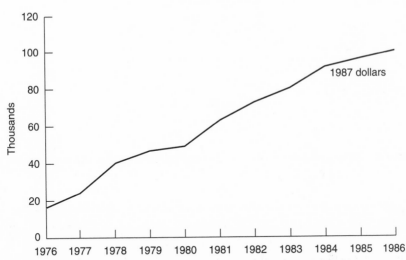

Based on claims-made coverage, Urban Institute, a Vanderbilt University, nationwide survey.

Figure 8–2. National Malpractice Insurance Premiums

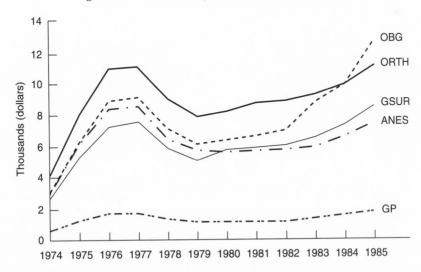

Note: 1987 dollars
Unpublished data from annual HCFA survey, analyzed by authors.

Source: James S. Kakilik and Nicholas M. Pace, *Costs and Compensation Paid in Tort Litigation* (Santa Monica, CA: Rand Corporation, 1986).

Table 8–1. Real Median Malpractice Premiums (1990 $)

1985	$ 8,445
1986	$ 9,964
1987	$11,335
1988	$11,160
1989	$11,307
1990	$10,400
Percent of gross revenue, 1990: 3.7%	

Source: Medical Economics, November 4, 1991, p. 145.

3. The courts have extended liability to protect from harm not only patients or clients but others ("third parties") who may be injured by patients' actions.

The intimate nature of their relationship with patients makes psychiatrists and other mental health professionals particularly vulnerable. However, the style of psychiatric practice makes it unlikely that exposure will approach that pertaining to such high-risk physicians as obstetricians or neurosurgeons. The greater the reliance on technology, the greater the risk. Technology reduces the danger of treatment and enhances its success, but its failure will more readily entail liability. In the absence of technology, the physician must exercise discretion, which is less likely to be regarded in law

Figure 8–3. Median and Mean Premiums Per Medical Specialty (1990 $)

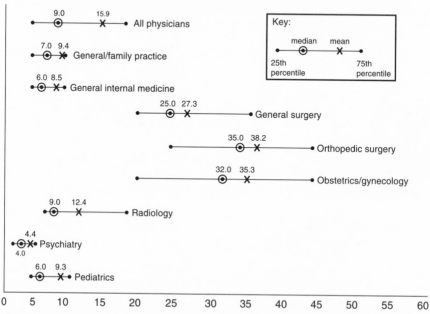

Source: AMA Center for Health Policy, *Physician Marketplace Statistics* (Chicago, American Medical Association), 1990, p. 58.

Table 8–2. Median Medical Malpractice Premiums in Populous States, 1990

State	Median	Percent of Gross Revenue
California	$10,000	3.3
Florida	$11,610	4.7
Illinois	$14,000	4.8
New Jersey	$11,860	4.4
New York	$13,000	5.1
Ohio	$ 8,800	2.9
Pennsylvania	$ 8,800	4.2
Texas	$ 9,670	3.0
All U.S.	$10,400	3.7

Source: Medical Economics, February 3, 1992, p. 49.

as negligent.[6] Within psychiatric practice, there is greater risk of liability in the administration of electroconvulsive therapy than there is with psychotherapy, unless the patient is thereby placed in unsafe confinement or outraged.[7] In formal terms, the defendant can often rely on the defense of error of judgment, asserting that the clinical decision was made following competent consideration of all relevant factors.[8] The courts defer to professional judgment but condemn mechanical error. Also retarding the growth of psychiatric malpractice is the maintenance of an intimate, long-term relationship with the patient, now lost in many areas of episodic, specialized medical care (and accounting, to some degree, for the rise of litigation).[9] It is no coincidence

Table 8–3. Expected Awards at Verdict

	Relative Award		Relative Probability of Plaintiff Winning		Relative Expected Award	
	NC	C	NC	C	NC	C
Auto liability	0.10	0.35	1.74	1.94	0.17	0.68
Product liability	1.00	0.81	1.26	1.33	1.26	1.08
Government	0.36	0.70	1.28	1.45	0.46	1.02
Medical malpractice	1.00	1.00	1.00	1.00	1.00	1.00
Predicted probability of plaintiff winning in medical malpractice cases			0.35	0.33		

Key: NC indicates the regression did not include other case characteristics. C indicates the regression includes other case characteristics.
Source: R. Bovbjerg, F. Sloan, A. Dor, and C. R. Hsieh, "Juries and Justice: Are Malpractice and Other Personal Injuries Created Equal?" *Law and Contemporary Problems,* 54, no. 1 (Winter 1991): 5–42.

that a large segment of psychiatric malpractice comprises cases of sexual exploitation wherein the relationship between clinician and patient has been poisoned.

In this chapter we do not attempt to analyze the liability of persons and institutions under §1983 of the Civil Rights Act (42 U.S.C.). Note, however, that if the person or institution acting under color of state law denies the plaintiff constitutional rights, liability will follow.[10]

THE DOCTOR–PATIENT RELATIONSHIP

Once a doctor–patient relationship is established, it will generate a phalanx of legal obligations:

1. A duty to render reasonably competent medical care
2. A duty to obtain informed consent
3. A duty to keep confidential information generated within, and for the purpose of, that relationship
4. A duty to protect others who may be injured by the patient, where the relationship bestows potential control by the physician over the patient's risk-producing behavior

The Initiation of the Contract

It is crucial to determine if and when a contractual relationship has been established. In most instances this is apparent: The patient has consulted a physician who has agreed to render services for a fee. However, payment is not necessary;[11] gratuitous services will attract a duty. Even though the standard of care may reflect their gratuitous quality, the courts usually construe the relationship to impose the duties described above. On the other hand, only rarely will they find that the physician was obliged to provide a particular result.[12] First-year law students study the case of the promised result of a "nose job" as an example of this odd breed of cases.[13] Putting this category aside, courts are usually indifferent about classifications permitting medical malpractice actions to be brought in tort (negligence, etc.) or for breach of contract (breach of implied warranty).[14]

More contentious is the point at which a relationship begins. The onset is usually denoted by a voluntary assumption of responsibility.[15] However, assumption of responsibility will sometimes be tenuous. In *O'Neill v. Motefiore Hospital,* it was held that a jury might find a relationship based upon a telephone call that arranged a subsequent appointment.[16] In another case, presence at the threshold of the waiting room sufficed.[17] Federal legislation (COBRA), which was designed to combat the dumping of patients by hospitals, imposes obligations on hospital staff to render medical care to emergency patients.[18]

The Termination of the Contract

Once the relationship ends, the physician owes no further obligation to render treatment. Obligations of confidentiality will, however, continue. The actual termination of the relationship can be problematical. Physicians who act unilaterally and without cause to end a relationship hazard liability for *abandonment,* a tort that does not require support by expert evidence. Abandonment may also be found if the physician uses poor judgment or does not diligently attend the patient. The issue, then, is whether the physician has supplied a reasonable standard of care. It will be reasonable care, rather than intentional abandonment, that demands expert evidence.

If the patient considers that the relationship is continuing, the physician must notify him of an intention to bring the relationship to an end and must ensure that necessary arrangements are made for alternative care. The mental health professional should be alive to this requirement and exercise great care if the patient is dependent on him for continuing care. A patient cannot be abandoned solely for the reason that he no longer has means of payment. Alternatives must be explored.[19] However, a therapist is not required to work for free.[20]

A particular concern in psychiatric practice is the obligation not to treat a patient beyond the point of benefit: Treatment is a paltry substitute for living.[21] But the patient may resist termination; failure to refer to another clinician in such circumstances may constitute negligence. Part of the therapist's duty of informed consent is the duty to apprise the patient of alternative therapies, including suspension of an ongoing regimen.[22]

The Responsibility of the Consultant

Clinicians often examine patients on behalf of a third party, such as a government agency. Clearly, consultants owe a contractual duty to the party employing them. However, negligence in the examination may cause the examinee physical, emotional, or economic harm. For instance, the clinician may fail to diagnose a serious psychological condition, causing the patient to suffer continuing harm. Some courts answer this claim by holding that, since his duty was solely to the employer, the clinician assumed no responsibility toward the claimant.[23] Other courts, however, have found that a duty subsisted when a condition should have been diagnosed.[24] In principle, the duty may be owed if the person being examined reasonably relied upon the examination to uncover a psychological condition. If it is known that the examination is for a limited purpose (e.g., to prepare expert testimony on a specific issue), no duty is owed. In some instances, if a duty would interfere with the proper functioning of courts or government agencies, immunity may be bestowed.[25] In *Howard v. Drapkin,* the defendant psychologist was asked, in the context of a custody dispute, to evaluate claims of sexual abuse against the child's father. The mother brought an action against the psychologist for negligent and intentional emotional distress and professional negligence. The appellate court found that the psychologist was immune from liability since the evaluation was conducted in a judicial setting in order to aid in the settlement of litigation.[26] In a similar case, the court relied upon the lack of physician–patient relationship between the father and physician, and the public policy of airing child abuse, to find that the physician owed no duty to the father for negligent misdiagnosis of child abuse.[27]

In terms of practical advice, the mental health clinician should apprise the examinee of the nontherapeutic nature of the examination, thus destroying the basis for reliance. At the same time, the examinee must authorize the clinician to disclose to the employer information gathered in the course of his examination.[28] If the clinician should examine and prepare reports for forensic purposes, he should seek advice concerning his immunity.

A negligent clinician may cause an examinee economic harm if the examination is the basis for denying the examinee due benefits, employment, or insurance coverage. The courts are divided on this issue.[29] In some circumstances, the examinee may sue the employer of the examining clinician, but this would usually require that there had been a contract between them. Since the loss is economic in nature, the courts will usually require both a close finding of assumption of responsibility and a high likelihood of economic loss.

The establishment of the doctor–patient relationship generates four kinds of duty. We shall now address these duties in more detail within the context of clinical practice.

The Duty to Render Reasonably Competent Care

This duty is implied in all clinician–patient relationships. The courts are reluctant to uphold agreements to the contrary. They have found that such a relationship is "affected by the public interest" and that contractual freedom must be circumscribed if the patient is to be protected.[30]

The duty obliges professionals to perform their tasks with the skill and care of the ordinary competent practitioner.[31] Medical practitioners are required to perform to the level of the reasonable specialist.[32]

In one notorious case, the Washington State Supreme Court held that ophthalmologists who had complied with the professionally accepted practice would nevertheless be held liable as a matter of law for failing to apply a simple, straightforward test that would have revealed the plaintiff's serious eye condition.[33] The decision has been severely criticized, and the courts have reemphasized their usual deference to professionally established standards.[34] The standard of care in mental health is complicated by its competing conceptual models. These models entail different treatment regimens, as in the well-known case *Osheroff v. Chestnut Lodge* (1982), where the arbitration panel had the formidable task of comparing the efficacy of psychotherapy with that of psychopharmacology. The courts take account of the varying and developing paradigms of practice by determining that due care has been taken and reasonable skill applied if, in the exercise of professional judgment, the treatment or procedure has conformed with that accepted by reputable, respectable, and reasonable experts.[35] It follows that "a physician does not incur liability merely by electing to pursue one of several recognized courses of treatment."[36]

The standard of care is established by professional practice and therefore requires expert evidence (see Chapter 11). In the United States, the courts have accepted the "community" or "locality" rule, [37] requiring that the physician be judged by the professional standard in his own locality.[38] This rule implies that expert evidence should be garnered from that locality.[39] However, this rule often frustrated legitimate claims, because plaintiffs could not get experts. Further, the rule was inconsistent with the emergence of national standards.[40] Many courts have accepted a national standard tempered by the availability of resources in disadvantaged areas.[41] Some state legislatures have retained the locality test or variants of it, and some scholars have questioned the desirability of a monolithic standard,[42] citing its inconsistency with the actual diversity of practice across the country.[43]

The question of whether a clinician has breached the duty is judged by the standard of knowledge at the time the breach took place. Clinicians are required to stay abreast of developments.[44] A licensed or certified clinician is held to the appropriate professional standard in accordance with the patient's expectation that competent care will be rendered. The courts are loath to find contributory negligence or assumption of risk in these circumstances.[45]

In some circumstances, expert evidence will not be necessary. The prime example is sexual contact with patients. This is unarguably negligent, if not outrageous. However, even in cases involving sexual exploitation, expert evidence will often be presented for the purpose of emphasizing the gross departure from professional standards.[46]

CAUSATION

In order to succeed, the plaintiff must prove that the clinician's breach proximately caused him harm. Many actions will founder on the shoals of this requirement. Consider the following case: Dr. *A* engages in a lengthy course of psychoanalysis with *B*. The treatment is unsuccessful. *B* now argues that his condition in fact demanded drug treatment. Even if *B* can show that Dr. *A* was negligent in not prescribing drugs, he must in addition prove that the drug treatment would have been successful.[47] Similarly, if Dr. *A* misdiagnoses *B*'s psychiatric condition, *B* must prove either (1) that in the absence of the misdiagnosis *B* would have received treatment that would have alleviated his condition, or (2) that he would have acted so as to avoid the harm that befell him.[48] In both instances, the law requires *B* to prove that, on the balance of probabilities, Dr. *A*'s negligence was the cause of the condition or harm that befell him. *B* will fail, therefore, if the evidence shows that the alternative treatment or correct diagnosis would have had a less-than-51-percent chance of alleviating his condition or safeguarding him. Some courts have found liability in such circumstances, but most do not.[49] Without entering into the nuances of this debate, it can be said that the damage caused to *B* may be defined as a *lost chance of success* or *loss of opportunity*.[50] If evidence is available that the misdiagnosis reduced *B*'s chances of alleviating his condition or avoiding harm by an estimable proportion, the proportion may be valued and recovery obtained.[51]

Probabilistic causation, in contrast to the traditional *preponderance* rule, has the potential of increasing clinicians' exposure to liability for malpractice suits based on alternative treatment or misdiagnosis. The probabilistic causation rule is designed both to deter malpractice and to spread compensation to the injured. The rule runs the risk of being overdeterrent, however, if it is applied only to those cases where proof fails to show a greater-than-51 percent chance.[52]

INFORMED CONSENT

The doctrine of informed consent imposes an obligation on medical practitioners to disclose to their patients information pertinent to a proposed procedure, operation, or therapy. Though affecting only a small number of litigated medical malpractice cases, this doctrine is now an important branch of the law, probably because the doctrine erodes the predominance of professional decision-making in establishing liability. We have seen that traditional malpractice liability turns on the failure of the physician to comply with professionally established norms. However, the doctrine of informed consent, which was designed to protect the individual patient's autonomy, bases liability not on *the physician's failure to comply with a professional standard* but rather on *the patient's need for information about a proposed therapy or procedure.*[53]

The former has been described as *the professional rule,* and the latter *the patient rule.* The professional rule incorporates an "inherently paternalistic and authoritarian . . . rule of disclosure" and has encouraged many jurisdictions to reject it. The "patient rule" builds on the "unquestioned principle" of a patient's "'right to exercise control over his or her body by making an informed decision concerning whether to submit to a particular medical procedure." Thus, the clinician has the obligation "to disclose to the patient all material risks involved in the procedure."[54]

This doctrine, which has so strongly emerged in the last thirty years, has venerable antecedents. Individualistic right was asserted in the ancient form of action in *trespass,* where the law's concern was to protect a person's interest in bodily integrity, property and movement (discussed in Chapter 7). The modern law of *battery* requires consent to physical invasion. However, liability for failure to obtain informed consent is grounded today on breach of the physician's *duty of care.* The battery action remains available nevertheless, and may be appropriate if there has been no consent at all.

Consent is stringently demanded when the treatment presents a risk of the vitals of autonomy, for example if the patient was deliberately sterilized after having consented to a different operation,[55] or when the patient is treated as a guinea pig in an experiment. In *Kaimowitz v. Dept. of Mental Health* (1973), the plaintiff, an involuntarily detained mental patient, was scheduled to undergo psychosurgery for aggressive behavior. The erosion of his free will in the coercive institutional environment, and the nature of the operation, was held to preclude free and voluntary consent.[56] Another case, *Mink v. University of Chicago,* further demonstrates the stringency of the informed consent rule. Diethylstilbestrol was administered to the plaintiff and other women during pregnancy. The subjects were not told that they were part of a double blind experiment conducted in order to determine the effectiveness of the drug in preventing miscarriage. Since the resulting injuries (cervicovaginal malignancies) were suffered not by the plaintiff women themselves but by their offspring, a negligence action could not be supported—the gist of a negligence action being damage to the plaintiff. However, a battery action, as pointed out in Chapter 7, requires a finding not of material damage but, rather, of invasion of bodily integrity. Such invasion had occurred; therefore, the plaintiffs were found to have given no consent, for they were ignorant of the experiment to which they had been subjected.[57] If the subject of the experiment is a minor, a very strong presumption rests against a finding of informed consent; even consent by parents or guardians will not be sufficient, unless the treatment is for the minor's benefit.[58]

The strictures surrounding experimentation directly implicate psychological or behavioral research on human subjects. As a result of abuses such as those occurring in the Tuskegee Syphilis Study,[59] among others, human subject research is now closely regulated in order to ensure full and free consent. Congress has created two regulatory mechanisms under the Department of Health and Human Services. The Food and Drug Act of 1938[60] and the National Research Act of 1975[61] empower the Secretary to regulate the protection of human subjects. A number of states have similar regulations covering subject facilities.[62] If the research involves planned deception, the researchers must defer consent, seek a waiver, and inform the subjects' proxy.

The "patient rule"—that is, the disclosure of sufficient information to protect the patient's autonomy—has been the subject of much commentary. Most cases are concerned with disclosure of risk.[63] Disclosure is generated by the patient's need to know, but the *scope* of disclosure requires the detailing of *material risks*.[64] A risk is material "when a reasonable person, in what the physician knows or should know to be the patient's position, would be likely to attach significance to the risks or cluster of risks in deciding whether or not to forgo the proposed therapy."[65] *The risks that should be disclosed are not only those generically linked with the therapy or procedure, but also those related to the physician himself and his capacity to perform the procedure or treatment.* In one case, a surgeon failed to disclose his alcoholism;[66] in another, a surgeon failed to reveal that he had HIV infection.[67] The scope of disclosure is reflected also in the causation requirement. The plaintiff must prove that nondisclosure of material risks caused the condition of which he complains. In order to protect physicians from selective hindsight, some courts have found that the test should turn on whether a reasonable person in the plaintiff's situation would have heeded the disclosure and would not have proceeded.[68] Other courts have insisted that the introduction of the scope of disclosure undermines the gist of the action—the protection of *that* patient's autonomy.[69]

All courts recognize that disclosure is not required in the following circumstances:

1. An emergency in which harm from failure-to-treat is imminent and outweighs the potential danger of the treatment[70] (In these circumstances a relative's consent, if possible, ought to be obtained.)

2. When material risks are either known to the patient or so obvious as to justify the presumption that the patient is aware of them[71]
3. If, by disclosing material risks, the patient's physical or psychological well-being might suffer harm[72]

The third exception—*therapeutic privilege*—is the most vexed. Therapeutic privilege must be carefully circumscribed lest it devour the disclosure rule itself.[73] It is clearly appropriate if the patient would probably become so ill or distraught that rational thought would be impossible, treatment hindered, or psychological damage sustained.[74] Indeed, to disclose information in the face of these hazards may itself constitute malpractice.[75] The physician may not, however, employ the privilege and withhold information merely because he fears the patient would otherwise refuse therapy thought to be desirable.

Therapeutic privilege is particularly troublesome for mental health clinicians, since the consenting patient's capacity to reason may be defective. Indeed, if the psychiatric condition is sufficiently serious, the patient may be found incompetent. In such circumstances, other authorities or the court must exercise informed consent on behalf of the patient. The competent adult cannot be bypassed in this way, however; clinicians must decide how much to disclose, taking into account the possible effect of such disclosure.

An emancipated minor should be accorded the full degree of informed consent. The consent that should be accorded to a mature but unemancipated minor presents issues the law has not resolved. Chapter 3 described how the evolution of case and statute law has afforded minors a greater role in making decisions about their own health care. To be consistent with this, clinicians should consult state law. However, for all patients over thirteen years of age, they should obtain formal informed consent, recognizing the minor's independent decision-making capacity. For example, Illinois statute Ill.—S.H.A. ch 91§ 3-501(a) states:

> Any minor fourteen years of age or older may request and receive counseling services or psychotherapy on an outpatient basis. The consent of the parent, guardian, or person in loco parentis shall not be necessary to authorize outpatient counseling or psychotherapy.

Depending on the nature of the procedure, it may not be necessary (or desirable) to obtain formal parental consent. Again, state legislation on abortion may require parental notification or judicial "bypass." The usual presumption is that the minor has the right to decide, if he or she is sufficiently mature.[76]

A psychotherapeutic relationship is the very type of close interaction that the doctrine of informed consent is designed to foster. Informed consent should entail something more than the pressing of a sterile list of risks upon a passive patient—as it too often does.[77] It is a collaborative endeavor preparing the way for a joint therapeutic venture.[78] However, if the patient's transference can be manipulated so as to ensure compliance with the clinician's agenda, then voluntariness, the essence of informed consent, may be illusive.[79] A psychotherapist, for example, may be reluctant to disclose the risks of treatment for fear that trust will be flawed at the outset.[80] The courts are sensitive to the need for balance and are unlikely to find a failure to disclose unless the therapist has arrogated to himself decisions about the course of therapy. Actually, plaintiffs will have difficulty proving, first, that they would have chosen differently had the risks been disclosed, and, second, that harm resulted from their uninformed choice.

What are the elements of disclosure? The therapist should discuss *alternative therapeutic modalities* and their pros and cons. This requirement has recently occasioned an ideological battleground in the aforementioned *Osheroff v. Chestnut Lodge*. In this case, following seven months of inpatient psychotherapy, a depressed patient was transferred from one hospital to another, where antidepressant medication proved successful.[81]

The *purpose, nature, benefits* and *dangers* of the recommended treatment must be explained.

The *implications of not engaging in the therapy* must be disclosed. This discussion can educate the patient about his capacity for choice.[82]

The therapist ought to communicate to the patient the legally mandated requirement for disclosure to appropriate authorities of what would otherwise be confidential information, and to persons as mandated by the state or for the protection of third persons.[83] In Massachusetts, the licensing provisions for psychologists require this declaration at the outset of a professional consultation.[84]

A psychiatrist cannot withhold information about tardive dyskinesis for fear that it will deter the patient from undertaking neuroleptic therapy.[85] However, mental illness may deprive the patient of the capacity to weigh the pros and cons of therapy. In such a case, therapeutic privilege and discretion call for the stabilization of treatment before disclosing the risk of tardive dyskinesia.

Though case law concerning informed consent has focused on risk description, the *fiduciary nature* of the therapeutic relationship goes beyond risk disclosure and requires that the relationship be one of trust and collaboration. For this reason, in *Moore v. Regents of University of California* the California Supreme Court found that a physician's duty to obtain informed consent was breached when he did not disclose to the plaintiff patient his economic interest in extracting body tissues for the purposes of creating a cell line. The court stated the duty as follows:

> [A] physician who is seeking a patient's consent for a medical procedure must, in order to satisfy his fiduciary duty and to obtain a patient's informed consent, disclose personal interests unrelated to the patient's health, whether research or economic, that may effect his medical judgment.[86]

In this case, the court found that the plaintiff had failed to show that the breach had caused any harm. Legal doctrine is likely to change, however, in the direction of finding that the criterion of causation need not be satisfied if the *fiduciary obligation* has been breached.[87]

State legislation has been enacted in response to the doctrine of informed consent. At the urging of insurers and professional medical organizations, several legislatures (e.g., in Alabama) have replaced the "patient rule" with the "professional rule." The following New York statute accepts the "professional rule" and sets forth other limiting requirements:

1. Lack of informed consent means the failure of the person providing the professional treatment or diagnosis to disclose to the patient such alternatives thereto and the reasonably foreseeable risks and benefits involved as a reasonable medical practitioner under similar circumstances would have disclosed, in a manner permitting the patient to make a knowledgeable evaluation.

2. The right of action to recover for medical malpractice based on a lack of informed consent is limited to those cases involving either (a) nonemergency treatment, procedure or surgery, or (b) a diagnostic procedure which involved invasion or disruption of the integrity of the body.

3. For a cause of action therefor it must also be established that a reasonably prudent person in the patient's position would not have undergone the treatment or diagnosis if he had been fully informed and that the lack of informed consent is a proximate cause of the injury or condition for which recovery is sought.

4. It shall be a defense to any action for medical malpractice based upon an alleged failure to obtain such an informed consent that:
   (a) the risk not disclosed is too commonly known to warrant disclosure; or
   (b) the patient assured the medical practitioner he would undergo the treatment, procedure or diagnosis regardless of the risk involved, or the patient assured the medical practitioner that he did not want to be informed of the matters to which he would be entitled to be informed; or
   (c) consent by or on behalf of the patient was not reasonably possible; or
   (d) the medical practitioner, after considering all of the attendant facts and circumstances, used reasonable discretion as to the manner and extent to which such alternatives or risks were disclosed to the patient because he reasonably believed that the manner and extent of such disclosure could reasonably be expected to adversely and substantially affect the patient's condition.[88]

Informed consent is often obtained via a monotone listing of risks. Although the "mechanical" approach may be decried, mental health professionals concerned about liability understandably turn to it. If certain procedures are inherently risky, the mental health clinician should implement a written consent form, supplemented, if necessary, by verbal advice noted on the patient's file. Figure 8–4 presents an example of an informed consent form designed for minors.

INFORMED CONSENT FOR METHYLPHENIDATE (RITALIN)

Patient's Name: _____ Date: _____
Age: _____

I have discussed the following matters with Dr. _____,
face to face (___) or by telephone (___):

1. Indications (check)

_____ Attention deficit
_____ Overactivity
_____ Impulsivity
_____ Aggressiveness

2. Administration (check)

By tablet (___) in separate doses or by skin patch (___)

3. Anticipated Benefits (check)

_____ Improved concentration
_____ Increased activity
_____ Decreased impulsivity
_____ Decreased aggressiveness or irritability

4. Side Effects (check)

_____ Headache
_____ Drowsiness
_____ Poor appetite
_____ Insomnia
_____ Rebound overactivity
_____ Slower rate of growth (rare)
_____ Abnormal movements (rare)

5. Drug Interactions (check)

_____ Heterocyclic antidepressants
_____ Monoamine oxidase inhibitors
_____ Anticonvulsants
_____ Ephedrine
_____ Pseudoephedrine

6. Alternative Treatments (check)

_____ Behavior modification

7. The Outcome of Providing No Treatment (check)

_____ Growing out of the problem
_____ Continuing problems with learning and
      self-control

After considering the above matters, I consent (___) (assent
(___) to treatment with methylphenidate (ritalin).

Patient's Signature: _____

Date: _____

Parent's Signature: _____

Date: _____

Parent's Signature: _____

Date: _____

Figure 8–4. Sample Informed Consent Form

233

DUTY OF CONFIDENTIALITY

The courts have recognized that confidentiality is the cornerstone of psychotherapy. As one court said:

> Under what circumstances can a person be expected to reveal sexual fantasies, infantile memories, passions of hate and love, one's most intimate relationship with one's spouse and others except upon the inferential agreement that such confessions will be forever entombed in the psychiatrist's memory, never to be revealed during the psychiatrist's lifetime or thereafter? The very needs of the profession itself require that confidentiality exist *and be enforced*.[89]

If a therapist should disclose confidential information, he will be liable to the patient for damages. Two issues are of importance with regard to this duty: (1) What is its source?[90] (2) When may confidential information be disclosed?

Though the courts sometimes confuse the two conceptions, the *duty of confidentiality* should be distinguished from the *right of privacy*. If *A* is in a psychotherapeutic relationship with Dr. *B*, Dr. *B* will breach her duty of confidentiality to *A* if she discloses information to *X*, unless either *A* consents or Dr. *B* is justified in making the disclosure. It cannot be said that Dr. *B* has invaded *A*'s privacy since *A* voluntarily conveyed the information to Dr. *B*. If *X* were to broadcast the information on television, it might be actionable as a breach or invasion of privacy. *A* would then have the burden of proving the outrageousness of the publication, a factor in which may be the way that *X* came by the information. *Humphers v. First Interstate Bank of Oregon* illustrates the distinction between the duty of confidentiality and the right to privacy. As a young woman, the plaintiff had given birth to a baby girl, whom she immediately gave up for adoption. She had been attended by a Dr. Mackey. Twenty-one years later, Dawn Kastning, the adopted daughter, sought to make contact with her natural mother. As the hospital records were sealed, she approached Dr. Mackey, who agreed to help her. Mackey wrote a letter falsely stating that he recalled prescribing DES to the mother. Relying on the letter, the hospital allowed Dawn to copy the records, thus to locate her mother. The mother, Donna Humphers, sued for damages against Mackey, claiming to have suffered emotional distress, embarrassment, and inability to function normally. The court conceded that Humphers had "privacy interest" but held that privacy was not the appropriate cause of action. The doctor "had not pried into a confidence but had failed to keep one."[91] Liability stemmed rather from the duty of confidentiality, an obligation beyond the scope of the general duty of people not to invade each other's privacy.

The duty of confidentiality arises from the relationship. Sometimes the courts have found that the duty is implied in the contract between physician and patient.[92] This is bolstered by the ethical obligations imposed on physicians to maintain confidentiality. Other courts have found the source of the duty neither in contract nor in extrinsic ethical objectives, but rather in the nature of the relationship itself.[93] However the courts may decide the issue, it is plain that the social purpose of confidentiality is to promote the candid revelation of intimate facts during psychotherapy. Assured of confidentiality, the patient will explore matters that are vital to the ends of treatment. It is for this general reason that the Supreme Court found that liability for breach of confidence is not superseded by the First Amendment right of free speech.[94]

DISCLOSURE

Once the duty of confidentiality is established, the following question arises: In what circumstances may private information be disclosed?

Private information may be disclosed if the patient consents to it or if its disclosure is justifiable. A patient has no cause for complaint if he has fully and freely consented to the disclosure. Sometimes the purpose of the examination is the release of information to such third parties as courts, prospective employers, disability agencies, or insurance companies. In these circumstances, the nature of the relationship implies consent, but the prudent clinician will nevertheless obtain written consent to the scope of the disclosure.[95] Within the usual relationship entered into for the purposes of treatment, the courts are loath to accept that the patient has consented unless there is clear evidence he has done so. In *Doe v. Roe,* the complainants, Mr. and Mrs. Doe, had been Roe's patients for many years. Eight years after the termination of the therapeutic relationship, Roe published a book which reported "verbatim and extensively the patients' thoughts, feelings, and emotions, their sexual and other fantasies and biographies, their most intimate personal relationships and the disintegration of their marriage."[96] The defendant argued that the plaintiffs had consented to the publication. The court was quick to reject any such defense, given the potential influence of transference, and pointed to the lack of weight that can be accorded oral consent when patient and therapist are engaged in a course of treatment.

If the patient is a minor, a conflict will arise should the minor and parents differ on the issue of disclosure. A parent, for example, may oppose disclosure if it would tend to incriminate him in the commission of child abuse. Contrariwise, parents may desire disclosure if the information would tend to clear them of child abuse charges. The courts have held that parents may not act in a manner inconsistent with the interests of their children. Thus, even in the face of a statute allowing parents to consent to the release of a minor's treatment records, a guardian *ad litem*'s refusal to do so should be heeded.[97]

The justifications for disclosure are complicated. Information transmitted within the confines of the relationship must be disclosed if state legislation mandates it. For example, statutes may require the reporting of *sexually transmitted diseases*[98] and *reasonable suspicion of child abuse*.[99] Reportable conditions are closely defined in some states, while in others the terms "child abuse" and "neglect" are left for the courts to interpret. Moreover, it is often unclear whether "mental injury" is included in the definition of "abuse," whether the abuse must be current, or whether incidents in the past should be reported. If the therapist is treating a pedophile, for example, must he report incidents that occurred long before? In some jurisdictions it will be necessary to assess the present risk of harm. In Maryland, for example, therapists treating ped-ophiles are required to report only abuse occurring from the time of the commence-ment of treatment.[100] The recipient of the report differs from state to state.[101]

As discussed in Chapter 6, failure to report according to child abuse statutes may involve the therapist in liability for damages to an abused child (e.g., *Landeros v. Flood*).[102] Liability may arise from failure to diagnose that the plaintiff child has been or is being abused, or for not reporting suspected abuse in accordance with the statute. In this case, the professional standard relates to the diagnosis of abuse, whereas the terms of the statute relate to reporting. Liability actions are more likely to succeed if there has been a failure to report.[103]

Courtroom testimony may also mandate disclosure. Information disclosed within the doctor–patient relationship generally enjoys no special privilege when evidence is being adduced. Indeed, refusal to testify may put the witness in contempt of court.[104] Some statutes, however, bestow testimonial privilege. Accordingly, confidential in-formation may not be disclosed in those states without the consent of the patient. Note that *testimonial privilege adheres to the patient, not the therapist*. A number of states provide expressly for testimonial privilege with regard to information generated in the psychotherapist–patient relationship.[105]

Testimonial privilege is narrowly construed, because it undermines the imperative that the court should have access to the fullest information.[106] Hence, a patient claim-ing privilege must actively assert the right lest he be taken to have waived the right to claim it.[107] The courts may find that information must be disclosed when the rela-tionship has been established at the behest of a state agency for the purposes of eval-uating child protection, adoption, and related matters.[108] For testimonial privilege to apply, the patient must have voluntarily consulted the clinician, since it is only in this circumstance that the privilege will be relevant to the social purpose of encouraging free discussion within a therapeutic relationship. However, testimonial privilege must yield to compelling state interests, for example, when disclosure would throw light on child abuse.[109] Indeed, some state child abuse statutes specifically carve out an ex-ception to testimonial privilege.[110] The same imperative to ascertain true facts requires testimony by people ancillary to the clinician who have been entrusted by the clini-cian with confidential information.[111]

Departing from statutory regimes, the common law may impose the duty to pro-tect a third party, discharged, for example, by the issuance of a warning to that party and the reporting of the danger to law enforcement officials. The well-known *Taras-off* decision (see next section) imposes a duty to protect in circumstances where the psychiatrist should reasonably know that a patient poses a danger to an identified third person, for example, a threatened spouse.[112] Some decisions cast the duty more broadly. In these circumstances, disclosures of information is justified.[113]

In the notorious *Menendez* case, one of two brothers accused of murdering his par-ents had disclosed his guilt to his psychotherapist. The court found that this informa-tion could be discovered because the psychotherapist had justifiably disclosed the information to his own wife and his paramour, fearing that their lives could be en-dangered by the aggressive brother. Since it was via this indirect route that the information had fallen into the hands of the prosecution, there was no impediment to its production in court.[114]

A mental health clinician is not subject to an action for invasion of privacy if he discloses an imminent danger to the patient and others and divulges confidences to the patient's employer.[115]

Disclosure may sometimes be justified when there is no duty to an endangered third person. Dr. *A*, while treating *B* for psychological problems, discovers that Dr. *C*, when previously treating *B*, engaged in sexual relations with *B*. May Dr. *A* disclose this information? Arguably, Dr. *A* owes no duty of care to Dr. *C*'s patients, but he does have an ethical obligation to report the improper behavior to the appropriate state licensure authority.[116] The justifiability of such a disclosure is firmly established in those states where the legislatures have made actionable the sexual exploitation of patients.[117]

An issue of some difficulty is raised in respect of minors. We have previously noted the growing recognition of the independent capacity of minors to consent to health care (see Chapter 3). The requirement for parental consent has therefore been weakened with respect to "mature" minors. That being so, would a clinician breach the duty of confidentiality by reporting a minor's consultation to his parents? In the case of an emancipated minor, unless consent for parental reporting were obtained, such disclosure would be a breach of confidentiality.[118] If the minor is unemancipated but mature, the situation is unclear. Since impecuniosity precludes many minors from independently seeking medical care, the problem has not been the center of judicial attention. However, it remains a crucial issue for physicians who must steer between the Scylla of parental consent and the Charybdis of the patient's right to confidentiality.[119] It is certain that parental consent does not predominate when the parent is accused of child abuse.[120] More generally, however, confidentiality should be respected if disclosure to parents would deter the minor from seeking appropriate care.[121] The right to control disclosure of medical information is coextensive with the ability to consent to medical treatment.[122] In many states, with the lowering of the age of medical consent from the age of majority to fourteen or fifteen years, many unemancipated adolescents have been enabled to make their own decisions about disclosure.[123] The American Psychiatric Association has recommended that minors over twelve be protected by confidentiality requirements.[124]

ENDANGERED THIRD PARTIES

As already described, the establishment of a clinician–patient relationship generates a set of duties by the clinician toward the patient. But in a way hitherto unanticipated, that relationship also imposes a duty of care toward third parties. In recent years the law has begun to obligate clinicians to take affirmative steps to protect others from harm. If Dr. *A* prescribes for *B* a drug that has a soporific effect but fails to warn him against driving a car, Dr. *A* will be liable if *B* sustains injuries in an accident after falling asleep at the wheel. If *C*, a pedestrian, is run down by the drowsy *B*, the courts will often find Dr. *A* liable to *C*.[125] The extension of the third-party duty to *C* relies on the reasoning that the failure to warn *B* against driving foreseeably endangers pedestrians.

Liability may also stem from a psychiatrist's failure to keep a disturbed patient confined when the latter's pharmacotherapy poses risks to others.[126] In an Oregon case, *Cain v. Rijken,* the deceased was killed in an automobile accident caused by the negligence of a man who was under the care and jurisdiction of the Oregon Psychiatric Security Review Board (PSRB) after he had been found not guilty for a crime by reason of insanity.[127] Still suffering from mental illness and affected by medication, the patient (who had been allowed leave from the hospital) speeded through an intersection, killing two pedestrians. The Oregon Supreme Court held that the PSRB had a duty toward parties reasonably endangered by patients within the board's jurisdiction. A psychiatrist owed a duty of care to protect third parties from the violent acts of his patient who, while involuntarily committed for violent and suicidal behavior, was not adequately supervised, and after escaping committed a violent crime.[128]

The extension of the duty of care becomes more contentious when a clinician must breach the duty of confidentiality in order to guard third parties against harm. For example, a physician who finds that a patient is HIV positive may have a duty to warn the patient's sexual partners if the patient should refuse to cooperate in communicating the danger.[129] This type of duty parallels the ethical duty to act to protect others who might be infected by patients with transmissible disease.[130] State legislation may modify the legal duty, as in California, where there is no duty to disclose; however, disclosure to a specified set of people is encouraged by granting the physician immunity.[131]

Even more contentious is the duty imposed under the holding of the California Supreme Court in *Tarasoff v. Regents of the University of California.* In this case, Prosenjit Poddar had been an outpatient under the care of Drs. Gold and Moore at a hospital administered by the University of California. Poddar shot and repeatedly stabbed Tatiana Tarasoff, killing her. The wrongful death action brought by Tatiana's parents accepted as fact that Gold and Moore had made a decision that Poddar should be committed for observation in a mental hospital. Dr. Moore had orally notified campus police that he would request commitment, and later followed this with a written request. After interviewing Poddar, the campus police released him because he appeared rational and promised to stay away from Tatiana. The plaintiff's parents asserted that the clinicians and police owed their daughter a duty of reasonable care either to warn them and her of the danger posed by Poddar, or to confine Poddar.[132] It was accepted for the purposes of the appeal that the clinicians had known of Poddar's threats and should reasonably have predicted the danger he posed to Tatiana.

When the appeal (*Tarasoff I*) was first heard, the California Supreme Court held that the clinicians owed a duty to warn the Tarasoffs but that, under California statute, they were immune from liability for failure to confine Poddar.[133] Similarly, the campus police were immune. The American Psychiatric Association and other mental health organizations sought to intervene to have the case reheard. The court acceded and, in *Tarasoff II*, handed down a decision that, in terms of underlying rationale, mirrored its decision in *Tarasoff I*. However, the court widened its scope in enunciating the duty owed by therapists in these circumstances. The *duty to warn* was subsumed in a wider *duty to protect* Tatiana from the danger Poddar posed. While this version of the duty was simply a generalization of the duty described in *Tarasoff I*, the mental health community was concerned with its portents. What protective measures would suffice?

Tarasoff is a momentous decision for tort jurisprudence. It imposes a positive duty to protect another despite the weight of the obligation of confidentiality. The court stated the duty thus:

> Once a therapist does in fact determine, or under applicable professional standards reasonably should have determined, that a patient poses a serious danger of violence to others, he bears a duty to exercise reasonable care to protect the foreseeable victim of that danger.[134]

This will translate to a duty to warn, even though confidentiality must be breached. The extent to which the therapeutic relationship might be impaired was outweighed by the costs to victims of violence should warnings not be given. The public interest in containing violence pointed to a duty to warn.

Tarasoff has generated a legion of academic commentaries. It has excited courts to cogitate upon its limits,[135] and prompted legislatures to define the limits of the duty to protect third parties. In *Tarasoff*, the duty was owed to an *identified victim*.[136] When the threat is not pointed but general, some courts have refused to apply *Tarasoff*. In *Thompson v. County of Alameda*, James, a juvenile offender, was released into his mother's custody even though it was known that he had a history of violence and had indicated that, if released, he would take the life of a young child in the neighborhood. Within twenty-four hours, he had carried out his threat, killing the plaintiff's son.[137] The court agreed with the trial court that no duty of care obtained in these circumstances. The extent of warning, with its negation of the rehabilitative regimes, and its probable ineffectuality as a guard against violence, convinced the majority of the court to distinguish this case from *Tarasoff*.[138]

However, not all courts have limited the duty.[139] Steps beyond warning may be necessary—for example, confinement.[140] A wide duty is cast if the clinician should open the way for a patient to commit violent crimes. In *Lundgren v. Fultz*, Fultz, a paranoid schizophrenic, was obsessed with guns. He was treated as an inpatient by Dr. Cline and eventually released from hospital. After Fultz had brandished guns at a student demonstration, the police confiscated his weapons and referred him back to Cline. Fultz asked the police to return his guns after treatment was completed. The police refused to do so unless Cline would give them a letter that Fultz was cured. Cline duly reported that Fultz had recovered, and the guns were returned. Three weeks later, Fultz entered a restaurant near the university and shot and killed a random victim, Ruth Lundgren. The court found that a duty to prevent the return of the guns should be imposed since the risk of violence outweighed any claim for professional discretion in treatment. To block return of the weapons would have been a direct and effective means of avoiding the violent result. In contrast, it was stated, warnings are problematical, for they add to "the stigma of mental illness while contributing little to public protection."[141]

The duty has been taken to its limit in cases of violence against persons. The courts have found that public interest in the integrity of the therapeutic relationship takes precedence when the threat is to the patient himself or to property. In *Bellah v. Greenson,* the court found that *Tarasoff* should not apply when a psychiatrist had failed to warn a patient's parents that she had suicidal propensities and was running risks by consorting with heroin addicts.[142]

Tarasoff and its progeny have occasioned bitter debate. The court in *Tarasoff* anticipated criticism by addressing the issue of whether a psychotherapist was under a duty to *predict* dangerousness. In *Tarasoff,* prediction was not disputed, because the court decided the appeal on a point of law, thus assuming that the defendant clinicians had predicted Poddar's dangerousness. The defendants could have argued that a reasonable clinician could not have predicted that Poddar would carry out his threats even though he was sufficiently dangerous to justify the consideration of commitment. Nevertheless, the issue of predictability is opened in such cases, and there is concern that the courts, not conversant with psychiatric practice, might too readily assume that violence can be accurately predicted.[143] Clinicians, however, have rarely been held liable merely for failing to predict violence.[144] The standard for prediction is gauged by expert evidence. Principled, detailed, and documented consideration concerning dangerousness will aid in showing compliance with the professional standard.[145] Nevertheless, clinicians continue to be confused about the limits of *Tarasoff.* The balancing of confidentiality against the protection of the public is a heavy burden, at a time of subtle and fluctuating legal doctrine.[146]

In an effort to clarify and limit the *Tarasoff* doctrine, twelve state legislatures have enacted legislation following a model law propounded by the American Psychiatric Association's Council on Psychiatry and Law.[147] California legislation, for example, provides that therapists are immune from liability to warn "except where the patient has communicated to the psychotherapist a serious threat of physical violence against a reasonably identifiable victim or victims."[148] The act goes on to prescribe the means by which the duty to warn may be discharged.[149]

While legislation provides some comfort, there is still room for uncertainty. For example, the California legislation addresses itself to a duty to warn.[150] However, the duty to protect third parties may go beyond issuing a warning and open questions as to the class of persons to whom the duty is owed. In fact, the number of cases involving *negligent release or discharge* exceed those involving the *duty to warn.*[151] Only those who can gain therapeutic benefit should be hospitalized.[152] If therapeutic benefit is unlikely, steps short of hospitalization (e.g., warnings to the police) will discharge the clinician's duty of care.

The following practical steps may reduce liability exposure:

1. If the patient is already hospitalized voluntarily, consider whether civil commitment is required. Take precautions against elopement, consider limiting visitation

and leave, and do not discharge the patient unless you are convinced that the risk of violence has diminished. If in doubt, ask for a consultation.

2. If a potentially violent hospitalized patient elopes or fails to return from leave, seek consultation from a colleague and from the hospital's attorney. If the risk of harm is significant, inform the local police and the police department of the place where the patient lives, by telephone and certified letter. If there are people (e.g., family, friends, or acquaintances) who could be in danger, warn them (a) by telephone, (b) through the police, or (c) by certified letter.

3. If you warn a third party by telephone or letter, take care to divulge only as much information as necessary to let them know they are at risk. For example:

"In the course of my professional duties, it has come to my attention that John Smith has feelings of anger towards you, and that he has made threats to harm you. On (date), John Smith eloped from this hospital and is at large in the community. I have informed the police at_____."

4. If the patient is an outpatient, attempt to deal with the problem in therapy. Seek consultation from a colleague and consult your attorney. If you regard the risk of violence as serious, consider hospitalizing the patient on a voluntary basis or after emergency commitment. Recall the necessity that therapeutic benefit could result from hospitalization. Consider whether close observation at home is preferable to hospitalization. Document the rationale for your final decision.

5. If the risk is serious but hospitalization not feasible, inform the police and the endangered third party by telephone and certified letter. Let the patient know that it is your professional and legal duty to do so. Try to enlist the patient's cooperation by allying yourself with his or her ego controls. If it is possible, let the patient be present when you telephone the police and the third party, and allow him or her to read the contents of the letters sent to the endangered third party and the police.

SEXUAL RELATIONS WITH PATIENTS

It has been stated that at least 15 percent of malpractice cases relate to sexual activities.[153] A nationwide survey of psychiatrists indicated that 7.1 percent of male respondents and 3.1 percent of female respondents admitted sexual contact with their patients.[154] These statistics may underreport the true prevalence.[155] Awareness is growing that psychiatrists are not the only professionals involved in improper sexual relationships with clients. Some states have specifically legislated a criminal offense for psychotherapists who engage in sexual activity with patients during treatment.[156] The Minnesota and Wisconsin statutes are the most precise in dealing with the problem.

As noted in Chapter 7, liability for sexual relationships may extend beyond the patient to others who are affected.[157] The gravity of ethical and legal censure supports an extension of the duty to third parties such as spouses and children.[158]

The courts have roundly rejected attempts to justify sexual relations with patients.[159] Sometimes it is argued that the sexual relationship arose after the therapeutic relationship. A polling of psychiatrists found that a surprising proportion (27 percent) regarded sex as permissible provided the patient was no longer a patient.[160] However, adjudicated cases are uniform in finding that the cessation of a professional relationship does not open the door to a sexual relationship. Residual transference persuades the courts that sexual relations are below the standard of proper professional behavior.[161] It may be argued that there is no harm in sexual relations, but the courts are aware that profound psychological disturbance can result. Furthermore, a relationship outside the professional sphere points to the therapist's failure to deal with the patient's emotions.[162] Finally, the courts have firmly rejected the defense that the patient consented to the sexual acts.[163]

Sexual misconduct may also result in action by the state's professional and regulatory agencies. Courts have upheld the authority of regulatory bodies to revoke licenses on this basis.[164]

To the weight of professional censure, license revocation, and malpractice liability may be added the doubtful insurance cover for damage awards made on the ground of sexual misconduct. The scope of coverage is primarily determined according to the wording of an insurance policy. Some courts have found that sexual misconduct falls outside the range of activities for which the standard policy provides coverage,[165] an interpretation encouraged by public policy, which condemns the practice.[166] Other courts, employing the usual presumption of coverage, have expected insurers to exclude coverage explicitly, finding that the usual wording of malpractice policies encompasses sexual misconduct.[167] Another interpretation suggests that the insurance policy obliges the insurer to defend the insured (though not necessarily to pay damages if liability should be found).[168] In line with increasing concern about sexual misconduct, many insurance policies have been rewritten to exclude such coverage. However, revisions do not spell the end of the forensic game, since plaintiffs wanting to maximize the chance of coverage (and compensation) will couch their actions in terms of garden variety negligence, instancing sexual misconduct as but one of a number of ways in which the defendant's practice fell below the standard of competence.[169] In such cases, improper sexual contact may be construed as incompetent management of the transference relationship.[170]

ABUSIVE OR OUTRAGEOUS TREATMENT

The clinician–patient relationship carries with it an implied consent by the patient for the application of accepted and usual therapeutic procedures. However, if the clinician uses an unusual therapy, a heavy burden falls upon him to demonstrate that it conforms to accepted norms of professional practice. In *Hammer v. Rosen,* the defendant psychiatrist, Dr. Rosen, had gained a reputation for his dramatic treatment of schizophrenic patients. In order to establish communication, he often had physical contact with patients, with varying degrees of force. Remarking on the "fantastic" nature of the treatment, the appeals court found that the matter should have been submitted to the jury, although the plaintiff had not adduced any evidence that the treatment breached the professional standard of care.[171] Judicial suspicion of treatments that abuse or assault patients is exemplified by *Abraham v. Zaslow.* Dr. Zaslow originated "rage reduction" therapy, a treatment designed to break down resistance by applying extensive physical stimulation to an immobilized patient in order to reduce the repressed compulsion to escape. Although the treatment was originally designed for autistic children, Dr. Zaslow applied it to disturbed adults. With telling effect, Mrs. Abraham testified, "I was tortured including choking, beating, holding and tying me down and sticking fingers in my mouth." The therapy was held to be outrageous malpractice.[172]

These cases exemplify a wider principle: Patients have a right to expect that clinician practice will follow accepted professional norms. Exceptional treatments tantamount to assault, battery, false imprisonment, or invasion of privacy are presumptively unlawful and actionable as intentional torts or negligence.[173] To be justified in applying such a treatment, the clinician must show a punctilious regard for the patient's or guardian's full and informed consent and must be prepared to support the procedure by reference to respected expert opinion.[174]

LIABILITY TO THIRD PARTIES

We have canvassed the major portion of liability to third parties (i.e., those persons not within a clinician–patient relationship). We noted that liability to third parties turns on establishing the existence of a clinician–patient relationship so binding as to allow control over the actions of the patient who injures the third party. Liability then rests on a voluntary undertaking by the clinician toward the patient. The law imposes no obligations in the absence of such an undertaking.

In some circumstances, the law encourages the formation of a beneficial relationship by requiring a lesser standard or, by legislation, bestowing an immunity when a ("good samaritan") physician treats the victim of an accident.[175]

The third party may be a fellow clinician. Clinicians may be appointed to hospital peer review committees concerned with the credentialing of clinicians for staff privileges. An aggrieved applicant may bring a suit against members of the committee. Various actions at common law are available (e.g., conspiracy, interference with business relation, or defamation). Such actions are rarely successful, since the courts usually find that the members of such committees are immune.[176] It is also possible to bring suit under the federal antitrust legislation, an action with some attraction given the statutory mandate of treble damages. However, peer review functions are encouraged under the Health Care Quality Improvement Act,[177] which provides immunity for bona fide peer review.[178] For example, immunity is bestowed upon a psychiatrist who cooperates in providing information to hospital peer review regarding another physician's misconduct.[179]

LIABILITY CONTEXTS

In this section we discuss two contexts—medication and suicide—in which the law is well developed and liability exposure significant. In both contexts, we endeavor to give a thumbnail sketch of the law in order to provide some insight into its complexity and the way it accommodates to changing scientific knowledge and professional norms in the field of child mental health.

Medication

The points in the medication of a patient at which negligence is most likely to occur are as follows:

1. The diagnosis of the psychiatric disorder
2. The adoption of an appropriate rationale for drug therapy
3. The choice of a particular drug to treat the patient's psychiatric disorder
4. Inquiry concerning a past history of excessive therapeutic response, severe side effects, or allergic reaction to the drug in question or to related drugs
5. The search for coexistent medical conditions which would contraindicate the medication in question or indicate the need for caution in its use
6. Obtaining informed consent
7. The administration of an appropriate dose of the drug in question, by an approved route
8. The prescription of drugs in combination, or the addition of a drug or drugs to an existing medication regimen
9. The choice of a drug not approved by the FDA, or the use of a drug in a way, or for a purpose, that deviates from what is recommended in the package insert or *Physician's Desk Reference*
10. Monitoring the therapeutic effect and side effects of the medication
11. Ceasing the medication after a therapeutic effect has been achieved, or maintaining long-term medication at a higher-than-necessary dosage

DIAGNOSTIC ERROR

The physician must distinguish organic disease from functional disorder and, within the latter, differentiate the major psychoses from each other and from other Axis I and II conditions. The physician who admits patients to a psychiatric hospital must be alert for signs that could indicate a toxic condition. In *Hirshberg v. State,* for example, a patient who had taken an overdose of salicylates died after having been hospitalized without adequate physical examination, special investigations, or proper precautions. The hospital was found liable.[180] A source of significant future liability in this category is misdiagnosis of tardive dyskinesia. In *Faigenbaum v. Cohen,* the plaintiff claimed that Dr. Cohen had failed to diagnose dyskinesia, mistaking it for Huntington's chorea. Other psychiatrists also failed to diagnose the condition and the patient's neuroleptic regime was continued. The court awarded damages of more than $1 million for brain damage suffered as a result of the misdiagnosis.[181]

The physician who fails to diagnose the patient accurately (for example, by missing psychosis when it is present or by confusing bipolar disorder with schizophrenia) may found treatment on a false premise and thus be open to a liability suit. However, there have been few actions on these grounds; lawyers are reluctant to pursue such cases in view of reputedly widely varying expert opinion concerning the most appropriate treatment for different psychiatric conditions. As child psychiatry becomes more empirically based, it is likely that such actions will increase in frequency.

FAILURE TO MEDICATE WHEN APPROPRIATE

If medication is an available and efficacious alternative to other forms of treatment, the clinician's duty is to inform the patient and permit the decision to be the patient's own against the background of the clinician's advice (see p. 231). Vying schools of psychiatric practice may make this duty difficult to implement, but the plaintiff's autonomy right imposes the obligation.

INAPPROPRIATE RATIONALE FOR TREATMENT

Psychotropic drugs are sometimes prescribed in order to control inmates in correctional institutions or hospitals for the mentally retarded. These situations warrant close scrutiny; the physician may have been induced to medicate the patient by the urgings of harassed staff rather than the medical needs of the patient, a practice which has been specifically criticized in at least one class action suit and one malpractice case.[182]

CHOICE OF INAPPROPRIATE OR UNAPPROVED DRUG

Malpractice can be found when the physician orders a drug inadequate to treat the patient's disorder (e.g., a benzodiazepam for major depressive disorder) or prescribes a drug for which there are less risky alternatives (e.g., a neuroleptic for anxiety disorder).

A different problem arises when the clinician prescribes a drug that is not approved by the FDA for use by children or, if approved, a drug that is restricted to a monitored trial or to testing protocols (e.g., clozaril in schizophrenia). Undoubtedly the risk of malpractice is greater if approved guidelines have not been followed. The clinician should reserve such medication for cases in which conventional treatment has failed. He should also document a risk-benefit analysis, seek expert consultation, and obtain specific informed consent. The clinician should not prescribe drugs that have not been approved by the FDA unless they are part of an authorized test with monitoring protocols.

FAILURE TO OBTAIN A MEDICATION HISTORY

The patient's medication history should be ascertained by interview, by review of medical records, and by telephone contact, if required, with other clinicians. The physician may be held liable for excessive side effects, allergic reactions, idiosyncratic responses, or drug interactions, if these could have been anticipated after reasonable inquiry.

FAILURE TO DETECT CONTRAINDICATIVE CONDITIONS

The physician may fail to check for conditions or disorders that would render the patient vulnerable to severe side effects. For example, preexisting subthyroidism may be overlooked when lithium is prescribed. Each class of psychotropic drug requires a standard workup involving medical history, physical examination, review of past medical records, and special investigations. If a contraindicative condition is uncovered but the medication is still considered advisable, a risk-benefit analysis should be documented, an expert consultation obtained, and specific informed consent recorded. Hospitals should mandate standard diagnostic workups for all psychotropic drugs.

INAPPROPRIATE DOSAGE OR ROUTE OF ADMINISTRATION

The *Physician's Desk Reference (PDR)* includes the information found in all official drug package inserts, together with manufacturers' information concerning drug products that have no insert. In *Mulder v. Parke Davis & Co.,* the court held that a departure from PDR guidelines represented a *prima facie* case of negligence.[183] The mental health clinician can defend the departure by showing an adequate reason for it.[184] In one case, the package insert was found to be not only good evidence of the standard of care in the prescription of the drug but "*essential* in determining the possible lack of care of a doctor where the issue involved is injury from the administration of a drug."[185] In order to protect themselves from liability claims, drug manufacturers publish information concerning all reported adverse reactions, however rare, and are conservative in the dosages they recommend. In some circumstances, it may be good clinical practice to regard the risk of particular adverse reactions as insignificant or to exceed the recommended dosage. However, before doing so, seek a consultation and locate references in the literature that would support the proposed medication regime.

An intravenous or intramuscular route of administration carries an increased risk or adverse response, particularly if the patient is predisposed to side effects as a result of hepatic, renal, cardiac, or brain dysfunction. The clinician should be cautious if such conditions are detected. Parenteral administration should generally be reserved for emergencies or long-term depot treatment.

POLYPHARMACY

Psychotropic cocktails increase the risk of adverse reactions. They are most likely to be prescribed when psychotic outpatients are slow to respond or in general hospitals and residential centers that have inadequate structure or staffing. On the other hand, drug combinations (e.g., of an antidepressant with a neuroleptic) are sometimes more efficacious than one drug alone.[186] Nevertheless, the clinician should record a risk-benefit analysis before prescribing multiple psychotropics.

FAILURE TO MONITOR TREATMENT

The case of *Clites v. Iowa* illustrates negligent failure to monitor psychotropic med-ication, in addition to a number of other errors.[187] The plaintiff, a mentally retarded patient, was admitted to a state residential facility at the age of eleven. Between the ages of seventeen and twenty-two he was treated with various psychotropic drug com-binations, until tardive dyskinesia was noticed. The appellate court held that the hos-pital had failed to document behavior sufficiently aggressive or self-abusive to warrant neuroleptic treatment; that the medication appeared to be designed primarily for the staff's convenience; that the practice of prescribing polypharmacy was substandard; that the treatment had not been monitored adequately by a physician; that "drug hol-idays" should have been employed; that the staff had been too slow in recognizing the patient's dyskinesia; and that informed consent had not been sought from the pa-tient's parents. Damages of $760,000 were affirmed. The mere development of tar-dive dyskinesia, without the procedural failure occurring in *Clites,* would not form a successful basis for a lawsuit.[188]

Adequate monitoring of drug effects requires baseline and regular mental status examinations, physical examinations, vital signs, and laboratory testing, in accor-dance with the pharmacology of the drug and its potential side effects. "Drug holi-days" should be considered if long-term medication is required. Physicians run a serious risk if they write p.r.n. orders for potent drugs, if they "phone in" prescrip-tions without examining their patients, or if they provide multiple repeat refills.

CAUSATION

In each of the above categories the plaintiff faces the burden of proving that the clini-cian's breach caused his psychiatric deterioration or that some harm would have been avoided if alternative medications or procedures had been adopted. If the plaintiff proves that an alternative medication or therapy would have had a 40 percent chance of avoiding the psychiatric condition, he must fail. As noted above, some authorities now open the possibility of obtaining damages even though it is less probable than not that the alternative medication or therapy would have been successful. While it is not yet the generally accepted rule, some courts will accept the argument that the plaintiff should be compensated for a *lost chance* if evidence can establish it.[189] If the prevailing doctrine does change, it is likely to widen the scope of liability for such breaches.[190]

When a *wrongful death* action is brought against a clinician for the suicide of a patient, specialized causation issues arise. These are discussed in the next section.

Suicide

Liability for suicide accounts for the greatest number of malpractice suits against psychiatrists and the highest percentage of settlements and verdicts paid by insurers.[191] For adolescents, suicide is the third most common cause of death, following accidents and homicide.[192] Attempts vastly outnumber successful suicides (possibly by 25–50 to 1). Youth suicide has received special attention. In the decade 1970–80, 49,496 people fifteen to twenty-four years old committed suicide. Within that decade the suicide rate of young people increased 40 percent, whereas the rate was stable for the remainder of the population. Males were mainly responsible for the increase (50 percent); the female rate increased by only 2 percent.[193]

Actions brought for suicide will usually be on the basis of *wrongful death,* in which relatives bring suit for the negligently caused death of the deceased patient. It has been suggested that the liability should be strict, because the negligence standard has failed to offer the psychiatric patient a viable means of recovery.[194] Sometimes, after a failed suicide, the plaintiff patient will bring an action for injuries sustained in the suicide attempt.

As a general matter, liability requires the plaintiff to show that a competent clinician should have foreseen that the deceased would attempt suicide.[195] Expert evidence is necessary to establish the standard of care[196] and the causal link between the negligence and the suicide.[197] The degree of control that could have been exercised will be critical. If patients are hospitalized, they can be appropriately monitored and the environment made secure. If patients are not hospitalized, control is mitigated, although clinicians must make principled decisions about whether or not to hospitalize. A conversation should be conducted with patients with a view to whether voluntary admission would be appropriate;[198] if suicide signals and symptoms are clear, and if there is imminent danger, the patient may be involuntarily admitted. Recall that involuntary admission will attract the full panoply of constitutional rights discussed in Chapter 10.

A careful, principled consideration of the risks of suicide will go far in providing clinicians with the defense that they exercised their discretion in a proper professional manner and should not be held liable for a mere error of judgment.[199] Failure to document reasons for a transfer to nonsuicidal status risks a finding of negligence.[200] The "Assessment of Suicide Risk" set forth in the Appendix to this Chapter, if followed and documented, may reduce exposure to liability.[201] Plaintiff's counsel will be unable to point to any failure to weigh important pros and cons, and hence will have difficulty in demonstrating a lack of proper professional discretion. In some cases the mental health clinician may not have access to information concerning the risk of suicide. In the absence of a duty to elicit the information himself, he will not be liable, but it is likely that the person who should have supplied the information will be held liable.[202]

Active assistance in a suicide will attract criminal law sanctions prohibiting suicide assistance and homicide.[203] Mental health clinicians are unlikely to face directly the ethical and legal dilemmas of disconnecting life support systems or ceasing to feed persons with terminal illnesses or no chance of recovering higher brain functions, although they may be consulted by persons contemplating seeking the assistance of physicians to aid them in terminating their lives.[204] The conflict at the center of this debate is a familiar one in the interaction of psychiatry and law: individual autonomy and family privacy versus the state's interest in sustaining life.[205] Here, as in other areas, the decision point between these interests will shift from time to time and is difficult to locate.[206] With regard to children on whose behalf life-and-death decisions must be made, it is necessary to take account of their lack of capacity. Accordingly, a child's expressed desires in the event of being reduced to a nonsentient state will not be accorded the same autonomy as in the case of an adult.[207] As *parens patriae,* the state could have reason to intervene. The physician could not safely proceed merely upon instructions from parents or guardians.

In wrongful death actions, the defendant is likely to argue that, in law, the act of the deceased caused the death. If the act is regarded as voluntary, the law will assign responsibility to the deceased rather than the physician.[208] However, if the suicide is the very thing that the clinician should have foreseen, he may be liable.[209] Other precipitating factors will not necessarily insulate the defendant from liability.[210] Similarly, in an action against a hospital based on its failure to prevent a suicide, the court rejected the argument that suicide constituted contributory negligence.[211] The plaintiff's wrongful death action will be enhanced if he can show that the suicide resulted from a psychiatric condition, caused, for example, by medication malpractice, that gave rise to an irresistible self-destructive impulse.[212]

The plaintiff will fail if he is unable to prove that the deceased would not have committed suicide had the clinician applied reasonable care. As in the above cases, liability may be extended if the courts are prepared to relax the traditional preponderance of evidence burden of proof. In *Gaido v. Weiser,* the plaintiff's deceased husband had been under the care of the defendant, Dr. Weiser. The deceased had been hospitalized for a suicidal condition and released when Dr. Weiser undertook to monitor his condition. The plaintiff claimed negligence on the ground that Dr. Weiser had failed to consult with the deceased prior to a scheduled appointment, despite having learned that the patient's psychiatric condition had relapsed. Although the defendant was found negligent, the plaintiff failed to prove that the negligence had caused the suicide.[213] The court, however, offered the opinion that the case could have fitted the "lost chance" theory. This theory would have allowed the plaintiff to recover damages on the basis that, had an earlier appointment been made, there was a chance that the deceased would have survived.

Hospitals are a common target of litigation for suicide. Liability stems from their *vicarious responsibility* for the torts of employees perpetrated in the course of employment. Liability has often been based on the staff's failure to supervise a patient properly,[214] to provide secure physical conditions,[215] or to release a patient from hospital care prematurely.[216] The greater the risk of suicidal behavior, the greater the care required;[217] hence, one-to-one supervision in a closed ward may be indicated.[218] It is generally sufficient for the hospital to adopt safety measures recommended by the attending physician.[219]

Actions against outpatient clinicians will typically arise from alleged failure to diagnose and treat. However, diagnosis involves such specialized professional judgment that courts are reluctant to find liability.[220] Although treatment can be more readily reviewed for adequacy, it too is highly discretionary, requiring the balancing of imponderables.[221] If obvious signals are ignored, liability will readily follow.[222] But since control is attenuated in outpatient practice, a duty to take affirmative steps to prevent suicide is less likely.[223] For example, a mental health facility was not responsible for the suicide of an outpatient from an overdose of Sinequan, when it had not been informed of the deceased's Valium intake or marital discord.[224] Moreover, in the outpatient context, plaintiffs will find it difficult to show that a breach of duty (failure to diagnose or treat) was the cause of the suicide, for it is just as likely that the patient would have committed suicide even if properly diagnosed or treated.[225] The argument may be made that the mental health clinician should have done more to protect the suicidal patient from himself; however, a positive duty to protect is rejected. The mental health clinician's duty may go no further than offering the best advice. To expect clinicians to exercise greater dominion over outpatients would impose intolerable burdens.[226] The issue of control is directly raised if the plaintiff proposes that the patient should have been involuntarily committed.[227] The mental health clinician's duty will be guided, though not determined,[228] by statutes governing the commitment of patients. Often the powers of the clinician are limited, for example, if the patient has opted for voluntary hospitalization.[229] In these circumstances the public policy expressed in the relevant statute overrides professional judgment in setting the standard of care. The duty will be one of inquiring and giving advice,[230] and will extend to advising caregivers of dangers (e.g., warning parents of suicide plans).[231] Failure to commit will result in liability if professional judgment clearly supports hospitalization and the decision not to admit is taken for reasons that ignore the welfare of the patient.[232]

Hospitalization

During the past ten years, there has been an increase in the number of psychiatric beds for children and adolescents, and more child psychiatrists have begun to work in inpatient settings. At the same time, liability issues have been exacerbated by the awareness that hospitals are attractive litigation targets and by a greater recognition that patients have the right to be informed of their rights.[233] Hospitalization presents a number of situations in which the clinician is at risk of liability.

SUBSTANDARD ADMISSION EVALUATION

The physician may fail to admit a suicidal or violent patient who subsequently harms himself or others. Such an error might be actionable if the physician had failed to evaluate the patient adequately (for example, by assessing mental status or reviewing the patient's past history for dangerous behavior). The assessment of suicide or violence risk is set forth in the Appendix to this chapter.

On the other hand, a physician who causes a patient to be admitted to a psychiatric hospital without proper evaluation might be sued for *negligent diagnosis* or *false imprisonment*.

WRONGFUL COMMITMENT

A person wrongfully committed or not released at a stipulated time will have an action for *false imprisonment*. False imprisonment is the direct restraint of liberty of movement without legal justification. The action rests against those restricting his freedom contrary to his will. A patient may leave an institution unless he has been restrained by due process of the law or by authority of parent or guardian. A person with a right to leave was clearly imprisoned when apprehended, brought back, locked and taped in a restraint chair, and denied access to a telephone despite requests to leave. A person inappropriately restrained in a ward for the insane may have a claim for punitive damages.[234]

An initially lawful detention may become unlawful if the institution fails to comply with statutes requiring court authorization. In *Johnson v. Greer* the defendant lawfully took the plaintiff into emergency custody after he had voluntarily sought out the police and complained of hearing voices and music. After twenty-four hours, further detention should have been authorized by court order, but the plaintiff was detained (i.e., falsely imprisoned) without court order for five days.[235]

Liability may also arise for failure to conduct "meaningful hearings" concerning continued commitment. In one case, plaintiff was confined for fifty years without treatment, following an original diagnosis of hebephrenic schizophrenia.[236]

Parents or guardians may admit unemancipated minors against their will, in accordance with the parental duty to protect the life and health of offspring.[237] In applying this law, the Alabama Supreme Court, in *R.J.D. v. Vaughan Clinic,* considered that health care providers should be able to rely on parental consent. An action for false imprisonment usually requires that the person detained be aware of his detention.[238] However, if a person is so drugged as to be unaware of what is happening, false imprisonment may be maintained.[239] Furthermore, false imprisonment is constituted by fraud or trickery, although the threat of divine retribution (made in order to induce a person to stay in a religious commune) implicates the First Amendment and is not actionable. Knowingly to induce another to act to his detriment is separately actionable as *fraudulent misrepresentation* or *deceit*. Thus, to misrepresent a country retreat as a congregation of socially concerned persons rather than an occasion for religious indoctrination would be actionable if the attendees so deceived suffered harm.[240]

A person falsely imprisoned may recover damages for *loss of dignity* and *emotional distress* in addition to injuries sustained as a direct result of the imprisonment.[241]

An action related to false imprisonment is *malicious prosecution.* Such an action is constituted if one person, in spite or bad faith, invokes legal processes to arrest or detain another. A clinician filing an application for involuntary commitment must be free from ulterior motive or bad faith. In *Pendleton v. Burkhalter* the defendant physician filed a lunacy complaint in order to oust the plaintiff's deceased husband from the administration of a hospital. This wrongful act, perpetrated to injure the deceased, constituted malicious prosecution.[242]

Hospitals and staff must be punctilious in checking the basis for commitment. Court orders may be necessary or consent of the patient or parents and guardians carefully noted. Medical admissions with respect to minors should provide for review of the medical or psychiatric justification of the admission. In *R.J.D.,* for example, the dissenting justice of the Alabama Supreme Court was concerned that psychiatric hospitalization had been employed for the purpose of obstructing a minor's romance rather than for legitimate medical or psychiatric reason.

NEGLIGENT DIAGNOSIS

The failure to distinguish organic disease from psychiatric disorder, to differentiate functional psychosis from other psychiatric disorders, or to discriminate between the major psychoses could be actionable if it resulted from inadequate or inept diagnostic investigation and if it could be shown to have caused harm to the patient.

FAILURE TO PROTECT OR CONTROL A SUICIDAL, VIOLENT, OR SEXUALLY AGGRESSIVE PATIENT

Hospitals assume a duty of care toward patients who have a potential for suicide or violence. The psychiatrist must assess the danger competently, ensuring that hospital staff take adequate precautions to prevent a suicidal, violent, or sexually predatory patient from doing harm to himself or others. Past medical records should be scrutinized, and referring agents and parents questioned, concerning suicide potential, violence, or sexually aggressive proclivities. In accordance with the imminence of the risk, housing in a secure unit, confinement to a single room, close observation, a search of clothing and personal effects, and removal of all dangerous objects (e.g., belts, mirrors), may be required. Staff should check that medication is swallowed. It is essential that the degree and nature of risk be clearly communicated to all staff who care for the patient. The importance of careful documentation cannot be overstressed. Timely, clear, legible, pertinent, thorough, dated, timed, and signed records are the key to communication and the best proof that hospital and staff have exercised reasonable care. In *Abille v. United States,* after a psychiatrist reclassified a patient from suicidal to less dangerous, the patient committed suicide. The finding of negligence against the defendant hinged upon the psychiatrist's failure to keep records explaining the decision to reclassify, even though it was conceded that, in the circumstances, his decision might have been reasonable.[243]

What if the patient refuses to cooperate with the admitting psychiatrist, who consequently does not elicit and diagnose imminent suicide risk? In *Skar v. City of Lincoln, Nebraska,* a recalcitrant patient injured himself in a suicide attempt. The court found for the defendant, holding that the patient had a duty to cooperate with his physician as far as he was able.[244] However, it is essential in such a case that the psychiatrist record the questions put to the patient and the patient's responses or failure to respond.

NEGLIGENT RELEASE OR DISCHARGE OF A SUICIDAL OR VIOLENT PATIENT

A patient may harm himself or others while on pass in the grounds of the hospital, on leave with relatives or friends, after discharge, or after absconding from hospital. Was the tragedy foreseeable by a reasonably prudent psychiatrist? That is a question the courts seek to answer. In doing so, they are aware that the safety of the public must be balanced against the need to rehabilitate patients, that reasonable, calculated risks must often be taken, and that bona fide errors of clinical judgment are unavoidable.[245]

Increasing pressure by Health Maintenance Organizations, Medicaid agencies, and other insurers has raised the specter of premature discharge against medical advice forced by withdrawal of funding. The clinician should be aware that legal responsibility for any harm that consequently befalls the patient or community may be placed on his or her shoulders. Hospitals and private clinicians who collaborate with Health Maintenance Organizations would be wise to draw the line. If a third party forces premature discharge against medical advice, the clinician should protest vigorously in the medical record and by telephone and letter to the insurer, rather than allow the patient to go. The risk may be so great that the hospital should bear the cost of continued hospitalization. This matter is further discussed later in this chapter.

FAILURE TO PROTECT SUSCEPTIBLE PATIENTS FROM HARM

A hospital will be liable if it permits a patient to be placed in a situation where he or she may foreseeably be harmed by another. If the person perpetrating the harm is an employee of the hospital, liability may be found on the basis of vicarious liability, or directly, on the ground that the hospital has failed to monitor the conduct of its staff. Liability is clear if the hospital had notice that its employee had a propensity toward harmful conduct or, having learned of the conduct, condones or ratifies it. In *Samuels v. Southern Baptist Hospital,* a hospital was found liable for its employee's sexual assault on a sixteen-year-old psychiatric patient.[246]

The hospital may also be liable even if the patient is harmed by a person not employed by it. For example, a hospital is liable if it allows a physician who is known to have the propensity to harass patients and staff sexually to have access to susceptible patients.[247] A chronically schizophrenic patient of low intelligence who, while hospitalized, becomes pregnant by another patient and who gives birth to a mentally retarded infant may bring an action against the physician and hospital. The court may be prepared to award punitive damages.[248] Indeed, a hospital has been found liable for a sexual assault perpetrated upon a sedated patient by a trespasser.[249] If the hospital or institution is operated by the state, *sovereign immunity* may be asserted, but the defense would probably fail.[250] The defense of sovereign or governmental immunity has a reduced importance in contexts where government provides services that are incidentally governmental, that is, where private enterprise could easily have delivered them without the exercise of governmental discretion.[251] Claims against federal hospitals, such as those administered by the Veterans Administration and its physicians, must be brought within the requirements of federal law, under which the federal government has waived immunity subject to significant exceptions.[252]

FAILURE TO PROTECT ENDANGERED THIRD PARTIES

If a patient absconds from hospital and there is reason to suspect that a third person is placed in jeopardy thereby, it is the psychiatrist's duty to take whatever steps are required in order to protect the community. This duty, which is strongly reinforced in the *Tarasoff* decision, has been discussed earlier in this chapter.

WRONGFUL INJURY

A patient injured by staff who use excessive force while subduing him or her may have a claim against the hospital for battery or wrongful injury. Wrongful injury may also be claimed when one patient is harmed by another whom the staff did not control; however, the plaintiff would have to establish that the hospital was derelict in its duty to control the violent or sexually aggressive patient. We discuss this liability in Chapter 7.

Seclusion and restraint present serious liability risks. They represent legitimate management techniques when the risk of harm is imminent and there are no alternatives, but they should not be used in order to compensate for understaffing. Physical control should be time-limited, and the patient should be examined by a physician if the maximum permissible time (e.g., one hour) requires extension. Seclusion and restraint should never be ordered *p.r.n.* (i.e., as the need arises). Close quality assurance tracking is required in order to flag the excessive use of physical controls.

IMPROPER TREATMENT

Treatment may be administered against the patient's will in an emergency, or if the patient has been adjudicated incompetent. In other circumstances, a mature minor and his or her legal guardian, or the legal guardian alone (in the case of immature minors), must give informed consent to treatment. This matter was discussed in more detail earlier in this chapter. Erroneous choice of treatment, the use of an unapproved treatment, and the failure to monitor side effects were also discussed earlier in this chapter. The hospital is directly liable for a failure to provide supports sufficient to manage the problems that accompany the procedures it offers.[253] Staffing must be adequate, and equipment must be suitable for preferred services.[254]

IMPROPER RELEASE OF INFORMATION FROM MEDICAL RECORDS

The comments to be made in this section are relevant to both hospital and outpatient practice. Traditionally, privilege has applied to all private communications between patient and doctor, including the medical record. However, in recent times the confidentiality of the medical record has been invaded ("polluted") by a number of bodies. Third-party insurers, for example, have access to patients' records in order to ensure that medical costs are legitimate. Nevertheless, the unauthorized disclosure of confidential information from a patient's record could be actionable on the ground of breach of confidentiality. Medical records should be kept in a secure place on the ward or in the medical records department, in order to bar access to unauthorized people. The patient or legal guardian must give written consent for the transfer of information to legitimate professionals or agencies (e.g., other involved clinicians, attorneys, hospitals, schools, social welfare departments, and insurance companies). See the section in this chapter on communication of information for a further discussion of this subject.

DEFAMATION

Defamation involves communication by one party to a second about a third that damages the reputation of the third party. In child psychiatry, defamation is most likely to occur when carelessly written medical records are released. For example, a patient may have been described in the record as a "psychopath" or "malingerer," labels that could be extremely damaging in the hands of employers or creditors. Clinicians who gossip about patients over coffee or in elevators put themselves at risk of liability on the grounds of defamation or breach of confidentiality. Defamation is discussed further later in this chapter.

LIABILITY FOR COMMUNICATION OF INFORMATION

We have already described the duty to maintain confidentiality. We refrained at that point from discussing defamation since, in contrast to confidentiality, the liability associated with defamation does not arise from the clinician–patient relationship but rather is owed to the world at large. A person is liable in defamation if he *publishes a defamatory statement* about another person. A mental health clinician's report, either oral or written, is actionable defamation when it makes reference to somebody in a way that, as an ordinary person would find, traduces his reputation (by holding him up to ridicule, shame, or obliquy) or tends to make people shun him. The term "publication" refers to the communication of words to a third person. Words directed to a patient outside the hearing of anyone else are not actionable; for example, if Dr. *A* in a private consultation with patient *B* calls *B* a "neurotic," Dr. *A* will not be liable for defamation (although abusive language may give cause of an action for *intentional infliction of emotional distress*). If Dr. *A* should write to *B*'s employer describing *B* as a "neurotic," this could be actionable in defamation. Such an action is one of *strict liability,* in the sense that the publisher need not have intended the material to defame any particular person. Indeed, the publisher may have thought that he was writing about a purely fictional character. The plaintiff will have a good action if a reasonable reader could identify him as the person referred to and would regard the material as defamatory. In an illustrative case, a newspaper innocently published a photograph captioning a couple as husband and wife. The real wife had an action based upon the imputation that her acquaintances could conclude she was "living in sin."[255]

Liability may be too stringent, given the requirements of free speech under the First Amendment. In *Gertz v. Robert Welch, Inc.,* the Supreme Court held that the plaintiff must establish the defendant to have been at fault—that is, careless in making the publication—at least when the defamation is of "public concern."[256] Usually, however, a mental health clinician will have published material of purely private concern, in which case the common law operates free of the constraints imposed under the *Gertz* case.[257] It follows that references to characters in fiction may identify people sufficiently to allow them to bring a defamation action. In *Bindrim v. Mitchell,* Dr. Bindrim, a licensed psychologist, employed "nude marathon group therapy" as a means of inducing people to shed their psychological inhibitions. The defendant, Gwen Davis Mitchell, registered for the treatment, telling Bindrim she did so for therapeutic purposes only, after signing an agreement not to disclose information. Later she wrote the novel *Touching,* which depicted the principal character ("Dr. Simon Herford") employing nude marathon therapy. Bindrim brought a defamation action against the author and her publishers. (A suit for breach of confidentiality could also have been brought.) The fictional character "Herford" was portrayed as having an appearance different from that of Bindrim, but a reasonable reader who knew of Bindrim's therapeutic technique could reasonably conclude that Herford and Bindrim were "one and the same."[258]

Interests in communication of information are accommodated by several defenses. For example, *substantial truth* is a good defense. Another defense of significance for the mental health clinician is *qualified or conditional privilege*. If Dr. *A* were to report patient *B* as having "borderline personality disorder" to another psychiatrist, Dr. *C,* to whom *B* has been referred, Dr. *A* would have a good defense of *conditional privilege*. Dr. *A* has a duty and interest to report such matters, and Dr. *C* has a reciprocal duty and interest to receive the report.[259] If, however, Dr. *A* conveys this information to others who have no such duty and interest, the privilege will be lost. If, in making such a report, Dr. *A* has a motive other than to inform Dr. *C*, his action could be construed as malicious.[260]

Similar reasoning obtains when information about patients is communicated in hospital peer review committees. Provided this information is necessary, it will attract conditional privilege. The courts recognize that conditional privilege is required if patient welfare is to be protected "by assuring the free exchange of information during the deliberations of medical review committees."[261] Note that some statutes provide immunity from such suits.[262]

Testimony given in court or in court documents attracts an *absolute privilege*.[263] A letter written by a psychiatrist to an attorney in a child custody case was given absolute privilege when the psychiatrist treated the late wife and children, the subject of the dispute. The letter was directed to the applicant's attorney and written as "a professional child psychiatrist to be used . . . only for the purpose of the Dolan child custody case."[264] No action may be based upon such statements unless they are completely outside the broadly defined subject matter addressed by the court.[265] If the same statements are made outside the court or in documents other than those related to the litigation, they will be actionable.

A common issue is *malice*. If malice is proved by the plaintiff, it will destroy any conditional privilege.[266] Proof of malice may be adduced from evidence of overt self-interest, excess distribution, knowledge of falsity, and reckless disregard for the truth.[267] In *Katz v. Enzer,* the defendant psychiatrist had written to the State Board of Psychology that the plaintiff social worker was overstepping the permissible bounds of her practice. This was clearly an occasion of privilege, but relevant to the issue of malice were the defendant's personal animus in seeking advantage for his practice and his "excessive distribution" of the same letter to members of the Jewish congregation to which they both belonged.[268] If a serious charge is involved, malice is constituted unless care is taken to garner the truth. Hence, on account of malice, Blue Cross/Blue Shield, as administrator of Medicare benefits, lost its privilege when it circulated unfounded assertions that a plaintiff podiatrist had been convicted of a crime.[269] Vituperative language reflects the mind of the author and is relevant to the issue of malice. The reporting clinician should attempt to corroborate the truth of statements at issue; take care that reports are sent only to those who have a duty to receive them; couch the report in a professionally accepted style; avoid snide, derogatory, or offensive characterizations of other people; and not stray beyond pertinent issues.

Allied to defamation is the possible *emotional distress* action arising from a divulgence of information about a patient. In a widely cited New Zealand case, *Furniss v. Fitchett,* a physician furnished to a patient's husband a certificate stating that his wife was suffering from a mental illness. At the time it was foreseeable that the husband might use the certificate in order to shock the wife. It was held that the physician was liable for the wife's emotional distress.[270] On the other hand, information disseminated as a result of judicial proceedings will attract immunity.[271]

As discussed earlier, liability in negligence may be established when the mental health clinician, having examined a person, tenders advice that financially harms him. This may occur in the employment context.[272]

The corollary to liability for communication is *liability for noncommunication.* This arises when Dr. *A* gathers information about patient *B.* Does *B* have a right to the information so gathered? The *right to access* is usually conceived as an aspect of the *right to privacy,* which enables someone to control information about himself. However, in respect of medical records, the courts have refused to find that the patient has a property right or a constitutional right to the medical information. When plaintiffs wished to obtain unrestricted access to their psychiatric records in order to complete a book about their experiences, the court denied the request.[273] However, records may be made available if the information is needed for a legitimate reason, such as litigation.[274]

Some states have enacted legislation allowing patients who have undergone psychotherapy access to their records. In Illinois, the Mental Health and Development Disabilities Confidentiality Act of 1979[275] provides that any recipient of mental health and developmental disabilities services "shall be entitled, upon request, to inspect and copy [his/her] record or any part thereof." This right is given to a recipient who is twelve years of age or older. This and similar legislation allows excision of the therapist's "personal notes," including:

1. Information disclosed to the therapist in confidence by other persons on condition that such information would never be disclosed to the recipient or other persons
2. Information disclosed to the therapist by the recipient which would be injurious to the recipient's relationships to other persons
3. The therapist's speculations, impressions, hunches, and reminders

Thus, by restricting access to the patient's *official record,* these statutes make it possible for therapists to regulate the amount of information made available to the patient. California legislation is less detailed, granting a patient access to his records unless, in the view of the physician or proper administrative officer, release of such records to the patient would not "serve his best interests."[276]

LIABILITY UNDER NEW HEALTH STRUCTURES

Much of the law has been established against a background of traditional medical practice. Duties to patients and the standard of care were articulated within the paradigm of fee-for-service, a system undergirded by health insurance and enjoyed by most people through the employment relationship.[277] The giant public health schemes, Medicare and Medicaid, were grafted onto the fee-for-service model. However, both private and public systems have created incentives for overutilization, increasing costs to such an extent that public policy has been enjoined. Along with other medical costs, mental health care costs have risen steadily (see Figure 8–5). A long battle to contain costs in both public and private health care spheres has ensued. Blumstein has described the different objectives of cost containment as follows: eliminating "unnecessary" care that is harmful to patient welfare; promoting efficiency through "waste" control; promoting cost-conscious decision-making that balances cost against quality and discourages utilization of services that are of relatively low benefit; and redistributing medical care costs from employers, payors, or providers to patients (or vice versa). Unfortunately, redistribution often pays little attention to its impact on the demand for and consumption of medical care.

Cost-containment can take the form of alternatives to the fee-for-service model or of controls upon utilization. Examples of the former are health maintenance organizations and some preferred provider networks. These organizations are designed to provide services on the payment of a capitation fee. A health maintenance organization has an incentive to economize on the provision of services, which it does by deflecting services from hospitalization and specialist care and, theoretically, by

Figure 8–5. Mental Health Costs

U.S. companies, average cost per employee

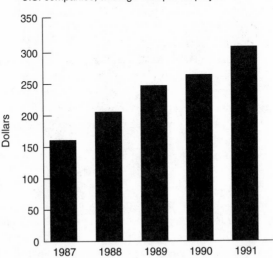

encouraging preventative health care. Recently, with employers flinching at the cost of medical insurance, and encouraged by the Federal Employee Retirement Income Security Act (ERISA), "managed care" has proliferated. Managed care departs sharply from the traditional consumer-choice, fee-for-service model.[278] For example, for routine care, employees may be restricted to services provided in company-run clinics by staff who act as "gatekeepers" to expensive care. Citing failings in the quality of mental health care delivered by companies that manage health care benefits for major companies, the American Psychological Association has developed its own model plan.[279]

The control-of-utilization incentive strategy presumes the fee-for-service model but provides mechanisms to review the provision of services. The mechanism of control may be financial, as when a set payment is determined by classification of the service under a Diagnosis Related Group (DRG).[280] Control may be by peer review. Peer review organizations, for example, may apply restrictions as to eligibility, scope of coverage, fee limits, hospital reimbursement limits, and utilization review requirements (e.g., preadmission certification, continued stay review, and retrospective review). Both types of strategy collide with the traditional standard of care. If they are to operate within a health maintenance organization or comply with peer review organization guidelines, clinicians will be forced to take account of matters extraneous to patient welfare. In some managed care situations, clinicians are employed by the patient's employer, and conflicts of interest arise. The financial incentives to restrict services imposed by health maintenance organizations are not consistent with the way courts typically expect medical practitioners to operate.[281]

A large literature has developed concerning the standard of care. Is the standard to be maintained despite changes in practice? Can it be said that, in opting for cheaper services, the consumer has forfeited his right to the fee-for-service standard? When the consumer has exercised choice in selecting the mode of delivery of his health care, it is more likely that the courts will accommodate a reduced standard of care. But the less apparent the choice and the greater the consumer's ignorance, the more the courts will insist upon a traditional standard. Over time, it is probable that the medical and legal culture will appreciate that universal standards are illusory. A harbinger of the cultural change is the burgeoning doctrine that health care is an economic good interchangeable with other goods,[282] and the acknowledgement that medical practice, for all its posturings, varies throughout the nation.[283] The rapidly changing scene confronts mental health professionals with a distressing lack of clarity and has prompted a search for practice guidelines.[284]

The injection of new actors into medical decision-making prompts the question of their liability. A patient objecting to a medical intervention (or its denial) may sue not only the physician but also the organization with whom the physician is associated, the utilization review body, or the payor who relies upon that mechanism.[285]

A physician was traditionally viewed as the quintessential independent contractor. According to legal doctrine, the organizations with which he was associated (e.g., the hospitals in which he had privileges) were not vicariously liable for his malpractice. With the passing of hospital charitable immunity and the policy in tort law of spreading losses to "deep pockets" (*enterprise liability*), the traditional rule has waned. Hospitals and other health care entities, such as health maintenance organizations, are increasingly subject to liability for malpractice, even though the negligent clinician is not an employee of the entity. Hospitals have been viewed as undertaking to provide services and to oversee their staff, failure at which may lead to liability.[286] Elsewhere, courts have found hospitals liable when they have held themselves out as offering services, usually in emergency rooms and radiology departments, even though the services are rendered by a nonemployee.[287] This liability has been extended to such other entities as HMOs.[288] In these cases, the entity may be said to be providing medical services. In the next group of cases, although the entities do not purport to provide services, they are held liable because their functions influence medical decision-making.

Payors of medical services increasingly monitor and control the medical services provided to persons whose medical bills they are paying. To what extent do the mechanisms designed to promote cost control implicate payors in liability? The foundational case is *Wickline v. State of California.* The principal question addressed in *Wickline* was the legal responsibility of the payor (the State of California under its Medi-Cal program) for harm caused to a patient when the cost containment program compromised a treating physician's medical judgment.[289] The cost containment program used prospective utilization review, which required authorization before the rendering of medical care. In this case, Mrs. Wickline was being treated by her family physician, who requested a consultation from a vascular surgeon. The surgeon diagnosed Mrs. Wickline has having arteriosclerosis obliterans, causing occlusion of the abdominal aorta. He recommended an arterial graft. Medi-Cal authorized the surgical procedure and ten days' hospitalization. Following surgery, Mrs. Wickline had a stormy convalescence. The surgeon advised that it was medically necessary for Mrs. Wickline to remain in hospital for eight days beyond her authorized discharge date, an extension requiring approval from Medi-Cal. The initial reviewer, an on-site nurse, felt unable to accede to the request and referred the application to a Medi-Cal consultant, a board-certified general surgeon. The treating surgeon's application was approved for four days only, and Mrs. Wickline was discharged without further appeal. After discharge, complications cost her the leg.

The court determined that the state owed Mrs. Wickline a duty of care, the standard of which was established by its statutory obligation to measure the "medical necessity" of the length and level of care. No breach of the duty was found. The prime responsibility was sheeted home to the vascular surgeon who had acceded to the Medi-Cal determination when his medical judgment was otherwise.

Although *Wickline* holds that the payor owes a duty of care, it leaves many questions unanswered. The duty finding was heavily influenced by earlier California case law and broadly couched statutory provisions. In the absence of both, it could be argued that a utilization review agency or payor would owe no duty of care. In a subsequent case that did not involve Medi-Cal, the same California court found that it was at least "arguable" that a utilization review agent and payor owed a duty of care. In *Wilson v. Blue Cross of Southern California,* Howard Wilson was admitted to a

Los Angeles hospital suffering from depression, drug dependency, and anorexia. His treating physician determined that he needed three to four weeks in hospital. Ten days after admission, Wilson's insurance company announced it would pay for no more hospital care. Wilson was discharged, having no means other than insurance to pay for care. He subsequently committed suicide. The trial court granted a summary judgment in favor of the defendant insurance company and utilization reviewer. However, an appeal court found that it was arguable that the defendants owed duties to the deceased and that their breaches caused his death.[290] In this case, the insurer (Blue Cross) had an arrangement whereby a firm, Western Medical, performed concurrent utilization review for "medical necessity." However, the insurance contract contained no utilization review provision (indeed, it provided that the attending physician should determine length of the stay short of thirty days). The liability of the insurer was therefore straightforward. Did the refusal to fund the hospitalization constitute breach of contract? This seemed clearly the case. The only question remaining was whether the breach was the proximate cause of the decedent's death. As for Western Medical, no justification was found to immunize it from liability. The court confirmed that liability could adhere beyond the attending or treating physician to those who make medically insensitive financial decisions.

The *Wilson* case warns insurers and utilization reviewers. But questions remain about the ability of those parties to make contractual arrangements under the policy for utilization review. If, in *Wilson,* the policy had contained a provision for utilization review, and if the terms of that provision had been adhered to, a summary judgment for the defendants could have been justifiable. However, this is not the end of the problem. In *Wickline* and *Wilson* the courts assume that the utilization review accorded with medical standards. The "medical necessity" of the hospitalization required payor and reviewer to make a medically sensitive decision. Is it necessary that the decision be medically sensitive? This question arises if the policy had stipulated utilization review without requiring the reviewer to consider medical needs. In such a case, the courts would probably interpret the policy as requiring medical decision-making. However, a contract could be written so as to require no reference to medical needs. Although the courts may require a medically sensitive decision by the payor or reviewer, to what extent would cost concerns be allowed to influence that decision? In *Wickline,* the court described the utilization decision as not "corrupting" the medically correct decision; but this comment gives little guidance. Even if one were to concede that the payor has a duty to be medically sensitive, the issue of proximate cause will continue to be a sticking point. In *Wilson,* the plaintiffs still had to prove that the refusal to approve continued hospitalization proximately caused the decedent's suicide.[291]

Cost containment raises another issue for the mental health clinician (and all medical practitioners), an issue arising from the well-established duty of informed consent. In *Moore v. Regents of University of California,* a patient brought an action against his physicians when, without his knowledge, they created a cell-line from his removed spleen and exploited it commercially. The plaintiff asserted that he should recover on two bases: (1) that his property had been taken and (2) that informed consent had not been obtained for the use of his cells in this way. The first objection raises thorny legal and moral issues about property rights that need not detain us. The second also raises difficult issues. Usually the doctrine of informed consent involves disclosure of risks connected with a medical procedure or therapy. In *Moore* there was no dispute about the disclosure of risks related to the spleen operation. However, Moore claimed that the defendants had the obligation of disclosing the extraneous financial and research interests they possessed in treating the plaintiff. After reviewing the law, the court stated the duty thus:

> These principles lead to the following conclusions: (1) a physician must disclose personal interests unrelated to the patient's health, whether research or economic, that may affect the physician's professional judgment; and (2) a physician's failure to disclose such interests may give rise to a cause of action for performing medical procedures without informed consent or breach of fiduciary duty.[292]

As mentioned above, under some cost containment arrangements, treating physicians and other health care professionals are given financial incentives to modify medical judgments. For example, HMO "gatekeeper" physicians may be rewarded if they divert patients from high-cost hospitalization and specialist services. Clearly, their duty is to disclose the interest. More generally, economic constraints that qualify or influence medical decision-making should be disclosed, for these matters are material to patients' decision-making.[293]

The law stemming from *Wickline* through *Wilson* and *Moore,* urges health professionals to advocate for their patients while keeping them informed. They should not quietly cave in to payors' decisions. The doctrine of informed consent may foster patient choice sufficiently to permit courts to enunciate a more flexible application of the standard of care.

REFORM OF THE LAW

The pressures of liability have led to legal reforms and to suggestions for others.[294] Some reforms touch aspects of liability; for example, abbreviating the time limitation within which an action must be commenced, or changing the rules for assessing damages (e.g., capping damages either *in toto* or in respect of the pain and suffering component). Other changes are designed to replace litigation with other forms of dispute resolution.[295] Some recommendations are systemic: They would abolish the common law fault system and replace it with a no-fault liability scheme.[296] Others would encourage contractual alternatives to tort.[297] Courts have responded to some law reform efforts by finding that they are unconstitutional under either federal or state law.[298] A mosaic has been created, and we shall not begin to describe it. Mental health clinicians should be aware of the flux and complexity of the current environment. Legislative initiatives may modify case law, as in *Tarasoff* liability, or more generally affect liability exposure, as the capping of damage awards, while the courts will attempt to accommodate the law to modern conditions.

CONCLUSIONS

Clinical practice is fraught with error, and error can have serious consequences. However, defensive psychiatry is no answer, for timidity also puts clinicians at risk of negligent malpractice. How, then, can they avoid litigation?

The best precaution is to do careful clinical work while fully apprising the patient and family of the diagnosis, the treatment plan, and the progress of therapy. Many malpractice suits arise from a neglect of this simple principle. Hospitals, in particular, provide many opportunities for failed communication, particularly when the attending physician delegates to other members of the team the responsibility for keeping parents informed of their children's progress. A good therapeutic alliance is the key to both good medicine and the avoidance of lawsuits. Used for this purpose, informed consent is transformed from an empty legalism into the foundation of a true collaboration.

"If it wasn't written down, it didn't happen." The clinician should keep a good record of the rationale for treatment. Progress notes should be timely, regular, dated, timed, and signed. Whenever a course of action is problematic, a risk-benefit analysis should be undertaken and documented, and a consultation obtained. If you disagree with a trainee's documented diagnosis, investigation plan, or treatment plan, note that you disagree and insert your amended diagnosis and plan. If you merely sign off on a trainee's notes, you could be concurring with erroneous observations, diagnosis, or treatment. One of the commonest errors is to raise a diagnostic question but not to follow through by investigating it; or, having ordered investigations, to lose sight of the results. Note any discrepancies between the nurses', the therapist's, and the physician's progress notes. If there is such a discrepancy try to account for it. Do not allow a nursing progress note concerning suicide risk to go unremarked. If you detect an error in your notes, do not erase it. Draw a line through the error, write "error," and date and sign your correction in the margin. Do not criticize or argue with other professionals or agencies in your notes, and avoid gratuitous or extravagant commentary (e.g., "This child has had an appalling home life.").

Before a particular medication is commenced, be careful to check that the patient harbors no conditions and is taking no drugs that would contraindicate it. Inquire for previous allergic or idiosyncratic reactions to drugs. Avoid polypharmacy. Monitor the progress of medication regularly. In long-term medication, "drug holidays" should be considered. Follow recommended guidelines for dosage and administration, unless there are good reasons for departing from them. Avoid prescribing medication "p.r.n." or with automatic refills, and be careful about responding to telephone requests for repeat prescriptions. Suicide risk should be considered, and only small amounts of the drug prescribed, if necessary. Hospitals should check that potentially suicidal patients are not hoarding medication.

When a patient is admitted to hospital, the risk of suicide or violence should be assessed, and the degree of risk should be linked to sets of nursing precautions to be activated automatically when the clinician indicates the risk. Every attempt should be made to obtain past records and scan them for risk factors.

If you will be unavailable in case of an emergency, the name of a fully informed substitute physician should be provided to the patient. Do not terminate treatment unilaterally without preparing the patient, giving adequate notice, and providing him or her with the names of other clinicians or agencies who could help.

In outpatient practice, the duty to protect is clearly activated when a patient makes a specific threat to harm a specified victim. When possible, incorporate the protection in therapy. Psychotherapy, hospitalization, and medication may be both more protective and more therapeutic than warning a foreseeable victim or alerting the police.

Do not record psychodynamic speculations in the clinical record; those unconscious incestuous strivings may come back to haunt you. You may consider keeping your psychotherapy *process notes* separate from the official *progress notes*. Be vigilant to avoid the unauthorized disclosure of confidential information to external agencies by gossiping about patients or by publishing articles about them without adequately disguising their identity. Obtain parents' consent before releasing reports to external agencies. Blanket consent forms obtained during the rush of admission may not hold legal water.

In conclusion, remember that the law has no wish to penalize physicians for honest errors. Its purpose is to protect patients from being harmed by reckless, careless, or incompetent clinical practice and, if they have been so harmed, to compensate them for injury. In most successful suits for negligent malpractice, the errors are glaring. Attention to the safeguards described in this chapter will protect clinicians from litigation while allowing them to practice nondefensive psychiatry.

APPENDIX TO CHAPTER 8

A. ASSESSMENT OF VIOLENCE

The risk of violence must be assessed in the following situations:

1. When the risk of violence is raised during outpatient evaluation or treatment
2. When a potentially violent patient presents for admission to hospital
3. When the leave or discharge from hospital of a potentially violent patient is being considered, or when such a patient elopes

The factors to be considered can be grouped into the following six areas (see p. 268):

1. Demographic factors
2. The violent threat
3. Past history
4. Psychological factors
5. The social environment
6. The therapeutic alliance

Do not merely sum the positive and negative items; their weighting and combination will differ in different cases.

1. *Demographic factors. Older, male, lower SES* patients from *disadvantaged ethnic groups* which have a *cultural tradition of masculine defensiveness* are at greater risk of violence.

2. *The violent threat.* Has the patient *directly expressed a violent threat* or threats toward another, by word or message? Does the potential victim have a *provocative relationship* with the patient which could engender hostility? Does the patient have a *plan* for harming the victim, and does he have *access to lethal weapons?*

3. *Past history.* Is there a *past history of violent threats or actions?* Does the patient have a *history of being victimized* in early life by child abuse? Has the patient a *history of serious head injury, epilepsy, or neurological impairment?* Does the patient have a *history of alcohol or drug abuse?*

4. *Psychological factors.* Is the patient prone to cope with anxiety or hostility by *externalizing* or *projecting* it in the form of *impulsive, explosive actions, suspicious*

vigilance, or frank *persecutory delusions?* Is the patient's *intelligence below average?* Is there evidence of *sensorial impairment?* Is the patient subject to *alcohol or substance abuse?*

5. *The social environment.* Are the patient's *family or caretakers able and willing to control* the patient? Is there evidence of family psychopathology in the form of *rejection, neglect, physical or sexual abuse,* or *family violence?* Is *parental mental or physical health* impaired?

6. *The therapeutic alliance.* Has the patient *lost* or *terminated* a *therapeutic relationship?* Is he *competent* and *motivated* to enter into one?

7. *Resources.* Factors which may protect against violence or enhance self-control are as follows. *Younger, female, caucasian, religious, middle-class* patients are at less risk. If there has been a threat of violence, a *threat without plan or identified victim,* in a patient *without access to lethal means,* is of relatively lower concern, particularly if the patient has *obsessional traits, low subjective urge,* and *above average intelligence.* A *secure family* without major psychopathology or mental or physical ill health is protective, as is a *positive relationship with a therapist* or the *motivation* and *competence* to enter into one.

8. *A hypothetical high-risk case.* The patient is an intoxicated seventeen-year-old, male, Hispanic youth from an impoverished family living in an urban ghetto. He has been brought to the emergency room by police because he was acting belligerently in a local bar. During the interview, he threatens to kill his allegedly unfaithful fiancée and her supposed lover by stabbing them to death. He has a police record involving numerous episodes of juvenile violence and is known to be a heavy user of alcohol and street drugs. He definitely has access to knives and other weapons. At interview he is highly emotionally aroused, threatening, hostile, and suspicious. He says he is directed by an inner voice to take vengeance for the insult to his honor. His family is chaotic and afraid of him. He has no therapist and, at the interview, no desire to seek help.

More risk variables are offered in R. I. Simon, "The Duty to Protect in Private Practice," in J. C. Beck, ed., *Confidentiality Versus the Duty to Protect: Forseeable Harm in the Practice of Psychiatry* (Washington: APA, 1990), p. 25.

B. ASSESSMENT OF SUICIDE RISK

A suicide risk–resource analysis is required when the clinician must decide whether the risk of suicide is *imminent* and *serious.* This decision is most often required in the following situations:

1. When the possibility of suicide is raised in the course of ambulatory or inpatient treatment
2. When a new patient presents for voluntary or involuntary hospitalization
3. When leave or the discharge of a potentially suicidal patient is being considered

In these circumstances, it is important for the clinician to record the pros and cons upon which the clinical decision is based. The Suicide Risk–Resource Checklist

A VIOLENCE RISK-RESOURCE CHECKLIST

RISK FACTORS	Check if applies	RESOURCES	Check if applies
A. DEMOGRAPHIC FACTORS			
1. Age: 15 years or older	[ ]	1. Age: Less than 15 years	[ ]
2. Sex: Male	[ ]	2. Sex: Female	[ ]
3. Race: Black, Hispanic	[ ]	3. Race: Caucasian	[ ]
4. SES: Low	[ ]	4. SES: Middle or high	[ ]
B. THE VIOLENT THREAT			
5. Explicit threat to identified person: Yes	[ ]	5. Explicit threat to identified person: No	[ ]
6. Potential victim -- rejecting, depriving, threatening, provocative	[ ]		
7. Plan: Yes	[ ]	7. Plan: No	[ ]
8. Access to lethal means: Yes	[ ]	8. Access to lethal means: No	[ ]
C. PAST HISTORY			
9. Previous violence: in threat or action	[ ]	9. Previous violence: None	[ ]
10. Neurological impairment: Yes	[ ]		
11. Of having been victimized: Yes	[ ]		
12. Drug or alcohol abuse: Yes	[ ]		

	Check if applies		Check if applies
D. PSYCHOLOGICAL FACTORS			
13. Paranoid or externalizing ideation	[ ]		
14. Hallucinations: Command or violent	[ ]		
15. Internal controls: Poor	[ ]	15. Internal controls: Adequate	[ ]
16. Subjective urge to violence: strong	[ ]	16. Subjective urge: Low	[ ]
17. Intelligence: Low	[ ]	17. Intelligence: Above average	[ ]
18. Sensorium: Impaired	[ ]		
E. THE SOCIAL ENVIRONMENT			
19. Security: Unable to control	[ ]	19. Security: Able to control	[ ]
20. Pathology: Rejection, violence, abuse, neglect	[ ]	20. Pathology: None	[ ]
21. Health: Mental or physical illness in caretakers	[ ]	21. Health: Good	[ ]
F. THE THERAPEUTIC ALLIANCE			
22. Loss: Recent severance or negative transference	[ ]	22. Intact alliance	[ ]
23. Competence: Incompetent	[ ]	23. Competent to form alliance	[ ]
24. Motivation: Resistant	[ ]	24. Motivation to form alliance	[ ]

(p. 272) is designed as an aide-memoir. It provides a convenient means of rapidly scanning the risk factors relevant to such decisions.

The checklist is divided into six sections, incorporating twenty-five items. These items cannot be equally weighted, because their relative valence and combination will differ according to the particular circumstances and characteristics of each case. Do not merely sum the risks and resources. Consider their weight and combination in each case.

The factors to be considered can be classified under six headings:

1. Demographic factors
2. The suicide attempt
3. Physical factors
4. Psychological factors
5. The social environment
6. The therapeutic alliance

1. *Demographic factors. Older white males* are at greater risk.

2. *The suicide attempt.* Pay close attention to the suicide attempt, if one has occurred. *Lethal means* involves hanging, gassing, jumping from a height, drowning, knife or gunshot wound, using a motor vehicle for suicidal purposes, self-poisoning, major overdose, or other concerted attempt at self destruction. Remember that, to a child who is ignorant of pharmacology, ten aspirins may represent a lethal dose.

Greater risk attaches to suicide attempts which were *planned* and *concealed,* although *impulsiveness* (e.g., drinking and driving wildly after an argument) can also be very dangerous.

The *intent* of the patient should be explored from suicide notes, prior conversations with family and friends, and the patient's recollection of the attempt. Did the patient truly *wish to die, sacrifice himself, expunge shame, exit permanently from an intolerable existence, find peace,* or *be reunited with a lost love one?* Was the suicide attempt a response to *command hallucinations?* On the other hand, did the suicide attempt represent a communication of the *need for help* or a *desire to punish someone?* Is the patient *able to grasp the finality of death?* Does he or she fantasize that *resurrection* is possible?

3. *Past history.* A history of a *previous attempt or attempts* adds to the risk of future suicide. The *means and intent of previous attempts* might also predict the seriousness of future attempts.

Some patients have given up on the future as a result of *chronic illness or handicap. Alcohol and drug abuse* increases the risk potential of other factors since the intoxicated adolescent may take desperate risks or express suicidal impulses that would otherwise be controlled. Is the patient *intoxicated* at the time of the examination? Is he or she *likely to resort to drugs or alcohol* if you do not hospitalize him or her?

4. *Psychological factors.* Does the mental status examination reveal or confirm the presence of *depressive affect, despair, hopelessness,* or the *vegetative signs* associated with *melancholia?* Is there evidence of *psychosis* with mental disorganization, abnormal perception, or delusional thinking? Can you detect evidence of *command*

hallucinations instructing the patient to kill or injure himself or to take serious risks (e.g., to fly from the roof of a building)? Is there evidence of *mental confusion, obtundation,* or *delirium* suggestive of an organic confusion or acute psychotic condition? Does the patient's history indicate *poor internal controls* with impulsiveness or explosive behavior when under stress? Is the patient preoccupied with *suicidal ideation* or with the *desirability of death?*

5. *The social environment.* The resources and deficiencies of the family or caretakers are very relevant to the determination of suicide risk. Are the family able to provide a *safe environment?* Are the parents able to cooperate with each other? Are they willing or competent to get rid of, or secure, all potentially lethal agents or suicide (e.g., prescription drugs, poisons, weapons)? Are they prepared or able to watch the patient closely, and be emotionally available to him or her in times of stress? On the other hand, is there evidence of *parental rejection, neglect, physical, sexual, or emotional abuse, mental illness, severe personality disorder, substance abuse,* or *physical illness or handicap* of a severity that would render the caretakers unable to provide adequate security and emotional sustenance to an acutely disturbed child?

Has there been a recent *loss* or *the severance of an important relationship,* such as the death of a close relative or beloved family pet, loss of contact with a concustodial parent, or the departure of close older sibling or special friend? Such an event may represent the "last straw" to an isolated, troubled child.

Pay special attention to *peer relations.* Particularly vulnerable is the isolated, alienated, persecuted, or rejected youngster, or the patient who has withdrawn from contact with peers. *Has a love relationship been threatened or severed?* Does the patient feel intolerably *guilty* or *ashamed* before his family or peers, as a result of some action or dereliction, or an undisclosed sexual problem? *Being ashamed before the family* is a particularly powerful emotion in Asian patients.

Is there a *family history of suicide?* A positive family history may reflect (1) an inherited propensity for psychiatric disorder, which increases suicide risk, or (2) a family tradition of committing or attempting suicide in stressful circumstances. Suicidal parents may unwittingly act as *suicide models.*

6. *The therapeutic alliance.* It is crucial to determine whether the patient has, or has lost, an adequate *therapeutic relationship.* Is the patient capable of forming an alliance? Do you believe the patient, if he promises to cooperate? Has he been reliable in the past? Is he prepared to sign a "suicide contract"? Although such contracts have no legal status, they are a useful clinical index of the patient's cooperativeness.

To some extent, the reverse of the risk factors can operate as mitigating factors. For example, a suicide attempt associated with the *desire to communicate a need for help* indicates that the patient is still potentially available to other people. A *competent family,* free of serious mental, physical, or personality disorder, is the most powerful protective factor. *A network of caring friends* who can be mobilized is also protective. The *capacity for internal control,* accentuated for example in obsessional patients, may impede direct suicidal action and may be activated if the patient has, or wants, a therapeutic relationship. Finally, an *existing adequate therapeutic alliance* or the *competence or motivation to seek one* is a mitigating factor.

The following stereotype describes a situation of extreme risk. The patient is a seventeen-year-old caucasian male who was discovered making his second suicide attempt by hanging, while intoxicated, in a remote part of the woods near his home. His family is chaotic. The father is psychotic and alcoholic and the mother chronically physically ill. One sibling has died by suicide and one by allegedly accidental gunshot wound. The patient's suicide was planned, and he intended to do away with himself. He has no friends, is persecuted at school, and was recently greatly upset by the death of a beloved grandmother. Mental status examination reveals severe depression with agitation, despair, and vegetative signs. He is preoccupied with the idea of dying and joining his grandmother. At times he hears the voice of his grandmother begging him to join her. He has had no recent mental health contact and rejects the offer of therapy.

A less risky situation is posed by the following example. The patient is a fourteen-year-old girl who swallowed ten aspirin tablets in the bathroom at home, after an argument with her mother about permission to go out with a boyfriend on a weeknight. She told her mother about the overdose an hour after it had occurred, and the mother brought her to the emergency room at once. The parents have been separated for three years, but both of them remain close to the patient, and neither suffers from serious mental, personality, or substance use disorder. The parents and child are in good physical health. The patient reveals no psychotic or melancholic symptoms. She says she did not really want to die, but that she was angry with her mother for not listening to her and for restricting her too much. She accepts the need for therapy, promises not to attempt suicide without calling you, and agrees to return for an outpatient appointment on the following day.

SUICIDE RISK-RESOURCE CHECKLIST

RISK FACTORS	Check if applies	RESOURCES	Check if applies
A. DEMOGRAPHIC FACTORS			
1. Age: 15 years or older	[ ]		
2. Sex: Male	[ ]		
3. Race: Caucasian	[ ]		
B. THE SUICIDE ATTEMPT			
4. Means:		4. Non-lethal means	[ ]
Potentially lethal	[ ]		
5. Location: Concealed	[ ]	5. Overt location	[ ]
6. Manner: Planned	[ ]		
7. Expressed intent: Death	[ ]	7. Desire for help,	
8. History		attention	[ ]
(Previous attempt (s))	[ ]		
C. PAST HISTORY			
9. Health: Chronic illness,			
handicap	[ ]		
10. Substance use:			
Alcohol, drugs	[ ]		
D. PSYCHOLOGICAL FACTORS			
11. Depression:			
Hopelessness	[ ]		
12. Psychosis: Mental			
disorganization	[ ]		
13. Hallucinations:			
Command	[ ]		
14. Internal controls: Poor	[ ]	14. Obsessionality	[ ]
15. Ideation: Suicide, death	[ ]		
16. Sensorium: Impairment	[ ]		
E. THE SOCIAL ENVIRONMENT			
17. Security:		17. Competent family	[ ]
Unable to protect	[ ]		
18. Pathology: Rejection,		18. Absence of pathology	[ ]
abuse, neglect	[ ]		
19. Health: Parental			
mental or physical			
illness	[ ]		
20. Loss: Recent	[ ]		
21. Isolation: Withdrawal,		21. Friendship network	[ ]
alienation, persecution or			
rejection by peers	[ ]		
22. Family history:			
of suicide	[ ]		
F. THE THERAPEUTIC ALLIANCE			
23. Loss: Recent		23. Intact alliance	[ ]
severance	[ ]		
24. Competence:		24. Competent to form	
Incompetent	[ ]	alliance	[ ]
25. Motivation:		25. Motivated to form	
Resistant	[ ]	alliance	[ ]

CHAPTER 9

JUVENILE DELINQUENCY

LEGAL PRINCIPLES
Historical Introduction

A t the beginning of the nineteenth century, the common law held that children younger than seven years of age were incapable of committing a crime. It was presumed that, from seven to fourteen, the child could not be held legally responsible for wrongdoing; however, this presumption might be overcome if it could be established that the child was capable of criminal intent. Individuals over fourteen were considered fully responsible.

Minors charged with offenses were generally dealt with in the same manner and accorded the same rights and protections as adults. As a result, many adolescents were jailed with hardened criminals, while others were consigned to poorhouses, workhouses, or other public institutions. As the nineteenth century progressed, however, with rapid industrialization, intense urbanization, and massive European migration, benevolent forces emerged. Gradually the states began to try adolescents separately from adults and to separate offenders in special institutions known as "houses of refuge" or "reformatories."[1]

The Creation of the Juvenile Justice System

In 1899 the Illinois Juvenile Court Act established the first juvenile code, a model system soon replicated in other states. The Illinois act emerged from reform efforts inspired by the unfortunate experience of children in criminal courts. Juvenile justice became distinguished by its rehabilitative, rather than punitive, aim, and juvenile court proceedings were deemed civil rather than criminal in character.[2]

The rehabilitative goal that shaped the juvenile justice system differed significantly from the aims of criminal justice. Accordingly, the language of criminal justice was modified to avoid the stigma attached to criminal proceedings. "Arrested" became "taken into custody"; a "trial" was called a "hearing"; "crime" was changed to "delinquency"; "conviction" to "adjudication"; "sentence" to "disposition"; and "prison" to "training school." The proceedings were characterized as "civil" because the state's

273

actions were based upon its *parens patriae* authority to act as a surrogate parent in the child's interest rather than as an adversary.[3] The *parens patriae* doctrine provided that a child should have a right merely to custodial care, not liberty. If a child were delinquent, the state could intervene as *parens patriae* in order to relieve the parents of their custodial responsibilities. Applying this rationale, the courts deprived juveniles of the procedural rights that are fundamental to adult criminal proceedings. The state's assertion of its *parens patriae* power was based upon the morally benevolent premise that youth do not deserve to be punished for violations of the law.[4] Informal juvenile court proceedings were designed to provide flexibility unknown in the criminal courts. Juvenile courts, for example, could order supervision in children's homes, lengthy apprenticeships, placement in foster homes, or transfer to hospitals or residential facilities. The paternalistic juvenile court judge was empowered to act in the best interests of the child by exercising wide discretion during the hearing and at disposition.

The Juvenile Justice System Reevaluated

During the civil rights movement of the early 1960s, expanded constitutional protections for minorities of criminals paved the way for the juvenile court to formalize its procedures in accordance with constitutional requirements. By the 1960s two kinds of protest had emerged, each from an opposite pole of the political compass.

On the left, civil libertarians attacked infringements on due process inherent in the existing system. Justice Fortas noted in *Kent v. United States* that "there is evidence, in fact, there may be grounds for concern that the child receives the worst of both worlds; that he gets neither the protections accorded to adults nor the solicitous care and regenerative treatment postulated for children." Juvenile justice was described in the landmark case *In re Gault* as a "kangaroo court," which consigned youth, without constitutional safeguards, to juvenile prisons where they were often confined for longer periods than adults who had committed similar offenses.

On the other hand, citizens concerned for law and order were outraged by the inexorable rise of juvenile crime, the decay of American cities, the difficulty of integrating urban immigrants, the growth of an underclass, the weakening of the education system, and an apparent deterioration in traditional family values. Rehabilitation, they contended, had "failed." Since "nothing works," it was time to "get tough" and give "hard-core" youthful criminals their "just desserts" by implementing proportional sentencing and "fitting the punishment to the crime."

The Development of Procedural Requirements

Eventually the two kinds of protest combined to topple the informal rehabilitative model and to substitute, in part, a legalistic system that aims at diversion, deinstitutionalization, and retribution. However, as will be seen, the older benevolent model has not been entirely discarded.

Several judicial decisions acted as a watershed in the transmogrification of the juvenile court. The most famous of these decisions, *In re Gault,* signaled that the juvenile court must become a real court and implement constitutional safeguards. A year prior to *Gault,* however, in *Kent v. United States,* the Supreme Court acknowledged the problems created by the *parens patriae* doctrine and questioned the lack of constitutional guarantees in the juvenile justice system.

Actually, *Kent v. United States* was only tangentially concerned with the juvenile justice system. The case concerned a sixteen-year-old juvenile who, while still on probation for housebreaking and attempted robbery, had been taken into custody on charges of burglary and rape. Psychiatric and psychological evaluation revealed severe psychopathology. Kent's counsel requested that the juvenile court retain jurisdiction and that Kent receive treatment. The juvenile court judge held no hearings and made no findings, however, but waived jurisdiction and transferred the case to adult court. The statute authorizing such actions required only that a "full investigation" be completed prior to transfer. The Supreme Court held:

There is no place in our system of law for reaching a result of such tremendous consequences without ceremony—without hearing, without effective assistance of counsel, without a statement of reasons. It is inconceivable that a court of justice dealing with adults, with respect to a similar issue, would proceed in this manner.[5]

Thus, before a juvenile court may waive jurisdiction and transfer the case to adult court, the defendant must be afforded counsel, a formal hearing, access to all relevant records, and a statement of reasons for the transfer to adult court. These safeguards rest upon constitutional rights to procedural due process and the assistance of counsel. *Kent* paved the way for the landmark decision *In re Gault* by raising, but declining to answer, the wider question as to whether the constitutional guarantees governing criminal proceedings must be applied in the juvenile court.

It was in *In re Gault* that the Supreme Court determined for the first time that "neither the Fourteenth Amendment nor the Bill of Rights is for adults alone." *In re Gault* concerned a fifteen-year-old boy on probation for stealing who had been taken into custody and charged with making a lewd telephone call. The boy's parents were not notified of his arrest; neither the boy nor his parents were informed of the charges; no witnesses were produced by the state at the evidentiary hearing; the youth was not provided access to counsel; and he had no opportunity to summon or cross-examine witnesses. The judge committed the youth to a state training school until he reached twenty-one years of age, allowing no appeal. An adult convicted of the same offense would have been sentenced to a maximum fine of fifty dollars or up to two months in prison. The Supreme Court reversed and remanded the case on the ground that the Bill of Rights and the Fourteenth Amendment ought to apply in juvenile court proceedings. The Court stated:

Failure to observe the fundamental requirements of due process [in delinquency proceedings] has resulted in instances . . . of unfairness to individuals and inadequate or inaccurate findings of fact and unfortunate prescriptions of remedy. Due process of law is the primary and indispensable foundation of individual freedom. It is the basic essential term in the social compact which defines the rights of the individual and delimits the powers which the state may exercise.[6]

The Court held that due process required juvenile proceedings to afford defendants the assistance of counsel, advance notice of specific charges, the right to confront and cross-examine witnesses, and privilege against self-incrimination. However, the Court stopped short of requiring all the protections provided in adult proceedings. A jury trial, for example, was not required.

Kent and *Gault* transformed the juvenile system. *Gault* scotched the belief that the limitation of due process was consistent with the benevolent aim of juvenile justice. After *Gault,* in *In re Winship,* the Supreme Court held that the standard of proof required in the adjudication of juvenile cases must be "beyond a reasonable doubt," reasoning that, when a youth's liberty is at stake, due process required that the standard of evidence necessary for a conviction be as exacting as that applied in adult proceedings.[7] However, in *McKeiver v. Pennsylvania,* the Supreme Court rejected the contention that a jury was constitutionally required in juvenile hearings.[8]

Juvenile proceedings steadily became more adversarial as juvenile rights, such as the right to an attorney, became entrenched; but the Supreme Court was reluctant to extend all constitutional rights assured in adult proceedings to juveniles. To do so, it was feared, would totally jettison the rehabilitative, protective model and would open juvenile hearings to a fully adversary process. In *Winship* and *McKeiver,* the Supreme Court's analysis focused on whether *Gault*'s requirement that juvenile proceedings meet the "essentials of due process and fair treatment" was in accordance with the Fourteenth Amendment. These decisions thus defined the limits of *Gault* instead of extending additional rights to juveniles.

In *Breed v. Jones* the Supreme Court determined that the Fifth Amendment's Double Jeopardy Clause applies in juvenile proceedings.[9] The Fifth Amendment requires that a criminal defendant be tried only once for the same offense. The Court noted that, although juvenile proceedings are "civil" in nature, the potential consequences of adjudication are just as severe as in criminal proceedings. The Court held that the Double Jeopardy Clause protected a juvenile from being criminally prosecuted for an offense after a juvenile court had already adjudicated it.

On the other hand, in *Schall v. Martin,* the Supreme Court held that *Gault*'s requirement of the "essentials" of due process and fair treatment did not preclude preventive detention of a potentially dangerous juvenile. The Court stated that the array of constitutional protections accorded to adult criminal proceedings do not entirely apply to juvenile proceedings. The state, as *parens patriae,* was held to have an interest in promoting the best interests of the child, a requirement that created a "fundamental difference" between juvenile proceedings and adult criminal trials.

The Juvenile Justice and Delinquency Prevention Act

The landmark decisions noted above extended constitutional rights to minors, a class of citizens who formerly had none. Juvenile code revisions followed soon afterward.

Since 1970 almost every state has substantially revised its code in order to provide precise guidelines for the exercise of discretion by juvenile judges. In 1974 the federal Juvenile Justice and Delinquency Prevention Act became law, demonstrating congressional concern over the extent of youth crime. Through this legislation, federal grants are provided to state and local authorities in order to promote delinquency prevention and education, to obviate the imprisonment of juveniles in adult jails by creating or expanding alternate programs, to deinstitutionalize status offenders, and to establish guidelines for the diversion and treatment of acts by children that would be federal crimes if committed by adults. The act offers incentive to the states by conditioning and monitoring the federal funding in such a way as to encourage the removal of juveniles from adult correctional facilities and the development of local programming for serious offenders. Amendments to the act are designed to protect the public from the serious delinquent. For example, the 1981 amendment permits juvenile courts to imprison status offenders who violate court orders (e.g., by absconding from court-ordered placement).

In 1971 the Institute of Judicial Administration at New York University Law School instigated a project to frame Juvenile Justice Standards. In 1973 the American Bar Association became co-sponsor of the project. Twenty of the twenty-three volumes from this project contain standards and commentary approved by the ABA House of Delegates, and provide guidelines and comments for local, state, and federal juvenile justice proceedings and enforcement policies.[10]

Legal Proceedings in Delinquency Cases

Juvenile delinquency hearings are categorized as *quasi-criminal;* that is, although they have some of the characteristics of criminal cases, there are significant differences. The following stages describe the process:

1. Apprehension
2. Diversion
3. Pretrial detention hearing
4. Probable cause hearing
5. Transfer to adult court
6. Adjudicatory hearing
7. Dispositional hearing
8. Appeal

APPREHENSION

Juvenile codes generally grant law enforcement officials broad discretion in taking juveniles into custody. Typically, the substantive standards concerning the legality of an arrest are the same for juveniles and adults.[11] Juveniles, however, may be apprehended for conduct (e.g., truancy) that would be noncriminal for an adult. Juveniles are taken into custody according to the laws of arrest.[12] The laws of arrest are determined by common law rules and state statutes subject to the constitutional requirements of the Fourth and Fourteenth Amendments.

The courts have held that Fourth Amendment protections apply to juvenile arrest proceedings.[13] The Fourth Amendment governs the issuance and execution of arrest warrants and provides that "no warrants shall issue, but upon probable cause." A distinction must be drawn between arrests made with a judicially issued warrant and warrantless arrests. In order to obtain the issuance of an arrest warrant, a law enforcement official must establish before a court the "probable cause" that a person whose arrest is sought has violated the law.[14] "Probable cause" is a level of certainty greater than mere suspicion but less than a preponderance of the evidence.

The majority of arrests of both children and adults are warrantless, as they occur in public places.[15] A warrantless arrest of any person is legal if the law enforcement officer has good reason to believe (again the term "probable cause" is used) that a crime has occurred and that that person has committed it.[16] Common law principles authorizing warrantless arrests of minors are broader for alleged felonies than for misdemeanors; thus, warrantless arrests occur more often when serious crimes are suspected.[17]

In *Miranda v. Arizona,* the Supreme Court held that a person in custody must be notified (1) that he has the right to remain silent; (2) that anything he says could be used against him; (3) that he has the right to an attorney and to have the attorney present during interrogations; and (4) that an attorney will be appointed for him if necessary.[18] *Miranda* warnings must be given to juveniles held in custody.[19] However, special problems arise in determining a juvenile's *Miranda* rights. Courts are often faced with questions about whether a juvenile may waive his *Miranda* rights, whether a request to see parents or a probation officer is, in effect, a request to see an attorney, and whether a child must be specifically informed that his confession could be used against him in an adult criminal proceeding rather than in juvenile court. It is permissible for juveniles to waive these rights, but only if they do so "voluntarily, knowingly, and intelligently."[20] Because of concern that, if a youth does not understand the consequences of waiving *Miranda* rights, the waiver might not meet the "voluntary" requirement, judges must take the "totality of circumstances" into account.[21] The totality of circumstances involves consideration of the appellant's age, the environment in which the interrogation occurred, the duration of interrogation, and the presence of (or request for) parents.

DIVERSION

Diversion is designed to minimize a juvenile's involvement in formal proceedings in order to avoid stigma and other unfavorable sequelae.[22] Actually, diversion usually occurs prior to the probation officer's formal determination to divert juvenile proceedings. For example, citizens often decide not to report crimes, and the police also divert many youths rather than take them into custody. If detained after apprehension, a youth must be brought before a Family Court or Juvenile Court within a time allotted by statute, typically seventy-two hours. At this point, a *judicial detention hearing* must be held and the decision is made to release the juvenile or to keep him in custody prior to a *hearing on the merits.*[23] If the juvenile is a repeat or serious offender, the court may order *pretrial detention* in order to protect the public or prevent the youth from running away.

In order to decide whether to divert the accused, the probation staff will investigate the nature of the alleged offense; the age, previous record, psychiatric history, and school adjustment of the juvenile; the capacity of the family to supervise the juvenile; and the juvenile's attitude to the offense. The screening usually incorporates an informal *intake conference,* at which the information is reviewed and decisions made about diversion. Juveniles are usually not entitled to legal counsel during the intake conference, nor may prosecutors file a complaint over the objection of intake staff.[24] Diversion can lead to such interventions as remedial education, psychiatric hospitalization, outpatient therapy, family counseling, drug and alcohol abuse treatment, or vocational training. Approximately half of the total number of juveniles brought to the attention of juvenile and family courts are handled at intake without the filing of formal judicial proceedings, thus reducing court backlog and congestion. Dangers loom, however, when administrators are given wide discretion. The low visibility of diversion in such a large system could allow for discriminatory and arbitrary action by the state without due regard for individual rights.[25]

PRETRIAL DETENTION HEARING

After apprehension, in most cases, the juvenile is released without bail to the care of his parents. However, serious offenders who might run away or whose parents cannot be reached may be judged in need of detention pending the adjudication hearing.

In *Schall v. Martin,* the Supreme Court upheld a New York law that authorized pretrial detention for delinquents at serious risk of committing further crimes. The Court did not require that the pretrial detention of a juvenile meet adult standards of due process, although subsequently it upheld a provision of the 1984 Bail Reform Act that authorized pretrial detention of adults charged with serious felonies who present a threat to the safety of others.[26] Pretrial detention has been the subject of extensive litigation, particularly when juveniles were kept in adult prisons.[27] Today, suspects are usually detained in detention centers, temporary shelters, foster homes, group homes, or their own homes. Incarceration with adults, however, is most likely to recur when the juvenile is detained before trial. The Juvenile Justice and Delinquency Prevention Act provides that no juvenile be detained or committed to any adult prison. Furthermore, the ABA Juvenile Justice Standards criticize "interim detention of accused juveniles in any facility or part thereof also used to detain adults."[28] As of 1980, however, only five states had prohibited the detention of youths in adult facilities.[29] Spurred by the incentive of monitored federal funding under the Juvenile Justice and Delinquency Prevention Act, by 1987 the majority of states had complied with the requirements prohibiting detention of children in adult facilities.[30] Between 1983 and 1989, the number of juveniles admitted to adult prisons was cut in half.[31]

Unfortunately, nationwide interest in building new adult facilities to obviate over-crowding is siphoning funds from equally overcrowded juvenile correction systems.[32] Annual funding for adult prisons has doubled since 1986, while expenditures for juvenile facilities have grown by only one-third in the same time. Severe overcrowding in juvenile facilities forces nonviolent offenders to be incarcerated with violent offenders, sometimes three and four youths being housed in rooms designed for one.

PROBABLE CAUSE HEARING

This hearing is often combined with the pretrial detention hearing. The probation officer who usually presides may decide against filing a petition for adjudication if there is no probable cause or if the petition would not be in the child's best interests (for example, if the child would be better managed in a mental health facility). If the arrest was without judicial authorization, the Fourth Amendment requires a prompt judicial hearing to test the reasonableness of the belief that the minor was guilty of the offense for which he was arrested and detained.[33] The court may act in one of four ways: release the child; divert the child; file a petition to have the case adjudicated; or file a petition to transfer the case to adult court.

TRANSFER TO ADULT COURT

A *transfer hearing* must be separate from, and must antedate, an adjudicatory hearing.[34] At a transfer hearing, the juvenile court judge decides whether the accused will be tried as a juvenile by juvenile proceedings, or whether to waive jurisdiction and have the youth tried as an adult. Following *Kent,* there must be a hearing on this issue, at which the juvenile is entitled to counsel, the child's attorney must have access to relevant records, and the judge must explain why he has waived juvenile court jurisdiction. The burden of proof required varies with the jurisdiction. Most courts require the state to establish by a preponderance of evidence that the child should be tried as an adult. Even though the burden is on the state, the child has a right to present evidence.[35] In deciding whether to transfer the juvenile to adult court, the judge will consider the following matters:

1. Age (the minimum age varies in different states)
2. Prior record
3. The seriousness of the alleged offense (i.e., whether it was against person or property)
4. The manner in which the offense was committed (e.g., whether it was aggressive or premeditated)
5. Psychiatric and medical history
6. Current psychiatric and medical status
7. Amenability to treatment

8. The availability of suitable rehabilitative programs
9. The safety of the public[36]

In general, the court is more likely to waive jurisdiction if the accused is older, has a record of recidivism, is charged with a serious crime, has no disorder or impairment of body or mind, and is thought not to be amenable to treatment in the juvenile facilities available. This matter will be discussed further in the section on clinical evaluation.

ADJUDICATORY HEARING

Juvenile proceedings are instigated by the filing of a petition alleging that a child is delinquent, in need of supervision, or neglected. The petition can be filed by law enforcement officials, probation officers, victims, or other interested parties. The petition details the charges in order to establish the jurisdiction of the court and to provide notice to the juvenile and his family of the allegations being made. Once a petition is filed, a hearing will be scheduled, notice of which the juvenile must receive.[37]

At the adjudicatory hearing, the juvenile court decides, beyond a reasonable doubt, whether the alleged act or acts were committed. The juvenile has the right to counsel. The state presents evidence of the juvenile's guilt. The juvenile's counsel cross-examines adverse witnesses and presents evidence on his or her behalf. Some states permit hearsay in limited circumstances. Next, the judge determines whether the minor should be adjudicated delinquent. Following *Gault*, the accused must be provided with due process safeguards (not as extensive as those given to adults), including a criminal standard of proof (beyond a reasonable doubt)[38] but not trial by jury.[39]

In order to avoid stigmatization, juvenile hearings and their records are closed to the public. However, First Amendment considerations restrict the ability of any state to prohibit the publication of information. In *Smith v. Daily Mail Pub. Co.* the Supreme Court held that a newspaper could not be criminally punished for publishing truthful and lawfully obtained information about a juvenile.[40] The Supreme Court recently applied *Daily Mail* guidelines in holding that a publisher was not liable in tort for disclosing the identity of a rape victim in a case in which the information had been mistakenly made public by the police.[41]

DISPOSITIONAL HEARING

The juvenile court has a range of available dispositions, all of which are at least partially rehabilitative in aim, for example: dismissal; restitution and fines; suspension of action contingent on good behavior; probation; community service; psychiatric hospitalization; placement in a foster home, group home, or other open residential center; and confinement in a secure facility. State and municipal agencies may be ordered to provide therapy, and parents may be ordered to participate in treatment or otherwise to cooperate in the rehabilitation of the juvenile. Despite the Juvenile Justice and Delinquency Prevention Act, however, some states persist in jailing some juvenile offenders. A number of class action suits have hammered out protections for juveniles confined in correctional facilities; these are discussed in Chapter 10. The sentence applied to a juvenile cannot exceed the maximum allowed under the United States Sentencing Guidelines applicable to analogous crimes committed by adults.[42]

APPEAL

Courts have held that equal protection under the Fourteenth Amendment requires that a juvenile's rights to appeal should be similar to those of an adult in criminal proceedings.[43] However, as with all due process rights, juveniles are not entitled to all the appeal rights that apply to criminal appeals. Typically, juvenile court statutes require that a disposition or "final judgment" be made before a juvenile can appeal a delinquency determination. It follows that, in most cases, a juvenile is not allowed an interlocutory appeal and thus may not appeal directly from the adjudication hearing.

Status Offenders

The term "status offense" refers to misbehavior that is subject to legal sanction in minors but would not be considered criminal in adults. Statutory descriptions of this misbehavior have to do with conduct typical of childhood rather than criminality. The most common status offenses are truancy, violating curfew, running away from home, habitual disobedience, and exposure to vice, moral danger, or depravity (i.e., gambling, mixing with older criminals, and premature sexual activity). Statutes refer to status offenders as "wayward," "incorrigible," or "ungovernable," or as "children in need of services" (CHINS), "juveniles in need of services" (JINS), "people in need of services" (PINS), "minors in need of services" (MINS) or "children in need of assistance" (CHINA).

The authority of the family court to deal with status offenders has come under fire. Criticisms call for the decriminalization of status offenses and the deinstitutionalization and diversion of status offenders.[44] Commentators have protested the practice of taking status offenders into custody under the benevolent cloak of rehabilitation, only to confine many of them along with felons in correctional institutions, prisons, or closed psychiatric hospitals. Moreover, the definition of "status offense" has been criticized by commentators as so unclear (e.g., "in danger of leading a dissolute life") that the relevant statutes should be *void for vagueness* and thus unconstitutional.[45] Conflicting Supreme Court decisions have made the law so turbid as to hamper the preparation of an adequate defense.[46] Others have complained that these statutes fault children and cause them to be unfairly stigmatized by juvenile proceedings when, in most cases, their misbehavior is the result of family dysfunction. The ABA Juvenile Justice Standards and the Office of Juvenile Justice and Delinquency Prevention urge elimination of the jurisdiction.[47]

The Supreme Court has not ruled on the due process rights of status offenders, and lower courts are divided. In all delinquency cases, juveniles are entitled to such "essentials of due process" as the right to counsel.[48] The required standard of proof is "beyond a reasonable doubt." Regarding the procedural rights of status offenders, however, the states are not uniform. Many require a lower standard of proof, such as a preponderance of the evidence (reasonable factual basis).[49] Moreover, some statutes expressly authorize the admissibility of evidence that procedural due process rights would exclude from a delinquency hearing.[50]

Legal proceedings for status offenders parallel the sequence for delinquents: intake, diversion or pretrial detention, hearing on probable cause, adjudicational hearing, and dispositional hearing. Diversion may involve returning the child to the family, relatives, or third parties; referral to a mental health facility; filing a petition for neglect, abuse, or dependency; foster care placement; or emancipation. Dispositional alternatives range from admonishment, through placement at home under probation or placement in a foster home or group home, to referral to an outpatient or inpatient mental health facility. Placements are supposed to be the least restrictive appropriate, as close to home as possible, and capable of providing adequate educational, medical, and social services.[51]

The population of status offenders overlaps those of delinquent and mentally ill children. All three groups are likely to come from families disorganized by parental conflict, child abuse, substance abuse, or psychiatric disorder. Social pathology of this magnitude defies legal remedies. A health plan devoting adequate funds for diagnostic, therapeutic, rehabilitative, and preventative services would ameliorate these problems to some extent. No such plan is in sight.

DEFINITION, EPIDEMIOLOGY, AND PREDICTION
Definition

The term "juvenile delinquency" refers to illegal acts or omissions on the part of minors that would be considered criminal if exhibited by adults.

Types of Offense

Delinquent acts may be committed against property (e.g., theft, automobile theft, breaking and entering, burglary, vandalism, or arson), against the person (e.g., assault, robbery, homicide, or rape), against the self (e.g., the use of illicit drugs), against governmental interests (intimidation of witnesses, bribery, and treason), or in violation of rules or ordinances (e.g., possession of a concealable weapon or speeding in a motor vehicle). The most detailed statistics are available for index offenses, that is, the serious offenses of homicide, aggravated assault, rape, robbery, burglary, theft, auto theft, and arson.

Epidemiologic Indices

The *delinquency rate* of a population refers to the number of delinquent acts committed per person during a specified time (e.g., a calendar year).

$$\text{Delinquency rate} = \frac{\text{No. of delinquent acts per year}}{\text{Population}}$$

The *prevalence of delinquency* refers to the number of delinquent persons in that population.

$$\text{Prevalence} = \frac{\text{No. of delinquents}}{\text{Population}}$$

The *incidence of delinquency* refers to the number of delinquent acts committed on average by each delinquent person during the specified time.

$$\text{Incidence} = \frac{\text{No. of delinquents acts}}{\text{No. of delinquents}}$$

The *delinquency rate* is a function of both prevalence and incidence:

$$\text{Delinquency rate} = \text{Prevalence} \times \text{Incidence}$$

$$= \frac{\text{No. of delinquents}}{\text{Population}} \times \frac{\text{No. of delinquent acts}}{\text{No. of delinquents}}$$

$$= \frac{\text{No. of delinquents acts}}{\text{Population}}$$

As Farrington (1987) points out, the fourth crucial index is *delinquency career length*.

$$\begin{array}{l}\text{No. of delinquent} \\ \text{acts committed by} \\ \text{a cohort up to the} \\ \text{eighteenth birthday}\end{array} = \text{Prevalence} \times \text{Incidence} \times \begin{array}{l}\text{Delinquency} \\ \text{career length}\end{array}$$

Epidemiology studies the influence of historical trends, age, sex, race, class, and urbanization upon delinquency rate, prevalence, incidence, and career length. A detailed review of these matters is beyond the scope of this book; the reader is referred to Farrington (1987, 1988), Rutter and Giller (1984), Wilson and Hernstein (1985), Gordon (1976a), Visher and Roth (1986), and Hindelang, Hirschi, and Weiss (1981). This section will describe the sources of statistical data for delinquency and address the following questions:

1. What are the rate, prevalence, and incidence of delinquency in the United States?
2. Has there been an increase in delinquency?
3. What are the relationships between delinquency and historical trends, age, sex, ethnicity, and urbanization?

Sources of Data

Each of the following sources of data has its advantages and deficiencies:

1. Official records
2. Self-reports
3. Victim reports
4. Informant reports
5. Direct observation

OFFICIAL RECORDS OF ARRESTS AND CONVICTIONS

Official records are the most commonly used source of data. Unfortunately, they suffer from the following drawbacks: (1) most offenses are undetected; (2) records are kept with variable completeness and reliability; (3) the patterns of arrest and conviction may vary from place to place and from time to time (e.g., in response to political pressure); (4) there may be systematic biases in favor of arresting or convicting certain social groups (e.g., blacks); and (5) official records are kept primarily for administrative purposes, not research. The Federal Bureau of Investigation has reported to it data from local law enforcement agencies upon which it collects statistics: the Uniform Crime Reporting (UCR) arrest statistics.

SELF-REPORT SURVEYS

In self-report surveys, respondents are asked whether they have committed delinquent acts during a specified period of time. The drawbacks to self-report include the following: (1) an indefinite number of delinquents may be missing because they are in custody; (2) juveniles may forget, suppress, or exaggerate their delinquencies; (3) trivial delinquencies may be overrepresented; and (4) there may be differential validity according to race (blacks being underreporters).

VICTIM REPORTS, INFORMANT REPORTS, AND DIRECT OBSERVATION

Although these sources of data have been less commonly used, they could potentially provide information supporting the data from official statistics and self-reports.

Historical Trends

Between 1961 and 1976, the number of juvenile court cases per 1,000 population between ten and seventeen years of age rose, year by year, from 20 to 40. The delinquency rate has been increasing more rapidly than the increase of population.[52] During the 1980s crime related to violence became a more significant component of juvenile crimes than property-related crime. This was evident not only among disadvantaged minority youth in urban areas but in all races, social classes, and life-styles. In 1990 the violent crime arrest rate reached an historical high of 430 per 100,000 juveniles; that rate was 27 percent higher than the 1980 rate.[53] Concern has been voiced for the future, considering that the ten-to-seventeen population group is projected to increase significantly between 1990 and 2000, and family stability is likely to deteriorate.[54]

Age Trends

In 1983 the rate of arrest of males for index offenses increased from 4.2 per 100 at 13–14 years to a peak of 7.7 at seventeen. The peak for females was 1.6 at sixteen. The male peak for violent offense rates is eighteen, and for nonviolent offenses, seventeen years of age. The equivalent female peaks are twenty and sixteen. Self-report surveys suggest that the peak prevalence of index offenses occurs between fifteen and seventeen.

Sex Trends

In 1983, the male:female ratio for index crime arrests increased from 3.7 at 13–14 years to a peak of 5.2 at eighteen years. At sixteen, the ratio was highest for burglary (15.8) and robbery (14.6) and lowest for theft (2.7). The average male offender has more recorded delinquencies than the average female offender. Self-report surveys put the gender ratio for prevalence at between 2.5 and 3.0; the most serious offenses have the highest gender ratios. Gender ratios for whites tend to be higher than those for blacks. There is some evidence that the ratio has declined in recent year. Gender differences may be related to biological differences, to sex-related differences in child-rearing, to differential opportunity resulting from different sex-role behavior (e.g., associating with a gang), or to differential reporting or diversion.

Racial Trends

For index crime arrests, the black:white ratio is 4.5 at ten years of age and 3.8 at seventeen. This ratio is higher for females than for males. Delinquency rates are strikingly lower for Asians. Self-report surveys yield lower sex ratios than official crime reports, possibly because of underreporting by black subjects. In general, ethnicity ratios are lower than sex ratios. The reason for ethnic differences can be sought in such factors as poverty, the greater prevalence among blacks of father-absent single-parent families, poorer parental supervision, and lower school attainment. It is likely that black–white differences are dependent on differences in SES and school attainment.

Table 9–1 breaks down arrest rates between different crimes and racial classifications. The decline in arrest rates for the "other" category is explained by the large increase in the numbers of Asian juveniles, the least crime-prone group among juveniles.[56]

Class Trends

The relationship between socioeconomic status and delinquency has been reviewed by Braithwaite (1981), Hindelang, Hirschi, and Weiss (1979), and Loeber and Dishion (1983). Social class is only weakly related to general delinquency. Snyder and Patterson (1987) conclude that the association is mediated through family dysfunction.

Urbanization Trends

Urban and suburban minors are more likely to appear in juvenile court than are rural minors. To some extent, this difference may reflect differential arrest rates; if there

Table 9–1. **Percent Changes in Juvenile Arrest Rates for Crimes Related to Violence, United States, 1990 over 1980***

Offense	All Races	White	Black	Other
Violent crime total	27.3	43.8	19.2	−53.4
Murder	87.3	47.5	145.0	−45.4
Forcible rape	36.7	85.9	8.5	−66.0
Robbery	−7.5	12.3	−15.6	−67.4
Aggravated assault	63.7	59.2	88.9	−38.8
Weapon law violations	62.6	57.6	102.9	−48.1
Drug abuse total	−20.1	−47.6	158.6	−77.0
Heroin/Cocaine	713.4	251.1	2,372.9	126.8
Marijuana	−66.0	−66.7	−47.5	−80.1
Synthetic	−26.5	−34.1	144.7	−77.4
Nonnarcotic	−5.5	−34.6	223.3	−87.5

* Arrest rate per 100,000 for the age group 10–17.
Source: Uniform Crime Reports for the United States, 1991 (Washington: FBI, U.S. Department of Justice, 1991).

are no local juvenile court or facilities, the police may be reluctant to take a minor into custody. Furthermore, there are more police in urban areas.

THE PREDICTION OF DELINQUENCY

In a series of papers, Loeber and Stouthamer-Loeber (1986, 1987) and Stouthamer-Loeber and Loeber (1988) have described the results of a meta-analysis of the literature concerning the prediction of delinquency from juveniles' earlier behavior and environment. In order to gauge the relative predictive power of different variables, Loeber and Stouthamer-Loeber employed a statistic, Relative Improvement over Chance (RIOC), that corrects the association between predictor and outcome variables by accounting for chance associations (calculated from baserates):

$$\text{RIOC} = \frac{\text{Total correct} - \text{chance correct}}{\text{Maximum correct} - \text{chance correct}} \times 100$$

According to the RIOC, in order of predictive power, the following behavioral variables were associated with later adjudications for delinquency:

1. Drug use
2. Stealing
3. Aggression
4. General problem behavior (e.g., disruptiveness, destructiveness)
5. Truancy
6. Poor educational achievement
7. Lying

Compositive behavioral indices (e.g., the index reported by Spivack and Cianci, 1987) have a greater predictive power than single behaviors do. Furthermore, the predictive power of behavior was increased if it was of early onset, frequent, diverse, and evident in more than one setting.

In order of predictive power, the following environmental variables were associated with delinquency:

1. Poor parental supervision
2. Deviant peers (only one study)
3. Lack of parental involvement
4. Poor discipline
5. Parental absence
6. Low SES (weak)
7. Poor parental health (weak)

In general, behavior is a better predictor than environment. As with behavioral predictors, composite environmental scales outdo single variables. The greater power of composite scales supports both Rutter's (1978) model of cumulative risk and Buikhuisen's (1979) probabilistic model (which postulates the interaction of predisposing, facilitating, and inhibiting factors).

Studies of delinquency prediction have three potential uses: to stimulate research into causal associations; to identify children at risk for delinquency who could benefit from preventative treatment;[56] and to help the courts and juvenile justice staff decide the best management for different kinds of offender.

THE CLINICAL CLASSIFICATION OF DELINQUENCY

Up to this point, delinquency has been discussed as though it were homogeneous. However, a considerable body of research and clinical observation indicates that delinquency is heterogeneous and that offenders can be categorized into subtypes. In general, two kinds of typology have been described: empirical and clinical.

Empirical Typologies

Empirical typologies are derived from the multivariate analysis of behavioral ratings and other measures of behavior. A large number of studies (reviewed by Quay, 1986a, 1986b, 1987) concur in isolating four behavioral factors or dimensions from the behavior ratings of populations of delinquents:

1. *Unsocialized aggression* (aggressiveness, disobedience, disruptiveness, lack of consideration for others)
2. *Socialized aggression* (association with delinquent peers, gang loyalty, group delinquency)
3. *Attention deficit* (lack of concentration, impersistence, hyperactivity, impulsiveness, immaturity)
4. *Anxiety-withdrawal-dysphoria* (anxiety, hypersensitivity, sadness, shyness, social withdrawal)

It should be stressed that the above factors are dimensions of behavior, not types of person. Despite the fact that the appropriate mathematical technique for establishing a taxonomy of persons is cluster analysis,[57] numerous researchers have used behavioral factors as though they referred to types of delinquent. For example, unsocialized aggressive delinquents are said to cause more disciplinary problems in institutions, to do less well in a "work-release" program,[58] to be more recidivist,[59] to have poorer adult outcome,[60] to be less able to inhibit responses in order to avoid punishment,[61] to be more likely to seek novelty and complexity,[62] to have poorer interpersonal skills,[63] and to be less responsive electrodermally.[64]

Clinical Typologies

Clinical typologies are based upon clinicians' intuitive classification of people and are usually influenced by an explicit or implicit theoretical viewpoint. In the field of delinquency, there has been an interplay between empirical and clinical approaches.

Sullivan, Grant, and Grant (1957) and Warren (1969), who introduced the California I-Level system of classification, recognized nine different delinquent subtypes. The purpose of I-Level typing is to match the offender to the most appropriate treatment. The nine subtypes were subsequently condensed to three:

1. *Passive-conformist* (responding with immediate compliance to whoever has power)
2. *Power-oriented* (responding to an identified power group of other delinquents and attempting to outwit authority in order to usurp power)
3. *Neurotic* (prone to feelings of inadequacy and guilt, either conscious or acted out)[65]

Weiner (1982) subdivides delinquents into the following categories:

1. *Sociological.* Those delinquents who are influenced by, and loyal to, their associates in a delinquent gang. In this group, delinquency may be a *conforming* or a *masculine proving* response to peer pressure. The sociological group is equivalent to the *socialized aggressive* type of the empiricists and to the *dyssocial, sociosyntonic, sociological,* or *subcultural* type of other clinical classifications.

2. *Characterological.* The characterological group is equivalent to the *unsocialized aggressive* group in the empirical typology. Other virtually synonymous terms are *impulse-ridden, antisocial, sociopathic, psychopathic,* or *affectionless.* Characteristic of this group are the inability to feel guilt, remorse, or empathy; gross egocentrism; incapacity for close, reciprocal relationships; inability to sustain life goals; poor capacity for planning; inability to profit from experience; impulsivity; and sensation-seeking.

3. *Neurotic.* Those who become delinquent not in order to conform with a gang or because they have deficient internal controls, but because they are attempting to resolve conscious or unconscious conflict or to externalize internal tension. This group is roughly equivalent to the *anxiety-withdrawal-dysphoria* group already described in the section on empirical classification. Rejection, loss, separation, and depression are said to be the ground from which their delinquency emerges, the delinquent act being, for example, the expression of a need for recognition, attention, or concern, of a need to express masculinity, or of an attempt to cope with depression. Parental fostering or reinforcement may aggravate the problem in some cases.

Two further (much smaller) groups can be split off from neurotic delinquency.

4. *Organic.* In a small number of cases, delinquent acts (particularly senseless, violent ones) are said to be associated with psychomotor epilepsy or "brain dysfunction." (This topic will be dealt with later.)

5. *Schizoid or Psychotic.* A small number of delinquents prove to be either schizoid or overtly psychotic (usually schizophrenic or paranoid; rarely manic).

Hinshaw, Lakey, and Hart (1993) review research indicating that there are two developmental pathways for delinquency (*childhood-onset* and *adolescent-onset*) and that comorbid attention-deficit disorder and academic underachievement are both associated with unfavorable outcome. Loeber and colleagues (1993) describe these developmental pathways: *authority-conflict* (stubbornness, defiance), *covert* (property damage, minor delinquencies), and *overt* (violence). The worst outcome was associated with escalation in all three pathways.

Summary

Research into etiology and outcome has been hindered by the presumption that delinquents are all from the same mold. Although the clinical classification of delinquents is far from satisfactory, there has been a useful interplay between the empirical and clinical approaches. However, cluster analyses of behavioral descriptions are required in order to determine whether a categorical typology is preferable to a dimensional model. A valid classification is clearly required, for it is evident that delinquents are not homogeneous. It is unlikely, for example, that unsocialized aggression has the same roots as neurotic or sociological delinquency.

ETIOLOGY AND PSYCHOPATHOLOGY

Research into the roots of delinquency falls into four general categories.

Sociological Research

SOCIAL SEGREGATION, SOCIAL DISORGANIZATION, AND THE CRIMINAL TRADITION

The sociological research of Shaw and McKay (1969) (reviewed by Gold, 1987) had its roots in the ecological theory of urbanization proposed by Park, Burgess, and McKenzie (1925). Shaw and McKay used as their dependent variables data from official delinquency records. They conducted detailed surveys of different areas and zones in Chicago with regard to relative social disorganization and criminal traditions, using such indices as median rents, the proportions of families on welfare, ethnic mix, infant mortality rates, rates of commitment to public mental institutions, and adult crime rates.

Shaw and McKay compared the delinquency rates of adjacent zones and documented the consistency of those rates, over time, in different areas. They found high correlations between delinquency and indices of social disorganization. They also found that when such social factors as the proportion of families on welfare were statistically removed, the effect of ethnicity was markedly reduced (though not entirely eliminated). In other words, although black and foreign-born residents were concentrated in those socially disorganized areas that had the highest delinquency rates, ethnicity was less powerful than social disorganization as a predictor of juvenile crime.

The ecological theory of delinquency was articulated in the following manner. The individuals, social classes, and ethnic groups that inhabit cities compete for the most desirable areas. In this competition, the most disadvantaged group are recent immigrants who tend to be relegated to decaying neighborhoods ("interstitial areas") near the inner city. The consequent socioeconomic segregation has two main results. First, the socially disadvantaged are less able to resist criminals, who thus find easy pickings. Second, the residents of poor areas are less able to prevent the encroachment of other people from culturally different backgrounds. Slums thus become both refuges for criminals and battlegrounds for competing ethnic groups. Crowded, disadvantaged, ethnically heterogeneous ghettos spawn criminogenic social organizations (e.g., youth gangs). Economically blocked from access to desirable amenities, some residents seek a criminal solution, while others tolerate their doing so. Nobody is unaffected by the local criminal tradition. Some resist it, some adapt to it, some are recruited by it.

The weakest part of this theory is the link between social disorganization and individual delinquency. Shaw and McKay suggested that socially disadvantaged families may be inefficient at teaching and supervising their children and that they lack access to community facilities (good schools, recreational opportunities) offering alternatives to crime. It is easy for youth in such families to slip out of social control.

The replications of, refinements of, and challenges to Shaw and McKay's ecological theory are reviewed by Gold (1987). The most telling critique alluded to a potential bias in their work toward disproving ethnic differences. In actuality, Shaw and McKay did not find that ethnicity makes no difference. Why is it, for example, that Asians have such a low delinquency rate compared to blacks? Ethnic groups do seem to have a differential vulnerability to crime, possibly as a result of variations in family cohesiveness. Furthermore, the validity of official records as an index of delinquency has been questioned (see below). Shaw and McKay may also have overestimated the social disorganization of the poor.

CULTURE CONFLICT

Sellin (1938) related the social disorganization of recently immigrated families to the confusion of immigrant parents and their children. Many recent immigrants come from homogeneous rural communities and must accommodate to a heterogeneous urban society in which they lack political power. As their children adapt to the new world, conflicts arise between the generations, and children slip out of control.

This theory was probably more relevant to the turn of the century, when immigration was at its peak. As immigrants assimilate, their delinquency rates drop. However, many blacks continue to be blocked from full participation in the society, with the result that delinquency rates remain high in the poorest black communities.

THE CRIMINOGENIC SOCIAL ORGANIZATION OF THE SLUM

Thrasher (1927) and Whyte (1955) have criticized Shaw and McKay's theory of social disorganization. They proposed that hierarchies of personal relationships and obligations cohere in the gangs, rackets, and politics of the slums. In other words, they contended, a culturally relative view is required. Some of the informal organizations that spring from the slums (gangs, for example) are conducive to crime and may be tolerated or supported by local residents.

Short (1963) has analyzed the street-corner gang, emphasizing the way in which antisocial values are transmitted to individuals through the peer group. Boys might be compelled to commit offenses, for example, in order to demonstrate courage and masculinity, and girls induced to steal in order to obtain goods to enhance their attractiveness.

Miller (1958) has analyzed the lower-class values ("focal concerns") that facilitate, and are imbedded in, the organization of the gang, for example: the preoccupation of gang members with "toughness" and the capacity to outwit others, the desire for autonomy and status, the hunger for excitement, and the belief that life is dictated by "fate" or "luck" rather than planning.

BLOCKED OPPORTUNITY

Merton's (1957) analysis of American society asserted the social preeminence of pecuniary success. Cohen (1955) extended Merton's analysis to the microcosm of gangs, interpreting them as alternative status systems for slum youth who feel excluded from middle-class opportunities.

Cloward and Ohlin (1960) have emphasized the function of the gang as an illegitimate means to the acquisition of desirable amenities in a society that accords the highest status to affluence. In more stable slums, criminal organizations, the police, and business owners accommodate each other, giving youth opportunities for apprenticeship as criminals. In disintegrated areas, by contrast, the desire for status is channeled into gang activity and drug use.

However, field analyses of juvenile gangs[66] have not found the adherence to antisocial values suggested by Cloward and Ohlin. Some gangs appear to be oriented to fighting with other gangs, some to drug use, and others to "hell-raising." Rebellion against the middle-class system does not seem to be a prominent feature, although gang members do perceive themselves as excluded from the dominant society. Delinquent behavior appears to occur when status is threatened, when hedonistic opportunity outweighs the risk of being detected, or when group obligations apply. Juvenile gangs may be more loosely organized and less supportive socially than was originally thought. It is interesting to conjecture whether the apparent lack of cohesion is related to the recent widespread use of narcotics.

DIFFERENTIAL JUSTICE

An alternative approach suggests that differential delinquency rates are caused by variations in the activity of the police and the staff of the juvenile justice system. The chances of apprehension for crime are greater in densely populated inner-city areas where there is more police surveillance. Juvenile courts may deal differently with youths from a high crime area.[67] Furthermore, contact with the juvenile justice system may itself promote further delinquency.

SOCIAL CONTROL THEORY

Reckless (1961) and Hirschi (1969) propose that, within a well-integrated society, crime is contained by social pressure. However, if families fail to supervise and discipline their children, if social roles and limits become unclear, and if there is inadequate reward for positive accomplishment, the individual must fall back upon inner resources. When these are weak, crime is a possibility.

LABELING THEORY

"Labeling" or "secondary deviance" theories[68] propose that delinquency stems from giving a juvenile the label "delinquent." As suggested above, there is indeed evidence that delinquent attitudes can be hardened by legal processing, but this is likely to be contributory, rather than a primary cause. "Reactive" theories associated with Marxist criminology view delinquency as a "protorevolutionary response to class repression"—provocative and colorful, perhaps, but of no heuristic import.

Psychological Research

FAMILY INTERACTION AND SOCIAL LEARNING

Snyder and Patterson (1987) have reviewed cross-sectional and longitudinal research into the relationship between family variables and delinquency (as measured by official reports, self-report, and recidivism). The data consistently show that the following family variables are associated with delinquency: poor discipline, poor guidance, poor supervision, poor problem-solving, and intrafamilial stress and conflict. Sociodemographic factors such as low socioeconomic status, "broken homes," paternal absence, and parental criminality probably relate to delinquency via these family variables. The rapid increase in juvenile delinquency parallels the tripling in the number of single-parent families since 1950.[69]

Snyder and Patterson postulate that delinquent behavior is a form of defective socialization, arising first at home and subsequently via antisocial peers who are not countered by satisfactory adult models. Homes that produce delinquents are characterized by poor discipline. Parents fail to label behavior as unacceptable, fail to track unacceptable behavior in different settings, and fail to manage it in a consistent manner. Such parents are described as inconsistent, erratic, neglectful, lax, harsh, or punitive. Some parents are undiscriminating in what they label as unacceptable, responding with equal vigor to trivia and serious infractions. Others, though threatening and verbally harsh, fail to follow through. As a result, coercive interactions are generated, each party cajoling the other more and more loudly until one backs down or explodes. Aggressive children elicit harshness from their parents, who in turn teach the children to escalate coerciveness until the opposition caves in. Poor parental guidance is manifest in failure to label good behavior as desirable, failure to track behavior across situations, failure to reinforce good behavior, and failure to convey concern, support, and pleasure in the child's activity. As a result, delinquents do not acquire the normative values, interpersonal skills, and work habits required for success with peers, in school, and at work, and may be rejected by the very adults (e.g., teachers) whom they urgently need as models. Poor supervision is evident in the parents' lack of awareness of their children's activities and whereabouts, particularly as the child grows older. Thus, the child drifts unchecked toward undesirable peers. Of all parental variables, poor supervision has the strongest association with delinquency. The parents of delinquents are poor problem-solving models. Unresolved problems lead to high levels of family stress and conflict, with further impairment of problem-solving, irritability, defensiveness, blaming, and avoidance of responsibility. Snyder and Patterson point out that although these family variables are not mutually exclusive, they are not redundant: Despite some overlap, there is sufficient statistical distinction between them for each to contribute independently to delinquency. Nevertheless, multivariate composites of family variables predict delinquency better than single items (see below).

It is not clear how family dysfunction relates to delinquency. Experimental interventions are required to determine whether family dysfunction has a causal relationship to delinquency or whether family problems and juvenile delinquency are noncausal correlates. The latter could be the case, for example, if both family dysfunction and delinquency had strong genetic roots. Snyder and Patterson postulate a *transactional synthesis* as follows: Early coercive interactions between parent and child persist and escalate. As a result of irregular reinforcement, the child learns that the inconsistent parent can often be shouted down and defeated, and consequently fails to develop social and work skills. Obstreperous and egocentric when he goes to school, the child fails academically and is rejected by peers and teachers. Consequently, he drifts towards like-minded peers and, since he is inadequately supervised, begins to perpetrate offenses.

THE CONCEPT OF PSYCHOPATHY

The diagnosis of *psychopathy* or *sociopathy* has its roots in Pritchard's (1837) concept of "moral insanity." However, it was Cleckley (1955) who most clearly articulated its clinical features. Cleckley characterized the psychopath as follows: without delusions, hallucinations, or anxiety; superficially charming; unreliable and untruthful; lacking remorse; exhibiting poorly motivated antisocial behavior; unable to learn from experience; pathologically egocentric; emotionally shallow; likely to have a trivial sexual life; prone to extravagant misbehavior when drunk; and unable to follow any life plan. Cleckley suggested that the underlying defect might be a "semantic aphasia," which prevents the psychopath from integrating the formal, semantic, and affective components of language. The Washington University School of Psychiatry has promoted the concept that sociopathy is a distinct category of psychiatric disorder, possibly inherited in origin, on the basis of its consistent clinical picture, persistence across a lifetime, and frequent association with other disorders.[70]

Yochelson and Samenow (1976, 1977) and McCord and McCord (1964) describe the psychopath's cognitive patterns of manipulation, denial of responsibility, prevarication, self-delusion, and capacity to "cut off" or dissociate fear and danger signals. Dorr and Woodhall (1986) ascribe these characteristics to ego dysfunction, particularly in the areas of reality testing, judgment, regulation of drives and affects, object relations, adaptive regression, and synthetic functioning.

PSYCHOANALYTIC THEORIES OF DELINQUENCY

The contribution of psychoanalysis to understanding delinquency can be described under three headings: (1) the postulation of a relationship between crime and unconscious guilt or parental fostering; (2) descriptive analyses of the impaired ego and superego functioning of the delinquent; and (3) studies that relate "affectionless psychopathy" to parental deprivation and attachment disruption during early childhood.

Psychoanalytic theory initially related crime to the acting out of unconscious guilt (e.g., for repressed incestuous urges) in such a manner as to receive punishment and expiation.[71] Johnson and Szurek (1952) described the unconscious facilitation of deviant behavior by an ambivalent parent ("sanctions for superego lacunae"). Bowlby (1946, 1952) noted a connection between "affectionless psychopathy" and early multiple separations and institutional care. It has been difficult, however, to differentiate between the effects of parental discord, deviant childrearing, failure to form attachments, distortion of relationships, and bond disruption. It may be that bond disruption following discord has the most serious consequences in regard to later delinquency.[72]

Much psychoanalytic theorizing concerning delinquency has been descriptive (rather than causal) in nature. However, the work of the attachment theorists[73] has provided a framework for research that has led to a progressive refinement of the hypotheses of maternal deprivation, attachment disturbance, separation, bond disruption and loss, and the contribution of these factors to sociopathy.

Greenberg, Speltz, and DeKlyen (1993) postulate that disruptive behavior arises from three complementary processes: distorted affective-cognitive structures, disorganized attachment patterns, and the motivational consequences of attachment insecurity. These processes arise from neurobiological risk factors, adverse family ecology, inappropriate parenting practices, and disturbance in early attachment. Waters, Posada, Crowell, and Lay (1993) also point to a connection between early attachment disorganization and later disruptive behavior problems.

NEUROPSYCHOLOGICAL AND NEURODEVELOPMENTAL RESEARCH

The voluminous literature concerning the intelligence testing and neuropsychological assessment of juvenile delinquents has been reviewed by Quay (1987b) and Miller (1988). Delinquent populations subjected to intelligence testing have consistently yielded intelligence quotients about eight points below nondelinquents, a difference that persists when SES is controlled. This IQ difference is due primarily to deficiencies in verbal performance, particularly in word knowledge, verbally coded information, and verbal reasoning. Furthermore, the most aggressive, impulsive delinquents are likely to have the most marked discrepancies between verbal and performance intelligence. These verbal deficiencies, which probably antedate school entry, interfere with school adjustment, giving rise to vicious circles of coerciveness and oppositionalism between the child and his teachers. More detailed neuropsychological assessment suggests that delinquents' verbal deficits relate particularly to complex problem-solving, verbally mediated response regulation, verbal reasoning, and language skills.

Unfortunately, much of the research into lower-order personality constructs (reviewed by Arbuthnot, Gordon, and Jurkovic, 1987) has been marred by a tendency to treat delinquents as homogeneous. It may be for this reason that research into time orientation, impulsivity, sensation seeking, and locus of control has not produced consistent results. The finding that offenders have a negative, unclear, or discrepant self-concept has suggested that delinquency might be a defensive response to low self-regard, but available research does not clarify the direction of causality.

A number of cross-sectional studies indicate that the moral reasoning of juvenile offenders is relatively immature and that a disproportionate number of offenders are at a preconventional level.[74] Jurkovic and Prentice (1977) found this to be particularly true for the psychopathic (i.e., unsocialized aggressive) delinquent. Furthermore, Chandler (1973) found that serious delinquents had deficient role-taking abilities.

Miller (1988) relates the offender's egocentrism, hedonism, unreflectiveness, poor role-taking capacity, and deficient moral reasoning to a developmental "immaturity" (rather than "disorder") in the functioning of the frontal lobes and left cerebral hemisphere.

Biological Research

GENETIC FACTORS

After fifty years of neglect, the genetic theory of crime has undergone a renascence. New data from pedigree, twin, and cross-fostering studies point to a link between inheritance and criminality. Useful reviews of genetic research have been provided by Cadoret (1986), Trasler (1987), and Rutter and Giller (1984).

Pedigree studies are used to detect families in which the prevalence of a phenotype is unusually high, in order to suggest the mode of inheritance and to find related phenotypes that might have a familial association. Cross-fostering and twin studies are used to substantiate the genetic basis of a disorder and to estimate the relative contribution of genes and environment in the production of a phenotype.

Pedigree studies suggest a familial association between antisocial personality (in men), alcoholism (in men), and hysteria (in women).[75] Cross-fostering studies have found an increased prevalence of sociopathy or criminality in the adopted-away offspring of adults with antisocial personality and in the biological parents of adult sociopaths who had been adopted away as children.[76] Bohman (1983) detected an interaction between genetic and environmental factors: Unstable preadoption placement trebled the predictive power of the genetic factor alone. Bohman also found that criminality rates were much higher among the relatives of antisocial women than among those of men. Criminality, antisocial personality, and alcoholism are commonly confounded in these studies; however, recent research suggests that alcoholism and antisocial personality have separate modes of inheritance.[77]

Early researchers found large differences between monzygotic (MZ) and dizygotic (DZ) twins in the prevalence of adult criminality;[78] unfortunately, these studies are flawed by sampling problems, unreliable determination of zygosity, and the fact that twins tend to grow up in very similar environments. Trasler (1987) points out that, as larger and less biased samples have been collected, the differences between MZ and DZ concordance rates have shrunk. Christiansen (1977a, 1977b) found pairwise concordance rates of 33.3 percent in MZ twins and 10.9 percent in DZ twins, whereas Dalgard and Kringlen (1976) found concordance rates of 25.8 and 14.9 percent. In one of the few studies of juvenile (rather than adult) offenders, the concordance rates for MZ and DZ twins were 100 and 71 percent, respectively, suggesting a preponderant environmental influence.[79]

In summary, it appears that polygenic factors have a moderate influence on adult criminality, particularly recidivism; that adverse genetic and environmental factors interact; that alcoholism and antisocial behavior are often associated (although they are probably genetically separate); and that future research should concentrate on antisocial personality rather than on adult crime or juvenile delinquency.

CHROMOSOMAL ABNORMALITY

The association between chromosomal anomalies and antisocial personality, though of scientific interest, is of little practical import. The three abnormalities that have been implicated—47XXY, 47XYY, and an abnormally long Y chromosome (Trasler, 1987)—are uncommon.

Men with the XXY anomaly have Klinefelter's syndrome, a disorder associated with mental retardation, tallness, abnormal body proportions, gynaecomastia, and infertility. In subnormal populations the XXY syndrome tends to be associated with antisocial behavior, but it is rarely encountered among delinquents. The XYY anomaly (which is even less common than the XXY abnormality) is characterized by tallness and electroencephalographic abnormality. It does not appear to be associated with crimes of violence, as was originally thought, but rather with recidivism and minor property offenses. The long Y anomaly may also be associated with recidivism.

SOMATOTYPE

A number of studies in the United States and Great Britain have detected an association between delinquency and body build.[80] Institutionalized offenders tended to be mesomorphic (muscular), rather than ectomorphic (lean) or endomorphic (fat). More recent studies have not supported this association in noninstitutionalized delinquents.

PSYCHOSIS, EPILEPSY, AND BRAIN DYSFUNCTION

Lewis and Balla (1976) have criticized the diagnoses of "sociopathy" and "conduct disorder" on the ground that they obscure diagnostic complexity and heterogeneity. Using detailed interviewing, psychological testing, and neurological assessment, Lewis and her co-workers claim to have uncovered evidence of hidden schizophrenia, paranoia, epilepsy, and brain dysfunction in many severe delinquents.[81] These abnormalities are said to be particularly prevalent among violent delinquents: it is hypothesized that they are related to head trauma caused by child abuse.

It is probable that Lewis and associates are erroneously attributing the hallucinatory experiences, illogical thinking, amnesia, and "absences" of these severely disturbed delinquents to psychosis and epilepsy. Under severe stress, children with poorly integrated personality are prone to exhibit dissociative phenomena, with pseudohallucinations,[82] memory gaps, temporary lapses of concentration, suspiciousness, and explosive aggression. In some cases these phenomena appear to be residua of childhood posttraumatic stress disorder related to physical and sexual abuse.

On the other hand, the neuropsychological deficits and minor neurological signs described by Lewis and co-workers have been detected among juvenile delinquents (especially violent offenders) by other researchers and have been attributed to neurodevelopmental "immaturity" rather than to "brain damage." It is possible that the "brain dysfunction" described by Lewis does not represent pathology but, rather, a variant of normal functioning that is susceptible to being molded in the direction of delinquency.

BEHAVIORAL INHIBITION

Much of the psychophysiologic research into the autonomic nervous functioning of offenders stems from Mowrer's (1950) theory of social learning ("passive avoidance" or "aversive inhibitory conditioning"). Mowrer suggested that when a child is punished for misbehavior, he feels anxiety. After several repetitions of this sequence, a normal child learns to inhibit the offensive behavior and is reinforced by a reduction of anticipatory anxiety. For this to be learned, the child must have the following competencies: (1) to respond to punishment with anxiety; (2) to establish associative mental links between offensive actions and the punishments they evoke; (3) to inhibit offensive actions; and (4) to experience a consequent reinforcing reduction of anxiety. Mowrer's theory suggests that sociopaths have deficient capacity for aversive inhibitory learning.

Research into the possible explanation for this deficiency has been reviewed by Trasler (1987) and Hare (1986). Low levels of tonic arousal, low autonomic reactivity, and rapid habituation could be associated with the sensation-seeking of the typical psychopath, but the experimental evidence is insufficient to judge which of these explanations is correct. Several studies, however, suggest that psychopaths are less responsive autonomically to pain. Eysenck (1964) linked psychopathic behavior to extraversion and neuroticism. In Eysenck's theory, extraversion was associated with low conditionability and neuroticism with recidivism. However, evidence for a general factor of conditionability has not been forthcoming, and recent studies (reviewed by Farrington, Biron, and LeBlanc, 1982) have not consistently found an excess of extraverts among offenders.

In a prospective study of a high-risk group, Mednick (1974) found an association between delinquency and slow electrodermal recovery (EDRec). Mednick hypothesized that the EDRec is an index of the onset and offset of fear, a slow EDRec indicating poor reinforcement of inhibition by fear reduction. However, subsequent research has thrown some doubt upon the stability and validity of the EDRec.

Protective Factors

Only a proportion of those at risk for delinquency actually become offenders. Rutter and Giller (1984) have reviewed research into the following factors which appear to counteract the emergence of delinquency in high-risk groups: parental supervision, improved family circumstances, differential association, employment, and marriage.

PARENTAL SUPERVISION

As described below, poor parental supervision is an important predictor of delinquency. Good supervision involves a monitoring of peer group associations and has been found to counteract vandalism. There is suggestive evidence that if one parental relationship is sound, the child is less likely to develop conduct disorder.[83]

IMPROVEMENT IN FAMILY CIRCUMSTANCES

Rutter (1971) found that conduct problems abated in some children when they were separated from homes disrupted by parental discord and other family problems. Hetherington, Cox, and Cox (1978) found that children's problems tended to decrease when divorce restored domestic harmony, and to persist when parental discord continued following divorce.

DIFFERENTIAL ASSOCIATION

In a longitudinal study of four hundred high-risk London boys, West and Farrington (1973) found that high-risk but nondelinquent subjects tended to have social handicaps (e.g., low intelligence or unemployment) other than delinquency. It may be that some of these handicaps (e.g., social isolation) were protective against delinquency. However, when persistent offenders were compared with delinquents who ceased to offend in late adolescence, it was found that many of the latter had changed peer groups and were no longer associating with bad companions. Rutter and colleagues (1979) tentatively drew a similar inference from their study of the effect of different school environments. Dropping out of school sometimes allows the youth to change companions, as does moving away from a high-risk neighborhood.

EMPLOYMENT

Bachman, O'Malley, and Johnstone (1978) have found an association between unemployment and self-reported delinquency in a longitudinal study of two thousand adolescent boys.

MARRIAGE

The relationship between marriage and delinquency is double-edged. Early marriage is correlated with increased delinquency, probably as a result of the connections among delinquency, early sexual experience, and adolescent pregnancy.[84] However, there is some evidence that the delinquency rate abates after marriage.[85] In a prospective study, Rutter, Quinton, and Liddle (1983) found that compared with a control group of family-reared subjects, institution-reared youth were more likely to have contracted early and unsatisfactory marriages, which intensified their social impairments, psychiatric disorder, and antisocial behavior. However, it is possible that a later marriage to a nondeviant partner could be protective.

Rutter and Giller (1984) surmise that protective factors could exercise their beneficial effect in the following manner: (1) by generating a more favorable self-concept; (2) by preventing adverse peer group association; (3) by providing more satisfying educational experiences; (4) by encouraging later school-leaving; (5) by allowing later and more satisfactory marriage; and (6) by providing improved life opportunities.

Summary: The Etiology of Delinquency

Sociological research delineates the characteristics of high-risk environments, but it cannot determine why only some individuals in those environments become delinquent and why still fewer become recidivist adult criminals. It is too soon to synthesize the sociological theories of delinquency and relate them to individual psychology. More research is required to determine whether regional and zonal differences in delinquency rates are real or artificial, to relate social conditions to family stress, and to elucidate the vexed questions of differential justice and secondary deviance.

As with sociological research, much of the investigation of personality variables has been marred by a tendency to treat delinquency as homogeneous. Sociological research seems to apply best to "socialized," "dyssocial," or "sociosyntonic" delinquency; psychological and biological research is pertinent to the "characterological," "undersocialized," or "sociopathic" type of offender; whereas psychoanalytic and neuropsychiatric clinical studies are most applicable to the "neurotic," "psychotic," and "organic" subtypes.

A promising field of psychological research relates aberrant family interaction to the development in children of coerciveness and deviant peer relationships. It is interesting to conjecture whether the vicious circles of coercion that characterize these families might not have originated in an inherited tendency for children at risk to be impulsive, unreflective, and deficient in the capacity to profit from aversive experience. Social learning theory currently appears to be suspended between hypotheses that coerciveness is a consequence of intermittent reinforcement and deviant adult modeling and hypotheses that they result from an inherent defect in the child's behavioral inhibition. Whatever the explanation, one can predict a progressive convergence of genetic, neurodevelopmental, and social learning theories of sociopathy and unsocialized aggression. In the meantime, clinical research will continue to pursue the relationship of personality disorder and posttraumatic stress disorder to delinquency, and to investigate the roots of different kinds of violent and sexual offenses.

TREATMENT

During the 1970s a number of influential reviews appeared concerning the efficacy of different therapeutic interventions for juvenile offenders. In summary, Martinson (1974); Lipton, Martinson, and Wilks (1975); and McCord (1978) have concluded that no intervention has been demonstrated to be effective. Their negative conclusions spread pessimism among researchers and engendered nihilistic attitudes in the administrators of services for juvenile delinquents. In many ways, the situation resembles that surrounding the initial evaluations of preschool educational intervention programs for culturally disadvantaged children. Were these negative conclusions premature? Was the baby thrown out with the bathwater? The following discussion will address these questions by reviewing recent evaluations of the efficacy of institutional and community programs for the treatment, diversion, or deterrence of delinquents, and by noting those techniques of intervention that are the most promising.[86]

Institutional Treatment

Garrett (1985) has undertaken a meta-analysis of all controlled studies of institutional treatment. Meta-analysis employs a statistical computation, *effect size,* which enables the improvement yielded by an experimental treatment to be transformed to a standard metric for purposes of comparison.

The effect size of an experimental treatment is calculated as follows:

Experimental-Control Effect Size =
$$\frac{\text{Experimental Group Post-treatment Mean} - \text{Control Group Post-treatment Mean}}{\text{Standard Deviation of Control Group Post-treatment Scores}}$$

By this means of standardization, the reviewer can go beyond conventional analysis (which merely polls successes and failures) and address the *relative efficacy* of different treatment programs.

Garrett classified different institutional programs into four categories:

1. *Psychodynamic* (individual, group, and family psychotherapy)
2. *Behavioral* (contingency management, cognitive-behavioral therapy, guided group interaction, and positive peer culture)
3. *Life skills* (drug and alcohol counseling, academic skills, vocational training, and outdoor experience)
4. *Miscellaneous*

The overall treatment effect size on outcome measures was + .37, indicating that youths who received treatment did better than controls. The overall effect size was greater for females (+ .58) than for males (+ .35), and for younger (+ .69) than for older offenders (+ .35). Effect size diminished (but did not disappear) as experimental designs became more rigorous. Psychodynamic therapy, life skills therapy, and miscellaneous treatments were outperformed by behavioral treatments, particularly contingency management (+ .86) and cognitive-behavioral therapy (+ .56). However, family therapy (+ .81) performed well—better, for example, than individual psychotherapy (+ .14) and group therapy (+ .17). On the other hand, the average treatment effect size with regard to recidivism was + .13 (+ .10 for rigorous studies, and + .29 for less rigorous studies). The most impressive effects of treatment were on community adjustment (+ .72), psychological adjustment (+ .45), and academic performance (+ .42).

Garrett's analysis does not support the bald conclusion that "nothing works," although admittedly the impact of treatment on recidivism has not been impressive. Nevertheless, cognitive-behavior therapy, contingent management, and family therapy merit further investigation.

Quay (1987a) has reviewed the outcome of a number of major institutional programs, all of which were completed in the 1970s. No major program evaluation has been published in recent years. Although several of these programs produced behavioral improvements within the institution, none had an appropriate effect on recidivism following discharge.

Community-based Treatment

Gottschalk and colleagues (1987) have conducted a meta-analysis of ninety community intervention studies that involved juvenile offenders. The average intervention lasted twenty-two weeks and required forty-two hours of direct treatment. Measures of behavior, attitude, and recidivism were used to assess outcome, and the effect size was calculated. In all measures except the attitudinal, pre–post effect sizes exceeded experimental-control effect sizes. The confidence limits of all effect sizes (except the attitudinal) included zero, so the null hypothesis could not be rejected. The reviewers noted that greater effect size was associated with older studies, nonadjudicated youth, duration of treatment, and mode of treatment (behavioral, educational, and group therapy interventions being the most successful). The pessimistic conclusions of other reviewers[87] concerning the community treatment of juvenile offenders were not contraverted by this meta-analysis.

Gensheimer and associates (1986) conducted a meta-analysis of 103 community diversion studies and found no evidence for their efficacy overall. Similarly, in a review of diversion, deterrence, and wilderness programs, Basta and Davidson (1988) found no evidence for a positive effect. The latter reviewers noted serious methodological deficiencies in many of the studies they analyzed.

The Efficacy of Different Techniques of Treatment

The efficacy of the different therapeutic techniques that have been used in the treatment of delinquency has been reviewed by Gordon and Arbuthnot (1987).

INDIVIDUAL THERAPY

Of the modes of individual psychotherapy, neither individual casework nor psychodynamic psychotherapy been found effective in reducing recidivism. Individual behavior therapy has resulted in improvements in classroom behavior (e.g., better attendance, less disruptiveness, and better participation in classroom activities) but generally little or no reduction of recidivism.

GROUP THERAPY

Didactic treatment, discussion therapy, psychoanalytic treatment, and client-centered group therapy have not consistently resulted in attitude change and increased cooperativeness within institutions; they have had little or no effect upon recidivism. Positive results have been reported for cognitive-behavioral group therapy that has specifically targeted interpersonal problem-solving, impulsivity, role-taking, and moral reasoning.[88]

FAMILY THERAPY

Family psychotherapy based upon a systems model has been reported as reducing recidivism,[89] but methodological problems vitiate the reliance that can be placed on these studies. Several parental skills training interventions have reported success in reducing delinquency. Researchers at the Oregon Social Learning Center have developed a behavioral parent training method that can be implemented in family groups. Promising results have been reported.[90] Alexander and Parsons (1982), who targeted family communication, problem-solving, contingency contracting, limit-setting, and other interactional deficits in their community-based approach, have reported positive effects on recidivism.

Summary

In brief, the most promising techniques of therapy are (1) cognitive-behavior group therapy and (2) behavioral family therapy that targets parenting skills. The training of therapists and the integrity of the therapy in question require close attention; the goals of therapy need to be clear, discrete, and readily conveyed to the client and family; and the therapist needs special skills in overcoming resistance and engaging clients and families. The correct response to the question, "What works?" is to reframe it as, "What works, for which youths, in whose hands, under what conditions, and in what way?"[91] The simple answer "Nothing" is not acceptable.

THE FORENSIC EVALUATION OF JUVENILE OFFENDERS
Introduction

The forensic evaluation of juvenile offenders has been discussed by Guggenheim and Garmise (1985), Lewis (1980), Sacks and Sacks (1980), Petti (1980), Palombi (1980), Benedek (1985), and Melton *et al.* (1987).

The scope of forensic evaluation for a juvenile offender is broader than that for an adult. Despite *Kent, Gault,* and their progeny, the juvenile court retains a rehabilitative aim, requires a comprehensive evaluation, and seeks a composite treatment recommendation. Although the clinician may be asked to address the issues of "competency to stand trial" and "mental state at the time of the offense," the forensic clinician is more often called upon to evaluate "amenability to treatment." Juvenile court staff have broad discretionary powers in ordering diversion or disposition, and the forensic clinician can have a powerful influence on the final order.

Circumstances of Referral

Mental health clinicians become involved in forensic evaluations if they are employed in a court clinic, if they are requested to evaluate an offender as a consultant to the court, or if they are engaged by a private attorney for that purpose. Mental health consultations are most likely to be requested at the following times to elucidate the following questions:

1. *Prior to the disposition hearing.* Amenability to treatment? Appropriate disposition? Recommended treatment?
2. *Prior to a transfer hearing.* Amenability to treatment? Dangerousness? Competence to waive due process rights? Competence to stand trial? Mental state at the time of the offense?
3. *Prior to adjudication.* Competence to stand trial? Competence to waive due process rights? Mental state at the time of the offense? Recommended psychiatric treatment? Appropriate disposition?
4. *Prior to diversion.* Amenability to treatment? Appropriate diversion? Recommended treatment?

Issues at Stake in the Forensic Evaluation of Juvenile Delinquents

The issues likely to be at stake are as follows:

1. Diagnosis
2. Amenability to treatment
3. Recommended disposition
4. Dangerousness
5. Waiver to adult court

6. Competence to stand trial
7. Competence to waive *Miranda* or due process rights
8. Mental state at the time of the offense
9. Mitigating factors

DIAGNOSIS

What is the *categorical diagnosis* (DSM-III, Axes I, II, and III)? Aside from conduct disorder in its ubiquitous forms, is there evidence for such disorders as organic brain disorder, epilepsy, anxiety disorder, dissociative disorder, posttraumatic stress disorder, conversion disorder, schizophrenia, paranoid disorder, depression, bipolar disorder, or personality disorder (e.g., of borderline, narcissistic, or schizotypal type)? Is there evidence for a *developmental disorder,* for example in academic functioning?

What is the *biopsychosocial formulation,* and how does it relate to the delinquent behavior? Specifically, what physical or psychosocial factors have *predisposed* the child to delinquent behavior? What are the juvenile's *intelligence* and *learning capacity?* What (if anything) *precipitated* the delinquency? What *perpetuates* it (i.e., what physical, psychological, or social factors reinforce it or prevent it from being inhibited or extinguished)? What were the conscious and unconscious *purposes* for the delinquent act or acts? How did the offender come to be apprehended? What is the current *pattern* of psychopathological phenomena, and what *mode and level of coping* do they represent? What biological or psychosocial *strengths* or *reserves* do the child and family possess? What is the *prognosis* for the diagnosed psychiatric disorder, conduct disorder, personality disorder, or developmental disorder, with or without treatment?

AMENABILITY TO TREATMENT

Is the juvenile likely to cooperate in, and respond to, rehabilitation? Is he or she likely to cooperate in, and respond to, mental health treatment in the community, if this is appropriate? Is such treatment available or accessible?

RECOMMENDED DISPOSITION

What combination of diversional options, dispositional alternatives, or treatment possibilities would you recommend? If mental health treatment is required, in what kind of setting should it be undertaken (e.g., at an outpatient service, day treatment program, intensive community-based treatment program, residential treatment center, or psychiatric hospital)? What treatment or combination of treatments would be most appropriate (e.g., individual, group, or family psychotherapy, treatment for substance abuse, pharmacotherapy, or cognitive-behavioral therapy)? What is the rationale for your treatment recommendations?

Should the juvenile remain at home, be placed with relatives or other adults, or be managed in a foster home, group home, or closed institution? What special arrangements are needed for the juvenile's education? What alternative treatments or dispositions could be helpful? If more than one treatment plan is feasible, what are the advantages and disadvantages of the various alternatives? Does the juvenile have special physical or educational needs that would complicate treatment? Is the treatment you recommend available to the court?

DANGEROUSNESS

How dangerous is the youth likely to be to others (assaultiveness, homicidal ideation, sexual offenses), to property (destructiveness, arson), or to himself or herself (impulsivity, risk-taking, sexual provocativeness, propensity for running away, suicidality)? The assessment of dangerousness is discussed further in Chapter 8.

WAIVER TO ADULT COURT

The guidelines by which a juvenile judge considers the transfer of a juvenile to adult court have already been described. A clinician is sometimes asked to evaluate the offender in order to throw light upon the following criteria:

1. The juvenile's personality, physical and mental maturity, and psychiatric diagnosis
2. The juvenile's amenability to treatment in the community
3. The suitability for this juvenile of the programs and facilities available to the juvenile court

Benedek (1985) has described the evaluation of transfer cases. The juvenile's attorney should be consulted. The clinician must review all police reports, mental health and medical records, school reports, and other pertinent documents. The juvenile must be informed of the nature of the evaluation and must give informed consent to it.

COMPETENCE TO STAND TRIAL

The requirement of mental competence assures that defendant is able to understand the nature and effect of the proceedings, to provide necessary information for an adequate defense, and to assist in that defense. This issue is most likely to be raised prior to transfer to adult court. The historical evolution of the concept, its legal definition, and the methods of evaluating competency are discussed in standard forensic texts[92] and in special publications.[93] Incompetency is a much more frequent plea than "not guilty by reason of insanity."[94] This section summarizes relevant issues.

In *Pate v. Robinson* the Supreme Court held that, if a trial judge has a bona fide doubt concerning a defendant's competence, the defendant has a constitutional right to a psychiatric examination for competency regardless of whether the defense raises the issue.[95] In *Jackson v. Indiana* the Supreme Court ruled that a defendant who lacks the competence to stand trial must have the opportunity to be treated in order that he might attain it or, if improvement is not foreseeable within a reasonable time, that he be civilly committed or released.[96] Indeed, the state has an interest in bringing a defendant to trial and may, as discussed below, insist that treatment be administered.[97] The issue must be resolved before court proceedings are embarked upon. That hearing may place the burden of proving incompetency on the defendant. It is primarily a "medical and psychiatric determination."[98]

The standard test for competency to stand trial was articulated by the Supreme Court in *Dusky v. United States* (per curiam) as follows:

> The test must be whether [the accused] has sufficient present ability to consult with his lawyer with a reasonable degree of rational understanding—and whether he has a rational as well as factual understanding of the proceedings against him.[99]

The *Dusky* standards refer to *present ability,* and to *a reasonable degree of rational understanding*. The Court added another facet to this test in *Drope v. Missouri* by holding that the defendant must be able "to assist in preparing his defense."[100] In *Wieter v. Settle*,[101] the court adopted the American Law Institute's formulation of criteria to determine competency to stand trial, according to which the defendant must have:

1. Orientation to time, place, and person
2. Sufficient elementary mental process to apprehend that he is in a court of justice charged with a criminal offense
3. Understanding that there is a judge on the bench
4. Understanding that a prosecutor is present who will try to convict him of a criminal charge
5. Understanding that a lawyer will defend him against that charge
6. Understanding that he is expected to tell the lawyer the circumstances involved in the alleged violation, to the best of his mental ability
7. Understanding that a jury will determine his guilt or innocence
8. The effect of a guilty plea or a waiver of rights
9. The mental ability to participate in an adequate presentation of his defense

These standards thus combine (1) orientation, (2) an understanding of the criminal process, and (3) the mental capacity to remember and relate the circumstances surrounding the alleged offense. The purpose of the standards is to permit criminal proceedings only against those whose mental state enables them to defend themselves.[102] Robey's (1965) is the seminal work in this area. Nicholson and Johnson (1991) provide an up-to-date appraisal. As further elaborated by the Group for the Advancement of Psychiatry (1974), competency criteria involve the following capacities:

1. To understand his current legal situation
2. To understand the charges against him
3. To understand the facts relevant to his case
4. To understand the legal issues and procedures in his case
5. To understand the legal defenses available in his behalf
6. To understand the dispositions, pleas, and penalties possible
7. To appraise the likely outcomes
8. To appraise the roles of defense counsel, the prosecuting attorney, the judge, the jury, the witness, and the defendant
9. To identify the witnesses
10. To relate to defense counsel
11. To trust, and to communicate relevantly with, legal counsel
12. To comprehend instructions and advice
13. To make decisions after receiving advice
14. To maintain a collaborative relationship with legal counsel and to help plan legal strategy
15. To follow testimony for contradictions or errors
16. To testify relevantly and be cross-examined if necessary
17. To challenge prosecution witnesses
18. To tolerate stress at the trial and while awaiting trial
19. To refrain from irrational and unmanageable behavior at the trial
20. To disclose pertinent facts surrounding the alleged offense
21. To protect himself and utilize the legal safeguards available to him

A thorough discussion of studies and procedures used to determine competency in a juvenile court is found in Grisso, Miller, and Sales (1987). For a review of federal and state procedures refer to Brakel, Parry, and Weiner (1985).

In preparing a forensic report relating to competency, the clinician should exclude any comments by the patient concerning the offense; *competency refers to present mental function, not to mental state at the time of the offense* (see below). Competency is a relative matter; the same defendant may be competent to stand trial on a simple charge but incompetent with regard to a complex matter. Not all psychotic or mentally retarded defendants are incompetent, but most incompetent defendants are psychotic or mentally retarded.

In quest of information relevant to the criteria for competency, the clinician can ask the defendant direct questions (e.g., "What is the purpose of the judge?") or elicit clues indirectly (e.g., "Tell me what happened the last time you were in court."). Lipsitt, Lelos, and McGarry (1971), and McGarry and colleagues (1974) have developed a test (popularly known as the "McGarry Test") that includes both a competency screening sentence completion test (the Competency Screening Test) and a semistructured interview (the Competency Assessment Instrument) for those who fail the screen. The goal of these tests is to provide valid quantifiable criteria for the translation of clinical data into legal conclusions. Roesch and Golding (1980) report high intertester reliability after training on a similar interview. These instruments are not without critics, however. Melton and associates (1987), who have reviewed studies of the reliability and validity of a number of competency assessment techniques, suggest that none of them has sufficient proven psychometric rigor to be relied upon exclusively. Brakel (1974) has criticized the criteria on the ground that they substitute political judgment for objective clinical testing; Nottingham and Mattson (1981) assert that tests fail to screen false positives successfully.

If the defendant is found incompetent at clinical interview, the clinician should recommend what is required to render him competent and estimate how long it will take to do so. For example, does he require education from counsel concerning the legal process? Does he require psychiatric treatment in order to restore his capacity to cooperate with the counsel for his defense or to comport himself properly during the trial? The clinician may also make recommendations to judge and counsel about how best to communicate with the defendant. Finally, the clinician should avoid conclusory statements about the ultimate legal issue. He should speak instead to each of the criteria for competency, and leave the ultimate conclusion to the fact-finder.

It is not uncommon for the defendant in a homicide or other serious case to claim amnesia for the event. In *Wilson v. United States* it was held that amnesia *per se* does not bar the prosecution of a defendant.[103] The appropriate test is whether the amnesia substantially interferes with the defendant's capacity to perform functions "essential to the fairness and accuracy of a criminal proceeding such as to assist counsel in his own defense, to testify on his own behalf, or to give evidence concerning the alleged crime." Furthermore, the court held that if the performance of the function could be arranged in an alternative manner (e.g., by obtaining necessary information from sources other than from the amnesiac defendant), then the requirement of competence would be satisfied. The focus should be on the performance of the essential functions, not the defendant's mental state. In the *Wilson* decision, the court was apparently swayed by an awareness that amnesia is easy to fake, and malingering hard to diagnose.

Until recently it was a moot question whether competency could be engendered by forcefully administering psychotropic medication.[104] In *Riggins v. Nevada* the Supreme Court faced this issue in a case where the defendant, who had been convicted of murder and robbery, was forced by court order to take psychotropic medication. The defendant had argued that the drug should be suspended until the end of his trial, on the ground that the drug's effect on his demeanor and mental state would deny him due process. The state resisted his application, submitting that the drug was necessary to assure the defendant's competence to stand trial.[105] The Court gave a cursory order denying the application. The Supreme Court relied on its earlier decision in *Washington v. Harper* to decide that forcible administration of drugs is permissible only if it is found that the medication is medically appropriate and the least intrusive alternative, after consideration of the defendant's own safety and the safety of others. Furthermore, the state may justify medically appropriate involuntary administration of a drug if this is the least intrusive way to obtain an adjudication of the defendant's guilt or innocence.[106] The lower court's "laconic" order permitting administration did not address these criteria; hence, the Nevada Supreme Court's decision was reversed. It follows that the forcible administration of drugs to engender competence is permissible provided that medical appropriateness is determined and alternatives to drug administration are considered.[107]

COMPETENCE TO WAIVE *MIRANDA* OR DUE PROCESS RIGHTS

The Fifth Amendment has been held to render inadmissible any incriminating evidence compelled from the defendant by the state. In *Miranda v. Arizona* the Supreme Court ruled that a person has the right to counsel during interrogation, that he must be informed he has this right, that he has the right to remain silent, and that his statements may be used against him.[108] These rights apply to juveniles. In *Fare v. Michael C.* the Court held that a mature minor might validly waive his *Miranda* rights and indicated that a case-by-case determination was required, in accordance with "the totality of the circumstances."[109] Thus, it is conceivable that expert opinion might be requested to elucidate whether a particular juvenile in a particular situation had the competence to waive his *Miranda* or other due process rights.

Grisso (1981, 1983, 1986) has discussed this matter in detail. The clinician assessor must investigate whether the juvenile waived his rights *voluntarily, knowingly,* and *intelligently*—in other words, whether the waiver was coerced or induced in an improper manner, whether the juvenile was aware of the consequences of the waiver, and whether he had the capacity to weigh the consequences of his potential actions and to make an intelligent decision about what course of action was in his best interests. Grisso (1981, 1986) describes several standardized tests designed to assess the juvenile's current appreciation of the meaning of the *Miranda* warnings: The Comprehension of Miranda Rights (CMR), the Comprehension of Miranda Rights—True/False (CMR-TF), the Function of Rights in Interrogation (FRI), and the Gudjonsson Suggestibility Scale (GSS).[110] The first three of these instruments test the "knowingly" qualification of the competence in question and can be used to add further information to clinical assessment, intelligence testing, and school achievement. The GSS gives information concerning the juvenile's suggestibility to coercion or persuasion by those in authority and therefore relates to the "voluntarily" qualification. Medical issues that can becloud a juvenile's competence are fatigue, hunger, illness, intoxication, psychosis, delirium, and confusion.

MENTAL STATE AT TIME OF OFFENSE

A crime involves two elements:

1. A physical act, such as striking a victim (*actus reus*)
2. A level of intent to commit the specific criminal act (*mens rea*)

In other words, it is not a crime to have evil thoughts. The state must prove that the perpetrator both *intended* to perform a wrongful act and *actually committed* the act.[111] If the defendant did not or could not intend to commit the wrongful act, then even if he performed the act, it may be held that no crime was committed. The level of intent required varies in accordance with the crime committed; some crimes require a very high degree of intent and others a substantially lower degree. The capacity to intend to commit a crime can be compromised by mental disorder, impairment, or defect. In those circumstances, the defendant may assert insanity as an affirmative defense to the crime. The insanity defense focuses on whether the defendant should fairly be subject to criminal law proceedings.

This section, like the last, is a summary. The history of the law concerning legal insanity is exceedingly tortuous and continues to evolve today. For comprehensive accounts, the reader is referred to such texts as those by Brooks (1974), Goldstein (1967), Melton *et al.* (1987), Moran (1981), Slovenko (1973), Moore (1984), and Halleck (1980), and to monographs like that by Dix (1984).

INSANITY DEFENSES

Currently, in the United States, there are several defenses whereby the mental state of the defendant at the time of the crime will excuse him from criminal responsibility:

1. The M'Naghten standard
2. The "irresistible impulse" standard (usually combined with or supplementary to the M'Naghten standard)
3. The Model Penal Code (MPC)

1. *M'Naghten standard.* Under this standard, which was enunciated in the late nineteenth century by the English House of Lords, a defendant is exculpated if, "at the time of the committing of the act, the party accused was laboring under such a *defect of reason,* from *disease of the mind,* as not to know the *nature and quality* of the act he was doing, or that the *act was wrong.*"[112] The standard was articulated because of popular dissatisfaction that the jury's function, which had been to judge whether the accused knew right from wrong, led to unsatisfactory acquittals, even though those acquitted were locked away in a mental hospital.

In 1984, in response to the public outcry over the trial of John Hinckley,[113] Congress substantially codified M'Naghten. Several states have followed the federal lead.

2. *Irresistible impulse.* Aware of the purely cognitive nature of the M'Naghten standard, some states have added a *volitional clause,* allowing a defendant who knew he was doing "wrong" to plead insanity when the mental disease or defect prevented the defendant from *restraining his conduct.*

3. *Model Penal Code.* The MPC standard drafted by the American Law Institute softens and broadens the wording of M'Naghten, as follows: "(1) A person is *not re-*

sponsible for criminal conduct if at the time of such conduct *as a result of mental disease or defect* he *lacks substantial capacity* either *to appreciate the criminality* (*wrongfulness*) of his conduct *or to conform his conduct* to the requirement of law. (2) As used in this Article, *the terms mental disease or defect do not include an abnormality manifested only by repeated criminal or otherwise antisocial conduct.*"[114]

In the Model Penal Code, the phrase "lacks substantial capacity to" replaces the M'Naghten requirement of total lack of capacity, and "appreciate" replaces "know." The MPC standard is also neutral as to the word "criminality" or "wrongfulness." A majority of states have now adopted the MPC's first paragraph, and many the second as well. The 1984 Congressional action echoed an American Bar Association test that draws on the Code but rids it of a volitional element, thus aligning it more closely with M'Naghten.

VARIATIONS AND OBSERVATIONS

A small number of states (Montana, Idaho, and Utah), despairing of this imbroglio, have abolished the insanity defense, allowing the defendant to argue that he lacked the requisite *mens rea* rather than that he is not guilty by reason of insanity. A defendant may be found sane and a verdict entered of guilty but mentally ill (GBMI). If found GBMI, the defendant is likely (1) to be sentenced to a period of confinement and (2) to receive treatment in a psychiatric hospital for some or all of that time. The standard for GBMI usually derives from the standard for civil commitment in that state (see Chapter 10). The GBMI verdict, which is essentially a compromise between NGRI and "guilty," has received considerable attention since the Hinckley trial.[115]

The rule of longest standing is the M'Naghten "right–wrong" test. Some jurisdictions have supplemented the M'Naghten test with the "irresistible impulse" test. During the 1950s and early 1960s, the District of Columbia followed the *Durham* rule (or *product test*), under which the accused is not criminally responsible if his unlawful act is *the product of a mental defect*.[116] The *Durham* test was initially applauded by psychiatrists because it maximized the involvement of psychiatrically trained people in the legal determination of insanity. Eventually the *Durham* test was discarded because it failed to provide standards to guide the jury and required the jury to rely excessively upon an expert's classification of mental abnormality. This problem came to a dramatic head in 1957, when staff members of St. Elizabeth Hospital (which provided the District of Columbia with psychiatric experts) voted to categorize as "mental disease" personality disorders, including the so-called sociopathic personality. In *McDonald v. United States* the District of Columbia Court of Appeals agreed with those opposing *Durham*. ("What psychiatrists may consider a 'mental disease or defect' for clinical purposes where their concern is treatment, may or may not be the same as mental disease or defect for the jury's purpose in determining criminal responsibility.")[117] Consequently, in *McDonald,* mental disease or defect was redefined as including "any abnormal condition of the mind which substantially affects mental or emotional processes and substantially impairs behavior controls." Moreover, in *Washington v. United States* psychiatrists were enjoined from testifying to the ultimate issue (criminal responsibility).[118] Eventually, in *United States v. Brawner,* the D.C. Circuit broadly accepted the Model Penal Code Rule (with some variations).[119] A summary of the standards that apply in different states can be found in Favole (1983). Debate regarding the abolition of the insanity defense is found in Goldstein (1967) and in Morris, Bonnie, and Finer (1986).

MITIGATING FACTORS

Diminished Capacity

The doctrine of diminished capacity applies to the *mens rea* or intent aspect of a crime. *Mens rea* has several levels; culpability has been described as varying, for example, from "specific premeditated intent," through "specific knowledge," to "recklessness," and "negligence." As Melton and colleagues (1987) point out, it is possible to be mentally deranged yet to have the capacity to form specific intent. The defense of diminished capacity attempts to exclude culpability by contending, by aid of clinical testimony, that the defendant was unable to form specific intent at the time of an alleged crime. This leaves open the possibility that the defendant could be prosecuted for, and found guilty of, lesser charges.[120] Thus, diminished capacity is discussed under the rubric of mitigating factors; although, in striking at the *mens rea* requirement, it is a complete defense.

Diminished capacity should not be confused with *diminished responsibility,* a doctrine that aims to reduce the penalty for a crime on the ground that mental impairment has affected the defendant's cognition or volition, but not to the extent of causing legal insanity or diminishing the capacity to form *mens rea.*

No American court has accepted the doctrine of diminished responsibility. However, the doctrine of *diminished capacity* attracts some adherence and is codified in the Model Penal Code, Section 4.02(1).[121]

Automatism

The term "automatism" refers to undirected behavior beyond conscious control. The defense of automatism usually asserts that an alleged crime was committed (1) during an episode of sleepwalking; (2) in the period of confusion following head injury; (3) as a result of the metabolic instability caused by hypoglycemia, anoxia, or the involuntary ingestion of drugs; (4) during a dissociative fugue state; or (5) in association with an attack of epilepsy. Since such actions are not voluntary, the requirement of *actus reus* is not satisfied. Hence, while an insanity defense subjects the defendant to a risk of commitment, automatism does not have this effect and may result in outright acquittal. The prosecution bears the burden of negating a claim of autonomism beyond a reasonable doubt.

In some jurisdictions it has been held that the automatism defense does not apply if the defendant knew that he was subject to the predisposing condition and could have prevented it.[122] If a defendant's automatism results from a "disease of the mind," some jurisdictions allow it to be treated as insanity. Both sleepwalking and epilepsy have been held to be mental diseases.[123]

Intoxication

If a crime was perpetrated by a person who was *unknowingly* under the influence of drugs or alcohol, then that person could not have had *mens rea* and will usually be acquitted. If the accused is involuntarily intoxicated or suffered an unforeseeably excessive reaction to a voluntarily ingested intoxicant, then most courts will treat the defendant as if he were insane.[124] Voluntary intoxication leading to a criminal act may result in a reduction of a charge; for example, a charge of homicide may be reduced from first to second degree due to the defendant's outrageously reckless behavior.[125] However, many states have enacted statutory proscriptions against such reduction.

Sources of Data

As in all forensic evaluations, the mental health clinician should obtain full documentation, consult with the juvenile's attorney, and interview the juvenile, the parents, and any other informant who could provide pertinent information. Special investigations (e.g., medical consultation, laboratory studies, electroencephalography), psychological testing (e.g., intelligence, personality, neuropsychological or psychoeducational), and standardized competency interviews may be ordered or conducted in response to questions raised by the initial clinical evaluation. In some cases, transfer to a psychiatric hospital may be required in order to complete the evaluation.

Interviewing Juvenile Defenders

Adolescents caught up in the juvenile justice system have a number of common characteristics. Many are afraid of psychiatrists and fearful of being labeled "insane." Indeed, a juvenile may be more fearful of being found "crazy" than of being adjudicated delinquent. At the same time, many offenders are desperately unhappy and lonely, and will be responsive to a humane, friendly approach. For this reason, the forensic clinician should make it clear that the interview is meant to be investigative, not therapeutic, and should make sure that the youth appreciates this.

The clinician is likely to be separated from the offender by class and ethnic barriers. It is important to learn as much as possible about the living environment and social organization of the juvenile's neighborhood of origin and to become familiar with the vernacular of the one he is asked to assess. Though familiar with the juvenile's colloquialisms, the clinician should not mimic them (with the possible exception of occasional graphic turns of phrase).

The Forensic Report

The following is a suggested format for forensic reports concerning juvenile offenders.

I. *Identifying data.*

II. *Circumstances and purposes of referral.* Who referred the case? What stage has the case reached in the adjudication process? What issue or issues have you been asked to elucidate (e.g., diagnosis, amenability to treatment, recommended treatment, dangerousness, competence to stand trial, competence to waive due process rights, mental state at the time of the offense, mitigating factors, or suitability for transfer to adult court)?

III. *Sources of data.*

    A. List all *documents* reviewed, citing dates and signatures.

    B. List all *interviews,* nominating the interviewees, with the date and duration of each interview.

    C. List all *special investigations,* including psychological testing, with dates.

IV. *Review of documents.* Summarize the content of all documents.

V. *Informed consent.* Record the information conveyed to the juvenile in order to obtain informed consent for the interview. Emphasize that the juvenile was told that the interview was not therapeutic in purpose, but designed to provide information to the court, and that the juvenile understood what you told him or her.

VI. *Content of interviews.* Summarize the relevant content of the interviews with all informants, using direct quotes when they are pertinent to the issues at stake.

VII. *Results of special investigation.* Record the specific questions posed to the psychological consultant. Summarize the results of psychological testing with particular reference to the issues at stake in the case.

VIII. *Discussion of findings.* Integrate all findings pertinent to the issue or issues at stake in the case. Organize the discussion in accordance with each issue you have been asked to address. If some findings do not concur with others in regard to a particular issue, note the discordance, and attempt to weigh the significance and reliability of the discrepant findings. If you decide to disregard a particular finding, give your reasons for doing so. If not, set out the pros and cons for the issue, and let the court decide. For example, with regard to amenability to treatment, the evaluator might find that the offender has a psychiatric disorder potentially treatable in an outpatient service, and that a suitable outpatient service would be available, but that, on the other hand, neither the juvenile nor his or her family had been cooperative in outpatient treatment on a previous occasion. The clinician might then provide an assessment of the offender's current motivation for mental health treatment, given the juvenile's awareness of the alternatives.

IX. *Conclusions and recommendations.* End the report with a summary of your opinions concerning the legal issue or issues you were asked to elucidate and your recommendations for disposition, diversion, or treatment.

X. *Appendixes.* Append psychological test reports or other pertinent special investigations.

CHAPTER 10

THE RIGHTS OF INSTITUTIONALIZED CHILDREN

INTRODUCTION

Before 1850 the mentally ill were all but free of medical intervention. As indigents, they wandered about the country and camped in the centers of the cities. A few "lunatics" were kept out of sight at home, tended by relatives; while the "furiously mad" were incarcerated in jails or madhouses.[1] Some might say that since 1960, with the advance of legalism and fiscal constraints, the wheel has turned full circle.

After the civil war, the reported success of moral treatment in "retreats" for the insane (e.g., the York Retreat in England and the Hartford Retreat in Connecticut), together with the political advocacy of activists like Dorothea Dix, influenced legislators to build large asylums for the purpose of housing the insane. The asylum was conceived as a place of refuge insulated from the hullabaloo of city life, where fresh air, honest work, religious observance, and the ministrations of an alienist and his assistants could restore the insane to health. Unfortunately, one man's insulation is another's isolation. In time the asylum became the mental hospital, an exurban repository for the socially inept and unwanted, a hideaway for the incompetent physician, and a soft spot for the uncaring or corrupt attendant.

After 1950 the psychopharmacological revolution began to empty the mental hospitals and spurred the growth of the community mental health movement. Unfortunately, it left behind a sizable residue of patients resistant to both medical treatment and psychosocial rehabilitation. These unfortunates became the chronic inmates of stagnant backwaters, subdued with medication and tended by staff demoralized by interminable budget cuts.

The 1960s heralded a resurgence of libertarianism, with the promulgation of hyperbolic doctrines concerning the supposedly mythic nature of mental illness,[2] a justified concern for the welfare of the chronically ill, and challenges to the authority of psychiatric diagnosis.[3] Professionals, particularly psychiatrists, were depicted in the popular media as uncaring dupes or manipulative sadists, and mental hospitals as spiritual jails (as in the novel and film *One Flew over the Cuckoo's Nest*). The benevolence of the state was questioned, together with the good faith of its putative

318

functionary, psychiatry. Well-meaning but loosely conceived procedures for involuntary and voluntary commitment were scrutinized by the courts and found wanting;[4] the masterly therapeutic inactivity of the superintendents of the chronic public wards was deemed unacceptable;[5] and the right of the institutionalized to have a say in their own treatment was upheld.[6] As with children's rights (see Chapter 3), an era of benevolent neglect was succeeded by one of legalism,[7] coincident with the eagerness of state governments to cut mental hospital expenditures.[8] In many instances, chronic wards were emptied without good planning, and their inmates housed in slum hotels or left to shuffle about the cities, sleeping in hotels for the homeless or over gratings in the sidewalk.[9] Reluctant to expend their dwindling resources in courtroom argumentation, state institutions have allowed many acutely ill patients to leave hospital before mandatory judicial review, in effect discharging them to "die with their rights on."[10] A dearth of funds for clinical and nonclinical mental health services following hospitalization has exacerbated the problems of the mentally ill in the era of deinstitutionalization.[11]

The evolution of psychiatric hospitalization for children and adolescents must be understood against the backdrop of momentous therapeutic, social, economic, and legal changes in adult psychiatry. Up to the 1960s there were relatively few inpatient facilities for children and adolescents. Many disturbed younger patients were admitted to adult hospitals, usually with little or no modification of the milieu to fit their needs. Some wards of the state were admitted to public mental hospital children's units, where they stagnated, victims of parental abandonment, bureaucratic inertia, and clinical bankruptcy. A few who had sufficient funds and influence were admitted to prestigious specialized units.[12]

Since 1970 the psychiatric hospital has been transformed from a long-term custodial or rehabilitative model to one involving short-term stabilization.[13] Third party insurers, increasingly concerned about costs, have become more exacting in their scrutiny of bed utilization. Managed care and health maintenance organizations put pressure on psychiatric hospitals to conform to a model of acute medical–surgical care. Publicly funded units have also experienced administrative pressure to resist admission and hasten discharge.[14] The swing toward briefer hospitalization has not been supported by convincing evidence of greater efficacy; on the other hand, there was insufficient evidence for the efficacy of the more expensive rehabilitative model.

At the same time, the number of psychiatric beds for children and adolescents has expanded. Over the past decade the treatment of drug abuse has become a nationwide industry with thousands of treatment centers. Responding to a perceived market in the psychiatric and drug abuse treatment of children and youth, private hospitals opened psychiatric units and general hospitals converted pediatric beds to psychiatric use. The number of children and youth admitted to private psychiatric beds doubled between 1980 and 1986.[15]

Many of the reforms aimed at the welfare of psychiatric patients in hospitals arose from concern that state institutions were underfunded, when criteria for involuntary civil commitment were loose and custodial care was the rule.[16] The problems today are different. How can sufficient funds be found to allow patients to be hospitalized for emergency care, to stay long enough to be adequately diagnosed and stabilized, and to be prepared for discharge? After patients are stabilized, where can they be treated? Less restrictive treatment alternatives are badly needed in order to divert some acute patients before admission and to treat others following brief hospitalization.[17]

LEGAL PRINCIPLES PERTAINING TO PSYCHIATRIC HOSPITALIZATION

The state derives its power to confine and treat severely mentally ill people against their will from two doctrines:

1. *Parens patriae.* The state is obligated to protect the person and property of those of its citizens who are not competent to care for themselves.[18]
2. *Police power.* The state is obligated to protect the health and safety of its citizens.[19]

The state's authority to intervene with the mentally ill has been challenged on three constitutional grounds. Eighth Amendment "cruel and unusual punishment" and Fourteenth Amendment "equal protection" arguments have been criticized as theoretically unsound. Virtually all successful challenges flow from the due process clause of the Fourteenth Amendment. Due process requires the state to act fairly whenever it infringes upon liberties. The rights of an individual to exercise autonomy must be carefully weighed against the state's interest in curtailing his rights.[20] Thus, the state's paternalistic impulses and tutelary obligations must be tempered by an awareness that involuntary commitment is akin to incarceration.

Due process has two facets:

1. *Procedural due process* is represented by the formalized policies and procedures that safeguard the rights of individual patients. These policies and procedures "are meant to protect persons not from the deprivation, but from the mistaken or unjustified deprivation of life, liberty or property."[21] The Supreme Court has said that the following factors must be weighed in determining whether procedural protection accords with the Fourteenth Amendment:

a. The private interest that will be affected by the official action
b. The risk of an erroneous deprivation of such interest through the procedures used
c. The probable value, if any, of additional or substitute procedural safeguards
d. The government's interest, including the function involved and the fiscal and administrative burdens that the additional or substitute procedural requirement would entail[22]

Due process is a "flexible concept that varies with the particular situation."[23]

2. *Substantive due process* refers to the need for the state to have an explicit rationale if it is to justify the abridgment of individual freedom. The rationale should have the following features:

a. The state's purpose in abridging liberty must be legitimate
b. There must be a logical connection between the abridgment and its purpose
c. The intended outcome of the abridgment must outweigh the undesirability of curtailing individual freedom
d. The state should alienate no more of the individual's rights than is necessary to accomplish its legitimate purpose

In other words, due process incorporates a substantive component barring certain arbitrary, wrongful governmental actions "regardless of the fairness of the procedures used to implement them."[24]

Both procedural and substantive due process considerations are embodied in the following: the documented *procedures required for civil commitment;* those sections of mental health legislation that stipulate and define the *criteria for commitment* and continued confinement; and the *limitations and duties imposed on the state* in order to safeguard the patient's liberty interests during confinement. It is in this third realm that the constitutional rights of the confined individual and the constitutional obligations of the state are indistinct.

Numerous cases during the 1970s addressed unconstitutional conditions in state hospitals for the mentally ill and retarded, as well as in penal institutions for juveniles.[25] In several cases, the court imposed standards upon the institution and monitored its subsequent compliance. In *Wyatt v. Stickney,* for example, the court held that the rights of hospitalized patients included enjoyment of the outdoors, religious worship, interaction with the opposite sex, reasonably nutritious food, and safe and humane living conditions. In *Halderman v. Pennhurst State School and Hospital,* the Third Circuit affirmed the jurisdiction of the federal circuit court in compelling the State of Pennsylvania to comply with the terms of a final settlement agreement.[26] This agreement, entered into six years earlier, set detailed standards for the care and treatment of residents at a hospital for the mentally retarded. Other decisions have resulted in consent decrees, which essentially reformed the policies and procedures the state institutions involved.[27]

States have not been successful in pleading impecuniosity as an excuse for their failure to implement imposed remedies. Indeed, the Supreme Court recently upheld the power of the court to require the taxing authority to levy moneys in order to enforce constitutional rights.[28] At the same time, however, the Court has signaled that it might be receptive to proposals to change the terms of some consent decrees. Unforeseeable changes may require the modification of a decree if the ultimate goals of reform are to be realized.[29]

Grave violations of the constitutional rights of patients in many state institutions exposed by the above cases and others, coupled with the complacency of state officials, led Congress to pass the Civil Rights of Institutionalized Persons Act (CRIPA) in 1980. CRIPA empowered the Department of Justice to institute civil actions against the states on behalf of inmates of any state facility where a "pattern or practice" seriously deprived residents of their rights under the Constitution and caused them "grievous harm."[30]

CIVIL COMMITMENT
Standards for Commitment

For more than two decades a debate has raged over the proper standards for civil commitment of the mentally ill.[31] Where should the balance be struck between an individual's constitutional right to privacy and due process and the state's interest in taking care of the incapacitated? How far should the state go in asserting its *parens patriae* power over those who are mentally ill but refuse treatment? The subject compels nearly everyone: the lawmaker who faces impassioned demands from constituents to care for or get rid of homeless or dangerous indigents, all the while under pressure to curb social welfare spending; the civil libertarian who zealously guards hard-won individual rights; the psychiatrist who seeks to help those who would suffer without treatment; the parent who has failed to gain access for a child to sorely needed psychiatric care; and the patient who protests that he is being wrongfully kept in a mental hospital.

Those who argue for precise and circumscribed standards for involuntary civil commitment point to the abuses of individual rights that can occur in state institutions for the mentally ill and disabled. Conversely, those who urge paternalism decry the indecency of a system that permits psychotic individuals to live in peril on the streets, at the mercy of their untreated illnesses.[32]

Prior to 1970, in accordance with prevailing paternalistic doctrines, most states had enacted legislation that authorized involuntary civil commitment first for mentally ill people who were *dangerous* and second for those *in need of care and treatment but not competent to seek it.* Such broad standards vested physicians with substantial power to determine whether an individual should be confined against his will.

With the widespread social upheaval of the 1970s, however, came profound changes. Some publicly questioned the motives, methods, and effectiveness of psychiatry. The community health care movement sought treatment in less restrictive settings than the traditional hospital, and states slashed funding for mental hospitals. In 1969 California, leading legislative reform, passed the Lanterman–Petris–Short Act, narrowing commitment standards and establishing *dangerousness to self or others* as the essential criterion. Coincidentally, the vigorous representations of civil libertarians established new constitutional standards for the involuntary civil commitment of the mentally ill and disabled. The seminal case of *Lessard v. Schmidt* held that, in order to confine an individual in a mental hospital against his will, the state must prove that there was *an extreme likelihood that if the person is not confined he will do immediate harm to himself or others.* Such proof, the court said, could be found in a "recent overt act, attempt or threat to do substantial harm to oneself or another."[33] In 1975, the Supreme Court affirmed the dangerousness standard in *O'Connor v. Donaldson,* stating:

> A finding of "mental illness" alone cannot justify a State's locking a person up against his will and keeping him indefinitely in simple custodial confinement.

[T]here is still no constitutional basis for confining such persons involuntarily if they are dangerous to no one and can live safely in freedom.

[W]hile the State may arguably confine a person to save him from harm, incarceration is rarely if ever a necessary condition for raising the living standards of those capable of surviving safely in freedom, on their own or with the help of family or friends.[34]

Commitment laws were subsequently changed to conform to the constitutional requirements. Most revised statutes permitted commitment of the mentally ill only after a hearing eliciting clear and convincing evidence[35] that the person was either *dangerous to himself or others if unsupervised in the community* or *so gravely disabled that hospitalization was necessary for his survival.* Some states required, moreover, that the risk of harm to the patient or others be both *imminent* and *substantial,* that the potential harm be *serious,* and that, as evidence of the risk, *recent overt action* be cited. Under these more exacting standards treatment could be delivered to those who needed it but who were neither dangerous nor gravely disabled, only if they voluntarily accepted it. States cannot avoid these strictures by classifying patients as "voluntary." For example, mentally retarded adults admitted on application of parent or guardian are to be regarded as involuntarily committed and accorded due process.[36] In determining these grounds, aspects of the trial-based adjudicatory system have been required, for example adequate notice of the hearing.[37] However, the need for flexibility in the due process requirements for particular situations has persuaded the court to stop short of declaring that the patient has a right to legally qualified representation.[38]

Over the past decade a significant counterpressure to relax commitment standards has arisen. The growing problem of homelessness, the lobbying efforts of patient advocates, the frustration of families who were unsuccessful in obtaining adequate treatment for their relatives, and sensationalist assaults on the legalistic system have created dissatisfaction with the commitment laws. Much of the argument has been about the legal definitions of "dangerous" and "gravely disabled," for it is these criteria that determine whether people who are incapacitated by mental illness will receive the treatment they need.[39]

Considering the importance of the question, very little research has been done to test the impact of the wording of commitment laws on hospitalization of the mentally ill. So far, the few reported studies have not borne out the popular beliefs. Cleveland and colleagues (1989) concluded that even the strictest commitment standards are flexible enough to permit the hospitalization of those who are seriously ill and that the vast majority of those who do not meet commitment criteria voluntarily admit themselves. Other studies suggest that the state's administrative policies regarding commitment and admission are the true gatekeepers of the mental health system.[40]

Durham and LaFond (1985) contend that any gain from legislative reform would be stymied by inadequate funding. They studied the effect on the treatment of mentally ill of Washington's Involuntary Treatment Act (1979), a statute that broadened the scope of the state's police and *parens patriae* powers of commitment. As a result, *parens patriae* commitments soared, crowding out voluntary admissions. Without increased funding, treatment facilities were overwhelmed.

Civil commitment under the dangerousness criterion typically requires certification by two physicians that, due to mental illness, the patient is at substantial risk of harm to himself or others. Pointing to studies that indicate such predictions to be wrong more often than right,[41] psychiatrists have protested that they have no expertise at predicting dangerousness over the long term. Indeed, the American Psychiatric Association presented this argument to the Supreme Court as *amicus curiae* in the case of *Barefoot v. Estelle*.[42] The APA claimed that psychiatrists bring no special skill to the prediction of future dangerousness in a particular case; the most reliable predictors of future violent behavior are not psychiatric diagnosis and medical opinion but such statistical and actuarial data as age, sex, race, and a history of violence and drug or alcohol use. The APA objected to the presentation of statistically based predictions by psychiatrists, claiming that it dressed opinion in the cloak of medical expertise and was therefore prejudicial to the defendant.[43]

Monahan's conclusions have not been universally supported. Recent studies, using different predictive models, have obtained substantially better results in predicting dangerousness.[44] Contending that methodological errors invalidate earlier studies, Litwach and Schlesinger (1987) disparage an oversimplified generalization that psychiatrists cannot predict dangerousness. The courts, too, have been unswayed by the American Psychiatric Association's argument. In *Barefoot v. Estelle*, the Supreme Court permitted the jury to rely on the testimony of a psychiatrist who predicted that Barefoot posed a continuing threat to society, the determining factor in his capital sentence.[45] The following year, in *Schall v. Martin*, the Court affirmed its faith in predictions of short-term future dangerousness, provided the predicting expert is experienced and incorporates appropriate variables in the prediction.[46] In any case, this debate often confuses the prediction of "imminent risk of substantial harm" (as in civil commitment) with the prediction of violence at an *unspecified future time* (as in trials involving capital offenses). The question is whether, in capital offense trials, psychiatrists have sufficient expertise to predict, *with reasonable certainty*, whether a defendant will be dangerously violent in the future.

Most states retain some form of "medical" criterion for commitment certification (e.g., grave disablement, the incapacity for basic self-care, or the likelihood of deterioration). Some states (e.g., Washington, Alaska, North Carolina, Texas, Hawaii, and Arizona) have revised their commitment laws, broadening their definitions of constitutionally permissible criteria. Several states make provision for commitment to outpatient treatment in an attempt to divert from hospitals some chronic patients who refuse treatment; and almost all states require that the individual be treated in the least restrictive environment. Periodic review of commitment conforming to due process is required if the procedure is to pass constitutional due process muster.[47] The state has the burden of proving the grounds of dangerousness.[48]

The American Psychiatric Association favors a more paternalistic model[49] and recommends the following expanded criteria:

1. The person suffers from a severe mental disorder which causes substantial impairment of thought and behavior, and deprives him or her of the capacity for rational decisions concerning treatment.
2. The person's condition is potentially treatable in this facility, and hospitalization represents the least restrictive alternative.
3. The person refuses, or is incompetent, to consent to voluntary admission for treatment.
4. The person is incompetent to give informed consent to treatment.
5. As a result of the severe mental disorder immediate hospitalization is required because the person is (a) likely to cause harm to himself or suffer substantial mental or emotional deterioration, or (b) likely to cause harm to others.[50]

Most states have separate laws for the mentally ill, but for the developmentally disabled and persons addicted to drugs and alcohol substantial variation remains. Twenty-four states have separate, detailed provisions for the involuntary civil commitment of drug-dependent individuals.[51] In several states the "drug-dependent" commitment standards are arguably looser than the "mentally ill" standards, citing "drug dependence" and "need for treatment" as sufficient criteria. The looser requirements for committal of the "mentally retarded" than for the "mentally ill" under Kentucky legislation were challenged as a denial of equal protection. However, the Supreme Court rejected the argument on the grounds that the state had demonstrated a rational basis for making the distinction.[52]

The Commitment of Minors

Burlingame and Amaya's (1985) review of voluntary admission statutes for minors found that in 1982 twenty-six states either specifically provided for unilateral parental consent or made no mention of minors; twelve states required both parents' and minors' consent; in nineteen states minors could also admit themselves; and nineteen states required judicial or administrative review before or after the parental admission of minors. Although most states still subordinate the liberty interest of individuals under the age of eighteen to the parents' right of control over their children, the policy has been widely criticized as permitting unconstitutional infringement on the privacy and liberty of young people. Weithorn (1988) contends that a large proportion of recent juvenile admissions to psychiatric facilities are inappropriate. She argues for a diversion of resources to less restrictive venues.

The Supreme Court has sanctioned the voluntary commitment by parents or guardians of minors, without the minor's consent. The landmark case concerning the due process rights of minors is *Parham v. J.R.* This class action was brought on behalf of children who had been admitted to a Georgia State hospital on the application of their parents or guardians. J.R. was a child of borderline intelligence who had been removed from parental care at the age of three months. He had lived in seven foster homes and was eventually admitted to hospital for aggressive behavior. J.R. represented a class of agency children who had been "volunteered" into hospital, but for whom no adequate discharge placement could be found. In *Parham,* the appellees argued that, since minors' wishes were not considered, Georgia's voluntary admission procedures violated due process. Due process, they argued, required formal adversary hearings in which minors' liberty interests could be protected.

In writing the majority opinion, Chief Justice Burger conceded that hospitalization did indeed infringe upon a child's liberty interest; however, he argued, the state does not stigmatize children by hospitalizing them; rather it provides necessary treatment, mental illness itself being more stigmatizing than hospitalization. The argument that existing practice was open to parental abuse ("dumping") was regarded as not compelling; the contention that *some* parents might not act in their children's best interests was considered insufficient reason to supersede parental authority in *all* cases; most children were thought "simply not capable" of making such weighty decisions. Parents were regarded as retaining a substantial, if not dominant, role in decision making (unless there were neglect or abuse). The Chief Justice alluded also to the waste of professional time in adversary hearings, and the need to facilitate rather than obstruct the treatment of disturbed children. The admitting physician, described as a "neutral fact finder," was thought to be sufficient protection against illegitimate admissions by either parent or agency; furthermore, adversary hearings could aggravate existing tensions within families. In summary, the Court found Georgia's medical fact-finding process "reasonable and consistent with constitutional guarantees."[53]

Parham has engendered much criticism. Many of the Court's fundamental assumptions have been attacked. The premise that the interests of the parent or guardian and child are "inextricably linked," which was crucial to the Court's conclusions, ignores the dysfunction of many families and the part that intrafamilial conflict can play in a parent's decision to commit a child. The incidence of child abuse and neglect in the United States, not fully recognized until very recently, further undermines the facile assumption that parents are necessarily committed to their children's best interests. The *Parham* majority also underrated the deprivations of liberty and privacy and the stigmatization that the child might endure in a mental institution, the very matters that led to the Court's view that civil commitment results in a "massive deprivation of liberty,"[54] not justified by the diagnosis of mental illness alone.[55] Nevertheless, the Court concluded that the confinement of a teenager against his wishes was justified by the parent's desire to treat him, even without a due process provision to verify whether that child was, in fact, in need of treatment. In addition to the abuse, lack of privacy and autonomy, and physical restraint that a youth may face in a psychiatric hospital,[56] Kiesler has emphasized the costs of stigma in terms of loss of social and vocational opportunity.[57] In this vein, Zenoff and Zients (1983) argue, thorough legal safeguards are necessary. While commending state legislation for bridging the protection gap, Zenoff and Zients recommend even greater legal safeguards (e.g., frequent reviews, the right to seek release, and access to legal counsel).

Finally, *Parham* has been sharply criticized as a poor analysis of the plaintiff's procedural due process claims.[58] Simet observes that the majority made no attempt to identify the extent of error inherent in Georgia's commitment practices. While classic procedural due process analysis seeks to balance the interest of the individual in not being erroneously deprived of his constitutional rights against the state's interests, the *Parham* court made no such inquiry. The Chief Justice did not consider any alternative procedural course that might reveal erroneous commitment decisions, preferring to tolerate any level of error in the commitment of minors inherent in the state's commitment laws in order to preserve the status quo. O'Boyle (1984) attacks *Parham* frontally, arguing that other Supreme Court authorities favor procedural safeguards more stringent than those prescribed in *Parham*. O'Boyle decries the current uncertainty of the law in the face of the powerlessness of minors and recommends further Supreme Court action to safeguard the rights of minor mental patients.

In *Parham,* the fundamental problem was not the hospital's admission policy, although it formed the fulcrum of the constitutional law debate. Rather, the true social vice was the appalling state of Georgia's inpatient units for children.[59] Unfortunately, the fine points of constitutional law that were the subject of disputation obscured a profound and still unresolved problem in many public mental health systems.

The findings in *Parham* were subsequently extended to a Pennsylvania case, *Secretary of Public Welfare of Pennsylvania v. Institutionalized Juveniles,* in which similar issues were at stake. The safeguards authorized by the Supreme Court—that is, the function of the admitting physician as a "neutral fact finder"—were thought to offer sufficient protection of minors' liberty interests.[60]

The states, as already indicated, are free to impose more extensive due process safeguards than *Parham* requires. The California Supreme Court in *In re Roger S.* set forth the following procedural safeguards: (1) a minor has a right to a precommitment hearing before a neutral factfinder; (2) during this hearing he or she has the opportunity to be present, to be represented by counsel, to present evidence and to cross-examine witnesses; and (3) in order to be hospitalized, the hospital must show by a preponderance of the evidence that the minor is mentally ill or disordered, gravely disabled, or dangerous, and that the treatment for which he or she is confined is likely to be beneficial. In addition, a record of the proceedings, adequate for appellate review, must be kept.[61]

The exact role that the minor should play in the decision to admit him for psychiatric or drug abuse treatment is highly controversial, as attested to by the numerous model statutes for the psychiatric hospitalization of minors that have been proposed. The American Psychiatric Association, for example, recommends voluntary parental placement of children under sixteen, provided the treating or admitting physician can certify that the child is in need of hospitalization and provided a judge concurs that the child has a mental disorder and is in need of care or treatment. The American Psychological Association, conversely, emphasizes the child's rights, the capacity of many adolescents to consent, and the invasiveness of hospitalization. Most model statutes provide for more stringent commitment criteria and substantially more procedural protection than the Supreme Court has required.[62] In their review of the status of minors' rights in commitment statutes, Schmidt and Otto conclude that the states are beginning to distinguish between older adolescents and younger children in regard to their rights. In contrast to the model statutes, however, nineteen states had no statutory provision for periodic review of voluntarily hospitalized minors, and only seventeen states provided access to counsel or advocacy service.

Burlingame and Amaya (1985) are critical of the legalistic approach. They refer to judicial error; the taxing of parent-child and child-therapist ties; the inflammation of patients' manipulativeness, divisiveness, and omnipotence; and the problematic role of the child's counsel in adversary hearings. They conclude that judges lack the psychological expertise to render finely tuned judgments in complex, contested cases; that great discrepancies in maturity between adolescents of the same age make it impossible to specify an age beyond which the minor should be accorded the competence to give consent; and that mandatory judicial review after admission ought to provide sufficient safeguard against inappropriate hospitalization.

Watson (1980) commends the thrust of *Parham* toward "a more sound perception of the psychological state and privacy needs of families." In doing so, he relies heavily on Goldstein, Freud, and Solnit's (1979) *Before the Best Interests of the Child,* the gist of which is to recommend the limitation of legal intervention into family affairs. Watson concedes the seriousness of the legal starting point—the child's liberty interest in terms of constitutional due process. Nevertheless, he submits, a more rational examination would have explored the psychological nature of the family and child-rearing process and thus questioned the legitimacy of state intervention in family privacy. Watson cites the rich literature on the crucial role of parents in child development. On the other hand, he disagrees with the majority of the court in *Parham* in equating voluntary admission at the behest of guardians with that by parents; the preferable view, he thinks, is that of Justice Brennan, who contended that the weaker bond between guardian and child indicates the need for a more stringent preadmission procedure when guardians seek to admit minors.

THE RIGHTS OF INSTITUTIONALIZED PATIENTS
The Source of Rights

The courts have recognized that people involuntarily institutionalized by the state retain certain rights under the Constitution. The due process and equal protection clauses of the Fourteenth Amendment protect their liberty interest. Due process restrains the extent to which the state may confine them, and equal protection ensures equality of treatment at the hands of the state. The Eighth Amendment prohibits the state from subjecting institutionalized patients to conditions that a court would characterize as cruel or excessively punitive.

Though courts agree that involuntarily institutionalized persons retain protectable interests, they have defined neither the scope of these interests nor the standards by which to assess whether their rights have been abridged. The ambiguity of law in this area is especially apparent where the issue involves the rights of various classes of institutionalized persons (e.g., voluntarily or involuntarily committed; dangerous or not dangerous; adult or minor; mentally ill; or mildly or severely mentally retarded). Though any one of these handicaps can affect an individual's constitutional interests, the actual differentiation of rights among such classes has seldom been addressed by the courts.

Beyond those rights secured by the Constitution, institutionalized patients may be entitled to additional protection by virtue of state constitutions or statute. Some statutes, for example, provide that individuals committed to a state institution for the mentally ill are entitled to treatment in the least restrictive setting. Other commitment statutes provide for both care and treatment.[63] In several instances, however, legislatures have emasculated the rights they have granted by cutting the budget that supports them.

Least Restrictive Environment

One doctrine that the courts recognize with some consistency is "the least restrictive alternative." This doctrine is consistent with the substantive due process notion that the state may not deprive any individual of his or her liberty except to the extent that it is justified by a legitimate governmental purpose. Those courts that recognize a constitutional right to the least restrictive means of care or treatment argue that, among other opinions, it derives from *Shelton v. Tucker:*

> [E]ven though the governmental purpose be legitimate and substantial, that purpose cannot be pursued by means that broadly stifle fundamental personal liberties when the end can be more narrowly achieved. The breadth of legislative abridgment must be viewed in the light of less drastic means for achieving the same basic purpose.[64]

Under this doctrine, a hospitalized patient may not be involuntarily medicated, denied communication, physically restrained or confined, or retained within the institution, except so far as is necessary to meet relevant and legitimate state interests (such as to prevent harm to the patient or others).

Prior to 1970 the doctrine of the least restrictive alternative had been applied to individual commitment proceedings when the plaintiff sought to require the committing authority to consider alternatives less restrictive than hospitalization. In *Lake v. Cameron,* it was held that courts had a duty to inquire into available community resources and alternative courses of treatment for the indigent mentally ill patient. The decision stated: "Deprivations of liberty solely because of dangers to the ill persons themselves should not go beyond what is necessary for their protection."[65] The lower court holdings that adopted the *Lake v. Cameron* rationale seemed to be consistent with existing Supreme Court decisions of the time, although the Court had not yet addressed the question in regard to institutions for the mentally ill or retarded.

Beginning with *Wyatt v. Stickney,* the doctrine of least restrictive means was applied to the postcommitment treatment of mentally ill and retarded persons. The minimum constitutional standards set by the *Wyatt* court included the right of patients to be free from unnecessary or excessive medication, and from physical restraint and isolation.[66] Other courts have held that institutionalized patients have a right to the least restrictive alternative and have even specified conditions of confinement in accordance with the characteristics of the resident.[67] These decisions hold that, if the state restricts a person's liberty against his will to a greater degree than truly necessary or for nonlegitimate reasons (such as for the convenience of caretakers), it violates a substantive right protected by the due process clause.

To date, the Supreme Court has not recognized the "least restrictive alternative" claim as a judicially reviewable right. In *Youngberg v. Romeo,* the most recent occasion on which the question was considered, the Court pointedly avoided the "least intrusive means" analysis used by the lower court, asserting that the inmates of an institution for the mentally retarded were entitled only to a "liberty interest in safety and freedom from bodily restraint" and "freedom from unreasonable restraints."[68] The Court went on to caution that this and other constitutionally protected interests were not absolute but that they were to be balanced against the legitimate interests of the state (including lack of funds). Further, in determining whether the hospital had met its duty in protecting the liberty interest of the resident or patient, the Court deferred to the judgment of the professional as to whether the conditions of confinement or treatment were appropriate.

Lower courts have sharply diverged in their interpretations of the extent of the right which *Youngberg* labeled "freedom from unreasonable restraints."[69] Some have concluded that, consistent with the Court's assertion that its holding addressed only the claims of that particular case, the narrowest interpretation of "bodily restraints" (i.e., the restriction of physical movement) is the appropriate one.[70] Other courts, such as the Eighth Circuit Court of Appeals in *Association for Retarded Citizens v. Olson,* have chosen a more elastic definition of freedom from restraint.[71] They maintain that the "restraint" concept alluded to in *Youngberg* does not foreclose a broader interpretation of confinement and could imply any inappropriate deprivation of personal liberty. Thus, they argue, a committed patient may not be subjected to more restrictive conditions than those which an appropriate professional has deemed appropriate. It is clearly consistent with *Youngberg* that the state owes a duty to use reasonable means to prevent patients from committing suicide and to protect them from injury at the hands of fellow inmates.[72]

The Right to Treatment

The "right to treatment" movement arose from widespread concern about the merely custodial care of the mentally ill in some state institutions. In a series of early cases, some courts asserted that, as *quid pro quo* for deprivation of liberty, the confined patient must receive adequate treatment (i.e., equal protection). In *Rouse v. Cameron,* for example, Judge Bazelon held that a committed patient was entitled to treatment, and that the court had the authority to determine the adequacy of that treatment in light of present knowledge.[73] *Wyatt v. Stickney* asserted the right of involuntary patients to individual treatment;[74] and *Wyatt v. Aderholt* (which evolved from the previous case) affirmed the court's authority to articulate detailed minimum standards for adequate care.[75] Controversy over whether such standards should be set by courts rather than legislatures was later settled in favor of the courts. The guidelines advanced by the *Wyatt* cases are still heeded by the courts today, as evidenced by the Fifth Circuit's decision to follow *Wyatt v. Aderholt* in the case of *Savidge v. Fincannon*.[76] By 1986, however, the minimum standards set by *Wyatt* in 1972 had still not been met by the state of Alabama, and judicial supervision ceased. The courts appear to have retreated from their former more active role. Consent decrees may be successfully modified through certain strategies, when previously the orders were rigidly applied.[77] Nevertheless, consent decrees enjoined upon the states have led to some improvement in services.[78]

As a constitutional principle, the right to treatment has not been established. Indeed, in *O'Connor v. Donaldson* (1975), Chief Justice Burger trenchantly attacked the notion. In *Youngberg v. Romeo* the Supreme Court considered for the first time the Fourteenth Amendment rights of involuntarily committed mentally retarded patients. The Court held that the residents of a state institution for the mentally retarded did have due process rights, but to no more than *safe conditions, freedom from unreasonable restraints,* and *minimum training to prevent deterioration and enable self-protection.* The appellees were held to have "no constitutional right to training or 'habilitation' per se," only the right to have professional judgment exercised on their behalf. *In determining the minimal standard for training or rehabilitation, the courts must defer to professional opinion in order to determine what is reasonable;* external medical or judicial review is not necessary.[79] Despite the pulling back implied by *Youngberg,* the courts retain an interest in reviewing the legitimacy of the way hospitals reach decisions concerning such invasive procedures as electroconvulsive therapy, psychosurgery, and aversion therapy.[80]

Although it fell short of a constitutional right, it has been submitted[81] that the Federal Developmentally Disabled Assistance and Bill of Rights Act of 1975[82] affords the residents of mental institutions the right to require the states to provide "appropriate treatment" in "the least restrictive environment." This legislation, however, is a paper tiger, because it provides funds without imposing obligations on the states receiving these funds.

In summary, no constitutional right to treatment has been upheld, and other sources of rights have not been fruitful. The *Halderman* litigation exemplifies how difficult it is to develop rights from federal and state statutes.[83] Court-ordered consent decrees have not been completely successful, since the states lack the resources required to keep pace with the costs of implementing the decree. One result of the dilemma has been wholesale deinstitutionalization.[84] This may have been beneficial to some; but for many the return to society might have been premature.[85] Meanwhile, federal courts have been reluctant to infringe on what is seen as the proper concern of state legislatures.

The Right to Refuse Treatment

It is accepted in law that forced treatment invades an individual's liberty rights.[86] On the other hand, if medical staff are prevented from treating a committed patient, what was the point of committing him in the first place? The legal history of this dilemma is tortuous. It arises from the tension between the medical and judicial models of decision-making. Originally, the involuntary administration of drugs was viewed as a legitimate exercise of the state's *parens patriae* power. Now, however, the *sine qua non* for that exercise of power is the incompetence of the patient to decide for himself whether he wants treatment.[87] The state's interest in treating the patient is to be balanced against the patient's liberty interests.[88]

Debate over the right to refuse treatment arose only after most states had changed the justification for civil commitment from "need for treatment" to "dangerousness." The hospital was then regarded as a medical prison to which the dangerous mentally ill could be remanded until they spontaneously improved (or consented to treatment). On the other hand, since civil commitment requires both mental disorder and dangerousness, what is the justification for confinement to hospital if treatment is not provided for the disorder? Indefinite confinement without treatment is arguably a more serious invasion of liberty than briefer confinement with forced medical treatment.[89]

The argument in favor of a right to refuse treatment is rooted in the doctrine of informed consent. For consent to treatment to be valid, the patient must have sufficient information about the proposed treatment and its risks and potential benefits, must give consent voluntarily, and must be competent to make such a decision. In *Johnson v. Zerbst* the court insisted that consent to waive a constitutionally protected right must be "knowing, intelligent, and voluntary."[90] The more hazardous the treatment, the more exacting these safeguards should be. Any treatment regarded as experimental requires the most stringent informed consent.[91]

Since commitment does not render a person incompetent to consent, a distinction may be drawn between patients who are competent to consent and those who are not. For competent patients, forced treatment infringes on the purposes of informed consent—the maintenance of individual autonomy. In *Rennie v. Klein* the Third Circuit Court of Appeals considered the right to refuse antipsychotic drugs. The court upheld a constitutional right to refuse treatment. It asserted, however, that the patient does not have an absolute right to refuse; rather, due process should be imposed in the form of close medical reasoning.[92] For a challenge to be upheld, the professional reasoning involved must have substantially departed from "accepted professional practice or standards." As in *Parham*, judicial review was regarded as counterproductive. The court noted that commitment itself involved procedural safeguards lessening the risk of deferring to medical judgment. On remand after the Supreme Court decision in *Youngberg v. Romeo*, the *Rennie* court decided that the New Jersey criteria for involuntary medication satisfied the professional opinion standards. New Jersey applied three criteria: (1) the patient would be likely to harm himself and others if unmedicated; (2) the patient would be unlikely to improve unless medicated; (3) the patient would improve more slowly if not medicated than if he were medicated.

Many patients will not be competent to consent. In such cases, the courts and legislators have articulated two standards to permit medical care to be rendered: (1) *substituted judgment* (the decision that the person would have made had he been competent); and (2) a *best interests of the patient* judgment. Griffith (1991) and Welch

(1989) discuss the extensive case law and academic commentary surrounding these standards.

Incompetence will be of little importance if the state relies upon medical judgment. Here, the judgment of qualified medical experts is brought to bear on either (1) the substituted judgment of the guardian or the state as *parens patriae,* or (2) the balance among costs, benefits, and the best interests of the patient. If a guardian should refuse consent on the substituted judgment standard, the refusal may be overridden after adequate medical review (as enunciated in the *Youngberg* case).

However, some courts reject medical review and insist on a judicial inquiry. In *Rogers v. Commissioner of the Dept. of Mental Health,* the Massachusetts Supreme Judicial Court insisted that a judicial inquiry was necessary on the substituted judgment basis.[93] Similarly, in *Rivers v. Katz,* the New York Court of Appeals underlined the need for judicial review of the right to refuse treatment by holding that the court should review two matters: (1) whether the individual lacked capacity to exercise informed consent; and (2) whether the benefits of the proposed psychotropic drug outweighed its adverse effects.[94] The Wisconsin Supreme Court has taken the same approach.[95]

Rogers, Rivers, and *Gerhardstein* reflect a more stringent approach than the minimum required under the federal constitution. State common law, statutes, or constitutions have directed Massachusetts, New York, and Wisconsin to insist that the right to refuse be protected by judicial review. In *Cruzan v. Director, Missouri Dept. of Health,* the Supreme Court allowed Missouri considerable room to define the requirements surrounding the exercise of a person's right to refuse treatment.[96] It is unlikely that all the states will reduce restrictions to the minimum required under the Constitution.

In *Washington v. Harper,* the Supreme Court confirmed the federal constitutional deferential standard as a minimum constitutional requirement. This case concerned a prisoner housed in the psychiatric unit of Washington State Penitentiary. After Harper refused treatment for a manic-depressive disorder, the treating physician sought to override his objection. Unit policy allowed involuntary treatment only if the patient suffered from a mental disorder and was gravely disabled or posed a likelihood of serious harm to himself, others, or property. State policy entitled the patient to a hearing before a committee consisting of a psychiatrist, a psychologist, and the associate superintendent of the unit, none of whom would be involved in the patient's treatment. Other procedural rights were required, such as notice, the right to be heard and to present evidence, and periodic review.

> [A]n inmate's interests are adequately protected, and perhaps better served, by allowing the decision to medicate to be made by the medical professionals rather than a judge.[97]

In supporting the finding that the policy of the unit was sufficient to meet federal constitutional dictates, the Supreme Court reiterated the advantages of nonjudicial review discussed in *Parham.*

As Justice Blackmun points out in his concurring opinion, the Court's conclusion was difficult to reach because of the conflicting attitudes to the use of antipsychotic medication presented in the briefs filed by the American Psychiatric Association and the American Psychological Association. The American Psychiatric Association stressed the costs of barriers to administration of necessary medical care and expressed concern about diversion of scarce professional resources to "costly and unproductive judicial proceedings." Without medication, it was contended, hospitalization would be prolonged and physical restraint required. In contrast, the American Psychological Association attacked antipsychotic medication, asserting that these drugs have "grave effects, inherent potential for abuse, and an actual history of indiscriminate use by the psychiatric profession." The brief cited scientific literature stressing the costs over the benefits of these drugs.

Such conflict concedes no middle ground. Any court, including the Supreme Court, has an onerous task in coming to confident conclusions. It is to be expected that the case law on this matter will remain roiled.[98]

Despite the explicit adoption by the Supreme Court of the *Parham* medical review model, state courts have been reluctant to concede too much power to medical decision-makers. Thus, in *Williams v. Wilzack* the Maryland Court of Appeals, while accepting *Harper,* decided that medical review did not pass constitutional muster. Williams was an involuntary state psychiatric patient with paranoid schizophrenia who had been found not responsible for criminal conduct. Williams's psychiatrist had prescribed neuroleptic medication, but Williams refused the drug because he feared its side effects. Under the Maryland Code, patients had the right to refuse medication for the treatment of a mental disorder. Two exceptions were allowed. The first, not in issue, related to emergencies. The second prescribed medical review in nonemergency situations. Williams, with his lawyer, explained to the review panel his reasons for refusing to take the drug. The panel reviewed the treatment record and found Williams moderately hostile and suspicious. They determined that mental illness prevented Williams from making a rational decision, that neuroleptic medication was the least intrusive treatment likely to work, and that, without medication, he would probably deteriorate.

The Maryland Appeals Court found that Williams had been deprived of his due process rights under both the Federal Constitution and the Maryland Constitution. First, the court found that constitutional consideration demanded a strict reading of the Maryland statute. The court construed the statute to preclude forced administration of any drug for a purpose other than for the treatment of a mental disorder that rendered the patient dangerous to himself or others. No such finding was made in this case. Second, medical review had failed to afford Williams sufficient guarantees of notice, evidence, and legal advice, as required under *Harper.*[99]

While it may be argued that *Harper* does not require all these safeguards, it is plain that courts concerned about the forced administration of drugs will insist that medical review closely match these augmented procedural safeguards. Thus, if judicial review is not required, medical review must be exacting and legalistic in demonstrating the medical need and a showing that no less intrusive treatment would attain the same medical and institutional ends. *Williams* also indicated that judicial review of the medical panel must be available through administrative law. In *Harper,* the Supreme Court indicated no such necessity. Indeed, the judicial review requirement in *Williams,* with its pedantic recital of procedural due process steps, runs counter to the *Harper* court's insistence that cumbersome judicial inquiry should not unduly intrude upon principled medical decision-making. Spelling out the court's suspicions of forcible administration, a jail psychiatrist was found liable for administering Thorazine to a nonconsenting prisoner who was detained awaiting trial. The court found for the plaintiff-prisoner, even though the law is unclear and even though immunity would have been enjoyed had the drug been administered after conviction.[100]

Like tectonic plates, the medical and legal models of institutionalization grind away. For the lawyer, the consequence of the medical model is Solzhenitsyn's *Cancer Ward.* For the psychiatrist, the legalization of treatment decisions raises the specter of Times Square, where the untreated mentally ill "rot with their rights on."

THE RIGHTS OF MINORS IN PSYCHIATRIC HOSPITALS
Informed Consent

Do the right to treatment and the right to refuse treatment apply to minors admitted involuntarily or voluntarily to hospital? As articulated for adults in *Rouse* and *Wyatt* (and partly withdrawn in *Youngberg*), the right to treatment must be extended, at least in part, to minors. *Youngberg* mandated that safety, freedom from restraint, and self-help training were minimal requirements for the mentally retarded. It is not clear how much more than "minimally adequate training" is required to justify the confinement of nonretarded mentally ill minors. The 1980 *Standards for the Administration of Juvenile Justice* recommends a variety of educational, counseling, psychiatric, and psychological services.

Presumably, the right to refuse treatment extends to mature minors, but this matter has never been adjudicated. It would be difficult to determine a minor's competence to make such a decision. As discussed in Chapter 3, the capacity to consent to medical treatment is based upon (1) adequate information (and educability), (2) freedom from coercion or inducement, and (3) competence. Competence depends upon (1) the mental capacity to weigh the factors involved and reach a decision and (2) sufficient emotional freedom to be able to exercise the capacity for choice.

Weithorn and Campbell (1982) have shown that children of fourteen have the intellectual capacity to weigh the pros and cons of health care decisions and to make reasonable choices. It should be noted, however, that the Weithorn and Campbell study involved psychologically healthy, middle-class children who were asked to resolve simulated health care dilemmas. When psychiatrically disturbed minors are grappling with real decisions, the issues of *voluntariness* and *emotional freedom* must be taken into account.

Children are likely to be under considerable pressure to agree to admission to hospital or treatment. The combination of parental and medical authority is exceedingly difficult for most children to withstand, particularly if they are unused to independent decision-making. Children may be subjected to threat ("If you don't do what I say I'll put you in the training school."), coercion ("Either you come in voluntarily, or I'll have you committed."), false information ("It'll only be for a few days."), or inducement ("They'll give you a friend; and you can use their swimming pool."). A minor who agrees to admission in these circumstances has not exercised proper informed consent.

Also in question is the mentally ill child's emotional freedom to exercise his or her intellectual capacity to make a rational choice. If the goal-direction of thought is derailed by psychosis, or if psychotic delusions disrupt clear thinking, the patient may be incompetent to make health care decisions. The child affected by depression, severe emotional lability, incongruous emotions, or pathological euphoria may be too sluggish, pessimistic, capricious, expansive, or insouciant to be competent in this regard. The pathologically guilty child may accede to hospitalization because he perceives it as punishment. The manipulative adolescent may seek to control others by resisting admission, and to avoid personal issues by pitting one adult against another in administrative or courtroom skirmishes.

Given the variation in intellectual capacity among emotionally healthy adolescents, and given the almost certain impairment of the capacity to exercise free choice in circumstances of severe psychiatric disorder, what guidelines can be offered? The Supreme Court's decision in *Parham* asserted that constitutional considerations demanded no safeguards beyond the admitting physician's acting as a "neutral fact finder" in order to weed out abuses of the system. What abuses? The chief concerns of the *Parham* court related to (1) the "volunteering" of children for hospital by parents who were not acting in good faith but were "dumping" unwanted offspring, and (2) the "warehousing" of disturbed children by state agencies that lacked the resources or skill to provide less restrictive alternatives. In hospitals like those associated with *Parham*, the child might be kept for years, with little effective treatment. In those circumstances, the capacity of a hard-pressed admitting physician to discern and weed out systemic abuses may be questioned.

During the 1980s the rates of juvenile admissions to psychiatric hospitals rose while the numbers of minors institutionalized as status offenders declined. During this time, status offenders were deinstitutionalized, and strict procedures were established for the constitutional placement of juvenile delinquents. No data support the thesis that the juvenile population in correctional and psychiatric institutions are identical. However, in Tennessee 50 percent or more of admissions to public inpatient units for adolescents since 1985 have been referred from the courts for evaluation.

Our analysis of the right to refuse treatment drew upon the law as it relates to adults. Is that law applicable to minors? Case law relies upon the Supreme Court's reasoning in *Parham* as a justification for the medical review model. The courts would probably find that the adult cases decided in this way were highly persuasive in considering what to do about minors. Family privacy, strongly supported by *Parham*, would certainly support the adequacy of medical judgment in prescribing drugs for unwilling minors. On the other hand, if the minor were competent, some constitutional authorities, such as those providing access to contraceptives, might weaken the claim of parental hegemony. But what if the parents were to withhold consent? The situation here is even less clear. Family privacy would then disappear as an interest, favoring the administration of treatment. Under existing law, institutionalized adults are entitled to more rigorous due process rights than are minors. In adult cases this guarantee is a safeguard against abuse during treatment. It may be argued, therefore, that minors who have had no judicial due process review prior to admission deserve greater protection during treatment. Legal intervention may be justified in order to protect minors' rights despite the desirability of medical care.

In *Society for Good Will to Retarded Children. Inc. v. Cuomo,* the Second Circuit determined that a minor admitted voluntarily to a school for the mentally retarded had a constitutional right to safe conditions. The right to safety included the right to adequate supervision in order to prevent injury (whether self-administered or at the hands of other patients).[101] This would appear to be a minimal requirement.

Other potential abuses are quite different from those considered in *Parham.* During the last decade, as commercial hospital corporations have expanded and general hospitals have sought to fill vacant beds, psychiatric units for adolescents have proliferated. Admitting physicians, under pressure to maintain occupancy and encouraged by insurance coverage,[102] may be induced to hospitalize patients who could be treated in a less restrictive manner. Although the justification for admission is monitored by internal and external utilization review, the quality of such surveillance varies. In short, the most common abuse may not be the "dumping" of unwanted youth in "warehouses" but the unwarranted admission of some minors to expensive (albeit brief-stay) private hospitals. Clearly, in this circumstance, the admitting physician is not a "neutral fact finder."

A review of the guidelines for minors' admission to psychiatric hospitals must focus on two issues:

1. What are the appropriate age guidelines for the voluntary admission of minors?
2. What kind of review mechanism is required to prevent infringements on minors' constitutional rights during admission and treatment?

Recommended Age Guidelines

The following four guidelines are based upon empirical studies of the competence of children to make decisions about their own health, tempered by considerations of the effect of severe psychiatric illness on the capacity for rational choice.

1. Psychiatrically disturbed minors who are *fourteen years of age or older* should be considered competent to make decisions about admission and treatment, unless it is judicially determined that they are incompetent.[103] The clinician who thinks an adolescent is not competent to make such a decision should petition for civil commitment or for a judicial determination of incompetence. If civil commitment or an adjudication of incompetence cannot be obtained, the patient should not be admitted to the hospital. If he is already in hospital and does not want to be a voluntary patient, he should be discharged.

2. Children *younger than fourteen* should be considered incompetent. Civil commitment should not be required for minors less than fourteen years of age. A parent or guardian should have the power to admit such a child to hospital on a voluntary basis, even if the child disagrees, and to give informed consent to medical treatment. This decision should be monitored by an independent mental health advocate who could refer the case for judicial review if continued stay in hospital were considered not to be in the child's best interests.

3. If, despite serious danger of harm, a parent or guardian attempts to remove a voluntary minor patient from the hospital, or if the parent or guardian refuses medical treatment considered to be essential to the minor's mental or physical health, the attending physician has the option of petitioning the court to mandate continued hospitalization or special medical treatment, on the basis of medical neglect.

4. If a voluntary patient fourteen years of age or older petitions to leave the hospital, and the attending physician does not consider that there are sufficient grounds to petition for civil commitment, the patient should be allowed to leave.

Recommendations for External Review

We have noted, particularly in regard to admission and continued stay, that a minor in a private hospital may not be accorded some of the protections he would have enjoyed in a public setting. Economic pressures are such that medical decisions both at admission and during hospitalization cannot be neutral. Admission bias is mitigated by internal and external utilization review, but without additional monitoring these are suspect.[104] We suggest, therefore, that the *Parham* equilibrium between the medical and legal models be established through an assurance of neutrality in the decision-making process. In our view, mental health advocates should review admissions shortly after they occur. Hospitals would be obliged to provide all relevant documents, and the mental health advocate would have the right to interview hospital staff and the admitted minor and his family. If discrepancies are found, the advocate may petition the court for a hearing. Care would have to be taken to ensure that the official complied with all due process requirements.

If a minor stays in hospital for longer than two months, further independent review is required. If drugs or other invasive therapies are administered, they must be noted in the record, and details of disclosure and consent must be provided. If a minor or his parent decides that a treatment should be discontinued and the hospital disagrees, this should be reported to the mental health advocate, who should require that due process requirements be fully complied with. The requirements would encompass an independent representation of the minor's interests, and a hearing by a panel of disinterested reviewers would be called with adequate notice, affording an opportunity for the minor to present his views.

Public resources in this area are severely limited, so enforcement might be haphazard. However, neutral decision-making is a minimum constitutional requirement. The states should mandate it. Some commentators would regard these recommendations as pusillanimous and would urge full judicial review as a minimum.[105] But in our view, this would both undermine family privacy and impede medical treatment, interests strongly supported by *Parham*. In addition, the rights-based orientation has recently been attacked, with suggestions for a greater accommodation between the medical and legal models.[106] Ultimately, it is essential that the judges, attorneys, and physicians consider what is in the child's best interests. Some acutely disturbed children are best served in a restrictive environment, provided that that environment implements active treatment with the goal of early discharge to a less restrictive place. The child's and parent's constitutional rights and desires do not always coincide with what is in the child's best interests.

THE RIGHTS OF JUVENILES IN CORRECTIONAL INSTITUTIONS

During the past twenty years, juveniles in correctional institutions have received attention. The regulations of these institutions will often prescribe disciplinary guidelines. It has been held that institutions are obliged to post these guidelines and to give juveniles the opportunity to contest charges prior to their implementation.[107] However, the courts have avoided detailing such matters for fear that conflicting guidelines will emanate from different courts.[108] Presumably, juveniles have the same rights as adult prisoners to communicate with counsel or court and to have mail, telephone calls, and visits.[109]

In *Shookoff v. Adams,* the court held that the state was under an obligation to furnish incarcerated juveniles with meaningful access to the courts on the level enjoyed by incarcerated adults.[110] The principle of equivalence was departed from in *Schall v. Martin,* in which the Supreme Court found that adult standards need not govern the pretrial detention of a youth accused of delinquency.[111] However, the Supreme Court later determined that the adult standards could be altered to comport with those governing the juvenile.[112] The position with regard to searches is unclear. In *New Jersey v. T.L.0.* the Supreme Court reviewed Fourth Amendment protection against unreasonable search and seizure in public schools.[113] In finding a search reasonable, the court weighed institutional interests against privacy rights. In correctional institutions, the balance is weighed to an even greater degree in favor of the institution. It is probable that, provided a search flows from the need to administer an efficient correctional institution, it would be regarded as constitutionally reasonable.

In *Nelson v. Heyne* the court proscribed as "cruel and unusual punishment" the use of drugs without medical guidance for the purpose of institutional control.[114] In another case dealing with the administration of drugs, *Pena v. State Division for Youth,* the court found that the use of drugs for punitive purposes violated the Fourteenth Amendment.[115] The use of solitary confinement has been restricted by safeguards,[116] as has the use of physical restraints.[117] A number of decisions have upheld the juvenile offender's right to an education.[118] The rights of inmates with regard to diet, exercise, recreation, religion, medical care, and corporal punishment have also been articulated. Chief Justice Rehnquist has said that when "the State takes a person into its custody and holds him there against his will, the Constitution imposes upon it a corresponding duty to assume some responsibility for his safety and general well-being."[119]

The original impetus to create separate juvenile courts was the intention to protect minors from the corrupting influences of adult prisoners. The courts have warned about the incompatibility of mainstream prison incarceration and the rehabilitative purpose of the juvenile system.[120] Most legislation proscribes the commitment of delinquent minors to adult correctional institutions. Section 223(a)(14) of the Juvenile Justice and Delinquency Prevention Act provides that no juvenile will be detained or confined in any adult jail or lockup.[121] Once committed, a juvenile may be transferred to an adult institution, but only after a subsequent administrative or judicial decision.

Ironically, the minors most commonly incarcerated with adults are those who are being detained *before* trial. The ABA Juvenile Justice Standards deplores such a practice,[122] and some states prohibit it by legislation. The number of juveniles so detained has probably decreased in recent years.[123]

SUMMARY

In this chapter, we have traced evolving concepts regarding the rights of institutionalized children. The intensive legal activity of the last twenty years has stemmed from justified concerns that many minors were hospitalized involuntarily on flimsy grounds; that the quality of treatment in public institutions was often scandalously low; that patients were sometimes forcibly treated without due concern for their rights; and that minors' rights could be overridden when hospitalization was proposed, with the result that many unwanted children were being "dumped" or "warehoused" in institutions of poor quality.

The legal actions described in this chapter reflect a variety of colliding forces: the duty of the state to protect children and the mentally ill or retarded; the duty of the state to protect its citizens from being harmed by the mentally incompetent; the right of parents to care for their children without interference; the right of children to have a say in their own health care; the right of a citizen not to be confined without due process; the claim of confined patients to be adequately treated in exchange for their loss of liberty; the right of patients to refuse treatment, even though hospitalized involuntarily; and the right of juveniles in correctional institutions to be humanely treated. These legal actions have coincided with an increasing distrust of medicine and psychiatry, amplified by skirmishing between the guilds of psychiatry and psychology. At the same time, desirable reforms have been compromised by pressures on public and private medicine to restrain the spiraling costs of health care.

The Supreme Court has supported medical decision-making as the appropriate means of reconciling the disparate interests. Note, however, that the deference to medicine is resisted by many who fear that individual rights may be compromised. Thus, the medical decision model continues to attract criticism and scrutiny.

Perhaps the most deplorable development, abetted by the weakening of the community mental health movement, has been the capitulation of state psychiatric hospitals, leading to the abandonment of psychotic patients, untreated, to the streets. Corporate medicine, with its emphasis on profitability, brings a different set of concerns. In this chapter, we have proposed a beginning on the long road to realistic reform. A constructive resolution of these problems will be possible only if the mental health professions are prepared to represent their patients' needs in the forum of the courts, the legislatures, and the media of public information.

Notwithstanding this degree of flux, the following advances are evident: the revision of commitment standards; the assertion of a right to treatment; the acceptance of a right to refuse treatment; the articulation of standards for the care of the retarded; and the provision of safeguards for juveniles in correctional institutions.

CHAPTER 11

THE CHILD MENTAL HEALTH PROFESSIONAL AS EXPERT WITNESS

co-authored by Craig Iscoe

INTRODUCTION

This chapter introduces the reader to the function of the child mental health clinician as an expert witness in civil suits, criminal trials, and other court proceedings. The chapter begins with a brief overview of the pretrial and trial process and proceeds to the relationship between the expert clinician and the retaining attorney, the principles of forensic evaluation, the keeping of forensic records, the preparation of forensic reports, and an analysis of the importance of the adversary model to expert testimony. Finally, the chapter discusses pretrial conferences, depositions, the sequence of events in a trial, and the presentation of testimony in court.

Trial Process

Experts occupy a special role in the trial process. Unlike most witnesses, who are ordinarily not allowed to express opinions, experts are permitted to proffer opinions on matters within their expertise. The manner and scope of expert witness testimony are limited by the state or federal rules of evidence that apply to the court before which the witness appears. These rules of evidence, together with other state or federal rules (e.g., rules and statutes regarding civil procedure, criminal procedure, juvenile court proceedings and civil commitment), govern the pretrial and trial processes.

The judge presides over the trial and applies the rules in determining which evidence should be admitted. The judge makes all "findings of law" and resolves issues concerning which law should be applied in the particular case. In some trials, the judge is also the "finder of fact" who reaches a verdict that determines the outcome of the trial. In most cases, however, a jury will consider the evidence admitted and render the verdict.

Aside from the testimony of witnesses, *physical evidence* can be introduced at trial, such as weapons, letters, drugs, medical reports, and photographs. *Demonstrative evidence,* such as charts and diagrams, is also permitted. Each witness at a trial is questioned first on *direct examination* by the attorney for the party who called the witness and then *cross-examined* by the attorney for the opposing party. During cross-examination, the examining attorney probes for weaknesses in the witness's testimony, such as inconsistencies, factual errors, bias, or prejudice. The finder of fact, either judge or jury, considers the witness's responses to questions asked on direct and cross-examination in evaluating the *credibility* and *reliability* of the testimony. A witness is credible if he is perceived as telling the truth and reliable if he has accurately observed and reported the matters about which he has testified. The judge or jury first evaluates all the evidence introduced at the trial—testimonial, physical, and demonstrative—in light of the applicable legal standards, then reaches a verdict.

The Fact Witness

Most witnesses at a trial are *fact witnesses*. A fact witness is someone who has personally perceived or done something and who subsequently testifies to what he has seen, heard, felt, smelled, tasted, or done. In general, in order to be permitted to testify, a fact witness must exhibit the following characteristics: (1) He should have the capacity accurately to perceive, record, and recollect impressions of facts (the Federal Rules of Evidence now presume that a witness is competent)[1] (*physical and mental capacity*); (2) he should have personally perceived things having a tendency to establish a fact of consequence in the litigation (*personal knowledge*); (3) he should declare that he will tell the truth and appreciate the duty to tell the truth (*oath or affirmation*); (4) he should know the difference between truth, lie, and fantasy; and (5) he should have the capacity to comprehend questions and express himself understandably (*narration*).[2]

Even when competence is presumed, it may be questioned in an attempt to disqualify a witness, for example, on the basis of extreme youth or mental incapacity. However, many courts are reluctant to exclude a witness's testimony on the basis of incompetence, preferring rather to permit the witness to testify and allow the jury to come to its own conclusion about credibility and reliability. In assessing a witness's credibility, the jury looks to the content of the testimony and the witness's demeanor on the witness stand. Under most rules of evidence, the credibility of a witness may be challenged by the attorney for any party, including the party calling the witness (the sponsoring party will challenge its witness's testimony only if it turns out to be antithetical to that party's case).

In general, the cross-examiner may freely explore matters having to do with the witness's trustworthiness and bias, from financial interests to sexual preference, if such questions are relevant to the case. The witness's character and reputation for honesty are also relevant.[3] Counsel may attack a witness's credibility by introducing evidence of the witness's criminal conviction within the last ten years for a crime punishable by imprisonment for longer than one year, or for a crime involving dishonesty or false statements.[4]

A witness may be cross-examined concerning his capacity to observe and testify about events. Mental capacity can be affected by intellectual retardation, mental illness, brain dysfunction, and age. Psychiatric testimony about the witness may be admitted at the discretion of the court.[5]

The Expert Witness

Unlike a fact witness, who may not present his opinion, an *expert witness* is asked to testify precisely because his opinion is based on specialized knowledge, skill, experience, training, or education.[6] For example, a fact witness may testify that he saw a man on the street who appeared to be shouting at people who were not present, but he may not state that the man was suffering from a mental illness. In contrast, a mental health expert could testify that he had examined the man and his medical record, that he had determined that the man was experiencing auditory hallucinations, and that, in his opinion, the man was suffering from a mental illness. In offering testimony, the expert could also testify as a fact witness regarding his observations of the man, the results of any psychological tests personally performed, and other factual matters.

In federal court and many state courts, a party may call an expert witness whenever the expert's scientific, technical, or other specialized knowledge would assist the trier of fact to understand the evidence or determine a fact at issue.[7] Before a court will permit a person to testify as an expert, it must first find that the person has an acceptable level of knowledge, skill, experience, training, or education in the specialized field. Some courts have applied the *Frye* test,[8] requiring that expert testimony be deduced from generally accepted knowledge "in the particular field in which it belongs." The Supreme Court has now found that the test has been superseded by the Federal Rules of Evidence.[9] Scientific evidence is, however, subject to limits on its admissibility. The expert's testimony must be "scientific knowledge" or "technical or other specialized knowledge"; it must be supported by appropriate validation. Further, it must help the trier of fact to understand or determine a fact in issue. A number of indicia are relevant. Has the information been tested, or can it be? Has it been subjected to peer review and publication? What is the rate of error with the technique? What is its "general acceptability" within the relevant scientific community? This approach is likely to produce a similar result to *Frye*. For example, expert testimony on the hypothetical psychological profile of a child abuser may be excluded either because it is neither "generally accepted" nor "scientific knowledge" as measured by the indicia above. As discussed below, an expert should work closely with the attorney retaining him in order to ascertain the applicable standards of the court in which he proposes to testify.

Experts are often challenged on their qualification to present expert testimony. The lawyer for the opposing party may challenge an expert's credibility and reliability in the same way that he would challenge a fact witness. In this regard, the fact that an expert witness is being paid to appear in court bears upon his credibility, not his competence to testify.[10] Experts are seldom challenged on this basis, however, because ordinarily both sides call them, and each would be subject to the same attack.

Expert witnesses differ from fact witnesses in matters involving hearsay. Although there are some important exceptions,[11] fact witnesses are not permitted to testify to hearsay, that is, to report someone's out-of-court statement for the truth of the fact that the statement asserts. Special exceptions to state and federal rules of evidence, however, permit expert witnesses to present certain hearsay testimony. For example, Rule 803 of the *Federal Rules of Evidence* allows experts to present hearsay testimony regarding the following: (1) third-person statements from previous mental health, medical, education, legal, or military records concerning an individual's diagnosis, treatment, or achievements; (2) records of previous recollections or activities; (3) the statements of a third person about another when such statements are customarily obtained for the purpose of professional diagnosis (e.g., a history given by a parent about a child's development); and (4) "learned treatises" (i.e., authoritative scientific or technical publications that bear upon the issue at stake).

Unlike a fact witness, an expert is allowed to testify to hypothetical questions posed by either side. In a hypothetical question, the witness is asked to assume certain facts are true, then to draw a conclusion. The purpose of the question is to summarize information in such a way as to focus upon a particular issue. For example, the attorney might say, "Given X, Y, and Z, doctor, is it your opinion, with reasonable medical certainty, that Mr. Smith suffers from a mental illness? Is it your opinion that the mental illness, if present, is substantially related to [an event]?" A further discussion of hypothetical questions during cross-examination is presented later in this chapter.

The expert witness is expected to state his or her opinion "with reasonable [medical, scientific or clinical] certainty." The level of certainty varies in different states; those who propose to testify should ask the attorney for the retaining party the standard in that jurisdiction. In general, the "reasonable certainty" standard is equivalent to "more likely than not" or "consistent with what the majority of other clinicians would conclude, given the same information." The standard is elastic enough to allow wide judicial discretion. Most courts have not been persuaded by such commentators as Morse (1978b) and Faust and Ziskin (1988), who contend that evidence about mental health issues seldom, if ever, achieves the required standard of certainty. Somewhere in mid-spectrum are Melton and colleagues (1987), who, while conceding that clinical opinions may have been overvalued, argue that a clinician's specialized diagnostic techniques can provide useful information for the court to consider. The approach of the Supreme Court in the *Daubert* case (note 9 above) favors the admission of expert testimony and, in terms of the law, militates against the Morse and the Faust and Ziskin arguments.

THE FIRST CONTACT WITH THE REFERRING AGENT

When an attorney first contacts you about the possibility of your involvement in a particular case, you should immediately ascertain whether you are familiar with the case or have discussed it with an attorney for the other side. If you have discussed the case in much detail with one side, you will probably be precluded from working for the other side, even if the party who contacted you first did not retain you. After making the initial determination that there is no conflict, you should then address the following issues, either by telephone or, preferably, in a face-to-face meeting.

The Circumstances of the Case

Is it a civil, a criminal, or a juvenile case? What is the nature of the charge, complaint, or dispute? Who are the parties involved, and what led up to the current legal action? What previous legal actions have taken place?

The Legal Issue

What is the legal issue or question that you, as an expert, are being asked to elucidate? What are the legal elements of the issue in that jurisdiction (e.g., in a custody dispute, what is the definition of "the best interests of the child")? Do not expect that all attorneys will spontaneously inform you of the legal issue at stake. An attorney may tell you only that he wants "an evaluation." You should ascertain precisely what type of evaluation is required and how the attorney intends to use the information obtained from the evaluation.

Your Role

What are you being requested to do? If the attorney has requested an evaluation, does he want you to prepare a report or to refrain from doing so until you have discussed the results of your evaluation? Sometimes the attorney will want to hear your initial assessment of the case but will not want you to prepare a report. An unfavorable report may be open to discovery by the other side.

Is the attorney asking you to evaluate the quality of another clinician's report, as often occurs in a civil liability case? Will you be asked to help the attorney prepare a legal strategy in order to counter the other side's case? If so, will you be asked to evaluate the case and testify?

The Appropriateness of Your Handling the Case

Do you have sufficient experience in the area of law or clinical work involved? If the case turns, for example, upon detailed knowledge of the side effects of a particular psychotropic drug, upon the credibility of a child's allegation of abuse, or upon the intricacies of psychoeducational testing, be sure that you have sufficient credentials and experience to render an expert opinion on the matter.

Are you being requested to operate in an appropriate and professional manner? For example, in a custody dispute, it is rarely effective for you to evaluate only one party. Sometimes, for example, an attorney will advise a disputant to "get a mental health evaluation." Don't be involved in such an unprofessional consultation. Also, as already discussed, avoid acting as an expert witness if you are already treating or propose to treat the client involved.

The Scheduling of the Case

What is the anticipated date of trial? Do you have sufficient time to complete an evaluation and compose a report? If not, ask the attorney to request a continuance or decline the case. It is always inadvisable to rush an evaluation. You do a client no favor if you save time or money by omitting important steps in an evaluation or by curtailing your reasoning in a report.

Skeletons in the Closet

Apprise the retaining attorney of anything that could impede your being accredited as an expert. Are you fully qualified and licensed? If you are board eligible, for example, have you failed the board examinations? Have you ever had your license to practice or your clinical privileges revoked? Are you being sued (or have you ever been sued) for malpractice? Has a malpractice suit ever been decided against you? Have you ever been found guilty of a criminal offense? Have you written a textbook or scientific article on the issue in question? Though your publications are not necessarily skeletons, the retaining attorney should be aware of them in case the other side ferrets out statements from them that appear to counter your opinion in the case in question.

The Fee

Clarify your fees. Some clinicians charge a "package fee," which differs according to the issue involved. It can be difficult, however, to predict the time that will be required to peruse all the documents or complete all the interviews or tests required. It is preferable to estimate the time and quote a probable fee based on the cost per hour, indicating that the fee could be more or less depending upon the requirements of the particular case. You should inform the attorney or parents before you exceed your estimated fee.

It is legitimate to charge an hourly fee above that charged for an ordinary clinical evaluation. You should charge for all the time you spend perusing documents and preparing reports. Indicate also that you will charge separately, on a half-day or full-day basis, for giving testimony at a deposition or in court.

How will the bill be paid, and who will pay it? In tort cases, the attorney usually operates on a contingency fee and is responsible for all expenses. In other cases, the payor will be the parents of the child or children evaluated, a state agency, or an insurance company. Insurance companies and state agencies can be billed after the evaluation report is completed. However, attorneys and private individuals should be handled differently. One approach is to ask for the entire estimated amount at the outset and to adjust the bill up or down prior to releasing the report. A second approach is to ask for a retainer (e.g., 50 percent of the estimated bill) at the outset, the balance to be paid prior to your issuing the report. A third approach is to send the entire bill and request payment in full prior to issuing the report. The danger is that, if you bill the payor after you send an unfavorable report, you may find it difficult, if not impossible, to collect your fee. Attorneys understand the "money-up-front" approach, since they themselves often operate in that manner.

When you have agreed with the attorney or parent about the method of payment, set out the agreement in a letter. The letter should state that you have contracted to conduct a forensic evaluation and to provide a report with regard to a specified legal matter; in return, the payor agrees to compensate you with a fee (based on an hourly or package rate) to be paid in full in a particular way (e.g., with the entire estimated fee or part of it paid at the outset). You will also make clear in the letter that, if you are required to give testimony in court, there will be an additional charge of an estimated amount according to whether you are involved for a half a day, a full day, or longer. Send the letter by registered mail, asking for a letter of acceptance but indicating that, if you do not receive a letter of acceptance in a certain number of days, you will assume that the receiver agrees with the terms of the contract.

Documents

Ask the attorney to forward to you or to obtain consent and gather on your behalf whichever of the following documents are available and appropriate: witness reports; police reports; affidavits; records of previous arrests; confessions or other statements; interrogatories; prior court decisions, holdings or decrees; past medical or mental health reports; school, military, or occupational records; previous forensic mental health reports; depositions; and any other documents that you believe may be useful.

Legal Principles

If the attorney has not already done so, ask him or her to forward the statutes, ordinances, case law precedents, or rules of evidence that are relevant to the case in question. For example, what is the local case or statutory law with regard to the *Tarasoff* doctrine (see Chapter 8), the best interests of the child, or civil commitment? If you are unsure of it, ask the attorney.

LIABILITY ISSUES

As Guyer (1991) has observed, a forensic mental health evaluation is a specialized procedure designed to provide findings and opinions useful to the court or to a party to a legal proceeding. The forensic clinician's client may be the court, the person who is evaluated, or a third party. The "client" is defined as the one who receives the expert's "work product" (the forensic report or testimony) in exchange for a "consideration" (the payment of a fee). Difficulties may arise if the person examined is not the client or if the client has not given informed consent for the evaluation. The evaluator should make sure that the client or examinee understands the nature and purpose of the evaluation, the estimated fee, the potential risks and benefits of having (and not having) the evaluation, and the fact that the evaluation is not for therapeutic purposes but to provide information to the court. The client should also be informed that the expert's opinion will not necessarily be favorable and that whatever is said may be included in a report that could become a public record.

Clinicians are obligated by law to report to the authorities suspected child abuse or neglect. Failure to do so will open them to criminal and civil liability. Similarly, an unconsented disclosure of a case record opens the clinician to a suit on the basis of breach of confidentiality. Every clinician should be aware of the local statute or case law in this regard (see Chapter 8).

Civil liability suits following child custody evaluations are particularly likely when sexual abuse has been alleged by one side against the other. Such suits are usually based on assertions of negligent evaluation or bias. It is sometimes possible to anticipate cases that will result in litigation of this kind. Draft explicit contractual understandings and be meticulous in your informed consent and case recording procedures. Remember also to date, time, and keep notes on every telephone call, interview, and test procedure. Be sure to state explicitly that your evaluation is for the purposes of the child-custody dispute.[12]

THE EVALUATION

The details of evaluation procedures for different issues (e.g., custody disputes, juvenile offenders, civil liability) are described in the appropriate chapters. This section will deal with general issues and principles.

Obtain Informed Consent

Interview the party or parties to the litigation and obtain informed consent for the forensic evaluation. The Fifth Amendment requires that criminal defendants be warned that their statements to the clinician may be used against them.[13] Get an agreement on the fee. Make it clear to all clients that the evaluation is for legal, not therapeutic, purposes, that you cannot guarantee a favorable report, that anything disclosed may be incorporated in a report to the court that others will read, and that there are risks associated with undertaking the evaluation (or not doing so). Have the party or parties sign an informed consent form.

Be Thorough

Clinical evaluations are conducted to an extent required to reach a provisional or working diagnosis, which is often modified or extended in the course of treatment. In the usual clinical situation, patients tell the truth as well as they can. The forensic situation is different. Passions run high. People who are truthful in other situations are prone to shade or slant the facts, conceal information, or lie. For those reasons, the forensic evaluator cannot be satisfied with a single version of what purports to be true but should seek corroborative information whenever possible. Interviews with different informants, standard questionnaires and rating scales, formal psychological testing, and past medical, mental health, military, occupational, legal, or educational records can all yield useful information. When a child's mental health is at issue, for example, cross-validate your information as follows: by interviewing the parents (separately, if they are contesting custody); by interviewing the child; from standardized questionnaires completed by the parents, teacher, or other informants (if appropriate); from school, health, and mental health records; and from psychological testing of the child. If there is a marked discrepancy—for example, between the two parents—try to find which viewpoint is best supported by other data and seek an explanation for the discrepancy.

Select Your Evaluation Procedures to Match the Legal Issues in Question

The clinician should always consider the legal issues before the court in selecting the evaluation procedures to use. In custody litigation, for example, the best interests of the child are at stake. In order for the court to decide what is best for the child, it may be useful for it to have information concerning the following matters: the wishes of the parents and the child; the quality of the relationship between the child and each parent, siblings, and any other significant persons; the child's adjustment to his or her current home, school, or community; and the mental and physical health of everyone involved. In such situations, clinicians commonly select interviews, child behavior questionnaires, parental competency interviews and questionnaires, and psychological testing concerning the intelligence, school performance, mental health, and personality of the parents and child.

Remember that your ultimate task is to provide the court with information that illuminates the legal question at issue in the case. If competence to stand trial is involved, for example, your task will be to determine—primarily by interview—whether the defendant understands and appreciates the nature and implications of the charges against him and of pleading guilty or not guilty, whether he understands the function of the courtroom personnel, whether he can advise his attorney adequately, and whether the defendant is able to comport himself properly in court. The question is not whether he is mentally impaired, but whether such impairment, if any, would preclude a proper trial and, if so, whether the impairment could be remedied soon enough to permit him to be tried.

THE REPORT

Your report is of the greatest importance. A good report helps counsel prepare an effective legal strategy and can also play a major role in determining the outcome of the case. A poor report provides ammunition that will allow your testimony to be shot down in cross-examination. Sometimes your report will be so compelling that the opposing party settles the case before going to court. If the case does go to trial, your report may be entered into evidence and referred to by the judge or jury in rendering a decision. In any case, the quality of your report advertises your expertise. The following guidelines may be helpful.

Be Logical

The report should proceed from a description of the circumstances and reason for referral; through the sources of your data and the techniques involved in gathering them, a description of your findings, and a discussion of their relative weight; to a summary of your opinion with regard to the elements of the legal issue at stake. You should address the ultimate legal issue in a criminal case only if the attorney retaining you tells you that it is appropriate to do so.

Be Thorough but Succinct

Judge and juries do not like verbosity. Keep your report succinct, but cover all the issues.

Write Plainly

Avoid the passive voice, however modest it may seem. "I interviewed the defendant at. . ." is better than "The defendant was interviewed at. . ."

Avoid jargon. Rather than state that a woman has "borderline traits," you could describe her as having an uncertain sense of identity, poor control of emotions, great difficulty in sustaining close relationships, and a tendency to react to upsets in her personal life with suicidal threats or attempts.

Whenever you use a technical term, define it. For example, "He complained of auditory hallucinations, saying that, even when alone, he heard voices talking to him in a disparaging manner. Sometimes, the voices tell him to hurt other people or kill himself."

Try to avoid qualifying your statements with "weasel" words (e.g., "perhaps," "somewhat," "rather"). If something is uncertain, say so. If intensity must be indicated, use such words as "slight," "mild," "moderate," "marked," "severe," or "drastic."

Standardize the Format

Label the front cover of the report "Confidential" and entitle it "Forensic Evaluation Concerning (full name)," with the date of birth. Next, list the content of the report according to headings and pages. At the bottom righthand corner put your signature, name and title, and at the bottom lefthand corner put the date the report was prepared. Double-space the body of the report.

Use Headings

Under *Circumstances of Referral,* describe briefly who referred the case, the *dramatis personae,* previous judicial hearings or findings, if any, and the current legal situation.

Under *Purpose of Evaluation,* enumerate the legal issues addressed in the case.

Informed Consent summarizes, when appropriate, your discussion of consent issues with the person or persons being evaluated, their understanding that the evaluation has a legal, not a therapeutic, purpose, and their consent to the evaluation.

Sources of Data lists the documents reviewed (with title, date, and signature), interviews conducted (with subject, date, and duration of interview), and tests administered (with subject, date, duration, and name of tester).

Findings describes the information, observations, and results obtained from documents, interviews, psychological tests, and other sources. Use direct quotes when it will illustrate your point. For example: "When asked if she would prefer to live with her mother or her father, she said, 'My mother. I never want to see my father again.' "

In *Discussion of Findings,* weigh the relative merit and significance of the data with regard to the issues in the case. Consider the pros and cons of different hypotheses or explanations for the central facts of the case. For example, when evaluating a child's allegation of sexual abuse, discuss the pros and cons of the hypotheses that the allegation arises from misinterpretation, delusion, indoctrination, contagion, confabulation, suggestive interviewing, fabrication, or truth-telling (see Chapter 6).

In *Summary and Recommendations,* enumerate what you can state "with reasonable certainty." If you cannot give a particular opinion with reasonable certainty, say so. For example:

Therefore, with reasonable medical certainty, I offer the following opinion:

1. William Smith suffers from residual posttraumatic stress disorder of moderate degree.
2. The timing and pattern of the symptoms of this disorder indicate that it was precipitated by the automobile accident of (date).
3. The disorder seriously disrupts his sleep and interferes with his capacity to benefit from school, sustain friendships, and enjoy life.
4. There is no evidence that William Smith suffered from a psychological disorder or impairment prior to the accident in question.

It is not possible to predict with reasonable certainty whether the disorder will abate, persist, or be reactivated or aggravated by future traumatic events. Nevertheless, in order to facilitate recovery and avert impairment or recurrence I recommend . . .

Number the *Appendixes,* and include therein your full *curriculum vitae,* an abbreviated *curriculum vitae* designed to help the attorney frame qualifying questions, any transcripts from your evaluation that you deem important, the full psychological test report, and any scientific articles you consider of pertinence to the case.

Edit the Manuscript

Winnow out all psychobabble (e.g., "He will meet the needs of the patient." "She assumed the maternal role." "He experimented with drugs." "She acted out her conflicts." "She is codependent."); all "buzzwords" (e.g., "on the cutting edge," "on the cusp of . . ."); all vogue usages (e.g., "The trauma impacted his personality."); and clichés (e.g., "each and every one of us," "in this day and age").

Remember Your Audience

Above all, remember that you are writing for lawyers, not clinicians. Be as concise as possible. Be logical, progressing from question, through data, to discussion and conclusion. Distinguish reasonable opinion from speculation. Consider alternative explanations and weigh the evidence for or against them. Let clarity, thoroughness, logic, and succinctness be your watchwords.

Appendix 1 contains sample case reports on various legal issues.

RECORDS

Discard nothing. Keep your case records in hard-backed folders, the contents divided into the following tabbed sections:

1. Initial contact sheet and contract with referring agent
2. Record of all interviews and tests, with dates, duration, and charges
3. Your forensic evaluation report
4. Copies of the laws, statutes, regulations, or case precedents relevant to the case
5. Scientific articles relevant to the case
6. Legal documents concerning the case (e.g., interrogatories, answers, petitions, affidavits, depositions, previous judicial holdings)
7. Other documents (e.g., past child welfare, pediatric, mental health, psychological, or educational records)
8. Your case notes
9. Psychological test results (The psychologist should retain the raw data of all tests.)
10. Telephone messages (dated and timed)
11. All letters pertaining to the case
12. Informed consent and data release forms
13. Audiotapes, videotapes, transcripts, etc.

Blau (1984) advises that the initial contact sheet (item 1 above) record the following: (1) the date and time of initial contact with the attorney; (2) the attorney's name, address, and telephone number; (3) the names, addresses, and telephone numbers of plaintiff, defendant, and other attorneys involved in the case; (4) the facts of the case; (5) the legal issues involved in the case; (6) the anticipated date of trial, the court, and the judge appointed to try the case.

THE SUBPOENA

In most cases in which you are retained as an expert, you will receive a *subpoena* ordering you to appear in court. The Latin term *sub poena* means "under penalty." A *subpoena ad testificandum* ("for the purpose of testifying") is a writ issued by an attorney, agency, or judge to require a person to attend a court of law at a particular time in order to give testimony. A *subpoena duces tecum* (literally, "under penalty thou shalt take with thee") commands the witness to produce specified property or documents (e.g., medical records) at a trial.

As an expert, you will receive relatively few "surprise" subpoenas. Most of those you do receive will have been issued by the attorney who retained you, only because the judge has required the attorneys to subpoena all witnesses. The time you are requested to appear in court, as listed on the subpoena, is not as inflexible as may appear. Usually the subpoena stipulates the time to appear as the time the trial is scheduled to begin, rather than the time that you will actually be called. By telephoning the attorney named on the subpoena, whether or not it is the attorney who retained you, you will often be able to negotiate a mutually agreeable time.

Although a *subpoena ad testificandum* compels the witness to appear in court, it does not necessarily compel you to testify about someone in treatment unless the judge orders you to do so. If you receive a subpoena commanding you to testify or produce records concerning a patient, do not disclose confidential information without taking precautions. Inform the patient and his or her attorney, asking for their advice. Consult your own attorney concerning the risk of breaching confidentiality. Ask for a copy of the local law concerning privileged communications. Review the record for sensitive material. Your attorney or the retaining attorney may petition the court for a protective order to seal the record against the disclosure of private but irrelevant material. The attorney can ask the judge to review the record in order to determine whether sensitive information should remain inviolate. In some cases your attorney or the patient's attorney will file a petition to quash the subpoena on the ground of breach of privilege. If you remain uncertain, you can always appeal to the judge in court, asking for direction concerning privileged information. However, if you are commanded by the judge to testify concerning a privileged communication, you may not remain silent without running the risk of being held in contempt of court.[14]

THE PRETRIAL CONFERENCE

Prior to testifying at a trial or deposition, you and the retaining attorney should confer. Be sure to allow sufficient time for the conference, usually a minimum of one to two hours. Without such a meeting, the attorney will be hampered in preparing an effective strategy, and the expert witness will have no guidance in anticipating the sequence of questions in the direct examination or deposition, those aspects of expert testimony that are of particular relevance to the case, and the lines of attack likely to be adopted by the cross-examiner.

At the pretrial conference, clinician and attorney will discuss how the clinician will be qualified. They can next review the legal theory of the case, the way in which professional testimony bears upon it, and potential weaknesses, discrepancies, or inconsistencies in the expert's evaluation. The attorney may decide to bring out the flaws during direct examination so as to take the wind from the opposition's sails or, on the contrary, to steer clear of flaws in the hope they will be overlooked. The expert should be sufficiently critical concerning his own work to be able to discuss potential problems with the attorney. For example, when a plaintiff in a civil liability case has had a preexisting psychiatric disorder that was aggravated by a defendant's allegedly negligent act (see chapter 7), expert and attorney should prepare for the almost inevitable attack on this vulnerable position.

The attorney will familiarize the expert with the order of questions to be put in direct examination. Generally, questions are posed about the witness's qualifications, the witness's examinations, the tests undertaken or ordered, the findings of the evaluation, the expert's opinion (with reasonable certainty), and his recommendations for treatment or disposition. Testimony thus converges upon (but stops short of) the ultimate legal conclusion. The wise attorney and expert will not rehearse the precise wording of every question to be posed. Spontaneous answers are more persuasive than stilted recitations.

The attorney will define for the expert the local standard for reasonable certainty. In most jurisdictions, this elastic concept refers to a "more likely than not" opinion, or an opinion that, though falling short of absolute certainty, is likely to be shared by the majority of experts in the field. The attorney's explanation will help the expert decide whether it is possible to testify to a particular opinion with reasonable certainty; if not, the witness may be able to say no more than that the data are consistent with a particular inference (though also consistent with other plausible explanations).

If the attorney proposes to put a hypothetical question, its premises should be discussed. For example:

ATTORNEY: Assuming that the child has been physically abused, and that the abuse was the cause of the injuries already described, and assuming that the injuries were inflicted by one or both parents, do you think that there would be a risk of further abuse, in this case, if the child were returned to the care of the parents?

EXPERT: In my opinion, there is a definite risk.

ATTORNEY: What factors contribute to the risk?

EXPERT: The age of the child, the history of repeated abuse, the severity of the child's injuries, the parents' denial that abuse occurred, and the failure of the parents to accept therapy.

Finally, the expert should check the date, time, and place of the hearing; the probable duration of the testimony; and where to go to announce his arrival. In most cases, it is wise to schedule a half-day or full day, depending on the case.

PREPARING TO GIVE TESTIMONY AT A DEPOSITION OR TRIAL

Shortly before you give testimony or are deposed, prepare your mind and your papers as follows:

1. Organize your files into tabbed sections (see p. 354). Arrange the contents of each section in chronological order.

2. Prepare a flow chart of the case, setting out the salient events and their dates. Put it at the front of the case record.

3. Put your evaluation report close to the front of the record so that you may refer readily to the dates and duration of diagnostic procedures and the documents reviewed prior to preparing the report.

4. Review all documents concerning the legal issues involved in the case. Make sure you are clear about the questions at stake, for your direct and cross-examination will bear upon them. For example, in a parental competence hearing, the court will be less interested in whether the parent has mental illness than whether the mental illness impedes parenting, whether it could be reversed in a foreseeable time, and whether the parent could cooperate in a reunification plan.

5. Collate, review, and file relevant clinical and research literature. Review the relevant DSM III-R diagnostic categories. If you have published in the field, read your own material. The cross-examiner would be delighted to find an apparent inconsistency between your publications and your opinion in the case. If your opinion could be construed as inconsistent, prepare an answer for the possible question, for example:

WITNESS: Yes, it is true that I have written that schizophrenia is not necessarily a bar to parenting. However, I was referring to parents with mental illness that responds to medical treatment and to parents, moreover, who were prepared to accept treatment. Mrs. Smith has been neither responsive nor receptive to treatment.

6. Prepare yourself for a "learned treatise" attack (described below).[15] Review the literature relevant to general and particular avenues of attack. Prepare a counterargument if one can be sustained.

7. Prepare charts or illustrations if these will aid your testimony. If you do so, however, make sure that the graphics are large and clear and that each illustration is uncluttered. In testimony related to mental health or developmental psychology, it is usually preferable to rely upon oral presentation, illustrating your ideas with effective example or analogies.

CROSS-EXAMINER: Doctor, isn't schizophrenia the same as a split mind, a Jekyll and Hyde personality?

WITNESS: No. It is true that "schizophrenia" means "split mind" in Greek, but a better translation would be "shattered mind," a mind reduced to fragments, like a shattered mirror.

8. Finally, make sure the case has not been settled out of court or continued (i.e., postponed). Sometimes the attorney will have forgotten to tell you or the message will have gone astray. Recheck the time and probable duration of your testimony.

THE DEPOSITION

The term "discovery" refers to the procedures whereby litigating parties obtain from each other some of the information that they need to prepare for trial. The purpose of discovery is to ensure that there are relatively few surprises when the case is tried, since each side will have had the opportunity to understand the basis of its adversary's argument. Discovery also encourages parties to settle cases before trial once they have learned the relative strengths of their cases. The methods of discovery include an exchange of documents, health reports, and records, and, in civil cases, the posing of written interrogatories (i.e., lists of questions), the deposing of witnesses, and the mental health evaluation of parties to the case. Discovery is more limited in criminal cases than in civil cases. In federal and most state criminal cases, for example, interrogatories or depositions are not permitted.

At a deposition, the witness testifies out of court in the presence of the attorneys for the parties and a court reporter. Some depositions are videotaped. A witness is usually deposed in order to permit the parties to learn the substance of the prospective witness's testimony. Sometimes a deposition is required in order to obtain testimony from someone who could not be present at trial (for example, by reason of illness or distance from the trial location).

As discussed in the "Pretrial Conference" section of this chapter, the clinician should meet with the retaining attorney before a deposition. The attorney should explain the purpose of the deposition and the probable substance and sequence of questions, and should advise whether materials pertaining to the *attorney's work product* (those materials, records of interviews, statements, memoranda, correspondence, etc., generated exclusively for the purpose of the trial) should be discussed at the trial.[16] Privilege will be waived if materials are raised in evidence. Consult with the attorney for the party who has retained you before preparing any report concerning the conclusions you have reached after conducting a mental health examination. Such reports are usually *discoverable* (i.e., they must be turned over to the opposing party during discovery).[17] In a civil case, most of the notes in a patient's file will usually be discoverable, with the exception of the attorney's work product mentioned above.

Testifying at a deposition is substantially different from testifying at trial, because the goal of an attorney at a deposition is not, as it is at trial, to present evidence favorable to his side and to exclude or explain unfavorable evidence. Rather, at a deposition, an attorney will attempt to find out as much about his opponent's case as possible, particularly in regard to information that could be harmful to his party's position. Because neither the judge nor the jury is present at a deposition, there is no danger in eliciting testimony that would be harmful to a party if it were presented at trial. Consequently, the range of questions put to a deponent is usually far broader than it would be at trial.

In addition to the broader range of questions, the style of questioning is also different. The attorney for the opposing side will often ask the deponent broad, open-ended questions designed to elicit as much as possible about the strength of the case and the characteristics of the expert witness. For example, the attorney might ask, "Tell me about your first interview with [the client]." The attorney would then follow up with more precise questions. In contrast, at a trial the cross-examiner will usually ask narrow leading questions permitting only short, tightly focused responses. Another difference between a deposition and a trial is that at many depositions the attorney for the party sponsoring the expert will ask the expert few questions, on the rationale that the answers to such questions would only assist the other side in preparing for trial.

Although the formality that characterizes a trial appears to be relaxed at a deposition, be careful. The seemingly friendly atmosphere can tempt an unwary expert into making careless statements that will be used against him at trial. Treat a deposition as you would a court appearance. Be courteous and professional, but do not fraternize.

At a deposition, the lawyer for the party that has retained you will be present and may object to questions asked by the lawyer for the opposing side. It is common for the retaining attorney to object when the opposing attorney goes on a "fishing expedition"—a wide-ranging examination, beyond the proper scope of discovery, designed to rummage for weaknesses in the witness's personality, training, experience, or reasoning. Even if the attorney objects, you must still answer the question, unless the attorney instructs you not to answer. Because there is no judge present at a deposition, objections made at that time are usually not resolved during the deposition itself. If you have been instructed not to answer, the opposing party may ask the judge to issue an order compelling you to answer at a subsequent deposition. Prior to the trial, the attorneys will usually ask the judge to resolve disputes about the admissibility of questions that you answered at the deposition after objection.

Before or after the deposition, the retaining attorney may advise you to provide opposing counsel access to the patient's case record. If the retaining attorney so advises, you should remove any elements of the retaining attorney's work product from your file and inform counsel or the opposing party that you have done so. Remove nothing else, lest you obstruct justice by withholding evidence.

At the conclusion of the deposition, the retaining attorney should ask the reporter when the transcript of the deposition will be ready. Review the transcript very carefully, correcting any errors with signed marginal comments. Never sign the document without reading it. The inadvertent omission of the simple word "not," for example, will reverse your meaning. When you subsequently testify in court, you may be made to look careless, if not foolish. For example:

COUNSEL: Doctor, you just testified that Mr. Jones is not below average in intelligence. You recall testifying under oath at a deposition held on March 1, don't you?

WITNESS: Yes.

COUNSEL: In that deposition (*holding up the deposition and pointing to it*) you said he *is* below average in intelligence, didn't you?

WITNESS: No, the reporter must have transcribed the deposition incorrectly.

COUNSEL: But you reviewed that transcript for accuracy, didn't you?

WITNESS: Yes, I must have missed that error.

COUNSEL: Do you often make such careless mistakes? What other mistakes have you made in this case?

TESTIFYING IN COURT
Preparation

Before you appear in court to testify you should reread all the written material on which you will rely in your testimony. You should also carefully review any reports you have prepared, the transcript of your deposition, and the relevant sections of DSM III-R. In addition, refresh your memory of the legal issues at stake and the research literature on the matter. Identify any weaknesses in your argument and anticipate cross-examination on them. Prepare for a "learned treatise" attack (see under "Cross-examination" in this section).

Dress professionally in a manner befitting the seriousness of being an expert witness. Men should wear suits, sober shirts, and restrained ties; women skirted suits with tailored blouses or dresses with jackets. Avoid jangling jewelry, flashy rings, colorful ties, leisure suits, pant suits, sports jackets, blazers, two-toned shoes, and open-toed sandals. Eschew any apparel or ornament that might distract the judge or jury from listening to what you say.

Find out from the retaining attorney when to arrive at court, where to meet him, and, if necessary, how to announce your arrival to the judge. Do not expect to be heard at the cited time. The fact that such predictions are inevitably imprecise will be reflected in your bill (per half-day or full day). Do not enter the courtroom until you are instructed to enter.[18]

You should seek instructions from the retaining attorney on what, if any, testimony you should hear before you take the stand. Federal Rule of Evidence 615, and most state court rules, require the court, "at the request of a party," to exclude the witness from hearing evidence, a practice known as "invoking the rule on witnesses." On its face, this rule would appear to bar expert witnesses from hearing the testimony of any other witnesses. Sometimes, however, the court will permit one party's expert to be present during the testimony of the opposing party's expert(s) on the same issue or to hear the testimony of certain fact witnesses, on the ground that the opinion of one expert may be relevant to another expert's conclusions, just as the diagnosis of a patient by one physician may be relevant to a second physician's diagnosis.[19] Sometimes the court will permit an expert witness to be present in order to assist counsel in his examination of the opposing side's expert.

If a witness should violate an order of exclusion, the court can impose a variety of sanctions—for example, by prohibiting the witness from testifying or by holding him in contempt.[20] The court would also instruct the jury to weigh the credibility of the witness in view of his presence in court or his discussions with other witnesses.[21] Finally, the court could order a mistrial.[22]

The prudent approach is to avoid exposing yourself to others' testimony, even incidentally. Do not, therefore, cause yourself and the court problems by fraternizing with witnesses for either side. Do not discuss a witness's testimony with him. If you encounter witnesses in the corridors before the trial, confine your conversation to a courteous salutation. You are under no obligation to speak to the attorney for the opposing side and should do so only after consulting with the retaining attorney.

Before your testimony you may be invited to wait in a nearby office. You will often have to wait for some time. Bring with you material to read, or refresh your recollection from the case record. Try to relax.

The Order of Events in the Trial

In general, a jury trial will progress in the following stages.

JURY SELECTION

The lawyers will question potential jurors under a procedure called *voir dire* (in French, literally, "to see, to say"). Each side is permitted to eliminate a limited number of jurors by *peremptory challenge* (i.e., without stating why they have chosen to eliminate them). The court may excuse an unlimited number by *for cause challenge* (i.e., based upon a showing of bias or presumption).

SWEARING THE JURY

After the jury has been selected, the judge will swear and instruct its members concerning their duties in the case.

OPENING STATEMENTS

The prosecution (or the plaintiff) and the defendant will then make opening statements that outline what they believe the evidence will establish.

CASE-IN-CHIEF

In the next stage of the trial, the prosecution (or plaintiff) calls witnesses who support its position. After the prosecution (or plaintiff) has presented all its witnesses, it "rests its case." The defense then calls witnesses who present evidence to support its position. Witnesses for each side are questioned first by direct examination by the attorney for the party who sponsored them and then by cross-examination by the lawyer for the opposing party. Direct examination questions do not suggest the answer, while cross-examination questions do. Compare the following:

DIRECT EXAMINATION: Did you notice anything unusual about Mr. Jones when you first met with him? [Note that the question does not state that Mr. Jones did anything unusual or, if so, what it was.]

CROSS-EXAMINATION: Mr. Jones loudly proclaimed that he was the King of England when he first appeared in your office, didn't he?

REBUTTAL CASE

Evidence is then presented in rebuttal by the prosecution or plaintiff. The rebuttal cannot be used to introduce fresh evidence. The prosecution or plaintiff may introduce evidence not previously admitted only in response to the defendant's evidence. Expert witnesses sometimes testify during this phase of the trial. Occasionally the defense will be permitted to present a surrebuttal that presents evidence responsive to that which the prosecution or plaintiff introduced on rebuttal.

CLOSING ARGUMENTS

Following the presentation of all evidence by both sides, the prosecution (or plaintiff) presents its *opening closing argument*. The defense then presents its *closing argument*. The prosecution (or plaintiff) then presents its *rebuttal closing argument*.

JURY INSTRUCTIONS

The judge gives final instructions to the jury concerning the legal questions at issue in the case and the manner in which the jury should conduct its deliberations.

JURY DELIBERATIONS

The jury retires to consider its *verdict* or *decision* concerning guilt (in a criminal trial), liability and damages, or other issues (in civil actions). In many jurisdictions, the verdict or decision must be unanimous in both criminal and civil cases. If the jury cannot reach a verdict in a civil or criminal case, a new trial may be required.

POST-CONVICTION PROCEEDINGS

In criminal cases, a presentencing hearing will often be scheduled prior to sentencing and commitment. Expert witnesses may be called upon to testify in favor of or against mitigation of the sentence.

The Courtroom

The courtroom is usually arranged with the judge's bench raised above the rest of the room. To one side of the judge is the jury box. The witness box is on the side of the judge that is closer to the jury. At separate tables sit the prosecutor (or the plaintiff and his or her attorney), the defendant and his or her attorney, the clerk of the court, the bailiff or marshal, and the court reporter. Spectators sit in rows at the back of the court. In juvenile court, the witness often sits facing the judge, between the opposing attorneys.

The bailiff or marshal is usually the person who will tell you when to enter the courtroom. When you do, go directly to the witness stand, acknowledge the judge with a nod, face the clerk, and raise your right hand. The clerk will administer the oath or affirmation that you must take before testifying. The judge will ask you to be seated.

Qualification

After you have been sworn, the attorney who is to conduct the direct examination will ask you questions that will enable you to inform the court of your qualifications as an expert witness. The purpose of the question is not only to establish your qualifications but also to show that those qualifications are equal to or superior to those of other witnesses. You will have already forwarded, with your report, a copy of your full *curriculum vitae* and an abbreviated curriculum that deals with your training and experience relevant to the current case. With this, the attorney will construct a series of questions that elicit qualifying information, for example:

COUNSEL: Please state your name and address.

WITNESS: John Smith, 10 Lygon Place, Nashville, Tennessee

COUNSEL: Please tell the judge and the jury your educational background.

WITNESS: I received my bachelor's degree in biology from Duke University in 1971 and my MD from the University of Florida in 1975.

COUNSEL: Where did you receive your internship and residency training? [If you received any degrees with honors, you should so state.]

WITNESS: I completed my internship and residency training in general psychiatry at the University of Tennessee from 1980 to 1983. I completed my training in child and adolescent psychiatry, from 1983 and 1985, at Vanderbilt University.

COUNSEL: What other professional qualifications do you have?

WITNESS: I am board certified in general psychiatry and in child and adolescent psychiatry.

COUNSEL: What does it mean to be board certified?

WITNESS: To receive board certification in general psychiatry one must have practiced psychiatry for two years and then pass oral and written tests administered by the American Board of Psychiatry and Neurology. To be board certified in child and adolescent psychiatry, one must have practiced child and adolescent psychiatry for two years and pass oral and written tests in child and adolescent psychiatry administered by the American Board of Psychiatry and Neurology.

COUNSEL: What percentage of the members of the American Psychiatric Association are board certified in general psychiatry?

WITNESS: Approximately 70 percent.

COUNSEL: What percentage of the members of the American Psychiatric Association are board certified in child and adolescent psychiatry?

WITNESS: About 10 percent.

COUNSEL: Do you belong to any professional societies?

WITNESS: I am a member of the American Psychiatric Association, the American Academy of Child and Adolescent Psychiatry, and the Tennessee Academy of Child and Adolescent Psychiatry.

COUNSEL: What professional experience have you had?

WITNESS: I have been in the practice of child and adolescent psychiatry since 1985. In that capacity, I have treated inpatients and outpatients, and have consulted to pediatricians concerning patients in Vanderbilt University Hospital. As clinical assistant professor, I teach psychiatric residents.

COUNSEL: Have you had any experience diagnosing young children who are alleged to be the victims of child abuse?

WITNESS: I have encountered more than one hundred cases involving allegations of sexual abuse.

COUNSEL: Has a court ever found you to be an expert in matters involving allegations of sexual abuse?

WITNESS: Yes, on twelve occasions.

COUNSEL: In which courts have you testified as an expert?

WITNESS: In the United States District Court for the Middle District of Tennessee and the Southern District of Florida and in state courts in Tennessee, New York, and California.

COUNSEL: (*to the Court*) I submit that Dr. Smith is qualified as an expert in the diagnosis and treatment of children who are alleged to have been sexually abused.

Opposing counsel may challenge your qualifications on the grounds that you have not had adequate general training or experience, or that you have insufficient expertise in the legal area associated with the particular case. Psychologists and social workers must expect challenges on the basis of "lack of medical training." Clearly, if the case demands a knowledge of pharmacotherapy or some other specialized medical area, psychologists and social workers should recuse themselves, just as a psychiatrist should do if the details of psychological testing or of the child welfare system are involved. On the other hand, the evaluation of allegations of sexual abuse (other than pediatric examination), of psychological injury, of competency to stand trial, of cases prior to waiver to adult court, and of many other child mental health issues require specialized training and experience of the type available to psychologists, social workers, and psychiatrists alike.

You should also expect questions to show that you are not as well qualified as the opposing side's expert. For example:

COUNSEL: Doctor, you have received no special training in psychopharmacology beyond that given to every psychiatric resident, have you?

or

COUNSEL: Doctor, you are not board certified in forensic psychiatry, are you?

or

COUNSEL: Doctor, you said you had testified as an expert in twelve cases, didn't you? [Yes.] Each time you testified for the plaintiff didn't you?

If you have testified for both sides, it is useful for the retaining attorney to elicit that information (without making it appear that you are a "hired gun"). For example, if you have been asked to conduct a forensic examination by a particular side, you might keep records of how often you have actually given testimony for that side. These records would enable you to state that about 60 percent of the time you have conducted a psychological injury examination for the plaintiff you have been asked to testify for the plaintiff, whereas about 50 percent of the time you have conducted such an examination for the defendant you have been asked to testify for the defendant.

Sometimes, ostensibly to save time, the opposing side will "stipulate" to your qualifications—that is, decline to contest them. If your credentials are impressive, it is unwise for the retaining counsel to agree to the stipulation, because doing so will prevent the judge and jury from learning the details of your background. Ultimately, your qualification is a matter for the judge (who will decide whether or not you are qualified to be an expert in the particular case) and the jury (who will weigh your testimony against that of other experts) to decide.

The Demeanor of the Expert Witness

The cross-examiner would like to depict the expert witness in an unfavorable or unflattering light. He may try to show that the expert is ignorant, out of date, inexperienced, unprepared, careless, muddled, fallacious, illogical, irrelevant, biased, or mercenary. The persuasive expert conveys competence, authority, and a professionalism that indicates his opinion is based on the merits of the case, not directed by whoever is paying the fee. The witness who is unrattled in the face of impugnment will have the greatest influence on the judge and jury. Remember that, as an expert, you are not an advocate for one side against the other but, rather, an advocate for your opinion. Your task is to convey to the judge and jury the purpose of your evaluation, the thoroughness and accuracy of your data collection, the logic and impartiality of your reasoning, and the details of your opinion.

Just as in your written forensic evaluation report, speak clearly, avoiding technical terms and pompous phrases. When you must use a technical term, define it in lay terms, for example:

> WITNESS: I also found that the defendant had auditory hallucinations. He said that, when he was alone, especially at night, he would hear voices telling him he was a bad person and commanding him to hurt himself, commit suicide, or attack other people.

Sometimes, a metaphor or analogy will help to clarify a concept with which a lay audience is unfamiliar. Here are some examples:

> WITNESS: Hearing voices, in schizophrenia, is like having a distracting radio playing inside your head.

> WITNESS: Children who have been traumatized often play the same trauma game over and over again without resolving their upset. The game usually represents the traumatic experience or some part of it. In the same way, adolescents and adults will reenact again and again a theme that represents the original trauma or their attempt to overcome it. Like a record player needle stuck in a track, they replay the theme over and over.

Be as forthright as the data allow, avoiding equivocal or "weasel" words like "somewhat," "perhaps," "tends to," and "apparently." Contrast the following responses:

> WITNESS: The patient had an apparent tendency to experience auditory hallucinosis.

> WITNESS: Mr. X heard voices that weren't there.

Restrict your answer to the question asked. Avoid gratuitous comments; they give the cross-examiner ammunition to fire back at you.

> WITNESS: In my experience, traumatized adolescents sometimes deliberately injure themselves; but I've never done a controlled study . . .

COUNSEL: What is a controlled study?

or

COUNSEL: Why would a controlled study be desirable?

Sometimes the cross-examiner will endeavor to have you restrict your answers to "yes" or "no." If it is reasonable, do so. However, if a simple yes-or-no answer would not convey your proper meaning, you should say so. It is permissible, also, to appeal to the judge.

COUNSEL: Are schizophrenics dangerous? Answer "yes" or "no."

WITNESS: It is not possible to answer that question "yes" or "no."

COUNSEL: Just answer "yes" or "no."

WITNESS: (*to judge*) Your Honor, that is a complex question. I cannot answer it properly if I am restricted to "yes" or "no."

JUDGE: Then expand upon your answer, Dr. Smith.

or

JUDGE: You must answer "yes" or "no."

Eye contact conveys authority. Focus upon the examiner for the question, then, as you answer, turn and make eye contact with the jury (or the judge if there is no jury). Do not be too mechanical, however; direct your gaze from time to time at others in the court. Don't allow yourself to be transfixed and controlled by the cross-examiner.

Keep the audience awake. Breathe life into your voice. Accent important words. Dramatize your answer at key points:

WITNESS: It is true that *some* psychiatrists cast doubt upon the truth of *all* allegations of sexual abuse by children. The *majority* of experts, however, believe that most allegations are, indeed, *true*. False allegations are likely to occur in *predictable* situations. *This* case fits *none* of those situations.

When the cross-examiner tries to trap you into a damaging admission by having you testify that something improbable or remote could apply, you can handle it by conceding the point, then denying that it is likely.

COUNSEL: It is possible you made a mistake taking notes during your interview with Mr. Smith, isn't it?

WITNESS: It's possible, but unlikely. I take detailed notes and review them for accuracy soon after each interview.

It is almost inevitable that at some time during your testimony in a trial you will become aware that you made a mistake in answering an earlier question. Sometimes, if the error is serious, it is possible to ask permission of the judge to correct it.

> WITNESS: Your Honor, I am afraid I may have created a misconception by one of my previous answers. Could I be permitted to correct it?

Sometimes you will be allowed to do so, and sometimes your request will be denied. In any case, do not dwell on it. Shake it off and concentrate on the question at hand.

Inexperienced witnesses fear the specter of Perry Mason waggling his finger in their face, hissing questions, and reducing them to white-lipped stammering. If Perry oversteps the limits of propriety, opposing counsel can object, and the judge may admonish the cross-examiner. Actually, this kind of badgering is relatively uncommon. It usually indicates desperation and, moreover, runs the serious risk of alienating the jury. Much more to be feared is the courteous lawyer who gently guides you down a garden path before springing a trap. Another cross-examiner to recognize is the "down home" or "just plain folks" counsel who tries to depict you as a "hired gun" from the big city, a waffling pedant from the university, or an impractical elitist out of touch with real people.

However trying the inquisition, eschew gratuitous comments or ill-advised attempts at humor, and resist temptations to score off the examiner. The courtroom is an arena for lawyers. It is unlikely you can beat one at his own game. Sit up straight, make eye contact, lean toward the audience when you are making telling points, enliven your voice by varying its volume and stress, speak clearly and forthrightly without unnecessary qualifications, use metaphors or examples to illustrate complex ideas, and admit flaws or inconsistencies when it is appropriate to do so. Face inquisitional belligerence with calmness and reason. Provided your argument is viable, nothing could be more persuasive.

Direct Examination

The direct examination is your opportunity to inform the judge and jury of your findings and conclusions. Because you can present your testimony only by responding to what the retaining attorney asks you, his questions are vital. Although you should not be so familiar with each question that your answers seem rehearsed, you should work closely with the retaining attorney in preparing for the direct examination. Do not minimize your own importance in the process of preparing to testify. As an expert in your field, you will know far more about the substantive clinical issues than will the attorney who retained you. If the questions proposed by the attorney do not capture the essence of your findings, explain why they do not and suggest how they could be rephrased.

It is important that you explain to the retaining attorney any weaknesses or uncertainties in your findings. The attorney can do two things with this information. First, he may choose to bring out some or all of those weaknesses during his direct examination of you. In so doing, he will demonstrate to the judge and jury that he has nothing to hide and is completely confident in your testimony and the strengths of the case. Second, he can help you prepare for possible cross-examination questions.

In pretrial preparation, the attorney will have familiarized you with the sequence of questions to be asked in direct examination. Although the outline of direct examination will vary substantially from case-to-case, a rough outline could be as follows:

1. How did you come to be involved in the case?
2. How did you proceed with your professional assessment or evaluation?
3. What documents did you review?
4. What interviews/examinations did you conduct, on what dates, and for what duration?
5. What special investigations or tests did you order?
6. What were the findings/results of the examinations, investigations, and review of documents?
7. Based on the examinations/interviews/review of records and other information that you gathered, have you reached an opinion with reasonable certainty on the appropriate legal issues?
8. Could you please state that opinion?

When answering these questions, summarize the main points of the documentary review, interviews, and special investigations. Reserve direct quotes for observations that are particularly telling or illustrative of the points you are trying to convey. If you plan to give the DSM-III-R diagnosis, be sure you are prepared to handle cross-examination on the definition of the disorder in question. Do not speculate without making it clear that you are doing so. For example:

WITNESS: It would be speculative to predict the outcome in adulthood of sexual abuse in childhood. The scientific literature describes a range of possible outcomes.

Refreshing Your Memory During Direct or Cross-Examination

Experts often find it necessary to refer to their files or records in order to answer questions during direct or cross-examination. The adverse party is entitled to examine and, if necessary, obtain a copy of any written material to which a witness refers in answering a question. At its discretion, the court may exclude irrelevant material and order that the remainder be delivered to the opposing counsel. A witness may use written material in one of two ways, if he cannot remember a particular matter. First, he may use the material to "refresh" his recollection. If, for example, the expert cannot remember the date on which he first met with the person examined, he may ask to refer to his records. If the rules of evidence are strictly applied, the expert must then surrender the records and testify about the date, without referring to his records again on that matter.

Often, however, the rules are relaxed when the expert must rely on lengthy medical records. The court will then permit the clinician to keep the records in front of him and to refer to them repeatedly.[23]

Keep in mind that counsel conducting cross-examination may use the written material to which the expert refers in order to refresh his recollection. McCormick has stated:

> With the memorandum before him, the cross-examiner has a good opportunity to test the credibility of the witness's claim that his memory has been revived, and to search out any discrepancies between the writing and the testimony.[24]

Moreover, if an expert has used a document to refresh his memory, any privilege adhering to the contents of the document may be lost.[25] For these and other reasons, the less you have to refer to your records while testifying, the better. Observers are impressed by the spontaneous witness with an unaided, comprehensive grasp of the case. Conversely, they are irritated by one who riffles through papers in order to locate information.

If the written material does not refresh the expert's recollection, then counsel may try to have the relevant portion of the writing itself read to the judge or jury. For example, even after he refers to notes that he made two years earlier, immediately after he interviewed a patient, an expert may not find his memory "refreshed" as to the precise address at which the patient said he lived when he was a child or the names of the schools that he said he attended. That is, the expert still may not have an independent recollection of those facts, although he is certain that his notes accurately reflect what the patient told him. In such cases, if the expert testifies that he made the notes when the facts were fresh in his memory, or "contemporaneously," and that he took care to make the notes accurately, the notes may be read into the record as a "past recollection recorded." The notes themselves may not, however, be admitted as an exhibit unless they are offered by the opposing party.[26]

Cross-examination

The nature and quality of the cross-examination of an expert witness vary according to the type and strength of the case, the quality of the expert's testimony, the strength of the testimony presented by any experts called by the side conducting the cross-examination, and the quality, preparation, and style of the attorney conducting the cross-examination. The following section describes various methods of attack used by cross-examining attorneys. Most attorneys adopt several of these methods.

The examples given do not exhaust all the approaches an expert may face, and actual questioning may be more or less rigorous than that presented here. By thorough preparation, the expert can anticipate the thrust of most of the questions to be asked on cross-examination and can do much to reduce their impact. Furthermore, as discussed above, by forthrightly revealing weaknesses or uncertainties during direct examination, the expert can avoid the suggestion that he is concealing evidence or has lost objectivity.

The cross-examiner may use some or all of the following tactics in conducting his examination: (1) direct challenges to the expert's conclusions; (2) challenges to the expert's ability, qualifications, or motives; (3) learned treatise attacks, and (4) disconcerting tactics.

DIRECTLY CHALLENGING THE BASIS OF THE EXPERT'S OPINION

In the most effective challenge, the examiner impugns the expert's opinion squarely on the merits. Such attacks vary from case to case; but follow a general pattern. Many lawyers begin by challenging aspects of the expert's preparation. If, for example, the expert relied extensively on the subject's medical record while hospitalized, the examination might go as follows:

COUNSEL: Doctor, in reaching your diagnosis you found it important that John had experienced auditory hallucinations over some period of time, didn't you?

WITNESS: Yes, that was one factor in my diagnosis.

COUNSEL: But the only time you personally observed what you think were auditory hallucinations was when you interviewed him on November 3. Isn't that right?

WITNESS: Yes, but the medical records show that he suffered those hallucinations for six months.

COUNSEL: Doctor, there are only four notations of auditory hallucinations in the records for that six-month period, aren't there?

WITNESS: I would have to check the records.

COUNSEL: You can't recall the number of hallucinations without reviewing the records again?

WITNESS: No, I don't remember the precise number, but I do remember several instances of hallucinations.

COUNSEL: And you also don't recall who reported that John was suffering auditory hallucinations, do you?

WITNESS: I don't know the names of the mental health personnel, if that is what you mean.

COUNSEL: And you also don't know whether those persons were orderlies, nurses, or doctors, do you?

WITNESS: No, I am not certain.

COUNSEL: You don't know how much professional experience, if any, that those persons have, do you?

WITNESS: No.

COUNSEL: But if John had not suffered auditory hallucinations for an extended period, your diagnosis might have been different, isn't that right?

WITNESS: It's possible, but not likely.

COUNSEL: But it is possible, isn't it?

WITNESS: Yes.

In the preceding example, the attorney did no real damage to the expert's testimony, though he did succeed in making him appear poorly prepared. If the expert had become agitated during the examination, or had appeared pompous or officious on direct examination, then the damage would have been far greater.

The cross-examining attorney may also attempt to highlight the difficulty of making a particular diagnosis, for example:

COUNSEL: Doctor, you testified on direct examination that John cannot remember what happened on the day of the murder because he had psychogenic amnesia, didn't you?

WITNESS: Yes.

COUNSEL: And you said that you had made that diagnosis with a reasonable degree of medical certainty?

WITNESS: Yes.

COUNSEL: Doctor, you are familiar with the discussion of psychogenic amnesia in DSM III-R, aren't you?

WITNESS: Yes.

COUNSEL: And DSM III-R states: [*Counsel opens DSM III-R and reads*] "Malingering involving simulated amnesia presents a particularly difficult diagnostic dilemma. Attention to the possibility that the amnesia is feigned is crucial." That is what DSM III-R says isn't it?

WITNESS: I don't remember the exact words, but it says something to that effect.

COUNSEL: In this case, since John is charged with murder, it would definitely be in his interest to malinger, that is, to pretend that he had amnesia, wouldn't it?

WITNESS: That is a possibility. So I hypnotized John and conducted a comprehensive interview while he was under hypnosis, just as is recommended in DSM III-R.

COUNSEL: But isn't it true that DSM III-R also says that [*counsel again opens DSM III-R and reads*] "some people continue to malinger even under hypnosis or during an amobarbital interview," which you did not conduct.

WITNESS: I believe so.

COUNSEL: So you can't be certain that John isn't faking the amnesia, can you?

WITNESS: Nothing is certain.

Another approach has the attorney dissecting the expert's argument into its elements, and then scrutinizing each element in cross-examination. If doubt can be cast upon one or more of the elements, then the opinion may not stand. The cross-examiner can also put together the elements and test whether alternative conclusions could be drawn. This kind of cross-examination is best dealt with if you used hypothetico-deductive reasoning in the first place to reach your opinion.

COUNSEL: There are other possible explanations, aren't there?

WITNESS: I weighed the pros and cons for six possibilities before concluding that the child was telling the truth.

COUNSEL: What were those possibilities?

WITNESS: I considered and ruled out five possibilities: First, that the child's accusation was the product of a delusion. Second, that the mother and child shared a delusion. Third, that the mother or another person had inadvertently indoctrinated the child. Fourth, that the mother or another person had deliberately and mischievously indoctrinated the child. Fifth, that the child was confabulating or fabricating the allegation. I ruled out all five of these possibilities. That left me with the sixth and final possibility, that the child was truthful, and for that I found corroborative evidence.

COUNSEL: But any of those other explanations could have been correct, couldn't they?

WITNESS: I rejected them.

COUNSEL: But you could have been wrong, couldn't you?

WITNESS: Yes, it is possible.

COUNSEL: It is possible that the child made the whole thing up, isn't it?

WITNESS: Yes.

COUNSEL: And it's possible that the child is delusional, isn't it?

WITNESS: Very unlikely.

The most important thing to remember during a substantive challenge to your opinion is that you reached it for good reasons. If you are confident in your opinion and have performed your evaluation thoroughly and professionally, then you should be able to withstand substantive challenges. As discussed above, in preparing to testify you should work closely with the retaining attorney to identify possible weaknesses in your evaluation. If aware of those weaknesses, you will not be surprised by the cross-examination, and you will be prepared to handle it effectively. Moreover, you will have prepared the retaining attorney to ask appropriate questions on redirect examination. Those will strengthen your testimony and persuade the judge and jury of your thoroughness and professionalism.

CHALLENGES TO THE EXPERT'S ABILITY, QUALIFICATIONS, OR MOTIVES

Challenging the Expert's Credentials

Even though the expert has been qualified by the court, his or her credentials are fair game for a cross-examiner. It is for this reason that the clinician should have disclosed to the retaining attorney any potentially embarrassing aspects of his past, such as loss of licensure, failure to obtain board certification, ineligibility for board certification, outstanding malpractice suits or settlements, loss of privileges to practice in a hospital, or any other matter that might reflect unfavorably on the expert.

Challenging Professional Expertise

The cross-examiner may attack the witness's expertise on the basis of inadequacy or irrelevance. Be prepared for questions concerning the number of cases of a particular type that you have evaluated or concerning which you have testified. Sometimes, if you are highly experienced, the direct examiner will have already brought this out. However, even if you have not had extensive forensic experience with such cases, general clinical experience is pertinent to forensic expertise. For example:

COUNSEL: Doctor, you have never testified as an expert in child abuse, have you?

WITNESS: That is correct, but since I began practicing child and adolescent psychiatry in 1980, I have evaluated four to five cases of child abuse per year, that is, about forty cases in all.

COUNSEL: So you see a case of alleged child abuse only about once every two or three months?

Sometimes counsel will attempt to show that your experience is irrelevant to the case in question. For example, sociocultural background may be introduced as a red herring:

COUNSEL: How many Hispanic children who have allegedly been sexually abused have you evaluated?

WITNESS: None.

COUNSEL: The Hispanic family culture has many unique aspects that affect a diagnosis of child abuse, doesn't it?

WITNESS: Although I have evaluated no abused Hispanic children, I am familiar with Hispanic family culture. Basically, the effects of sexual abuse are similar, whatever the culture.

If your expertise is truly irrelevant to the case, however, you were unwise to have become involved in the first place.

Challenging Clinical Techniques

Psychologists can expect attacks on the reliability and validity of psychological testing, and psychiatrists will frequently be attacked on the ground that their diagnostic techniques or predictions are fallible. In order to cope with such challenges, the expert must be familiar with the field trials of DSM III-R or with the psychometric qualities of particular psychological tests.

COUNSEL: Isn't it true that field trials of *The Diagnostic and Statistical Manual of Mental Disorders III-R* showed that psychiatrists were very unreliable?

WITNESS: No. Psychiatrists actually agreed very well on the major diagnoses like schizophrenia, which, in my opinion, John suffers from. Most of the apparent disagreement was over details.

COUNSEL: But we are concerned with details in this case, aren't we?

WITNESS: Yes. I discussed those details in my testimony.

Imputing Bias

The cross-examiner may also attempt to impute bias. The crudest form of this challenge is to paint the expert as purely mercenary (i.e., a "hired gun").

COUNSEL: How much are you being paid for your testimony?

WITNESS: I am not paid for my testimony. I am paid for my evaluation, for the report I prepare, and for appearing in Court.

COUNSEL: Well, how much *are* you being paid? Are you reluctant to tell us?

WITNESS: Not at all. I charge for the time it takes to complete the evaluation, and for the time I spend in Court.

COUNSEL: How much is that?

WITNESS: It depends on how long you keep me.

COUNSEL: You still haven't told us how much you intend to charge.

WITNESS: I have not yet prepared the account. However, I estimate that I have spent about fifteen hours in conference, reviewing documents, interviewing people, and composing my report. It appears I will spend a half-day in court. I charge on the basis of $150 per hour for evaluation and $500 per half-day testifying in court.

COUNSEL: So you will make almost $3,000 for your work on this case?

WITNESS: Probably about that.

COUNSEL: And you wouldn't have made nearly that amount if your initial conclusion had been that the child had not been sexually abused, would you?

WITNESS: I doubt if there would have been any difference.

If you are asked why you charge more for forensic cases than for other cases, you should point out that forensic cases are more demanding, and that they require more experience.

More subtle (and effective) challenges are based upon the expert's past experience. A clinician who always testifies for one side will be seen as an advocate who is biased in favor of that side. Clinicians giving testimony in child custody disputes can expect to be asked if they are divorced and, if so, whether they disputed custody, and who won the dispute. Clinicians in child abuse cases have been asked if they, or their children or relatives, have ever been molested—an effective strategy when the expert appears to be a biased crusader. Needless to say, a clinician already treating a child who is the subject of litigation is likely to be impugned as overidentified with his or her client or standing to gain from a settlement. This imputation is virtually unanswerable.

THE "LEARNED TREATISE" ATTACK

One of the most celebrated and organized strategies for discrediting mental health professionals in general was developed by Ziskin. It is known as the "learned treatise" approach. The reader is referred to *Coping with Psychiatric and Psychological Testimony* (Ziskin and Faust, 1988a and b). This three-volume publication contains extensive reviews of the literature casting doubt on the scientific status of psychiatry and clinical psychology, the validity of psychiatric diagnosis, the reliability of clinical diagnosis and psychological testing, the capacity of clinicians to detect malingering or predict dangerousness, and the relevance of clinical experience and training to forensic expertise (see Chapter 1). The reader should keep in mind that Ziskin and

Faust do not present a balanced argument. They have written a polemic designed to be of use to cross-examining attorneys. This strategy is useful if only one side has called a clinical expert. If both sides have called experts, a general attack on the mental health professions will hurt both sides.

The attorney using this approach begins by attempting to have the witness attest that a particular article or book is authoritative. Avoid doing so, unless you truly believe the material to be authoritative. Clearly, it is important that the witness know the key articles in each critical field in order to rebut them, when it is possible to do so. Poythress (1980) has summarized counterarguments useful to a witness who is being "Ziskinized." Once an attorney finds himself embroiled in the give and take of a learned debate, he will soon lose both his own way and the attention of the jury.

The more effective learned treatise attack is one in which a book or article presents a viewpoint that squarely differs from your own. As before, the first approach is to reject the book or article as a learned treatise.

COUNSEL: Are you familiar with *The Comprehensive Textbook of Psychiatry* by Kaplan and Sadock?

WITNESS: Yes.

COUNSEL: You agree it is an authority in the field of psychiatry, don't you?

WITNESS: The book is widely read. However, it has many chapters, each of which is written by a different author or authors. Textbooks tend to be several years out of date by the time they reach publication. Also, textbooks are forced to generalize and may not contain information specific to a particular case. I would prefer to rely upon primary, up-to-date scientific articles and monographs. Which section of Kaplan and Sadock were you referring to?

Whether or not you find the article or book to be authoritative, the cross-examining attorney may continue to examine you on it, after getting you to concede, for example, that *The New England Journal of Medicine* is an authoritative publication and then asking you about an article recently published in this journal. When confronted with this approach, you should explain why you disagree with the conclusions of the article or why, despite these conclusions, you believe your diagnosis or conclusion is correct.

DISCONCERTING TACTICS

The cross-examiner may also attempt to confuse the witness. The attorney may use these disconcerting tactics at any time during examination of the witness and in conjunction with any of the other examination tactics discussed above. Some examples of these disconcerting techniques follow. The reader is referred to Brodsky (1991) for a more detailed account.

Posing Unanswerable Questions

The attorney may open by asking a question to which there is no clear answer. By laying down a pattern of such questions, he hopes to get you to convey ignorance and uncertainty. Witnesses should stand their ground.

COUNSEL: Doctor, psychologists and psychiatrists don't know the cause of mental illness, do they?

WITNESS: There are many kinds of mental illness. For some, we understand the causes. For others, we do not. There is seldom a single cause of mental illness.

COUNSEL: But experts do not know the precise cause of most mental illnesses do they?

WITNESS: As I said, there is seldom a single cause. For some kinds of mental illness we understand the causes, for others we do not.

Misquotation

The attorney may misquote you, add erroneous information, or quote out of context from your previous evidence, report, or deposition. Be alert to this. Correct misquotations. If necessary, ask to see the deposition, in order to check what you actually did say.

ATTORNEY: In your deposition you said that the plaintiff did *not* have posttraumatic stress disorder.

WITNESS: That is not what I said. What I said was that I found insufficient evidence in the medical record to justify the diagnosis of posttraumatic stress disorder.

Trivializing

In this ploy, the attorney will seek to have you agree that your evaluation was somehow casual, trifling, or unprofessional.

ATTORNEY: So you based your opinion upon a single interview of the patient?

WITNESS: (*calmly*) Not at all. My opinion is based upon an extensive review of the medical record, interviews of the patient and his mother and sister, a detailed case history, discussions with other psychiatrists who examined him, a mental status examination, the results of psychological testing, my training and reading of the scientific literature, and my clinical experience with other cases of a similar nature.

Requesting Definitions

Lawyers defer to authority. Anticipate that many will regard the *Diagnostic and Statistical Manual of Mental Disorders III-R* as akin to a book of statutes. It is important that you have a general grasp of the categories in the manual and a detailed recollection of factors in DSM III-R that relate to the diagnosis that you have made.

COUNSEL: (*holding DSM-III-R aloft*) What is the precise definition of posttraumatic stress disorder?

WITNESS: I have not committed the precise definition to memory. However, the diagnosis refers to a mental disorder precipitated by an exceptionally severe stress. The patient subsequently experiences flashbacks, intrusive memories, nightmares . . .

COUNSEL: It is correct that to be diagnosed as having posttraumatic stress disorder a patient must have the symptoms presented in five different categories, isn't it?

WITNESS: I believe so.

COUNSEL: Without consulting DSM III-R, you can't tell the jury which of those categories this patient met, can you?

Posing Absolutes

Beware of agreeing with absolutes, or appearing to do so.

COUNSEL: Schizophrenia is always associated with hallucinations and delusions, isn't it?

WITNESS: No. Those symptoms are indeed common in schizophrenia. However, in some cases, the patient keeps them from the examiner. In other cases, the symptoms are not apparent, and the diagnosis must be based on the other symptoms and signs of the disorder.

Seeking Inconsistencies

The cross-examiner will be delighted to find inconsistencies between what you are saying in cross-examination and what you have testified to before, in court or in de-

position. Thorough attorneys will have read your scientific papers in a search for opportunities to have you appear capricious or contradictory. You should review all of
your own publications before testifying.

COUNSEL: You have published a scientific article on the competence and credibility of the child as a witness, haven't you?

WITNESS: Yes, I have.

COUNSEL: Isn't it true that, *in your own article,* you describe how children can
make false accusations of sexual abuse?

WITNESS: Yes, but . . .

COUNSEL: Thank you Doctor, you have answered my question.

Note that in the example above the cross-examining attorney did not give the expert
an opportunity to explain the apparent inconsistency between his article and his testimony. That is a perfectly permissible cross-examination technique. Upon objection
by the retaining attorney that the witness was not permitted to complete his response,
however, the judge may permit the expert to continue testifying. If not, the retaining
attorney should provide the witness an opportunity to explain his response on redirect examination. For example:

RETAINING COUNSEL: Doctor, on cross-examination you tried to complete your answer to a question that Mr. Y asked you about an article that
you wrote, but he did not give you a chance to explain your
answer. What was it that you wanted to say?

WITNESS: I wanted to explain that it is true that older children occasionally make false accusations of sexual abuse. However,
this is relatively uncommon, and usually occurs in recognizable situations. Moreover, deliberate fabrications have
the earmarks of lying that are described in my paper. None
of those circumstances apply in *this* case.

Probing for Discomfort or Guilt

Skillful attorneys are quick to detect when a witness hesitates, stammers, or stumbles.
Compulsive or inexperienced witnesses come to court with the secret fear that they
might have blundered, omitted an important test or investigation, or failed to find a
key scientific article. Sometimes the attorney will go on a rambling hunt for such vul-
nerabilities. Lawyers refer to this style of attack as a "fishing expedition." Sometimes
they will play on a narcissistic expert's desire to show off his or her knowledge while
educating the court. At other times they are seeking to irritate the witness. Their purpose is to tempt the unwary witness into gratuitous comments that can then be seized

upon. When you answer a question, even when your response is lengthy, stay within the scope of the question and try to relate it to the case in hand. If you find that you made a mistake during your testimony, admit it, and explain why that mistake does not affect your ultimate conclusion.

Probing for Ignorance

It is wise to be up to date on the scientific literature. However, it is not possible to read everything in a field. Do not feel guilty if an obscure reference has escaped your attention.

COUNSEL: You are familiar with J. Smith's article on the reliability of projective testing published in *Annual Progress in Psychology* in 1981, aren't you?

WITNESS: No, I am not.

ATTORNEY: This review is regarded as an authoritative article in the field, isn't it?

WITNESS: Not that I am aware of. It could be out of date. If you would like me to review the article, I would be glad to give you an opinion on its merit.

Occasionally the cross-examiner will surprise the witness by asking for the origin of a familiar procedure.

ATTORNEY: Who originated the format for the psychiatric history?

WITNESS: No one person. The psychiatric history has been contributed to during the latter part of the nineteenth century and all of this century, by European, British, and North American psychiatrists.

Promoting Self-condemnation

A most effective technique is to lead the witness down a garden path of answers that progressively depict the expert's profession as fallible. Sometimes little can be done other than to agree with the cross-examiner.

COUNSEL: Dr. Jones, psychologists are not infallible, are they?

WITNESS: Certainly not.

COUNSEL: You are aware of the large body of scientific research showing that psychologists are often mistaken in their diagnoses, aren't you?

WITNESS: Yes.

The witness can often break the rhythm of these questions by conceding then denying the point.

COUNSEL: Dr. Jones, psychologists are not infallible, are they?

WITNESS: Certainly not. No scientist is infallible.

COUNSEL: You are aware of the large body of scientific research showing that psychologists are often mistaken in their diagnoses, aren't you?

WITNESS: I am. However, much of that research was done in artificial experimental situations unlike the way psychologists actually work.

Note that the witness has drawn counsel into deeper water. Only a confident (or rash) attorney will venture further. A similar gambit is the "not an exact science" question. In this, the attorney has the witness confirm an assertion that the witness's profession is not comparable with other "sciences."

COUNSEL: Doctor, psychiatry is not an exact science, is it?

A number of responses are possible (other than a lame "No"):

WITNESS: No science is exact. All sciences require the interpretation of data.

or

WITNESS: No branch of medicine is "exact." Psychiatric diagnosis is comparable in reliability with other branches of medicine, such as surgery and radiology.

or

WITNESS: The purpose of science is to find out the truth about the relationship between things and events. Medicine, psychiatry included, has the purpose of diagnosing and treating sick people. In doing so, physicians use methods derived from science. But medicine itself is not a science. No scientifically derived method of diagnosis or treatment can be absolutely exact. In fact, no science is absolutely exact.

By this stage, the attorney is probably out of his depth, and the witness has resumed control.

Introducing Unfamiliar Information

Sometimes the attorney will seek to unbalance you by introducing data with which you are unfamiliar or data from a field beyond your expertise. Stand your ground. Do not change your opinion on the stand.

COUNSEL: Would your opinion change if I told you that William has been tested elsewhere and found to have posttraumatic stress disorder?

WITNESS: I would have to review the test results. A diagnosis of posttraumatic stress disorder should never be based on psychological testing alone.

Hypothetical Questions

Hypothetical questions may be posed by either side. Their purpose is to allow counsel to summarize the premises of a case and to ask the expert witness what he would conclude from those premises. Counsel generally asks hypothetical questions at the end of direct examination in order to summarize, review, and emphasize the main points of the case that the witness has considered in reaching his opinion, and to reinforce the opinion. Essentially counsel says: "If A, B, and C were the case, what would your conclusion be?" For example:

COUNSEL: Therefore, Ms. Burns, allow me to put this question to you. If this child has indeed been physically abused, and if the perpetrator of the abuse was one or both of the parents, and if the parents deny the abuse and have, up to now, refused treatment, what would be your opinion about returning the infant to the parents' care at this time?

WITNESS: It would put the child at serious risk of further abuse.

The cross-examiner may pose hypothetical questions in order to challenge the expert's opinion, either by suggesting that there were different premises from the ones you have taken into account or by suggesting that an alternative conclusion would be reasonable from the original premises. Essentially, the cross-examiner will say (putting aside *your* premises, A, B, and C): "If W, X, and Y were the case, would you change your opinion?" or, "Even if A, B, and C were the case, would not E be a reasonable conclusion?" If counsel introduces premises you did not find or do not agree with, it is legitimate to point this out. However, you must answer the question:

WITNESS: Well, it's difficult for me to picture such a situation since I did not find W or X to be present. In fact, I found M and N, which contradict X.

However, if W, X, or Y had all been present, my conclusion might have
been A or B.

Before accepting a particular premise, however, make sure you know what it means.
Ask for further information if counsel introduces vague terms (e.g., "retarded," "insane," or "incompetent").

Redirect and the Cross-examination

Neither side can introduce new material during reexamination. During redirect, counsel will attempt to emphasize the strengths of your testimony and repair any damage the cross-examiner has inflicted. In your responses during redirect examination,
you should attempt to explain any of your responses to the cross-examination that
were incomplete or out of context. The retaining attorney should ask questions in
such a way as to permit you to elaborate upon your answers on cross-examination.
He may not, however, know all the points on which you would like to offer further
testimony to clarify your responses, so you should take advantage of any opportunity to do so.

Some judges may permit the cross-examiner to pursue any new points that came
out during redirect examination. If the judge does permit recross-examination, that
will usually end the questioning. Only rarely do judges allow re-redirect or re-recross-
examination.

The Conclusion of the Examination

When the examination is complete, the judge will tell you that you are excused. Collect your impedimenta and, with deliberation and dignity, thank the judge, nod to
the jury and both counsel, and leave by the door of entry. Do not linger in the courtroom listening to further proceedings; as a busy professional, you need to get back
to your job. Never leave the courtroom looking defeated or embarrassed, no matter
how severe the drubbing you have received. By the same token, do not leave in a
flush of triumph, emulating the legendary expert who left the stand beaming and
flashing a "victory" sign toward the plaintiff. Remember that you are above the adversarial fray. Your task has been to communicate an impartial opinion, not to "win"
the case.

The attorney's task is to represent the client vigorously, within the limits of professional ethics and the law. For that reason, he is bound to emphasize the strength of
his own case and to expose the other side's weaknesses. There is a playlike quality to
much of this, even though the stakes be high. Advocates who bristle at each other in
court may be the best of friends on the golf course. In the midst of the fray, remember that, as an expert, you are above partisanship. You may be surprised to find that
a hectoring cross-examiner will congratulate you after the trial for remaining gracious
and impartial under fire.

General Guidelines for the Expert Witness

The preceding sections address the role of the expert witness in considerable detail. The following precepts summarize the role of the expert witness:

BE AN INFORMANT, NOT AN ADVOCATE

The primary function of the expert is to provide information that will help the court in its determination of the ultimate legal issues. Experts do so by conveying, through their reports and testimony, impartial, well-reasoned opinions stemming from reliable data. It is legitimate for an expert to confer with the retaining attorney in order to help the latter argue the case in an effective manner. It is also legitimate for the expert to present his or her testimony in a clear, telling manner, within the limits of reasonable certainty. It is not legitimate to oversimplify complicated issues, to withhold inconsistencies from cross-examination, or to claim for data, inferences, or opinions a greater certainty than is scientifically warranted.

BE AN EVALUATOR, NOT A THERAPIST

Therapists identify with their patients. (If they did not, they should not be treating them.) Inevitably, the therapeutic relationship introduces a countertransference which erodes the reliability of clinical judgment for forensic purposes and opens the witness to impeachment on the ground of partiality. Furthermore, even when the patient has waived privilege, the trust required for effective therapy is compromised when the therapist must divulge private matters in open court.

WHO DEFENDS EVERYTHING DEFENDS NOTHING

No opinion is perfect, for the data upon which clinical opinions are based vary in reliability and validity. The certainty with which different inferences are made also varies, since some data are capable of more than one interpretation. The wise expert must honestly concede the potential fallibility or ambiguity of some aspects of his or her testimony. The retaining attorney may decide to bring out the weak points of an expert's reasoning during direct examination so as to take the wind out of the other side's sails.

DO NOT DOCTOR YOUR OPINION

Do not withhold or gloss over information that runs counter to your ultimate opinion. Weigh the relative merit and significance of the data that constitute the pros and cons of your opinion. Do not attempt to sustain a level of certainty higher than that which is warranted by the information you have gathered. This is particularly important in custody disputes. For example, you may be unable to recommend a clear parental preference; nevertheless, a thorough inventory of the favorable and unfavorable features of the proposed custodial alternatives is likely to be helpful to the court. Moreover, you will add to your reputation for impartiality.

THOROUGHNESS, CLARITY, AND REASONING ARE MORE INFLUENTIAL THAN OPINIONS

The detail, comprehensiveness, care, and impartial reasoning embodied in your report and testimony are more likely to sway the court than the vigor with which you advocate your opinion.

DO NOT PASS JUDGMENT ON THE ULTIMATE LEGAL ISSUE

Keep in mind that your role is not to decide the ultimate legal issue before the court, but rather to provide the court with information that will help it resolve the issue. Ultimate issues include questions of morality, values, and social policy that are not the province of clinicians but the proper domain of courts and legislators. With regard to some ultimate issues, such as the legal sanity of a criminal defendant, experts are expressly prohibited from expressing their opinions. Even when experts are permitted or required to give their opinions on the ultimate issue, such as competence to stand trial or fitness to be a parent, you should focus on the evidence that led you to reach your conclusion, not on the conclusion itself. Remember also that other experts who testify may disagree with your opinion on the ultimate issue and that the only opinion that is relevant at the end of trial is that of the jury or judge.

CROSS-EXAMINATION IS NOT A PERSONAL ATTACK

It is the task of the adversary counsel to question your qualifications, impugn your impartiality, throw doubt on the validity or accuracy of your data or diagnosis, seek errors and inconsistencies in your reasoning, and suggest alternative interpretations of the information elicited. Keep your composure. The cross-examiner who, despite a vigorous grilling, has not shaken you is likely at a later date to offer congratulations (or even to retain you in a subsequent case).

APPRECIATE THE ADVERSARY SYSTEM

As triers of fact, the judge or jury must assume that no crime or civil inequity has occurred. Procedural law employs the adversary system to expose and test the merit of each side's case, setting plaintiff or prosecution against defense. The two sides take turns, often generating (or professing) considerable heat—so much, in fact, that the judge will sometimes be constrained to admonish them. As a voice of nonpartisan reason, the expert witness should remain aloof from the prevailing clangor. Remember that the system is designed so that, when truth and justice collide, justice will prevail.

DO NOT RESTRICT YOURSELF TO FORENSIC WORK

The clinician who drops clinical work in favor of an exclusively forensic practice may be perceived to be a creature of the courts, a "hired gun." Judges and juries prefer witnesses who have had extensive clinical experience and who pursue active clinical careers.

SUMMARY

This chapter began with a distinction between a fact witness and an expert witness. The expert, in contrast to the lay witness, is permitted to draw inferences and give opinions within the area of his expertise. The expert witness should be an informant, not an advocate for one side against the other. Aware that no set of data is ever perfect, he should studiously avoid any shading or doctoring of the data. The thoroughness and clarity of the expert's reasoning are more persuasive than the vigor of his opinion. Appreciating the purpose of the adversary system—to expose and test each side's case—the expert learns that cross-examination is not a personal attack but a test of the elements of his reasoning and an opportunity to convey his opinion.

The expert's involvement usually begins when an attorney contacts the clinician to discuss the circumstances and scheduling of the case, the legal issues, the expert's role, and the fee. If you decide to become involved, keep detailed notes on every telephone and face-to-face communication. During the evaluation phase, you should obtain and meticulously record informed consent from the client or clients, studiously avoiding the evaluation of those you are treating or planning to treat. The evaluation converges upon the legal issue in question and involves the careful checking of data from several sources. The report of the evaluation should be logical, organized, edited, succinct, and tailored for the audience and purpose for which it was prepared. Buttressing the report is the discoverable, organized, tabulated evaluation record, with its case notes, test results, clinical documents, legal documents, and scientific literature.

Prior to testifying at deposition or in court, you and the attorney should confer in order to familiarize yourself with the sequence of questions to be put in direct examination and to anticipate the cross-examiner's probable direction of attack. You should also organize the file, prepare flowcharts, and refamiliarize yourself with the data, the case record, the legal issues, and the relevant scientific literature. Dress conservatively, arrive in court early, and ask where to wait. Do not fraternize with witnesses or opposing attorneys lest you be "contaminated" by them. Once the bailiff asks you to enter the court, take the stand and wait to be sworn. After you answer the qualifying questions and the judge qualifies you as an expert, the direct examination will continue along the lines already discussed in the pretrial conference. Convey impartiality, thoroughness, and a logically progressive argument. Avoid jargon and equivocations. Enliven your voice by varying stress and volume. Make eye contact with the jury from time to time, and lean forward as you make stronger points.

The cross-examiner's purpose is to cast doubt upon your competence, credibility, and impartiality. In order to do so, cross-examiners use a variety of tactics. The most effective challenges may be the ones to the substance of your opinions. You may also face challenges to your credentials, expertise, evaluation techniques, bias, or opinion or to the competence of the mental health professions in general. In addition, the cross-examiner may pose unanswerable questions; misquote your previous testimony; trivialize your evaluation; ask for definitions; search for inconsistencies, ignorance, or discomfort; or attempt to have you impeach yourself as fallible or unreliable. Expect hypothetical questions from either side, either to reinforce your opinion or to seek alternative explanations.

When you have completed your testimony, leave the court with dignity. Learn from your mistakes. Live to testify another day.

SAMPLE REPORTS

Case 1
Review of Medical Record Concerning
Justification for Hospitalization

This report illustrates a review of a medical record of an adolescent with regard to the justification of hospitalization and length of stay. The patient's father had accused the hospital of improperly admitting his daughter and was withholding payment.

In the case of *Metropolitan Hospital v. William Toohey*

REVIEW OF MEDICAL RECORD
Re: Tania Toohey
Admitted to Metropolitan Hospital
from 4/25/85 to 7/16/85

PURPOSE OF REVIEW

I was asked by Messrs. Smith & Jones, attorneys at law, to review the medical record of Tania Toohey's admission to Metropolitan Hospital (4/25/85–7/16/85) with regard to the following issues:

1. Was hospitalization necessary and reasonable?
2. Was the treatment provided adequate?
3. Was the length of stay in hospital (82 days) appropriate?

REVIEW OF RECORD

This thirteen-year-old single white female was admitted to and discharged from Metropolitan Hospital with the following diagnosis: conduct disorder of adolescence, socialized, nonaggressive. The behavior which occasioned her admission was stated to be: rebelliousness at home; drop-off in school performance; truancy from school; running away from home; and alcohol and marijuana abuse.

Reportedly, her parents had been divorced five years before, and she was in the custody of her mother. The second of three children, she had been closer to her father, prior to the divorce, than to her mother. However, her relationship with both par-

389

ents had deteriorated after she fell in with bad company, and began to drink and smoke marijuana. She is reported to have blamed her mother for the divorce and to have wavered about whether to leave her mother and live with her father.

The master treatment plan (4/26/85) is not adequately individualized. Nowhere in the records could I find a diagnostic formulation other than "conduct disorder." The essentials of treatment appear to have been group therapy with regard to her conduct problems and substance abuse, and individual psychotherapy with regard to her family problems and oppositionalism. Several interviews were undertaken with both mother and patient, but only one involving the father and the patient.

Progress during hospitalization was slow. Initially and sporadically throughout the entire hospitalization, the patient was avoidant and noncommunicative. At various times she was openly oppositional, flouting unit rules. On 5/6/85 it was noted that her father was antagonistic to hospitalization and that she did not want him to interfere with her treatment. By mid-April 1985 she was often excluded from group therapy because she had been restricted to her room for misbehavior. A previous suicidal attempt (undated) was noted on 5/14/85. At that time she began to speak about difficulties of communication between her mother and herself. By late May–early June 1985 she continued to be resistant to hospital rules, and to refuse to address her personal problems. This deterioration may have followed a family therapy meeting with her mother on 5/26/85. Her participation in group activities was minimal through the early part of June, and the patient became resistant to the unit point system. On 6/14/85, she stated that she felt rejected by her parents if "she stood up to" them. She described feeling "used" by her parents. She also began to express ambivalence toward living with her father. From mid-June until discharge in mid-July 1985, she made no apparent progress.

DISCUSSION

The admission of this patient to hospital was justified on the basis of her drinking and marijuana use, and her running away from home and school. As she was out of the control of her mother, outpatient therapy would not have been proper at that time.

Unfortunately, no adequate diagnostic formulation was presented (or at least documented) during hospitalization. The treatment foci ("abuse of THC and alcohol" and "conduct disorder") do not capture the essence of the patient's problem. As a consequence, the thrust of therapy—at least as documented—was superficial.

In my opinion, the patient suffered from both oppositional defiant disorder and substance use disorder, secondary to unresolved conflict concerning the separation and hostility between her parents. From time to time references are made to the patient's lack of communication with her mother, blaming of the mother for the divorce, protective feelings toward her father, and ambivalence about going to live with him. It is likely that her oppositionality, drinking, and marijuana use stem from her psychological inability to resolve these conflicting issues.

Given the reported opposition of the father to hospitalization and the apparent inability of the staff to arrange conjoint family therapy, it is unlikely that hospitalization could have been successful. Had intense individual psychotherapy focused on the unresolved conflict been instituted, it might have been possible to justify hospitalization for a period of four to five weeks. However, if the patient had remained un-invested in psychotherapy, as occurred during this hospitalization, earlier discharge should have been considered.

OPINION

1. Hospitalization was justified because the patient was truanting from school, taking alcohol and illicit drugs, and was out of her parents' control.
2. The diagnostic formulation and treatment plan, as documented, are inadequate.
3. Failing a more successful engagement of both parents in the treatment process, it is unlikely that hospital treatment could have succeeded. However, the attending physician could not have known this on admission.
4. Given the lack of investment of this patient in therapy, and the lack of parental support for it, discharge should have been considered at four weeks.

Case 2
Evaluation of Prospective Parents
Concerning Parental Competence

This report was undertaken at the request of a gynecologist who was concerned that, if artificial insemination were successful, the prospective parents might be incompetent and the child maltreated, thus putting the hospital and physician at risk of a malpractice suit on the grounds of wrongful birth. The gynecologist's concern was related to the report of a psychiatric illness in the prospective mother, during her adolescence.

CONFIDENTIAL
FORENSIC EVALUATION
Re: Victor M. Fitzhugh
Date of Birth: 9/2/52
and
Petra D. Fitzhugh
Date of Birth: 2/10/50

CIRCUMSTANCES OF REFERRAL

Mr. and Mrs. Fitzhugh were referred to me by Dr. Charles James, Director of the Division of Reproductive Endocrinology and Infertility, Metropolitan Hospital. The couple are requesting artificial insemination.

PURPOSE OF EVALUATION

To determine whether either of the couple suffers from psychiatric disorder or psychosocial impairment of such a type, or of such severity, as to preclude competent parenting.

INFORMED CONSENT

I explained to Mr. and Mrs. Fitzhugh that the evaluation was for legal, not therapeutic, purposes, that what they said to me might be put into a report to Dr. James, and that my opinion would have a bearing on whether artificial insemination would be recommended. They indicated that they understood the purpose of the evaluation and wanted me to proceed with it.

SOURCES OF DATA

Documentation

1. Medical record, Metropolitan Hospital, of admission of Petra N. Geraghty to Ward S5, from 4/10/67 to 5/19/67
2. Psychological evaluation report re Victor Fitzhugh, Metropolitan Hospital Department of Psychiatry, signed Harry Rumbaugh, Ph.D., 8/18/82

Interviews

1. Joint interview with Petra and Victor Fitzhugh, 4/25/90 (1 hour)
2. Interview with Petra Fitzhugh, 4/30/90 (1½ hours)
3. Interview with Petra Fitzhugh, 5/1/90 (2 hours)
4. Interview with Victor Fitzhugh, 5/1/90 (1 hour)
5. Interview with Victor Fitzhugh, 5/3/90 (2 hours)
6. Joint interview with Petra and Victor Fitzhugh, 5/22/90 (1 hour)
7. Joint interview with Petra and Victor Fitzhugh, 5/22/90 (1 hour)

Psychological Testing

1. Millon Clinical Multiaxial Inventory–II (MCMI–II), Minnesota Multiphasic Personality Inventory (MMPI), Adult-Adolescent Parenting Inventory (AAPI) on Victor Fitzhugh, scored 5/3/90
2. Millon Clinical Multiaxial Inventory–II (MCMI–II), Minnesota Multiphasic Personality Inventory (MMPI), Adult–Adolescent Parenting Inventory (AAPI) on Petra Fitzhugh, scored 5/3/90

FINDINGS

Interviews with Petra Fitzhugh

Mrs. Fitzhugh described a somewhat difficult childhood. Her parents separated when she was twelve months of age, following which she lived with her mother and had little further contact with her father. When she was five years of age, Mrs. Fitzhugh's mother remarried Stephen Geraghty, whose last name Mrs. Fitzhugh assumed. The mother's remarriage was initially happy, but it was eventually disrupted by her alcoholism and terminated in divorce. Mrs. Fitzhugh regarded her stepfather as her father and was always distrustful of her natural father. She greatly respected her stepfather but found it difficult to get close to him.

After completing High School in _____, she entered _____ College, where she qualified as a teacher of the deaf. She taught elementary school for three years, and returned to graduate school to complete a master's degree in speech and language pathology. She ultimately became a speech therapist and remains so to the present day.

Mrs. Fitzhugh has a wide variety of interests including music, dancing, reading, and walking. She attends church regularly. She reported that her physical health is good, that she has had no previous pregnancies, that she has had no serious illnesses, and that she does not smoke, seldom drinks alcohol, and has never used street drugs.

She reported that, at the age of seventeen, partly in reaction to not being able to attain a close relationship to her stepfather, she became depressed, attempted suicide, and was admitted to a metropolitan psychiatric inpatient unit for six weeks.

After discharge from the psychiatric unit, Mrs. Fitzhugh continued in outpatient psychotherapy. She denies having had any further suicidal ideation or making any further suicide attempt. She denies having had problems with drugs or alcohol. She considered that her initial depression improved in therapy and that she has had no depressive feelings for more than ten years. Specifically, she stated that she has not been depressed during the marriage; although she has experienced concern about whether artificial insemination would be approved.

When thirty years of age, she met her husband at a religious retreat. They fell in love, courted, and married after about six months. The marital relationship she described as "good." Initially, having both lived single lives until their thirties, the husband and wife were "independent" and somewhat "stubborn"; but they have negotiated compromises and now divide the labor at home according to which of them is the more efficient at a particular task.

Approximately fifteen months after marriage, the couple discussed having children and agreed to seek artificial insemination. If she has a child, Mrs. Fitzhugh proposes to remain home until the child is in elementary school, stating that her husband's income is sufficient for this.

Throughout my contact with her, Mrs. Fitzhugh exhibited a normal sensorium and no evidence of disorder in the process or content of thought. At no time did she appear depressed or emotionally inappropriate; nevertheless, she was anxious about the evaluation, being very concerned that I might consider that the psychiatric illness she had at the age of seventeen should preclude her from being granted permission for artificial insemination.

Interviews with Mr. Victor Fitzhugh

Mr. Fitzhugh reported a stable childhood in a religious family. From the age of about twelve years, he worked as a camp counselor and lifeguard. His upbringing was strictly religious. He was seldom rebellious either at home or at school. He attended _____ High School and subsequently _____ College, from which he graduated in 1975. His ambition at that time was to be a bible instructor, but he subsequently became interested in sales work. He is currently in charge of regional sales for a large computer company.

Mr. Fitzhugh's interests coincide with those of his wife: tennis, camping, traveling, reading, dancing. With her, he belongs to the Roman Catholic Church.

At the age of thirty-four, Mr. Fitzhugh met his future wife, and dated her over a period of approximately one year before marriage. Reportedly, their sexual relationship has been a happy one. The finding that he is probably sterile (due to a low sperm count) has caused no rift between them.

He described himself and his wife as strong-willed and independent but able to compromise and meld their views. It was after the solidity of the marriage had become apparent that Mrs. Fitzhugh asked if he would agree to having a child. He did so.

The couple own a home and a condominium. Mr. Fitzhugh said that his income ($60,000–$70,000 per year) will be sufficient if his wife ceases to work during the child's first five years (as planned).

Mr. Fitzhugh has had no significant physical illnesses or surgery. He has an occasional drink but denies smoking or drug-taking. He is in good psychological health, he states, and denies symptoms of anxiety, depression, elation, poor anger control, repetitious thoughts, or vegetative signs. He said that he and his wife did not plan to tell their child that he or she was the product of artificial insemination. If the child found out, they would acknowledge the fact. He cannot see that it would serve any purpose to tell the child about it unless the child becomes aware of it from another source.

Conjoint Interview

At this interview, I explored the couple's experience of and understanding of child care.

As described above, Mrs. Fitzhugh does not intend to work until the child starts elementary school. Each partner has had experience caring for children—Mr. Fitzhugh at camp, and Mrs. Fitzhugh with her younger sister.

To direct questions, the couple were able to discuss rationally their approach to limit-setting with a child aged two to three years, and their understanding of the developmental needs of an eight- to ten-year-old. With regard to major decisions, they described themselves as able to plan together. So far as division of labor is concerned, they see Mrs. Fitzhugh as paying the bills, cooking, and doing the housework, whereas Mr. Fitzhugh will do the yard work, look after the cars, plan major social events such as vacations, and initiate long-range financial planning.

Mrs. Fitzhugh echoed her husband's opinion about how much the child should be told of the facts of the artificial insemination (i.e., not at all).

Review of Documents

The medical record concerning Petra Geraghty indicated that she was admitted to the psychiatric unit of Metropolitan Hospital on 4/10/66 with a diagnosis of schizophrenic reaction (acute, undifferentiated) following a suicidal gesture. Comments were made in the chart that she was "hallucinating," but the details of the "hallucinations" were not documented, and they appear to have quickly receded. Initially, it was thought that the hospital course might be long. During hospitalization she received a low dose of neuroleptic medication. The patient was discharged, recovered, on 5/19/66. In retrospect, the diagnosis of schizophrenia is suspect.

Psychological Test Results

On the AAPI, Mrs. Fitzhugh indicated appropriate expectations of children, appropriate understanding of child development, and appropriate empathy with children's feelings. She valued alternatives to corporal punishment and appeared unlikely to use children to meet her own needs. The MCMI yielded a profile of a well-functioning individual with no major personality disturbance, but who may currently be undergoing psychosocial stress. Alternatively, the profile could be one of an individual who responds to questions as she would like things to be, rather than as they are. No evidence was found indicating an Axis I clinical disorder. The MMPI completed by Mrs. Fitzhugh yielded a profile of questionable clinical validity since she was apparently extremely reluctant to disclose personal information and tended to minimize personal faults.

On the AAPI, Mr. Fitzhugh provided a profile consistent with his having appropriate expectations of children and appropriate empathy and with his valuing of alternatives to corporal punishment, and not being prone to use children to meet his own needs. On the MCMI, Mr. Fitzhugh's profile was similar to that obtained from Mrs. Fitzhugh. Either he is a well-functioning individual who has no major personality disturbance but who is experiencing psychological stress, or his responses reflected wishful thinking rather than reality. On the MMPI, no axis I symptomatic pattern was noted, and the profile was within normal limits.

SUMMARY

Mrs. Fitzhugh had a somewhat disturbed childhood, characterized by a conflictual relationship with an alcoholic mother and a sense of distance from a respected stepfather. In contrast, she had little respect for her biological father, whom she scarcely saw after the age of four years. At the age of sixteen, Mrs. Fitzhugh had an acute psychiatric disturbance characterized by a suicide attempt and, reportedly, "hallucinations." No details are given of these hallucinations in the medical record. She was apparently treated with very small doses of a neuroleptic medication and discharged to outpatient treatment after relatively brief hospitalization.

There has been no recurrence of this acute disturbance over the past twenty-three years. At present, I can detect no evidence in Mrs. Fitzhugh of disturbed emotion, disturbance of thought, or perceptual disturbance that would indicate a residual schizophrenic illness. Indeed, her adult social and occupational adjustment have been excellent. I take her psychological test results to reflect appropriate parental attitudes but a degree of test defensiveness.

Mr. Fitzhugh had a stable childhood and adolescence. He appears to be socially well adjusted, occupationally successful, and psychologically stable. His psychological test results reveal appropriate parental attitudes and no evidence of acute psychiatric disorder, but a somewhat defensive attitude toward test-taking, as might be expected in these circumstances.

From both psychological testing and direct interviewing, it is apparent that this couple have had previous experience caring for children, that they have appropriate expectations of children at different ages, and that they are motivated by mutual affection and the normal desire to complete their family life.

RECOMMENDATION

Despite the history of adolescent psychiatric disorder in Mrs. Fitzhugh, and based upon my evaluation of the couple's current adjustment and parental capacity, I do not think there are grounds to deny Mr. and Mrs. Fitzhugh the opportunity for artificial insemination.

Case 3
Evaluation of Children and Their Parents
with Regard to Alleged Physical Abuse

In this case, two children's visitation with their jointly custodial father had been stayed, pending investigation of the allegation that he had been physically abusive toward one of them. The case illustrates the way in which such accusations can become inflamed by unresolved conflict between parents in the course of a bitter divorce. The report attempts to capture this, and to convey it to the court and the parents in a potentially therapeutic manner.

CONFIDENTIAL
FORENSIC EVALUATION
Re: Jesse Connors
Date of Birth: 4/24/82

CIRCUMSTANCES OF REFERRAL

Jesse Connors is the second child of Robert J. Connors and Teri A. Connors, a couple who separated in 1990 and who received their final divorce decree in March 1991. The divorced couple have joint custody of the two children. The children reside with the mother during the week and have visitation with the father one night per week and every second weekend. Visitation with the father was stayed in April 1991, following allegations that the father had physically abused the child. The case was referred to me for evaluation by Kenneth A. Davidson, Attorney at Law (address).

PURPOSE OF EVALUATION

1. To determine whether there is evidence to support the allegation that Robert J. Connors has been physically abusive toward his son, Jesse Connors
2. If so, to make recommendations to the court concerning future visitation

INFORMED CONSENT

On 4/23/91, prior to the evaluation, I explained to both parents that the evaluation would be for forensic and not therapeutic purposes. I explained to them that what they said to me might be incorporated in the report to the court, and that my purpose was to advise the court in the best interests of the child. They indicated that they understood the purpose of the evaluation and that they wanted me to proceed with it.

SOURCES OF DATA

In the course of the evaluation, I had access to the following documents: (1) affidavit from (name), Director, Early Education Program (address) (4/2/91); (2) final divorce order in the case of *Teri A. Connors vs. Robert J. Connors* (3/5/91); (3) order restraining Robert J. Connors from visitation with his two children (4/2/91); (4) motion to set aside temporary restraining order (4/6/91).

The following interviews were conducted: (1) joint interview with both parents (4/23/91, 1 hour); (2) interview with Mrs. Teri Connors (4/30/91, 1.5 hours); (3) interview with Mr. Robert Connors (5/1/91, 1.5 hours); (4) interview with Mrs. Teri Connors (5/8/91, 1 hour); (5) interview with Mr. Robert Connors (5/14/91, 1 hour); (6) interview with Jesse Connors (5/15/91, 1 hour); (7) interview with Jesse's sister, Tina Connors (5/15/91, 1 hour); (8) interview with both parents together with the two children (5/19/91, 1 hour).

FINDINGS

Review of Documents

The affidavit provided by (_____), Director of the _____
Early Education Program, describes how, on 4/1/91, Jesse Connors told her that he was apprehensive about visiting his father that evening, reportedly because his

father "spanks me when I am good . . . makes me stay in my room by myself for a long time . . . won't let me eat supper." Furthermore, reportedly, Mr. Connors "hurts me by making me get down and he gets on top of me with his knees on my back" and "spanks (me) with a stick and a rope."

Interviews

Mrs. Connors described how, prior to the preschool director's report, both children were often reluctant to visit their father. On one occasion when she telephoned them at the father's house, Jesse is said to have whispered into the telephone, "Do you remember what you said? Please come get me right now." On another occasion, Jesse telephoned his mother asking her to come and take his sister and himself home. Following the preschool director's report, Jesse repeated to his mother his complaints about his father, adding, "My Daddy won't even play with me or take us to McDonald's. Daddy doesn't play baseball with me. He makes me sit in my room. He whips me with a stick and a rope." Jesse also described how "Keith," a friend of the father, "wrestled" with him (Jesse) on a bed.

Mrs. Connors described Tina as being reluctant to visit her father at times. She complained that, on one occasion, the father insisted that Tina have a bath with Jesse and another boy (aged four and two years, respectively), in order to "save water." Furthermore, Mrs. Connors said, during February 1991 Mr. Connors neglected a fever suffered by Tina and a thumb cut sustained by Jesse. Since visitation has been stayed, Tina on one occasion is reported to have said, "I know it's time to go back. Please don't let me go." On another occasion Jesse is said to have told his mother, "You know my eyes swell and itch. My Daddy spanks me when I do and he says 'Don't cry.' My Daddy hollers at me all the time."

Mrs. Connors stated that, following her separation from her former husband, she has lived with her parents. Since November 1991 she has worked as a waitress for up to six days a week, with flexible hours. She describes her relationship with the maternal grandparents as close; however, this domestic arrangement will soon come to an end since the maternal grandparents plan to sell their present home in the near future.

Mrs. Connors described her childhood as having been happy. She stated that, as a child, she suffered from no serious physical or psychological illnesses and that she was not subject to alcohol or substance abuse. Reportedly she met her husband at the age of eighteen and married him when twenty years of age. Both pregnancies were planned and welcome. She said that the marriage began to deteriorate because her husband gave her little help in the house, would drink heavily on weekends, and became increasingly inconsiderate following the onset of his back trouble in 1989 (see below). By that time, reportedly, he had been unfaithful to her, was gambling excessively and extravagant, and was possibly involved in substance abuse. On at least one occasion, reportedly, he was excessively rough with the children. Eventually, in October 1990, she took the children and left. Relations between the parents have been tense and hostile since that time. However, Mrs. Connors avers that she has never derogated the father in front of the children; indeed, she acknowledges that they miss him and love him.

*   *   *

Mr. Connors stated that, between mid-1987 and mid-1990, he had a series of injuries and surgical operations, which significantly affected his life and personality. This difficult period began with an injury to his left ankle and a herniated cervical disc (March 1988), and removal of this disc (April 1988), followed by four months off work, a rerupture of the same disc (September 1988), an operation to fuse the affected vertebrae, then five months off work, surgery to his ankle (December 1988), injury to the lower back with rupture of a disc in the lower back (April 1989), and a compression fracture of the lower back and left ankle and an injury to the right knee. Reportedly, it was during his recuperation from the last injury that his wife became restless and left him. Eventually, despite marriage counseling, she left their home in October 1990, a time of severe emotional distress for him. Now, he says, he loves her no more. He accuses her of having "milked" the savings he received from workman's compensation and of pressing him for more and more cash, alimony, child support, and household appliances. It is his opinion that she is spitefully withholding the children from him.

Insofar as the allegations of physical abuse are concerned, he denies having used a stick or rope to punish his son. Once, two years ago, he says, he used a switch taken from a tree in the yard. He also admits to having used a belt to whip Jesse on one occasion. He admits to having wrestled with Jesse, in play, and suggests that this is why Jesse described his father as having put his "knees in his back." So far as the children's reluctance to visit him is concerned, "I just blow it off . . . they just tell stories." He reported that the children tell stories against their mother to him, but he ignores them. So far as Jesse's having cut his thumb in the bath is concerned, he said that he sought hospital care, having asked his former wife to come over. He made the counter-accusation that she had dropped Jesse on two occasions when he was a baby.

Asked his attitude to punishment for a five-year-old boy, he stated that he had not whipped Jesse with his pants down since October 1990. About once every two weeks, he thought, he had hit Jesse with his hand through his pants on the behind, for example when the boy had kicked his sister. For very serious infractions, he could be inclined to hit Jesse once on the behind with his pants down, or to use a belt. He pointed out that "whippings" had straightened *him* out when he was a child.

He went on to say that he offers praise and affection freely, in contrast to his own father, who was an unaffectionate man. Both his parents are alive and in good physical and mental health. He said the relationship between them was caring but not affectionate. Although he was infrequently physically punished, he was often scolded by his father.

After graduating from high school and a year in college, he was apprenticed as a carpenter and has worked in his father's business since that time. He met his future wife when he was nineteen years of age. They courted for two years, despite breaking up on several occasions. He states that there were no separations between them until, seven years after they were married, his wife left him in October 1990. After that, his love turned to hatred, and he and she have become virtually unable to speak to each other, even on the telephone.

He said that he drinks alcohol only during weekends, and the only drug he took was an analgesic for back pain. He denied any other recent contact with drugs. He denied current emotional problems. When asked what could be the motivation for the allegation of physical abuse, he wondered whether it had been promoted as "a malicious lie." Nevertheless, he believed that he and his former wife have similar attitudes toward discipline: If children transgress, for example, they should be deprived of a valued object, asked to go into time-out, or, if the infraction is severe (for example, if they hit each other), their "butts should be popped" with a hand.

Mr. Connors described himself as a much more emotional man than his own father. He was much affected by the recent death of his grandfather. He stated that children should "realize when they have done wrong." However, he believed in spending time with his children, flying kites, playing baseball, fishing, and supporting his daughter's more feminine pursuits. He also believed in conveying a strong faith in God.

Jesse was a little reluctant to separate from his mother and was prone to converse in a whining tone of voice. However, he quickly settled down and played spontaneously with the toys provided. He exhibited good vocabulary and excellent dexterity.

With regard to his parents, he said: "They got divorced . . . they won't live with each other any more. . . . I love my Daddy. . . . I like him. . . . I don't get to see him. (Do you want to?) Yes! (Why?) Because they got divorced. I used to spend nights with him, now Mommy said no. The doctors and presidents wanted to talk it out. I only want to spend time at Daddy's. (Do you love your Daddy?) Yes. (Why?) Well the presidents and the doctors are talking it out. I was in the office and I was doing a bad thing. I talked to the office lady. I said he whips me, but not all the time. (When did you say that?) I be bad. A belt or his hand or a switch or a rope. (When did that happen?) I don't know, a long time ago. (Did your Daddy do anything else to you?) No. (Did he punish you too much?) No. (Did you ever tell your Mommy to come and get you?) All the time I want to be with Daddy. (Did you ever telephone your Mommy to come and get you?) I didn't do it a lot! Twice—because I wanted to talk to her. (Did you miss your Mom?) Yes. (Who would you rather live with?) My Mommy. (Do you want to visit your Daddy?) Yes. I want to. (Did your Daddy ever hit you with a switch or a rope?) It was so long ago, I don't remember. (Why did you tell your teacher about your Daddy?) He spanked me. I wanted her to know. It's been so long—she didn't remember. Because I wanted her to know, because my Daddy is special."

Later in the interview, he told me that his ambition was to be a policeman and to arrest bad people. His three wishes in order were: (1) "to go back to Daddy's house"; (2) "to play with toys at Daddy's house"; (3) "that they be back together married." He said that his father has a girlfriend who is "real nice" and who has a child called "Jed." Asked to draw a person, he depicted a man "working being a carpenter." The man's name was "Rob." "Rob" is "sad" because "I can't come over to his house anymore." He indicated that the man was his father.

Tina, age six, separated easily from her mother and conversed spontaneously. Asked why she had come to see me, she said: "I don't understand why. Because people at court told me I couldn't see Daddy. . . . I wish I could be with Daddy instead of Mommy. I get cereal at Daddy's. He's fun. Mommy doesn't take us anywhere special like Chuck E. Cheese's. Daddy did it sixty-one times! . . . Jesse told the court that

Daddy was mean, then he said 'I'm just trickin'.' He said that 'cause Jesse thinks Daddy was giving us spankings. Daddy's not mean. Mommy's not mean."

Tina denied that she or Jesse had received excessive punishment before or after their parents had separated. With regard to the divorce, Tina did not know why her parents had separated. "Mommy said that Daddy could go out with his friends, but when he comes back she says, 'You can't.' He only goes out once a week."

Her three wishes were as follows: (1) "spend nights at Daddy's"; (2) "go to Florida with Daddy"; (3) "ride in an airplane." Asked to draw a person, she depicted a girl who is "seeing a man and wondering if they can go out on a date. . . . If Mommy goes out on a date with Daddy they kiss. (Do they still kiss?) No. They're divorced. They don't kiss nobody. Mommy has a friend—just a friend, not a boyfriend. (And Daddy?) Daddy has a girlfriend, Susan. She has a little kid. He spits up and plays in the bathroom with number two. He's scared of Daddy because he doesn't know him well. (What does the little girl in the picture need most?) A boyfriend, cause some people don't like marriage, but she wants to marry. She wants ten babies."

DISCUSSION

It is evident that hostility and tension continue between these parents. Their mutual antagonism is apparent from their demeanor when together, and from the separate accounts they give of their marriage and its breakup. Mr. Connors regards his former wife as having abandoned him and been unfaithful to him at a time when he was afflicted with physical infirmity and emotional stress. His love has turned to coldness. Mrs. Connors views her former husband as insensitive, inconsiderate, and immature. She left him because she foresaw no chance of any improvement in their relationship.

It is likely that the series of debilitating injuries and surgeries sustained by Mr. Connors during the last two years of the marriage significantly affected the relationship between the parents. Currently, despite the final divorce decree, there are continuing disputes about money. Over the telephone or when together, the parents either squabble or remain frigidly silent.

Caught between the two parents are the two children. Both children express strong affection for both parents. Tina, if anything, leans more in the direction of her father. Jesse dearly loves his father and plays comfortably in his presence but is closer to his mother. However, when the time comes to leave his mother to visit the father, Jesse becomes anxious and inclined to view the father as intimidating and insensitive. Unsurprisingly, these characterizations match the mother's concerns about the father. Neither child describes the father as overpunitive. Tina believes that Jesse exaggerated his allegations of abuse. Jesse hints that he did so.

CONCLUSIONS

Therefore, with reasonable medical certainty, I have the following opinions:

1. Robert J. Connors has not been physically abusive toward his son Jesse Connors.

2. Teri A. Connors has not indoctrinated Jesse to accuse the father of physical abuse and is not attempting to sabotage the relationship between them.
3. Jesse's allegation of physical abuse is related to a reluctance to leave his mother.
4. This reluctance is a manifestation of separation anxiety secondary to the family tensions surrounding the recent separation and divorce.

RECOMMENDATIONS

1. I have counseled the parents that, if they want joint custody to work, they must separate their personal tensions and disputes from their joint management of the children.
2. Neither parent should ever derogate the other in front of the children.
3. The mother should ensure that the transfer of the children from herself to the father is tension-free.
4. Mr. Connors should reserve physical punishment for very severe infractions, remember that a raised voice can be very intimidating to an anxious child, and use deprivation of toys or time-out as the preferred method of discipline.
5. The parents have similar spiritual and family values. They should appreciate that joint custody can be effective only if they collaborate in conveying these values to their children.

Case 4(a)
Preliminary Report Assisting
the Child Protection Department to Stay
Visitation Pending a Complete Evaluation

This emergency report illustrates how a timely (but preliminary) report can be used to halt visitation when sexual abuse is suspected. Note the caution implicit in the opinion and recommendations. The full evaluation is reported in Case No. 4(b).

CONFIDENTIAL
PRELIMINARY FORENSIC REPORT
Re: Denis Morris
Date of Birth: 5/3/84
and
Charly Morris
Date of Birth: 10/10/87

CIRCUMSTANCES OF REFERRAL

Denis and Charly Morris were referred to me by their caseworker, Mr. (name), Department of Social Services (_____) County, (State). The two children were originally removed from the home of their natural father in 1988 and placed in two foster homes before being transferred to the foster home of Mr. and Mrs. (name) on July 5, 1990. In November 1990 they were returned to the custody of the maternal grandmother. In December 1990 they were taken from the custody of the maternal grandmother and placed again in the (name) foster home. The Department of Social Services is seeking a stay of visitation with the maternal grandmother and mother, pending the completion of this evaluation.

PURPOSE OF EVALUATION

To determine if it is in the children's best interest to continue to have supervised visitation with the maternal grandmother and the father, and overnight visitation with the mother.

SOURCES OF DATA

In the course of this evaluation, I reviewed the following documents: court documents concerning the case; reports to the court from the Department of Social Services of (_____) County and (_____) County, (State); a report of the child investigation team from Metropolitan Hospital concerning the two children; a developmental screening and intake interview concerning Charly Morris (dated 10/18/89); progress notes concerning individual psychotherapy with Denis Morris conducted by (name), M.A., between 8/89 and 2/91; psychiatric reports over the same time completed by (name), M.D.; psychological testing of Denis Morris, 9/17/89, conducted by (name), M.A.; psychological report concerning the children's biological mother, Heather Morris, 6/9/90, signed (name); and psychological report concerning the biological father, Denis Morris, Sr., 4/12/90, signed (name), M.A.

Up to this point I have interviewed the foster parents jointly for one hour, and the two children each on two separate one-hour interviews. The foster parents have completed child behavior checklists on both children.

FINDINGS

Review of Documents

The development screen of Charly Morris conducted in September 1989 revealed that he had developmental delays in the area of communication. There is little else of significance in the record concerning Charly. However, on 3/14/91, Mr. (caseworker) reported to me that Charly had initiated fellatio with another child at the day care center which he attends. While performing fellatio, Charly is said to have bitten the other child on the penis, and the other child is said to have retaliated in kind. Charly is reported to have said, subsequently, that the maternal grandstepfather had performed fellatio on him and on his older brother Denis. Denis is reported to have said that the maternal grandmother had held Charly down while the maternal grandstepfather performed fellatio on Charly. This report was corroborated to me by the foster mother, Mrs. (name).

The psychotherapy progress notes completed by (therapist) contain statements by Denis that his father's friend "Mac," his father's friend "Rory," his brother Charly, the maternal grandstepfather, the maternal grandmother, two foster siblings, and his biological father had sexually interfered with him. The allegations allude to genital touching, fellatio, and anal intercourse.

Interviews

Mr. & Mrs. (name), the foster parents, reported to me that the two children currently visit their mother twice a month, overnight. They visit the father and maternal grandmother separately, once a week, the former for two hours and the latter for one hour, while supervised at the offices of the Department of Social Services.

Since December 1990, reportedly, Denis has been destructive, inattentive, hyperactive, disruptive in school, and prone to draw sexually explicit pictures. At the foster home he tends to be oppositional, defiant, and heedless. Since December 1990, reportedly, Charly has been hyperactive, weepy if thwarted, resistant to eating, and preoccupied with an imaginary friend ("Uncle Bobby"). The foster parents report that, prior to visitation with their mother, the children are ready to leave; after returning, however, their behavioral problems are aggravated. Furthermore, after weekly visitation with the maternal grandmother and father, the children are, reportedly, heedless and oppositional.

At interview, Charly was a sturdy four-year-old. He exhibited poor verbal articulation, immature syntax, an impoverished vocabulary, and limited receptive language skills. Shortly after the commencement of my first interview with him, he volunteered: ("You know what? George pulled my pants down and sucked on my barrel box.") He spoke about visiting his Daddy ("He buys me food.") and his grandmother ("She don't buy me no food!"). In my second interview with him, Charly was unable to tell the difference between truth and a lie. He spoke of his biological parents as "Daddy with the limp" and "Mommy with the long hair." He referred to his maternal grandmother as "Granny" and his maternal grandstepfather as "George." At this interview, he denied questions concerning his father's, his mother's, or his grandmother's having molested him. With regard to the maternal grandstepfather, he said: "I don't know what he do, he did something, I don't know any more." In general, his play was poorly organized, and he was highly distractible and destructive of the play materials.

Denis separated easily from the foster parents. He manifested no defect in receptive or expressive speech. His drawings of the human figure exhibited meticulous attention to the "belly button" area. In my second interview with him, he was able to distinguish adequately between the truth and a lie. He reported that the following people "touched (his) private parts": (1) "Daddy with the limp"; (2) "George"; (3) "Granny"; (4) "Mommy with the long hair"; (5) "Mac"; (6) "Rory." Using anatomically complete dolls, he demonstrated the following people (depicted by adult dolls) putting their mouths on the genital region of a boy doll: "Daddy," "Granny," "George," "Rory," "Mac," and "Mommy with the long hair." He denied that any of the following people had sucked his genital organ: "Mommy at home"; "Daddy at home"; "Charly at home"; Lester ("Don't know him") or his teacher Mrs. (name) ("No!"). When I suggested to him that children often got pains in the knees, he said: "A little bit. Sometimes. Not a lot." Toward the end of the interview he became excited and vigorously denied that anyone had told him to say that he had been sexually interfered with. Eventually he became so disorganized and hyperactive, jumping off and on the couch, that the interview was terminated.

Psychological Test Results

The child behavior checklist completed by the foster parents indicated that both children have a severe degree of psychiatric disturbance.

DISCUSSION

Charly's communicative skills are so deficient that his fragmentary report of having been sexually abused is not credible. In my opinion, in a legal sense, he is not a competent witness.

Taken together, the psychotherapy progress notes, the history given by the foster parents, and my interview with the child himself make it clear that Denis Morris has been sexually abused. He has reported sexual abuse at the hands of his biological father, two of the father's friends, the maternal grandstepfather, the maternal grandmother, and the biological mother.

Reports from the foster parents and my interviews with both children indicate that both children have a severe degree of psychiatric disturbance. In addition, Charly Morris is seriously delayed in language development.

According to the reports of the foster parents, the children's psychological disturbance is aggravated following visitation with the biological mother, biological father, and maternal grandmother.

CONCLUSIONS

With reasonable medical certainty, I have the following opinions:

1. Both children are seriously psychologically disturbed.
2. The psychological disturbance of both children is aggravated by visitation with their natural parents and maternal grandmother.
3. Denis Morris's behavior and statements are consistent with his having been sexually abused.
4. Charly Morris's language defects render him an incompetent witness.

RECOMMENDATIONS

In my opinion, visitation with the natural parents and the maternal grandmother should be stayed pending the completion of this evaluation. After the evaluation is complete, I will be in a position to give further recommendations.

Case 4(b)
Final Report Concerning the Credibility of Sexual Abuse
Allegations and the Cessation of Parental Visitation

A confusing case, in which two children, the natural parents (separated), and the grandmother make serious accusations and counter-accusations about each other. The opinion rendered reflects proper caution about the children's allegations, given uncertainty about whether their psychotherapist may have inadvertently caused the older child to exaggerate or embellish his allegations.

CONFIDENTIAL
FORENSIC EVALUATION
Re: Denis Morris
Date of Birth: 5/3/84
and
Charly Morris
Date of Birth: 10/10/87

CIRCUMSTANCES OF REFERRAL

Denis and Charly Morris were referred to me by their caseworker, Mr. (name), Department of Social Services, of (County), (State). The two children were originally removed from the home of their natural father in 1988. They were placed in two foster homes prior to eventual transfer to the foster home of Mr. and Mrs. (name) on 7/5/90. In November 1990 they were placed in the custody of their maternal grandmother. In December 1990 they were taken from the custody of the maternal grandmother and placed again in the (name) foster home.

PREVIOUS EVALUATION

This evaluation is to be combined with my previous evaluation of the above children (3/28/91). I have been asked to comment on the credibility of the allegations that the two children have been sexually abused and to recommend whether it would be in the children's best interest for visitation to be resumed.

SOURCES OF DATA

In addition to the sources described in the initial report, I interviewed Mr. Denis Morris, Sr. (5/28/91; 1½ hours), Mr. and Mrs. Brad Glenn (6/5/91; 1½ hours), and Mrs. Mary Morris-Garson (6/5/91; 1½ hours). I also had access to psychological evaluation reports prepared by (psychologist), Ph.D., Clinical Psychologist, concerning Charly Morris (4/27/91) and Denis Morris (4/27/91).

INFORMED CONSENT

Prior to interviewing Mr. Denis Morris, Sr.; Mr. and Mrs. Brad Glenn; and Mrs. Mary Morris-Garson, I explained to each of them (and ascertained that they understood) that the interview was for forensic purposes only; that it was not intended to be therapeutic; and that whatever they said to me might be conveyed to the court in a report.

FINDINGS

Psychological Test Results

On psychological testing, Charly obtained a full-scale IQ in the low average range. Personality testing suggested fearfulness, tension, and worry. He appeared to be a very needy child who required high levels of support and who is prone to become irritable and complaining if he feels deprived of attention. There was no direct evidence of sexual abuse in the psychological test protocol; however, he did state to the psychologist, "It was Brad who touched my private parts." An assessment of family relations indicated that he was psychologically involved and bonded virtually exclusively with the foster parents.

Psychological evaluation of Denis Morris indicated that the child had a full-scale intelligence in the average range. He was hyperactive, impulsive, anxious, and oppositional, with a sense of inner badness and a concern that others might treat him harshly. Psychological testing also revealed that he was preoccupied with sexual matters. At one point he expressed regret at having been touched by other people "on the private parts." Denis expressed hatred toward his father and described only a weak relationship with his biological mother. He is closely attached to his foster parents, whom he idealizes. This child's high anxiety, preoccupation with sexual themes, and hostility toward his parents are consistent with posttraumatic stress disorder.

Interviews

Denis Morris, Sr., of (Town), (State), is thirty years of age. He works as a truck driver and salesman for a produce company. After marrying in 1983, he separated from his wife in 1988, and divorced her in 1990.

His own father, a construction worker, was an alcoholic who on one occasion was jailed for possession of a sawed-off shotgun. His mother was killed in an accident in which he himself sustained a fracture of the left leg. He had two brothers, one of whom was killed by the police (in 1985) following a high-speed car chase. He described his family life as disrupted by his father's heavy drinking and by conflict between himself, his brothers, and his parents. He denied having been sexually abused. He and his brothers all spent time in foster care and also in juvenile and adult correctional institutions. Mr. Morris himself was admitted to (   ) school as an adolescent. In 1979 he was incarcerated for three years, reportedly for "attempt to commit a felony," in company with one of his brothers.

After dropping out of high school, he became seriously involved with drugs between the ages of fourteen and twenty-one. Reportedly, he met his wife in 1982 and married her after she become pregnant by him. After the birth of his son, Denis, Jr., he reportedly ceased to smoke marijuana or to drink alcohol and attempted to help his wife keep the house clean. However, the marriage deteriorated because his wife is said to have neglected the baby and the house and to have been unfaithful to him (on one occasion with his brother and on another with his boss). An additional disturbing factor in the marriage, according to Mr. Morris, was persistent interference by the maternal grandmother, who disliked him and wanted her daughter to leave him. Eventually, after Charly was born (1987), he punched his wife during an altercation about her relationship with another man. She then had him arrested for assault, and the couple separated for good.

After the separation the children lived with their mother, with the maternal grandmother and her boyfriend (Mr. Glenn), and with Mr. Morris. In 1988, when Denis, Jr., was living with his father, a friend of the father ("Mark") attempted to molest Denis. Mr. Morris heard Denis crying out, interceded between the would-be molester and his son, and ejected the man from the trailer in which Mr. Morris was living.

Mr. Morris is incredulous concerning Denis's accusations of sexual abuse against "Roger" (possibly Mr. Morris's brother), the maternal grandmother, the paternal grandmother, the mother, and himself. He wonders whether Denis "wants attention" or is being "coached." He burst into tears at this point, saying how much he wanted his children back. He criticized his former wife as a poor housekeeper and mother and berated his mother-in-law for having physically abused the children.

At this interview Mr. Morris was tense, self-righteous, hostile to his former wife and her mother, and anxious to impress me with his capacity to care for both his children.

*   *   *

Mrs. Ro Glenn, the maternal grandmother, and her husband, Mr. Brad Glenn, were interviewed together. Mrs. Glenn said that she had always disapproved of the marriage between the children's parents. She appreciated that Mr. Morris was an abusive man because she herself had experienced abuse in a previous marriage. She had observed that her daughter was afraid of Mr. Morris, who was an extremely jealous man. After the children were born, reportedly, their parents frequently left them with different people for up to two weeks at a time. In her opinion, neither parent is competent to care for children.

The maternal grandmother and stepgrandfather divorced when the mother was only five years of age after her stepfather left the maternal grandmother for another woman. Mrs. Glenn was left to raise five children by herself. Mrs. Glenn has no idea why her daughter (Mrs. Morris-Garson) became so disturbed, averring that she was loved even though she was born out of wedlock. Mrs. Glenn said that her daughter had been in psychiatric care between the ages of twelve and eighteen. She described her as a withdrawn, surly, uncommunicative child who became seriously involved with drugs from midadolescence onward. From an early age, reportedly, Mrs. Morris-Garson was sexually active, and she was raped at the age of twelve.

Mrs. Glenn described herself as having been physically (but not sexually) abused by her own father and having been forced to work at an early age. It is for this reason that she was especially concerned about Mr. Morris's abusiveness toward her daughter. However, she corroborated Mr. Morris's allegation that her daughter had been unfaithful to him.

Mrs. Glenn remarried in 1990, to Mr. Brad Glenn. The marriage is described as "wonderful."

Mr. Brad Glenn said that he was the third of six siblings raised on a farm. He left school after the tenth grade and became a crane operator and electrician. In 1968 he was involved in a car wreck, which killed his first wife and their two children. He remarried in 1970 for eighteen years but was eventually divorced in 1988. He became upset when he spoke of his second wife who, reportedly, left him "because (he) earned too little." He denied ever having trouble with the law; ever having taken alcohol, drugs; or ever having had psychiatric treatment. On the other hand, he had been "nervous" since the 1968 car wreck.

Mr. and Mrs. Glenn said that they had temporary custody of the children between October and December 1990. The children were returned to foster care because of accusations against Mr. and Mrs. Glenn, the father, and one of the father's friends. Mr. Glenn said that he felt justified in having "whipped" Charly ("not hard") for wetting the bed.

Both Mr. and Mrs. Glenn denied ever having been sexually abused themselves. Mrs. Glenn remembered that her daughter had accused her of having physically abused her, but she denied that this had ever occurred. On the other hand, reportedly, Mrs. Morris-Garson had physically abused both Denis and Charly, as well as neglecting them. Furthermore, reportedly, Mr. Morris sold drugs and used them heavily.

During the interview, Mr. and Mrs. Glenn expressed severe criticism of both Mr. Morris and his former wife, their daughter. Neither of them, they said, is fit to care for children.

*   *   *

Mrs. Morris-Garson said that her pregnancy with Denis was normal and her relationship to her then husband was a stable one at that time. Having found out that she was pregnant, she ceased taking drugs, reportedly, and has taken none since that time. Denis's infancy and early childhood were uneventful, aside from an attack of meningitis when he was six weeks old and frequent ear infections during the second year of his life. Her pregnancy and confinement with Charly were normal, as were Charly's infancy and early childhood. The parents separated when Denis was four years old and Charly one and a half years old.

Mrs. Morris-Garson reported that the identity of her father was never revealed to her by her mother. She described her mother, Mrs. Ro Glenn, as having been physically and emotionally abusive toward her. When she was four years of age, allegedly, her stepfather sexually molested her on a number of occasions; her mother refused to believe her when she reported these incidents.

During her middle childhood and adolescence she was sexually precocious. Her adolescence was a whirlwind of foster homes, running away, drug addiction, sexual escapades, psychiatric hospitals, and juvenile halls.

At the age of eighteen she met Denis Morris, Sr., and moved in with him in order to have a roof over her head. After Denis was born, however, having found that he had been unfaithful to her, she lost her love for Mr. Morris. She described him as a drug dealer and a criminal. During their marriage, reportedly, he frequently beat her until finally she had him arrested for assault.

Her strained relationship with the maternal grandmother continues to this day. Reportedly, the maternal grandmother married Mr. Glenn only in order to get Mrs. Morris-Garson's children. Reportedly, Denis accused the paternal grandmother of beating him and his father's friend ("Mark") of having attempted to sodomize him. Subsequently Denis accused his mother, the maternal grandmother, and the maternal grand-stepfather, of having sexually abused him. Mrs. Morris-Garson denied ever having sexually abused the children, saying "I love them too much." She doubted whether her mother or Mr. Brad Glenn would have sexually abused the children. She also doubted that her husband—physically abusive though he may have been—would sexually abuse children. Nevertheless, she complained that Mr. Morris was excessively slow to protect Denis from sexual abuse at the hands of "Mark."

Currently, having remarried, Mrs. Morris-Garson lives with her second husband, a construction worker, and two stepchildren. Reportedly, she and he have a close relationship, but it is sometimes strained by quarrels concerning her ten-year-old stepdaughter, who tends to manipulate her stepmother and to be "jealous" of her.

At this interview, Mrs. Morris-Garson impressed as a woman of average intelligence who has had an extremely disrupted early life. She is anxious to have her children back but is evidently struggling to stabilize her relationship with her second husband and stepchildren.

DISCUSSION

Psychological testing corroborates the observations recorded in my preliminary report. Charly Morris is a developmentally delayed child. His communication skills are so poor that little credence can be placed in what he says. In my opinion, he is not a competent witness. Though of average intelligence, Denis Morris, Jr., is an anxious, guilty, sexually preoccupied child. His psychological profile is consistent with emotional trauma caused by sexual abuse.

Denis Morris, Jr., has made allegations of sexual abuse against a number of people: his father's friend "Mark," his father's brother "Roger," his father, his mother, his paternal grandmother, his maternal grandmother, and the maternal grandmother's new husband. These allegations have come to light in a number of situations, but predominantly during individual psychotherapy. It is not clear, from reports of the psychotherapy, what form of questioning was used to elicit the allegations. It should be noted that Denis Morris, Jr., is quite suggestible and anxious. It is possible that he is confabulating or embellishing accusations of sexual abuse in order to elicit the concern of adults.

From the welter of mutual accusations made between mother, father, and maternal grandmother, each of whom is requesting custody of the children, a number of observations can be made. Both the mother and father had disrupted childhoods, followed by disturbed adolescent years characterized in the mother's case by early sexual activity and drug abuse and, in the father's case, by drug abuse, delinquency, and criminality. Born out of wedlock, the mother was and is rejected by the maternal grandmother. The maternal grandmother rejects both the mother and the father, criticizing them both as incompetent and neglectful parents. Neither the mother nor the father, nor the maternal grandmother, puts credence in the younger Denis Morris's allegations of sexual abuse, aside from the attempted rape by the father's friend "Mark."

The father lives alone in a trailer, works long hours from early morning, and is without household support. Although he has finished parenting classes and claims to be a competent housekeeper, he would have to rely heavily on day care if he were to resume custody of the children.

Mrs. Morris-Garson impressed as a still immature young woman who is struggling to cope with a new marriage and who is already having conflict with her stepdaughter. It is doubtful whether she has sufficient personal and marital stability at this point to be able to absorb the care of two additional children.

Mr. and Mrs. Glenn have exhibited physically abusive behavior toward Charly Morris.

OPINIONS AND RECOMMENDATIONS

With reasonable certainty, it is my opinion that:

1. Being developmentally delayed, particularly in language, Charly Morris is not a competent witness. However, his recent behavior is consistent with his having been sexually abused at some time in the past.
2. Denis Morris, Jr., is a seriously emotionally disturbed child. The pattern of his emotional disturbance is consistent with posttraumatic stress disorder following sexual abuse.
3. Denis Morris, Jr.'s, suggestibility and emotional neediness, together with uncertainty about the nature of the questioning that he has received to elicit allegations of sexual abuse, mitigate the credibility that can be accorded to his allegations of sexual abuse against family members. On the other hand, the original allegation of sexual abuse against the father's friend "Mark" has been corroborated by the father.
4. Prior to the cessation of visitation, both Charly Morris and Denis Morris, Jr., were emotionally disturbed following visitation with their mother, father, and maternal grandmother.

Accordingly, I offer the following recommendations:

1. Denis Morris, Jr., should continue to receive psychotherapy.
2. Charly Morris should be evaluated by a speech and language pathologist with regard to his need for speech therapy and language stimulation.

3. Visitation with the mother, father, and maternal grandmother should not be resumed for six months. At that time, the children's psychological status should be reviewed with a view to determining whether resumption of visitation is in their best interests.
4. Further interrogation of Denis Morris, Jr., concerning sexual abuse is inadvisable. Such material should be dealt with as it appears, spontaneously, in individual psychotherapy.

Case 5
Attempt by Maternal Custodian to Bar Paternal Visitation on the Ground of Sexual Abuse

In this case, the custodial mother moved from the home state in order to bar the father, whom she has accused of sexually molesting the child, from visitation. Two years have passed and the child's recollection of the alleged abuse is blurred and contaminated by recent events. Thus, the child's account of sexual abuse cannot be validated; nevertheless, alternative explanations do not hold up. The opinion and recommendations reflect the evaluator's caution.

CONFIDENTIAL
FORENSIC EVALUATION
Re: Michael Kenton
Date of Birth: 8/16/83
Mother—Catherine Kenton

CIRCUMSTANCES OF REFERRAL

The mother and father of the subject child were separated in May 1985 and divorced in February 1986. The mother was awarded sole custody and the father, supervised visitation. Between August 1986 and October 1986, the mother allowed unsupervised visits. These visits were stopped unilaterally by her in October 1986, on the ground that the father had sexually abused the child. This allegation of sexual abuse was subsequently evaluated with negative result by the local police, child protective services, and a private psychologist. The mother left the state of the child's birth and moved to (State). After locating her, in June 1989, the father requested a resumption of supervised visitation. The mother opposes this. At a hearing on the matter on 10/15/89, the matter was continued to 12/3/89, pending a forensic evaluation.

PURPOSE OF REFERRAL

1. To determine whether the subject child suffers from a psychiatric disorder; if so, to evaluate its severity and determine whether it could be related to past sexual abuse
2. To recommend treatment for the psychiatric disorder if present

3. To determine whether resumption of supervised visitation with the father would result in psychological harm to the child

SOURCES OF DATA
Documents

Here all legal documents, past mental health reports, and protective service reports are listed and dated.

Interviews

1. Interview with mother, 9/21/89 (1 hour)
2. Interview with Michael Kenton, 10/1/89 (1 hour)
3. Interview with Michael Kenton, 10/2/89 (1 hour)
4. Interview with Michael Kenton, 10/6/89 (1 hour)
5. Interview with mother, 10/8/89 (2 hours)
6. Interview with father, 11/12/89 (2½ hours)
7. Interview with paternal grandmother, 11/12/89 (1 hour) and 11/13/89 (½ hour)

Psychological Testing

1. Psychological testing conducted by Dr. _____ (psychologist), 10/5/90
2. Child Behavior Checklists completed by mother (10/1/89) and teacher (10/4/89)

INFORMED CONSENT

Prior to the interviews proper, both mother and father were separately informed of the forensic, nontherapeutic purpose of this evaluation, and gave consent for it to continue.

FINDINGS
Interviews

On 10/22/89, Mrs. Kenton told me that her son had been "raped" by his father on a number of occasions between August and October 1986. Reportedly, Michael did not disclose this until one month after the sexual molestation had ceased. After a number of investigations of the alleged sexual abuse (which, as described below, were negative), Mrs. Kenton moved from (State) to (State) in order to be close to her brother. Mrs. Kenton originally became suspicious that sexual abuse had occurred for the reasons set out in the next paragraph.

About one month after unsupervised visitation began (that is, in September 1986),

Michael is reported to have begun to act in a regressive fashion: He began to suck his fingers; he was depressed, angry, and aggressive toward other children; he exhibited nightmares about his father killing his mother and monkeys "getting" him; and he complained of abdominal pain. On two occasions, reportedly, his father brought him home with wet underwear. After visitation from his father, reportedly, he wanted to be bathed. On one occasion he is said to have said: "My father has a big pee pee." About one month after the mother stopped the visitation, reportedly, Michael commented to his mother, "My papa put his thing in my butt." Mrs. Kenton called the police and the child protective services. However, no physical evidence was noted on pediatric examination, and the child's allegations could not be validated by the police, the child protection service, or a private psychological counselor.

Reportedly, since coming to (State) in May 1987, Michael has been less aggressive, less cruel to animals, and less destructive. On the other hand, he has continued to stick things (e.g., a toothbrush) into his rectum, and to be hyperactive and disruptive in school. When he first arrived in (State) he was noticed to be trying to insert his finger into a dog's anus. On 10/08/89 following his three interviews with me, Mrs. Kenton noted that Michael had become anxious and clinging.

It should be noted that Michael has had no contact with his father for two years (except for the receipt of one present) and that his father is reportedly $11,000.00 in arrears on maintenance and child support payments.

Mrs. Kenton described how her father had died in a motor vehicle accident when she was two years of age. Her mother subsequently married a businessman who was an excellent provider but was too busy to develop a close relationship with his children. Mrs. Kenton has two stepbrothers and one stepsister. She said that she gets along well with all of them. Initially, neither her mother nor her stepfather was supportive to her concerning Michael's alleged sexual abuse by his father. However, over the last year they have become more helpful and understanding.

Mrs. Kenton graduated from (College), and subsequently qualified as an accountant. After moving to (State), she became involved with Mr. Kenton. Although, reportedly, the relationship was initially an exciting one, from the beginning Mr. Kenton is said to have been "very needy." Mrs. Kenton fell pregnant before the marriage and married Mr. Kenton when Michael was three months of age.

When Michael was about six months of age, Mrs. Kenton allegedly found a syringe in the house, confronted her husband, and discovered that he had been using narcotics. She referred him for help, and he underwent inpatient and outpatient treatment, reportedly without success. Mrs. Kenton claims Mr. Kenton was on probation for having had possession of marijuana, for which he had previously served eighteen months in jail. Mrs. Kenton said that, during the marriage, her husband had consorted with prostitutes. Mrs. Kenton stated that Mr. Kenton had told her that the paternal grandfather had beaten him "like a horse" when he was a child. She eventually separated from him in May 1985, when she discovered that he was having an affair with one of her friends. The divorce took place in February 1986.

Reportedly, between August and October 1986, Mr. Kenton picked his son up from a preschool on a number of occasions in order to bring him home. Mrs. Kenton noticed that the boy's underwear was wet on two occasions. The child commented on the size of his father's penis, and on one occasion Mrs. Kenton noticed "white stuff" escaping from the child's anus. Michael frequently asked to be bathed after seeing his father. He slept poorly, suffered from nightmares, became aggressive toward other children, and on one occasion made sexual sound effects in front of a preschool teacher. As a consequence, Mrs. Kenton stopped Michael from visiting his father. One month later, reportedly, Michael disclosed: "Do you know what Papa did to me? He put his thing (pointing to his genital) in my butt." He also said, "Papa gonna kill us if I told." The child showed the mother where his father had sodomized him ("Papa hurt my bottom near the trees"). On several occasions he noted, "Daddy will kill us."

Mrs. Kenton denies ever having taken illicit substances herself, aside from marijuana as a college student. She said that she seldom drank alcohol. After moving to (State) she obtained work as an accountant. She was in psychotherapy over a period of two years in (State) in order to deal with problems stemming from her marriage, but she has had no other mental health problems. Recently an intruder got into her bedroom holding a knife, but she screamed and he ran away. She has coped very well with the aftermath of this frightening event. Michael was unaware of the intruder at the time, but has learned about it since.

My contact with the child, Michael Kenton, during three one-hour interviews will now be presented. On all three occasions, Michael, an animated, husky young man of six years, separated readily from his mother and eagerly played with the toys (blocks, toy animals, toy cars and trucks) provided. Asked to draw something, he rendered a depiction of a ghost with knives who had been stabbed by a policeman in the abdomen and killed. Beside the ghost was a man bleeding from head wounds inflicted by the knife-wielding ghost. Michael then drew a man in Halloween costume, saying, "A car ran over him." Asked to draw a person, he produced a drawing of poor quality saying, "He is thinking about getting a son. He's gonna be a father. The father gets killed and is a ghost but is still a father." These figures were drawn in a distracted and careless manner.

Asked to draw his family, he depicted himself next to his mother. The following interchange took place:

INTERVIEWER: Is there anybody else in your family?

MICHAEL: All I've got is Mom.

INTERVIEWER: Where's you Dad?

MICHAEL: I don't have one. He's dead. Somebody broke into our house and killed him with a knife. He'd be a ghost if he came back.

Asked to draw a picture of his father, he depicted a man who had been stabbed and who was buried in a coffin in the ground. He said that he did not know who did it, but that "somebody broke into our house in (State). . . . He comes back—Mom sees him by herself when I am asleep. He comes out of the graveyard and does it. 'I'm always coming to you' (*said in a 'scary' voice*). He goes in and scares my Mom. He doesn't want to scare her. He wants to get back together and be a ghost. But Mom don't want to be dead. Momma told me he was dead."

At the initial interview, Michael was noted to have normal articulation and average language ability. He did not appear particularly hyperactive, but he was distractible and slapdash. His stories were poorly articulated and fragmentary, consisting mainly of desultory aggressive themes. He spoke of being the "strongest boy" in his class. ("Everybody punches me and I punch back. I win. One punch and they're down. I'm the leader. Mr. (_____) the teacher punched me and I punched him over on the desk.")

Toward the end of the interview, he went back to the story of his father's having died from stabbing and becoming a ghost: "A man broke in to get Mom's jewelry. Mom had a gun. The man threw the knife and stabbed him (the father) in the stomach. I was asleep." Asked again why he did not live with his father, he said, "Because my other father was bad. I got three fathers. Two are good and one was bad."

During the second interview, it was apparent that Michael was not inattentive if he was permitted to pursue his chosen interests. He was vocal and friendly, displaying an average vocabulary but poor graphic ability. The stories he produced concerned concatenated aggressive incidents rather than integrated themes. He began by enacting a series of scenes in which different animals attacked each other or human beings. During one of the altercations a deer "got" a goat in "a private spot" (he indicated the goat's anus). When asked about his "three fathers," he described them as: (1) his grandfather in (State); (2) his real father in (State); and (3) his father in (State). Asked to draw his real father, he colored in the outline of the man with black ink ("He's kinda dark") saying, "I don't like him; That's why I drew the down mouth."

When I asked him to draw what his real father did to him he said, "My pants weren't down—yes they were—they were down. It was in (State), inside a house, our house. Here's the thing he stuck—a little part of a man's arms that I broke off. It was blue. It was a play arm—off my toy. A blue toy arm he stuck in my bottom," and drew a yellow oval (representing his "bottom") inside which the "thing" had been "stuck."

Asked to illustrate what had happened, using adult male and child male anatomically explicit dolls, he showed the adult doll pushing a toy car into the anal region of the boy doll.

INTERVIEWER: What clothes did he have on?

MICHAEL: A short sleeve shirt, with rolled sleeves.

INTERVIEWER: What room was it in?

MICHAEL: My room.

INTERVIEWER: Where was Mommy?

MICHAEL: The same room. She beat him up. She wasn't there till she saw him sticking there! Then she stopped it.

INTERVIEWER: What did it feel like?

MICHAEL: Not good. It felt like a bad word.

INTERVIEWER: What bad word?

MICHAEL: Fuck! (Stamping the paper repeatedly with an ink-stamp.)

INTERVIEWER: Did it happen other times?

MICHAEL: Just one time. Case closed! (He indicated that he wanted to stop the interview at this point.)

Later, he stated that he did not like his father ("He's bad"). Asked if he would like to resume visits with his father, he said, "I wouldn't like. He'd hurt my Mom. He'd stay there at her home!"

INTERVIEWER: Would you like to see him?

MICHAEL: No! Not today!

INTERVIEWER: Would you like to see him tomorrow?

MICHAEL: No!

INTERVIEWER: What is "fuck"?

MICHAEL: Nobody is supposed to say it in front of my Mom . . . because she kicked my father out. She said—"Jerk, fuck."

INTERVIEWER: Why was your mother angry?

MICHAEL: Because he stuck a thing in my bottom in (State).

INTERVIEWER: Did it happen any other time?

MICHAEL: No. Mommy said, "One more time you mess up and I kick you out" and he did it. My Mommy she gets after me, gets mad, if I knock all my toys down. I got a chainsaw that cuts wood. Real cuttin'! It can chop anything. . . . I have picture of (father) and I shot at him.

INTERVIEWER: Are you angry?

MICHAEL: Real angry! I get army practice! I shot a lot of times!

INTERVIEWER: Why are you angry?

MICHAEL: I am angry because he stuck the thing in my bottom.

INTERVIEWER: What do you like about Daddy?

MICHAEL: Only the funny mustache. I called him "Jerk Ass." He said, "I'm gonna get you now, boy." I got this Chinese knife, a buck knife, and he has a play knife. He got the real little knife. . . . We fought and fought. I won, I knocked the sword out. I'm stronger than he is and he's weak. (He then drew a picture of the "weak father.") He's skinny in the arm. He lost his arm. He's got weak feet, a down mouth, he's crying and he's a dummy. Daddy was drunk and had a car accident.

The third and final interview was designed in order to terminate with the child. He spoke of school, played in an energetic and pleasurable way, making appropriate sound effects with fragmentary conversations. When asked why he had come to see me, he said: "I have problems at school. No other reason. I been bad—here today I been good. I was bad a long time ago. Johnny came—he kicked me and he punched me and I didn't tell the teacher. I kicked him."

I said that he had also come to see me in order to work out if he should visit with his father. He responded, "No. Because I don't like him. Because he did the thing I drew you last week . . . I wouldn't like. He'd hurt Mommy. Because he hurt her before. She yelled, 'Help!' because he was choking her, killing her. She's still alive. Daddy said, 'No way, Jose. I'm gonna chase her.' "

Asked if his father had done anything to him on any other occasion, he said, "No. I don't know. Oh yeah he did. He tried to do it. He hid the little man's arm. He had a knife ready for to do it, to hurt my bottom."

INTERVIEWER: Did he really?

MICHAEL: No. I found the knife and I stabbed him.

INTERVIEWER: Really?

MICHAEL: No. I just did this (making little stabbing movements). I barely stabbed him.

He then said that he wanted to see his chart, "because it has things in it that my father did to me." I reassured him that I would tell nobody about it except the judge. He said, "Okey dokey." The interview was terminated at this point.

In my interview with him on 11/12/89, Mr. Kenton presented in an intense, concerned manner. He said that he had not seen his son since May 1989. Despite the fact that he has written letters and sent presents, he has received no answer. He said that he had sent no child support ("What has that got to do with it? I have money deposited. I don't know where to send it. The court ordered me to pay child support and have visitation. I never got my right. I have $13,000.00 deposit in the bank for Michael.")

Mr. Kenton reported that his parents are alive and in good health. They separated in 1975 but are reported to be on good terms. Mr. Kenton, his father, and his brother work together in a family business. Mr. Kenton is the oldest of four children. All his siblings have been in good physical and mental health aside from a brother who had alcoholism (now recovered).

Mr. Kenton reported that his father, who had had a military background, emphasized discipline, which was "for the best."

Mr. Kenton reported that he completed elementary school, high school, and college education (four semesters) in (State). After leaving college, reportedly, he joined the family business.

Since his divorce from Mrs. Kenton, reportedly, Mr. Kenton has not remarried. He does not wish to marry again, but he lives with a girlfriend in (Town, State).

Mr. Kenton reported that he was in good general health. He denied having had psychiatric problems but admitted that he had had a serious difficulty with substance abuse between 1981 and 1986. In 1981 he spent eighteen months in prison for possession of marijuana. While in jail, he was introduced to narcotics. Following release from jail, he became a heavy user of narcotics, alcohol, and other drugs. However, after two years of treatment, in October 1986, he stopped using substances and reportedly has not used them since.

He met his future wife following his release from prison, and they lived together between February 1982 and May 1987. She fell pregnant in August 1983, and the couple married in December 1984, when the child was about three months of age. Reportedly, his wife wanted the marriage but he did not. ("I loved her, I cared for her, I gave her all she needed. Marriage is a piece of paper.") Mr. Kenton went on to say that he financed his wife's accounting business to the extent of $60,000.00, and gave her jewels, furs, trips, and a Mercedes Benz. However, reportedly, she failed in business and invented excuses, for example numerous body pains for which she used aspirin and smoked marijuana. Although he initially denied that his former wife had used "hard" drugs, he next said that she used cocaine and "crystal meth." He said that she was hostile to him, did not respect his attempt to rehabilitate himself from drugs, and was a poor housewife because she was often affected by drugs. Furthermore, although he himself was faithful to her, reportedly, she was not faithful to him. He also pointed out that although he and she separated initially in December 1986, she returned to live with him in February 1987, in spite of her allegations that he had sexually abused the child.

Reportedly, he learned of the first allegation in late 1986 when his brother asked him if he had ever molested Michael. He said that he had confronted the police and all the agencies to whom the complaint had been made. Reportedly, all agencies said that they found no proof that Michael had been sexually abused. When asked why his former wife would lie about him in such a malicious manner, he said his wife told many other lies during their relationship. Reportedly, she once told Mr. Kenton that Michael had told her that he (Mr. Kenton) had killed a dog in the Jacuzzi and had cleaned up the blood. Mr. Kenton also alleged that his former wife had a lesbian sister and that she had lived with "two gay guys" in (State). Furthermore, she once blamed him for lending her contraceptive diaphragm to another woman and was always ridiculously suspicious of him. On one occasion, reportedly, she alleged that another woman had altered all her clothing. He thought that she must be "mentally ill" and suffering from "hallucinations." Mr. Kenton also alleged that Mrs. Kenton had told him that her stepfather had "raped" her. On another occasion, reportedly, Mrs. Kenton said that she heard Michael (a three-month-old child) tell her, "Momma, give me the bottle." He went on to allege that there was nothing wrong with Michael (he was sure of this, even though he had not seen the child for two years) and that it is really his former wife who is "molesting the kid."

Reportedly, he does not want to take the child from his mother ("The child should stay with the mother"), but he wants his son to see him and his relatives. He said that he is saving child custody payments in order to support Michael in college. Asked why his wife appeared to hate him so much, he could only suggest that she was angry with herself because she had failed in business, and therefore displaced her anger onto him: "Addicts blame everyone but themselves. Addicts will do anything. She molests his (i.e., Michael's) brain." He added that Mrs. Kenton had made ridiculous claims that other members of his family had molested their children, and that his father had molested him.

When I discussed with him that his son currently showed evidence of emotional disorder, he denied that it could be so, stating that all that was required was for people to "treat (Michael) like a child."

Michael's paternal grandmother stated that she believed the allegation of sexual abuse made against her son was a lie. She described Mrs. Kenton as having been neglectful of her son, leaving him frequently in care of the father's family. The grandmother stated that Mrs. Kenton had said that her stepfather had "raped" her and that her mother (the maternal grandmother) had never cared for her.

Psychological Test Results

Psychological testing indicated a child of average intelligence with marked inattention, impulsivity, anxiety, and intensity of emotional expression. He appeared preoccupied with problems between his parents and alluded to having been sexually molested. The pattern of attention deficit and impulsivity was corroborated by school report.

DISCUSSION

From the psychological test results, the school reports, the mother's account of the child's behavior, and my observation of the child, it is apparent that Michael suffers from a psychiatric illness of moderate degree. The pattern of this illness is consistent with that of attention deficit disorder with an impulsive, aggressive component. In other words, he suffers from a syndrome of moderate severity characterized by poor concentration, distractibility, hyperactivity, impulsivity, and the tendency toward explosive aggressiveness. Moreover, there is evidence from psychological testing, from drawings, and from direct discussion with the child that Michael's emotionality, impulsivity, and aggressiveness are activated or aggravated by a remembrance of past sexual experiences, by exposure to violent scenes, by a continuing fear of confrontation and attack by the father, and by anxiety concerning the resumption of visitation with the father. These fears appear to have been exacerbated by the mother's recent encounter with an armed intruder (in August 1989), and by the child's disclosure to me of the sexual abuse which allegedly occurred in (State) prior to his coming to (State).

Michael said, very clearly, that he did not want to visit his father and that he was afraid his father might attack him or his mother. In fact, in his first interview with me, Michael depicted his father as stabbed to death and buried in a coffin. In subsequent interviews he expressed much hostility toward his father.

More than two years have passed since the alleged sexual abuse. Michael's remembrance of the abuse involves a single occasion during which an arm was broken off from a doll and inserted by the father into his anus. He made a vague allusion to a further occasion, involving a knife.

Alternative hypotheses which must be excluded are as follows:

1. The child is deluded.
2. The child is confabulating, or fabricating the story for an ulterior purpose.
3. The mother is deluded and has inadvertently indoctrinated the child with her own delusion.
4. The mother has fabricated the story and indoctrinated the child to tell it to me.
5. The child is telling the truth.

Psychotic delusions are virtually unknown in children of this age. Furthermore, the child has none of the characteristics of severe mental disorder that would be consistent with the diagnosis of a delusional condition.

Although children of this age are capable of telling lies, it would not be possible for a six-year-old child to fabricate a complex story of this kind and hold to it consistently. Complex, consistently held malicious fabrications are not likely until adolescence.

I found no evidence of severe mental disorder in the mother; thus the hypothesis that the mother is deluded can be dismissed.

If the mother had deliberately fabricated this story, I would have expected it to have been produced *in toto* at the time of the first allegation. The child would have displayed much less emotion, embarrassment, or shame about the allegation. I would not expect the allegation to have gone underground for more than two years and only now to be redisclosed in a piecemeal manner. The child's emotional disturbance is consistent with the allegation; and the child displayed appropriate emotions while telling me the story. Moreover, sexual abuse was both hinted at and directly alluded to during psychological testing.

Counterbalancing Mrs. Kenton's accusations, Mr. Kenton made serious allegations concerning his former wife. For example, he claimed that she was addicted to cocaine and methylamphetamine, that she was unfaithful to him, and that she was so mentally ill as to experience hallucinations (for example, that her baby could talk to her) and delusions (for example, that Mr. Kenton had had all her dresses altered to fit another woman). However, there was no evidence during my interviews with Mrs. Kenton of serious mental illness. Furthermore, I found unconvincing Mr. Kenton's explanation for why his former wife would make such serious accusations against him (that is, that she was angry and disappointed about her failure in business and had displaced the anger onto him).

In my opinion, alternative hypotheses concerning the sexual abuse allegations cannot be sustained; thus, the possibility that the sexual abuse took place cannot be dismissed.

SUMMARY AND RECOMMENDATIONS

Therefore, with reasonable medical certainty, I have reached the following conclusions:

1. There is clinical support for the allegation that the child has been sexually abused.
2. The child is adamant in not wishing to have visitation with his father.
3. The child suffers from a psychiatric disorder of moderate degree which has been aggravated by the fear of visitation from his father.
4. It is not possible to determine whether this psychiatric disorder was originally caused by the alleged sexual abuse; however, it has certainly been aggravated by unresolved conflict concerning sexual abuse.
5. If visitation with the father were to be resumed at this point, it is possible that the child could be psychologically harmed.

6. The child requires mental health treatment for the psychiatric disorder described above. The treatment required would involve weekly visits for a period of six to twelve months and would combine individual psychotherapy with parental counseling and, possibly, psychopharmacological treatment. The total cost of treatment would be $2,500–$5,000. I would recommend the following local child psychiatrists: (names and addresses).

7. I recommend that the advisability of paternal visitation be reevaluated in six months.

I declare under penalty of perjury according to the laws of the State of (_____) that the above is true and correct.

Case 6
Dispute over Custody on the Basis of Alleged Sexual Abuse

This report illustrates (1) the use of verbatim dialogue to convey the essence of the case, and (2) the way in which the "Discussion" section can weigh the pros and cons of alternative explanations for an allegation of sexual abuse.

CONFIDENTIAL
FORENSIC EVALUATION
Re: Jane Doe
Date of Birth: 1/11/77

CIRCUMSTANCES OF REFERRAL

The parents of the subject child, Jack Doe and June Doe, separated in 1983 and were subsequently divorced. Following the original divorce decree (in which custody of the child was awarded to the mother), there has been disputation concerning division of property and the right of the father to visit the child. Both mother and child have opposed the father's visitation.

In 1987 June Doe, Jane's mother, was found guilty of receiving stolen goods. She was incarcerated from February 1988 to April 1989. Prior to the mother's incarceration, Mr. Doe sought custody of the child, but Mrs. Doe and her daughter countered with an allegation that Mr. Doe had sexually abused Jane before the 1983 divorce. Mr. Doe was charged with aggravated sexual battery, a charge that was subsequently dropped because the statute of limitations was held to apply. During Mrs. Doe's incarceration, the Department of Human Services assumed custody of Jane and placed her with her maternal aunt and maternal grandmother. At present the Department of Human Services retains legal custody of the child, although she lives with her mother.

Mental health clinicians have differed as to the validity of Jane's allegations that she was sexually abused by her father. Jane continues to oppose visitation with her father.

PURPOSE OF EVALUATION

I have been asked to address the following questions:

1. Is Jane's story of sexual abuse credible?
2. What is the foundation for Jane's fear of visitation with her father?
3. Is it in Jane's best interest that visitation with her father be resumed?

INFORMED CONSENT

Prior to undertaking the examination, I explained to Mrs. Doe that the evaluation was for legal, not therapeutic, purposes and that anything she or her daughter told me might be included in a report for the court.

DOCUMENTS REVIEWED

1. Deposition of Belinda Smith, Ed.D., in the Chancery Court for Franklin County, Tennessee, dated 4/4/85
2. Motion to rescind final decree and grant new trial, dated September 1986, unsigned
3. Affidavit exhibit A, dated September 1986, unsigned
4. Order in the Chancery Court of Franklin County, Tennessee, undated (1986), unsigned
5. Report to Mr. Nelson Layne, attorney at law, from Belinda Smith, Ed.D., 10/8/87
6. "Statement in the matter of Jane Doe," signature indecipherable, dated 12/17/87
7. Petition for Temporary Custody of a Child, signed June Doe and Kathy Smith, dated 12/31/87
8. Order in the Chancery Court of Franklin County, Tennessee, signed L. F. Stirling, dated 9/2/88
9. Default judgment in the Chancery Court of Franklin County, Tennessee, signed Ed Packett, dated 6/21/88
10. Custody Order in the Chancery Court of Franklin County, Tennessee, signed L. F. Stirling, dated 6/21/88
11. Verbatim interview between Jane Doe and "Carol," dated 6/24/88, unsigned
12. Verbatim interview between Jane Doe and "Vicki Meckla," dated 12/18/87, unsigned
13. Tennessee School Achievement Testing Program, Stanford Achievement Test on Jane Doe, dated April 1988
14. Report to Judge H. Edwards, from B. James and S. Childers, concerning Jane Doe, dated 7/12/88
15. Verbatim interview between Jane Doe, C. Jimson, and S. Childers, dated 7/2/88, unsigned
16. Letter to Hon. Ed Packett concerning Jane Doe, signed L. F. Stirling, dated 7/1/88

17. Confidential court report to the Hon. L. F. Stirling concerning Jane Doe, prepared by C. Jimson, dated 8/22/88
18. Letter to Judge Stirling from Jane Doe, undated, signed "Jane"
19. Letter to Mr. B. James re: Jane Doe, signed Belinda Smith, Ed.D., dated 11/21/88
20. Letter to S. Childers re: Jane Doe, signed S. Teilor, M.A., dated 2/6/89
21. Report to S. Childers re: Jane Doe, signed Belinda Smith, Ed.D., dated 2/3/89
22. Letter to S. Childers re: Jane Doe, signed B. Thompson, M.S.W., dated 6/28/89

INTERVIEWS

1. Two interviews with Mrs. June Doe, 8/4/89 and 8/9/89 (each of 1 hour)
2. Two interviews with Jane Doe, 8/4/89 and 8/9/89 (each of 1 hour)

PSYCHOLOGICAL TESTING

Child behavior checklist concerning Jane Doe, completed by Mrs. June Doe, dated 8/4/89.

INTERVIEW WITH MRS. JUNE DOE

In my first interview with her, Mrs. Doe explained that, since she was released from prison (April 1989), Jane has lived with her, pending reversion of custody to her from the Department of Human Services. She stated that she filed for divorce from Mr. Doe in October 1983 and that the final decree was issued in December 1983. She said that she had filed for divorce as soon as Jane told her that her father had sexually abused her. This revelation, reportedly, followed a history of physical abuse by her former husband toward herself and her two sons.

In her initial revelation of sexual abuse to her mother, reportedly, Jane said that her father had touched her "pooh-pooh" (family name for "vagina"). Mrs. Doe said that she confronted her husband with this accusation and that he denied it. Reportedly, Jane subsequently revealed that sexual contact had occurred on more than one occasion, and specifically that her father had "rubbed her pooh-pooh" and made her "touch his pee-pee." At this point, the mother allegedly became convinced that Jane had not fabricated the story, and filed for divorce. She said that her husband had agreed to the divorce provided that he would not be charged with sexual molestation.

Following the divorce, in late 1984, Mr. Doe is reported to have become abusive to Mrs. Doe. On one occasion, reportedly, he stormed through the house looking for Jane. According to Mrs. Doe, Mr. Doe has at various times filed for visitation rights, denied that he consented to the divorce, and sought custody of Jane. In 1985 he was awarded six visitations, to be supervised by a clergyman. During these scheduled visitations, either Jane told her father that she did not wish to see him or refused to see him, or he failed to show up. Reportedly, in the five years following the divorce, Mr. Doe has sent his daughter no letters, no birthday presents, no Christmas presents, and no cards, and made no personal telephone calls.

Mrs. Doe stated that Jane has no current behavior problems. She is in grade seven at school and progressing well. Her ambition is to be a model. When younger, reportedly, she would "hit the floorboards" if a car like her father's passed by. If she saw her father, she would "turn pale." On one occasion she asked for a "bodyguard" lest he kidnap her. However, she has no nightmares and appears to have had no "flashbacks" involving unhappy memories.

INTERVIEW WITH JANE DOE

In my first interview with Jane, we discussed neutral topics. She was aware that I was interviewing her in order to assess whether visitation was advisable between her and her father (whom she spontaneously described as "stupid").

She said that she was progressing well in school. Her ambition is to be a model. She has numerous friends, no enemies, but no boyfriend. She enjoys reading, movies, hobbies, and country music.

She said that her parents were divorced in 1983. While they lived together, reportedly, screaming and fighting involved all members of the family. "Daddy picked on all of us. . . . He'd whip us all—for watching TV. He whipped us with a belt, saying 'Never turn the TV on without permission.' " Reportedly, he choked Mrs. Doe on one occasion, and "started bustin' on her."

Jane remembers having seen her father on one occasion since the divorce. On at least two other occasions, she said, he did not show up for a scheduled visitation. On more than one occasion she has point blank refused to see her father at the time of scheduled visitation. In her words, "I've tried to put it in the past."

She described her father in these terms: "Short, skinny, with brown hair and a mustache. Not handsome. The eyes glow like wild or crazy." Asked what she would do if visitation were ordered, she said: "I'd say I am not going to go." She would say this "because of the mean things that he did . . . because (she) is scared of him," and "because there is no telling what he might do." At this point, she described how, on one occasion, he chased her through their trailer. ("I hid from him. I was under the dresser. He grabbed me".)

She said that she did not know why her mother had been put in jail and did not want to know, because "I think it might be bad." Now that her mother is home with her it is "no different from before." She described her mother as affectionate and nonpunitive.

In my second interview with Jane, she said that, about three years ago, when she attended a scheduled visitation with her father, "I tried my best to ignore him. I focused on something else. He'd just set there." At those times, she felt "weird . . . I'd rather be somewhere else doing something else." Reportedly, her father stared for thirty minutes in silence, then threw a fit, cursed the pastor who was supervising the visit, and departed. She said she did not know why he was angry. With regard to the "weird" feeling (see above), she spoke of wanting to go home and not wanting even to look at her father. She remembered trying to block out feelings of fear when her father lived with the family and became angry. She said that remembrances of bad times returned to her "when I talk to you and when I see him." She reported that her father slapped her and her brothers and whipped them for playing in the backyard and watching TV. Asked if there was any other reason why she did not want to live with her father, she admitted that there was, but said that she did not really want to talk about it. She requested that I ask specific questions of her; but I explained that it would be preferable she should tell me the story in her own words. The following interchange then took place:

INTERVIEWER: When did the trouble begin?

JANE: He told Mike and Shannon (her brothers) to stay outside when my mother went shopping. He carried me to the bedroom. He forced me to come. He got my arm and jerked me. This was the first time. He said not to tell Mama or he would kill Mama or me or do whatever he had to.

INTERVIEWER: What happened then?

JANE: He pushed me on the bed, took my clothes off, started doing things that I did not want him to do. He took off all my clothes, and took off all his clothes, as far as I remember.

INTERVIEWER: When did this happen?

JANE: In the afternoon, one o'clock or two o'clock.

INTERVIEWER: Where did this happen?

JANE: In his bedroom—his and Mama's.

INTERVIEWER: What kind of bed was it?

JANE: A queen or a kingsize bed.

INTERVIEWER: Whose clothes came off first?

JANE: I think he took off mine.

INTERVIEWER: What happened then?

JANE: He forced me on the bed, he got on the bed and just . . .

INTERVIEWER: What happened then?

JANE: (no answer)

At this point the interviewer reemphasized the need for Jane to tell the story in her own words, even though she wanted him to ask questions of her.

INTERVIEWER: What did he do next?

JANE: He starts feeling me. He touched my private parts.

INTERVIEWER: Where are your private parts?

JANE: Below my belt and my breasts (she points to them).

INTERVIEWER: Do you mean your belly-button?

JANE: No.

INTERVIEWER: Can you give me the name of the female private part?

JANE: I don't know. That is where he touched me.

INTERVIEWER: Was he rough or gentle?

JANE: Rough.

INTERVIEWER: Did he touch you on the inside or the outside?

JANE: He touched me on the outside and put his finger on the inside.

INTERVIEWER: How did it feel?

JANE: It hurt.

INTERVIEWER: Did it cause you any injury?

JANE: No.

INTERVIEWER: What happened afterward?

JANE: It continued for one hour, putting his hands on my private part and touching my breasts.

INTERVIEWER: Did he do anything else?

JANE: He rolled around on top of me.

INTERVIEWER: What was he doing?

JANE: He grabbed me close to him and we rolled around a couple of times.

INTERVIEWER: What about his private part?

JANE: He made me feel it. He grabbed my arm and stuck it down there.

INTERVIEWER: Did anything happen to his private part?

JANE: It was bouncing around and then it got stiffer.

INTERVIEWER: Did anything come out of his private part?

JANE: No.

INTERVIEWER: Did he ever try to put his private part inside yours?

JANE: No.

INTERVIEWER: Did he talk during this?

JANE: He told me to shut up.

INTERVIEWER: Did he strike you?

JANE: He slapped me.

INTERVIEWER: How did it end up?

JANE: He got up and told me to put my clothes on.

Jane went on to say that there was another occasion upon which she was sexually abused. Reportedly, on the second occasion, events took place in a different order.

INTERVIEWER: Was it as long on the second occasion?

JANE: Shorter.

INTERVIEWER: Did he say anything?

JANE: Not to tell anyone or else he would kill me and Mama.

INTERVIEWER: How did you feel during this?

JANE: Scared.

INTERVIEWER: How do you feel now?

JANE: Scared and disgusted.

INTERVIEWER: Why disgusted?

JANE: I am mad. He shouldn't have done that. He is my father. It's just wrong.

INTERVIEWER: Why is it wrong?

JANE: Because I am his kid.

INTERVIEWER: Has your Mom given you any education about sex? About its purpose, what it is for?

JANE: Only in school, a little bit.

INTERVIEWER: Have you had your first period?

JANE: No. Mom's told me a little bit.

INTERVIEWER: Do you feel ready for it?

JANE: Not really.

INTERVIEWER: How do you feel about growing up?

JANE: I'd rather stay in high school.

INTERVIEWER: Do you want to get married and have kids?

JANE: I love kids, but I don't want to get married.

INTERVIEWER: What do you think about sex between boys and girls?

JANE: I don't think they should do it until they get married.

INTERVIEWER: Do you worry what your sexual life will be like?

JANE: I try not to think about it.

INTERVIEWER: What made you decide to tell your mother?

JANE: Someone at school, my best friend told me that men shouldn't do that kind of stuff to kids. A few weeks later I told my mother about what my father had done.

INTERVIEWER: Did you think it was your fault?

JANE: Sometimes, but then I thought it was just him, that he was mad at me. Now I think it is just *him*.

INTERVIEWER: Do you ever ask yourself why he did it?

JANE: He was mad and just thought it was me.

INTERVIEWER: Was he drunk when he did it?

JANE: No.

INTERVIEWER: Can you remember anything else about the room where it happened?

JANE: It had an air conditioner above the bed. The bed was made. He pulled the covers down. We layed on top of the bed. He pulled the blankets down and then just layed on the pillows.

INTERVIEWER: Where were your brothers?

JANE: Outside or in the mountains.

INTERVIEWER: Did anything else ever happen like that, that was upsetting or frightening?

JANE: When he whipped me.

INTERVIEWER: Can you tell us what happened when he chased you in the trailer?

JANE: When I saw Jack (i.e., the father), I hid underneath the desk and pulled the stool back. Under it I got as tight as I could and stayed there. He looked there; the last place was the desk. He pulled me by the hair and threw me on the bed. Mama was crying. I was crying and rolled up into a little ball. That is all I remember.

INTERVIEWER: What was he mad at?

JANE: He couldn't find me.

INTERVIEWER: Why was he there?

JANE: They were divorced. He was unwelcome.

INTERVIEWER: Maybe he missed his family.

JANE: No. He was mad.

INTERVIEWER: Do you remember any nice times with your dad?

JANE: No.

INTERVIEWER: Not one?

JANE: He would be gone on the truck.

INTERVIEWER: Did he give you any birthday or Christmas presents?

JANE:	I can't remember. When I was at Granny's, he and his mother came at Christmas time. I hid behind the stove. He had something then.
INTERVIEWER:	What is the difference between imagination and the truth?
JANE:	Imagination is staring into space, thinking. Things that are real are always there.
INTERVIEWER:	Maybe you're just angry with him and made it up.
JANE:	I wish he *would* get into trouble. I didn't make this up. If I did, I wouldn't want him to get into trouble.
INTERVIEWER:	Could it be that your Mom is angry and convinced you to make up the story?
JANE:	No. She only tells me to tell the truth. She would ask me every night if I wanted to see Jack. I'd say no and I would get mad at her for always asking.
INTERVIEWER:	Do you ever miss him at all? Even for a second?
JANE:	No.

Jane Doe is an attractive preadolescent female of at least average intelligence. Although initially reluctant to speak of private matters, during the second interview she was induced to speak relatively freely about the alleged sexual abuse. Her description of these matters involved a mixture of anger and embarrassment. Aside from at those times, she was not depressed or anxious, and her modulation of affect was normal. There was no disorganization of thinking, and no evidence of other psychiatric symptomatology.

RESULTS OF PSYCHOLOGICAL TESTING

On the Child Behavior Checklist, Mrs. Doe reported Jane to have average social competence and virtually no psychological symptomatology. The almost complete absence of all symptoms suggests that Mrs. Doe is presenting Jane in the best possible light. School achievement testing (April 1988) reveals satisfactory to above average academic achievement.

INTERVIEW WITH FATHER

I asked Mr. Childers to ask Mr. Doe if he would agree to being interviewed by me. Mr. Childers reported that, despite repeated attempts to contact the father, he was not able to do so.

REVIEW OF DOCUMENTS

I did not review any documents until after I had interviewed Jane Doe and her mother. In this section I report only those matters of direct relevance to the questions to be addressed by this evaluation.

In her deposition of 4/4/84, Dr. Smith alludes to Jane Doe's fear of her father ("I love him, but he is not my friend"), the father's alleged physical abuse of her siblings and her mother, and her fear that the father would hurt her or kidnap her from her mother. There is no indication in the deposition that Dr. Smith questioned Jane concerning sexual abuse. In the psychological test questionnaire filled out by Mrs. Doe concerning Jane, there is a suggestion that (as with the Child Behavior Checklist of 8/4/89) Mrs. Doe is exaggerating Jane's lack of psychological symptomatology.

In her report of 10/8/87, Dr. Smith stated that Jane had alleged that her father had attempted to touch her sexually when she was about five years of age. In a subsequent report (2/3/89), Dr. Smith gives the following reasons for disbelieving Jane's accusations of sex abuse against Mr. Doe:

1. Mr. Doe would have risked serious legal sanctions if he had sexually abused his daughter.
2. Mr. Doe has spent thousands of dollars in an effort to have visitation with his child.
3. Jane delayed reporting the alleged sexual abuse until a time when her mother was facing incarceration and the father was seeking custody.

The interview between Vicki Neckla and Jane Doe (dated 12/18/87) is generally consistent with Jane's report to me of the alleged sexual abuse. Several other reports corroborate Jane's extreme resistance to attending visitations scheduled with her father.

DISCUSSION OF FINDINGS

The following alternative hypotheses must be examined in this case:

1. The subject child is deluded.
2. The child is confabulating or fabricating sexual abuse for histrionic or malicious reasons.
3. The subject child has been indoctrinated by somebody else, possibly the mother, to falsely report sexual abuse.
4. The child's allegations are credible.

The first hypothesis can be dismissed. Delusions occur in two settings: (1) childhood psychosis or (2) when there is a psychotic delusion in a parent or caretaker that has been subsequently conveyed to the child. Neither Mrs. Doe nor Jane shows evidence of psychosis.

Confabulation is most likely to occur in an adolescent of histrionic or borderline personality who seeks the center of the stage for psychopathological reasons. There was no evidence, from the mother's description of the child or from my observation of the child, to indicate a personality disorder of this type and magnitude. On the contrary, aside from being fearful of forced visitation with her father, the subject child appears to be a psychologically normal preadolescent.

Fabrication is most likely to occur in a child of sociopathic or histrionic character, motivated by the desire for revenge or escape. Either or both these motives are conceivably present in this case; however, there is no evidence in Jane of the kind of histrionic or sociopathic personality which would be consistent with such extreme, malicious mischief-making.

The third hypothesis gives the greatest concern. Could Mrs. Doe have indoctrinated the child to falsify an allegation of sexual abuse? As Dr. Smith points out, formal allegations of sexual abuse were not made until the custody dispute arose. Dr. Smith stresses this, together with the four-year delay before the child reported the alleged sexual abuse. On the other hand, if the mother's report to me is correct, Jane initially reported sexual abuse in 1983, and, since the father initially agreed to the divorce, there was no need for the mother to lay charges against him. Dr. Smith's first-stated reason for disbelieving Jane's allegations—that Mr. Doe would have realized that he would run the risk of legal sanctions—carries little weight. If fear of apprehension were a valid consideration, few potential offenders would ever offend. Similarly, the assertion that the father has expended a lot of money in order to win custody or visitation carries little weight; sexual abuse and affection are not necessarily mutually exclusive.

Supporting the validity of the child's report to me and to others are the following factors:

1. The child's account of the alleged sexual abuse has remained relatively consistent over time.
2. The child's account to me of the alleged sexual abuse is internally consistent and contains no grossly improbable details.
3. The child gives incidental details of the alleged incident (for example, the air conditioner, the position of the coverlet, blankets, and pillows, and the father's conversation with her after the sexual abuse).
4. The child was initially reluctant to speak about the sexual abuse but was eventually able to do so without excessive use of leading questions on my part.
5. The child's affect during her recounting of the alleged sexual abuse was a mixture of embarrassment, anger, and disgust—a confused emotional state consistent with a valid account.

For the above reasons, I consider the child's account of the alleged sexual abuse to be internally consistent.

If the child's allegation of sexual abuse is valid, and if her remembrances of physical and emotional abuse toward her family by the father can be believed, I consider it would be psychologically harmful to the child to insist on further visitation. Even if the above allegations are not true, Jane's resistance to her father is so extreme that it would be fruitless to insist that they be reunited. One can only hope that, with maturity, the child will gain a broader perspective on what has happened.

OPINION

With reasonable medical certainty, I have reached the following conclusions:

1. The credibility of Jane Doe's allegations of physical and sexual abuse concerning her father is supported by their internal consistency, richness of detail, spontaneity, and consistency over time, together with the appropriateness of her affect as she reports the alleged abuse. Furthermore, there is no evidence to support hypotheses that the child is deluded, confabulating, lying, or indoctrinated by another person.
2. The subject child would be harmed by forced visitation with her father.
3. Visitation with her father should cease until such time as the subject child decides that she wishes it to resume.

Case 7
Forensic Evaluation of a Case Alleging Psychological
Injury Following a Motor Vehicle Accident

This report illustrates the use of depositions, medical documentation, psychological testing, and direct interviewing to counter another mental health clinician's forensic evaluation (which found evidence for severe mental disturbance). The presence of posttraumatic stress disorder, in particular, is in contention. The question is addressed by reviewing documents and depositions, interviewing the child in question and his mother, conducting a structured interview of the child and his mother with regard to posttraumatic stress disorder, and asking an unbiased clinical psychologist to test the child with the diagnosis of posttraumatic stress disorder in mind.

CONFIDENTIAL
FORENSIC EVALUATION
Re: Steven Soutar
Date of Birth: 6/3/81

CIRCUMSTANCES OF REFERRAL

On 3/9/89 Steven Soutar was a passenger in an automobile driven by his father, William Soutar, when the automobile was rear-ended by a semitrailer. Steven sustained a fracture of the left femur, which required him to be admitted to Metropolitan Hospital for a period of two months. On 4/6/89 he was removed from traction and placed in a spica cast. He was discharged home on 4/11/89 in stable condition and was treated as an outpatient. By July 1989 he was walking with a crutch. When examined on 4/22/90 he had no significant pain and was normally active; there was no appreciable inequality of the length of his legs; he had full motion of the hip and knee, but there was some residual wasting of the thigh. X-rays of the left femur showed excellent position and alignment of the fracture.

PURPOSE OF REFERRAL

To ascertain whether Steven Soutar has sustained psychological injury as a result of the accident described above, to determine the nature and extent of such injury, if any, and to recommend the type and extent of treatment required for it.

QUALIFICATIONS

My *curriculum vitae* is appended to this report.

INFORMED CONSENT

Mrs. Soutar, Steven's mother, was informed (and indicated that she understood) that evaluation was for legal, not therapeutic purposes, and that her observations to me might be included in a report to the court.

SOURCES OF DATA

Documents

I reviewed the following documents: discharge summary and medical record containing Steven Soutar's hospitalization at Metropolitan Hospital (3/9/89–4/10/89); report from (orthopedic surgeon), M.D., Metropolitan Surgical Group, Ltd. (7/26/90); follow-up records of the Metropolitan Surgical Group concerning Steven Soutar (4/30/89–11/18/89); report of psychological evaluation of Steven Soutar performed by Rose Schmidt, Ph.D. (4/3/91); deposition of Steven Soutar (4/6/91); deposition of William Soutar (4/6/91).

Interviews

In the course of the evaluation I undertook the following interviews: Mrs. Jessie Soutar (5/1/91, one and one-half hours); Steven Soutar (5/1/91, one and one-half hours). During these interviews, I administered a structured interview for adolescent post-traumatic stress disorder to both Steven and his mother (concerning Steven).

Psychological Testing

Psychological evaluation of Steven Soutar was undertaken by John Shand, Ph.D., on 5/1/91. Dr. Shand conducted his evaluation prior to my interviewing Steven and his mother.

FINDINGS

Review of Documents

The medical records concern the treatment and healing of a left femoral trochanteric fracture. They are summarized above.

The psychological evaluation conducted by Dr. Schmidt diagnosed Steven as suffering from posttraumatic stress disorder and dysthymia. Recommendations were made that Steven be referred for intensive individual psychotherapy and that the family receive family psychotherapy.

The deposition of Steven Soutar indicates that, although he is restricted from contact sports, Steven has no problems with his left leg at present. He denied having nightmares related to the accident but admitted being afraid of tractor-trailer trucks when in a motor vehicle driven by his mother.

Mr. Soutar, on being deposed, described the accident in detail, including the difficult two-hour extraction of Steven from the wrecked automobile. He reported that currently Steven has no problem with his left leg, other than stiffness. He said that Steven had a few nightmares in the aftermath of the accident, but these have completely subsided. He considered that his son had made a full and complete recovery. He reported that, in the ten to eleven days following the accident, his wife suffered from nausea and vomiting, after having sustained a hit on the head during the accident. Subsequent to the accident, his wife tends to become fearful when driving a vehicle in the vicinity of a truck. Other than that, reportedly, she has no psychological problems. Neither he nor his wife has sought psychological counseling for themselves or for Steven.

Interviews

Steven, a husky nine-year-old, appeared to be of above-average intelligence. Although initially somewhat jaded, apparently as a result of the flight from Illinois, he soon warmed to the examiner and related in an animated way. In my opinion, he was a reliable historian.

He began by describing the accident on 4/6/89. He remembered being in the back seat of the family automobile, and then waking in the car wreck with his feet bent and his left leg twisted and jammed behind the back seat of the car. He remembered no pain at first—more disorientation and anxiety. He did not know what was happening and, in fact, did not appreciate that he had been in a car wreck until he was taken to the hospital. He remembered the top of a car being removed, and that he was afraid as a blowtorch and "the jaws of life" were used to free his trapped leg. He remembered being afraid that he might die and asking his father: "Are we in hell, Dad?" He remembered wondering if he were in a dream and being reassured when one of his rescuers said: "You'll be okay, Steve."

He described his six-week hospitalization as "painful and boring," yet he was seldom scared, because he "knew what to expect." The last four weeks of the hospitalization were less boring, because he was able to use the hospital playroom. He remembered that his mother was nauseated and disoriented for approximately a week after the accident.

Steven described his recovery, following discharge from Metropolitan Hospital, as slow but steady and involving little pain. He was in a body cast for about two months, then on crutches, and then in a walker for about two weeks. He denied having feelings of frustration, fear, or nightmares. Currently, reportedly, he is allowed to engage in any activity except football. He said that in March 1991 he sustained a fracture of the right clavicle as a result of a fall while playing basketball. The same clavicle had been fractured previously when he was four years of age. He reported that currently he is not nervous except, while riding, when large trucks are close to the family automobile. He said that he is achieving a mixture of A's and C's at school, and that his school results did not deteriorate after the accident. He described age-appropriate recreational pursuits and friendships.

During the structured interview for posttraumatic stress disorder, Steven described no other single-event traumata apart from a minor dog bite (aged four years), several minor accidents, and the recent death of a school friend (as the result of a car accident). He reported that "occasionally" he had flashbacks to the accident when injuries of other children reminded him of his own experience. He denied nightmares, however, and denied ever acting or feeling as though the accident were recurring. He remembered feeling startled on one occasion when he heard the air brakes of a big truck. He remembered being upset when a school friend died as the result of a car accident. He said that, in order to escape thoughts or feelings about the event, he "thinks of something else." He remembered on one occasion trying to avoid thinking about a truck that was driving behind the family car. He denied any amnesia for the event (other than a few seconds before and after the impact), and denied loss of interest, feelings of detachment or estrangement, restricted range of affect, or the sense of having a foreshortened future. Other than the dreams already described, he denied insomnia, sudden wakening, inability to return to sleep after wakening, irritability, poor concentration, hypervigilance, or frequent startling. As described above, reminders of the event have occasionally caused him anxiety.

Mrs. Soutar gave the impression of being a reliable historian, neither exaggerating nor minimizing the effects of the accident. She recalled returning to consciousness herself approximately three hours after the accident. However, for ten to eleven days following the accident, she suffered from nausea, vomiting, and spatial disorientation. She reported that she is still afraid of trucks and accidents. At first, following the accident, she suffered from nightmares, but she seldom has nightmares now. She occasionally has restless sleep. Sometimes she worries that her life could be short. She denied flashbacks concerning the accident, depression, poor impulse control, loss of enjoyment, or restriction of activities. From time to time, admittedly, she feels "overtaxed."

She said she works as an administrative secretary at the (_____) Corporation, where her husband also works as a draftsman. She reported that she and her husband have been happily married for fifteen years.

She denied that Steven had deteriorated at school since the accident. However, he needs close attention and encouragement in his school work, for he is not an independent student. Mrs. Soutar reported that, since the accident, Steven has become more cautious, fears injury, and is something of a "back seat driver." As a result of underactivity, he has gained approximately 15 pounds since the accident.

During a structured interview for posttraumatic stress disorder administered concerning Steven, Mrs. Soutar confirmed Steven's account of his upset as a result of the recent death of a friend in a motor vehicle accident. She reported that, following the 1989 accident, Steven had recurrent dreams of being hit and of attempting to escape from a wreck. These dreams, which occurred approximately three times a week for several months, have now ceased. She denied that currently he actually feels as if the event were recurring. At times, however, he will show some distress, for example, when an airplane in which he is flying hits a pocket of air turbulence. So far as she knew, Steven did not try to avoid thinking about the accident; however, he would rather fly than drive and prefers to avoid expressways. So far as she knew, he had no amnesia for the event and had had no loss of interest, emotional detachment, restriction of affect, or sense of a foreshortened future, since the accident. She denied that, since the accident, he had exhibited sleep disturbance (other than initial nightmares). Since the accident, he has been slightly more irritable when frustrated. She denied that his concentration was impaired and said that he is hypervigilant only when reminded of the event, for example, if a truck comes too close to the motor vehicle in which he is riding.

Psychological Test Results

Psychological testing suggests that, aside from a situation-specific concern about future accidents, Steven is a generally well-adapted child devoid of significant psychopathology. Specifically, he showed no evidence on testing of the psychological "reexperiencing" required for the diagnosis of posttraumatic stress disorder. However, he perceived some difficulty with school work and was self-critical on that account. No evidence was elicited of clinically significant depression.

DISCUSSION OF FINDINGS

No evidence of posttraumatic stress disorder was elicited during the depositions of Steven Soutar and his father, by my interview with Steven Soutar and his mother, by structured interviews concerning posttraumatic stress disorder undertaken with Steven Soutar and his mother, or in the psychological testing of Steven Soutar. Steven does show mild situation-specific anxiety concerning trucks and expressways, and mild anxiety on being reminded of the accident (e.g., by the death of a friend). He has also been somewhat more cautious since the accident and has gained some weight as a result of enforced restriction of activity.

The above residual symptoms are to be expected following an event of this magnitude. On the other hand, Steven has been managed well medically, and his family has coped exceptionally well with his injury. The family is a stable one, and the marital relationship is close. There was a hint of some contagion of anxiety between mother and son when the mother is driving. This would not appear to be of serious magnitude. Steven appears to have some difficulty concentrating in school, but this problem, reportedly, antedated the accident.

OPINION

My opinion, with reasonable medical certainty, is as follows:

1. Steven Soutar does not currently suffer from posttraumatic stress disorder or dysthymia.
2. Although he suffered from anxiety dreams in the first months following the accident, these symptoms have largely subsided.
3. Aside from situation-specific fears, he has recovered psychologically from the emotional trauma of the accident.

RECOMMENDATIONS

In view of his continuing emotional recovery and his excellent management by his parents, I do not recommend that Steven or the family seek treatment for psychological disturbance.

Case 8
Forensic Evaluation of a Boy Severely Bitten by a Dog
in Regard to Alleged Psychological Injury

This case illustrates the complex interaction between an anxious mother, herself burdened by life stress and past injury, and a traumatized child.

CONFIDENTIAL
FORENSIC REPORT
Re: Victor Rogers
Date of Birth: 8/28/76

CIRCUMSTANCES OF REFERRAL

On July 29, 1984, I was asked by Evelyn V. Smith, attorney, to evaluate Victor Rogers. The office of Smith & Smith, as attorneys for the General Insurance Company of

America, is defending a suit brought by the boy and his parents against a neighbor whose dog allegedly bit the boy on the leg on February 8, 1982. The parents allege that the child suffered, and continues to suffer, emotional problems as a result of the psychologically traumatic incident.

PURPOSE OF EVALUATION

1. To determine whether Victor Rogers suffers from psychological disorder or impairment.
2. To determine whether, if present, the disorder or impairment was wholly or partly caused by the traumatic incident.
3. To estimate the cost of treatment required to remedy the disorder or impairment.

QUALIFICATIONS

My *curriculum vitae* is appended.

INFORMED CONSENT

Prior to my interviews with them and Victor, I indicated to the parents that the evaluation was for legal, not therapeutic, purposes and that what they and Victor told me might be included in a report for the court. They said that they understood and wished the interview to continue.

SOURCES OF DATA

Documents Reviewed

Listed here with date and name of signatory: The emergency room, medical, psychiatric, and speech and language evaluation of the above child, conducted after the alleged trauma, and the school progress, educational evaluation, and special education team reports prior to and subsequent to the alleged trauma.

INTERVIEWS

1. On 9/16/84, I interviewed Mr. Ronald and Mrs. Elaine Rogers for a period of one and one-half hours.
2. On 10/3/84, I interviewed Victor Rogers for a period of two hours.

Psychological Testing

Testing was undertaken by (psychologist), Ph.D., on 10/4/83.

FINDINGS

Review of Documents

The medical reports from Drs. X and Y indicate that Victor sustained an injury of the lower left leg, consistent with a dog bite, and that this injury subsequently became infected.

Dr. Z's reports concerning Victor Rogers and his mother indicate that, since 1983, Victor has suffered from a chronic stress disorder for which Dr. Z estimated he would require three to five years of further treatment. Dr. Z also stated that Mrs.. Rogers had been physically injured and emotionally affected by an automobile accident and that she was emotionally disturbed by the attack on her child. He described Mrs. Rogers as depressed, withdrawn, fearful, and subject to suicidal ideation. He diagnosed her as suffering from chronic post-stress disorder together with generalized anxiety, dysthymic disorder, and dependent personality disorder. Dr. Z expanded upon his evaluation in a subsequent report (dated 2/20/84), describing the mother's condition in 1983 as having involved nervousness, palpitations, shortness of breath, nausea, irritability, apprehensiveness, multiple fears, and, eventually, loss of appetite and sleep, withdrawal, hostility, and suicidal ideation. At that time (2/20/84), Victor was being seen on a weekly basis by Dr. Z and, although he was regarded as showing improvement, was still at times disruptive in school.

The psychological evaluation undertaken by Dr. (psychologist) on 5/1/82 and 5/6/82 described Victor as friendly and cooperative but subject to fatigue and apprehension during testing. Intelligence testing indicated average intelligence. Victor's short-term auditory memory was depressed, but no other evidence of neuropsychological impairment was detected. Personality testing revealed a picture of a fearful, insecure, oppositional child with inadequate emotional controls. Low self-esteem, depression, and anxiety of phobic quality were described. Dr. (psychologist) diagnosed chronic posttraumatic stress disorder.

In April 1984, two months after the dogbite, the Department of Special Services of the (_____) School System undertook a speech, hearing, language, and education evaluation of Victor Rogers, since retention in Grade 2 was being considered. The evaluation report depicted Victor as an anxious child distressed when asked to respond orally in class. Victor's classroom performance was described as inconsistent. Hearing and vision problems were apparent during kindergarten and first grade. These problems were subsequently corrected without improvement in the child's school performance. During the testing of March 1984, Victor was initially cooperative but required much encouragement and praise in order to ensure his concentration on tasks. His general information was deficient. Educational testing revealed underachievement in reading, arithmetic, and spelling. His visual memory, auditory discrimination, and recall of lowercase letters were below age- and grade-level expectations. He also had deficiencies in auditory processing, visual and auditory association, and auditory memory.

No conclusion was reached as to the specific cause of Victor's learning problems.

Interviews

As I was particularly interested to determine if Victor's school performance had deteriorated after the dogbite, I asked the parents to gather information from the schools Victor had attended. They were not able to assemble this information until September 1984; hence the delay in my providing this report. When they eventually arrived for the appointment on 9/16/84, they had not completed a number of questionnaires that my secretary had mailed them, though they subsequently did so.

Mr. and Mrs. Rogers related to the interviewer in an initially cautious but eventually open and cooperative manner. Mr. Rogers, forty-seven, is reportedly physically disabled as a result of coronary artery disease. Mrs. Rogers, thirty-eight, moves slowly as a result of injuries to her legs.

The parents supported each other during the interview and were in agreement on all major points. They described Victor as prone to outbursts during which he smashes or breaks his own or others' possessions. He is said to fight with neighboring children almost daily. The parents are most concerned, however, about Victor's nightmares. Approximately twice a week he wakes screaming. On several of these occasions he has dreamt that a dog chased him over a cliff. On most occasions he does not recall his nightmares after waking. However, he is often restless at night, banging on the wall while asleep. He will not go to bed alone and wants his parents to sleep with him. Victor has also exhibited a fear of unfamiliar dogs since the accident and has sometimes been aggressive to the family dog.

The parents report that Victor's school work has deteriorated and that he now requires remedial reading. He failed in all subjects in school in 1983–84 and is currently in a special class. As a result of his poor school progress, he was transferred from parochial school to public school in September 1984.

The parents reported that Victor was bitten by a dog on February 8, 1982. On the day before the dogbite, Mr. Rogers had been admitted to hospital, as an emergency, with his third heart attack. On the following day Victor was at home with his mother. Mrs. Rogers was actually telephoning the hospital cardiac intensive care unit when she heard her child crying for help. Going to Victor's assistance, reportedly, she found him face down on the ground, with a black Doberman Pinscher chewing his leg. Mrs. Rogers drove the dog off, rescued Victor, and took him to the emergency room of (_____) Hospital. Mrs. Rogers described herself as very disturbed by the incident. She recalled how the nurses were blaming her for upsetting her husband in the intensive care unit at the time she was on the telephone and heard Victor's screams.

In April 1979, prior to the incident with the dog, Mrs. Rogers, the paternal grandmother, and Victor, reportedly, were involved in a motor vehicle accident. An automobile drove onto a sidewalk, killing the paternal grandmother, and crushing the mother's legs against a seawall. Victor, aged two years at the time, was not injured; however, he was very upset, talking about the accident and exhibiting sleep disturbance for approximately six months afterward.

As a result of the injury to her legs, Mrs. Rogers required a number of operations. After microsurgery for arterial repair, she was hospitalized for two months, and remained in a cast for nine months. She still uses crutches. Additional orthopedic and gynecological operations followed in 1980 and 1981. Further operations are required, but Mrs. Rogers does not feel emotionally able to cope with them at present. Since the injury, reportedly, she has been emotionally disturbed and has attended Dr. (psychologist) for treatment of anxiety and depression, which, she considers, are subsiding. She said that by February 1982 she was beginning to recover, when her husband fell ill once again and Victor was bitten by the dog.

Following the dogbite, reportedly, Victor immediately began to exhibit fear of animals, especially dogs, and to suffer from night terrors and nightmares. He spoke obsessively about the dog, saying, "I like doggies. Why would the dog do that to me?" These symptoms persist and he has become increasingly aggressive and explosive. Even today, he sometimes complains that his leg hurts where the dog bit him.

Aside from the reported incident with the dog, Victor has been in good physical health. He is regarded as an athletic and vigorous child.

Mrs. Rogers reported that conception, pregnancy, delivery, and early development were in Victor's case uneventful. His developmental milestones were normal. Since the reported dogbite, he is said to have become more prone to disobedience, temper tantrums, fighting, inattention, low frustration tolerance, and irritability.

Mr. Rogers reported that he sustained his first heart attack in 1972, at the age of thirty-five. He worked until 1977, when, at the age of forty, he had a second heart attack. Victor was eight months old at that time. Mr. Roger's third heart attack occurred in 1982, when Victor was five. As described before, Victor was bitten by a dog four days after the father had been admitted to an intensive care unit. Currently, as a result of heart disease, reportedly, Mr. Rogers has lost 20 percent of his cardiac function and suffers from chronic angina pectoris. Cardiac surgery is said to be "out of the question." He is on social security disability.

Mrs. Rogers, at thirty-eight, studies social work at the local community college. She is totally disabled, on social security, as a result of the injuries sustained in the automobile accident of 1979. Prior to Victor's birth she worked as a secretary, but she has not worked since that time. She is uncertain if she will ever be able to return to work.

The parents report that, despite their many problems, their marriage has remained stable. They have had much support from their families.

Victor separated readily from his father and entered my office without demur. Physically big for his age, he was neatly dressed in a checked shirt, jeans, and boots. He has no disfiguring marks.

Victor related to the interviewer in a friendly, open and cooperative manner, conversing spontaneously, without anxiety. He exhibited no abnormality of activity level, movement, power, coordination, or balance. His speech was normal in articulation, tempo, and fluency, and his vocabulary appeared to be normal for his age. In mood, he was pleasant, cheerful, trusting, displaying apprehension only when speaking of his parents' illnesses. His concentration, orientation, and attention were within normal limits at this interview. No impulsiveness was noted. His long- and short-term memory appeared to be intact to clinical testing, and he was able to reason causally in a manner appropriate to his chronological age. He knew the present date and time but did not know his birthday ("two months ago"). He knew his address, telephone number, and the days of the week, but he did not know the months of the year. No abnormality was noted in the tempo or coherence of his thought processes. Aside from his complaint of repetitive nightmares and his anxiety about the health of his parents, he exhibited no abnormal preoccupations. He understood why he had been referred to me.

In regard to the reason for his coming, he said: "I tripped. The dog gets loose and sits on the steps. I tripped. He was loose. I tripped. The dog heard me, ran fast, got me. He was growling. My shoe was untied. I tripped. It bit my leg. Mom heard me, came outside, the dog growled." Uncertain about which leg had been bitten, he pointed tentatively to the right side. "It was hurt inside. The rescue came, catched the dog, and took the dog to a farm. I was in hospital for four hours. They wrapped my leg and I wore it for five or ten months. I went to the living room and lay down. Mom put stuff on it and wrapped it up to the knee. I lay on my couch and watched TV. I was away from school for two months. I had a cast on my leg for ten months."

At this point, he showed me the back of both calves. No scar was evident. He repeated that he had tripped before the dog bit him. He did not know that the dog was there because he could not see the dog before it bit him. Asked why it was that the dog bit him, he said, "Maybe it got mean trying to protect its puppies." Also, in regard to the reason for the dog bite, he said: "The people next door were mean to us. The man backed a truck at me and went over my bike and bent it. He (the man next door) said, 'I'm sorry,' after the dogbite. They trained the dog so nobody could break in."

In regard to his feelings about dogs today, he said: "I wake up sometimes and let our dog jump on my bed. Some dogs are nice to me." He spoke of his uncle's dog, which lets Victor pet him. On the other hand, whenever a dog growls at him, he feels "scared in the chest, and nervous."

He spoke about fighting other boys who "push and punch." "I gave another boy a black eye. His name was Eric and he was mean to me at school, wouldn't knock it off, so I punched him in the tooth." He went on to say that he did not like to fight, but other kids chase him. He spoke of seldom losing fights. ("I get 'em later.")

He said that he sometimes feels sad, for example when his fish died. He sometimes feels scared at night, when he thinks that somebody, perhaps a spy, might be watching him. He said that he has frequent nightmares of being chased by a large, black dog similar to the dog that actually bit him. The dog in the dream chases him over a cliff. He falls down and down and wakes up suddenly, feeling scared. He remembers calling out to his mother and father on occasions. He claims that he has the nightmare "about every week," his most recent having been the previous night. He thinks that on one occasion he walked in his sleep as far as the back steps.

Asked to draw a human figure, he produced an immature drawing of a boy, writing under it his name and address, with one letter reversal. He said that the drawing was of a boy ("like me") about eight years of age. The boy feels "strange" inside because "somebody is hiding under the chair and watching him. . . . When he turns around, nobody is there but there really is. . . . Somebody creeps closer and closer, aisle by aisle, to him. . . . He will sneak up and get him, make him sit on a seat and make him talk." He went on to speak about the boy being sad if his dog ran away, and sometimes angry because his dog bit him.

Asked to draw a picture of his family doing something together, he drew a picture of himself, his mother, his father, and the family dog, which the family are taking for a walk.

He spoke of being in the third grade and of liking school. He said that he is best at social sciences and science. He said he had good friends, no particular enemies, and no special ambition. He said that his father sometimes works, selling things for cable television. However, he is not well because he has a problem with his heart. "He can't run. He has a big stomach. He might get sick or something like now. He might get badly sick and he might die. He looks sick, sometimes, looks strange in the face, when his whole face goes all white."

His mother, too, he believes is not well. "A long time ago, it was a crazy guy in a taxi cab. I was four or five. The car came too close, the car ran up against her and put her on the wall. I opened the door and kicked the car." He went on to say that his mother was hurt in the legs and now has a big scar where she was injured. Reportedly, two months subsequently, the taxi driver died.

His mother was badly hurt in both legs and cannot feel with her left leg. "She was badly sick in hospital." He sometimes worries that his mother might get sick again. "This morning she was sick and I felt scared. I was scared she might get sick and go to hospital."

Psychological Test Results

A Child Behavior Checklist (CBCL) concerning Victor, completed by the parents on 9/8/84 and scored automatically, indicated normal involvement in social activities and responsibilities but below normal school progress. In regard to the total number and severity of behavior problems, the parents report on the CBCL that the child is very fearful and prone to nightmares. However, the total behavior problem score is not in the clinical range.

A Child Behavior Checklist completed by his teacher on 8/3/84 indicates that Victor is working hard, behaving appropriately, and happy in school, but that his school performance and learning are below average. The teacher reports that Victor is anxious, self-conscious, shy, unpopular, and prone to nervousness, twitching, and messiness. The teacher regards Victor as aggressive and corroborates the parents' description of learning and behavior problems.

DISCUSSION

The diagnostic questions to be answered in this case are as follows:

1. Does the child suffer from an emotional disorder?
2. If the child suffers from an emotional disorder, how serious is it?
3. What is the evidence that the disorder, if present, is the result of psychological trauma sustained at the time of the dogbite in 1982?
4. Does the child have a learning disability?
5. What is the evidence that the learning disability, if any, is associated with the psychological trauma of the dogbite in 1982?

6. If the learning disability is secondary to the emotional trauma of the dogbite, do it and the emotional disorder constitute a serious aggregate problem with regard to (a) past and current stress and (b) implications for future development?

The parents describe in Victor a symptom pattern, since the dogbite of 1982, of nightmares and night terrors involving attacks by dogs, together with a fear of strange dogs, and the recent appearance of destructiveness, impulsiveness, and aggressiveness. They associate these persistent symptoms with a deterioration in the child's school work.

It is impossible to be certain beyond a reasonable doubt that Victor's emotional problems are secondary to the dogbite. However, Victor's own description of his sleep disorder and the parents' description of the nightmares are consistent with the diagnosis of chronic posttraumatic stress disorder of moderate degree.

There is abundant evidence of impairment in learning. Psychoeducational testing undertaken in 1984 demonstrates erratic performance, impulsiveness, a constant need for encouragement during testing, and deficiencies in auditory short-term memory, visual short-term memory, and auditory association. Neuropsychological testing undertaken in 1982 did not reveal an underlying neuropsychological defect. Although the most likely cause of this impairment of learning is emotional, it is not possible to be certain whether it is caused by the dogbite.

It is important to point out that the whole family has been exposed to very severe stress since 1979. The mother has been totally disabled by an automobile accident and continues to suffer from the physical and psychological effects of that accident. The father has sustained three heart attacks and is now totally disabled. He was in an intensive care unit at the time of the dogbite in 1982. Although the parents report that they have coped well, there is evidence that Mrs. Rogers has suffered psychologically from the physical trauma that she sustained in 1979, from her worry about her husband's physical health, and from her worry about the dog's attack on her child. It is likely that the mother's anxiety and depression have tended to perpetuate the psychological after-effects in the child of the trauma of the dogbite. At this point it would not be possible to estimate the proportionate extent to which Victor's current emotional and learning problems are directly related to the trauma of the dogbite and to what extent they are secondary to the mother's emotional disturbance.

If the child's learning disability is indeed a psychological consequence of the dogbite, then it and the current emotional disorder constitute, in aggregate, a serious impairment of functioning. Both the emotional and the learning problems have proved resistant to psychiatric treatment and remedial education, and the latter, in particular, has serious implications for the child's educational, occupational, and psychological future.

SUMMARY

In my opinion, with reasonable medical certainty, Victor suffers from chronic posttraumatic stress disorder of moderate degree, caused by a dogbite sustained in 1982.

He also has a learning disorder which is probably of emotional origin and possibly, though less certainly, related to the aforementioned dogbite.

The anxiety of his mother concerning her husband's cardiac condition and her own health have (inadvertently) aggravated Victor's emotional problems. If the learning disorder and emotional disorder are aggregated, they have serious implications for Victor's future development. If the emotional disorder is considered alone, the implications are less serious, and the impairment is only moderate in degree.

RECOMMENDATIONS

1. Victor and his mother should continue in individual and family psychotherapy in order to alleviate the child's posttraumatic stress disorder, the mother's anxiety state, and the inadvertent vicious cycle that operates between them. One to two years of weekly psychotherapy are required. (Estimated cost: $10,000–$20,000)
2. Victor should receive private remedial teaching to address his academic deficits. (Estimated time and cost: one to two years, $2,000–$5,000)

Case 9
Forensic Evaluation of an Adolescent Admitted to Psychiatric Hospital by Court Order, Following a Hearing Concerning Delinquent Behavior

This case illustrates the usefulness of psychiatric hospitalization in diagnosing the roots of delinquency, motivating the patient to seek therapy, and providing recommendations to the Court. In this instance, there is a clear dynamic connection among unresolved psychological conflict, the need for peer acceptance, and dyssocial behavior.

CONFIDENTIAL
FORENSIC EVALUATION
Re: David Roberts
Date of Birth: 11/22/73

CIRCUMSTANCES OF REFERRAL AND REASON FOR EVALUATION

David Roberts is a seventeen-year-old white male who was admitted to Metropolitan Psychiatric Hospital on 6/16/91 per court order for psychiatric evaluation and recommendations concerning his recent delinquent behavior. The patient had previously been placed on probation from March 1990 to February 1991, following charges of burglary, theft, and vandalism. The patient's most recent offense involved burglary (unlawful entry into a pawn shop with the theft of approximately $15,000 in guns and jewelry).

INFORMED CONSENT

The patient was informed that he was being evaluated for the purpose of informing the court concerning his diagnosis and to provide recommendation to the court concerning his disposition. He gave permission for the evaluation to be completed.

SOURCES OF DATA

Documentation

1. Discharge summary, Metropolitan Hospital 11/02/88, (resident), M.D., Neurosurgery Service
2. Pediatric Genetics Consultation, 11/11/88, (physician), M.D.

Current Evaluation

1. Psychosocial Assessment, 6/20/91, A. (caseworker), C.M.S.W., Metropolitan Hospital
2. Psychiatric Interviews, 6/16/91–7/12/91, D. (name), M.D., Psychiatry Resident, Metropolitan Hospital
3. Daily observations 6/16/91–7/12/91, nursing staff and therapists, Metropolitan Hospital
4. Psychological evaluation, 7/24/91, M. (psychologist), Ph.D., Metropolitan Hospital
5. Educational Assessment, 7/28/91, S. (psychologist), M.S., Metropolitan Hospital

FINDINGS

Past Medical Records

David Roberts has a severe, congenital connective tissue disease (Ehlers-Danlos Syndrome), which weakens the walls of his blood vessels. In 1988 the patient, then aged fourteen years, was found to have a left internal carotid artery aneurysm, an acute life-threatening condition necessitating a complex, potentially fatal operation. Since recovery from the operation, the patient has been faced with a veritable Sword of Damocles: the potential recurrence of life-threatening complications (brain hemorrhage) at any time. In addition to the serious implications of this disease, he is extremely thin (he is 5'11" and weighs under 105 lbs.).

Psychosocial Assessment

Psychosocial assessment involved interviews by Ms. (caseworker), C.M.S.W., at Metropolitan Hospital, including David and his mother, followed by family therapy sessions one to two times per week lasting approximately one and one-half hours per session.

The patient's parents were divorced when the patient was five years old. His father has been neither emotionally involved nor financially supportive. Since his parents' divorce, the patient has had three stepfathers. David's mother, his present stepfather, and his maternal grandfather are supportive, but his mother, out of a sense of guilt concerning his chronic illness, has inadvertently reinforced and perpetuated the patient's self-indulgent, irresponsible behavior. Family therapy during hospitalization has focused on the patient's father's rejection and the mother's overinvolvement with the patient.

The patient's behavior began to deteriorate following his operation two and one-half years ago, evidently as a result of depression and hopelessness concerning his illness.

Psychiatric Interviews and Hospital Observations

Psychiatric interviews were conducted five times a week for twenty to sixty minutes per session. Early in the patient's hospital course, David denied the effect of his illness and family life upon him. However, as hospitalization progressed, he was able to reveal his fear and anger concerning his neglectful father, his resentment concerning his frail physique, and his fear and sense of injustice concerning his potentially fatal disease. Hospital observations by nursing staff and therapists substantiate these observations.

Psychological Test Results

Psychological testing indicates that David is of average intelligence. He is significantly depressed, with feelings of insecurity and self-doubt concerning his physical appearance and health. The patient has underlying hostility over unmet needs for attention and appears to be driven to maintain peer acceptance.

Educational Test Results

David does not have a significant learning disability and is capable of functioning in school at his level of intelligence. However, due to illness, he is two years behind his age group in grade level.

PSYCHIATRIC DIAGNOSIS

Axis I: 1. Oppositional-defiant disorder
          2. Dysthymia
Axis II: No diagnosis

Axis III: 1. Connective tissue disease (Ehlers-Danlos syndrome)
         2. Left internal carotid aneurysm resection
         3. Left Horner's syndrome

DIAGNOSTIC FORMULATION

The interplay of these diagnoses and their connection with David's delinquent activity are as follows. Throughout his life David has attempted to cope with a neglectful father and a frail physique. In addition, early in adolescence, he had to deal with his imminent death as a result of a potentially fatal illness. As a result, he has attempted to block out anger, pain, and depression. Because of his poor self-esteem, the patient is driven to seek peer approval and has been willing to go to extremes in order to gain social acceptance, even to the point of acceding to involvement in delinquency. Moreover, because of his mother's overprotective relationship with him, he has had few behavioral consequences for his irresponsible behavior. With continued appropriate treatment, Mr. Roberts is much less likely to commit future crimes. He is not regarded as a potentially dangerous person. At the time of discharge from hospital, he was motivated to seek help for his unresolved psychological problems.

RECOMMENDATIONS

1. In view of his susceptibility to peer influence, residential placement with others who have committed crimes could increase the likelihood of future criminal actions.
2. The patient should be returned home. The following recommendations could be included in the terms of probation.
3. He and his mother require family therapy, with a focus on behavioral control and emancipation.
4. He requires individual psychotherapy in order to enhance his insight into the connection between his poor self-image and his felonious actions.
5. He requires appropriate medical follow-up, with routine ophthalmology, neurosurgery, cardiology, and internal medicine appointments.

Case 10
Evaluation of an Adult with Regard to His Mental State
at the Time of an Offense, and for Factors that
Might Mitigate Sentence

The defendant has been found guilty of one homicide and is about to be tried for another to which he has confessed and pled guilty. This evaluation first seeks to determine whether there is any support for the defense of legal insanity. However, its main purpose is to determine whether there is sufficient connection between the defendant's disturbed early life and the homicide to mitigate a sentence of death. The dynamic formulation builds a case linking homosexual rape in early adolescence to conflict about homosexual impulses, revenge fantasies, substance abuse, criminality, and the enactment of revenge fantasies following life stress.

CONFIDENTIAL
FORENSIC EVALUATION
Re: Harry H. Portent
Date of Birth: 7/5/65

CIRCUMSTANCES OF REFERRAL

Harry H. Portent has been found guilty of first degree homicide of William Yando in (city) committed on March 9, 1990. He is currently awaiting sentence after having pleaded guilty to the homicide of Richard Barrett, in (city), committed on March 6, 1990. Mr. Portent was referred to me by his attorneys Messrs. J. Smith and K. Jones.

PURPOSE OF EVALUATION

1. To determine if there is evidence supporting a defense of legal insanity at the time of the homicide of Richard Barrett
2. To determine if there are psychological factors that might mitigate the sentence for a capital offense

SOURCES OF DATA

At the request of his attorneys, Messrs. J. Smith and K. Jones, I interviewed Harry H. Portent at the Metropolitan Security Prison on October 25, October 28, and November 8, 1990. Each interview lasted approximately three hours. The purpose of these interviews was to evaluate whether psychiatric influences deriving from the defendant's background were operative during the commission of the alleged murder of Richard Barrett on 4/6/90.

In addition to the interviews, I reviewed the records of the defendant's attendance and school performance at the Metropolitan County Schools for grades 1–8 (1971–1980). I also reviewed records of the defendant's attendance at (name) Mental Health Center (1/21/78–2/25/78), and his hospitalization at (_____) Hospital (3/21/80–4/15/80), his emergency treatment at (_____) Hospital (7/3/81), and his hospitalization at (_____) Hospital (7/3/81–9/10/81) and (_____) Psychiatric Hospital (4/3/82–8/19/82). I had access to investigators' reports on the family backgrounds of both the defendant, Harry Portent, and his girlfriend, Gertrude R. Green. I also reviewed an (undated) statement made to the police by Gertrude Green.

Based on the information available to me, I am of the opinion that the alleged crime against Richard Barrett can be understood to have resulted, in part, from psychological conflict and psychosocial impairment stemming from the defendant's background and development.

MENTAL STATUS

Mr. Portent was cooperative throughout the three interviews. He gave the impression of striving to be honest with himself and with me concerning the facts of his life and his motivation. On several occasions, he insisted that he did not want his behavior explained on the basis of "craziness."

Throughout the interviews, his concentration and memory were intact and his thought processes coherent and goal-directed. There was no evidence of psychotic thought disorder. He displayed a sober, even somber, demeanor during the second and third interviews when discussing the offenses for which he is being charged. When recounting the incident of sexual molestation during his childhood (see below), he manifested tension, his face coloring and his respirations accelerating and deepening.

He was generally self-derogatory, describing himself as having been an "unproductive" human being. On several occasions he said that he deserved punishment. He said that he frequently had suicidal ideation and that, if it were left to him, he would do away with himself. Throughout the interviews, he manifested great difficulty reconciling his contrary views of his mother and girlfriend, his homosexual tendencies, and his feelings about homosexual men.

FAMILY HISTORY

Henry Portent is the older of two children by his mother, Karen Dottle, and his father Henry Portent, Sr. He has a younger brother by this relationship, now aged twenty-three years. Mrs. Dottle had been married previously and had had three sons by this union: Marcus, thirty-one; Frederick, thirty; and Jerry, twenty-seven. During his seventeen-year-long relationship with the defendant's mother, Mr. Portent, Sr., was married to another woman by whom he had five children. When Mrs. Dottle terminated her relationship with Harry Portent, Sr., she married a Mr. Dottle, with whom she has remained for the last ten years.

The defendant described himself as having had a close relationship with a father he idealized, but a conflictual relationship with his mother. He regards his mother as having been unfair to his father and as having terminated her relationship with the father merely because the latter could no longer support her financially. Mr. Portent described bitterly the way, during his adolescence, his mother had discarded the father for another man. According to the records, the marriage to Mr. Dottle was unexpected and occurred while Mr. Portent, Jr., was hospitalized at (_____) Hospital. Mr. Portent is aware, however, that his father had adamantly refused to divorce his legal wife and marry the defendant's mother. The defendant described himself as having been his father's favorite. He related this to his relatively greater comfort in the company of men. ("My mother gave up on me when my father didn't. My mother felt lost. My father never gave up even when I went to prison.") He was bitter about the fact that, even though it was months after his father's funeral, his family had only recently revealed to him that the father had died.

During the defendant's childhood, the family changed residence on at least six occasions. As a result, he attended at least five schools. He said that he had been a good student, never having failed a subject until after grade six. He said that, in the seventh grade, his school work and attendance deteriorated catastrophically. He began to run away from home, sniff gas and glue, and refuse to eat. He said that he could not get along with people because he did not feel "right" being around them and did not "fit in." His drug use and delinquent behavior began immediately following the summer school vacation of 1977.

The investigator's report corroborates the defendant's description of his family background and early development. However, Mrs. Dottle and her family describe the relationship between Mr. Portent, Sr., and Mrs. Dottle as having been abusive. For reasons that are not clear, when the defendant was eleven years of age, Mrs. Dottle and her children were forced to give up their home and to move to a trailer in a crime-ridden part of town. At this time, Mrs. Dottle was forced to work, and the children were left largely unsupervised.

Shortly after this move, the rift between the parents was widened when the mother discovered that the father was having a sexual affair with her sister. It is evident, therefore, that the sexual trauma to be described in the next section of this report followed immediately after increasing parental dissension, the loss of the family home due to poverty, and the mother's discovery of the father's infidelity.

The defendant's account of the rapid deterioration in his behavior following the summer of 1977 is borne out, independently, by the mother's history, by the school records, and by the record from (_____) Community Mental Health Center.

SEXUAL HISTORY

The defendant reported that, during the summer of 1977, at the age of twelve, he was picked up by an older man and sexually abused. He described having been kissed, undressed, rubbed all over, masturbated, fellated, having a finger inserted in his anus, and being forced to fellate his molester. The molester also attempted to penetrate him anally. He said that he told nobody about this event for many years, until he met Gertrude Green (see below).

The defendant recounted, with shame, how subsequently to his being sexually abused, he had sexually molested his younger brother, and that he had attempted to engage in sexual activity with a young female cousin. These acts occurred within a short time of his own molestation and caused him further loss of self-esteem.

Mr. Portent engaged in consensual homosexual activity during his first adult incarceration (1983–1986). Following his release from a Florida prison in 1988, he lived on two occasions with male homosexuals, and approximately a year before the alleged murder of Richard Barrett, he began to earn money as a male prostitute. Despite extensive homosexual experience (which includes stripping in a homosexual bar), the defendant does not see himself as being "gay." Significantly, he did not allow his family to have any knowledge of his homosexual activity and took care to preserve their view of him as a heterosexual.

The most important woman in his life has been Gertrude Green, an adolescent runaway, whom he picked up in downtown Metropolis in March 1988. His relationship to Gertrude Green was cemented when he found that she had experienced sexual abuse as a child. It was this that led to his confiding his own carefully guarded secret to her. Harry Portent and Gertrude Green lived together beginning in March 1988, sometimes in the residences of homosexual men. He described his love for Gertrude as possessive, and he was much concerned about rumors that she had acted as a prostitute in the past. It was partly to keep an eye on her (lest she betray him) that he gave up regular work and began to work as a homosexual prostitute.

EVENTS PRIOR TO THE OFFENSE

At the time of the Barrett homicide in April 1989, Harry Portent and Gertrude Green were living with his brother, Jerry, and sister-in-law, Tammy, and their two children. Reportedly, Gertrude confided in Tammy that Mr. Portent was "gay." Tammy mentioned this to her husband, who confronted Mr. Portent with the accusation. An argument ensued between Gertrude Green and Harry Portent, and Mr. Portent was told by his brother that he was no longer welcome in the brother's home.

Following two impulsive trips to Florida within one week, Mr. Portent lost his construction job. On the verge of leaving his brother's house, jobless, and shamed before his family, Mr. Portent found himself subject to a number of external and internal stresses which, given his unresolved psychological conflicts, contributed significantly to the disinhibition of his aggressive impulses.

DISCUSSION

The homicide of Richard Barrett can be explained by the progressive unfolding of Harry Portent's psychopathology: from his *predisposition* to personality disorder as a result of a disturbed and distorted childhood; through the decisive *trauma* of homosexual molestation in preadolescence; to a rapidly progressive *deterioration*, during adolescence and young manhood, caused by the spiraling interaction of substance abuse, school failure, and crime; culminating in a *disintegration* of his personality shortly before the homicide in question. Each of these steps will now be discussed, in detail.

Predisposition

1. There is a heavy loading of alcoholism, psychological illness, and criminality among the defendant's first- and second-degree relatives. People with this family background have an increased risk of developing alcoholism, substance abuse, and criminal behavior. They may also be genetically more vulnerable to emotional trauma during childhood.

2. The defendant is the older of two sons born of an irregular union between his unmarried mother and an already-married father. His father refused to leave his legal wife, by whom he had five children. In spite of this, the unstable relationship between the defendant's parents continued for seventeen years.

3. The refusal of Harry Portent, Sr., to leave his legal wife caused increasing conflict between himself and the defendant's mother. There were many quarrels between

the parents, some of which involved violence. The defendant denies that his father abused his mother, but the mother and other family members attest to it.

4. In contrast to the younger son of this union, the defendant was his father's favorite. The father indulged him, undermined the mother's attempt to discipline him, and rescued him from punishment for delinquent behavior. Parental dissension created a barrier between the defendant and his mother, a barrier reflected in the defendant's current distrust of women. On the other hand, the defendant idealized his father and remains the only family member who blames the mother for the family's problems.

5. The defendant's idealization of and identification with his hypermasculine father is reflected in his greater emotional comfort in the company of men and his desire for their attention and approval. By the same token, the betrayal of his trust in men by the man who molested him (see below) intensified the posttraumatic disturbance which commenced at the outset of his adolescence and persists to this day.

6. A further significant factor is the defendant's father's expressed homophobia. Harry must have been aware of this. Given his idealization of his father and desire to emulate him, great conflict would be created by his later sexual identity problems.

7. Although his father was able to support two households during the earlier part of the defendant's childhood, he later became ill and was unable to do so. However, even before he was disabled, the mother and her children were cast into poverty, lost their home, and were forced to move to a trailer in a crime-ridden part of town. At this time, the mother was working, and the children were largely unsupervised.

8. An additional factor, denied by the defendant but attested to by his mother and siblings, was the widening of the rift between his mother and father when the mother discovered the father in the trailer (from which the children had been locked out) in a sexual affair with her own sister. This event occurred in the summer of 1977, when the defendant was eleven years and ten months of age, shortly before the homosexual rape to be described in the next section.

9. Though average in school and presenting no serious behavior problems by preadolescence, the defendant was a temperamental youth who idealized his psychologically absent father, who was estranged from his increasingly desperate mother, and who tended to exploit the conflict and poor communication between them.

Trauma

1. Just before his twelfth birthday, in the August between sixth and seventh grade, the defendant was kidnapped and violently molested by an adult male. The molestation involved fondling, kissing, forced fellatio by and of the perpetrator, digital penetration, and attempted anal intercourse. He told nobody about his molestation until thirteen years after the event, initially for fear of retaliation, but eventually because of his shame and conflict about it.

2. The trauma produced a pervasive distortion in an already vulnerable personality. The defendant's desire for the approval of father substitutes continued, but he remained (and remains) deeply conflicted about homosexual tendencies which he has denied, repressed, and projected upon others. A homosexual identity would be in-

consistent with the hypermasculine ideal with which he had identified; furthermore, as a homosexual, he would be rejected by his family.

3. His fear during the sexual attack transmuted to rage, and he fantasied encountering, capturing, torturing, and killing the original perpetrator. These fantasies, and other fantasies of sexual aggression, preoccupied him during his adolescence and young manhood.

4. His failure to resolve the trauma was further manifested in his identifying with the aggressor and reenacting the trauma by sexually molesting his younger brother (using threats to prevent the younger child from disclosing the abuse) and attempting to molest a female cousin.

Deterioration

1. The defendant began to fail at school, truant, and run away from home for the first time, early in the school year following the summer during which the trauma occurred. Preoccupied with undisclosed conflict, alienated from his peers by shame and self-hatred, he was unable to attend to his schoolwork and dropped farther and farther behind his schoolfellows.

2. He began to allay anxiety, shame, and rage, first with inhalants and later with depressant drugs such as valium, quaalude, alcohol, and marijuana. Heavy marijuana use has persisted until the present day.

3. His mother declared bankruptcy when she was unable to pay the costs of a lawsuit resulting from damages perpetrated by the defendant during a runaway escapade.

4. During midadolescence, his estrangement from his long-suffering mother was aggravated when she renounced the father and married the stepfather. The defendant regarded the marriage as a final betrayal, refused to accept the stepfather, allied himself with his father in trying to destroy the marriage, terrorized the mother and stepfather, and was ejected by his mother from the family home.

5. Partly in order to finance his substance abuse, partly to gain acceptance by a deviant peer group, and partly in order to discharge the tension and self-hatred resulting from sexual abuse, the defendant became increasingly involved in breaking, entering, and stealing, and, eventually, in kidnapping and armed robbery. His conduct was quite beyond parental control, and his adolescent years were spent in mental hospitals, juvenile residences, correctional institutions, and the like.

6. In prison he learned to maintain his shaky sense of masculinity, yet to obtain sexual release, through homosexual contact. He did so by defending himself violently against being "pushed around like a punk" by other prisoners and by emulating the jailhouse creed that, while a masculine man may honorably allow himself to be fellated, he should not fellate others or be the receptive partner in homosexual intercourse.

7. The defendant learned from fellow prisoners that "easy money" could be obtained from "queers" by "hustling" them. After he met his girlfriend, Gertrude Green, he operated as a homosexual prostitute when in need of money. He was briefly employed as a male stripper and lived with two homosexual men whose attention he enjoyed. Nevertheless, he continued to deny the homosexual side of his personality, ostensibly regarding homosexual activity either as a purely commercial transaction

or as a bid for nonsexual attention from adult males. He continued to split his attitude toward male homosexuals between wanting them tortured and killed as child molesters and appreciating individual homosexuals as kind and generous people. While his homosexual clients remained impersonal, he could maintain his contempt and disdain for them as a class.

8. The tendency to split and keep apart discordant entities has persisted to the present day. He splits his bad mother ("the whore") from his idealized father. He splits the homosexual side of his personality from the hypermasculine side, that part of him which is capable of violent attack and daring crime. And he regards homosexual men as both child molesters who deserve to be killed and as decent human beings. In a brief space of time, during the one conversation, he will switch from one side of his ambivalence to the other.

9. In 1988 he fell in love with Gertrude Green, an adolescent female runaway who both reciprocated his affection and was prepared to be dominated by him. Part of his attraction to her was his awareness that she had been sexually abused as a child. She was the first person to whom he confided the story of his homosexual rape. Nevertheless, although he prefers women to men sexually, he has never been emotionally comfortable with women. As he sees it, women are mercenary beings ("whores") who will betray men unless kept happy with a constant supply of gifts and money. The equation of his girlfriend to his mother (as a loving but mercenary "whore") is clear. On one occasion, he arranged a *ménage à trois* of which he was the centerpiece, his girlfriend and a homosexual lover vying for his affection. This unstable situation represented the temporary achievement of a childhood fantasy. However, his homosexual activities eventually created problems between his resentful girlfriend and himself and led directly to the next stage of his development.

10. One of the reasons for his involvement in homosexual prostitution ("easy money") was his need to stay beside (and keep an eye on) Gertrude Green. He was intensely jealous and possessive of her, fearing that she might have been a "prostitute" and that she would betray him with other men.

11. Thus, the defendant entered the final stage, a man whose images of himself and others were internally split into irreconcilable opposites: hypermasculine criminal/homosexual lover; idealized father/unavailable father; and long-suffering mother/mercenary whore. Moreover, beneath these discrepancies, there simmered an unresolved conflict concerning sexual abuse, associated with a pathological need to turn the tables and seek revenge against the man who originally attacked him and put him in fear of death. As he learned in prison, violence was the best defense against passivity.

Disintegration

1. The final episode began when his girlfriend, apparently resentful about his past homosexual activity, told his brother's wife that he was "gay." The sister-in-law told his brother, and the brother informed the defendant that he and his girlfriend were no longer welcome and must leave the house. This rejection repeated the defendant's experience of having been thrown out of the family home by his mother when he was fifteen years of age. Even worse, his homosexuality (which he had kept strictly secret

from his family) was now overt, and he felt exposed and ashamed at the revelation of his double life, a life inconsistent with his hypermasculine façade.

2. His psychological turmoil following these shocks is revealed in his wildly driving backward and forward between (State) and (State) and his formulation of the final criminal plan.

3. His decision to solicit a homosexual and kill the first one who went with him can be interpreted as a need to regain control in a situation of shame regarding the exposure of his homosexuality, his rejection by his family, and a persistent doubt about the true allegations of his girlfriend. He consciously hoped that his determination to go through with the homicide would impress his girlfriend and tie her to him emotionally.

4. Nevertheless, his confused motivation during the killing is revealed in his attempting to rationalize it by taking goods and a bankcard number from the victim, by the wavering of his motivation before the killing, and by covering the victim's face with a pillow, reportedly in order to prevent the victim from seeing and later identifying Gertrude Green. According to the defendant, he ultimately killed the victim after Gertrude Green pointed out that the victim would be able to identify him.

5. The killing itself can be interpreted as a reenactment of unresolved sexual abuse trauma, an enactment of revenge fantasies stemming from the original abuse, the projection of self-loathing onto the victim, and an attempt to revive for himself and his girlfriend the masculine image which had been his chief defensive façade against denied homosexual tendencies.

6. Confused motivation is evident in the subsequent Yando homicide, which is, in many ways, a repetition of the Barrett killing. Although he was not pressed for funds, in a hare-brained scheme to discover Yando's automatic teller number, he drove backward and forward from (_____) to (_____) on two occasions and was apprehended there.

SUMMARY

In summary, with reasonable medical certainty, it is my opinion that there is a causative link between the defendant's delinquent adolescence, adult criminality, and, in particular, the alleged homicide of Richard Barrett. On the other hand, there is no psychiatric evidence to support the defense that, at the time of the offense in question, the defendant was unable to appreciate the criminality of his action or to conform his conduct to the requirements of the law.

LANDMARK CASES

INTRODUCTION

The field of children's mental health law has developed through an accumulation of many cases and statutes. Our purpose in including a section of leading cases is to provide readers with ready access to a number of them that have been influential in the development of the law. While these cases are discussed in the text, their full factual richness cannot be described there. Case law is not a sterile declaration of legal principle but an intricate, often difficult, application of rules and policies to social reality. Indeed, a thorough investigation of the history and actual implications of particular cases makes for some of the very best writing in law and psychiatry. We cannot undertake an exhaustive canvassing of the background of each case. However, we can, in short compass, give a fairly thorough review of the facts of these cases and their holdings.

Many candidates for leading cases present themselves in the course of writing a book of this nature. We have attempted here to give a sampling of those cases.

PLYLER, SUPERINTENDENT, TYPER INDEPENDENT
SCHOOL DISTRICT, ET AL.
V.
DOE, GUARDIAN, ET AL.,
457 U.S. 202 (1982)

FACTS

In May 1975 the Texas legislature revised its educational laws to withhold from local school districts any state funds for education of children who were not "legally admitted" into the United States. The revision also authorized local school districts to deny enrollment in their public schools to children not "legally admitted" to the country. This and other cases involve constitutional challenges to those provisions. The class actions were brought on behalf of school-age children of Mexican origin residing in Smith County, Texas, who could not establish that they had been legally admitted into the United States.

HOLDING

The Court reasoned that the children were persons under the Fourteenth Amendment of the Constitution. The Fourteenth Amendment was designed to afford its protection to all within the boundaries of a state. The Court differentiated the situation of adults from children. Even if the state were to find it expedient to control the conduct of adults by acting against their children, legislation directing the onus of a parent's misconduct against children does not comport with fundamental concepts of justice. The provision here had an effect of discriminating against a legal characteristic over which children had little control.

Although public education was not a right granted to individuals by the Constitution, it rises to a significant level of importance. Public schools are a "vital civic institution for the preservation of a democratic system of government." (*Abington School District v. Shempp,* 374 U.S. 203 (1963)).

The Court found that undocumented aliens could not be treated as a suspect class, nor was education a fundamental right, and consequently the strict scrutiny standard could not be applied to this discrimination. However, imposition of a lifetime hardship on a discrete class of children not accountable for their disabling status is of such magnitude that to be justified the state must show that it furthered "some substantial goal." The Court then turned to the state objectives that were said to support the discriminatory policy.

The state argued that the classification furthered an interest in the "preservation of the state's limited resources for the education of its lawful residents." No evidence was shown that education of the children of illegal aliens would burden the state's economy. Nor could it be shown that the barring of these children from local schools would improve the quality of education provided by those schools. Lastly, it was not shown that these children would be less likely to contribute later to the welfare of the state than the children of lawfully resident persons.

Justice Powell's concurrence is particularly trenchant. He found that the state's denial of education to these children bore no substantial relation to any substantial state interest.

The dissent of Chief Justice Burger, joined by Justices White, Rehnquist, and O'Connor, focused on the point that the Court had trespassed upon assigned functions of the political branches of government: The effect of the majority's decision was to make policy for the states. The Chief Justice found that the Equal Protection Clause of the Fourteenth Amendment did not mandate identical treatment of different categories of persons. He found that the distinction drawn by Texas was based not only upon its own legitimate interests but on classifications established by the federal government in its immigration laws and policies. Although no suspect class or fundamental right was divined in this case, the Chief Justice characterized the majority's reasoning as patching together "bits and pieces of what might be termed quasi-suspect class and quasi-fundamental rights analysis." He finds this a result-oriented approach. The dissenters give latitude to the state to determine the means to legitimate ends. The means are rational, although they may not be good policy.

MICHAEL M.

V.

SUPERIOR COURT OF SONOMA COUNTY
(CALIFORNIA, REAL PARTY IN INTEREST),
450 U.S. 464 (1981)

FACTS

Sharon was a sixteen-and-a-half year old female who, on the night of question, was waiting with her sister at a bus stop. Michael M. was one year and eighteen days older. Michael and two friends approached Sharon and her sister. Michael and Sharon, who had already been drinking, moved away from the others and began to kiss. After being struck in the face for rebuffing the Petitioner's initial advances, Sharon submitted to sexual intercourse with Michael. A complaint was filed alleging that Michael had had sexual intercourse with a female under the age of eighteen in violation of a California statute. The question before the Supreme Court was whether the statute violated the Equal Protection Clause of the Fourteenth Amendment, in that the statute discriminated on the basis of sex, because only females may be victims and only males may violate the section.

HOLDING

The majority, Justice Rehnquist joined by Chief Justice Burger and Justices Stewart and Powell, concluded that the statute did not violate the Equal Protection Clause of the Fourteenth Amendment. The Court found that gender-based classifications are not "inherently suspect" so as to be subject to the so-called strict scrutiny standard of review, but will be upheld if they bear a "fair and substantial relationship" to legitimate state ends. A statute will be upheld where gender classification is not invidious but rather realistically reflects the fact that the sexes are not similarly situated in certain circumstances. In this case it was found that the California statute revealed the state's interest in the prevention of illegitimate teenage pregnancies. The state protects women from sexual intercourse and pregnancy at an age when the physical, emotional, and psychological consequences are particularly severe. Most of the significant harmful and identifiable consequences of teenage pregnancy fall on the female, and accordingly the legislature acts well within its authority when it elects to punish only the participant who by nature suffers few of the consequences of his conduct. Moreover, a gender-neutral statute would frustrate the state's interest in effective enforcement since a female would be less likely to report violations of the statute if she herself would be subject to prosecution. Neither is the statute impermissibly overbroad because it makes unlawful sexual intercourse with prepubescent females, incapable of becoming pregnant. Other reasons would support the ban, but generally nothing in the Constitution limits the scope of the statute to older teenagers.

The dissent (Justice Brennan, with whom Justices White and Marshall agreed) concentrated their reasoning on the standard of review to be adopted by the Court. Was the statute substantially related to the achievement of the state's goal of avoiding teenage pregnancies? It was suggested that the statutory rape law was initially designed to further outmoded sexual stereotypes rather than to reduce the incidence of teenage pregnancies. It was only with the incoherence of this end that the avoidance of pregnancy goal was invented.

WISCONSIN V. YODER,
406 U.S. 205 (1972)

FACTS

Yoder and Miller were members of the old order Amish religion, and Yutzy was a member of the conservative Amish Mennonite church. They resided in Green County, Wisconsin. Wisconsin's compulsory school attendance law required them to cause their children to attend public or private school until the age of sixteen, but the members of the Amish church declined to send their children, fourteen and fifteen years of age, to public school after they completed the eighth grade. The children were not enrolled in any private school or within any recognized exception to the compulsory attendance law. The defendants were charged, tried, and convicted of violating the compulsory attendance law and fined $5.00 each. The defendants argued that the application of the law violated their rights under the First and Fourteenth Amendments to the Constitution. Testimony showed that the Respondents believed, in accordance with the tenets of the old order Amish communities, that their children's attendance at high school, public or private, was contrary to the Amish religion and way of life. They believed that by sending their children to high school they would not only expose themselves to the danger of being shunned by the church community but, as found by the county court, also endanger their own salvation and that of their children. Evidence confirmed the convictions of these beliefs.

HOLDING

Chief Justice Burger delivered the opinion of the Court, in which Justices Brennan, Stewart, White, Marshall, and Blackmun joined. Justices Stewart, Brennan, and White filed concurring opinions. Justice Douglas filed an opinion dissenting in part. The majority premised its opinion on the proposition that only those interests of the highest order and those not otherwise served can overbalance legitimate claims to free exercise of religion. The state's interest in universal compulsory education is not absolute to the exclusion or subordination of all other interests. The Court found that, in unchallenged testimony, the requirement of compulsory formal education after the eighth grade would gravely endanger if not destroy the free exercise of Amish religious beliefs.

As a principle, even religious activities are subject to regulation by states in the exercise of their power to promote health, safety, and general welfare, and by the federal government in the exercise of its delegated powers. The Court required an examination of the interests that the state seeks to promote by its requirement for compulsory education to age sixteen and the impediment to those objectives that would flow from recognition of the claimed Amish exemption.

The Court found that more than a parental interest was involved in this case. The interests of parenthood were combined with the free exercise of religion claim, and thus the state was required to show more than just a "reasonable relation to some purpose within the competency of the state" to sustain the validity of the compulsory attendance law under the First Amendment. It may be that parental decisions would jeopardize health or safety of the child or have potential for significant social burdens, in which case a state regulation would pass Constitutional muster. But in this case the Amish had introduced persuasive evidence undermining the state arguments that the regulation was supported in terms of the welfare of the child and society as a whole.

TINKER ET AL.

V.

DES MOINES INDEPENDENT COMMUNITY
SCHOOL DISTRICT ET AL.,
393 U.S. 503 (1969)

FACTS

In December 1965 a group of adults and students in Des Moines held a meeting in the home of the Eckhardt family. The group determined to publicize objections to the war in Vietnam and their support for a truce by wearing black armbands during the holiday season and by fasting on December 16 and New Year's Eve.

Principals of the Des Moines schools became aware of the plan, and on December 14 they met and adopted a policy that any student wearing an armband to school would be asked to remove it and, if he refused, would be suspended until he returned without an armband. On December 16 Mary Beth and Christopher Eckhardt wore armbands, and John Tinker wore his the next day. They were all sent home and suspended from school until they would come back without their armbands. They did not return to school until after the planned period for wearing armbands had expired, that is, until after New Year's Day. The children, through their fathers, brought an action under Section 1983 asking for an injunction to restrain the school officials and members of the school boards from disciplining the children and sought nominal damages.

HOLDING

The opinion of the Court was delivered by Justice Fortas. The Court found that the wearing of armbands was a type of symbolic act that was within the free speech clause of the First Amendment. It was closely akin to pure speech, which the court had repeatedly held was entitled to comprehensive protection under the Constitution. The Constitutional rights of students and teachers are maintained in the school context. Against this must be balanced the need for the comprehensive authority of the states and of school officials consistent with Constitutional safeguards to prescribe and control conduct in schools.

In this case the punishment went to expression of opinion when accompanied by any disorder or disturbance. The speech or action did not intrude upon the work of the schools or the rights of other students. It was important in this case that the ban did not prohibit the wearing of all symbols of political or controversial significance. Justice Fortas stated that in our system "state operated schools may not be enclaves of totalitarianism. School officials do not possess absolute authority over their students. Students in school as well as out of school are 'persons' under our Constitution. They are possessed of fundamental rights which the state must respect just as they themselves must respect their obligations to the state."

STATE V. YOUNG,
525 N.E.2D 1363 (1988) (SUPREME COURT OF OHIO)

FACTS

The question before the court was whether the state, consistent with the First Amendment, may outlaw private possession of child pornography. The Defendants were convicted for possession of child pornography. The statute provided in pertinent part:

(A) No person shall do any of the following:

(3) possess or view any material or performance that shows a minor who is not the person's child or ward in a state of nudity, unless one of the following applies:

(a) the material or performance is sold, disseminated, displayed, possessed, controlled, bought or caused to be brought into this state or presented for a bona fide artistic, medical, scientific, educational, religious, governmental, judicial, or other proper purpose, by or to a physician, psychologist, sociologist, scientist, teacher, person pursuing bona fide studies or research, librarian, clergyman, prosecutor, judge, or other person having a proper interest in the material or performance.

(b) the person knows that the parents, guardian, or custodian has consented in writing to the photographing or use of the minor in a state of nudity and to the manner in which the material or performance is used or transferred.

The Defendants contended that the statute was overbroad because it encompassed activities that constitute exercise of constitutionally protected expression under the First Amendment.

HOLDING

The court found that the First Amendment must remain inviolate. However, this did not conflict with the finding that obscenity is not protected by the First Amendment. Likewise, child pornography is not protected. The state has a compelling interest in the protection of children. Reasonable laws prohibiting the exploitation of children may be passed by the state legislature to ensure that interest.

ANNA J. V. MARK C.,
286 CAL. RPTR. 369 (CAL. APP. 4 DIST. 1991)

FACTS

Mark and Crispina were a married couple who desired to have their own child. Crispina had had her uterus removed in 1984. She nevertheless had the ability to produce ova and the couple eventually considered surrogacy. In 1989 Anna heard about Crispina's plight from a co-worker and offered to be a surrogate for her and Mark. On January 15, 1990, Mark, Crispina, and Anna signed a contract, which provided that an "embryo" created by the sperm of Mark and the egg of Crispina would be implanted in Anna and the child born would be taken into Mark and Crispina's home "as their child." Anna agreed she would relinquish "all parental rights" to the child in favor of Mark and Crispina. In return, Mark and Crispina would pay Anna $10,000 in a series of installments, the last to be six weeks after the child's birth. They were also to pay a $200,000 insurance policy on Anna's life. The zygote was implanted January 19, 1990. Less than a month later, an ultrasound confirmed that Anna was pregnant. Relations deteriorated between the two sides. Mark learned Anna had not disclosed she had suffered several stillbirths and miscarriages. Anna was upset because Mark and Crispina did not do enough to obtain the required insurance policy. She also felt abandoned during the onset of premature labor in June. In July, Anna sent Mark and Crispina a letter demanding the balance of the payments due her or else she would refuse to give up the child. Mark and Crispina responded with a lawsuit seeking a declaration that they were the legal parents of the unborn child. Anna filed her own action to be declared the mother of the child, and the two cases were eventually consolidated, with Anna's case being made the lead. The child was born on September 19, and blood samples were obtained from both Anna and the child for analysis. The blood tests excluded Anna as the genetic mother of the baby. The parents agreed to a court order providing the child would remain with Mark and Crispina on a temporary basis with visits by Anna.

HOLDING

In order to resolve the question of maternity, the court applied the language of the Uniform Parentage Act. That legislation turned on blood tests, and thus the court found that Anna was excluded as the natural mother of the child. Although a person may establish that she is the natural mother by demonstrating that she gave birth to the child, that is not a sufficient test. The court further found that the statute under which Anna was declared not to be the natural mother was constitutional. The court also discussed questions of surrogate contracts that were not central to the holding in the case.

COY V. IOWA,
487 U.S. 1012, 101 L.ED.2D 857 (1988)

FACTS

In August 1985, John Avery Coy was arrested and charged with sexually assaulting two thirteen-year-old girls earlier that month while they were camping in the back-yard of the house next door to him. Coy entered their tent after they were asleep, wear-ing a stocking over his head, and shined a flashlight into their eyes and warned them not to look at him. Neither was able to describe his face. The prosecution made a mo-tion pursuant to a then recently enacted statute to allow the girls to testify either via closed-circuit television or behind a screen. The trial court approved the use of a large screen to be placed between Coy and the girls during their testimony. Coy's counsel objected strenuously to the use of the screen, based on his Sixth Amendment con-frontation right. He argued that although the device might succeed in its apparent aim of making the witnesses feel less uneasy in giving their testimony, the confrontation clause directly addressed this issue by giving criminal defendants the right to face-to-face confrontation. Coy also argued that his right to due process was violated since the procedure would make him appear guilty and thus erode the presumption of in-nocence. The trial court rejected both constitutional claims, though it instructed the jury to draw no inference of guilt from the presence of the screen.

HOLDING

Justice Scalia delivered the opinion of the Court in which Justices Brennan, White, Marshall, Stevens, and O'Connor joined. Justice O'Connor filed a concurring opin-ion, in which White, J., joined. Justice Blackmun filed a dissenting opinion in which Chief Justice Rehnquist joined.

The Court found that the confrontation clause guarantees a defendant a face-to-face meeting with witnesses appearing before the trier of fact, that is, the jury. It was admitted that insistence upon confrontation would have a profound effect upon the witness standing in the presence of a person. Face-to-face presence may upset the truthful rape victim or abused child. But that may, by the same token, confound and undo the false accuser or reveal a child coached by a malevolent adult. In the absence of individualized findings that these particular witnesses, the raped girls, needed any special protection, the denial of the right to confrontation could not be sustained.

The dissenters found that because the girls testified under oath in full view of the jury and were subjected to unrestricted cross-examination, there could be no argu-ment that their testimony lacked sufficient indicia of reliability.

Both the Court's opinion and that of the dissent stressed the significance of the state's interest. It cited reported incidence of child molestation in the United States and the difficulties of prosecuting child abuse cases. To force confrontation may undermine the truth-finding function of the trial itself and cause psychological injury to the child. These were good reasons why an absolute insistence upon confrontation could not be supported, but a right conditioned on appropriate factual findings could.

HART V. BROWN,
289 A.2D 386 (CT. 1972) (SUPERIOR COURT OF CONNECTICUT)

FACTS

The plaintiffs in this case were Peter and Eleanor Hart, the parents and natural guardians of Katheleen and Margaret Hart, minors and identical twins, age seven years and ten months. The defendants were practicing physicians licensed in Connecticut. Katheleen was a patient in the Yale New Haven Hospital awaiting a kidney transplant. It was found reasonably probable that if the procedure did not occur she would die and that successful kidney transplants had been done in the past upon minor patients. The physicians were unwilling to take as kidneys for the transplant the kidneys of the parents. The physicians were, however, willing to operate on the children as to transplant a kidney from one to the other, but only if the court declared that the parents or the guardians *ad litem* had the right to give consent to the operation. In more detail, the facts were that Katheleen was a minor suffering from hemolytic uremic syndrome. This disorder of the kidneys causes clots within the small blood vessels. After certain procedures, a biopsy disclosed a new and more disastrous lesion, malignant hypertension that the physicians found could prove fatal. A bilateral nephrectomy was performed with the removal of both kidneys to control the situation. As of that date, Katheleen became a patient with fixed uremia with no potential kidney function and required dialysis treatments twice weekly. The prospect of survival was, because of her age, at best questionable. It was medically advised that she not continue this dialysis therapy, but rather must have a kidney transplant. One type of kidney transplant was a parental homograph, which presents severe problems of rejection. A transplant from the twin, however, would have a much higher chance of success. A psychiatrist who examined the donor gave testimony that the donor had a strong identification with her twin sister. He also testified that if the expected successful results were achieved there would be an immense benefit to the donor in that the donor would be better off in a family that was happy than in a family that was distressed and in that it would be a very great loss to the donor if the donee were to die from her illness. A clergyman also gave evidence which was weighed by the court.

HOLDING

The court found that it needed to balance the rights of the natural parents and the rights of minor children. Because of the great medical progress in this field, natural parents would be able to substitute their consent for that of minor children only after a close independent and objective investigation of their motivation and reasoning. Finding that the proposed transplant was not experimental but a medically accepted therapy, the court found that the parents could give consent on behalf of the minor. In the circumstances the court found that the natural parents of minors should have the right to give their consent to the kidney transplant procedure when their motivation and reasoning are favorably reviewed by community representation, which includes a court of equity.

PROCANIK V. CILLO,
478 A.2D 755 (N.J. 1984) (NEW JERSEY SUPREME COURT)

FACTS

In June 1977 Mrs. Procanik, during the first trimester of her pregnancy with Peter, consulted Dr. Cillo and told him that she had "recently been diagnosed as having measles and did not know if it was german measles." Dr. Cillo examined Mrs. Procanik and ordered "tests for german measles known as Rubella Titer tests." The results were indicative of past infection of rubella. Instead of ordering further tests, Dr. Cillo negligently interpreted the results and told Mrs. Procanik that she had nothing to worry about because she had become "immune to german measles as a child." In fact, the past infection disclosed by the tests was the german measles that had prompted Mrs. Procanik to consult the defendant doctors.

Ignorant of what an accurate diagnosis would have disclosed, Mrs. Procanik allowed her pregnancy to continue and Peter was born on December 26, 1977. Shortly thereafter, on January 16, 1978, he was diagnosed as suffering from congenital rubella syndrome. As a result of the doctor's negligence, Mr. and Mrs. Procanik were deprived of the choice of terminating the pregnancy, and Peter was "born with multiple birth defects" including eye lesions, heart disease, and auditory defects. The infant plaintiff sought damages for his pain and suffering and for his "impaired childhood." A plea for expenses arising from medical nursing and related health care services was included at a later time. Peter's parents also sought damages for their emotional distress for the extraordinary medical expenses attributable to Peter's birth defects. However, their claim was barred by the two-year statute of limitations under New Jersey law. It followed that the only claim available was that of Peter himself, that is, a wrongful life claim.

HOLDING

The New Jersey court had previously held that parents would have a right of action in the circumstances where a physician's negligence had deprived them of the choice of opting for an abortion. However, the wrongful life action was more controversial, because the child himself or herself was arguing that an abortion should have been performed, which necessarily would mean, if reasonable professional care had been exercised, that the child would not exist. Could nonexistence be described as a preferable state to a life, albeit impaired? The New Jersey court allowed the wrongful life action. The court confirmed that they would give extraordinary medical expenses incurred by parents on behalf of a birth-defective child. At the same time, recovery of the cost of extraordinary medical expenses by either the parents or the infant, but not both, was consistent with the principle that the doctor's negligence vitally affects the entire family. It appeared unjust to the court to allow an action by the parents and not by the child. The court held that a child or his parents may recover special damages for extraordinary medical expenses incurred during infancy and that the infant may recover those expenses during his majority. Although the court conceded that there may be logical problems with the result, justice demanded it, as did the fulfilling of the objectives of the tort system, the compensation of injured parties, and the deterrence of future wrongful conduct.

EISEL V. BOARD OF EDUCATION OF MONTGOMERY COUNTY, 597 A.2D 447 (MD. 1991) (COURT OF APPEALS OF MARYLAND)

FACTS

Nicole Eisel was a thirteen-year-old student at Sligo Middle School in Montgomery County. She and another thirteen-year-old girl consummated a murder-suicide pact in November 1988. The complaint stated that Nicole had become involved in Satanism, causing her to have an "obsessive interest in death and self-destruction." During the week prior to the suicide, Nicole told several friends and fellow students that she intended to kill herself. Some of these friends reported Nicole's intentions to their school counselor, Morgan, who relayed the information to Nicole's school counselor, Jones. Morgan and Jones then questioned Nicole about the statements, but Nicole denied making them. Neither Morgan nor Jones notified Nicole's parents or the school administration about Nicole's alleged statements of intent. Information in the record suggested that the other party to the suicide pact shot Nicole before shooting herself. The murder-suicide took place on a school holiday in a public park at some distance from the middle school.

HOLDING

The court found a sufficient relationship established between the school through its counselors and the deceased student to give rise to an affirmative duty on the part of the defendant, School Board, to use reasonable means to prevent the suicide and in particular to warn the parents. Of importance in establishing the relationship was the fact that the suicide was by an adolescent. Here the parent, if warned, could have exercised custody and control over Nicole and reduced the possibility of suicide. A duty to warn, the court found, would not impose an undue burden on schools, especially in light of the documented dangers of teenage suicide.

TARASOFF V. REGENTS OF UNIVERSITY OF CALIFORNIA, 551 P.2D 334 (1976) (SUPREME COURT OF CALIFORNIA)

FACTS

The plaintiffs alleged that in this case Poddar was a voluntary outpatient receiving therapy at Cowell Memorial Hospital. Poddar informed Moore, his therapist, that he was going to kill an unnamed girl, readily identifiable as Tatiana Tarasoff, when she returned home from spending the summer in Brazil. Moore, with the concurrence of Dr. Gold, who had initially examined Poddar, and Dr. Yandell, assistant to the director of the department of psychiatry, decided that Poddar should be committed for observation in a mental hospital. Moore orally notified officers Atkinson and Teel of the campus police that he would request commitment. He then sent a letter to the police chief requesting the assistance of the police department in securing Poddar's confinement.

The officers took Poddar into custody but, satisfied that Poddar was rational, released him on his promise to stay away from Tatiana. The psychiatrist, it was alleged, failed to notify the parents of Tatiana that her daughter was in "grave danger from Posenjit Poddar." Shortly after Tatiana's return from Brazil, Poddar went to her residence and killed her.

HOLDING

As explained in Chapter 8, the California Supreme court on two occasions addressed the issues that arose in this case. The police officers were immune from liability under a California statute. The only question for the court was one of law: Did the defendant psychiatrists have a duty of care in negligence to safeguard Tatiana? The claim in this case by the plaintiffs, Tatiana's parents, was that this duty was breached when the defendant psychiatrists failed to warn them or Tatiana of the danger that Poddar posed. We discuss the holding in this case at some length in the book. The dilemma for the court in finding a duty to take affirmative steps to protect Tatiana was that the implementation of the duty demanded that the defendants breach their duty of confidentiality to the patient. The court, however, found that the public interest in avoiding violence of this kind outweighed the confidentiality interest. It is to be noted that the court does not address the difficult issue of the predictability of violence. In this case, it was assumed that the defendants had made an assessment that Poddar did pose a threat to Tatiana. The only question, then, was whether a duty of care could be found and how that duty of care should be couched.

FRANKLIN V. GWINNETT COUNTY PUBLIC SCHOOLS, 112 S.CT. 1028 (1992)

FACTS

Christine Franklin was a student at North Gwinnett High School in Gwinnett County, Georgia, between September 1985 and August 1989. It was alleged that she was subjected to continual sexual harassment beginning in the autumn of her tenth-grade year (1986) from Andrew Hill, a sports coach and teacher employed by the school district. Among other allegations, Franklin asserted that Hill engaged her in sexually oriented conversations in which he asked about her sexual experiences with her boyfriend and whether she would consider having sexual intercourse with an older man; that Hill forcibly kissed her on the mouth in the school parking lot; that he telephoned her at home and asked if she would meet him socially; and that on three occasions in her junior year Hill interrupted a class, requested that the teacher excuse her, and took her to a private office where he subjected her to coercive intercourse. It was further alleged that when the school became aware of and investigated Hill's sexual harassment of Franklin and other female students, teachers and administrators took no action to halt it and discouraged Christine Franklin from pressing charges against Hill. Hill resigned on condition that all matters pending against him be dropped, whereupon the school closed its investigation.

The plaintiff brought an action seeking damages under Title IX of the Education Amendments of 1972 (20 U.S.C. §§1681-1688), which prohibited exclusion from participation in, and denial of, or discrimination under, any educational program or activity receiving federal assistance. The question for the Court was whether Title IX was enforceable through an implied right of action in the person who has suffered injury resulting from a breach of the section. (Title IX contained no words granting an express right to bring a damages action.)

HOLDING

The opinion of the Court reasons that a presumption applies in favor of appropriate relief. The defendant school board argued that the presumption should not apply for three reasons. In the first place, it was urged that an award of damages would violate constitutional separation of powers principles because it would unduly expand the federal court's power in a sphere properly reserved to the executive and legislative branches. The Court found that the courts had a historic authority to award appropriate relief in cases brought before them. Second, it was argued that the presumption should not apply because Title IX was enacted pursuant to Congress's Spending Clauses power. In this case, intentional discrimination was alleged, and the previous authority in *Pennhurst State School and Hospital v. Halderman,* 451 U.S. 1 (1981), held only that remedies were limited under spending clause statutes where the alleged violation was *unintentional.* Third and last, it was argued that any remedy should be limited to back pay and prospective relief. These remedies, however, were found by the Court to be clearly inadequate. The same result was reached by Justice Scalia, with whom Chief Justice Rehnquist and Justice Thomas concurred. This opinion signals a concern with the expansion of private rights under judicial interpretation of Congressional legislation.

HOFFMAN V. BOARD OF EDUCATION OF THE CITY OF NEW YORK, 400 N.E.2D 317 (N.Y. CT. APP. 1979)

FACTS

Daniel Hoffman entered kindergarten in the New York City School System in September 1956. Shortly thereafter, he was examined by Monroe Gottsegen, a certified clinical psychologist in the school system, who determined that the plaintiff had an intelligence quotient (IQ) of 74 and recommended that he be placed in a class of children with retarded mental development. Dr. Gottsegen was, however, not certain of his findings. The apparent reason for this uncertainty was that the plaintiff suffered from a severe speech defect, which had manifested itself long before the plaintiff entered the school system. The plaintiff's inability to communicate verbally made it difficult to assess his mental ability by means of the primarily verbal Stanford Binet Intelligent Test administered by Dr. Gottsegen. As a result, Dr. Gottsegen recommended that the plaintiff's intelligence "be reevaluated within a two-year period so that a more accurate estimation of his abilities can be made." Daniel continued to perform poorly on standardized achievement tests. He was not retested as had been recommended by Dr. Gottsegen. In 1968 Daniel was transferred to the Queens Occupational Training Center (OTC), a manual and shop training center for retarded youths. The following year, after his mother's request, the plaintiff's intelligence was retested. Under the Wechsler Intelligence Scale for Adults (WAIS), he had a full-scale IQ of 94. As a result, he was no longer qualified to be enrolled in the OTC program.

Daniel commenced an action against the Board of Education, alleging that the Board was negligent in its original assessment of his intelligence ability and that the Board negligently failed to retest him pursuant to Dr. Gottsegen's earlier recommendation. A jury awarded the plaintiff damages in the amount of $750,000.

HOLDING

The Court of Appeals of New York found that the holdings of the lower court should be reversed. The court reasoned that courts should not substitute their judgment, or the judgment of the jury, for the professional judgment of educators and government officials actually engaged in the complex and often delicate process of educating children in school. It found that courts should intervene in the administration of the public school system only in the most exceptional circumstances involving "gross violations of defined public policy." To allow judicial second-guessing of this kind would be to open the door to an examination of the propriety of each of the procedures used in the education of every child in the school system. The court was not the proper forum to test the validity of the educational decision to place a particular student in one of the many educational programs offered by schools in New York. If review be desired, the court found that it should be done via review of professional education judgment through the administrative processes provided for in legislation.

IN RE WINSHIP,
397 U.S. 358 (1970)

FACTS

Winship, a twelve-year-old boy, had entered a locker and stolen $112 from a woman's pocketbook. He was charged with delinquency on the ground that his act, "if done by an adult, would constitute the crime or crimes of Larceny." The trial judge acknowledged that the proof may not establish guilt beyond a reasonable doubt, but rejected Winship's contention that such proof was necessary. The trial judge relied upon a New York statute that provided that any determination in a juvenile hearing must be based on a preponderance of the evidence. In a subsequent dispositional hearing, Winship was ordered to be placed in a training school for an initial period of eighteen months subject to annual extensions of his commitment until his eighteenth birthday, six years in his case. The New York Court of Appeals affirmed by a four-to-three vote the constitutionality of the New York statute. The question for the Court was whether the Fourteenth Amendment extended to require proof beyond a reasonable doubt, the usual criminal standard.

HOLDING

The Court found that proof beyond a reasonable doubt was required by the Due Process Clause of the Fourteenth Amendment in criminal trials as among the "essentials of due process and fair treatment." This requirement extended to the judicatory stage of a juvenile trial where the charge turns upon an act that would constitute a crime if committed by an adult. The courts relied upon *In re Gault* (see below) to find that the constitutional protection extended to minors. The Court found that the extension of this requirement would not destroy the beneficial aspects of juvenile process. Furthermore, the Court found that the difference between the reasonable doubt and preponderance standards was substantial and not tenuous.

A dissenting opinion was filed by Chief Justice Burger, with whom Justice Stewart concurred. Justice Black dissented in a separate opinion.

IN RE GAULT,
387 U.S. 1 (1966)

FACTS

On Monday, June 8, 1964, at about 10:00 A.M., Gerald Frances Gault and a friend, Ronald Lewis, were taken into custody by the sheriff. Gerald at the time was subject to a six-month probation order, which had been entered in February 1964 as a result of his having been in the company of another boy who had stolen a wallet from a lady's purse. The police action on June 8 was taken as a result of a complaint by a neighbor of the boys, Mrs. Cook, about a telephone call made to her in which the caller or callers made lewd or indecent remarks. As the Court put it, these remarks were of the "irritatingly offensive, adolescent, sex variety." Gerald's mother and father were at work when he was picked up by the police. No notice that Gerald was being taken into custody was left at the home. No other steps were taken to advise the parents that their son had, in effect, been arrested. Gerald was taken to the Children's Detention Home. When his mother arrived home at about 6:00 P.M., Gerald was not there. His older brother was sent to look for him at the trailer home of the Lewis family. He apparently learned that Gerald was in custody. The parents repaired to the Detention Home. The deputy probation officer, Flagg, who was also superintendent of the Detention Home, told Mrs. Gault why Gerald was there and said that a hearing would be held in the juvenile court at 3:00 P.M. the following day, June 9. Flagg filed a petition with the court on the hearing day. It was not served on the Gaults. Instead, none of them saw this petition until a *habeas corpus* hearing on August 17, 1964. The petition to the court of June 9 made no reference to any factual basis for the judicial action it initiated. It appeared that at the juvenile hearing Gerald was questioned by the judge about the telephone call. There was conflict as to what was said. His mother recalled that Gerald said that he had only dialed Mrs. Cook's number and handed the telephone to his friend Ronald. Officer Flagg recalled that Gerald had admitted making the lewd remarks. Judge McKee testified that Gerald "admitted making one of these [statements]." At the conclusion of the hearing, the judge said he would think about it. Gerald was taken back to the Detention Home. On June 11 or 12, after having been detained since June 8, Gerald was released and driven home. There is no explanation in the record as to why he was kept at the Detention Home or why he was released. At 5:00 P.M. on the day of Gerald's release, Mrs. Gault received a note signed by Officer Flagg informing her of a further date and time to consider "Gerald's delinquency." That hearing was held but was not attended by Mrs. Cook, the complainant. As a result of this hearing, a "referral report" was made which was filed with the Court but was not disclosed to Gerald or his parents. At the conclusion of the hearing, the judge committed Gerald as a juvenile delinquent to the state industrial school "for a period of his minority [that is, until 21] unless sooner discharged by due process of law." No appeal was permitted in juvenile cases.

HOLDING

The Court found that due process requirements under the Fourteenth Amendment extended to juveniles, stating that under the Constitution "the condition of being a boy does not justify a kangaroo court." The summary procedure, as well as the long commitment, was possible because Gerald was fifteen years of age instead of over eighteen years of age. The Court pointed out that the particular offense, if he had been over eighteen, would have carried a maximum punishment of $5–$50 or imprisonment in jail for not more than two months. Instead, he was committed to custody for a maximum of six years. The Court found that due process requires written notice to be afforded the child and his parents or guardian and that such notice must inform them "of the specific issues that they must meet" and must be given "at the earliest practicable time, and in any event sufficiently in advance of the hearing to permit preparation." Notice in this case was neither timely nor adequate, nor was there waiver of the right to constitutionally adequate notice. The child and his parents must also be advised of their right to be represented by counsel, and if they are unable to afford counsel, that counsel will be appointed to represent the child. Mrs. Gault's statement at the *habeas corpus* hearing that she had known that she could employ counsel was not "an intentional relinquishment or abandonment" of that right. Another constitutional privilege that must be invoked is the privilege against self-incrimination. The admission by a juvenile must not be used against him in the absence of clear and unequivocal evidence that the admission was made with knowledge that he was not obliged to speak and would not be penalized for remaining silent. Juvenile proceedings to determine delinquency that may lead to commitment in a state institution must be regarded as criminal for the purposes of the privilege of self-incrimination. Absent a valid confession, a juvenile in such proceedings must be afforded the rights of confrontation and sworn testimony of witnesses available for cross-examination.

ROE V. WADE,
410 U.S. 113 (1973)

FACTS

Jane Roe was a single woman residing in Dallas County, Texas, when she instituted a federal action in March 1970 against the District Attorney of the county. She sought a declaratory judgment that the Texas criminal abortion statutes were unconstitutional and requested an injunction restraining the defendant from enforcing the statutes. She alleged that she was unmarried and pregnant and that she wished to terminate her pregnancy by abortion "performed by a competent licensed physician under safe clinical conditions." She submitted that she was unable to get a "legal" abortion in Texas because her life did not appear to be threatened by the continuation of a pregnancy and that she could not afford to travel to another jurisdiction in order to secure a legal abortion under safe conditions. She claimed that the Texas statutes were unconstitutionally vague and that they abridged her right of personal privacy protected by the First, Fourth, Fifth, Ninth, and Fourteenth Amendments. John and Mary Doe filed a companion complaint to that of Roe. They submitted that if Jane were to become pregnant they would want to abort the fetus. The Court found that the Does did not have standing to sue, although Roe did.

HOLDING

The Court found that the state criminal statutes disregarded the stage of pregnancy and other interests involved and thus violated the Due Process Clause of the Fourteenth Amendment, which protects against state action the right of privacy, including a woman's qualified right to terminate her pregnancy. The state cannot override that right. It has legitimate interests in protecting both the pregnant woman's health and the potentiality of human life, each of which interests grows and reaches a "compelling" point at various stages of the woman's approach to term. In the first stage prior to approximately the end of the first trimester, the abortion decision and its effectuation must be left to medical judgment of the pregnant woman's attending physician. For the stage subsequent to approximately the end of the first trimester, the state in promoting its interest in the health of the mother may, if it chooses, regulate the abortion procedure in ways that are reasonably related to maternal health. For the stage subsequent to viability, the state in promoting its interest in the potentiality of human life may, if it chooses, regulate and even proscribe abortion except where necessary in appropriate medical judgment for the preservation of the life or health of the mother. The state may define the term "physician" to mean only a physician currently licensed by the state and may proscribe any abortion by a person who is not a physician so defined.

As we note in the book, the Supreme Court in *Carey* (see below) has substituted the more flexible test of whether the abortion statute imposes an unreasonable burden on the woman's right to choose. Thus, the rigid tripartite division is overruled.

NEW YORK V. FERBER,
458 U.S. 747 (1982)

FACTS

Paul Ferber, the proprietor of a Manhattan bookstore specializing in sexually oriented products, sold two films to an undercover police officer. The films were devoted almost exclusively to depicting young boys masturbating. Ferber was indicted on two counts for violating New York laws controlling dissemination of child pornography. After a jury trial, Ferber was acquitted of the two counts of promoting obscene sexual performance but found guilty on two counts that did not require proof that the films were obscene. Ferber's convictions were affirmed by the Appellate Division of the New York State Supreme Court. The New York Court of Appeals reversed, holding that the New York statute violated the First Amendment. The United States Supreme Court granted certiorari, presenting a single question for the Court:

> To prevent the abuse of children who are made to engage in sexual conduct for commercial purposes, could the New York state legislature, consistent with the First Amendment, prohibit the dissemination of material which has children engaged in sexual conduct, regardless of whether such material is obscene?

HOLDING

The Court found that the statute in question did not violate the First Amendment as applied to the states through the Fourteenth Amendment. In reaching this conclusion, the Court found that the states are entitled to greater leeway in the regulation of pornographic depictions of children for the following reasons:

1. The legislative judgment is that the use of children as subjects of pornographic materials is harmful to the psychological, emotional, and mental health of the child.
2. The obscenity standard established by the Court in prior First Amendment decisions was not a satisfactory solution to the child pornography problem.
3. The advertising and selling of child pornography provided an economic motive for, and are thus an integral part of, the production of such materials, an activity illegal throughout the nation.
4. The value of permitting live performances and photographic reproductions of children engaged in lewd exhibitions is exceedingly modest if not *de minimis*.
5. When an identifiable class of material such as that covered by the New York statute bears so heavily and persuasively on the welfare of children engaged in its production, the balance of competing interests is clearly struck and it is permissible to consider these materials as without First Amendment protection.

PRINCE V. MASSACHUSETTS,
321 U.S. 158 (1944)

FACTS

Betty M. Simmons was a nine-year-old girl legally in the custody of her aunt, Sarah Prince. Mr. and Mrs. Prince and all their children were Jehovah's Witnesses. Both Mr. and Mrs. Prince and Betty testified that they were ordained ministers. Mrs. Prince was accustomed to go out each week onto the streets of Brockton, Massachusetts, to distribute *Watchtower* and *Consolation*. She had permitted the children to engage in this activity but had been warned against it by the school attendance officer, Mr. Perkins. On the evening in question, Mrs. Prince had first refused to take her children with her in her activities, but they pleaded and were allowed to go. While downtown, Mrs. Prince permitted the children to "engage in the preaching work with her upon the sidewalks." Betty and Mrs. Prince took positions about 20 feet apart near the street intersection. Betty held up her hand for passersby to see copies of *Watchtower* and *Consolation*. From her shoulder hung the usual canvas magazine bag, on which was printed "Watchtower and Consolation 5¢ per copy." No one accepted a copy from Betty that evening, and she received no money, nor did her aunt. But on other occasions Betty had received funds and had given out copies. About 8:45 P.M., Mr. Perkins approached Mrs. Prince. He inquired about Betty's identity, but Mrs. Prince refused to give Betty's name. However, she offered that the child attended the Shaw School. Mr. Perkins referred to his previous warnings and said he would allow them five minutes to get off the street. Mrs. Prince admitted that she had supplied Betty with the magazines, saying, "Neither you nor anyone else can stop me. . . . This child is exercising her God-given right and her constitutional right to preach the gospel, and no creature has a right to interfere with God's command." Mrs. Prince and Betty then departed. The only question remaining for the Court was whether the statute that prohibited children from selling newspapers, magazines, and periodicals was valid. Mrs. Prince was charged with having committed breaches of this act. Mrs. Prince rested her defense squarely upon freedom of religion under the First Amendment.

HOLDING

The Court found that the statute did not violate the First Amendment. The power of the state to control the conduct of your children is broader than its power over adults. The Court found that the family was not beyond regulation in the public interest as against a claim of religious liberty. The state as *parens patriae* may restrict the parents' control by requiring school attendance, by regulating or prohibiting the child's labor, and in many other ways. Its authority is not nullified merely because the parent grounds a claim on the child's course of conduct on religion or conscience.

The *Prince* case is important for its statement of the powers of the state vis-à-vis children. However, its holding must now be considered in light of the *Yoder* case and later Supreme Court decisions concerning the regulation of religious practices. If a law applies neutrally and is not intended to strike at a particular religion, then its constitutionality may be upheld under the First Amendment.

KENT V. UNITED STATES,
383 U.S. 541 (1966)

FACTS

Morris A. Kent, Jr., came under the authority of the Juvenile Court of the District of Columbia in 1959. He was then fourteen. He was apprehended as a result of several housebreakings and an attempt to snatch a purse. He was placed on probation in the custody of his mother, who had been separated from her husband since Kent was two years old. Juvenile Court officials interviewed Kent from time to time during the probation period and accumulated a "social service" file on him. On September 10, 1961, an intruder entered the apartment of a woman in the District of Columbia. He took her wallet. He raped her. The police found latent fingerprints in the apartment. They were developed and processed. They matched the fingerprints of Morris Kent, taken when he was fourteen years old and under the jurisdiction of the Juvenile Court. About 3:00 P.M. on September 5, 1961, Kent was taken into custody by police. Kent was then sixteen and therefore subject to the "exclusive jurisdiction" of the Juvenile Court. He was still on probation to that court as a result of the 1959 proceedings. Upon being apprehended, Kent was taken to police headquarters, where he was interrogated by police officers. He admitted his involvement in the offense that led to his apprehension and volunteered information concerning similar offenses involving housebreaking, robbery, and rape. His interrogation proceeded from 3:00 P.M. to 10:00 P.M. the same evening. The following day, Kent's mother retained counsel. Kent was detained at the Receiving Home for almost a week. During that time he was not arraigned, and no determination was made by a juvenile officer of probable cause for the apprehension. Despite Kent's counsel's arguments that the Juvenile Court should retain jurisdiction, the Juvenile Court judge, having held no hearing, determined that "(after) full investigation I do hereby waive" jurisdiction of Kent and directed that he be held for trial for the alleged offenses. No reasons were given for the waiver. Kent was indicted in the District Court. He moved to dismiss the indictment on the ground that the Juvenile Court's waiver was invalid. The District Court overruled the motion, and the petitioner was tried. He was convicted on six counts of housebreaking and robbery but acquitted on two rape counts by reason of insanity. On appeal, the petitioner raised, among other things, the validity of the Juvenile Court's waiver of jurisdiction. The United States Court of Appeals for the District of Columbia found that the procedure leading to the wavier and the waiver order were valid.

HOLDING

The Supreme Court found that the Juvenile Court order waiving jurisdiction and remitting the petitioner Kent for trial in the District Court was invalid. The Court found that the Juvenile Court's latitude in determining whether to waive jurisdiction was not complete. It must comply with "procedural regularity sufficient in the particular circumstances to satisfy the basic requirements of due process and fairness, as well as compliance with the statutory requirement of 'full investigation.' " The *parens patriae* philosophy of the Juvenile Court may not be taken as an "invitation to procedural arbitrariness." The juvenile, in light of his statutory and constitutional rights, was entitled to a hearing, to access for his counsel to social records and probation or similar reports presumably considered by the Juvenile Court, and to a statement of the reasons for the Juvenile Court's decision sufficient to enable meaningful appellate review of the decision.

CAREY V. POPULATION SERVICES INTERNATIONAL, 431 U.S. 678 (1977)

FACTS

New York education law made it a crime (1) for any person to sell or distribute any contraceptive of any kind to a minor under sixteen; (2) for anyone other than a licensed pharmacist to distribute contraceptives to persons sixteen or over; and (3) for anyone, including licensed pharmacists, to advertise or display contraceptives. Population Planning Associates was a corporation engaged in the mail order retail sale of nonmedical contraceptives. No limit was in place to prevent sales of products to persons under any particular age. New York officials threatened enforcement of the legislation, and the company challenged the constitutionality of the legislation. A three-judge district court declared the statute unconstitutional under the First and Fourteenth Amendments insofar as it applied to nonprescription contraceptives and enjoined its enforcement as so applied.

HOLDING

The Court confirmed that the right to privacy in decisions affecting procreation extends to minors as well adults. Prohibition could not be justified by the state's interest in protecting children's health. The prohibition of any advertisement or display of contraceptives that sought to suppress completely any information about the availability and price of contraceptives could not be justified on the ground that advertisements of contraceptive products would offend and embarrass those exposed to them and that permitting them would legitimize sexual activity by young people. These are classically not justifications validating suppression of expression protected by the First Amendment, and here the advertisements in question merely state the availability of products that are not only entirely legal but constitutionally protected.

HAZELWOOD SCHOOL DISTRICT V. KUHLMEIER, 484 U.S. 260 (1988)

FACTS

Spectrum was written and edited by the Journalism II class at Hazelwood East High School. The newspaper was published every three weeks or so during the 1982–83 school year. More than 4,500 copies of the paper were distributed during that year to students, school personnel, and members of the community. Emerson, the teacher in charge of the journalism class, delivered proofs of the May 13 edition to Headmaster Reynolds, who objected to two of the articles scheduled to appear in that edition. One of the stories described three Hazelwood East students' experiences with pregnancy; the other discussed the impact of parental divorce on students at school. Reynolds was concerned that, although the pregnancy story used false names "to keep the identity of these girls a secret," the pregnant students might be identifiable from the text. He also believed that the article's references to sexual activity and birth control were inappropriate for some of the younger students of the school. In addition, Reynolds was concerned that a student identified by name in the divorce story had complained that the father "wasn't spending enough time with my mom, my sister, and I" prior to the divorce and described other intimate family matters. Reynolds believed that the student's parents should have been given the opportunity to respond to these remarks or consent to their publication. He was unaware that Emerson had deleted the student's name from the final version of the article. Three former school students who were staff members of *Spectrum* brought an action contending that school officials had violated their First Amendment rights by deleting two pages of the articles from the May 13, 1983, issue. The District Court found that no First Amendment violation had occurred. The Court of Appeals reversed.

HOLDING

The Court found that the students' First Amendment rights were not violated. The Court found that the First Amendment rights of students in public schools are not coextensive with the rights of adults in other settings and must be applied in light of the special characteristics of the school environment. A school need not tolerate student speech that is inconsistent with its basic educational mission, even though the government could not censor similar speech outside the school. The school newspaper here could not be characterized as a forum for public expression. School facilities may be deemed to be public forums only if the school authorities have by policy or practice opened the facilities for indiscriminate use by the general public or by some segment of the public, such as student organizations. The officials did not evince any intention to open the paper's pages to indiscriminate use by its student reporters or by its student body generally. Accordingly, school officials were entitled to regulate the paper's contents in any reasonable manner. Educators do not offend the First Amendment by exercising editorial control over the style and content of student speech in school-sponsored expressive activities, so long as their activities are reasonably related to legitimate pedagogical concerns. The Court found that the school principal had acted reasonably in this case.

BROWN V. BOARD OF EDUCATION OF TOPEKA,
347 U.S. 483 (1954)

FACTS

A number of cases were consolidated from the states of Kansas, South Carolina, Virginia, and Delaware. In the Kansas case, the plaintiffs were black children of elementary school age residing in Topeka. They brought an action in the United States District Court for the District of Kansas to enjoin enforcement of a Kansas statute that permitted but did not require cities of more than 15,000 of population to maintain separate school facilities for black and white students. Under that authority, the Topeka Board of Education elected to establish segregated elementary schools. Other public schools in the community, however, were operated on a nonsegregated basis. The District Court found that segregation in public education had a detrimental effect upon black children but denied relief on the ground that black and white schools were substantially equal in respect of buildings, transportation, curriculum, and the educational qualifications of teachers. The cases brought from other states had a similar factual background. The segregation in those cases was alleged to deprive the plaintiffs of the equal protection of the laws under the Fourteenth Amendment. The lower courts had applied the "separate but equal" doctrine announced by the United States Supreme Court in *Plessy v. Ferguson*, 163 U.S. 537.

HOLDING

The Supreme Court unanimously held that the segregation of children in public schools solely on the basis of race, even though the physical facilities and other "tangible" factors may be equal, deprives the children of the minority group of equal educational opportunities. Separate educational facilities were inherently unequal. Thus the term "separate but equal" had no place in the field of public education. It is to be noted that the Court relied upon evidence as to the adverse psychological impact on blacks flowing from the legally sanctioned separation of the races in education.

INGRAHAM V. WRIGHT,
430 U.S. 651 (1977)

FACTS

James Ingraham and Roosevelt Andrews were students enrolled in a junior high school in Dade County, Florida. Ingraham was in the eighth grade and Andrews in the ninth. Corporal punishment was widely used as a means of maintaining discipline in school. A Florida statute authorized limited corporal punishment by way of negative inference proscribing the use of "degrading or unduly severe punishment" by teachers. Ingraham, because he was slow to respond to his teacher's directions, was subjected to more than twenty licks with a paddle while being held over a table in the principal's office. He suffered a hematoma requiring medical attention, keeping him out of school for several days. Andrew was paddled several times for minor infractions. On two occasions he was struck on his arms, once depriving him of the full use of his arm for a week. The question before the Supreme Court was whether the punishment in these cases fell within the constitutional proscription under the Eighth Amendment of cruel and unusual punishment and under the Fourteenth Amendment of procedural due process.

HOLDING

The Eighth Amendment proscription of cruel and unusual punishment does not apply to disciplinary corporal punishment in public schools. The opinion of the Court refers to the historical context of the Eighth Amendment as designed to protect those convicted of crimes.

In respect of the Fourteenth Amendment due process claim, the Court found that the school was not required to give notice or hearing prior to the imposition of corporal punishment, since the practice was authorized and limited by the common law. No deprivation of substantive rights was possible so long as the corporal punishment remained within the limits of the common law privilege. The Florida scheme, considered in light of the openness of the school environment, afforded sufficient protection against unjustified corporal punishment of schoolchildren. If the punishment were found to be excessive, those responsible would be held liable in damages or would be subject to criminal penalties. A constitutional requirement imposing additional administrative safeguards would intrude into the area of educational responsibility that lies primarily with public school authorities. Prior procedural safeguards require a diversion of educational resources, and school authorities may abandon corporal punishment as a disciplinary measure rather than incur the burdens of complying with procedural requirements. Incremental benefit of invoking the Constitution to impose prior notice and hearing cannot justify those costs.

DESHANEY V. WINNEBAGO COUNTY DEPARTMENT OF SOCIAL SERVICES, 109 S.CT. 998 (1989)

FACTS

Joshua DeShaney was born in 1979. In 1980 a Wyoming court granted his parents a divorce and awarded custody of Joshua to his father, Randy DeShaney. The father shortly thereafter moved to Wisconsin, taking the infant with him. He entered into a second marriage, which also ended in divorce. Winnebago County authorities first learned that Joshua DeShaney might be a victim of child abuse in January 1982, when his father's second wife complained to police that at the time of their divorce he had previously "hit the boy causing marks. He was a prime case for child abuse." The Winnebago County Department of Social Services interviewed the father, but he denied the accusations and the Department did not pursue them further. In January 1983 Joshua was admitted to a local hospital with multiple bruises and abrasions. The examining physician suspected child abuse and notified the Department, which immediately obtained an order from a Wisconsin Juvenile Court placing Joshua in temporary custody of the hospital. Three days later the County convened an *ad hoc* "Child Protection Team" consisting of a pediatrician, a psychologist, a police detective, the county's lawyer, several Department caseworkers, and various hospital personnel, to consider Joshua's situation. The team decided that there was insufficient evidence of child abuse to retain Joshua in the custody of the court. The team, however, recommended several measures to protect Joshua, including enrolling him in a preschool program, providing his father with certain counseling services, and encouraging his father's girlfriend to move out of the home. Randy DeShaney entered into a voluntary agreement with the Department in which he promised to cooperate with them in accomplishing these goals. Joshua was returned to the custody of his father. A month later emergency room personnel called the Department caseworker handling Joshua's case to report that he had once again been treated for suspicious injuries. The caseworker concluded that there was no basis for action. For the next six months the caseworker made monthly visits to the DeShaney home, during which she observed a number of suspicious injuries on Joshua's head; she also noticed that he had not been enrolled in school and that the girlfriend had not moved out. The caseworker recorded these incidents in her files, along with continuing suspicions that someone in the DeShaney household was physically abusing Joshua. She did nothing more, however. In November 1983 the emergency room notified the Department that Joshua had been treated once again for injuries that they believed to be caused by child abuse. On the caseworker's next two visits to the DeShaney home, she was told that Joshua was too ill to see her.

In March 1984 Randy DeShaney beat four-year-old Joshua for the last tragic time. He fell into a coma, was operated on, but suffered brain damage of such severity that he was expected to spend the remainder of his life in an institution for the profoundly mentally retarded. The operation revealed a series of brain hemorrhages caused by trauma over a long period of time.

Joshua's mother brought an action under Section 1983 alleging that the Department had deprived Joshua of his liberty without due process of the law in violations of the Fourteenth Amendment.

HOLDING

The Due Process Clause of the Fourteenth Amendment imposes no affirmative obligations on the state to provide the general public with adequate protective services, except where a "special relationship" is created. When the state takes a person into its custody and holds him there against his will, the Constitution imposes a corresponding duty to assume responsibility. However, no such duty was established in this case, since the harm suffered by Joshua did not occur while he was in the state's custody, but rather while he was in the custody of his natural father. When Joshua was returned to his father's custody, he was placed in no worse position than he would have been in if the Department had not acted at all.

BURNETTE V. WAHL,
588 P.2D 1105 (OR. 1978) (SUPREME COURT OF OREGON)

FACTS

The plaintiffs in this case were five minor children, aged two to eight, who, through their guardian, brought actions against their mothers for emotional and psychological injury caused by failure of those mothers to perform their parental duties to the plaintiffs. The plaintiffs' claim was solely for emotional or psychological damage resulting from failure to support, nurture, and care for the children. In this respect, the claim was unusual and depended upon the implication of private rights of action from various state legislation designed to protect the welfare of children. The question was one of law as to whether the statutes would sustain the implication of such rights of action.

HOLDING

The majority of the court found that a cause of action may be created by the court for an act or omission which violates a statute. In deciding whether to create such a cause of action, the court should take account of the policy of the legislation.

The dissenting opinion of Justice Linde is important. This well-regarded jurist puts greater emphasis on the declaration of policy by the legislature in enacting the statute for the protection of children and would imply a right of action from that legislation. Justice Linde's view accords with that of the Restatement (Second) of Torts, Section 874(A).

IN THE MATTER OF BABY M,
537 A.2D 1227 (N.J. 1988) (SUPREME COURT OF NEW JERSEY)

FACTS

In February 1985 William Stern and Mary Beth Whitehead entered a surrogacy contract. The contract stated that Stern's wife, Elizabeth, was infertile, that the couple wanted a child, and that Mrs. Whitehead was willing to provide that child as mother with Mr. Stern as the father. The contract provided that, through artificial insemination, using Mr. Stern's sperm, Mrs. Whitehead would become pregnant, carry the child to term, bear it, and deliver it to the Sterns, and they were out to do whatever was necessary to terminate her maternal rights so that Mrs. Stern could thereafter adopt the child. Mrs. Whitehead's husband, Richard, was also a party to the contract, but Mrs. Stern was not. Mr. Whitehead promised to do all acts necessary to rebut the presumption of paternity under the Parentage Act. Mrs. Whitehead was paid $10,000 by Mr. Stern upon delivery of the baby.

The Sterns had met while Ph.D students at the University of Michigan and, because of financial considerations, had decided to defer starting a family. Before her family was begun, Mrs. Stern learned that she might have multiple sclerosis and that the disease in some cases renders pregnancy a serious health risk. Mr. Stern was very much concerned to continue his blood line, since most of his family had been destroyed in the Holocaust. Contact was made with Mrs. Whitehead, artificial insemination was provided, pregnancy achieved, and birth given to Baby M on March 27, 1986. Mrs. Whitehead, however, felt such a bond to the child that she did not want to part with her. Nevertheless, she gave over the child to the Sterns. Mr. Stern filed a complaint seeking enforcement of the surrogacy contract when Mrs. Whitehead, having subsequently been given the child for a short period in order to alleviate her grief, failed to relinquish her to the Sterns.

HOLDING

The court held that the surrogate parenting contract was illegal under laws prohibiting the use of money in connection with adoptions. No valid termination of parental rights was affected, and therefore no adoption could follow. The mother was entitled to retain her rights as mother of the child, since she was never found to be unfit but was affirmatively found to be a good mother of her other children. The court also found that constitutional protections surrounded the right to companionship of a child with his or her mother. It is to be noted that the court did not find that a surrogacy arrangement was illegal where no money changed hands. It called for legislative regulation of this difficult and ethically charged area.

The issue then reverted to one of custody between Whitehead (the mother) and Mr. Stern (the father) and his wife. The court referred to expert evidence in respect of the custody issue and found that the predominant view was that the best interests of the child were served by granting custody to the Sterns. However, Mrs. Whitehead was entitled to visitation.

FARE V. MICHAEL C., 442 U.S. 707 (1979)

FACTS

Michael C. was implicated in the murder of Robert Yeager. The murder occurred during a robbery of the victim's home on January 19, 1976. A small truck registered in the name of Michael C.'s mother was identified as having been near the Yeager home at the time of the killing, and a young man answering Michael C.'s description was seen by witnesses near the truck and near the home shortly before the murder.

Acting on this information, Van Nuys, California, police took Michael C. into custody at approximately 6:30 P.M. on February 4. At that time he was sixteen and one-half years old and on probation to the Juvenile Court. He had been on probation since the age of twelve and approximately a year earlier had served a term in a youth corrections camp under the supervision of the Juvenile Court. He had a record of several previous offenses, including burglary of guns and purse-snatching, stretching back over several years. Police officers began to interrogate Michael at the police station. In a tape-recorded conversation in which Michael and the police officers were the only participants, Michael was informed that he had been brought in for questioning in relation to the murder and fully advised of his Miranda rights. The following conversation occurred:

QUESTION: Do you understand all these rights as I have explained them to you?

ANSWER: Yeah.

QUESTION: Okay. Do you wish to give up your right to remain silent and talk to us about this murder?

ANSWER: What murder? I don't know about no murder.

QUESTION: I'll explain to you which one it is if you want to talk to us about it.

ANSWER: Yeah, I might talk to you.

QUESTION: Do you want to give up your right to have an attorney present while I talk about it?

ANSWER: *Can I have my probation officer here?*

QUESTION: Well, I can't get hold of your probation officer right now. You have a right to have an attorney.

ANSWER: How I know you guys won't pull no police officer in and tell me he's an attorney?

QUESTION: Huh?

ANSWER: [How I know you guys won't pull no police officer in and tell me he's an attorney?]

QUESTION: Your probation officer is Mr. Christiansen?

ANSWER: Yeah.

QUESTION: Well, I'm not going to call Mr. Christiansen tonight. There's a good chance we can talk to him later, but I'm not going to call him right now. If you want to talk to us without an attorney present, you can. If you don't want to, you don't have to. But if you want to say something, you can, and if you don't want to say something, you don't have to. That's your right. You understand that right?

ANSWER: Yeah.

QUESTION: Okay, will you talk to us without an attorney present?

ANSWER: Yeah. I want to talk to you.

Michael C. then proceeded to answer questions put to him by officers and to make statements and draw sketches that incriminated him in the Yeager murder. Charges were brought against Michael C. largely on the basis of these statements. He moved to suppress the statements and sketches he gave the police during the interrogation on the basis that the statements had been obtained in violation of Miranda, in that his request to see his probation officer at the outset of questioning constituted an invocation of his Fifth Amendment right to remain silent just as if he had requested the assistance of attorney.

HOLDING

The Supreme Court found that the California Supreme Court had erred in finding that the respondent's request for his probation officer was an invocation of his Fifth Amendment rights. The Court came to this conclusion on the basis that the Miranda rule was based on the unique role of the lawyer in the adversary system of criminal justice. A probation officer, despite a relationship of trust and cooperation with the juvenile, was not capable of effective legal advice sufficient to protect juvenile's rights during police investigation. Furthermore, the request for the probation officer could not be construed as a request to remain silent as guaranteed under the Fifth Amendment. Therefore, the Court concluded that Michael C. had waived his Fifth Amendment rights voluntarily in this case.

PARHAM V. J.R.,
442 U.S. 584 (1979)

FACTS

This was a class action brought by children treated in a Georgia mental hospital against Georgia mental health officials. The children sought a declaration that Georgia's procedures for voluntary commitment of children under the age of eighteen years to state mental hospitals violated the Due Process Clause of the Fourteenth Amendment. The facts in respect of two individual plaintiffs were addressed by the Court. In the case of J.L., who had died at the time of the Supreme Court's decision, the boy was admitted in 1970 at the age of six to the Central State Regional Hospital in Milledgeville, Georgia. Prior to his admission, J.L. had received outpatient treatment at the hospital for more than two months until his mother requested that the hospital admit him indefinitely. The admitting physician interviewed J.L. and his parents. He learned that J.L.'s natural parents were divorced and his mother had remarried. He also learned that J.L. had been expelled from school because he was uncontrollable. He accepted the parents' representation that the boy had been extremely aggressive and diagnosed the child as having a "hyperkinetic reaction of childhood."

J.L.'s mother and stepfather agreed to participate in family therapy during the time their son was hospitalized. Under this program, J.L. was permitted to go home for short stays. Apparently his behavior during those visits was erratic. After several months the parents requested discontinuance of the program. In 1972 the child was returned to his mother and stepfather on a furlough basis, that is, he would live at home but go to school at the hospital. The parents found that they were unable to control J.L. to their satisfaction, and this created family stress. Within two months, they requested his readmission to Central State, and they relinquished their parental rights to the county in 1974.

Although several hospital employees recommended that J.L. be placed in a special foster home with a "warm, supportive, truly involved couple," the Department of Family and Children's Services was unable to place him in such a setting. In 1975 J.L. filed a suit requesting an order for the court to place him in a less drastic environment suitable to his needs.

In the case of J.R., the boy was declared a neglected child by the county and removed from his natural parents when he was three months old. He was placed in several different foster homes in succession prior to his admission to Central State Hospital at the age of seven.

Immediately preceding his hospitalization, J.R. received outpatient treatment at a county mental health center for several months. He began attending school but was disruptive, and unable to conform to normal behavior patterns. J.R.'s seventh set of foster parents requested his removal from their home. The Department then sought his admission to Central State. The agency provided the hospital with a complete sociomedical history at the time of his admission. In addition, three separate interviews were conducted with J.R. by the admission team of the hospital. It was determined that he had borderline intellectual retardation and that he suffered from "unsocialized, aggressive reaction of childhood." It was recommended unanimously that he would "benefit from the structured environment" of the hospital and would "enjoy living and playing with boys of the same age." J.R.'s progress was reexamined periodically, and unsuccessful attempts were made by the Department to place him in foster homes.

Georgia law provided for the voluntary admission to state regional hospitals of children such as J.L. and J.R. Admission began with an application for hospitalization signed by "parent or guardian." Upon application, the superintendent of each hospital was given power to admit temporarily any child for "observation and diagnosis." If after observation the superintendent finds "evidence of mental illness" and that the child is "suitable for treatment" in the hospital, then the child may be admitted for such a period under such conditions as is authorized by law. The mental health statute also provided for discharge of voluntary patients. This was to be done at the request of a parent or guardian or where the child had recovered from mental illness or sufficiently improved to the extent that hospitalization was no longer desirable.

The District Court held that Georgia's statutory scheme was unconstitutional because it failed to protect adequately the plaintiffs' due process rights and that due process included at least the right after notice to an adversary-type hearing before an impartial tribunal.

HOLDING

In a long opinion, the Supreme Court held that the District Court had erred in holding unconstitutional the state's procedures for admission of children and that Georgia's medical fact-finding processes were consistent with constitutional guarantees. This conclusion depended upon the observation that under a due process claim the Court must balance (1) the private interest that will be affected by official action, (2) the risk of an erroneous deprivation of such interest through the procedures used and the probable value of additional or substitute procedural safeguards, and (3) the state's interests, including the fiscal and administrative burdens that additional or substitute procedural requirements would entail. The Court emphasized the parental interest in acting on behalf of children. Although they did not have absolute discretion to institutionalize a child, parents retained plenary authority to seek such care for their children subject to independent medical judgment. In respect of the state's interest, procedural obstacles may be costly and may discourage the mentally ill or their families from seeking psychiatric assistance. The Court addressed the risk of error inherent in parental decision and considered that it was sufficiently great to require inquiry by a "neutral fact-finder" to determine whether the statutory requirements for admission were satisfied. The initial admission decision needed to be reviewed periodically. However, nothing required the neutral fact-finder to be legally trained or a judicial or administrative officer. Nor should the physician be required to conduct a formal or quasi-formal adversary hearing. The Court could see no special advantage in a more formal judicial-type hearing over a thorough psychiatric investigation followed by periodic review of the child's condition. Thus, it followed that Georgia's practices comported with minimum due process requirements.

The Supreme Court lays down minimum due process requirements, and nothing prevents a state from imposing more thoroughgoing requirements. We observe, in the text, that a number of states require more detailed review. Note also the differentiation between the request for admission by the child's natural parents and admission by his guardians. The majority of the Court deemed that this different status should make no difference. However, see the view of Justice Brennan dissenting in part on this point.

PLANNED PARENTHOOD OF SOUTHEASTERN PENNSYLVANIA V. CASEY, 112 S.CT. 2791 (1992)

FACTS

In this case, the Supreme Court considered the fundamental constitutional issue raised in *Roe v. Wade,* 14 U.S. 113, discussed previously. At issue were five provisions of the Pennsylvania Abortion Control Act of 1982, as amended in 1988 and 1989. The act required that a woman seeking an abortion give her informed consent prior to the abortion procedure. It specified that she be provided with certain information at least twenty-four hours before the abortion is performed. For a minor to obtain an abortion, the act required the informed consent of one of her parents but provided for a judicial bypass option if the minor did not wish to, or could not, obtain a parent's consent. Another provision of the act requires that unless certain exceptions applied, a married woman seeking an abortion must have signed a statement indicating that she had notified her husband of her intended abortion. The act exempted compliance with these three requirements in the event of a "medical emergency" defined under the act.

HOLDING

The Court found that *Roe v. Wade,* in its central holding, should be retained and reaffirmed. The Court recognized that a reexamination of the principles was called for because of subsequent decisions casting doubt on the meaning and reach of *Roe*'s central holding. The Court found that in order to protect the central right recognized by *Roe,* while at the same time accommodating the state's profound interest in potential life, an "undue burden" standard should be employed. An undue burden exists, and therefore the provision of law is invalid, if its purpose or effect is to place substantial obstacles in the path of a woman seeking an abortion before the fetus attains viability. Accordingly, the rigid trimester framework in *Roe* was rejected. To promote the state's interest in potential life throughout pregnancy, the state may take measures to ensure that the woman's choice is informed. Measures designed to advance this interest should not be invalidated if their purpose is to persuade the woman to choose childbirth over abortion. These measures must not be an undue burden on the right. The state may enact regulations to further the health and safety of the woman seeking an abortion but may not impose unnecessary health regulations that present substantial obstacles to a woman seeking an abortion. The state may not prohibit any woman from making the ultimate decision to terminate her pregnancy before viability.

Applying the undue burden standard, the Court found that the spousal notification requirement was unconstitutional, while the other requirements were constitutional. In respect of the statute's parental consent provision, the Court found that this was consistent with pervious decisions of the Court involving such requirements. It was reasonably designed to further the state's important and legitimate interest in "the welfare of its young citizens, whose immaturity, inexperience, and lack of judgment may sometimes impair their ability to exercise their rights wisely."

These views were maintained against trenchant dissents by Justices Scalia and Chief Justice Rehnquist, who were joined by Justices White and Thomas. These Justices rejected *Roe v. Wade* as a guiding authority.

The retention of *Roe v. Wade,* it may be noted, will involve the federal courts and ultimately the Supreme Court in review of states' abortion statutes in light of the articulated undue burden test. It is clear that the parental consent requirement will be constitutionally permissible if accompanied by a judicial bypass.

SCHALL V. MARTIN,
467 U.S. 253 (1984)

FACTS

A class action was brought on behalf of all juveniles detained under the provisions of the New York Family Court Act. This act authorized pretrial detention of juvenile delinquents based on a finding that there was a "serious risk" that the child "may before the return date commit an act which if committed by an adult would constitute a crime." Gregory Martin was arrested on December 13, 1977, and charged with first-degree robbery, second-degree assault, and criminal possession of a weapon based on an incident in which he, with two others, allegedly hit a youth on the head with a loaded gun and stole his jacket and sneakers. Martin was in possession of the gun when he was arrested. The incident occurred at 11:30 P.M. The defendant was fourteen years old at the time, and therefore came within the jurisdiction of New York's Family Court. Martin had lied to the police about where, and with whom, he lived and was consequently detained overnight. A petition of delinquency was filed, and Martin made an initial appearance in the Family Court on December 14, accompanied by his grandmother. The Family Court judge, citing possession of a loaded weapon, the false address given to the police, and the lateness of the hour as evidence of lack of supervision, ordered Martin to be detained. Some five days later a probable cause hearing was held at which probable cause was found to exist for all the crimes charged. On December 27–29, Martin was found guilty on the robbery and criminal possession charges and was adjudicated a delinquent and placed on two years' probation. The court cited other similar cases where the court had ordered detention of juveniles. The District Court struck down the statute as permitting detention without due process and ordered release of Martin and other members of the class. The Second Circuit Court of Appeals affirmed, holding that, since the vast majority of juveniles detained under the statute either had their cases dismissed before adjudication of delinquency or were released after adjudication, the statute was administered not for preventive purposes but to impose punishment for unadjudicated criminal acts. Therefore the statute was unconstitutional.

HOLDING

The Supreme Court found that the provision was not invalid under the Due Process Clause of the Fourteenth Amendment. It reached this conclusion by finding that preventive detention under the statute served a legitimate interest of the state in protecting both the juvenile and society from the hazards of pretrial crime. The section's procedural safeguard provided sufficient protection against erroneous and unnecessary deprivations of liberty. The section required notice, a hearing, and a statement of facts and reasons to be given to the juvenile prior to any detention and a formal fact-finding hearing to be held within a short time thereafter. The Court could find no merit in the argument that the risk of erroneous and unnecessary detention was too high despite these procedures. There was nothing inherently unattainable about a prediction of future criminal conduct. Such prediction is an experienced one based on a host of variables that cannot be readily codified. Moreover, the Court ruled that the postdetention procedures—*habeas corpus* review, appeals, and motions for reconsideration—provide a sufficient mechanism for correcting, on a case-by-case, basis any erroneous detention.

NOTES

CHAPTER 1
THE MENTAL HEALTH PROFESSIONS AND THE LAW

1. Slovenko, 1991.
2. Huber, 1991.
3. See Kuhn, 1970, for discussion on the philosophy of science.
4. Posner, 1987.
5. Tribe, 1971; Robinson and Abraham, 1992, p. 1486, referring to the "traditional hostility of courts to statistical and probabilistic evidence . . . in favor of individual, 'clinical'-type evidence."
6. *McCleskey v. Kemp*, 481 U.S. 279 (1987).
7. Manicas and Secord, 1983. But in areas where causation is notoriously difficult to establish, the courts may rely on generalized scientific studies. American Law Institute Study, 1991, Vol. 2, pp. 383–439. For criticism of the common law's particularistic treatment, see Saks and Blanck, 1992.
8. The emphasis on rights is paradoxical, since it occurs against the background of a society that is philosophically relativistic. This style of discourse contended in the eighteenth century with classical republicanism, which centered on the ideal of citizenship, conceived as the exercise of civic virtue and participation in the common good. See Pocock, 1975.
9. See *Cruzan v. Director, Missouri Dept. Health*, 497 U.S. 261 (1990). For a survey of the legal, medical, and ethical issues see White, 1992.
10. Gutheil and Appelbaum, 1982.
11. The Supreme Court bowed to those concerned in finding that the right to confrontation is subject to caveats. *Maryland v. Craig*, 497 U.S. 836 (1990).
12. See Chapter 8.
13. *Parham v. J.R.*, 442 U.S. 584 (1979). For an example of the criticism see LaFond and Durham, 1992, pp. 125–26.
14. Moore, 1984, p. 113.
15. *Ibid.*, p. 423.
16. *Ibid.*, p. 424.
17. Skinner, 1971.
18. *Ake v. Oklahoma*, 470 U.S. 68 (1985).
19. Szasz, 1961.
20. Fleming and Maximov, 1974.
21. Morse, 1978a, p. 560.
22. See Bonnie and Slobogin, 1980 (a detailed and well-considered rejoinder to critics). For an ethical argument in support of the psychiatric role in the vexed area of the death penalty, see Mossman, 1992.

23. The power of psychiatry and psychology in the law has varied with the social temper of the times, see LaFond and Durham, 1992, pp. 29–34 (dividing eras into the progressive, liberal, and neoconservative).
24. See Coady, 1992, Chapter 16.
25. Morse, 1978b.
26. Lipkin, 1990.
27. Although some may argue they should occupy an important place in the policies promoted by the law; see Wexler, 1990. For a range of perspectives, see Ogloff, 1992.
28. *Daubert v. Merrell Dow Pharmaceuticals*, 113 S.Ct. 2786 (1993).
29. In addition to the reasoning of the Supreme Court in *Daubert*, see Bonnie and Slobogin, 1980, pp. 461–95, and Hoge and Grisso, 1992.
30. Morris, 1982, p. 56.
31. For an agenda see Bonnie and Slobogin, 1980, pp. 496–522.
32. American Psychiatric Association Task Force, 1984.
33. Appelbaum, 1990.
34. In Chapter 9 we briefly discuss the defense of insanity, a prime example of the juxtaposition of nuanced professional knowledge brought to the categorical ends of the administration of justice. See also LeFond and Durham, 1992, pp. 34–45; Morris, 1982; and Schopp, 1991.
35. See Chapter 2.
36. *Brown v. Board of Education*, 349 U.S. 294 (1955).
37. Allport *et al.*, 1953.
38. Rosen, 1972, p. 174.
39. Bonnie and Slobogin, 1980, p. 522.
40. Hafemeister and Melton, 1987.
41. Weiss, 1987.

CHAPTER 2
THE LEGAL SYSTEM

1. Holmes, 1881, p. 36.
2. *Roe v. Wade*, 410 U.S. 113 (1973); *Planned Parenthood of Southeastern Pennsylvania v. Casey*, 112 S.Ct. 2791 (1992), discussed in Chapter 3.
3. See Chapter 3.
4. *Canterbury v. Spence*, 464 F.2d 772 (D.C. Cir. 1972). For discussion, see Chapter 8.
5. See, e.g., Code of Alabama §6-5-484, "Degree of Care Owed to Patient."
6. *Helling v. Carey*, 519 P.2d 981 (Wash. 1974). See discussion, Chapter 8.
7. *Gates v. Jensen*, 595 P.2d 919 (Wash. 1979).
8. *Southern Pacific Co. v. Jensen*, 244 U.S. 205, 222 (1917).
9. The role and nature of precedent are discussed later in this chapter.
10. *Teeters v. Currey*, 518 S.W.2d 512 (Tenn. 1974). For limitation period in child abuse, see 9 A.L.R. 5th. *O'Neal v. Division of Family Services*, 821 P.2d 1139 (Utah 1991) holds that limitation period continues to run and is not tolled after gaining of majority, but if the plaintiff proves that he has repressed the memory of the abuse and the fact of the abuse is corroborated, the statute may be tolled, *Meiers-Post v. Shafer,* 427 N.W.2d 606 (Mich. App. 1988).

11. Lacey and Haakonsson, 1991.

12. Ball, 1975.

13. *United States v. Hudson and Goodwin*, 11 U.S. (7 Cranch) 32 (1812).

14. *Erie R. Co. v. Tompkins*, 304 U.S. 64, 78 (1938).

15. *DeShaney v. Winnebago County Department of Social Services*, 489 U.S. 189 (1989). See Chapter 3 for further discussion.

16. *Brown v. Board of Education*, 349 U.S. 294 (1955).

17. *Taylor v. Ledbetter*, 818 F.2d 791 (11th Cir. 1987); *K.H. v. Morgan*, 914 F.2d 846, 932 (7th Cir. 1990); *Norfleet v. Arkansas Dept. of Human Services*, 989 F.2d 289 (8th Cir. 1993).

18. *In re Gault*, 387 U.S. 1, 13 (1967).

19. *Parham v. J.R.*, 442 U.S. 584, 624–25 (1979).

20. *West Virginia State Board of Education v. Barnette*, 319 U.S. 624 (1943).

21. *United States v. Eichman*, 496 U.S. 310 (1990).

22. *Tinker v. Des Moines Independent Community School District*, 393 U.S. 503 (1969).

23. *Pierce v. Society of Sisters*, 268 U.S. 510 (1925). Within schools, the Supreme Court has dealt with the question of whether a school newspaper is protected, like public forum newspapers, from the school's (i.e. the state's) editorial and censorial powers. When a school principal censored a high school newspaper before it was published, the Court of Appeals found the students' right to freedom of speech had been violated, because the paper was the students' public forum. *Kuhlmeier v. Hazelwood School District*, 795 F.2d 1368 (8th Cir. 1986). However, the Supreme Court reversed this decision, deciding that schools could reasonably regulate the contents of school-sponsored publications. *Hazelwood School District v. Kuhlmeier*, 484 U.S. 260 (1988).

24. *Chaplinsky v. New Hampshire*, 315 U.S. 568 (1942).

25. *Brandenburg v. Ohio*, 395 U.S. 444 (1969). The exceptions are narrowly construed. *R.A.V. v. St. Paul, Minn.*, 112 S.Ct. 2538 (1992).

26. In *New York v. Ferber*, 458 U.S. 747, 749 (1982), the Supreme Court unanimously upheld a New York statute that prohibited persons from "knowingly promoting sexual performances by children under the age of 16 by distributing material that depicts such performances." The Supreme Court noted the moment of the problem dealt with by the statute, and that government regarded the prevention of the exploitation of children as an objective of "surpassing importance." When material is found to be obscene—i.e. appeals to the prurient interest, is offensive to community standards and lacks artistic, literary, or other value—it is not protected by the First Amendment. Its "slight social value . . . is always outweighed by the compelling interest of society, as manifested [by its] laws." Obscenity rulings can apply to recordings as well as pictures, books, and films. *Skyywalker Records, Inc. v. Navarro*, 739 F. Supp. 578 (S.D. Fla. 1990). The state may not, however, discriminate on the basis of political view in proscribing some behavior and not other, see *R.A.V. v. St. Paul, Minn.*, 112 S.Ct. 2538 (1992).

27. *Wallace v. Jaffree*, 472 U.S. 38 (1985).

28. *Lee v. Weisman*, 112 S.Ct. 2649, 2659 (1992). But Cf. *Jones v. Clear Creek Independent School Dist.*, C.A. 5, No. 89-2638, November 24, 1992 (finding that coercion disappears if school officials allow students to choose by majority vote to include student's prayer in graduation ceremony).

29. *Wisconsin v. Yoder*, 406 U.S. 205 (1972).

30. *Employment Division, Oregon Department of Human Resources v. Smith*, 494 U.S. 872 (1990).

31. *Buchanan v. Warley*, 245 U.S. 60 (1917).

32. *Shelley v. Kraemer*, 334 U.S. 1 (1948).

33. *Lochner v. New York*, 198 U.S. 45 (1905), was the seminal case.

34. *United States v. Carolene Products Co.*, 304 U.S. 144 (1938); *Olsen v. Nebraska*, 313 U.S. 236 (1941).

35. *Planned Parenthood of Southeastern Pennsylvania v. Casey*, 112 S.Ct. 2791 (1992). See Chapter 3 for discussion.

36. *Coolidge v. New Hampshire*, 403 U.S. 443, 449 (1971).

37. *In re Gault*, 387 U.S. 1 (1967); *Kent v. United States*, 383 U.S. 541 (1966). See Chapters 3 and 10.

38. *Reed v. Reed*, 404 U.S. 71 (1971).

39. *In re Gault*, 387 U.S. 1, 13 (1967); *Planned Parenthood of Central Missouri v. Danforth*, 428 U.S. 52 (1976); *Goss v. Lopez*, 419 U.S. 565 (1975).

40. *Carey v. Population Services International*, 431 U.S. 678 (1977).

41. *Planned Parenthood of Southeastern Pennsylvania v. Casey*, 112 S.Ct. 2791 (1992).

42. *United States v. Kantor*, 677 F. Supp. 1421 (C.D. Cal. 1987).

43. See note 29 above; see also *Pierce v. Society of Sisters*, 268 U.S. 510 (1925); *Stanley v. Illinois*, 405 U.S. 645, 651 (1972); *Ginsberg v. New York*, 390 U.S. 629, 639 (1968); *Prince v. Massachusetts*, 321 U.S. 158, 166 (1944); *Meyer v. Nebraska*, 262 U.S. 390, 399 (1923).

44. *Bonner v. Moran*, 126 F.2d 121, 122 (D.C. Cir. 1941).

45. See, for example, *People ex rel. Wallace v. Labrenz*, 104 N.E.2d 769 (Ill. 1952).

46. *Parham v. J.R.*, 442 U.S. 584 (1979).

47. *Williams v. Wilzack*, 573 A.2d 809 (Md. App. 1990).

48. Watson, 1980.

49. Sunderman, 1989.

50. *Coolidge v. New Hampshire*, 403 U.S. 443 (1971).

51. *Oliver v. United States*, 466 U.S. 170, 179 (1984).

52. *New Jersey v. T.L.O.*, 469 U.S. 325 (1985); *State in Interest of T.L.O.*, 463 A.2d 934 (N.J. 1983) (see Chapter 3). We discuss arrest of juveniles in Chapter 9.

53. *Bivens v. Six Unknown Named Agents of Federal Bureau of Narcotics*, 403 U.S. 388 (1971). An example of another right the breach of which is actionable by damages is the Supreme Court decision in *Estelle v. Gamble*, 429 U.S. 97 (1976), wherein a prison official's "deliberate indifference" to inmate's "serious medical need" was actionable as a breach of the Eighth Amendment's proscription of cruel and unusual punishment.

54. 42 U.S.C.A. §1983.

55. *Smith v. Daily Mail Pub. Co.*, 443 U.S. 97 (1979).

56. *Prejean v. Blackburn*, 743 F.2d 1091 (5th Cir. 1984).

57. *Walton v. Arizona*, 110 S.Ct. 3047 (1990); see also *Richmond v. Arizona Department of Corrections*, 61 L.W. 4013 (1992).

58. E.g., *Morales v. Turman*, 535 F.2d 864 (5th Cir. 1976), reversed by 430 U.S. 322 (1977).

59. *Ingraham v. Wright*, 430 U.S. 651, 687 (1977).
60. Read *et al.*, 1982.
61. *County of DuPage v. Harris*, 231 N.E.2d 195 (Ill. App. 1967).
62. *Chi., Ind. & L. Ry. Co. v. United States*, 219 U.S. 486 (1911).
63. *Cipollone v. Liggett Group*, 112 S.Ct. 2608 (1992).
64. *Bob Jones University v. United States*, 461 U.S. 574 (1983).
65. Harris, 1972, p. 158.
66. *Ibid.*, p. 160.
67. Oleszek, 1989, p. 271.
68. *Patrick v. Burget*, 486 U.S. 94 (1988).
69. Oleszek, 1989, pp. 50–51.
70. Annual Report, Dir. Admin. Ofc. of the United States, Appendix 1, Table A1 (1989).
71. 28 U.S.C. 1253.
72. Gunther, 1991, p. 62, n. 15.
73. Sigler, 1968, p. 193.
74. *Bellotti v. Baird*, 428 U.S. 132 (1976); *L. v. Matheson*, 450 U.S. 398 (1981); *Ohio v. Akron Center for Reproductive Health*, 497 U.S. 502 (1990); *Planned Parenthood of Southeastern Pennsylvania v. Casey*, 112 S.Ct. 2791 (1992).
75. *Martin v. Hunter's Lessee*, 14 U.S. (1 Wheat.) 304 (1816).
76. 28 U.S.C. §1257.
77. McCormick, 1984, §185.
78. *State v. Jurgens*, 424 N.W.2d 546, 555 (Minn. App. 1988).
79. Federal Rules of Evidence (Fed. R. Evid.) 402.
80. McCormick, 1984, §185.
81. Fed. R. Evid. 403.
82. *State v. Axford*, 409 N.W.2d 893 (Minn. App. 1987).
83. *Trower v. Jones*, 520 N.E.2d 297, 300 (Ill. 1988).
84. Fed. R. Evid., 701.
85. *Ibid.*, 702.
86. *Ibid.*
87. McCormick, 1984, §13.
88. *Goodrich v. Tinker*, 437 S.W.2d 882 (Tx. Civ. App. 1969).
89. McCormick, 1984, §14.
90. Fed. R. Evid., 703. The role of expert evidence is much debated in the legal literature; see R. J. Allen and J. S. Miller, The Common Theory of Experts: Deference or Education?, 87 Nw. U. L. Rev. 1131 (1993).
91. *State v. Middleton*, 657 P.2d 1215 (Or. 1983).
92. *State v. Moran*, 728 P.2d 248, 253 (Ariz. 1986). See Chapter 6 for discussion of these evidentiary rules in child maltreatment cases.
93. *State v. Loebach*, 310 N.W.2d 58, 64 (Minn. 1981).
94. *In re Cheryl H.*, 200 Cal. Rptr. 789 (Cal. App. 1984).
95. Fed. R. Evid., 801.
96. McCormick, 1984, §245.
97. *Briney v. Williams*, 242 N.E.2d 132 (Ind. App. 1968). See discussion in Chapter 12.
98. Ohio Rev. Code Ann, §2151.35(F). See Chapter 7 for discussion.
99. Fed. R. Evid. 803.

100. *Johnston v. Ohls*, 457 P.2d 194 (Wash. 1969).
101. *State v. Wagner*, 508 N.E.2d 164 (Ohio App. 1986).
102. *Wilson v. Bodian*, 519 N.Y.S.2d 126 (App. Div. 2d Dept. 1987).
103. McCormick, 1984, §62.
104. *Idaho v. Wright*, 497 U.S. 805 (1990).
105. Knapp, 1987; Epstein and Martin, 1989.
106. The privilege has come under attack as reducing the probability that illegal acts will be deterred. See Kaplow and Shavell, 1989.
107. Fed. R. Evid., 504 (proposed but rejected). See Uniform Rules of Evidence, p. 503.
108. McCormick, 1984, §98.
109. *Bond v. District Court*, 682 P.2d 33 (Colo. 1984).
110. *State v. Hansen*, 743 P.2d 157 (Or. 1987).
111. *Grosslight v. Superior Court*, 140 Cal. Rptr. 278 (Cal. App. 1977).
112. See *Addington v. Texas*, 441 U.S. 418 (1979).
113. *Womack v. Eldridge*, 210 S.E.2d 145 (Va. 1974).
114. *Speiser v. Randall*, 357 U.S. 513 (1958).
115. *In re Winship*, 397 U.S. 358 (1970).
116. *Leland v. Oregon*, 343 U.S. 790 (1952).
117. *Patterson v. New York*, 432 U.S. 197 (1977).
118. *Mullaney v. Wilbur*, 421 U.S. 684 (1975).
119. Genn, 1987; Sloan *et al.*, 1993.
120. *Maryland v. Craig*, 497 U.S. 836 (1990).
121. *Planned Parenthood of Southeastern Pennsylvania v. Casey*, 112 S.Ct. 2791 (1992).
122. *Roe v. Wade*, 410 U.S. 113 (1973).
123. *Casey*, at 2798. Chief Justice Rehnquist and Justice Scalia were, however, scathing in their criticism of the majority's novel approach to *stare decisis*. *Casey*, at 2860–67.
124. Harvard Medical Practice Study Group, 1990. See discussion in Weiler, 1991.
125. *Muller v. Oregon*, 208 U.S. 412 (1908); *Brown v. Board of Education*, 349 U.S. 294 (1955). The fact-laden "Brandeis brief" (named after the brief submitted by Louis Brandeis in *Muller* concerning labor legislation) was most effectively used in *Brown* to convince the Justices that educational development of black children would be stunted in segregated school systems. Relying on social science data presented by the attorneys arguing for desegregation, the Court concluded that "separate but equal" educational systems actually created some inferior schools.
126. Updike, 1986, p. 286.

CHAPTER 3
THE RIGHTS OF CHILDREN

1. Alston *et al.*, 1992.
2. 43 Corpus Juris Secundum (C.J.S.) §108, 371.
3. *Cidis v. White*, 336 N.Y.S.2d 362 (N.Y. D.C. 1972).
4. Compare *Honeycutt v. Wichita*, 796 P.2d 549 (Kan. 1990) (child of six years and four months not necessarily incapable of negligence) with *Strong v. Allen*, 768

P.2d 369 (Okla. 1989) (A "child under the age of seven years or in the absence of evidence establishing capacity, one between the ages of seven and fourteen years, is *presumed incapable of negligence*").

5. Cal. Civ. Code §4606 (West 1988).
6. Guggenheim, 1984, p. 94.
7. Landsman and Minow, 1978, pp. 1138–53.
8. Bremner, 1970–74; Horowitz and Davidson, 1984.
9. Zelizer, 1985.
10. Pollock, 1983.
11. Minow, 1990, p. 284.
12. *Chapsky v. Wood*, 26 Kan. 650 (1881).
13. *Prince v. Massachusetts*, 321 U.S. 158, 165 (1944).
14. Strasburg, 1984.
15. Skolnick, 1975.
16. *Kent v. United States*, 383 U.S. 541 (1966).
17. *In re Gault*, 387 U.S. 1 (1967).
18. *In re Winship*, 397 U.S. 358 (1970).
19. *Morales v. Turman*, 535 F.2d 864 (5th Cir. 1976), reversed by 430 U.S. 322 (1977).
20. *Gesicki v. Oswald*, 336 F. Supp. 371 (S.D.N.Y. 1971).
21. Minow, 1990, p. 285.
22. The classic work is Piaget, 1932. For commentary see Flavell, 1963. For contemporary insights see Committee on Child Psychiatry, 1989.
23. Mullin, 1990.
24. *Thompson v. Oklahoma*, 487 U.S. 815 (1988).
25. *Stanford v. Kentucky*, 492 U.S. 361 (1989).
26. *Kent v. United States*, 383 U.S. 541 (1966); *In re Gault*, 387 U.S. 1 (1967).
27. *Hodgson v. Minnesota*, 853 F.2d 1452 (8th Cir. 1988), affirmed, 497 U.S. 417 (1990).
28. *Stanford v. Kentucky*, 492 U.S. 361 (1989).
29. Hentoff, 1988; Fink, 1986, p. 265. Recent surveys, however, show that the public has not completely renounced the possibility of rehabilitating juveniles. Fink, 1986, at 263, quoting *Breed*. Furthermore, empirical data refute the popular ideas of crisis. The nation's violent crime problem has not changed since the 1960s. Offenders younger than eighteen still account for no more than 10 percent of all FBI-indexed violent crimes and 20 percent of all violent crime arrests. National Council of Juvenile and Family Court Judges, 1984.
30. Horowitz and Davidson, 1984.
31. *In re Gault*, 387 U.S. 1 (1967); *Parham v. J.R.*, 442 U.S. 584 (1979).
32. *Fare v. Michael C.*, 442 U.S. 707 (1979).
33. *Carey v. Population Services International*, 431 U.S. 678 (1977); *Planned Parenthood of Central Missouri v. Danforth*, 428 U.S. 52 (1976); *Bellotti v. Baird*, 443 U.S. 622 (1979); *L. v. Matheson*, 450 U.S. 398 (1981).
34. Gunther, 1972.
35. *Fare v. Michael C.*, 442 U.S. 707 (1979).
36. *People v. Castro*, 462 N.Y.S.2d 369 (Sup. Ct. 1983).
37. *Juvenile Dept. of Lane County v. Gibson*, 718 P.2d 759 (Or. App. 1986); *Ex rel. Riley*, 653 F.2d 1153 (7th Cir. 1981).

38. *Bellotti v. Baird*, 443 U.S. 622 (1979); *L. v. Matheson*, 450 U.S. 398 (1981); *Planned Parenthood of Central Missouri v. Danforth*, 428 U.S. 52 (1976); *Carey v. Population Services International*, 431 U.S. 678 (1977); *Hodgson v. Minnesota*, 853 F.2d 1452 (8th Cir. 1988), affirmed, 497 U.S. 417 (1990).

39. *Planned Parenthood of Southeastern Pennsylvania v. Casey*, 112 S.Ct. 2791 (1992).

40. *Griswold v. Connecticut*, 381 U.S. 479 (1965); *Eisenstadt v. Baird*, 405 U.S. 438 (1972); *Carey v. Population Services International*, 431 U.S. 678 (1977).

41. Warboys, 1988.

42. Calabresi, 1982.

43. 42 U.S.C. §1983.

44. *Wilder v. Virginia Hospital Association*, 496 U.S. 498 (1990).

45. 42 U.S.C. §§620–28, 670–79(a).

46. 1980 U.S. Code Cong. and Admin. News 1448, 1450 (96th Cong., 2d sess.).

47. 42 U.S.C. §671(a) (15).

48. *Suter v. Artist M*, 112 S.Ct. 1360 (1992). In *LaShawn A. v. Kelly*, 990 F.2d 1319 (D.C. Cir. 1993), the court found that D.C. legislation relating to abuse and neglect created a private cause of action for children in the foster care system.

49. *Artist M. v. Johnson*, 917 F.2d 980 (7th Cir. 1990).

50. H.R. 11, passed July 2, 1992. Note also the right of action prescribed in legislation in *LaShawn A. v. Kelly*, 990 F.2d 1319 (D.C. Cir. 1993).

51. *Burnette v. Wahl*, 588 P.2d 1105 (Or. 1978).

52. *Franklin v. Gwinnett County Public Schools*, 112 S.Ct. 1028 (1992); see Justice Scalia at 1038–39.

53. Education Amendment of 1972 §901–9, as amended 20 U.S.C.A. §§1681–88.

54. Moss, 1985.

55. Jameson and King, 1989.

56. English, 1988.

57. Herr, 1991.

58. *DeShaney v. Winnebago County Department of Social Services*, 489 U.S. 189 (1989).

59. *Ibid.*, at 1012.

60. Tribe, 1989; Zipursky, 1990; Eaton and Wells, 1991.

61. *Eugene D. v. Karman*, 889 F.2d 701 (6th Cir. 1989); *Lux v. Hansen*, 886 F.2d 1064 (8th Cir. 1989). See also *Salyer v. Patrick*, 874 F.2d 374 (6th Cir. 1989); *Babcock v. Tyler*, 884 F.2d 497 (9th Cir. 1989).

62. *Baltimore City Department of Social Services v. Bouknight*, 493 U.S. 549 (1990).

63. *LaShawn A. v. Dixon*, 762 F. Supp. 959 (D.D.C. 1991). On appeal, *LaShawn A. v. Kelly*, 990 F.2d 1319 (D.C. Cir. 1993), the Court dismissed the appeal of the defendant department and upheld the remedies granted to the plaintiff children. However, the court did not reach the question of constitutional rights but found that the children had a good cause of action arising from the District of Columbia's statutes and regulations providing a scheme for the protection and care of foster children.

64. 18 U.S.C. §2252(a) (1977).

65. 136 Cong. Rec. §4729–30.

66. *New York v. Ferber*, 458 U.S. 747 (1982).

67. *Osborne v. Ohio*, 525 N.E.2d 1363 (1988).
68. *State v. Fan*, 445 N.W.2d 243, 246–47 (Minn. App. 1989).
69. *United States v. Brooks*, 841 F.2d 268 (9th Cir. 1988), cert. denied, 487 U.S. 1227 (1988); *Nelson v. Moriarty*, 484 F.2d 1034 (1st Cir. 1973).
70. *Powell v. Texas*, 392 U.S. 514, 535–36 (1968); *Lambert v. California*, 355 U.S. 225, 228 (1957); *State v. White*, 464 N.W.2d 585 (Minn. App. 1990).
71. 18 U.S.C. §2251(d), §2252(b) (1988). Note Civil RICO provides (§2251 and §2252) that, among other things, sexual exploitation of children is a predicate act giving rise to liability for treble damages and attorneys fees.
72. Strang, 1990. Cf. *United States v. X-Citement Video Inc.*, 61 L.W. 2396 (9th Cir. 1992) (element of knowledge of the minority of at least one of the performers who engage in the specific conduct).
73. E.g., Cal. Penal Code §266j, §266k, §267, §309. See West, 1988.
74. E.g., Cal. Veh. Code §12513.
75. *Naprstek v. Norwich*, 545 F.2d 815 (2d Cir. 1976).
76. *Waters v. Barry*, 711 F. Supp. 1125 (D.C. Cir. 1989).
77. In *International Society for Krishna Consciousness v. Lee*, 112 S.Ct. 2701 (1992), the Supreme Court found that the state-owned airport could be regulated to prohibit solicitation.
78. Schoepflin, 1989.
79. *Amalgamated Food Employees v. Logan Valley Plaza*, 391 U.S. 308 (1968); *Marsh v. Alabama*, 326 U.S. 501 (1946).
80. *Hudgens v. NLRB*, 424 U.S. 507 (1976).
81. *Public Utilities Comm'n v. Pollak*, 343 U.S. 451 (1952).
82. *Pruneyard Shopping Center v. Robins*, 447 U.S. 74 (1980).
83. *Dallas v. Stanglin*, 490 U.S. 19 (1989).
84. *Aladdin's Castle v. City of Mesquite*, 630 F.2d 1029 (5th Cir. 1980), reversed on other grounds 455 U.S. 283 (1982).
85. Public Law No. 98-363 (1984).
86. *Stanley v. Georgia*, 394 U.S. 557 (1969).
87. *ABA Juvenile and Child Welfare Law Reporter* 9 (April 1990): 30.
88. *Osborne v. Ohio*, 525 N.E.2d 1363 (1988).
89. *Stanley v. Georgia*, 394 U.S. 557 (1969).
90. *Jacobson v. United States*, 112 S.Ct. 1535 (1992) (government agents spent two and a half years persuading accused to buy child pornography). These statutes may have the effect of facilitating the conviction of child abusers since they are likely to be in possession of child pornography. Potuto, 1987. Others disagree. "Note," *William and Mary Law Review* 29 (1987): 187, 209-13.
91. *Ginsberg v. New York*, 390 U.S. 629, 641 (1968).
92. *Pope v. Illinois*, 481 U.S. 497 (1987).
93. *American Booksellers v. Webb*, 919 F.2d 1493 (11th Cir. 1990), cert. denied, 111 S.Ct. 2237.
94. *F.C.C. v. Pacifica Foundation*, 438 U.S. 726 (1978).
95. *Carlin Communications v. F.C.C.*, 749 F.2d 113 (2d Cir. 1984) ("*Carlin I*").
96. *Carlin Communications v. F.C.C.*, 787 F.2d 846 (2d Cir. 1986) ("*Carlin II*").
97. *Carlin Communications v. F.C.C.*, 837 F.2d 546 (2d Cir. 1988) ("*Carlin III*").
98. *Sable Communications of California v. F.C.C.*, 492 U.S. 115 (1989).

 99. *Dial Information Services v. Thornburgh*, 938 F.2d 1535 (2d Cir. 1991).
100. *Carey v. Population Services International*, 431 U.S. 678 (1977).
101. *Michael M. v. Superior Court of Sonoma County*, 450 U.S. 464 (1981).
102. *Fleisher v. City of Signal Hill*, 829 F.2d 1491 (9th Cir. 1987).
103. *Doe v. Taylor Independent School District*, 975 F.2d 137 (5th Cir. 1992).
104. *D.R. v. Middle Bucks Area Vocational Technical School*, 972 F.2d 1364 (3d Cir. 1992). See notes 141–42 below, detailing the conflicting authorities.
105. *Pierce v. Society of Sisters*, 268 U.S. 510 (1925).
106. *Wisconsin v. Yoder*, 406 U.S. 205 (1972).
107. *Plyler v. Doe*, 457 U.S. 202 (1982).
108. *Ingraham v. Wright*, 430 U.S. 651 (1977).
109. *Cunningham v. Beavers*, 858 F.2d 269 (5th Cir. 1988).
110. *Johnson v. Horace Mann Mutual Ins. Co.*, 241 So. 2d 588 (La. App. 1970); see also *Baker v. Owen*, 395 F. Supp. 294 (M.D. N.C. 1975) (due process protections set forth).
111. *Goss v. Lopez*, 419 U.S. 565 (1975).
112. *West Virginia State Board of Education v. Barnette*, 319 U.S. 624 (1943); but cf. *Sherman v. Community Consolidated School Dist. 21 of Wheeling Township*, CA 7, No. 91-1684, Nov. 20, 1992 (Illinois statute construed to allow willing students to pledge allegiance found constitutional).
113. *Hazelwood School District v. Kuhlmeier*, 484 U.S. 260 (1988).
114. *Tinker v. Des Moines Independent Community School District*, 393 U.S. 503 (1969).
115. *Kuhlmeier*, 484 U.S. 260 (1988). Cf. *Chandler v. McMinnville School District*, L.W. 2294 (1992) (finding that students' complaint covering a ban on badges containing the word "scab" during a teacher's strike could be sustained as violating the First Amendment; the speech was not inherently disruptive to school activities and did not carry the school imprimatur).
116. *Planned Parenthood of Southern Nevada v. Clark County School District*, 441 F.2d 817 (1991).
117. Minow, 1990.
118. *Board of Education, Island Trees Union Free School District No. 26 v. Pico*, 457 U.S. 853 (1982).
119. O'Neil, 1981.
120. Diamond, 1981.
121. *Lemon v. Kurtzman*, 403 U.S. 602 (1971), aff'd 411 U.S. 192 (1973).
122. *Engel v. Vitale*, 370 U.S. 421 (1962).
123. *Brandon v. Board of Education of Guilderland Central School District*, 635 F.2d 971 (2d Cir. 1980).
124. *Lubbock Civil Liberties Union v. Lubbock Independent School District*, 669 F.2d 1038 (5th Cir. 1982); *Lee v. Weisman*, 112 S.Ct. 2649 (1992); but cf. when school officials allow students by vote to include prayer, *Jones v. Clear Creek Independent School Dist.*, C.A. 5, No. 89-2638, Nov. 24, 1992.
125. *Doe v. Shenandoah County School Board*, 737 F. Supp. 913 (W.D. Va. 1990).
126. *New Jersey v. T.L.O.*, 469 U.S. 325 (1985).
127. *T.J. v. State*, 538 So.2d 1320 (Fla. App. 1989).
128. *Commonwealth v. Carey*, 554 N.E.2d 1199 (Mass. 1990).

129. *United States v. Mendenhall*, 446 U.S. 544 (1980).

130. *California v. Hodari*, 111 S.Ct. 1547 (1991).

131. *Brown v. Board of Education*, 349 U.S. 294 (1955).

132. *Bray v. Lee*, 337 F. Supp. 934 (D. Mass. 1972).

133. *Mississippi University for Women v. Hogan*, 458 U.S. 718 (1982).

134. *Grimes v. Cavazos*, 786 F. Supp. 1184 (S.D. N.Y. 1992).

135. *Franklin v. Gwinnett County Public Schools*, 112 S.Ct. 1028 (1992).

136. *D.R. v. Middle Bucks Area Vocational Technical School*, 972 F.2d 1364 (3d Cir. 1992) (the Court followed the reasoning in *DeShaney*, see above, finding that the school and student relationship did not supply a special relationship that would impose positive duties on the school to protect the welfare of its students). In accord, see *Maldonado v. Josey*, 61 L.W. 2199 (10th Cir. 1992), and *J.O. v. Alton Community School District*, 909 F.2d 267 (7th Cir. 1990). But cf. *Stoneking v. Bradford Area School District*, 882 F.2d 720 (3d Cir. 1989), finding school district liable for maintaining a policy, practice, and custom with deliberate indifference to the consequences when a student was sexually abused by a teacher.

137. *Doe v. Taylor Independent School District*, 975 F.2d 137 (5th Cir. 1992) (also applying *DeShaney*, but forging the affirmative duty of protection from state compulsion to attend school and custody assumed by school officials over school pupils).

138. *Ingraham v. Wright*, 430 U.S. 651 (1977).

139. Ratner, 1985.

140. *Peter W. v. San Francisco Unified School District*, 131 Cal. Rptr. 854 (Ct. App. 1976); *Donohue v. Copiague Union Free School District*, 391 N.E.2d 1352 (1979); McBride, 1990.

141. *Hoffman v. Board of Education of the City of New York*, 400 N.E.2d 317 (Ct. App. 1979).

142. *DeRosa v. City of New York*, 517 N.Y.S.2d 754 (N.Y. App. Div. 1987); *Agostine v. School District of Philadelphia*, 527 A.2d 193 (Pa. 1987); *Doe v. Board of Education of Montgomery County*, 453 A.2d 814 (Md. App. 1982).

143. *Snow v. State*, 469 N.Y.S.2d 959 (N.Y. App. Div. 1983).

144. 20 U.S.C. §§1401–62 (1988).

145. 42 U.S.C.A. §§11421–432 (West Supp. 1991).

146. 11 ABA Juvenile & Child Welfare Law Reporter, 64 (June 1992).

147. *In re Phillip B.*, 156 Cal. Rptr. 48 (Ct. App. 1979).

148. Report, 1 Security Access to Health Care: Report 22 (1983).

149. English, 1988.

150. *Curran v. Bosze*, 566 N.E.2d 1319 (Ill. 1990). For an excellent discussion of the interrelationship of the two standards see Welch, 1989, pp. 1628–38.

151. *In re Grady*, 426 A.2d 467, 472 (N.J. 1981). See also *Ruby v. Massey*, 452 F. Supp. 361 (D. Conn. 1978); *In re Guardianship of Hayes*, 608 P.2d 635 (Wash. 1980); *In re Moe*, 432 N.E.2d 712 (Mass. 1982); *Strunk v. Strunk*, 445 S.W.2d 145 (Ky. 1969), discussed in Chapter 8. The issues are explored and recommendations made in New York State Task Force on Life and the Law, March, 1992.

152. Annas *et al.*, 1990.

153. 42 U.S.C.A. §1395dd (1986).
154. In *Stevison v. Enid Health Systems, Inc.*, 920 F.2d 710 (10th Cir. 1990), a mother claimed that the defendant hospital had failed to provide her daughter with an appropriate screening examination required under COBRA. A hospital does not violate the act's provisions by directing by radio an ambulance to go elsewhere; see *Johnson v. University of Chicago Hospitals*, 61 L.W. 2400 (7th Cir. 1992).
155. *Wilder v. Virginia Hospital Association*, 496 U.S. 498 (1990).
156. 42 U.S.C. §1396(a)(10)(A)(i)(III) and §1396(d)(n)(2).
157. *Harris v. McRae*, 448 U.S. 297 (1980).
158. *Planned Parenthood of Central Missouri v. Danforth*, 428 U.S. 52 (1976).
159. *Planned Parenthood of Southeastern Pennsylvania v. Casey*, 112 S.Ct. 2791, 2821 (1992).
160. *Ibid.*, at 2832.
161. Alabama, Alaska, Arizona, Arkansas, California, Colorado, Delaware, Florida, Georgia, Idaho, Illinois, Indiana, Kentucky, Louisiana, Maryland, Massachusetts, Michigan, Minnesota, Mississippi, Missouri, Montana, Nebraska, Nevada, New Mexico, North Dakota, Ohio, Pennsylvania, Rhode Island, South Carolina, South Dakota, Tennessee, Utah, Washington, West Virginia, Wyoming. Embree and Dobson, 1991. In 1991 the National Abortion Rights Action League reported that fifteen of those thirty-five states actively enforced parental involvement legislation: Alabama, Arizona, Indiana, Louisiana, Massachusetts, Michigan, Minnesota, Missouri, North Dakota, Ohio, Rhode Island, South Carolina, Utah, West Virginia, Wyoming. *Ibid.*, citing National Abortion Rights Action League, *Who Decides? A State-by-State Review of Abortion Rights* (1991). With the recent Supreme Court decision in the Pennsylvania case, *Casey v. Planned Parenthood*, 112 S.Ct. 2791 (1992), one would suppose that Pennsylvania could be added to that list, and that decision could also pave the way for new statutes or revised enforcement of old statutes in other states. In addition to those states which require parental involvement in minors' abortion decisions, three states have legislation that mandates counseling in which parental involvement may be required: Connecticut, Maine, Wisconsin. Embree and Dobson, 1991, p. 60.
162. *Planned Parenthood Ass'n of the Atlanta Area, Inc. v. Miller*, 934 F.2d 1462, 1480–81 (11th Cir. 1991).
163. *Zbaraz v. Hartigan*, 776 F. Supp. 375 (N.D. Ill. 1991).
164. *Planned Parenthood of Southeastern Pennsylvania v. Casey*, at 2807.
165. *Carey v. Population Services International*, 431 U.S. 678 (1977).
166. *Doe v. Irwin*, 615 F.2d 1162 (6th Cir. 1980).
167. Friedman, 1992.
168. Robertson, 1983.
169. Scott, 1986.
170. See Brown *et al.*, 1986.
171. *Zoski v. Gaines*, 260 N.W. 99 (Mich. 1935).
172. *State v. Perricone*, 181 A.2d 751 (N.J. 1962).
173. *In re Seiferth*, 127 N.E.2d 820 (N.Y. 1955).
174. Ala. Code tit. 22, §22-8-3.

175. *Greenspan v. Slate*, 97 A.2d 390 (N.J. 1953).
176. *Newmark v. Williams*, 588 A.2d 1108 (Del. 1991).
177. *In the Matter of McCauley*, 565 N.E.2d 411 (Mass. Sup. Jud. Ct. 1991).
178. *In re Sampson*, 317 N.Y.S.2d 641 (N.Y. Fam. Ct. 1970).
179. *Custody of a Minor*, 393 N.E.2d 836 (Mass. 1979).
180. Todres *et al.*, 1977; Steinfels and Steinfels, 1976; Shaw *et al.*, 1977.
181. *In re Infant Doe*, No. GU 8204-004A (Cir. Ct. Monroe County, Ind. April 12, 1982).
182. See above, at note 149, and English, 1988.
183. *Lacey v. Laird*, 139 N.E.2d 25 (Ohio 1956). English courts have recently shown a willingness to order treatment against the express wishes of emancipated minors. See *In re R* [1991], 4 All E.R. 177, and *Re W (a minor) Child in Care: Medical Treatment* [1992] 3 W.L.R. 758. In the former case the court ordered psychotic medication for a girl aged fifteen and in the latter ordered treatment for anorexia nervosa, in both cases against the will of the minors.
184. Weithorn, 1984.
185. *Ibid.*; Cady, 1979.
186. See *Lawson v. Brown*, 349 F. Supp. 203 (W.D. Va. 1972); *Brumfield v. Brumfield*, 74 S.E.2d 170 (Va. 1953).
187. *Kent v. United States*, 383 U.S. 541 (1966); *Parham v. J.R.*, 442 U.S. 584 (1979).
188. *Kent v. United States*, at 566–67.
189. *Addington v. Texas*, 441 U.S. 418, 429 (1979).
190. *Parham v. J.R.*, at 607–8.
191. Roth *et al.*, 1977; Meisel, 1979.
192. Ferguson, 1978; Grisso and Vierling, 1978; Schowalter, 1978; Wald, 1979; Wald and Freidman, 1976; and Weithorn and Campbell, 1982.
193. Weithorn, 1984.
194. Weithorn and Campbell, 1982.
195. Rotter, 1966.
196. 48 Fed. Reg. 9814, 9819 (1983).
197. Capron, 1973; Capron, 1974.
198. For wider ethical concerns see Fried, 1974; Calabresi, 1969. For a discussion of the impact of recent changes see Freedman, Fuks, and Weijer, 1993.

CHAPTER 4
THE EDUCATIONAL RIGHTS OF HANDICAPPED CHILDREN

1. *Pennsylvania Ass'n. for Retarded Citizens v. Pennsylvania*, 343 F. Supp. 279, 294 (E.D. Pa. 1972), summarizing the testimony of Dr. Ignacy Golberg, President's Committee, Mental Retardation 1969 Annual Report, N.T. at 10–15 (Hearing of August 12, 1971) (hereinafter *PARC*).
2. The terms "disabled" and "exceptional" have come to replace "handicapped." The term "handicap" has increasingly fallen into disfavor, as is evident from the fact that Congress replaced it with the word "disability" in the 1990 amendments of the EHA. Education for All Handicapped Children Act, 20 U.S.C.A. §§1400-1485 (1990); Individuals with Disabilities Education Act, 20 U.S.C.A. §1400(a) (1990).

3. *PARC*, at 294.
4. Taylor, 1983. See also Engel, 1991, pp. 181–84; Bowe, 1980, pp. 7, 10.
5. *PARC*, at 297.
6. *Ibid.*, at 294, n. 42.
7. *Buck v. Bell*, 274 U.S. 200, 207 (1927).
8. *Watson v. City of Cambridge*, 32 N.E. 864 (Mass. 1893).
9. *Beattie v. Board of Education of City of Antigo*, 172 N.W. 153, 154 (Wis. 1919).
10. *Board of Education v. Rowley*, 458 U.S. 176, 191 (1982) (". . . many of these children were excluded completely from any form of public education or were left to fend for themselves in classrooms designed for education of their non-handicapped peers").
11. *Beattie.*
12. *Thomas v. Cincinnati Board of Education*, 918 F.2d 618, 619 (6th Cir. 1990); Bell, 1982. See also *Rowley*, 102 S.Ct. 3034 (1982); *PARC*, at 279; Engel, 1991.
13. H.R. Rep. 332 at 10, 94th Cong., 1st Sess. (1975) Education for All Handicapped Children Act of 1975.
14. *Brown v. Board of Education*, 349 U.S. 294 (1955).
15. *Ibid.*, at 395.
16. Engel, 1991, p. 171.
17. See Section 504 of the Rehabilitation Act of 1973, 29 U.S.C.A. §794 (1990); Amendments to the Elementary and Secondary Education Act of 1965, Pub. L. No. 89-750, 80 Stat. 1191, 1204-8 (1966) (establishing a Bureau of Training and Education for Handicapped Students in the Office of Education and offering grants to states to improve and develop handicapped education programs); Amendments to the Elementary and Secondary Education Act of 1965, Pub. L. No. 91-230, 84 Stat. 121, 175-88 (1970) (establishing the National Advisory Committee on Handicapped Children and reauthorizing state grants to improve educational programs). For a brief discussion of this early legislation, see Engel, 1991, p. 171.
18. 29 U.S.C.A. §794 (1990).
19. 45 C.F.R. §84.31-84.39 (1981) defines "appropriate education" as a program that is "designed to meet individual educational needs of handicapped persons as adequately as the needs of non-handicapped persons are met."
20. PARC; *Mills v. Board of Education*, 348 F. Supp. 866 (D.D.C. 1972).
21. *PARC*, at 279.
22. *Ibid.*, at 282; 24 Purd. Stat. §13-1375.
23. *PARC*, at 282; 24 Purd. Stat. §13-1304.
24. *PARC*, at 296.
25. *Ibid.*, at 297.
26. *Ibid.*, at 296. See also Arnett, 1989. The *PARC* opinion also cites The President's Committee on Mental Retardation, where the committee stated: "Some three-quarters of this nation's retarded people could become self-supporting if given the right kind of training early enough." 1969 Annual Report at 17. 343 F. Supp. at 296, n. 50.
27. *Mills*, at 868.
28. *Ibid.*, at 878.
29. *Ibid.*, at 876.

30. *Ibid.*, at 880–83.
31. 20 U.S.C.A. §1400(b) (1), (3), (4).
32. 20 U.S.C.A. §§1400-1485; this act was renamed the Individuals with Disabilities Education Act in 1990.
33. 20 U.S.C.A. §1400(c) (1988). See also *Thomas v. Cincinnati Board of Education*, 918 F.2d 618, 619 (6th Cir. 1990); *Honig v. Doe*, 484 U.S. 305, 310 (1988) (discussing the legislative history behind the act); H.R. Rep. 332, 94th Cong., 1st Sess. 2 (1975); 34 C.F.R. §300.550(b) (1990) ("Each public agency shall insure: 1. That to the maximum extent appropriate, handicapped children, including children in public or private institutions or other care facilities, are educated with children who are not handicapped."); S. Rep. No. 168, 94th Cong., 1st Sess. 13 (Senate Committee enumerates six specific purposes for the bill).
34. 20 U.S.C.A. §1400. See also Rothstein, 1990.
35. *Honig v. Doe*, 484 U.S. 305, 310 (1988).
36. *Thomas*, at 619.
37. N. Jones, 1991, pp. 48–49.
38. See Engel, 1991.
39. 20 U.S.C.A. §1400.
40. Zirkel, 1983.
41. Engel states that "the significant substantive rights guaranteed by the EHA were . . . delineated far less carefully than the procedural steps by which they were to be protected." Engel, 1991, p. 173.
42. The vagueness of these terms has resulted in a great deal of litigation when parents disagree with the school board regarding the meaning; see *Board of Education v. Rowley*, 458 U.S. 176 (1982); *Honig v. Doe*, 484 U.S. 305 (1988); *Greer v. Rome City School District*, 950 F.2d 688 (11th Cir. 1991); *Polk v. Central Susquehanna Intermediate Unit 16*, 853 F.2d 171 (3d Cir. 1988); *Thomas v. Cincinnati Board of Education*, 918 F.2d 618 (6th Cir. 1990); *A.E. v. Independent School Dist. No. 25*, 936 F.2d 472 (10th Cir. 1991); *In re Conklin*, 946 F.2d 306 (4th Cir. 1991); *Irving Independent School Dist. v. Tatro*, 468 U.S. 883 (1984); *Williams v. Gering Public Schools*, 463 N.W.2d 799 (Neb. 1990).
43. 20 U.S.C.A. §1400(a) (20).
44. See *Thomas v. Cincinnati Board of Education*, 918 F.2d 618, 620-621 (6th Cir. 1990), for a discussion of the procedural safeguards provided to parents.
45. See Engel, 1991, p. 178, citing Neal and Kirp, 1985, p. 72, n. 39.
46. 20 U.S.C.A. §1401(a) (20).
47. *In re Conklin*, 946 F.2d 306, 312 (4th Cir. 1991). See Engel, 1991, referring to the IEP as "the child's ticket to an 'appropriate' education."
48. 20 U.S.C.A. §1414(a) (5).
49. 20 U.S.C.A. §§1415(b) (1) (A)–(C); 20 U.S.C.A. §1415(e) (2)–(3); see *Thomas*, 918 F.2d 618, 621, for a discussion of these safeguards, and Bell, 1982, for further discussion.
50. 20 U.S.C.A. §1415(b) (1) (A).
51. *Ibid.*, §1415(b) (2), (c)–(e).
52. *Ibid.*, §1415(b) (2). Parents may be represented at the administrative hearing by counsel, and they may present witnesses, such as mental health or educational experts. A trained, impartial referee presides over the hearing. The rules of evi-

dence prevail, and each of the disputants has the right to present and cross-examine witnesses. The standard of proof is a "preponderance of evidence," the burden of proof lying with the party seeking a change in the IEP. The decision of the hearing must be provided in writing, setting out findings of fact and decisions, no later than forty-five days after the hearing has been requested. The costs of the hearing are borne by the local educational authority.

53. *Ibid.*, §1415(e) (1)–(2).
54. *Lester H. v. Gilhool*, 916 F.2d 865 (3d Cir. 1990); *Jefferson County Bd. of Educ. v. Breen*, 853 F.2d 853 (11th Cir. 1988); *Todd D. v. Andrews*, 933 F.2d 1576 (11th Cir. 1991); and *Burr v. Ambach*, 863 F.2d 1071 (2d Cir. 1988); *Babb v. Knox County School Sys.*, 965 F.2d 104 (6th Cir. 1992) (removal by parents from public to private facility was in the child's best interests and, after exhaustion of remedies, the parents could recover the costs of the change).
55. 20 U.S.C.A. §1415(d) (1).
56. P.L. 99-372; 20 U.S.C.A. §1415(c) (4)–(f) (1986).
57. The legislation responded to *Smith v. Robinson*, 468 U.S. 992 (1984), deciding that because EHA was an exclusive remedy, attorney fee recovery drawn from other parallel statutes was inapplicable.
58. *Eggers v. Bullitt County School Dist.*, 854 F.2d 892 (6th Cir. 1988).
59. *Angela L. v. Pasadena Independent School Dist.*, 918 F.2d 1188 (5th Cir. 1990).
60. *Ibid.*, at 1995. See also *Field v. Haddonfield Bd. of Educ.*, 769 F. Supp. 1313 (D.N.J. 1991) (holding that although "main goal" of residential placement not achieved, issues settled in favor of parents were significant), and *Krichinsky v. Knox County Schools*, 963 F.2d 847 (6th Cir. 1992) (a similar holding).
61. Nouryan and Weisel, 1990, pp. 415–16 (setting forth factors courts will consider in reviewing fees).
62. GAO, "Special education: The attorney fees provision of Public Law 99-272," Washington, D.C., November 1989.
63. Nouryan and Weisel, 1990.
64. 20 U.S.C.A. §1415(e) (3).
65. See Engel, 1991, p. 176, stating that "a deaf child has special needs quite unlike those of a mentally retarded child. Even the single label 'mentally retarded' encompasses a broad spectrum of widely divergent needs. A system of regulations that prescribed a specific program for each type of handicap would inevitably ignore important differences among individuals."
66. See Note, 1979, *Harvard Law Review*.
67. 20 U.S.C.A. §1401(a) (1) (A); now referred to as "children with disabilities."
68. 20 U.S.C.A. §1401(a) (18).
69. 20 U.S.C.A. §1401(a) (17).
70. Not defined in 20 U.S.C.A. §1401(a).
71. 20 U.S.C.A. §1401(a) (1) (A) (i).
72. See Engel, 1991, pp. 180–92, discussing Sacks, 1985.
73. "Serious emotional disturbance" is defined as a severe, long-duration impedance to education caused by (1) an inability to learn not explicable by intellectual, sensory, or health factors; (2) an inability to build or sustain satisfactory interpersonal relationships; (3) inappropriate behavior or feelings; (4) pervasive unhappiness or depression; or (5) a tendency to develop physical symptoms or

fears associated with personal or school problems. 34 C.F.R. §300.5(b) (8). However, this attempt to clarify the term has had little real effect.

74. Engel, 1991, p. 183, states: "Physically disabled persons are viewed with fear and revulsion because they occupy an anomalous social position." Of recent concern is the issue of whether children with AIDS ought to be regarded as handicapped. Section 504 of the Rehabilitation Act was amended in 1974 to protect "those who are regarded as impaired" as well as those who are actually impaired.

75. 20 U.S.C.A. §1401(a) (18).

76. *Board of Education v. Rowley*, 458 U.S. 176 (1982).

77. *Rowley v. Board of Education*, 483 F. Supp. 528, 534 (S.D.N.Y. 1979).

78. Taylor, 1983.

79. *Board of Education v. Rowley*, 458 U.S. 176.

80. *Board of Education v. Rowley*, 458 U.S., at 206. The Court stated that the EAHCA "was more to open the door of public education to handicapped children on appropriate terms than to guarantee any particular level of education once inside." *Ibid.*, at 3049.

81. *Knight v. District of Columbia*, 877 F.2d 1025, 1029 (D.C. Cir. 1989); *Williams v. Gering Public Schools*, 463 N.W.2d 799 (Neb. 1990); *Daniel R.R. v. State Board of Education*, 874 F.2d 1036, 1047 (5th Cir. 1989); *Abrahamson v. Hershman*, 701 F.2d 223, 228 (1st Cir. 1983); *Matta v. Board of Educ.*, 731 F. Supp. 253, 254 (S.D. Ohio 1990); *Lascari v. Board of Educ.*, 560 A.2d 1180, 1189 (N.J. 1989).

82. See Taylor, 1983, p. 1659.

83. *Valerie J. v. Derry Cooperative School Dist.*, 771 F. Supp. 483 (D.N.H. 1991).

84. See Huefner, 1991.

85. *Polk v. Central Susquehanna Intermediate Unit 16*, 853 F.2d 171, 179 (3d Cir. 1988). See *In re Conklin* (note 47 above), for such an interpretation.

86. *Polk*, at 181–85. H. Rep. No. 332, 94th Cong. at 13 (1975) explains that a fundamental tenet of the act is that "each child requires an educational plan that is tailored to achieve his or her maximum potential." In *Rowley v. Board of Education*, 483 F. Supp. 528 (S.D.N.Y. 1979), affirmed, 632 F.2d 945 (2d Cir. 1980), at 3948, n. 23, the Supreme Court recognized that a goal of the act was to promote self-sufficiency; but see *Timothy W. v. Rochester, New Hampshire School District*, 875 F.2d 954 (1st Cir. 1989), seeming to hold that educational benefit is irrelevant.

87. *Board of Education v. Diamond*, 808 F.2d 987, 991 (3d Cir. 1986).

88. *Burke County Bd. of Educ. v. Denton*, 895 F.2d 973, 980 (4th Cir. 1990); *Evans v. District No. 17*, 841 F.2d 824, 831 (8th Cir. 1988); *Brown v. Wilson County School Bd.*, 747 F. Supp. 436, 442 (M.D. Tenn. 1990).

89. Iowa Code Ann. §281.2 (West 1982).

90. *Buchholtz v. Iowa Dept. of Public Instruction*, 315 N.W.2d 789 (Iowa 1982).

91. For a summary of the state requirements and arguments as to why the standards exceed the FAPE floor, see *In re Conklin*, 946 F.2d 306, 320–21 (4th Cir. 1991).

92. *Babb v. Knox County School Sys.*, 965 F.2d 104 (6th Cir. 1992); see also *Clevenger v. Oak Ridge School Board*, 744 F.2d 514 (6th Cir. 1984).

93. 20 U.S.C.A. §1401(a) (17). In *Zobrest v. Catalina Foothills School Dist.*, 61 L.W. 4641 (1993), the Supreme Court decided that the school district was required

to provide a sign-language interpreter for the deaf child and that the Free Exercise Clause of the First Amendment did not bar the service within a Roman Catholic school.

94. 20 U.S.C.A. §1401(a) (16)–(17).

95. See *Irving Independent School Dist. v. Tatro*, 468 U.S. 883 (1984) (parents seek to have school board provide child with "clean intermittent catheterization"). *Tatro* takes its logic from *Rowley*. The *Tatro* test was applied in *Doe v. Smith*, 897 F.2d 1340, 1341 (6th Cir. 1989).

96. *Tatro*, 104 S.Ct. 3371.

97. *Ibid.*, at 3378.

98. *Ibid.*, at 3376.

99. Id. at 3377.

100. 20 U.S.C.A. §1412(5) (B).

101. See Engel, 1991, pp. 176–77.

102. See *ibid.*, p. 175.

103. Gartner and Lipsky, 1987, p. 374.

104. Biklen, 1982.

105. Larrivee and Cook, 1979.

106. *Ibid.*, p. 371.

107. *Daniel R.R. v. State Board of Education*, 874 F.2d 1036 (5th Cir. 1989); *Greer v. Rome City School District*, 950 F.2d 688 (11th Cir. 1991).

108. *Daniel R.R.*, at 1048; *Greer*, at 696.

109. *Greer*, at 696.

110. *Ibid.*, at 696–97.

111. *Greer*, at 696; *Daniel*, at 1048.

112. Voeltz *et al.*, 1982.

113. Biklen, 1982.

114. *In re Gault*, 387 U.S. 1 (1967).

115. P.L. 99-457, 100 Stat. 1145 (1986).

116. 100 Stat., at 1146.

117. P.L. 102-119 (1991), section 14 amending section 677. 105 Stat. 587, 597.

118. 100 Stat., at 1155–59.

119. *Ibid.*, at 1159–72.

120. *Ibid.*, at 1162–68.

121. 20 U.S.C.A. §1400; P.L. 101-476 (1990).

122. 20 U.S.C.A. §1401(a) (1) (A) (1990); 20 U.S.C.A. §1412(5) (B) (1990).

123. P.L. 102-119; 105 Stat. 587.

124. 105 Stat., at 598.

CHAPTER 5
CHILD CUSTODY DISPUTES

1. U.S. National Center for Health Statistics, National Estimates of Marital Dissolution and Survivorship, Vital and Health Statistics (1990).

2. Hacker, 1983.

3. *Loving v. Virginia*, 388 U.S. 1 (1967).

4. *Reynolds v. United States*, 98 U.S. 145 (1879).

5. *Baker v. Nelson*, 191 N.W.2d 185 (Minn. 1971).

6. *Marvin v. Marvin*, 557 P.2d 106, 116–21 (Cal. 1976).

7. *Griswold v. Connecticut*, 381 U.S. 479 (1965).

8. *Hathaway v. Worcester City Hospital*, 475 F.2d 701 (1st Cir. 1973).

9. *Planned Parenthood of Southeastern Pennsylvania v. Casey*, 112 S.Ct. 2791 (1992).

10. *In re Sampson*, 317 N.Y.S.2d 641 (N.Y. Fam. Ct. 1970).

11. See, e.g., *Schumm v. Schumm*, 299 A.2d 423 (N.J. Super. 1973); *Ross v. Ross*, 400 A.2d 1233 (N.J. Super. Ct. 1979); *Dowling v. Dowling*, 679 P.2d 480 (Alaska 1984).

12. Moore, 1985; Reskin, 1985.

13. P.L. 102-521.

14. Elster, 1989. For a complete primer on this issue, see Maccoby and Mnookin, 1992.

15. Foster and Freed, 1964.

16. *Carter v. Carter*, 144 A. 490, 492 (Md. App. 1929).

17. *Shelley v. Westbrooke*, 37 Eng. Rep. 850 (1917).

18. *Brenneman v. Hildebrandt*, 119 S.W. 452, 453 (Kan. Ct. App. 1909).

19. 70 ALR 3d 262, 274-275.

20. *Horst v. McLain*, 466 S.W.2d 187, 187 (Mo. Ct. App. 1971).

21. See *Chester v. Municipality of Waverly*, 62 C.L.R. 1, 17 (Austl. 1939).

22. *Helms v. Franciscus*, 2 Bland. Ch. 544 (Md. 1830).

23. *Miner v. Miner*, 11 Ill. 35, 40 (1849).

24. 2&3 Vict., c. 54.

25. *Ex parte Devine*, 398 So. 2d 686 (Ala. 1981); *King v. Vancil*, 341 N.E.2d 65 (Ill. App. Ct. 1975); *State v. Watts*, 350 N.Y.S.2d 285 (N.Y. Fam. Ct. 1973); *Pusey v. Pusey*, 728 P.2d 117 (Utah 1986).

26. Scott, 1992.

27. *J.B. v. A.B.*, 242 S.E.2d 248 (W.Va. 1978); *Gordon v. Gordon*, 577 P.2d 1271 (Okla. 1978), *cert. denied* 439 U.S. 863.

28. *Park v. Park*, 610 P.2d 826 (Okla. App. 1980).

29. *Isaacs v. Isaacs*, 358 S.E.2d 833 (W.Va. 1987).

30. T.C.A. §36-6-101(d).

31. Garrett, 1990, §24–26.

32. *Chapsky v. Wood*, 26 Kan. 650 (1881); *Finlay v. Finlay*, 148 N.E. 624 (N.Y. Ct. App. 1925).

33. *M.E.D. v. J.P.M.*, 350 S.E.2d 215, 219 (Va. App. 1986).

34. *Ibid.*, at 220.

35. *David M. v. Margaret M.*, 385 S.E.2d 912, 923 (W.Va. 1989); *In re Maxwell*, 456 N.E.2d 1218, 1222 (Ohio App. 1982).

36. 41 ALR 4th 1129, 1135–36 §2(b).

37. Mnookin, 1975, pp. 257–58.

38. *Ibid.*, pp. 260–61.

39. Mnookin, 1985.

40. Reppucci, 1984.

41. Elster, 1989.

42. Pearson and Ring, 1983; Weitzman and Dixon, 1979.

43. *Marriage of Estelle*, 592 S.W.2d 277 (Mo. App. 1979); *Bah v. Bah*, 668 S.W.2d 663 (Tenn. Ct. App. 1983).
44. Klaff, 1982.
45. Mnookin and Kornhauser, 1979.
46. Mnookin, 1985.
47. Lowery, 1981.
48. Weitzman and Dixon, 1979.
49. 24 Am Jur 2d *Divorce and Separation*, §987.
50. Garrett, 1990, §24–25.
51. See, e.g., Cal. Civ. Code §4600.5 (West 1983); Conn. Gen. Stat. §46.b–56a (1981).
52. *McClain v. McClain*, 716 P.2d 381 (Alaska 1986), interpreting Alaska Stat. §25.20.060 (1982).
53. *Beck v. Beck*, 432 A.2d 63, 71 (N.J. 1981).
54. *Marriage of Bush*, 547 N.E.2d 590, 598 (Ill. App. 1989).
55. 92 ALR 2d 691, 698 (1963).
56. E.g., *Kaehler v. Kaehler*, 18 N.W.2d 312, 314 (Minn. 1945).
57. 92 ALR 2d, at 698–700. See Foster and Freed, 1979.
58. Steinman *et al.*, 1985.
59. E.g., Ohio Rev. Code Ann. §3109.04(A) (1989).
60. E.g., Conn. Gen. Stat. §46-56 (1981).
61. E.g., Cal. Civ. Code §4600.5(b) (1983).
62. E.g., La. Civ. Code Ann. art. 146(c) (1983).
63. See Roman and Haddad, 1978.
64. *In re Baby M*, 537 A.2d 1227, 1263 (N.J. 1988).
65. See Mo. Stat. §452.400.2 (1986).
66. *DiStefano v. DiStefano*, 401 N.Y.S.2d 636 (N.Y. App. Div. 1978).
67. *Gallo v. Gallo*, 440 A.2d 782 (Conn. 1981).
68. *J.L.P. (H.) v. D.J.P.*, 643 S.W.2d 865 (Mo. App. 1982).
69. *M.E.D. v. J.P.M.*, 350 S.E.2d 215 (Va. App. 1986).
70. *J.P. v. P.W.*, 772 S.W.2d 786 (Mo. App. 1989).
71. *K.J.B. v. C.M.B.*, 779 S.W.2d 36 (Mo. Ct. App. 1989).
72. *Suttles v. Suttles*, 748 S.W.2d 4217 (Tenn. 1988).
73. *Mittwede v. Mittwede*, 490 S.W.2d 534 (Tenn. App. 1969).
74. *Radford v. Matczuk*, 164 A.2d 904, 909 (Md. 1960).
75. See, e.g., Benedek and Benedek, 1977; *Pierce v. Yerkovich*, 363 N.Y.S.2d 403 (Fam. Ct. 1974).
76. Group for the Advancement of Psychiatry, 1980.
77. Chesler, 1986; Fineman, 1988.
78. West, 1988.
79. *Graves v. Wooden*, 291 S.W.2d 665, 669 (Mo. Ct. App. 1956).
80. *In re State in Interest of Black*, 283 P.2d 887 (Utah 1955).
81. *Feldman v. Feldman*, 358 N.Y.S.2d 507 (N.Y. App. Div. 1974).
82. *Harrison v. Harrison*, 359 So. 2d 266 (La. App. 1978).
83. DuCanto, 1967.
84. *Alberto B. v. Rosa O.*, 423 N.Y.S.2d 111 (N.Y. Fam. Ct. 1979).

85. *In the Interest of Bachelor*, 508 P.2d 862, 865 (Kan. 1973).

86. *Palmore v. Sidoti*, 466 U.S. 429 (1984).

87. *Gould v. Gould*, 342 N.W.2d 426 (Wis. 1984).

88. *Marriage of Grandinetti*, 342 N.W.2d 876 (Iowa App. 1983).

89. *Sanborn v. Sanborn*, 465 A.2d 888 (N.H. 1983).

90. *Stapley v. Stapley*, 485 P.2d 1181 (Ariz. App. 1971).

91. *Gluckstern v. Gluckstern*, 151 N.E.2d 897 (N.Y. Ct. App. 1956).

92. *Harris v. Harris*, 343 So. 2d 762 (Miss. 1977).

93. *Vazquez v. Vazquez*, 443 So. 2d 313 (Fla. App. 1983).

94. *Grayman v. Hession*, 446 N.Y.S.2d 505 (N.Y. App. Div. 1982).

95. *Wojnarowicz v. Wojnarowicz*, 137 A.2d 618 (N.J. Super. Ct. 1958).

96. *Witmayer v. Witmayer*, 467 A.2d 371, 376 (Pa. Super. 1983), citing with approval *In re Custody of Pearce*, 456 A.2d 597 (Pa. Super. 1983).

97. *Child's Wishes as Factor in Awarding Custody*, 4 ALR 3d 1396 (1965).

98. *Lundell v. Lundell*, 387 N.W.2d 654 (Minn. App. 1986).

99. *In re Snyder*, 532 P.2d 278 (Wash. 1975) (finding of incorrigibility); *In re Polovchak*, 454 N.E.2d 258 (Ill. 1983) (PINS statute). Recently the courts have been active; see *Wall Street Journal* September 28, 1992, p. B14.

100. E.g., *Flaherty v. Smith*, 274 N.W.2d 72 (Mich. App. 1978); *DuPont v. DuPont*, 216 A.2d 674 (Del. 1966).

101. See, e.g., *Beck v. Beck*, 432 A.2d 63 (N.J. 1981); *Auge v. Auge*, 334 N.W.2d 393 (Minn. 1983).

102. *Johnson v. Lundell*, 361 N.W.2d 125, 128 (Minn. App. 1985).

103. *Theriot v. Huval*, 413 So. 2d 337, 341 (La. App. 1982).

104. McFadden, 1983.

105. *Christian v. Randall*, 516 P.2d 132 (Colo. App. 1973).

106. *J.P. v. P.W.*, 772 S.W.2d 786 (Mo. App. 1989).

107. 24 Am. Jur. 29 §1011.

108. *Bloss v. Bloss*, 711 P.2d 663, 664–65 (Ariz. App. 1985).

109. See, e.g., *McIntyre v. McIntyre*, 452 So. 2d 14 (Fla. App. 1984).

110. See, e.g., *In re Baby M*, 537 A.2d 1227, 1265-1270 (N.J. 1988).

111. See, e.g., N.J. Stat. Ann. §9:17-44 (West 1983).

112. Ariz. Rev. Stat. Ann. §25-218 (1991); Utah Code Ann. §76-7-204 (1990).

113. Ark. Code Ann. §9-10-201 (Michie 1987); W.Va. Code §48-4-16 (1992). See also Charo, 1988, and Wadlington, 1992–93, setting forth the state responses, discussing the Uniform Status of Children of Assisted Conception Act, and suggesting legislative models.

114. Wash. Rev. Code §26.26.260 (1986); Mich. Comp. Laws Ann. §722.861 (West 1968).

115. *In re Baby M*, 537 A.2d 1227, 1240-41 (N.J. 1988). See Wadlington, 1992–93.

116. *Surrogate Parenting v. Commonwealth*, 704 S.W.2d 209 (Ky. 1986). Similarly, the California Supreme Court in *Johnson v. Calvert*, 61 LW 2721 (1993), found that the genetic mother was the natural mother, the determination turning on the intention of the parties under the surrogacy agreement. Nothing in public policy invalidated such agreements.

117. *Surrogate Parenting*, at 213.

118. Ky. Rev. Stat. Ann. §199.590 (Michie 1991).
119. *Anna J. v. Mark C.*, 286 Cal. Rptr. 369, 386 (Cal. App. 1991).
120. The court is discomforted by its decision and thus attempts to base its reasoning on objective guideposts like the Uniform Parentage Act. But the argument is made that the genetic test denies women's experience. See Rothman, 1989.
121. A Canadian commission is due to report shortly on these and other matters flowing from reproductive technologies: *Canadian Royal Commission on New Reproductive Technologies*. For a discussion, see Martin *et al.*, 1993.
122. *Stiver v. Parker*, 975 F.2d 261 (6th Cir. 1992).
123. Loveless, 1989.
124. Gardner, 1989.
125. *Rosendorf v. Blackmon*, 800 S.W.2d 377 (Tex. Ct. App. 1990).
126. Schetky and Benedek, 1985. See also Gardner, 1987, suggesting criteria for measuring the reliability of sexual abuse allegations.
127. 24 Am Jur 2d *Divorce and Separation* §1002.
128. See e.g., *Bates v. Wishart*, 512 So. 2d 977 (Fla. App. 1987); *Ely v. Casteel*, 341 So. 2d 730 (Ala. Ct. Civ. App. 1977).
129. *Wrecsics v. Broughton*, 426 A.2d 1155 (Pa. Super. Ct. 1981).
130. *Johnson v. Johnson*, 681 P.2d 78 (Okla. 1984).
131. *Adoption of M.J.C.*, 590 N.E.2d 1095 (Ind. Ct. App. 1992).
132. *Looper v. McManus*, 581 P.2d 487 (Okla. Ct. App. 1978).
133. See, e.g., *Theodore R. v. Loretta J.*, 476 N.Y.S.2d 720 (N.Y. Fam. Ct. 1984).
134. *Stricker v. Stricker*, 474 So. 2d 1146 (Ala. Civ. Ct. App. 1985).
135. *Matter of C.E.R.*, 796 S.W.2d 423 (Mo. App. 1990).
136. *Layton v. Foster*, 460 N.E.2d 1351 (N.Y. 1984); *In re Nearhoof*, 359 S.E.2d 587 (W.Va. 1987).
137. *Bond v. Yount*, 734 P.2d 39 (Wash. App. 1987).
138. Senior, Gladstone, and Nurcombe, 1982.
139. Schetky and Haller, 1983.
140. "Comment: Thompson v. Thompson—The Jurisdictional Dilemma of Child Custody Cases Under the Parental Kidnapping Prevention Act," *Pepperdine Law Review* 16 (1989): 409, 429.
141. U.S. Const. Art. IV, §1.
142. "Comment: Thompson v. Thompson," pp. 411–12. Schuetze, 1989.
143. UCCJA §§1–28, 9 U.L.A. 116-70 (1979).
144. "Comment: Thompson v. Thompson," p. 415.
145. 28 U.S.C. §1738A.
146. *In re Marriage of Diehl*, 582 N.E.2d 281 (Ill. App. Ct. 1991). See generally Lewin, 1981.
147. See *M.A.B. v. R.B.*, 510 N.Y.S.2d 960, 965 (Sup. Ct. 1986).
148. *J.L.P. (H.) v. D.J.P.*, 643 S.W.2d 865 (Mo. App. 1982); *Matter of J.S. & C.*, 342 A.2d 90 (N.J. Super. 1974).
149. *Jacobson v. Jacobson*, 314 N.W.2d 78 (N.D. 1981).
150. *S.L.H. v. D.B.H.*, 745 S.W.2d 848 (Mo. App. 1988).
151. See, e.g., *Bezio v. Patenaude*, 410 N.E.2d 1207 (Mass. 1980); *DiStefano v. DiStefano*, 401 N.Y.S.2d 636 (N.Y. App. Div. 1978).

152. *Marriage of Ashling*, 599 P.2d 475 (Or. Ct. App. 1979); *White v. Thompson*, 569 So. 2d 1181 (Miss. 1990) (custody granted to paternal grandparents; mother unfit to have custody, use of marijuana, general neglect, and immoral conduct with live-in female lover); *In re Marriage of Williams*, 563 N.E.2d 1195 (Ill. App. 1990) (mother's lesbian relationship a relevant factor among others).
153. *M.A.B. v. R.B.*, 510 N.Y.S.2d 960 (Sup. Ct. 1986).
154. Garrett, 1990, §24–7.
155. E.g., *In re Marriage of Diehl* (note 148 above) (appeal court affirming trial court's order giving custody to father taking account of mother's lesbian relationship).
156. E.g., R. Green, 1978; Hoeffer, 1981; Mandel, Hotvedt, and Green, 1979; Kirkpatrick, Smith, and Roy, 1981.
157. Hall, 1978; K. Lewis, 1980.
158. E.g., McDermott, 1968; Neubauer, 1960.
159. Wallerstein and Kelly, 1980b; Kalter and Rembar, 1981.
160. E.g., Neal, 1983; Springer and Wallerstein, 1983; Young, 1983.
161. E.g., Biller, 1974; Hetherington, Cox, and Cox, 1978a, 1978b; Hodges, Wechsler, and Ballantine, 1979.
162. Kurdek, Blisk, and Siesky, 1981; Pett, 1982.
163. Hetherington, Cox, and Cox, 1978a, 1978b; Wallerstein, 1977.
164. Bahr, 1983; Hetherington, Cox, and Cox, 1978a; Johnson *et al.*, 1991.
165. Hetherington, Cox, and Cox, 1978a; Colletta, 1979, 1983; Guidubaldi and Perry, 1984.
166. Kopf, 1970.
167. Bloom, Asher, and White, 1978; Hetherington, Cox, and Cox, 1978a.
168. E.g., Felner *et al.*, 1985; Hetherington, Cox, and Cox, 1979a; Wallerstein, 1977; Rutter, 1981.
169. E.g., Wallerstein and Kelly, 1980a, 1980b.
170. E.g., Felner, Farber, and Primaveri, 1980; Rutter, 1981.
171. *Higgins v. Higgins*, 629 S.W.2d 20, 22 (Tenn. App. 1981).
172. American Bar Association, 1990.
173. *In re Baby M*, 537 A.2d 1227, 1260-61 (N.J. 1988).
174. E.g., Ziskin and Faust, 1988a, 1988b, 1988c; Morse, 1978a, 1978b.
175. Lowery, 1981.
176. Grisso, 1986.
177. Grisso, 1986.
178. Ziskin and Faust, 1988b.

CHAPTER 6
FORENSIC EVALUATION IN CASES OF CHILD MALTREATMENT

1. Braun, 1989. The actions are possible because the limitation period has effectively been extended in some jurisdictions; see Kanovitz, 1992, p. 1202. Virginia Acts ch. 674, Va. Code Ann. S. 8.01-249 (1950), the retrospective aspect of which was declared unconstitutional in *Starnes v. Cayouette*, 419 S.E.2d 669 (Va. 1992). See also *Petersen v. Bruen*, 792 P.2d 18 (Nev. 1990) finding that the

limitation period statute does not bar child abuse actions. But see *O'Neal v. Division of Family Services*, 821 P.2d 1139 (Utah 1991), holding that the limitation period is not tolled either because of mental incompetence or lack of discovery.

2. *Prince v. Massachusetts*, 321 U.S. 158 (1944).
3. Kempe *et al.*, 1962.
4. National Center on Child Abuse and Neglect, 1988.
5. Daro and Mitchel, 1989. For a comprehensive study of the prosecution of child sexual abuse, see Gray, 1993. For an appraisal of professional errors see Howitt, 1993.
6. 42 U.S.C. §5706(g) (4) (1978).
7. 16 N.J.S.A. §9:6-8.9 (1987).
8. *People v. Ewing*, 140 Cal. Rptr. 299 (App. 1977).
9. *State v. Tanner*, 675 P.2d 539 (Utah 1983). See also *People v. Nelson*, 561 N.E.2d 439 (Ill. 1990).
10. *People v. Hernandez*, 168 Cal. Rptr. 898, 902 (Ct. App. 1980).
11. *State v. Lucero*, 647 P.2d 406 (N.M. 1982).
12. E.g., *Application of Auster*, 100 N.Y.S.2d 60 (Sup. Ct. 1950).
13. *Wisconsin v. Yoder*, 406 U.S. 205 (1972).
14. *Prince v. Massachusetts*, 321 U.S. 158, 170 (1944).
15. Okla. Laws 1990, Ch.165, Section 2.
16. *Walker v. Superior Court*, 222 Cal. Rptr. 87 (Cal. App. 1986).
17. *In re Stephen W.*, 271 Cal. Rptr. 319 (Cal. App. 1990).
18. *Matter of Stefanel Tyesha C.*, 556 N.Y.S.2d 280 (App. Div. 1990).
19. Brown and Riley, 1984.
20. Patton, 1990.
21. 42 U.S.C.S. §§5101-5106 (1974).
22. See, e.g., Fla. Stat. §827.07(3) (1979).
23. See, e.g., N.J.S.A. §9:6-88.13 (1987).
24. Ten Bensel, 1984.
25. *State v. Grover*, 437 N.W.2d 60 (Minn. 1989).
26. *Borne v. Northwest Allen County School Corp.*, 532 N.E.2d 1196 (Ind. App. 1989); *Fischer v. Metcalf*, 543 So. 2d 785 (Fla. App. 1989).
27. *Landeros v. Flood*, 551 P.2d 389 (Cal. 1976).
28. See, e.g., N.J.S.A. §9:6-8.13 (1987).
29. *Rubenstein v. Baron*, 529 A.2d 1061 (N.J. Super. 1987).
30. *Dominguez v. Kelly*, 786 S.W.2d 749 (Tex. Ct. App. 1990).
31. *State v. Hill*, 556 A.2d 1325 (N.J. Super. 1989).
32. *State v. R.H.*, 683 P.2d 269 (Alaska App. 1984).
33. Assessments of abuse within child custody proceedings also attract immunity or defenses; see *Howard v. Drapkin*, 271 Cal. Rptr. 893 (Cal. Ct. App. 1990); *Vineyard v. Kraft*, 828 S.W.2d 248 (Tex. Ct. App. 1992).
34. *Landeros v. Flood*, 551 P.2d 389 (Cal. 1976); for further discussion, see Chapter 9.
35. *In re Clark*, 281 S.E.2d 47 (N.C. 1981).
36. *Lassiter v. Department of Social Services*, 452 U.S. 18 (1981).

37. McCormick, 1984; for a comprehensive review of the law, see Myers, 1992.

38. Federal Rules of Evidence (Fed. R. Evid.), 601.

39. Bulkley, 1986, pp. 5–23.

40. Dziech and Schudson, 1992, Chapter 3.

41. E.g., *State v. Bellotti*, 383 N.W.2d 308 (Minn. App. 1986); Ohio Rev. Code Ann. §2151.35(F).

42. *Johnston v. Ohls*, 457 P.2d 194 (Wash. 1969); Fed. R. Evid. 803(2).

43. *Goldade v. State*, 674 P.2d 721 (Wyo. 1983); *Davis v. State*, 569 So. 2d 1317 (Fla. App. 1990); *White v. Illinois*, 112 S.Ct. 736 (1992); Fed. R. Evid. 803(4). Exceptions to the hearsay rule beyond these may contravene the confrontation clause: *Idaho v. Wright*, 497 U.S. 805 (1990).

44. *White v. Illinois*, 112 S.Ct. 736, 742 (1992). Talk in sleep not reliable: *State v. Zimmerman*, 829 P.2d 861 (Idaho 1992).

46. *White v. Illinois*, 112 S.Ct. 736, 743 (1992), but compare *Garza v. State*, 828 S.W.2d 432 (Tex. Ct. App. 1992) (finding that necessity is an essential element to admitting hearsay evidence).

46. *Idaho v. Wright*, 497 U.S. 805, 818-21 (1990).

47. *Ibid.*, at 3151.

48. Orfinger, 1989.

49. *Hall v. State*, 415 S.E.2d 158 (Ga. 1991) (father murdered son in front of his daughters; affection shown by daughters at funeral explained by expert evidence of repression and denial of traumatic event).

50. E.g., *State v. Moran*, 728 P.2d 248, 252 (Ariz. 1986).

51. *People v. Beckley*, 456 N.W.2d 391, 404 (Mich. 1990).

52. *People v. Izzo*, 282 N.W.2d 10 (Mich. App. 1979); *United States v. Azure*, 801 F.2d 336 (8th Cir. 1986).

53. *In re Cheryl H.*, 200 Cal. Rptr. 789 (Cal. App. 1984).

54. Fed. R. Evid. 403. Admission of testimony of child abuse syndrome to explain delay in reporting has been ruled reversible error: see *Hellstrom v. Commonwealth*, 825 S.W.2d 612 (Ky. 1992); *Commonwealth v. Evans*, 603 A.2d 608 (Pa. Super. Ct. 1992). But see *State v. Payton*, 481 N.W.2d 325 (Iowa 1992), and *State v. Fox*, 480 N.W.2d 897 (Iowa Ct. App. 1991), approving admission of expert testimony to explain delayed disclosure.

55. *Coy v. Iowa*, 487 U.S. 1012, 1020, 1021, 2802–3 (1988).

56. *Maryland v. Craig*, 497 U.S. 836, 844–45 (1990).

57. *Ibid.*, at 852.

58. *White v. Illinois*, 112 S.Ct. 736, 744 (1992). Justice Thomas, joined by Justice Scalia, suggests that the Confrontation Clause jurisprudence is ripe for reconsideration.

59. Other commentators have recommended more sensitive rules. See Brustein, 1989, and Yun, 1983.

60. Patton, 1990.

61. *In re Jessica B.*, 254 Cal. Rptr. 883, 893 (Cal. App. 1989).

62. *Matter of Vance A*, 432 N.Y.S.2d 137 (N.Y. Fam. Ct. 1980).

63. "No Place to Call Home—Discarded Children in America: A Report of the Select Committee on Children, Youth, and Families," U.S. House of Rep-

resentatives, 101st Cong. 1st sess. (Washington: Government Printing Office, 1989).

64. E.g., *Taylor v. Ledbetter*, 818 F.2d 791 (11th Cir. 1987).

65. *Smith v. Organization of Foster Families for Equality and Reform*, 431 U.S. 816 (1977).

66. *Haselhorst v. State*, 485 N.W.2d 180 (Neb. 1992) (foster child sexually assaulted plaintiffs' children).

67. E.g., the Child Abuse Prevention and Treatment and Adoption Reform Act of 1978, 42 U.S.C. §§5101-5118 (1988); the Adoption Assistance and Child Welfare Act of 1980, AACWA, Pub. L. No. 96-272, 94 Stat. 504 (1980), 42 U.S.C. §670 (1980).

68. 42 U.S.C. ch. 7.

69. 20 U.S.C. §1400. See Chapter 4.

70. AACWA, Pub. Law No. 96-272, note 67 above.

71. "No Place to Call Home," and Magid and McKelvey, 1987, pp. 150–59.

72. Wisdom, 1989; Pollock *et al.*, 1990.

73. *Sanders v. Oklahoma*, 811 P.2d 910 (Okla. Ct. App. 1991).

74. See, for example, *Ex rel. Jones*, 567 So. 2d 664 (La. Ct. App. 1990) (termination of schizophrenic mother's rights, where children lived on street and expert evidence showed that mother was unable to care for children indefinitely; no need to persist in reunification of parent and child where parent shows no interest in return).

75. *Ex rel. M.W.*, 796 P.2d 66 (Colo. Ct. App. 1990) (termination despite condition stabilized on medication).

76. *Lassiter v. Department of Social Services*, 452 U.S. 18 (1981).

77. *Santosky v. Kramer*, 455 U.S. 745 (1982).

78. Huard, 1956, pp. 745–46.

79. 455 U.S. 745 (1982).

80. *Lehr v. Robinson*, 463 U.S. 248 (1983); *Caban v. Mohammed*, 441 U.S. 380 (1979); *Quilloin v. Walcott*, 434 U.S. 246 (1978); *Stanley v. Illinois*, 405 U.S. 645 (1972).

81. Sorosky *et al.*, 1984, pp. 211–14.

82. L. Smith, 1986, pp. 536–38.

83. Three states have completely open records to all adoptees over the age of eighteen: Alabama, Alaska, and Kansas. Twenty-one states have voluntary registers to match adoptees with birth parents.

84. *Griffith v. Johnston*, 899 F.2d 1427 (5th Cir. 1990).

85. Brooks, 1991, describes the federal role in permanency planning for special needs children, present weaknesses, and possible remedies.

86. American Humane Association, 1981.

87. E.g., Gil, 1970; Galdston, 1965; Garbarino, 1977; Kempe, 1973.

88. E.g., Steele, 1970; Galdston, 1965.

89. Starr *et al.*, 1984; Horowitz and Wolcock, 1981; Green, 1976; Green *et al.*, 1980.

90. Burgess and Conger, 1977; Gaensbauer and Mrazek, 1981; Gaensbauer and Sands, 1979; Reid, 1986; Wassermann *et al.*, 1983; Hyman, 1981.

91. Belsky, 1980.

92. Elmer and Gregg, 1967; Martin *et al.*, 1974; Morse *et al.*, 1970.

93. Galdston, 1965.

94. Johnson and Morse, 1968; Aber *et al.*, 1989.

95. George and Main, 1979; Green *et al.*, 1974.

96. Shaheen *et al.*, 1968.

97. Hannaway, 1970.

98. Whitten, Pettit, and Fischoff, 1969; Whitten, 1981.

99. Harris, 1982.

100. Fischoff, Whitten, and Pettit, 1971.

101. Elmer, 1960; J. Moore, 1982; MacCarthy, 1974.

102. Newberger *et. al.*, 1977.

103. MacCarthy, 1974; Bullard *et al.*, 1967; Oates and Yu, 1971.

104. Rosenn, Loeb, and Jura, 1980.

105. Gordon and Jameson, 1979.

106. Kotelchuk, 1980.

107. Schmitt, 1981.

108. Cantwell, 1980.

109. Martin and Walters, 1982.

110. Martin, 1981.

111. Burgess, 1979; Burgess and Conger, 1978.

112. Meadow, 1977, 1982; Rogers *et al.*, 1976.

113. Committee on Sexual Offenses against Children and Youth, 1984.

114. E.g., Fromuth, 1986; Finkelhor, 1979; Wyatt, 1985; Fritz, Stoll, and Wagner, 1981.

115. James and Meyerding, 1977; Silbert and Pines, 1981; Weisberg, 1985.

116. McCormack, Janus, and Burgess, 1986.

117. Goodwin, McCarthy, and DiVasto, 1981; Summit and Kryso, 1978.

118. Groth and Burgess, 1979.

119. Langevin *et al.*, 1983.

120. Putnam, 1985; Putnam *et al.*, 1986.

121. Grapentine *et al.*, 1990.

122. Lewis and Sarrell, 1969; Kempe and Kempe, 1978; Browning and Boatman, 1977; Weiss and Berg, 1982; Asher, 1988.

123. E.g., Tsai and Wagner, 1978; Courtois, 1979; Justice and Justice, 1979; De-Young, 1982.

124. E.g., Tsai, Feldman-Summers, and Edgar, 1979; Russell, 1984; Bagley and Ramsey, 1985.

125. E.g., Courtois, 1979; Finkelhor, 1979.

126. Weinberg, 1955.

127. E.g., Finkelhor, 1979; Lukianowicz, 1972.

128. Meiselman, 1978; Finkelhor, 1979.

129. Herman, 1981.

130. Lukianowicz, 1972; Herman, 1981.

131. Meiselman, 1978.

132. Kaufman, Peck, and Tagiuri, 1954; Goodwin, McCarthy, and DiVasto, 1981; Summit and Kryso, 1978.

133. Meiselman, 1978; Sgroi, 1982a.

134. Sgroi, 1982a.

135. McIntyre, 1981; Taubman, 1984.
136. Asher, 1988.
137. Lerman, 1988.
138. Cammaert, 1988.
139. Haugaard and Reppucci, 1988.
140. E.g., Grapentine *et al.*, 1990; Stone, 1981.
141. E.g., Kluft, 1984; Spiegel, 1984; Greaves, 1980.
142. Finkelhor, 1979; Russell, 1983.
143. Casnoff, 1986; Finch, 1973.
144. Mrazek, 1981; Marvasti, 1986; McCarthy, 1986.
145. Renshaw, 1982.
146. Green, 1988.
147. Attorney General's Commission on Pornography, 1988.
148. E.g., Ross, 1986; Johnston, 1989; Marron, 1988.
149. E.g., in Jordan, Minnesota, and Manhattan Beach, California.
150. Braun, 1986.
151. Finkelhor, 1979; Fritz, Stoll, and Wagner, 1981; Bell and Weinberg, 1981.
152. Muram, 1989a.
153. Muram, 1989b; Muram and Elias, 1989.
154. Emans *et. al.*, 1987.
155. McCann *et al.*, 1989; McCann *et al.*, 1990.
156. Goodman, Golding, and Haith, 1984.
157. Kohlberg, 1976.
158. Melton, 1981.
159. Dent and Stephenson, 1979.
160. Fivush, 1984.
161. Bahrick, Bahrick, and Wittlinger, 1975.
162. Goodman, Hepps, and Reed, 1986.
163. E.g., Goodman and Reed, 1986; Goodman and Aman, 1987.
164. Horowitz, 1976.
165. *Hawaii v. Kim*, 645 P.2d 598 (Haw. 1982).
166. E.g., *People v. Fogarty*, 446 N.Y.S.2d 91 (App. Div. 1982); *State v. Fitzgerald*, 694 P.2d 1117 (Wash. App. 1985).
167. Arntzen, 1970, 1982, 1983; Undeutsch, 1982.
168. Raskin and Steller, 1989; Steller, 1989.
169. Achenbach and Edelbrock, 1983.
170. MacFarlane and Krebs, 1986. In addition to the references below, see Skinner and Berry, 1993.
171. White *et al.*, 1986; Jampole and Weber, 1987; Leventhal *et al.*, 1989; Sivan *et al.*, 1988.
172. E.g., as recommended by Sgroi, Porter, and Blick, 1982.
173. DiLeo, 1973; Koppitz, 1968.
174. Kanovitz, 1992.
175. Bavolek, 1984.
176. Green and Schetky, 1988.
177. Blick and Porter, 1982.
178. Goodman *et al.*, 1987.

179. Berliner and Barbieri, 1984.
180. Runyan *et al.*, 1987.

CHAPTER 7
PSYCHOLOGICAL TRAUMA AND CIVIL LIABILITY

1. Keeton *et al.*, 1984, secs. 1–2. On the difficulties of definition, see the classic treatise of T.A. Street, 1906, pp. xxv–xxix.
2. *Garratt v. Dailey*, 279 P.2d 1091 (Wash. 1955).
3. The jurisprudential aspects of intentional action are well explored by Moore, 1984, pp. 77–81.
4. 279 P.2d 1091 (Wash. 1955).
5. Restatement (Second) of Torts §8A (1965) (hereinafter Restatement).
6. *Talmage v. Smith*, 59 N.W. 656 (Mich. 1894). The transferred intent doctrine is a specific example of a principle that usually the law will not visit the consequences of a mistake on the innocent party.
7. *McGuire v. Almy*, 8 N.E.2d 760 (Mass. 1937). Provided caregivers or the insane person was in a position to alter his harm-producing activity prior to the act, liability will follow, see Landes and Posner, 1987, pp. 130–31.
8. *Breunig v. American Family Ins. Co.*, 173 N.W.2d 619 (Wis. 1970).
9. Restatement §435B, Illus. 1.
10. *Fisher v. Carrousel Motor Hotel*, 424 S.W.2d 627 (Tex. 1967).
11. *Mohr v. Williams*, 104 N.W. 12 (Minn. 1905).
12. *Western Union Telegraph Co. v. Hill*, 150 So. 709 (Ala. App. 1933).
13. Keeton *et al.*, 1984, sec. 12 at 54–55; see also *Harris v. Jones*, 380 A.2d 611, 614 (Md. 1977).
14. See, e.g., *State Rubbish Collectors Ass'n v. Siliznoff*, 240 P.2d 282 (Cal. 1952).
15. See *Harris v. Jones*, 380 A.2d 611 (Md. 1977).
16. *Slocum v. Food Fair Stores*, 100 So. 2d 396 (Fla. 1958).
17. *Taylor v. Vallelunga*, 339 P.2d 910 (Cal. App. 1959).
18. *Great Atlantic & Pacific Tea Co. v. Roch*, 153 A. 22 (Md. App. 1931).
19. *Harris v. Jones*, 380 A.2d 611 (Md. 1977).
20. Pfeuffer, 1990.
21. *Chiles v. Chiles*, 779 S.W.2d 127 (Tex. Ct. App. 1989) (rejecting the availability of the tort in the divorce context); an action may be brought by children against parents in federal court despite the exclusion of "domestic relations" in the jurisdiction of federal courts. *Ankenbrandt v. Richards*, 112 S.Ct. 2206 (1992).
22. *Kirker v. Orange County*, 519 So. 2d 682 (Fla. App. 1988). See also below, at note 53.
23. *The Florida Star v. B.J.F.*, 491 U.S. 524 (1989).
24. *Chambon v. Celender*, 780 F. Supp. 307 (W.D. Pa. 1992).
25. See *Cohen v. Cowles Media Co.*, 111 S.Ct. 2513 (1991); the action for breach of confidence is discussed in Chapter 8.
26. *Murray v. McMurchy*, [1949] 2 D.L.R. 442 (B.C. Sup. Ct.).
27. *Jones v. Fisher*, 166 N.W.2d 175 (Wis. 1969); *Joyce-Couch v. DeSilva*, 602 N.E.2d 286 (Ohio Ct. App. 1991), respectively.
28. *Pacific Mut. Life Ins. Co. v. Haslip*, 111 S.Ct. 1032 (1991).

29. Keeton *et al*. 1984, sec. 16, at 109.
30. See cases cited below, note 97.
31. *O'Brien v. Cunard Steamship Co.*, 28 N.E. 266 (Mass. 1891).
32. Restatement §62, Illus. 3.
33. *Ibid.*, §282.
34. *Heaven v. Pender*, 11 Q.B.D. 503 (1883).
35. Moore, 1984, pp. 81–84.
36. See, generally, Cane, 1987.
37. *Palsgraf v. Long Island Railroad*, 162 N.E. 99 (N.Y. 1928).
38. *Linder v. Bidner*, 270 N.Y.S.2d 427 (Sup. Ct. 1966).
39. *Silberstein v. Cordie*, 474 N.W.2d 850 (Minn. Ct. App. 1991).
40. See *Tarasoff v. Regents of University of Cal.*, 529 P.2d 553 (1974), aff'd in part, rev'd in part, 551 P.2d 334 (1976), discussed in Chapter 8.
41. *Eisel v. Board of Education of Montgomery County*, 597 A.2d 447 (Md. 1991).
42. *Nally v. Grace Community Church of the Valley*, 763 P.2d 948 (Cal. 1988).
43. *Whetham v. Bismarck Hospital*, 197 N.W.2d 678 (N.D. 1972).
44. *Dillon v. Legg*, 441 P.2d 912 (Cal. 1968).
45. Keeton *et al.*, 1984, §54, p. 366.
46. *Ibid.*, pp. 362–63.
47. *Corgan v. Muehling*, 574 N.E.2d 602 (Ill. 1991); for discussion of liability for sexual relations, see Chapter 9.
48. *Doe v. Woodbridge Nursing Pavillion*, Ill. Cook County Cir. (Jan. 15, 1992). See note 215, Chapter 8.
49. *Johnson v. Ruark Obstetrics & Gynecology Assoc.*, 395 S.E.2d 85, 97 (N.C. 1990). *Ford v. Aldi, Inc.*, 832 S.W.2d 1 (Mo. App. 1992) (necessary to show that the alleged emotional distress is medically diagnosable and severe enough to be considered medically significant).
50. Restatement 2d §436A. The Supreme Court of Virginia has restricted recovery by demanding that the plaintiff prove causation by "clear and convincing" evidence: *Womack v. Eldridge*, 210 S.E.2d 145 (Va. 1974). For burden of proof, see Chapter 2.
51. In *Ochoa v. Superior Court*, 703 P.2d 1 (Cal. 1985), the court found that *Dillon* did not require contemporaneous viewing of "brief and sudden occurrence"; the factors were guidelines only. But in *Thing v. LaChusa*, 771 P.2d 814 (Cal. 1989), the court insisted that the criteria were limiting tests for recovery of emotional distress by bystanders. The law is well developed, albeit uncertain, elsewhere in the Anglo-American legal system, see *Alcock v. Chief Constable of the South Yorkshire Police* [1991], 4 A11 E.R. 907 (House of Lords, Engl.) (emotional distress suffered by relatives of victims of a riot at a soccer game).
52. *Molien v. Kaiser Foundation Hospitals*, 616 P.2d 813 (Cal. 1980).
53. Keeton *et al.*, 1984, p. 362.
54. *Strachan v. John F. Kennedy Memorial Hospital*, 538 A.2d 346 (N.J. 1988).
55. Another well-recognized, albeit minority, exception is the death telegram rule. Recovery may be made against a telegraph company that negligently transmits a message announcing death. See *Johnson v. State*, 334 N.E.2d 590 (N.Y. App. 1975). The federal rule allows recovery if physical harm results: *Kaufman v. Western Union*, 224 F.2d 723 (5th Cir. 1955).

56. *Marlene F. v. Affiliated Psychiatric Medical Clinic, Inc.*, 770 P.2d 278 (Cal. 1989).
57. *Schwarz v. Regents of University of California*, 276 Cal. Rptr. 470 (Cal. App. 1990).
58. A mother and child may be treated as one unit and a duty owed to both. Thus in *Anisodon v. Superior Court*, 285 Cal. Rptr. 539 (1991), a mother had an action for negligent infliction of emotional distress when the defendant's negligence had caused her child to be born a spastic quadriplegic.
59. *Hagerty v. L&L Marine Services*, 788 F.2d 315, 318 (5th Cir. 1986). The asbestos cases are discussed in *Mauro v. Raymark Indus.*, 561 A.2d 257 (N.J. 1989).
60. *Petriello v. Kalman*, 576 A.2d 474 (Conn. 1990).
61. *Johnson v. West Virginia University Hospitals*, 413 S.E.2d 889 (W.Va. 1991).
62. *Adams v. Johns-Manville Sales*, 783 F.2d 589 (5th Cir. 1986).
63. E.g., *In re Moorenovich*, 634 F. Supp. 634 (D. Me. 1986). In *Gerardi v. Nuclear Utility Services, Inc.*, 566 N.Y.S.2d 1002 (Sup. Ct. 1991), the Court upheld a claim for emotional distress for anxiety attendant to a lifetime of medical monitoring.
64. See Restatement §402A. For a discussion of these cases, see Dworkin, 1984, and Gale and Groyer, 1986.
65. *Endresz v. Friedberg*, 248 N.E.2d 901 (N.Y. Ct. App. 1969).
66. Gordon, 1965; Meadows, 1992. For a recent case allowing recovery for wrongful death and allowing damages for loss of society, see *Seef v. Sutkus*, 583 N.E.2d 510 (Ill. 1991).
67. Brown *et al.*, 1986.
68. *Harbeson v. Parke-Davis, Inc.*, 656 P.2d 483 (Wash. 1983); *Arche v. U.S. Dep't of Army*, 798 P.2d 477 (Kan. 1990) (joining twenty other jurisdictions), but cf. *Atlanta Obstetrics & Gynecology Group v. Abelson*, 398 S.E.2d 557 (Ga. 1990) (denying wrongful birth action).
69. In *Arche*, the court declined to award damages for emotional distress in an effort to limit damages.
70. *Procanik v. Cillo*, 478 A.2d 755 (N.J. 1984); *Lloyd v. North Broward Hosp. Dist.*, 570 So. 2d 984 (Fl. Dist. Ct. App. 1990).
71. *Curlender v. Bio-Science Laboratories*, 165 Cal. Rptr. 477 (Cal. App. 1980); *Lloyd*, 570 So. 2d 984; *Passoulas v. Ramey*, 450 So. 2d 822 (Fla. 1984).
72. *Hartke v. McKelway*, 526 F. Supp. 97 (D.D.C. 1981); *Cowe v. Forum Group, Inc.*, 541 N.E.2d 962 (Ind. Ct. App. 1989) (liability for failure of a mental health institution to prevent rape and subsequent pregnancy of a resident).
73. *United States v. Carroll Towing Co.*, 159 F.2d 169 (2d Cir. 1947).
74. For a case exploring this issue, see *Roberts v. Louisiana*, 396 So. 2d 566 (La. App. 1981).
75. *C.T.W. v. B.C.G.*, 809 S.W.2d 788 (Tex. Ct. App. 1991).
76. See e.g., Restatement §283A.
77. *Morby v. Rogers*, 252 P.2d 231 (Utah 1953) (violation of statute by thirteen-year-old boy did not displace the child standard of care).
78. See, e.g., *Robinson v. Lindsay*, 598 P.2d 392 (Wash. 1979), where a thirteen-year-old child was held to an adult standard of care when the snowmobile he was driving injured another child in an accident.

79. Restatement §431–33; see also *Anderson v. Minneapolis St. P. & S. St. M. R.R. Co.*, 179 N.W. 45 (Minn. 1920).

80. See, e.g., *In re "Agent Orange" Product Liability Litigation MDL No. 381*, 597 F. Supp. 740 (E.D. N.Y. 1984).

81. The foundation case is *Summers v. Tice*, 199 P.2d 1 (Cal. 1948).

82. *Res ipsa loquitur* was applied; see below, at note 119.

83. *Ybarra v. Spangard*, 154 P.2d 687 (Cal. 1944).

84. Nace, 1991.

85. See *Bartolone v. Jeckovich*, 481 N.Y.S.2d 545 (Sup. Ct. 1984), and *Miley v. Landry*, 582 So.2d 833 (La. 1991) (psychiatric illness precipitated by negligent act).

86. The drug company must supply an adequate warning to physicians prescribing the drug: *Sterling Drug v. Yarrow*, 408 F.2d 978 (8th Cir. 1969); *Reaves v. Ortho Pharmaceutical Corporation*, 765 F. Supp. 1287 (D.C. Mich. 1991) (rule applied to oral contraceptive). But compare *O'Gilvie v. International Playtex*, 821 F.2d 1438 (10th Cir. 1987) (tampon manufacturer liable for toxic shock syndrome death where doctor misdiagnosed condition as scarlet fever).

87. *Haselhorst v. State*, 485 N.W.2d 180 (Neb. 1992).

88. See also *Crowley v. Spivey*, 329 S.E.2d 774 (S.C. App. 1985) (finding grandparents liable to father of deceased children when they negligently failed to supervise their daughter, the children's mother, allowing her to shoot and kill the children). But compare *Rozycki v. Peley*, 489 A.2d 1272 (N.J. Super. 1984) (parents of boys who were physically and sexually abused by defendant's husband brought suit against her alleging that her knowledge of the husband's pedophilia imposed a duty on her to warn the children and their parents; the court found no duty because of the importance of the marital relationship and its subversion if a duty were found). *Tarasoff v. Regents of University of Cal.*, 529 P.2d 553 (1974), aff'd in part, rev'd in part, 551 P.2d 334 (1976), discussed extensively in Chapter 8, is a further example of liability imposed to protect third parties from intentional and malicious acts of third parties.

89. *Anderson v. Sears, Roebuck & Company*, 377 F. Supp. 136 (E.D. La. 1974).

90. *Platt v. McDonnell Douglas*, 554 F. Supp. 360 (E.D. Mich. 1983).

91. *Sharman v. Evans*, 138 C.L.R. 563 (Austl. 1977) (High Court of Australia) (the court must allow for "mental suffering, including the anguish [induced by] knowledge that her life expectancy has been substantially reduced").

92. The issue is controversial. In *McDougald v. Garber*, 536 N.E.2d 372 (N.Y. App. 1989), the majority, against a trenchant dissent, concluded that "cognitive awareness is a prerequisite to recovery for loss of enjoyment of life."

93. *Hibpshman v. Prudhoe Bay Supply, Inc.*, 734 P.2d 991, 994 n.11 (Alaska 1987); *Hay v. Medical Center Hosp.*, 496 A.2d 939, 942 (Vt. 1985); *Ueland v. Pengo Hydra-Pull Corp.*, 691 P.2d 190, 191 n.1 (Wash. 1984).

94. See, e.g., *Ferriter v. Daniel O'Connell's Sons, Inc.*, 413 N.E.2d 690 (Mass. 1980); *Berger v. Weber*, 303 N.W.2d 424 (Mich. 1981).

95. *Hibpshman*, at 997; *Theama v. City of Kenosha*, 344 N.W.2d 513, 518 (Wis. 1984).

96. *Reighley v. International Playtex, Inc.*, 604 F. Supp. 1078, 1081 n.1 (D. Colo. 1985); *Hibpshman*, at 992.

97. The trend began with the Massachusetts case of *Ferriter v. Daniel O'Connell's Sons, Inc.*, and was continued in *Reighley*, at 1081; *Hibpshman*, at 992; *Hay*, at 946; and *Ueland*, at 193. But see *Barton-Malow Co., Inc. v. Wilburn*, 547 N.E.2d 1123 (Ind. App. 3 Dist. 1989) (Hoffman J. noting that since 1980 only six jurisdictions other than Massachusetts have recognized the loss of parental consortium action).

98. *Hay*, at 941; *Ueland*, at 192 (a child may still pursue a wrongful death cause of action if the parent is killed).

99. *Hay*, at 944; *Ueland*, at 195; *Theama*, at 520–21.

100. *Reighley*, at 1083; *Theama*, at 520.

101. *Theama*, at 522; *Belcher v. Goins*, 400 S.E.2d 830 (W.Va. 1990) (eighteen-year-old nonhandicapped child not entitled to consortium claim).

102. *Reighley*, at 1084; *Hibpshman*, at 997; *Hay*, at 943; *Ueland*, at 195.

103. Restatement §895 A-E.

104. See *Gelbman v. Gelbman*, 245 N.E.2d 192 (N.Y. Ct. App. 1969); *Williams v. Williams*, 369 A.2d 669 (Del. 1976). See generally Tobias, 1989.

105. *Mahnke v. Moore*, 77 A.2d 923 (Md. 1951).

106. *Martens v. Martens*, 167 A. 227 (N.J. 1933).

107. Restatement §895G, Comment d–i (1979).

108. *Mahnke*, 77A. 2d 923.

109. *Peoples Bank of Bloomington v. Damera*, 581 N.E.2d 426 (Ill. App. 1991) (committing suicide not contributory negligence in action against psychiatrist based on breach of duty to safeguard against suicide).

110. South Carolina and Tennessee are the latest states into the fold of comparative fault; see *Nelson v. Concrete Supply Co.*, 399 S.E.2d 783 (S.C. 1991), and *McIntyre v. Balentine*, 833 S.W.2d 52 (Tenn. 1992).

111. Harper, James, and Gray, 1986, p. 386.

112. *Blackburn v. Dorta*, 348 So. 2d 287 (Fla. 1977).

113. Robinson, 1986a, discusses the cases and suggests that the courts should permit more freedom in contracting out of liability.

114. *Winterstein v. Wilcom*, 293 A.2d 821 (Md. Spec. Ct. App. 1972) (allowing contracting out by owner of drag racing site).

115. Restatement 2d §496C, illus. 1.

116. *Honeycutt v. Wichita*, 796 P.2d 549 (Kan. 1990) (six-year-old child).

117. *Greenman v. Yuba Power Products*, 377 P.2d 897 (Cal. 1963).

118. *Robertson v. Sixpence Inns of America, Inc.*, 789 P.2d 1040 (Ariz. 1990).

119. *Farber v. Olkon*, 254 P.2d 520 (Cal. 1953).

120. The California Supreme Court distinguished its decision in *Ybarra v. Spangard*, 154 P.2d 687 (Cal. 1944), on the basis that electric shock treatment induced bodily convulsions, while in *Ybarra* the appendix operation gave rise to no risk of the paralysis from which the plaintiff suffered following the operation's completion.

121. Weiler, 1991, p. 23.

122. *Ravi v. Williams*, 536 So. 2d 1374 (Ala. 1988) (finding negligence in failing to remove all sponges despite taking usual steps to ensure removal).

123. Achenbach and Edelbrock, 1983.

124. Herjanic and Campbell, 1977.

125. Achenbach and Edelbrock, 1983.
126. Van Eerdewegh *et al.*, 1982.
127. Rutter, 1966; Lifschitz *et al.*, 1977.
128. Respectively, Burke *et al.*, 1982; Ziv and Israeli, 1973; Gleser *et al.*, 1981; McFarlane, 1987.
129. Respectively, Gislason and Call, 1982; Wisely *et al.*, 1983; Pynoos & Eth, 1984; Senior *et al.*, 1982; Green, 1983; Terr, 1983.
130. Terr, 1979, 1981a, 1981b, 1983, 1988.
131. Robins and O'Neal, 1953.
132. Green, 1983.
133. Nurcombe *et al.*, 1994.
134. Rutter, 1983; Dohrenwend and Dohrenwend, 1978.
135. Andrews and Tennant, 1978; Brown and Harris, 1978; Paykel, 1978.

CHAPTER 8
MALPRACTICE

1. Sloan *et al.*, 1991, pp. 4-7, reports an upsurge of claims in the mid-1950s. Medical malpractice is not just a twentieth-century phenomenon; see DeVille, 1990.
2. Robinson, 1986b; Danzon, 1985.
3. Weiler, 1991, p. 2.
4. For surveys of the data, see Weiler, 1991; Wiener, 1992, pp. 394–404. For commentary, see Schuck, 1991.
5. Weiler, 1991.
6. Grady, 1988; Weiler, 1991, p. 45.
7. E.g., *Baker v. United States*, 343 F.2d 222 (8th Cir. 1965); *Doctors Hospital v. Kovats*, 494 P.2d 389 (Ariz. App. 1972); *Schrempf v. State*, 487 N.E.2d 883 (N.Y. 1985). For specific coverage of psychiatric malpractice see Smith, 1986.
8. *Schrempf v. State* (the line between medical judgment and deviation from good medical practice is not easy to draw, particularly in cases involving psychiatric treatment). This observation is born out by data reported by Bencivenga, 1992.
9. Sloan *et al.*, 1993, pp. 50–71; Mechanic, 1975.
10. Cf. *Monahan v. Dorchester Counseling Center, Inc.*, 961 F.2d 987 (1st Cir. 1992) (distinguishing tort and constitutional law).
11. *DuBois v. Decker*, 29 N.E. 313 (N.Y. App. Div. 1891).
12. The law imposes no duty to rescue, even though a physician has the skill and opportunity to effect the rescue. If, however, the physician embarks on the rescue, he must perform to a level of reasonable care and skill. For discussion of rationale, see Levmore, 1986.
13. *Sullivan v. O'Connor*, 296 N.E.2d 183 (Mass. 1973) (plaintiff contracted for a nose like Hedy Lamar's; she ended up with a definite hump on its bridge).
14. Cf. *Dennis v. Allison*, 698 S.W.2d 94 (Tex. 1985).
15. *Hurley v. Eddingfield*, 59 N.E. 1058 (Ind. 1901).
16. *O'Neill v. Montefiore Hospital*, 202 N.Y.S.2d 436, 439–40 (App. Div. 1960).
17. *Lyons v. Grether*, 239 S.E.2d 103 (Va. 1977).
18. *Stevison v. Enid Health Systems, Inc.*, 920 F.2d 710 (10th Cir. 1990); *Power v.*

Arlington Hospital, 800 F. Supp. 1384 (E.D. Va. 1992) (cap on damages under state law does not limit damages under the statute).

19. *Christy v. Saliterman*, 179 N.W.2d 288 (Minn. 1970).
20. Simon and Sadoff, 1992, pp. 32–33.
21. Simon, 1982.
22. See *Osheroff v. Chestnut Lodge et al.*, Maryland Health Claims Arbitration #82-262 (1982), and *Hicks v. United States*, 368 F.2d 626 (4th Cir. 1966). For a thorough discussion of the place of informed consent in psychiatry see Lidz *et al.*, 1984.
23. *Lotspeich v. Chance Vought Aircraft*, 369 S.W.2d 705 (Tex. Civ. App. 1963); *Johnston v. Sibley*, 558 S.W.2d 135 (Tex. Civ. App. 1977); *Lo Dico v. Caputi*, 517 N.Y.S.2d 640 (N.Y. App. Div. 1987); *Meinze v. Holmes*, 532 N.E.2d 170 (Ohio App. 1987); *Rogers v. Horvath*, 237 N.W.2d 595 (Mich. App. 1975); *Ervin v. American Guardian Life Assur.*, 545 A.2d 354 (Pa. Super. 1988).
24. *Betesh v. U.S.*, 400 F. Supp. 238 (D.D.C. 1974).
25. *Mullen v. McKnelly*, 693 S.W.2d 837 (Mo. App. 1985).
26. *Howard v. Drapkin*, 271 Cal. Rptr. 893 (Cal. Ct. App. 1990).
27. *Vineyard v. Kraft*, 828 S.W.2d 248 (Tex. Ct. App. 1992).
28. King, 1986, p. 33, tenders similar advice.
29. *Davis v. Tirrell*, 443 N.Y.S.2d 136 (N.Y. Sup. Ct. 1981) (no duty); *Olson v. Western Airlines*, 191 Cal. Rptr. 502 (App. 1983) (duty).
30. *Tunkl v. Regents of the University of California*, 383 P.2d 441 (Cal. 1963).
31. *Robbins v. Footer*, 553 F.2d 123 (D.C. Cir. 1977).
32. *Henning v. Thomas*, 366 S.E.2d 109 (Va. 1988); *Stepakoff v. Kantar*, 473 N.E.2d 1131 (Mass. 1985). See Chapter 7 for a discussion of standard of care.
33. *Helling v. Carey*, 519 P.2d 981 (Wash. 1974).
34. *Barton v. Owen*, 139 Cal. Rptr. 494 (Ct. App. 1977).
35. *Furey v. Thomas Jefferson University Hospital*, 472 A.2d 1083 (Pa. Super. Ct. 1984); *Duckworth v. Bennett*, 181 A. 558 (Pa. 1935) (requiring adoption by a considerable number of physicians), cited with approval in *D'Angelis v. Zakuto*, 556 A.2d 431 (Pa. 1989); *Downer v. Veilleux*, 322 A.2d 82 (Me. 1974); *Koch v. Gorrilla*, 552 F.2d 1170 (6th Cir. 1977).
36. *Downer v. Veilleux*, 322 A.2d 82, 87 (Me. 1974).
37. *Small v. Howard*, 128 Mass. 131 (1880). See Pearson, 1978, p. 528.
38. McCoid, 1959.
39. *Carbone v. Warburton*, 94 A.2d 680 (N.J. 1953).
40. *Hardy v. Brantley*, 471 So. 2d 358 (Miss. 1958).
41. *Hall v. Hilbun*, 466 So. 2d 856 (Miss. 1985).
42. Blumstein, 1991, p. 37.
43. Wennberg, 1984, p. 6.
44. *Roe v. Minister of Health* [1954] 2 Q.B. 66; [1954] 2 A11 E.R. 131 (C.A.). This is also an ethical requirement; see American Psychiatric Association, 1986, Section 5(1), p. 7.
45. *Weil v. Seltzer*, 873 F.2d 1453 (D.C. Cir. 1989); *Windisch v. Weiman*, 555 N.Y.S.2d 731 (1990); *Jensen v. Archbishop Bergan Mercy Hosp.*, 459 N.W.2d 178 (Neb. 1990).

46. Such evidence will enhance the quantum of damages. Punitive damages have generally been denied, but compare *Greenberg v. McCabe*, 453 F. Supp. 765 (E.D. Pa. 1978). For the role expert evidence in disciplinary hearings, see Hymans, 1992.

47. *Dick v. Lewis*, 506 F. Supp. 799 (D.N.D. 1980), aff'd 636 F.2d 1168 (8th Cir. 1981) (need to prove that failure to perform caesarean section caused cerebral palsy). See also *Fitzgerald v. Manning*, 679 F.2d 341 (4th Cir. 1982). The hypothetical is similar to the facts in *Osheroff v. Chestnut Lodge et al.*, Maryland Health Claims Arbitration #82-262 (1982), discussed in Klerman, 1990.

48. The latter situation is the more common, as where a patient is placed in a physical environment where he injures himself: *Pisel v. Stamford Hosp.*, 430 A.2d 1 (Conn. 1980). This may go to suicide: *Bornmann v. Great SW. Gen. Hosp.*, 453 F.2d 616 (5th Cir. 1971).

49. *Waffen v. United States, Dept. of Health & Human Services*, 799 F.2d 911 (4th Cir. 1986); *Hurley v. United States*, 923 F2d 1091 (4th Cir. 1991); *Karl v. Oaks Minor Emergency Clinic*, 826 S.W.2d 791 (Tex. Ct. App. 1992); *Dumas v. Cooney*, 1 Cal. Rptr. 2d 584 (Ct. App. 1991).

50. *Falcon v. Memorial Hospital*, 462 N.W.2d 44 (Mich. 1990).

51. *Herskovits v. Group Health Cooperative*, 664 P.2d 474 (Wash. 1983).

52. For argumentation on this point see Kaye, 1982, and Shavell, 1987, p. 117.

53. *Canterbury v. Spence*, 464 F.2d 772, 784 (D.C. Cir. 1972). This question is still keenly debated and remains unsettled in England: *Sidaway v. Bethlehem Royal Hospital* [1985] A.C. 871 (H.L.). The purposes of the doctrine are set forth in Capron, 1974.

54. *Pauscher v. Iowa Methodist Medical Center*, 408 N.W.2d 355 (Iowa 1987).

55. *Murray v. McMurchy* [1949] 2 D.L.R. 442 (B.C. Sup. Ct.).

56. *Kaimowitz v. Dept. of Mental Health*, No. 73-19434-AW (Mich. Cir. Ct., Wayne County, July 10, 1973).

57. *Mink v. University of Chicago*, 460 F. Supp. 713 (N.D. Ill. 1978).

58. Burger, 1968; Capron, 1973.

59. Jones, 1992. For discussion see Caplan *et al.*, 1992.

60. 21 U.S.C. §355.

61. 42 U.S.C. §§2891–92.

62. West's Ann. Cal. Penal Code §§2670–78; N.Y.: McKinney's Pub. Health Law §§2440–46. Some argue that the regulation may be too stringent, but IRB regulations are criticized as too lax.

63. For example, the risk that a sterilization operation may fail: *F. v. R.* (1983), 33 S.A. St. R. 189 (S. Ct. S.A.); or the risk of HIV-infected blood: *Kozup v. Georgetown University*, 663 F. Supp. 1048 (D.D.C. 1987).

64. *Scott v. Bradford*, 606 P.2d 554 (Okla. 1979).

65. *Canterbury v. Spence*, 464 F.2d 772, 787 (D.C. Cir. 1972).

66. *Hidding v. Williams*, 578 So. 2d 1192 (La. App. 1991).

67. *Estate of Behringer v. Medical Center at Princeton*, 592 A.2d 1251 (N.J. Super. 1991); see also Lieberman and Derse, 1992, supporting requirement of disclosure.

68. *Canterbury v. Spence*, 464 F.2d 772 (D.C. Cir. 1972).

69. *Scott v. Bradford*, 606 P.2d 554 (Okla. 1979).

70. *Canterbury v. Spence*, 464 F.2d 772, 788 (D.C. Cir. 1972).

71. *Pauscher v. Iowa Methodist Medical Center*, 408 N.W.2d 355 (Iowa 1987).
72. *Ibid.*
73. *Canterbury v. Spence*, 464 F.2d 772 (D.C. Cir. 1972).
74. *Sard v. Hardy*, 379 A.2d 1014 (Md. 1977).
75. *Natanson v. Kline*, 350 P.2d 1093, 1103 (Kan. 1960).
76. Wadlington, 1973.
77. Wadlington, 1984.
78. Katz, 1984; for full historical treatment, see Faden and Beauchamp, 1986.
79. Simon, 1987, p. 103.
80. Epstein, 1978; Robitscher, 1978.
81. Maryland Health Claims Arbitration #82-262 (see note 47 above).
82. *Truman v. Thomas*, 611 P.2d 902 (Cal. 1980).
83. Barnum, 1990, p. 101.
84. Mass. Gre. Law ch. 112 §129A.
85. *Barclay v. Campbell*, 704 S.W.2d 8 (Tex. 1986); see generally Simon and Sadoff, 1991, p. 110.
86. *Moore v. Regents of University of California*, 793 P.2d 479, 152 (Cal. 1990).
87. This argument depends on the courts accepting that the fiduciary relationship generates a class of remedies beyond those usually associated with tort liability. For discussion, see Gurry, 1984.
88. New York Public Health Law §2805-d (1975).
89. *Doe v. Roe*, 400 N.Y.S.2d 668 (N.Y. Sup. Ct. 1977). Emphasis in original.
90. Although the emerging rule strongly favors an action, some courts have refused to recognize an action in tort. See *Mikel v. Abrams*, 541 F. Supp. 591 (W.D. Mo. 1982); *Logan v. District of Columbia*, 447 F. Supp. 1328 (D.D.C. 1978); *Collins v. Howard*, 156 F. Supp. 322 (S.D. Ga. 1957); *Quarles v. Sutherland*, 389 S.W.2d 249 (Tenn. 1965).
91. *Humphers v. First Interstate Bank of Oregon*, 696 P.2d 527 (Or. 1985).
92. *Ibid.*
93. *Horne v. Patton*, 287 So. 2d 824 (Ala. 1973).
94. *Cohen v. Cowles Media Company*, 111 S.Ct. 2513 (1991) (liability of newspaper for disclosing identity of plaintiff informant after undertaking of confidentiality).
95. Reisner, 1985.
96. *Doe v. Roe*, 400 N.Y.S.2d 668 (N.Y. Sup. Ct. 1977).
97. *State v. S.H.*, 465 N.W.2d 238 (Wis. App. 1990).
98. *Stenger v. Lehigh Valley Hospital Center*, 609 A.2d 796 (Pa. 1992). For a contemporary discussion, see Appelbaum and Appelbaum, 1990.
99. *Whalen v. Roe*, 429 U.S. 589, 602 n. 29 (1977); for discussion see Barnum, 1990, p. 77.
100. Md. 1987, ch. 635 §2(b).
101. A useful table has been compiled by the Clearinghouse on Child Abuse and Neglect Information, cited and extracted in Barnum, 1990, Table 2.
102. *Landeros v. Flood*, 551 P.2d 389 (Cal. 1976). An attorney is not obliged to report when the information comes to him covered with client–attorney privilege, but if the information indicating the likelihood of future abuse is derived otherwise he has a duty to report. Mosteller, 1992.

103. Recall the discussion of negligence *per se* in Chapter 7.
104. *In re Lifschutz*, 467 P.2d 557 (Cal. 1970).
105. Cal. Evid. Code §1014 provides the patient of psychotherapy with the privilege to refuse to have confidential communications disclosed. There are two common schemes of privilege. The first provides privilege as modeled by attorney–client privilege. See N.Y. Civil Practice Laws & Rules §4507 (McKinney 1984). The second scheme provides privilege with qualifications. See Mich. Comp. Laws §330.1748 (1990); Mont. Code Ann. §630.140 (1988); Ala. Code §26-18-7 (1984), allowing disclosure when ordered by courts; Alaska Stat. §08.86.200(a) (1988), requiring disclosure of known child abuse.
106. Wigmore, 1985, §2286.
107. *Inabnit v. Berkson*, 245 Cal. Rptr. 525 (Cal. App. 1988) (construing the California provisions).
108. *Adoption of Embick*, 506 A.2d 455 (Pa. Super. 1986).
109. *People v. Caplan*, 238 Cal. Rptr. 478 (Cal. App. 1987).
110. *State v. Hansen*, 743 P.2d 157 (Or. 1987) (finding the exception to apply whether or not the evidence supports a finding of abuse).
111. *In the Matter of C.P.*, 543 N.E.2d 410 (Ind. App. 1989).
112. *MacDonald v. Clinger*, 446 N.Y.S.2d 801 (App. Div. 1982).
113. *Davis v. Lhim*, 335 N.W.2d 481 (Mich. App. 1983). Informed consent doctrine requires that the psychiatrist inform the patient that he will have a duty to disclose information of this kind if it is transmitted to him. The duty of informed consent in the psychiatric context protects important social values; see Lidz *et al.*, 1984, p. 7.
114. *Menendez v. Superior Court*, 279 Cal. Rptr. 521 (App. 1991). The California Supreme Court confirmed, holding that the taped notes were not privileged because of the dangerous patient exception, but that the notes of the session after the warning were privileged because warning was not necessary to avoid harm; 834 P.2d 786 (1992).
115. *Davis v. Monsanto*, 627 F. Supp. 418 (S.D. W.Va. 1986).
116. American Psychiatric Association, 1989, Section 2.
117. Cal. Business & Professions Code §729 (West 1990); Ill. Ann. Stat. Ann. ch. 70 para. 801 (Smith-Hurd 1989); Minn. Stat. Ann. §148A.01 *et seq.* (West 1989).
118. Simon, 1987.
119. American Psychiatric Association, 1989, Section 4, Ann. 7, simply suggests, rather unhelpfully: "Careful judgment must be exercised by the psychiatrist in order to include, when appropriate, the parents or guardian in the treatment of a minor. At the same time the psychoanalyst must assure the minor proper confidentiality."
120. *In the Matter of C.P.*, 543 N.E.2d 410 (Ind. App. 1989).
121. Stromberg *et al.*, 1988: "It is also important that adolescents be able to depend upon a promise of confidentiality in counseling, to the full extent permitted by law. Many adolescents fear, more than anything else, their parents' reactions to learning of pregnancy, drug abuse, or mental problems—and will avoid seeking help rather than risk disclosure."
122. Simon, 1987, p. 142.
123. *Ibid.*, pp. 142–43.

124. American Psychiatric Association, 1978, §3(a).
125. Cf. *Joy v. Eastern Maine Medical Center*, 529 A.2d 1364 (Me. 1987); *Kirk v. Michael Reese Hospital and Medical Center*, 483 N.E.2d 906 (Ill. App. Ct. 1985), rev'd, 513 N.E.2d 387 (Ill. 1987).
126. *Petersen v. State of Washington*, 671 P.2d 230 (Wash. 1983).
127. *Cain v. Rijken*, 717 P.2d 140 (Or. 1986).
128. *Tamsen v. Weber*, 802 P.2d 1063 (Ariz. App. 1990).
129. *Estate of Behringer v. Medical Center at Princeton*, 592 A.2d 1251 (N.J. Super. 1991), suggesting this in dicta. See also Hermann and Gagliano, 1989; Appelbaum and Appelbaum, 1990.
130. Appelbaum and Appelbaum, 1990.
131. Cal. Health and Safety Code, §199.25(a) (b) & (c).
132. *Tarasoff v. Regents of University of California*, 529 P.2d 553 (1974), aff'd in part, rev'd in part, 551 P.2d 334 (1976).
133. *Tarasoff (I)*, 529 P.2d 553 (1974).
134. *Tarasoff (II)*, 551 P.2d 334, 347 (1976).
135. Some courts have rejected any *Tarasoff* duty: *Currie v. U.S.*, 644 F. Supp. 1074 (M.D.N.C. 1986); *Sharpe v. South Carolina Dept. of Mental Health*, 354 S.E.2d 778 (S.C. App. 1987); *Shaw v. Glickman*, 415 A.2d 625 (Md. App. 1980).
136. Another case of a clear duty to an identified victim is *Johnson v. State*, 447 P.2d 352 (Cal. 1968), where the state placed a known violent juvenile in the plaintiff's home without any warning about his propensities.
137. *Thompson v. County of Alameda*, 614 P.2d 728 (Cal. 1980).
138. To similar effect, see *Novak v. Rathnam*, 505 N.E.2d 773 (Ill. App. 1987).
139. *Nova Univ., Inc. v. Wagner*, 491 So. 2d 1116 (Fla. 1986) (liability for negligently permitting dangerous juveniles to flee); *Hamman v. County of Maricopa*, 775 P.2d 1122 (Ariz. 1989) (distinguishing *Brady v. Hopper*, 570 F. Supp. 1333 [D. Co. 1983], aff'd, 751 F.2d 329 [10th Cir. 1984]).
140. *Lipari v. Sears, Roebuck & Co.*, 497 F. Supp. 185 (D. Neb. 1980); *Hamman v. County of Maricopa*, 775 P.2d 1122 (Ariz. 1989); *Perreira v. State*, 768 P.2d 1198 (Colo. 1989).
141. *Lundgren v. Fultz*, 354 N.W.2d 25, 29 (Minn. 1984).
142. *Bellah v. Greenson*, 146 Cal. Rptr. 535 (Cal. App. 1978), but cf. *Peck v. Counselling Service of Addison County*, 499 A.2d 422 (Vt. 1985) (duty to warn father of patient son's wish to burn down father's barn).
143. *Hedlund v. Superior Court of Orange County*, 669 P.2d 41, 48–49 (Cal. 1983), per Justice Mosk dissenting; Stone, 1976.
144. See *Hedlund*, finding liability in a negligent failure to diagnose; generally, Beck, 1990, p. 10.
145. *White v. United States*, 780 F.2d 97 (D.C. Cir. 1986).
146. Wise, 1978.
147. See, for example, Colo. Rev. Stat. §13-21-117 (1986); Idaho Code §6-1902 (1991); Ind. Code §34-4-12.4-2 (1987); Ky. Rev. Stat. Ann. §202A.400 (1986); La. Rev. Stat. Ann. §9:2800.2 (West 1986); Mass. Gen. L. ch. 112 §129A (1989); Mich. Comp. Laws §330.1946 (1989); Minn. Stat. §148.975 (1986); N.H. Rev. Stat. Ann. §330-A:22 (1987); Tenn. Code Ann. §33-10-302 (1989).
148. Cal. Civil Code §43.92.

149. See legislation listed above, note 147.

150. See Cal. Civil Code §43.92(b).

151. *Chrite v. United States*, 564 F. Supp. 341 (E.D. Mich. 1983); *Tamsen v. Weber*, 802 P.2d 1063 (Ariz. App. 1990); Simon and Sadoff, 1992, p. 237.

152. Appelbaum, 1988a.

153. Perr, 1986. See also Gartrell *et al.*, 1986. For a thorough review, see Schoener *et al.*, 1989; see also Pope, 1990.

154. Gartrell *et al.*, 1986; Wolinsky, 1991.

155. Simon and Sadoff, 1992, p. 165.

156. 1990 Fla. Sess. Law Serv. ch. 90-70 §1(4) (a) (1991); Minn. Crim. Code §§609.341(17)-(20), 609-344(g) (v), (h)-(j), 609.344 (1987) (Supp. 1991); N.H. Rev. Stat. Ann. §632-A:2 Part VII (Supp. 1986); Wis. Stat. Ann. §§940.22(2), 940.255(2) (b) (West Supp. 1990); Colo. Rev. Stat. §18-3-405.5 (Supp. 1990); N.D. Cent. Code §12.1-20-06.1 (1987); and Maine, Rev. Stat. Ann. tit. 17-A §253(2) (1), 2255 (Supp. 1990).

157. *Figueiredo-Torres v. Nickel*, 584 A.2d 69 (Md. 1991) (duty to husband of the patient). But cf. *Homer v. Long*, 599 A.2d 1193 (Md. Ct. Spec. App. 1992) (no action available to nonpatient husband for breakup of marriage).

158. *Mazza v. Huffaker*, 300 S.E.2d 833 (N.C. Ct. App. 1983) (liability on theory of *de facto* abandonment).

159. See Robertson, 1988. *Roy v. Hartogs*, 366 N.Y.S.2d 297 (Civ. Ct. 1975) signaled the judicial attitude that sexual behavior was unacceptable and unjustifiable. The case became celebrated with the publication of the book *Betrayed* (1976), published by the plaintiff and Lucy Freeman.

160. As reported by Simon and Sadoff, 1992, p. 171.

161. *Noto v. St. Vincents Hospital*, 537 N.Y.S.2d 446 (Sup. Ct. 1988); *Whitesell v. Green*, No. 38745 (Honolulu Dist. Ct. Nov. 19, 1973).

162. *Corgan v. Muehling*, 574 N.E.2d 602 (Ill. 1991); *Landau v. Weiner*, 105 Sol. J. 1008 (1961); Pope, 1990.

163. *Noto v. St. Vincents Hospital*, 537 N.Y.S.2d 446 (Sup. Ct. 1988).

164. *Dorsey v. Board of Regents*, 449 N.Y.S.2d 337 (N.Y. App. Div. 1982); *Solloway v. Dept. of Professional Regulations*, 421 So. 2d 573 (Fla. App. 1982); see Hymans, 1992.

165. *St. Paul Fire & Marine Insurance Co. v. Mitchell*, 296 S.E.2d 126 (Ga. App. 1982).

166. *Hartogs v. Employers Mutual Liability Insurance Co. of Wisconsin*, 391 N.Y.S.2d 962 (Sup. Ct. 1977). For a thorough discussion of the insurance issue, see Jorgenson, Bisbing, and Sutherland, 1992.

167. *L.L. v. Medical Protective Co.*, 362 N.W.2d 174 (Wis. App. 1984); *Mazza v. Medical Mutual Insur. Co. of North America*, 319 S.E.2d 217 (N.C. 1984). In *Roe v. Federal Insurance Co.*, 587 N.E.2d 214 (Mass. 1992), the court held that a dentist was not covered for sexual misconduct distinguishing psychotherapist and gynecologist cases, where the risk of sexual advances is present.

168. *Standlee v. St. Paul Fire & Marine Insur. Co.*, 693 P.2d 1101 (Idaho App. 1984).

169. *South Carolina Medical Malpractice Liability Insur. v. Ferry*, 354 S.E.2d 378 (S.C. 1987).

170. *L.L. v. Medical Protective Co.*, 362 N.W.2d 174 (Wis. App. 1984).

171. *Hammer v. Rosen*, 165 N.E.2d 756 (N.Y. Ct. App. 1960).
172. *Abraham v. Zaslow*, No. 245862 (Santa Clara County Sup. Ct. October 26, 1970), San Francisco, Cy. Sup. Ct. 1972, reported in *New York Times*, July 5, 1972, p. 27, and *A.P.A. Monitor*, 1973.
173. *Woods v. U.S.*, 720 F.2d 1451 (9th Cir. 1983).
174. See *Estate of Berthiaume v. Pratt*, 365 A.2d 792 (Me. 1976) (describing the limits of physician's privilege to photograph, touch, and invade privacy of patient on day of his death).
175. A rush of legislation was enacted following the 1959 California legislation: *Matts v. Homsi*, 308 N.W.2d 284 (Mich. App. 1981); "Comment," *Southwest Law Journal* 31 (1977):695.
176. *Spencer v. Community Hospital of Evanston*, 408 N.E.2d 981 (Ill. App. 1980) (protection when acting in good faith, without malice). See also *Limjoco v. Schenck*, 486 N.W.2d 567 (Wis. Ct. App. 1992) (presumption of good faith not overcome by evidence that physicians had a personal grudge and potential of economic gain).
177. 42 U.S.C. §§11101 *et seq.*; for discussion, see Horner, 1990.
178. For discussion of immunity, see *Austin v. McNamara*, 731 F. Supp. 934 (Cal. D.C. 1990).
179. Stromberg *et al.*, 1988, pp. 219–20.
180. *Hirshberg v. State*, 42 U.S.C. §11111 (1989).
181. *Faigenbaum v. Cohen*, 1982 Mich. Wayne County Court; see also Taub, 1982.
182. Respectively, *Nelson v. Heyne*, 355 F. Supp. 451 (N.D. Ind. 1972), aff'd, 491 F.2d 352 (7th Cir. 1974), and *Clites v. State of Iowa*, 322 N.W.2d 917 (Iowa Ct. App. 1982).
183. *Mulder v. Parke Davis & Co.*, 181 N.W.2d 882 (Minn. 1970); see also *Thompson v. Carter*, 518 So. 2d 609 (Miss. 1987).
184. *Salgo v. Leland Stanford University*, 317 P.2d 170 (Cal. App. 1957); *Stafford v. Nipp*, 502 So. 2d 702 (Ala. 1987).
185. *Mueller v. Mueller*, 221 N.W.2d 39, 43 (S.D. 1974). Emphasis added.
186. Simon, 1987.
187. *Clites v. State of Iowa*, 322 N.W.2d 917 (Iowa Ct. App. 1982).
188. Perr, 1985.
189. *Herskovits v. Group Health Cooperative*, 664 P.2d 474 (Wash. 1983); *McKellips v. St. Francis Hospital*, 741 P.2d 467 (Okla. 1987); *Aasheim v. Humberger*, 695 P.2d 824 (Mont. 1985); *Thompson v. Sun City Community Hosp., Inc.*, 688 P.2d 605 (Ariz. 1984), allowing full recovery when plaintiff had less than 50 percent chance of recovery. See also *DeBurkarte v. Louvar*, 393 N.W.2d 131 (Iowa 1986), allowing recovery by the plaintiff for the percentage of lost chance for which the doctor is deemed responsible.
190. The courts have had a varied experience in dealing with scientific evidence establishing causal links between drugs and subsequent medical conditions. See M. Green, 1992; Latin, 1987.
191. "Psychiatry Claims Closed 1980–1985," *Psychiatric News* 22 (April 3, 1987):11.
192. P. Moore, 1986.
193. Davidson and Linnoila, 1989, pp. 2–9.

194. Farrow, 1978.
195. *Dobbs v. Smith*, 514 So. 2d 871 (Ala. 1987); *McNamara v. Honeyman*, 546 N.E.2d 139 (Mass. 1989) (liability to a patient exhibiting suicidal tendencies placed on fifteen-minute checks rather than continual observation).
196. *Rudy v. Meshorer*, 706 P.2d 1234 (Ariz. App. 1985) (expert psychiatric evidence necessary to establish breach of duty).
197. *Vinchiarello v. Kathuria*, 558 A.2d 262 (Conn. App. 1989); *Nieves v. New York*, 458 N.Y.S.2d 548 (App. Div. 1983).
198. This may be part of open discussion about suicide plans, Simon and Sadoff, 1992, p. 123.
199. *Topel v. Long Island Jewish Medical Center*, 431 N.E.2d 293 (N.Y. 1981); *Centeno v. City of New York*, 358 N.E. 520 (N.Y. App. Div. 1976). The unpredictability of liability is a cause for concern, see Coleman and Shellow, 1992.
200. *Abille v. United States*, 482 F. Supp. 703 (N.D. Cal. 1980).
201. See also Simon and Sadoff, 1992, p. 122, and, for description of common characteristics and risk factors, pp. 125–26.
202. *Huntley v. State*, 464 N.E.2d 467 (N.Y. Ct. App. 1984).
203. E.g., Ariz. Rev. Stat. Ann. §13-1103 (1989); Fla. Stat. Ann. §782.08 (West 1976); N.Y. Penal Law §125.15 (1984); Cal. Penal Code §187(a) (West 1988). A wide debate exists between suicide and euthanasia; for an excellent discussion see Fletcher, 1988; also Rachels, 1986; Quill *et al.*, 1992. For legally based analyses, see Young, 1992; Zima, 1992.
204. For a thorough cross-cultural and international discussion see Berger and Berger, 1990.
205. *Cruzan v. Director, Missouri Dept. of Health*, 497 U.S. 261 (1990); for a survey see Eaton and Larson, 1991. For a review of public perceptions, see Blendon *et al.*, 1992.
206. See Note, 1992, *Harvard Law Review*, arguing for the legality of physician-assisted suicide providing a balance of patient and state interests; but cf. Clark, 1992, arguing the importance of weighing the presence of psychiatric illnesses, e.g. depression, in determining the rationality of a decision to commit suicide. See also Quill *et al.*, 1992.
207. *Strunk v. Strunk*, 445 S.W.2d 145 (Ky. 1969). See New York State Task Force on Life and the Law, 1993.
208. *Weathers v. Pilkinton*, 754 S.W.2d 75 (Tenn. App. 1988).
209. *Fernandez v. Baruch*, 244 A.2d 109 (N.J. 1968); for discussion of this problem, see V. Schwartz, 1971.
210. *Bell v. New York City Health and Hospital*, 456 N.Y.S.2d 787 (Sup. Ct. 1982).
211. *Tomfohr v. Mayo Foundation*, 450 N.W.2d 121 (Minn. 1990); see also *Mochen v. State*, 352 N.Y.S.2d 290 (App. Div. 1974).
212. *Fuller v. Preis*, 322 N.E.2d 263 (N.Y. Ct. App. 1974); *Krieg v. Massey*, 781 P.2d 277 (Mont. 1989) (no liability for failing to remove gun from possession of suicide victim); Morse, 1967.
213. *Gaido v. Weiser*, 558 A.2d 845 (N.J. 1989).
214. *Texarkana Memorial Hospital v. Firth*, 746 S.W.2d 494 (Tex. Ct. App. 1988); *Kent v. Whitaker*, 364 P.2d 556 (Wash. 1961) ("duty of exercising reasonable care to safeguard and protect a patient with known suicidal tendencies from in-

juring herself"); *Brandvain v. Ridgeview Instit.*, 372 S.E.2d 265 (Ga. App. 1988).
215. *Kates v. State*, 261 N.Y.S.2d 988 (N.Y. Claims 1965).
216. *Bates v. Denney*, 563 So. 2d 298 (La. App. 1990).
217. *Bramlette v. Charter-Medical-Columbia*, 393 S.E.2d 914 (S.C. 1990).
218. In contradistinction, if no indication of suicidal tendencies is known to the hospital, it is not liable for injuries sustained in a suicide attempt; see *Clements v. Swedish Hospital*, 89 N.W.2d 162 (Minn. 1958) (plaintiff a car accident victim, irrational but with no signs of suicidal tendencies).
219. *Klein v. Reynolds*, 291 N.E.2d 446 (Ohio 1972).
220. *Paddock v. Chacko*, 522 So. 2d 410, 414 (Fla. App. 1988); *Johnson v. United States*, 409 F. Supp. 1283 (M.D. Fla. 1976).
221. *Bell v. New York City Health and Hospital*, 456 N.Y.S.2d 787 (Sup. Ct. 1982).
222. *Weatherly v. State*, 441 N.Y.S.2d 319 (Ct. Cl. 1981).
223. *King v. Smith*, 539 So. 2d 262 (Ala. 1989).
224. *Chavin v. West Jefferson Health Center*, 597 So. 2d 134 (La. App. 1992).
225. *Vinchiarello v. Kathuria*, 558 A.2d 262 (Conn. App. 1989) (suicide by overdose of Asendin); *Nieves v. New York*, 458 N.Y.S.2d 548 (App. Div. 1983) (release of patient with self-inflicted wounds).
226. *Paddock v. Chacko*, 522 So. 2d 410, 415 (Fla. App. 1988).
227. *Stepakoff v. Kantar*, 473 N.E.2d 1131 (Mass. 1985).
228. *Naidu v. Laird*, 539 A.2d 1064, 1072 (Del. 1988).
229. For a discussion of these restrictions, see Chapter 10: see also Smith, 1991, p. 222.
230. *Farwell v. Un*, 902 F.2d 282 (4th Cir. 1990).
231. *Eisel v. Board of Education of Montgomery County*, 597 A.2d 447 (Md. 1991) (school counselors' liability for failure to warn parents of student's suicidal statements).
232. *Tabor v. Doctors Memorial Hospital*, 563 So. 2d 233 (La. 1990) (patient admitted with overdose of alcohol and quaaludes; physician unwilling to admit because family did not supply $400 deposit when informed by staff this could be waived). Cf. *Weathers v. Pilkinton*, 754 S.W.2d 75 (Tenn. App. 1988).
233. Beginning December 1, 1991, all hospitals, nursing facilities, hospice programs, and health care maintenance organizations that serve Medicare and Medicaid patients must provide all their new adult patients with written information describing the patient's rights under state law to make decisions about medical care, including their right to execute a living will or durable power of attorney. As amended November 1990, Omnibus Budget Reconciliation Act, Pub. L. No. 101-508, 104 Stat. 1388 (1990). The purpose is to help implement a right that has been universally recognized: the right to refuse any and all medical interventions, even life-sustaining interventions. The challenge is to use these forms to foster communication between doctor and patient as well as respect for the patient's autonomy. The challenge is particularly troublesome when applied to psychiatric admissions; how far is it viable to give certain patients the right to issue advance directives as to treatment? Spielman, 1992.
234. *Big Town Nursing Home, Inc. v. Newman*, 461 S.W.2d 195 (Tex. Civ. App. 1970).

235. *Johnson v. Greer*, 477 F.2d 101 (5th Cir. 1973).
236. *Texas Dept. of Mental Health & Mental Retardation v. Petty*, 817 S.W.2d 707 (Tex. Ct. App. 1991).
237. *R.J.D. v. Vaughan Clinic*, 572 So. 2d 1225 (Ala. 1990) (the majority cited in support *Parham v. J.R.*, 442 U.S. 584 [1979]).
238. *Parvi v. City of Kingston*, 362 N.E.2d 960 (N.Y. 1977).
239. *Murray v. Ministry of Defence* [1988], 2 A11 E.R. 521 (H.L.).
240. *Molko v. Holy Spirit Assn.*, 762 P.2d 46 (Cal. 1988) (such claims have raised the admissibility of the psychiatric basis of brainwashing).
241. *Johnson v. Greer*, note 235 above.
242. *Pendleton v. Burkhalter*, 432 S.W.2d 724 (Tex. Civ. App. 1968).
243. *Abille v. United States*, 482 F. Supp. 703 (N.D. Cal. 1980).
244. *Skar v. City of Lincoln, Nebraska*, 599 F.2d 253 (8th Cir. 1979).
245. *Higgins v. State*, 265 N.Y.S.2d 254 (Sup. Ct. 1965).
246. *Samuels v. Southern Baptist Hospital*, 594 So. 2d 571 (La. App. 1992). Sexual harassment has accumulated a considerable body of law: an employer will be liable in damages for the harassment of supervisory personnel provided the supervisor had apparent control over the situation complained of, see *Lehmann v. Toys "R" Us*, 132 N.J. 587, 626 A.2d 445 (1993).
247. *Copithorne v. Framingham Union Hosp.*, 520 N.E.2d 139 (Mass. 1988) (liability to employed technologist drugged and sexually assaulted by physician with staff privileges, *a fortiori* liability to patient, see Judge Lynch's dissent). See Chapter 7.
248. *Adams v. Murakami*, 813 P.2d 1348 (Cal. 1991).
249. *Young v. Huntsville Hospital*, 595 So. 2d 1386 (Ala. 1992).
250. *Department of Health & Rehabilitative Services v. Whaley*, 574 So. 2d 100 (Fla. 1991) (youth sexually assaulted by two youths with a history of assault; no immunity for placing youth in dangerous circumstances).
251. *Freidman v. State*, 493 N.E.2d 893 (N.Y. Ct. App. 1986).
252. For discussion of this waiver and the liability of employed physicians, see *United States v. Smith*, 111 S.Ct. 1180 (1991).
253. *Hernandez v. Smith*, 552 F.2d 142 (5th Cir. 1977).
254. Respectively, *Horton v. Niagara Falls Memorial Medical Center*, 380 N.Y.S.2d 116 (App. Div. 1976); *Emory University v. Porter*, 120 S.E.2d 668 (Ga. App. 1961).
255. *Cassidy v. Daily Mirror* [1929] 2 K.B. 331 (CA).
256. *Gertz v. Robert Welch, Inc.*, 418 U.S. 323 (1974).
257. *Dun & Bradstreet v. Greenmoss Builders*, 472 U.S. 749 (1985).
258. *Bindrim v. Mitchell*, 155 Cal. Rptr. 29 (Cal. App. 1979).
259. *Toogood v. Spyring*, 1 C.M.&R. 181, 149 Eng. Rep. 1044 (1834).
260. *Sindorf v. Jacron Sales Co.*, 341 A.2d 856 (Md. Spec. App. 1975). Statutes granting immunity for reporting of child abuse do not constitute a defense unless the report is made to the stipulated body under the statute: *Searcy v. Auerbach*, 980 F.2d 609 (9th Cir. 1992) (psychologist liable in defamation in report to father that the child had been abused while in the custody of the mother).
261. *Sibley v. Lutheran Hospital of Maryland, Inc.*, 709 F. Supp. 657 (D.C. Md. 1988) (chairman of privileges committee has conditional privilege).

262. For example, the Health Care Quality Improvement Act, see note 177 above.

263. *Rogers v. Janzen*, 711 F. Supp. 306 (E.D. La. 1989).

264. *Dolan v. Von Zweck*, 477 N.E.2d 200 (Mass. App. 1985). See also *Vineyard v. Kraft*, 828 S.W.2d 248 (Tex. Ct. App. 1992) (no duty to father for misdiagnosis of child abuse), and *Lavit v. Superior Court*, 839 P.2d 1141 (Ariz. Ct. App. 1992).

265. Veeder, 1909. An excellent case for viewing the protection of mental health clinicians from liability for testimony in court and repeated out of court is *Rosenberg v. Helinsky*, 616 A.2d 866 (Md. 1992).

266. *Sibley v. Lutheran Hospital of Maryland, Inc.*, 709 F. Supp. 657 (D.C. Md. 1988) (burden on plaintiff).

267. *Hughley v. McDermott*, 530 A.2d 13 (Md. Spec. App. 1987).

268. *Katz v. Enzer*, 504 N.E.2d 427 (Ohio App. 1985).

269. *Simonds v. Blue Cross–Blue Shield*, 629 F. Supp. 369 (W.D. Mich. 1986).

270. *Furniss v. Fitchett* [1958], N.Z.L.R. 396. In another case, *Barnes v. Commonwealth* (1937), 37 S.R. (N.S.W.) 511, the defendant informed the plaintiff (incorrectly) that her husband was in a mental asylum. The plaintiff was distressed and recovered upon the premise that the defendant had a duty not to convey incorrect information.

271. Cf. *Howard v. Drapkin*, 271 Cal. Rptr. 893 (Cal. App. 1990).

272. *Davis v. Tirrell*, 443 N.Y.S.2d 136 (N.Y. Sup. Ct. 1981).

273. *Gotkin v. Miller*, 514 F.2d 125 (2d Cir. 1975).

274. *Palmer v. Durso*, 393 N.Y.S.2d 898 (Sup. Ct. 1977).

275. 740 I.L.C.S. 110/1-17.

276. West's Ann. Cal. Code §5328.9.

277. The history is eloquently described in Starr, 1982.

278. Jensen and Grabel, 1988.

279. R. Winslow, "Psychologist Group Courts Corporations," *Wall Street Journal*, August 18, 1992, p. B1.

280. The extension of the DRG to psychiatric specialist hospitals would place them at a high level of financial risk when compared with general hospitals, but suggestions have been made to achieve integration by mitigating the risks; see Dada et al., 1992. In child and adolescent psychiatry see Stevenson et al., 1987.

281. See below for examination of these structures in terms of informed consent. Note that the fee-for-service system may itself contain perverse incentives, such as patient overservicing, that may diminish the patient's welfare.

282. E.g., Blumstein, 1981, and Note, 1985.

283. Wennberg and Grittelsohn, 1973; Wennberg, 1984. And indeed internationally see L. Payer, 1988. *Medicine and Culture: Varieties of Treatment in the United States, England, West Germany, and France.* New York: Holt.

284. Learned commentators differ on the issue of how far the present articulation of the standard of care allows for different practice standards under the new strategies. See Morreim, 1989, 1987; Note, 1985, *Harvard Law Review.* Cf. Hall, 1991, 1988. For discussion of practice guidelines, see Brennan, 1991.

285. Griner, 1991.

286. *Johnson v. Misericordia Community Hospital*, 301 N.W.2d 156 (Wis. 1981).

287. *Jackson v. Power*, 743 P.2d 1376 (Alaska 1987).

288. *Sloan v. Metropolitan Health Council of Indianapolis*, 516 N.E.2d 1104 (Ind. App. 1987); *Boyd v. Albert Einstein Medical Center*, 547 A.2d 1229 (Pa. Super. Ct. 1988).

289. *Wickline v. State*, 239 Cal. Rptr. 810 (Cal. App. 1986).

290. *Wilson v. Blue Cross of Southern California*, 271 Cal. Rptr. 876 (Cal. App. 1990).

291. Weiler, 1991, pp. 124–25, makes the argument that liability should be channeled to hospitals and away from physicians. This would introduce economies in litigation or give hospitals an incentive to police behavior of physicians. A similar argument could be marshaled to impose (or channel) liability to payor for physicians' negligence. Thus payors would monitor physicians' behavior, and claimants could economize on litigation costs.

292. *Moore v. Regents of University of California*, 793 P.2d 479, 150 (Cal. 1990).

293. For recent discussion, see Miller, 1992. An important but legally technical question remains relating to the duty as enunciated in *Moore*. It must be proved that the plaintiff would have acted otherwise if informed, and that if he had acted otherwise, he would not have suffered his consequent loss. But in *Moore* he would have probably gone ahead with the operation, and it may be said he suffered no loss. However, the duty is of a fiduciary kind where it is arguable that a remedy of accounting for profits should be available. Thus relying upon fiduciary law (not pure tort law), a satisfactory remedy may be fashioned that gives a patient an accounting for profits.

294. For a review, see Qual, 1986.

295. GAO/HRD, 1991.

296. Weiler, 1991, pp. 114 ff.

297. American Law Institute, 1991, pp. 517 ff.

298. *Smith v. Department of Insurance*, 507 So. 2d 1080 (Fla. 1987) (striking down cap on noneconomic losses).

CHAPTER 9
JUVENILE DELINQUENCY

1. Binder, 1987.

2. *In re Gault*, 387 U.S. 1 (1967).

3. *Kent v. United States*, 383 U.S. 541 (1966).

4. Mack, 1909.

5. *Kent v. United States*, 383 U.S. 541 (1966).

6. *In re Gault*, 387 U.S. 1 (1967).

7. *In re Winship*, 397 U.S. 358 (1970). See Chapter 2 for discussion of burden of proof.

8. *McKeiver v. Pennsylvania*, 403 U.S. 528 (1971).

9. *Breed v. Jones*, 421 U.S. 519 (1975).

10. Mnookin, 1978. See National Advisory Committee for Juvenile Justice and Delinquency Prevention, 1980.

11. *Ibid.*

12. E.g., Tex. Fam. Code §52.01(a) (2).

13. *Lanes v. State*, 767 S.W.2d 789 (Tex. Ct. App. 1989).

14. *Katz v. United States*, 389 U.S. 347 (1967).
15. *United States v. Watson*, 423 U.S. 411 (1976); but cf. *Payton v. New York*, 445 U.S. 573 (1980) (warrant required for private place arrests).
16. *A Minor Boy v. State*, 537 P.2d 477 (Nev. 1975).
17. LaFave, 1965.
18. *Miranda v. Arizona*, 384 U.S. 436 (1966).
19. *State v. Whatley*, 320 So. 2d 123 (La. 1975).
20. *In re Riley*, 301 S.E.2d 750 (N.C. Ct. App. 1983).
21. *Fare v. Michael C.*, 442 U.S. 707 (1979); Ferguson and Douglas, 1970.
22. Roberts, 1989; Vito and Wilson, 1985.
23. *Schall v. Martin*, 467 U.S. 253 (1984).
24. *In re Anthony S.*, 341 N.Y.S.2d 11 (Fam. Ct. Rich. 1973).
25. Nejelski, 1976, pp. 115–16. Maron, 1975; Cohen, 1985, pp. 52–55, argues that the results of diversion are perverse in sweeping into the system those who formerly would not have been proceeded with, thus stigmatizing them.
26. *United States v. Salerno*, 481 U.S. 739 (1987). Custody of juvenile aliens who may be deportable is constitutionally permissible; conditions of custody must meet a standard that is decent and humane but need not meet the standard of the best interests of the child; see *Reno v. Flores*, 113 S.Ct. 1439 (1993).
27. *D.B. v. Tewksbury*, 545 F. Supp. 896 (D. Or. 1982).
28. Standards relating to juvenile delinquency and sanctions: IJA-ABA Joint Commission, 1980.
29. King, 1980.
30. *Youth Law News*, September–October 1987.
31. *Sourcebook of Criminal Justice Statistics*, 1989.
32. *Wall Street Journal*, September 6, 1991.
33. *Gerstein v. Pugh*, 420 U.S. 103 (1975); *Moss v. Weaver*, 525 F.2d 1258 (5th Cir. 1976).
34. *Kent v. United States*, 383 U.S. 541 (1966).
35. *In re Doe*, 519 P.2d 133 (N.M. App. 1974).
36. Gasper and Katkin, 1980.
37. *In re Gault*, 387 U.S. 1 (1967). Typically the notice must be twenty-four hours. Some states require more, e.g., Tennessee, three days' notice, Tenn. Code Ann. §37-223(a); if the petition is served out of the jurisdiction, more time (five days) must be given.
38. *In re Winship*, 397 U.S. 358 (1970).
39. *McKeiver v. Pennsylvania*, 403 U.S. 528 (1971).
40. *Smith v. Daily Mail Pub. Co.*, 443 U.S. 97 (1979).
41. *The Florida Star v. B.J.F.*, 491 U.S. 524 (1989); but cf. *In re A Minor*, 595 N.W.2d 1052 (Ill. 1992) (upholding constitutionality of protections of disclosure of identity of child abuse victims in juvenile proceedings).
42. *United States v. R.L.C.*, 112 S.Ct. 1329 (1992).
43. *Matter of Brown*, 439 F.2d 47 (3d Cir. 1971); *In re N.*, 112 Cal. Rptr. 89 (Ct. App. 1974). The conclusion in these cases is drawn from *Griffin v. Illinois*, 351 U.S. 12 (1956), where the right of appeal was made available to all persons, including the indigent.
44. LaTessa, Travis, and Wilson, 1984; Rosenberg, 1983.

45. Katz and Teitelbaum, 1983; see Martin, 1992.
46. *Mailliard v. Gonzalez*, Mo. 50424 N.D. Cal. Fed. 7 (1971), vacated and remanded, 416 U.S. 918 (1974); *Gesicki v. Oswald*, 336 F. Supp. 371 (S.D. N.Y. 1971).
47. Vito and Wilson, 1985; Murray, 1983.
48. *In re Gault*; *Winship*.
49. N.C. Gen. Stat. §7A-574 (Supp. 1987).
50. Cal. Welf. & Inst. Code §701 (West 1984 and Supp. 1988).
51. Binder, 1989.
52. Flanagan *et al.*, 1980.
53. *Uniform Crime Reports for the United States* (Washington: FBI, U.S. Department of Justice, 1991), p. 279 (hereinafter referred to as *UCR* 1991).
54. *Ibid.*, pp. 289–90.
55. *Ibid.*, p. 283.
56. Loeber, Dishion, and Patterson, 1984.
57. Maxwell, 1971.
58. Quay and Levinson, 1967.
59. Quay and Love, 1977.
60. Henn, Bardwell, and Jenkins, 1980.
61. Newman, Widom, and Nathan, 1985.
62. Skrzypek, 1969.
63. Panella and Henggeler, 1986.
64. Borkovec, 1970.
65. Palmer, 1974.
66. E.g., Gordon *et al.*, 1963.
67. Hagan, Gillis, and Chan, 1978.
68. Plummer, K. 1979. Misunderstanding labelling perspectives. In D. Downes and P. Rock (Eds.), *Deviant Interpretations*. London: Martin Robertson.
69. *UCR* 1991, p. 279.
70. Woodruff, Goodwin, and Guze, 1974; Guze, 1976.
71. Friedlander, 1947.
72. Rutter, 1971.
73. Bowlby, 1969, 1973, 1980.
74. E.g., Jennings, Kilkenny, and Kohlberg, 1983.
75. E.g., Cadoret, 1978; Cloninger, Reich, and Guze, 1975.
76. E.g., Bohman, 1983; Mednick, Gabrielli, and Hutchings, 1984; Crowe, 1974; Schulsinger, 1977.
77. Cadoret *et al.*, 1985.
78. E.g., Lange, 1928.
79. Rosanoff, Handy, and Plessey, 1934.
80. E.g., Sheldon, Stevens, and Tucker, 1940; Glueck and Glueck, 1956; Gibbons, 1963.
81. Lewis, Shanok, and Balla, 1979; Lewis *et al.*, 1979; Lewis *et al.*, 1982.
82. Scharfetter, 1980.
83. E.g., Rutter, Quinton, and Liddle, 1983.
84. Knight, Osborne, and West, 1977.
85. Bachman, O'Malley, and Johnstone, 1978.

86. See also the radical criticism leveled by Cohen, 1985.
87. E.g., Levitt, 1971; Romig, 1978.
88. For example, Sarason and Ganzer, 1973 (problem-solving); E.g. Camp *et al.*, 1977, and Kendall and Finch, 1978 (impulsivity); Chandler, 1973 (role-taking); Arbuthnot and Faust, 1981 (moral reasoning).
89. E.g., Beal and Duckro, 1977; Stringfield, 1977.
90. Patterson, Chamberlain, and Reid, 1982.
91. Melton *et al.*, 1987. See Gensheimer and Mayer, 1987 for community based intervention.
92. E.g., Brooks, 1974; Melton *et al.*, 1987; Gutheil and Appelbaum, 1982; Curran, McGarry, and Shah, 1986.
93. E.g., Group for the Advancement of Psychiatry, 1974.
94. Morris, 1982.
95. *Pate v. Robinson*, 383 U.S. 375 (1966).
96. *Jackson v. Indiana*, 406 U.S. 715 (1972). For discussion, see Morris, 1982, pp. 38 ff.
97. *Riggins v. Nevada*, 112 S.Ct. 1810 (1992).
98. *Medina v. California*, 112 S.Ct. 2572, 2588 (1992).
99. *Dusky v. United States*, 362 U.S. 402 (1960).
100. *Drope v. Missouri*, 420 U.S. 162 (1975).
101. *Wieter v. Settle*, 193 F. Supp. 318 (W.D. Mo. 1961).
102. Bennett, 1985.
103. *Wilson v. United States*, 391 F.2d 460 (D.C. Cir. 1968).
104. Bennett, 1985; Melton *et al.*, 1987.
105. *Riggins v. Nevada*, 112 S.Ct. 1810 (1992).
106. *Washington v. Harper*, 494 U.S. 210, 1815 (1990). This case is discussed in Chapter 10. Not all courts have found that state constitutions allow the same scope for the administration of antipsychotic drugs. See *Louisiana v. Perry*, 61 L.W. 2288 (1992) (finding that the involuntary administration of drugs to an incompetent prisoner to ensure competency for execution was unconstitutional under the Louisiana Constitution as violating the petitioning prisoner's right to privacy).
107. Id. at 1815. See also *Donaldson v. District Court of Denver*, 847 P.2d 632 (Col. 1993) setting forth the criteria for administration of the antipsychotic drug Prolixin.
108. *Miranda v. Arizona*, 384 U.S. 436 (1966).
109. *Fare v. Michael C.*, 442 U.S. 707 (1979).
110. Gudjonsson, 1984.
111. LaFave and Scott, 1986.
112. *M'Naghten's Case*, 8 Eng. Rep. 718 (H.L. 1843).
113. 18 U.S.C.A. §17; *United States v. Hinckley*, 672 F.2d 115 (D.C. Cir. 1982); Low, Jeffries, and Bonnie, 1986; Slovenko, 1983.
114. M.P.C. §4.01.
115. The effect of the plea is subject to uncertainty and has engendered criticism. See *People v. Crews*, 522 N.E.2d 1167 (Ill. 1988); Slovenko, 1983, p. 373 (one might as well have a verdict called "guilty but flat feet").
116. *Durham v. United States*, 214 F.2d 862 (D.C. Cir. 1954).

117. *McDonald v. United States*, 312 F.2d 847 (D.C. Cir. 1962).

118. *Washington v. United States*, 390 F.2d 444 (D.C. Cir. 1967).

119. *United States v. Brawner*, 471 F.2d 969 (D.C. Cir. 1972).

120. *Commonwealth v. Walzack*, 360 A.2d 914 (Pa. 1976); but cf. *Johnson v. State*, 439 A.2d 542 (Md. 1982).

121. See *Hendershott v. People*, 653 P.2d 385 (Colo. 1982); the doctrine has been endorsed by the American Bar Association in its Criminal Justice Mental Health Standard 7-6.2, 1987.

122. E.g., *People v. Decina*, 138 N.E.2d 799 (N.Y. 1956).

123. *Tibbs v. Commonwealth*, 128 S.W. 871 (Ky. App. 1910); *People v. Higgins*, 159 N.E.2d 179 (N.Y. 1959).

124. M.P.C. §2.08(5) (c).

125. *State v. Propst*, 161 S.E.2d 560 (N.C. 1968).

CHAPTER 10
THE RIGHTS OF INSTITUTIONALIZED CHILDREN

1. Bromberg, 1959; Grob, 1966, 1973.

2. Szasz, 1961.

3. Rosenhan, 1973; Grob, 1991.

4. *Donaldson v. O'Connor*, 493 F.2d 507 (5th Cir. 1974), vacated on other grounds, 422 U.S. 563 (1975).

5. *Wyatt v. Stickney*, 344 F. Supp. 387 (M.D. Ala. 1972).

6. *Rogers v. Okin*, 821 F.2d 22 (1st Cir. 1987).

7. Savitsky and Karras, 1984.

8. Braun *et al.*, 1981.

9. Borus, 1981; Talbott, 1981; Rossi, 1989; Lewis, Roger, and Rosenburg, 1991.

10. Treffert, 1973.

11. Johnson, 1990; Grob, 1991.

12. Nurcombe, 1989.

13. *Ibid.*

14. Torrey, 1988.

15. Schwartz, 1989.

16. Gruenberg and Archer, 1979, describe this as "the demise of state responsibility for the seriously mentally ill and the current crisis of abandonment."

17. Nurcombe, 1989; Grob, 1991.

18. *Rogers v. Okin*, 821 F.2d 22 (1st Cir. 1987), see Chapter 3.

19. Schwartz, 1972.

20. See *Donaldson v. O'Connor*, 493 F.2d 507 (5th Cir. 1974), vacated on other grounds, 422 U.S. 563 (1975).

21. *Carey v. Piphus*, 435 U.S. 247, 259 (1978). For application, see *In re Miller*, 585 N.E.2d 396 (1992).

22. *Mathews v. Eldridge*, 424 U.S. 319, 335 (1976).

23. *Zinermon v. Burch*, 494 U.S. 113, 127 (1990).

24. *Daniels v. Williams*, 474 U.S. 327, 331 (1986).

25. See *Wyatt v. Stickney*, 344 F. Supp. 387 (M.D. Ala. 1972); *New York State Ass'n. for Retarded Children, Inc. v. Rockefeller*, 357 F. Supp. 752 (E.D.N.Y. 1973);

Morales v. Turman, 535 F.2d 864 (5th Cir. 1976), reversed by 430 U.S. 322 (1977).

26. *Halderman v. Pennhurst State School and Hospital*, 901 F.2d 311 (3d Cir. 1990) (enforcement of settlement).

27. *New York State Ass' n for Retarded Children, Inc. v. Carey*, 706 F.2d 956 (2d Cir. 1983); *Ricci v. Okin*, 781 F. Supp. 826 (D. Mass. 1992).

28. *Missouri v. Jenkins*, 491 U.S. 274 (1989).

29. *Rufo v. Inmates of Suffolk County Jail*, 112 S.Ct. 748 (1992).

30. 42 U.S.C.A. §1997.

31. For general discussion, see Reisner, 1985.

32. Endicott and Newell, 1990.

33. *Lessard v. Schmidt*, 349 F. Supp. 1078, 1093 (E.D. Wis. 1972).

34. *Donaldson v. O'Connor*, 493 F.2d 507 (5th Cir. 1974), vacated on other grounds, 422 U.S. 563 (1975).

35. See *Addington v. Texas*, 441 U.S. 418 (1979) (discussing the constitutionally established minimum standard of proof in proceedings for involuntary commitment).

36. *Doe v. Austin*, 848 F.2d 1386 (6th Cir. 1988).

37. *Doremus v. Farrell*, 407 F. Supp. 509 (D. Neb. 1975).

38. *Vitek v. Jones*, 445 U.S. 480 (1980).

39. For general discussion, see Hermann, 1986 and Bonovitz and Guy, 1979.

40. Fisher, Pierce, and Appelbaum, 1988; Durham and LaFond, 1985.

41. Monahan, 1981. Lidz, Mulvey, and Gardner, 1993, found that clinical judgment has been undervalued in previous research, but they are relatively inaccurate predictors of violence. This is especially so with women.

42. *Barefoot v. Estelle*, 463 U.S. 880 (1983).

43. Brief *amicus curiae* for the American Psychiatric Association, *Barefoot v. Estelle*, No. 82-6080 (1982).

44. Sepejak, Menzies, and Webster, 1983; Klassen and O'Connor, 1988; Lidz, Mulvey, & Gardner, 1993 (data suggest that accuracy can be improved; faulty base rate information may be origin of errors; greatest error predicting violence in women). On the ethics of risk assessment testimony, see Grisso and Appelbaum, 1992; for criticism, see Litwack, 1993.

45. *Barefoot v. Estelle*, 463 U.S. 880 (1983).

46. *Schall v. Martin*, 467 U.S. 253 (1984).

47. *Lynch v. Baxley*, 386 F. Supp. 378 (M.D. Ala. 1974); *Wyatt v. King*, No. 3195-N (M.D. Ala. 1991).

48. *In re Dickson*, 469 N.W.2d 357 (Neb. 1991).

49. Stromberg and Stone, 1984a.

50. See Stromberg and Stone, 1984b, for detailed elaboration and justification; for criticism, see Schmidt, 1985.

51. Garcia and Keilitz, 1991.

52. *Heller v. Doe*, 113 S.Ct. 2637 (1993).

53. *Parham v. J.R.*, 442 U.S. 584 (1979).

54. *Humphrey v. Cady*, 405 U.S. 504 (1972).

55. *Donaldson v. O'Connor*, 493 F.2d 507 (5th Cir. 1974). See also *Commonwealth v. Hubert*, 430 A.2d 1160, 1162 (Pa. 1981); *Eubanks v. Clarke*, 434 F. Supp. 1022, 1028 (E.D. Pa. 1977).

56. Schwartz, 1989.

57. Kiesler and Sibulkin, 1987.

58. Simet, 1982.

59. Stone, 1987.

60. *Secretary of Public Welfare of Pennsylvania v. Institutionalized Juveniles*, 442 U.S. 640 (1979).

61. *In re Roger S*, 569 P.2d 1286 (Cal. 1977).

62. Schmidt and Otto, 1988.

63. E.g., Colo. Rev. Stat. §27-10-116 (Supp. 1988); S.D. Codified Laws Ann. §27A-12-11 *et seq.* (Supp. 1990); Texas Rev. Civ. Stat. Ann. art. 5547-300, §§7, 11 (Vernon Supp. 1990).

64. *Shelton v. Tucker*, 364 U.S. 479, 488 (1960).

65. *Lake v. Cameron*, 364 F.2d 657, 660 (D.C. Cir. 1966).

66. *Wyatt v. Stickney*, 344 F. Supp. 387 (M.D. Ala. 1972).

67. E.g., *Goodwin v. Shapiro*, 545 F. Supp. 826 (D.N.J. 1982); *New York State Ass'n. for Retarded Children, Inc. v. Rockefeller*, 357 F. Supp. 752 (E.D.N.Y. 1973); *Negron v. Ward*, 458 F. Supp. 748 (S.D.N.Y. 1978).

68. *Youngberg v. Romeo*, 457 U.S. 307, 319, 321 (1982)

69. *Ibid.* at 321.

70. *Society for Good Will to Retarded Citizens v. Cuomo*, 737 F.2d 1239 (2d Cir. 1984).

71. *Association for Retarded Citizens v. Olson*, 713 F.2d 1384 (8th Cir. 1990).

72. See, respectively, *Gann v. Delaware State Hospital*, 543 F. Supp. 268 (1982); *Welsch v. Likins*, 373 F. Supp. 487 (D. Minn. 1974). The duty is reinforced by the Supreme Court's decision in *Helling v. McKinney*, 61 LW 4648 (1993), finding that prisoners may use the Eighth Amendment to sue custodians over adverse long-term effects of exposure to secondhand tobacco smoke.

73. *Rouse v. Cameron*, 373 F.2d 451 (D.C. Cir. 1966).

74. *Wyatt v. Stickney*, 344 F. Supp. 387 (M.D. Ala. 1972).

75. *Wyatt v. Aderholt*, 503 F.2d 1305 (5th Cir. 1974).

76. *Savidge v. Fincannon*, 836 F.2d 898 (5th Cir. 1988).

77. *Rufo v. Inmates of Suffolk County Jail*, 112 S.Ct. 748 (1992).

78. Mills, Cummins, and Gracey, 1983.

79. See notes 34 and 70 above.

80. See *Scott v. Plante*, 532 F.2d 939 (3d Cir. 1976); *Gundy v. Pauley*, 619 S.W.2d 730 (Ky. Ct. App. 1981).

81. *Pennhurst State School and Hospital v. Halderman*, 465 U.S. 89 (1984).

82. 42 U.S.C. §6000 *et seq.*

83. *Halderman v. Pennhurst State School and Hospital*, 673 F.2d 647 (3d Cir. 1982); *Pennhurst State School and Hospital v. Halderman*, 465 U.S. 89 (1984).

84. Borus, 1981.

85. Garcia *et al.*, 1989.

86. *Bowers v. Hardwick*, 478 U.S. 186 (1986).

87. *Rogers v. Okin*, 821 F.2d 22 (1st Cir. 1987).

88. *Youngberg v. Romeo*, 457 U.S. 307 (1982); Rappaport and Parry, 1986.

89. Appelbaum, 1988a, 1988b, and generally Appelbaum and Hoge, 1986.

90. *Johnson v. Zerbst*, 304 U.S. 458 (1938).

91. Annas, Glantz, and Katz, 1977; see also Chapter 8.

92. *Rennie v. Klein*, 462 F. Supp. 1131 (D.N.J. 1978), *vacated*, 458 U.S. 1119 (1982).

93. *Rogers v. Commissioner of the Department of Mental Health*, 458 N.E.2d 308 (Mass. 1983). See Gutheil, 1985.

94. *Rivers v. Katz*, 495 N.E.2d 337, 344 (N.Y. 1986).

95. *Jones v. Gerhardstein*, 416 N.W.2d 883 (Wis. 1987); see generally Brooks, 1987.

96. *Cruzan v. Director, Missouri Dept. of Health*, 497 U.S. 261 (1990).

97. *Washington v. Harper*, 494 U.S. 210, 211 (1990). States may require a more rigorous standard; see *Louisiana v. Perry*, 61 L.W. 2288 (1992).

98. In *Riggins v. Nevada*, 112 S.Ct. 1810 (1992), the majority of the Supreme Court applied the *Harper* case to the forcible administration of drugs to a defendant prior to conviction. For discussion, see Chapter 9.

99. *Williams v. Wilzack*, 573 A.2d 809 (Md. App. 1990).

100. *Bee v. Greaves*, 744 F.2d 1387 (10th Cir. 1984).

101. *Society for Good Will to Retarded Children, Inc. v. Cuomo*, 737 F.2d 1239 (2d Cir. 1984).

102. Nurcombe, 1989.

103. Weithorn, 1984; Grisso and Vierling, 1978.

104. For a discussion of the state schemes and suggestions for reform, see M. C. Sperber, "Short-Sheeting the Psychiatric Bed," *American Journal of Law and Medicine* 18 (1992): 251.

105. Hollar, 1989.

106. Wexler, 1990.

107. *Santana v. Collazo*, 533 F. Supp. 966 (D.P.R. 1982), aff'd in part and vacated and remanded in part, 714 F.2d 1172 (1st Cir. 1983).

108. *In re Owen*, 295 N.E.2d 455 (Ill. 1973).

109. *W. v. Louisiana*, 437 F. Supp. 1209 (E.D. La. 1976), aff'd, 622 F.2d 804 (5th Cir. 1980); *Morales v. Turman*, 535 F.2d 864 (5th Cir. 1976), reversed by 430 U.S. 322 (1977).

110. *Shookoff v. Adams*, 750 F. Supp. 288 (M.D. Tenn. 1990).

111. *Schall v. Martin*, 467 U.S. 253 (1984).

112. *United States v. Salerno*, 481 U.S. 739 (1987).

113. *New Jersey v. T.L.O.*, 469 U.S. 325 (1985).

114. *Nelson v. Heyne*, 355 F. Supp. 451 (N.D. Ind. 1972), aff'd, 491 F.2d 352 (7th Cir. 1974).

115. *Pena v. New York State Division for Youth*, 419 F. Supp. 203 (S.D. N.Y. 1976).

116. E.g., *Santana v. Collazo*, 533 F. Supp. 966 (D.P.R. 1982), aff'd in part and re-manded and vacated in part, 714 F.2d 1172 (1st Cir. 1983); *Inmates of Boys' Training School v. Affleck*, 346 F. Supp. 1354 (D. R.I. 1972).

117. *Youngberg v. Romeo*, 457 U.S. 307 (1982); *W. v. Louisiana*, 437 F. Supp. 1209 (E.D. La. 1976), aff'd, 622 F.2d 804 (5th Cir. 1980).

118. E.g., *Inmates of Boys' Training School v. Affleck*, 346 F. Supp. 1354 (D. R.I. 1972); *Nelson v. Heyne*, 355 F. Supp. 451 (N.D. Ind. 1972), aff'd, 491 F.2d 352 (7th Cir. 1974); *Morales v. Turman*, 535 F.2d 864 (5th Cir. 1976), reversed by 430 U.S. 322 (1977).

119. *DeShaney v. Winnebago County Department of Social Services*, 489 U.S. 189, 200 (1989).
120. *Inmates of Boys' Training School v. Affleck*, 346 F. Supp. 1354 (D. R.I. 1972).
121. Pub. L. 93-415 (1974).
122. §10.2, 96 (1980).
123. Mnookin and Weisberg, 1989.

CHAPTER 11
THE CHILD MENTAL HEALTH PROFESSIONAL AS EXPERT WITNESS

1. Fed. R. Evid. 601.
2. Graham, 1991, p. 379.
3. Fed. R. Evid. 608.
4. Fed. R. Evid. 609; *United States v. Lester*, 749 F.2d 1288 (9th Cir. 1984).
5. *United States v. Pacelli*, 521 F.2d 135 (2d Cir. 1975); *Hamling v. United States*, 418 U.S. 87 (1974).
6. Fed. R. Evid. 702.
7. *Ibid.*
8. *Frye v. United States*, 293 F. 1013 (D.C. Cir. 1923).
9. *Daubert v. Merrell Dow Pharmaceuticals*, 113 S.Ct. 2786 (1993).
10. *United States v. Persico*, 832 F.2d 705 (2d Cir. 1987).
11. For example, exceptions are prescribed for child abuse cases where hearsay statements are made by victims and the children because of incompetence or unavailability do not give direct evidence; see *Stevens v. People*, 796 P.2d 946 (Colo. 1990) (applying the Colorado statute); *Davis v. State*, 569 So. 2d 1317 (Fla. App. 1990) (applying the Florida statute). Other exceptions permit fact witnesses to give hearsay testimony of the declarant's statements that are (1) present sense impressions, (2) excited utterances, or (3) descriptions of then existing mental, emotional, or physical conditions. Fed. R. Evid. 803(1)–(3).
12. See Chapter 8, notes 224, 225, and 233; *Howard v. Drapkin*, 271 Cal. Rptr. 893 (Cal. Ct. App. 1990), discussed in Chapter 8, note 26.
13. *Estelle v. Smith*, 451 U.S. 454 (1981).
14. *In re Lifschutz*, 467 P.2d 557 (Cal. 1970).
15. Ziskin and Faust, 1988a, 1988b; see also Chapter 1.
16. An attorney's work product is qualifiedly privileged from discovery, see *Hickman v. Taylor*, 329 U.S. 495 (1947); *United States v. Nobles*, 422 U.S. 225 (1975).
17. Federal Rules of Civil Procedure (FRCP), no. 35.
18. Fed. R. Evid. 615, pertains to exclusion of witnesses.
19. Graham, 1991, p. 593, citing Fed. R. Evid. 703.
20. *United States v. Smith*, 578 F.2d 1227 (8th Cir. 1978).
21. *Holder v. United States*, 150 U.S. 91 (1893).
22. *United States v. Pollack*, 640 F.2d 1152 (10th Cir. 1981).
23. *Goings v. United States*, 377 F.2d 753 (8th Cir. 1967).
24. McCormick, 1984, §9, p. 20.
25. *Bailey v. Meister Brau, Inc.*, 57 F.R.D. 11 (N.D. Ill. 1972).
26. Fed. R. Evid. 803(5).

BIBLIOGRAPHY

Abarbanel, A. 1979. Shared parenting after separation and divorce, *American Journal of Orthopsychiatry* 49:320–29.

Abel, G.; J. Becker; W. Murphy; and B. Flanagan. 1981. Identifying dangerous child molesters. In R. B. Stuart, ed., *Violent behavior: Social learning approaches to prediction, management and treatment*. New York: Brunner/Mazel.

Aber, J.; J. Allen; V. Carlson; and D. Cicchetti. 1989. The effects of maltreatment on development during early childhood: Recent studies and their theoretical, clinical, and policy implications. In D. Cicchetti and V. Carlson, eds., *Child maltreatment: Theory and research on the causes and consequences of child abuse and neglect*. New York: Cambridge University Press.

Achenbach, T., and C. Edelbrock. 1983. *Manual for the child behavior checklist and revised behavior profile*. Burlington, VT: Queen City Printers.

Adams-Tucker, C. 1982. Proximate affects of sexual abuse in childhood: A report on twenty-eight children, *American Journal of Psychiatry* 139: 1252–56.

Ahrons, C. 1980. Joint custody arrangements in the postdivorce family, *Journal of Divorce* 3:189–205.

Alexander, J., and B. Parsons. 1982. *Functional family therapy*. Monterey, CA: Brooks/Cole.

Allen, V., and D. Newtson. 1972. Development of conformity and independence, *Journal of Personal and Social Psychology* 22: 18–30.

Allport, F.; G. Allport, C. Babcock; V. Bernard; *et al.* 1953. The effects of segregation and the consequences of desegregation, *Minnesota Law Review* 37: 427–43.

Alston, P.; S. Parker; and J. Seymour, eds. 1992. *Children, rights, and the law*. New York: Oxford University Press.

American Bar Association. 1990. Ethics and advocacy: Emerging issues for guardians ad litem, *Lawyers for Children*, p. 65. American Bar Association, Washington D.C.

American Humane Association. 1981. *National study on child neglect and abuse reporting*. Englewood, CO: American Humane Association.

American Law Institute. 1991. *Enterprise responsibility for personal injury*. Vols. I and II. Philadelphia: American Law Institute.

———. 1986. *The principles of medical ethics, with annotations especially applicable to psychiatry*. Washington: American Psychiatric Association. Section 5(1), p. 7.

———. 1984. *Task Force on the Role of Psychiatry in the Sentencing Process*. Washington, D.C.: American Psychiatric Association.

———. 1978. Model law of confidentiality of health and social service records. Washington: American Psychiatric Association.

Anderson, S.; C. Bach; and S. Griffith. 1981. Psychosocial sequelae in intrafamilial victims of sexual assault and abuse. Paper presented at the Third International Conference on Child Abuse and Neglect, Amsterdam, Netherlands.

Andrews, G., and C. Tennant. 1978. Life event stress and psychiatric illness, *Psychological Medicine* 8: 545–49.

Annas, G.; S. Law; R. Rosenblatt; and K. Wing. 1990. *American health law*. Boston: Little, Brown.

Annas, G.; L. Glantz; and B. Katz. 1977. *Informed consent to human experimentation: The subject's dilemma*. Cambridge, MA: Ballinger.

Appelbaum, K., and P. Appelbaum. 1990. The HIV antibody-positive patient. In J. Beck, ed., *Confidentiality versus the duty to protect: Foreseeable harm in the practice of psychiatry*. Washington: American Psychiatric Press.

Appelbaum, P. 1990. The parable of the forensic psychiatrist: Ethics and the problem of doing harm. *International Journal of Law and Psychiatry* 13: 249–59.

———. 1988a. The new preventive detention: Psychiatry's problematic responsibility for control of violence, *American Journal of Psychiatry* 145: 779–85.

———. 1988b. The right to refuse treatment with antipsychotic medications: Retrospect and prospect, *American Journal of Psychiatry* 145: 413–19.

———. 1982. The Supreme Court looks at psychiatry, *American Journal of Psychiatry* 141: 827–35.

Appelbaum, P., and S. Hoge. 1986. The right to refuse treatment: What the research reveals, *Behavioral Sciences and the Law* 4: 279–92.

Arbuthnot, J., and D. Faust. 1981. *Teaching moral reasoning: Theory and practice*. New York: Harper & Row.

Arbuthnot, J.; D. Gordon; and G. Jurkovic. 1987. Personality. In H. C. Quay, ed., *Handbook of juvenile delinquency*. New York: Wiley.

Arnett, L. 1989. Mootness and the Education for All Handicapped Children Act: Timely decision saves judicial and social costs—Honig v. Doe, 108 S.Ct. 592 (1988), *University of Cincinnati Law Review* 57:1101–22.

Arntzen, F. 1983. *Psychologie der Zeugenaussage: Systematik der Glaubwurdigkeitsmerkmale*. München: Beck.

———. 1982. Die Situation der forensischen Aussagepsychologie in der Bundesrepublik Deutschland. In A. Trankell, ed., *Reconstructing the past: The role of psychologists in criminal trials*. Stockholm: Norstedt.

———. 1970. *Psychologie der Zeugenaussage*. Gottingen: Gogrese.

Asher, S. 1988. The effects of childhood sexual abuse: A review of the issues and the evidence. In L. Walker, ed., *Handbook on sexual abuse of children: Assessment and treatment issues*. New York: Springer.

Attorney General's Commission on Pornography. 1988. *Final report*. 2 vols. Washington: U.S. Government Printing Office.

Bachman, J.; P. O'Malley; and J. Johnstone. 1978. *Adolescence to adulthood: Change and stability in the lives of young men*. Volume VI of *Youth in transition*. Ann Arbor: Institute for Social Research, University of Michigan.

Bagley, C. 1969. Incest behavior and incest taboos, *Social Problems* 16: 505–19.

Bagley, C., and R. Ramsey. 1985. Disrupted childhood and vulnerability to sexual assault: Long term sequels with implications for counselling. Paper presented at the Conference on Counselling the Sexual Abuse Survivor. Winnipeg, Canada.

Bahr, S. 1983. Marital dissolution laws: Impact of recent changes for women, *Journal of Family Issues* 4: 445–66.

Bahrick, H.; P. Bahrick; and R. Wittlinger. 1975. Fifty years of memory for names and faces: A cross-sectional approach, *Journal of Experimental Psychology* 104: 54–75.

Ball, M. 1975. The play's the thing: An unscientific reflection on courts under the rubric of theatre, *Stanford Law Review* 28: 81–115.

Barnum, R. 1990. Managing risk and confidentiality in clinical encounters with children and families. In J. Beck, ed., *Confidentiality versus the duty to protect: Foreseeable harm in the practice of psychiatry*. Washington: American Psychiatric Press.

Basta, J., and W. Davidson. 1988. Treatment of juvenile offenders: Study outcomes since 1980, *Behavioral Sciences and the Law* 6: 355–84.

Bavolek, S. 1984. *Handbook for the adult–adolescent parenting inventory*. Schaumberg, IL: Family Development Associates.

Beal, D., and P. Duckro. 1977. Family counseling as an alternative to legal action for the juvenile status offender, *Journal of Marriage and Family Counseling* 3: 77–81.

Beck, J. 1990. Current status of the duty to protect. In J. Beck, ed., *Confidentiality versus the duty to protect: Foreseeable harm in the practice of psychiatry*. Washington: American Psychiatric Press.

Becker, J., and M. Kaplan. 1988. Assessment and treatment of the male sex offender. In D. Schetky and A. Green, eds., *Child sexual abuse: A handbook for health care and legal professionals*. New York: Brunner/Mazel.

Bell, A., and M. Weinberg. 1981. *Preliminary data: Childhood and adolescent sexuality in the San Francisco study*. Bloomington, IN: Institute for Sex Research.

———. 1978. *Homosexualities: A study of human diversity*. New York: Simon & Schuster.

Bell, E. 1982. (Note) Disciplinary exclusion of handicapped students: An examination of the limitations imposed by the Education for All Handicapped Children Act of 1975. *Fordham Law Review* 51: 168–95.

Belsky, J. 1980. Child maltreatment: An ecological integration, *American Psychologist* 35: 320–35.

Bencivenga, D. 1992. Your first malpractice suit, *The Psychiatric Resident*, November–December, pp. 12–26.

Benedek, E. 1985. Waiver of juveniles to adult court. In D. Schetky and E. Benedek, eds., *Emerging issues in child psychiatry and the law*. New York: Brunner/Mazel.

Benedek, E. and Schetky, D. 1985. Allegations of sexual abuse in child custody and visitation disputes. In D. Schetky and E. Benedek, eds., *Emerging Issues in Child Psychiatry and the Law*. New York: Brunner/Mazel.

Benedek, R., and E. Benedek. 1980. Participating in child custody cases. In D. Schetky and E. Benedek, eds., *Child psychiatry and the law*. New York: Brunner/Mazel.

———. 1977. Post divorce visitation: A child's right, *Journal of the American Academy of Child Psychiatry* 16: 256–71.

Bennett, G. 1985. A guided tour through selected ABA standards relating to incompetence to stand trial, *George Washington Law Review* 53: 375–413.

Berger, A., and J. Berger, eds. 1990. *To die or not to die? Cross-disciplinary, cultural, and legal perspectives on the right to choose death*. New York: Praeger.

Berliner, L., and M. Barbieri. 1984. The testimony of the child victim of sexual assault, *Journal of Social Issues* 40: 125–37.

Berman, A., and D. Kirsh. 1982. Definitions of joint custody. *Family Advocate*, 5: 2–4.

Berry, G. 1975. Incest: Some clinical variations on a classical theme, *Journal of the American Academy of Psychoanalysis* 3: 151–61.

Bess, B., and Y. Janssen. 1982. Incest: A pilot study, *Hillside Journal of Clinical Psychiatry* 4: 39–52.

Biklen, D. 1982. The least restrictive environment: Its application to education. In G. Melton, ed., *Legal reforms affecting child and youth services.* New York: Haworth Press.

Biller, H. 1974. *Paternal deprivation: Family, school, sexuality and society.* Lexington, MA: Lexington Books.

Billingham, R.; A. Sauer; and L. Pillion. 1989. Family structure in childhood and sexual attitudes and behaviors during late adolescence. Paper presented at the Annual Meeting of the National Council on Family Relations, New Orleans.

Binder, A. 1989. Juvenile diversion. In A. Roberts, ed., *Juvenile justice: Policies, programs and services.* Chicago: Dorsey.

———. 1987. An historical and theoretical introduction. In H. Quay, ed., *Handbook of juvenile delinquency.* New York: Wiley.

Blau, T. 1984. *The Psychologist as Expert Witness.* New York: Wiley.

Blendon, R.; U. Szalay; and R. Knox. 1992. Should physicians aid their patients in dying? The public perspective, *Journal of American Medical Association* 267: 2658–62.

Blick, L., and F. Porter. 1982. Group therapy with female adolescent incest victims. In S. Sgroi, ed., *Handbook of clinical intervention in child sexual abuse.* Lexington, MA: Lexington Books.

Block, J.; J. Block; and P. Gjerde. 1988. Parental function and the home environment in families of divorce, *Journal of the American Academy of Child and Adolescent Psychiatry* 27: 207–13.

Bloom, B.; S. Asher; and S. White. 1978. Marital disruption as a stressor: A review and analysis, *Psychological Bulletin* 85: 867–94.

Blumstein, J. 1991. Health care delivery and tort: Systems on a collision course?. In Elizabeth Rolph, ed., *Conference Proceedings.* Dallas, Texas, June. Santa Monica, CA: Rand Corporation. No. 3524-ICJ.

Blumstein, J. 1981. Rationing medical resources: A constitutional, legal, and policy analysis, *Texas Law Review* 59: 1345–1400.

Bohman, M. 1983. Alcoholism and crime: Studies of adoptees, *Substance Alcohol Actions Misuse* 4: 137–47.

Bonnie, R., and C. Slobogin. 1980. The role of mental health professionals in the criminal process: The case for informed speculation, *Virginia Law Review* 66: 427–522.

Bonovitz, J., and E. Guy. 1979. Impact of restrictive civil commitment procedures on a prison psychiatric service, *American Journal of Psychiatry* 136: 1045–48.

Borkovec, T. 1970. Autonomic reactivity to sensory stimulation in psychopathic, neurotic and normal delinquents, *Journal of Consulting and Clinical Psychology* 35: 217–22.

Borus, J. 1981. Deinstitutionalization and the chronically mentally ill, *New England Journal of Medicine* 305: 339–42.

Bowe, F. 1980. An overview paper on civil rights issues of handicapped Americans: Public policy implications. In *Civil Rights Issues of Handicapped Americans: Public Policy Implications*. Washington: U.S. Commission on Civil Rights.

Bowlby, J. 1980. *Attachment and loss*. Vol. III: *Loss, sadness and depression*. New York: Basic Books.

———. 1973. *Attachment and loss*. Vol. II: *Separation: Anxiety and anger*. London: Hogarth.

———. 1969. *Attachment and loss*. Vol. I. London: Hogarth.

———. 1952. *Maternal care and mental health*. Geneva: World Health Organization.

———. 1946. *Forty-four juvenile thieves: Their characters and home-life*. London: Baillere, Tindall & Cox.

Bowman, M. 1983. Parenting after divorce: A comparative study of mother custody and joint custody families, *Dissertation Abstracts International* 44: 578A.

Brainerd, C., and P. Ornstein. 1991. Children's memory for witnessed events: The developmental backdrop. In J. Doris, ed., *The suggestibility of children's recollections*. Washington: American Psychological Association.

Braithwaite, J. 1981. The myth of social class and criminality reconsidered, *American Sociological Review* 46: 36–57.

Brakel, S. 1974. Presumption, bias, and incompetency in the criminal process, *Wisconsin Law Review*, 1974: 1104–30.

Brakel, S.; J. Parry; and B. Weiner. 1985. *The mentally disabled and the law*. 3d ed. Chicago: The Foundation.

Braun, B. 1989. Psychotherapy of the survivor of incest with dissociative disorder, *Psychiatric Clinics of North America* 12: 307–24.

———. 1986. Issues in the treatment of multiple personality disorder. In B. Braun, ed., *Treatment of multiple personality disorder*. Washington: American Psychiatric Press.

Braun, P., *et al.* 1981. Overview: Deinstitutionalization of psychiatric patients: A critical review of outcome studies, *American Journal of Psychiatry* 138: 736–49.

Brayden, R.; W. Altemier; T. Yeager; and D. Muram. 1990. Interpretations of colposcopic photographs: Evidence for competence in assessing sexual abuse. Unpublished manuscript, Department of Pediatrics, Vanderbilt University, Nashville.

Bremner, R. 1970–74. *Children and Youth in America: A Documentary History*. 3 vols. Cambridge: Harvard University Press.

Brennan, T. 1991. Practice guidelines and malpractice litigation: Collision or collusion? *Journal of Health Politics, Policy and Law* 16: 67–85.

Briere, J. 1984. The effects of childhood sexual abuse on later psychological functioning: Defining a post–sexual-abuse syndrome. Paper presented at the Third National Conference on Sexual Victimization of Children, Children's Hospital Medical Center, Washington, D.C.

Brodsky, S. 1991. *Testifying in court: Guidelines and maxims for the expert witness*. Washington, D.C.: American Psychological Association.

Bromberg, N. 1959. *The mind of man: A history of psychotherapy and psychoanalysis*. New York: Harper.

Bronfenbrenner, U. 1979. *The ecology of human development: Experiments by nature and by design*. Cambridge, MA: Harvard University Press.

Brooks, A. 1987. The right to refuse antipsychotic medications: Law and policy, *Rutgers Law Review* 39: 339–76.

———. 1974. *Law, psychiatry, and the mental health system.* Boston: Little, Brown.

Brooks, S. 1991. Rethinking adoption: A federal solution to the problem of permanency planning for children with special needs, *New York University Law Review* 66: 1130–64.

Brown, G., and T. Harris. 1978. *Social origins of depression: A study of psychiatric disorder in women.* London: Tavistock.

Brown, H.; M. Dent; M. Dyer; C. Fuzzell; A. Gifford; A. Kasselberg; J. Workman; and M. Cooper. 1986. Legal rights and issues surrounding conception, pregnancy, and birth, *Vanderbilt Law Review* 39: 597–850.

Brown, L., and J. Riley. 1984. Agency procedures with child abuse reports, *Juvenile and Family Court Journal*, Winter, pp. 45–46.

Browning, D., and B. Boatman. 1977. Incest: Children at risk, *American Journal of Psychiatry* 134: 69–72.

Brustein, S. 1989. *Coy v. Iowa*: Should children be heard and not seen? *University of Pittsburgh Law Review* 50: 1187–1208.

Buchanan, C.; E. Maccoby; and S. Dornbusch. 1991. Caught between parents: Adolescents' experience in divorced homes, *Child Development* 62: 1008–29.

Buikhuisen, W. 1979. An alternative approach to the etiology of crime. In S. Mednick and S. Shoham, eds., *New paths in criminology: Interdisciplinary and intercultural.* Lexington, MA: Lexington Books.

Bulkley, J. 1986. Analysis of legal reforms in child sexual abuse cases. In H. Davidson and R. Horowitz, eds., *Legal advocacy for children and youth: Reforms, trends and contemporary issues.* Washington: National Legal Resource Center for Child Welfare Programs, American Bar Association.

Bullard, D.; M. Dexter; H. Glaser; M. Heagarty; and E. Pivchik. 1967. Failure to thrive in the neglected child, *American Journal of Orthopsychiatry* 37: 680–90.

Burger, W. 1968. Reflections on law and experimental medicine, *U.C.L.A. Law Review* 15: 436–42.

Burgess, A., and L. Holmstrom. 1979. *Rape: Crisis and recovery.* Bowie, MD: Brady.

Burgess, A.; A. Groth; and M. McCausland. 1981. Child sex initiation rings, *American Journal of Orthopsychiatry* 51: 110–19.

Burgess, R. 1979. Project interact: A study of patterns of interaction in abusive, neglectful, and control families, *Child Abuse and Neglect* 3: 781–91.

Burgess, R., and R. Conger. 1978. Family interaction in abusive, neglectful, and normal families, *Child Development* 49: 1163–73.

Burke, J.; J. Borus; B. Burns; K. Millstein; and M. Beasley. 1982. Changes in children's behavior after a natural disaster, *American Journal of Psychiatry* 139: 1010–14.

Burlingame, W., and M. Amaya. 1985. Psychiatric commitment of children and adolescents: Issues, current practices, and clinical input. In D. Schetky and E. Benedek, eds., *Emerging issues in child psychiatry and the law.* New York: Brunner/Mazel.

Byrne, J., and E. Valdiserri. 1982. Victims of childhood sexual abuse: A follow-up study of a noncompliant population, *Hospital and Community Psychiatry* 33: 938–40.

Cadoret, R. 1986. Epidemiology of antisocial personality. In W. Reid, D. Dorr, J. Walker, and J. Bonner, eds., *Unmasking the psychopath: Antisocial personality and related syndromes*. New York: Norton.

———. 1978. Psychopathology in adopted-away offspring of biologic parents with antisocial behavior, *Archives of General Psychiatry* 35: 176–84.

Cadoret, R.; T. O'Gorman; E. Troughton; and E. Haywood. 1985. Alcoholism and antisocial personality: Interrelationships, genetic and environmental factors, *Archives of General Psychiatry* 42: 161–67.

Cady, F. 1979. Emancipation of minors, *Connecticut Law Review* 12: 62–91.

Calabresi, G. 1982. *A common law for the age of statutes*. Cambridge, MA: Harvard University Press.

———. 1969. Reflections on medical experimentation, *Daedalus* 98 no. 2: 387–405.

Cammaert, L. 1988. Nonoffending mothers: A new conceptualization. In L. Walker, ed., *Handbook on sexual abuse of children: Assessment and treatment issues*. New York: Springer.

Camp, B.; W. van Doornick; S. Zimet; and N. Dahlen. 1977. Verbal abilities in young aggressive boys, *Journal of Educational Psychology* 69: 129–35.

Cane, P. 1987. *Atiyah's Accidents, Compensation and the Law*. London: Weidenfeld & Nicolson.

Cantwell, H. 1980. Child neglect. In C. Kempe and R. Helfer, eds., *The battered child*. 3d ed. Chicago: University of Chicago Press.

Caplan, E.; P. King; and J. Jones. 1992. Twenty years after: The legacy of the Tuskegee Syphilis Study, *Hastings Center Report* 22: 29–43.

Capron, A. 1974. Informed consent in catastrophic disease research and treatment, *University of Pennsylvania Law Review* 123: 340–438.

———. 1973. Legal considerations affecting pharmacological studies in children, *Clinical Research* 21: 141–50.

Cavallin, H. 1966. Incestuous fathers: A clinical report, *American Journal of Psychiatry* 122: 1132–38.

Chandler, M. 1973. Egocentrism and antisocial behavior: The assessment and training of social perspective-taking skills, *Developmental Psychology* 9: 326–32.

Charo, A. 1988. Legislative approaches to surrogate motherhood, *Law, Medicine and Health Care* 16: 96–112.

Chasnoff, I. 1986. Maternal neonatal incest, *American Journal of Orthopsychiatry* 56: 577–80.

Chesler, P. 1986. *Mothers on trial*. New York: McGraw-Hill.

Christiansen, K. 1977a. A preliminary study of criminality amongst twins. In S. Mednick and K. Christiansen, eds., *Biosocial bases of criminal behavior*. New York: Garnder.

———. 1977b. Seriousness of criminality and concordance among Danish twins. In R. Hood, ed., *Crime, criminology and public policy*. New York: Free Press.

Clark, D. 1992. "Rational" suicide and people with terminal conditions or disabilities, *Issues in Law and Medicine* 8: 147–66.

Clarke-Stewart, A.; W. Thompson; and S. Lepore. 1989. Manipulating children's interpretations through interrogation. In "Can children provide accurate eyewitness reports?" Symposium at biennial meeting of the Society for Research in Child Development, Kansas City, Missouri.

Cleckley, H. 1955. *The mask of sanity*. 3d ed. St. Louis: Mosby.

Cleveland, S.; E. Mulvey; P. Appelbaum; and C. Lidz. 1989. Do dangerousness-oriented commitment laws restrict hospitalization of patients who need treatment? A test, *Hospital and Community Psychiatry* 40: 266–71.

Cloninger, C.; T. Reich; and S. Guze. 1975. The multifactorial model of disease transmission, III: The familial relationship between sociopathy and hysteria (Briquet's syndrome), *British Journal of Psychiatry* 127: 23–32.

Cloward, R., and L. Ohlin. 1960. *Delinquency and opportunity: A theory of delinquent gangs*. Glencoe, IL: Free Press.

Coady, C. 1992. *Testimony: A philosophical study*. Oxford: Clarendon Press; New York: Oxford University Press.

Coddington, R. 1972. The significance of life events as etiologic factors in the diseases of children, II: A study of a normal population, *Journal of Psychosomatic Research* 16: 205–13.

Cohen, A. 1955. *Delinquent Boys*. New York: Free Press.

Cohen, R., and M. Harnick. 1980. The susceptibility of child witnesses to suggestion: An empirical study, *Law and Human Behavior* 4: 201–10.

Cohen, S. 1985. *Visions of social control: Crime, punishment and classification*. New York: Polity Press.

Cohn, A. 1979. Essential elements of successful child abuse and neglect treatment, *Child Abuse and Neglect* 3: 491–96.

Coleman, P., and R. Shellow. 1992. Suicide: Unpredictable and unavoidable—Proposed guidelines provide rational test for physician's liability, *Nebraska Law Review* 71: 643–93.

Colletta, N. 1983. Stressful lives: The situation of divorced mothers and their children, *Journal of Divorce* 6: 19–31.

———. 1979. The impact of divorce: Father absence or poverty? *Journal of Divorce* 3: 27–35.

Committee on Child Psychiatry, Group for the Advancement of Psychiatry. 1989. *How old is enough?: The ages of rights and responsibilities*. New York: Brunner–Mazel.

Committee on Sexual Offenses Against Children and Youth. 1984. *Sexual offenses against children*. Ottawa: Canadian Government Publishing Center.

Conte, J., and J. Schuerman. 1987. Factors associated with an increased impact of child sexual abuse, *Child Abuse and Neglect* 11: 201–11.

Courtois, C. 1979. The incest experience and its aftermath, *Victimology* 4: 337–47.

Cowan, D. 1982. Mother custody versus joint custody: Children's parental relationships and adjustment, *Dissertation Abstracts International* 43: 726A.

Crowe, R. 1974. An adoption study of antisocial personality, *Archives of General Psychiatry* 31: 785–91.

Curran, W.; A. McGarry; and S. Shah. 1986. *Forensic psychiatry and psychology: Perspectives and standards for interdisciplinary practice*. Philadelphia: F. A. Davis.

Dada, M.; W. White; H. Stokes; and P. Kurzeja. 1992. Prospective payment for psychiatric services, *Journal of Health Politics, Policy and Law* 17: 483–508.

Dale, P.; E. Loftus; and L. Rathbon. 1978. The influence of the form of the question on the eyewitness testimony of preschool children, *Journal of Psycholinguistic Research* 7: 269–77.

Dalgard, O., and E. Kringlen. 1976. A Norwegian twin study of criminality, *British Journal of Criminology* 16: 213–32.

Danzon, P. 1985. *Medical malpractice: Theory, evidence, and public policy*. Cambridge: Harvard University Press.

Daro, D., and L. Mitchel. 1990. *Current trends in child abuse reporting and fatalities*. Chicago: National Committee for Prevention of Child Abuse.

Davidson, H., and K. Gerlach. 1984. Child custody disputes. In R. Horowitz and H. Davidson, eds., *Legal Rights of Children*. Family Law Series. Colorado Springs: Shepard's/McGraw-Hill.

Davidson, L., and M. Linnoila, eds., 1989. *Report of the Secretary's Task Force on Youth Suicide*. Washington: United States Department of Health and Human Services.

Davies, G. 1991. Concluding remarks. In J. Doris, ed., *The suggestibility of children's recollections*. Washington: American Psychological Association.

Dawson, P. 1981. The psychology of eyewitness testimony: Developmental study of long-term memory fulfillment. Unpublished doctoral dissertation, New School for Social Research, New York.

Dent, H., and G. Stephenson. 1979. An experimental study of the effectiveness of different techniques of questioning child witnesses, *British Journal of Social and Clinical Psychology* 18: 41–51.

Derdeyn, A. 1975. Child custody consultation, *American Journal of Orthopsychiatry* 45: 791–801.

DeVille, K. 1990. *Medical malpractice in nineteenth-century America: Origins and legacy*. New York: New York University Press.

DeYoung, M. 1984. Counterphobic behaviors in multiply molested children, *Child Welfare* 63: 333–39.

———. 1982. *Sexual victimization of children*. Jefferson, NC: McFarland.

Diagnostic and statistical manual of mental disorders (DSM-III-R). 1987. Washington: American Psychiatric Association.

Diamond, D. 1981. The First Amendment and public schools: The case against judicial intervention, *Texas Law Review* 59: 477–528.

DiLeo, J. 1973. *Children's drawings as diagnostic aids*. New York: Brunner/Mazel.

Dix, G. 1984. Criminal responsibility and mental impairment in American criminal law: Response to the Hinckley acquittal in historical perspective. In D. Weisstaub, ed., *Law and mental health: International perspectives*. Vol. I. New York: Pergamon.

Dixon, K.; L. Arnold; and K. Calestro. 1978. Father–son incest: Underreported psychiatric problem? *American Journal of Psychiatry* 135: 835–38.

Dohrenwend, B. S., and B. P. Dohrenwend. 1978. Some issues in research on stressful life events, *Journal of Nervous and Mental Disease* 166: 7–15.

Dorr, D., and P. Woodhall. 1986. Ego dysfunction in psychopathic psychiatric inpatients. In W. Reid, D. Dorr, J. Walker, and J. Bonner, eds., *Unmasking the psychopath: Antisocial personality and related syndromes*. New York: Norton.

DuCanto, J. 1967. Mental illness and child custody, *Journal of Family Law* 7: 637–43.

Duncan, E.; P. Whitney; and S. Kunen. 1982. Integration of visual and verbal information in children's memories, *Child Development* 53: 1215–23.

Durham, M., and J. LaFond. 1985. The empirical consequences and policy implications of broadening the statutory criteria for civil commitment, *Yale Law and Policy Review* 3: 395–446.

Dworkin, T. 1984. Fear of disease and delayed manifestation injuries: A solution or a Pandora's box? *Fordham Law Review* 53: 527–77.

Dziech, B., and C. Schudson. 1992. *On trial: America's courts and their treatment of sexually abused children*. Boston: Beacon Press.

Eaton, T., and E. Larson. 1991. Experimenting with the "right to die" in the laboratory of the states, *Georgia Law Review* 25: 1253–1326.

Eaton, T., and M. Wells. 1991. Governmental inaction as a constitutional tort: *DeShaney* and its aftermath, *Washington Law Review* 66: 107–67.

Edwall, G., and N. Hoffman. 1988. Correlates of incest reported by adolescent girls in treatment for substance abuse. In L. Walker, ed., *Handbook on sexual abuse of children: Assessment and treatment issues*. New York: Springer.

Elmer, E. 1960. Failure to thrive: Role of the mother, *Pediatrics* 25: 717–25.

Elmer, E., and G. Gregg. 1967. Developmental characteristics of abused children, *Pediatrics* 40: 596–602.

Elster, J. 1989. *Solomonic judgments: Studies in the limitations of rationality*. Cambridge and New York: Cambridge University Press.

Emans, S.; E. Woods; N. Flagg; and A. Freeman. 1987. Genital findings in sexually abused symptomatic and asymptomatic girls, *Pediatrics* 79: 778–85.

Embree, M., and T. Dobson. 1991. Parental involvement in adolescent abortion decisions: A legal and psychological critique, *Law and Inequality Journal of Theory and Practice* 10: 53–79.

Emery, R. 1988. *Marriage, divorce, and children's adjustment*. Newbury Park, CA: Sage.

———. 1982. Interparental conflict and the children of discord and divorce, *Psychological Bulletin* 92: 310–30.

Engel, D. 1991. Law, culture, and children with disabilities: Educational rights and the construction of difference, *Duke Law Journal*, pp. 166–205.

English, A. 1988. Legal issues in health care for children and adolescents, *Fourth National Conference on Children and the Law*, 11-61, ABA National Legal Resource Center for Child Advocacy.

Epstein, E., and M. Martin. 1989. *The attorney-client privilege and the work-product doctrine*. 2d ed. Chicago: American Bar Association.

Epstein, G. 1978. Informed consent and the dyadic relationship, *Journal of Psychiatry and the Law* 6: 359–62.

Evans, S.; J. Reinhart; and R. Succop. 1972. Failure to thrive, *Journal of the American Academy of Child Psychiatry* 11: 440–57.

Everett, C. 1983. Family assessment in child custody disputes, *Journal of Marital and Family Therapy* 4: 343–53.

Eysenck, H. 1964. *Crime and personality*. Boston: Houghton Mifflin.

Facaros, N. 1988. Comment: Reorchestrating the *Lenrich* requiem for free expression in privately owned shopping centers under the Oregon constitution, *Oregon Law Review* 67: 467–94.

Faden, R., and T. Beauchamp. 1986. *History and theory of informed consent*. New York: Oxford University Press.

Farrington, D. 1988. Advancing knowledge about delinquency and crime: The need for a coordinated program of longitudinal research, *Behavioral Sciences and the Law* 6: 307–31.

———. 1987. Epidemiology. In H. Quay, ed., *Handbook of juvenile delinquency*. New York: Wiley.

Farrington, D.; L. Biron; and M. LeBlanc. 1982. Personality and delinquency in London and Montreal. In J. Gunn and D. Farrington, eds., *Abnormal offenders, delinquency, and the criminal justice system*. New York: Wiley.

Faust, D., and J. Ziskin. 1988. The expert witness in psychology and psychiatry, *Science* 241: 31–35.

Favole, R. 1983. Mental disability in the American criminal process: A four-issue survey. In J. Monahan and H. Steadman, eds., *Mentally disordered offenders: Perspectives from law and social science*. New York: Plenum.

Felner, R.; S. Farber; M. Ginter; M. Boike; and E. Cowen. 1985. Family stress and organization following parental divorce or death, *Journal of Divorce* 4: 67–76.

Felner, R.; S. Farber; and J. Primaveri. 1980. Transitions and stressful life events: A model for primary prevention. In R. Price, R. Ketterer, B. Bader, and J. Monahan, eds., *Prevention in mental health: Research policy and practice*. Beverly Hills, CA: Sage.

Felner, R., and L. Terre. 1987. Child custody dispositions and children's adaptation following divorce. In L. Weithorn, ed., *Psychology and child custody determinations*. Lincoln: University of Nebraska Press.

Ferguson, B., and A. Douglas. 1970. A study of juvenile waiver, *San Diego Law Review* 7: 39–54.

Ferguson, L. 1978. The competence and freedom of children to make choices regarding participation in research: A statement, *Journal of Social Issues* 34: 114–21.

Finch, S. 1973. Sexual abuse by mothers, *Medical Aspects of Human Sexuality* 7: 191–97.

Fineman, M. 1988. Dominant discourse, professional language, and legal change in child custody decisionmaking, *Harvard Law Review* 101: 727–74.

Fink, J. 1986. Juvenile delinquency legislation: Punishment in vogue. In H. Davidson and R. Horowitz, eds., *Legal advocacy for children and youth: Reforms, trends, and contemporary issues*. Washington, DC: American Bar Association, National Legal Resource Center for Child Welfare Programs.

Finkel, M. 1988. The medical evaluation of child sexual abuse. In D. Schetky and A. Green, eds., *Child sexual abuse: A handbook for health care and legal professionals*. New York: Brunner/Mazel.

———. 1979. *Sexually victimized children*. New York: Free Press.

Finkelhor, D., and A. Browne. 1988. Assessing the long-term impact of child sexual abuse: A review and conceptualization. In L. Walker, ed., *Handbook on sexual abuse of children: Assessment and treatment issues*. New York: Springer.

———. 1985. The traumatic impact of child sexual abuse, *American Journal of Orthopsychiatry* 55: 530–41.

Fischer, M. 1983. Adolescent adjustment after incest, *School Psychology International* 4: 217–22.

Fischoff, J.; C. Whitten; and M. Pettit. 1971. A psychiatric study of mothers of infants with growth failure secondary to maternal deprivation, *Journal of Pediatrics* 79: 209–15.

Fisher, R., and W. Ury. 1981. *Getting to yes*. New York: Houghton Mifflin.

Fisher, W.; G. Pierce; and P. Appelbaum. 1988. How flexible are our Civil commitment statutes? *Hospital and Community Psychiatry* 39: 711–12.

Fivush, R. 1984. Learning about school: The development of kindergartners' school scripts, *Child Development* 55: 1697–1709.

Flanagan, T.; M. Hindelang; and M. Gottfredson, eds. 1980. *Sourcebook of criminal justice statistics—1979*. Washington: U.S. Government Printing Office.

Flavell, J. 1963. *The developmental psychology of Jean Piaget*. Princeton, NJ: Van Nostrand.

Fleming, J., and B. Maximov. 1974. The patient or his victim: The therapist's dilemma, *California Law Review* 62: 1025–68.

Fletcher, J. 1988. The courts and euthanasia, *Law, Medicine and Health Care* 15: 223–30.

Foster, H., and D. Freed. 1979. Joint custody: A viable alternative? *Trial* 15: 26–31.

———. 1964. Child custody (Part 1). *New York University Law Review* 39: 423–43.

Francis, J. 1987. Incidence of father–son incest. Paper presented at the annual meeting of the American Psychiatric Association, Chicago.

Freedman, B.; A. Fuks; and C. Weijer. 1993. In loco parentis: Minimal risk as an ethical threshold for research upon children. *Hastings Center Report* 23(2): 13–19.

Fried, C. 1974. *Medical experimentation: Personal integrity of social policy*. New York: North-Holland Publishing Co.

Friedlander, K. 1947. *The psychoanalytic approach to juvenile delinquency*. London: Routledge & Kegan Paul.

Friedman, S. 1992. *The law of parent–child relationships: A handbook*. Chicago: American Bar Association.

———. 1988. A family systems approach to treatment. In L. Walker, ed., *Handbook on sexual abuse of children: Assessment and treatment issues*. New York: Springer.

Friedrich, W.; A. Urquiza; and R. Beilke. 1986. Behavior problems in sexually abused children, *Journal of Pediatric Psychiatry* 11: 47–57.

Fritz, G.; K. Stoll; and N. Wagner. 1981. A comparison of males and females who were sexually molested as children, *Journal of Sex and Marital Therapy* 7: 54–59.

Fromuth, M. 1986. The relationship of childhood sexual abuse with later psychological and sexual adjustment in a sample of college women, *Child Abuse and Neglect* 10: 5–15.

Furrow, B. 1978. Defective mental treatment: A proposal for the application of strict liability to psychiatric services, *Boston University Law Review* 58: 391–434.

Furstenberg, F.; S. Morgan; and P. Allison. 1987. Paternal participation and children's well-being after marital dissolution, *American Sociological Review* 52: 695–701.

Gaensbauer, T., and D. Mrazek. 1981. Differences in the patterning of affective expression in infants, *Journal of the American Academy of Child Psychiatry* 20: 673–91.

Gaensbauer, T., and K. Sands. 1979. Distorted affective communications in abused/neglected infants and their potential impact on caretakers, *Journal of the American Academy of Child Psychiatry* 18: 236–50.

Gagnon, J. 1965. Female child victims of sex offenses, *Social Problems* 13: 176–92.

Galdston, R. 1965. Observations on children who have been physically abused and their parents, *American Journal of Psychiatry* 122: 440–43.

Gale, F., and J. Groyer. 1986. Recovery for cancerphobia and increased risk of cancer, *Cumberland Law Review* 15: 723–44.

GAO/HRD. 1991. *Medical malpractice: Alternatives to litigation.* Washington: General Accounting Office.

Garbarino, J. 1977. The price of privacy in the social dynamics of child abuse, *Child Welfare* 56: 565–75.

Garcia, S.; E. Drogin; R. Batey; and R. Spana. 1989. Institutionalized delinquents and maladjusted juveniles: A psycholegal systems analysis, *Nebraska Law Review* 68: 261–91.

Garcia, S., and I. Keilitz. 1991. Involuntary civil commitment of drug-dependent persons with special reference to pregnant women, *Mental and Physical Disability Reporter* 15: 418–20.

Gardner, R. 1989. Differentiating between bona fide and fabricated allegations of sexual abuse of children, *Journal of the American Academy of Matrimonial Lawyers* 5: 1–25.

———. 1987. *The parental alienation syndrome and the differentiation between fabricated and genuine child sex abuse.* Cresskill, NJ: Creative Therapeutics.

———. 1982. *Family evaluation in child custody litigation.* Cresskill, NJ: Creative Therapeutics.

Garrett, C. 1985. Effects of residential treatment on adjudicated delinquents: A meta-analysis, *Journal of Research in Crime and Delinquency* 22: 287–308.

Garrett, W. 1990. *Divorce, alimony and child custody.* Norcross, GA: Harrison.

Gartner, A., and D. Lipsky. 1987. Beyond special education: Toward a quality system for all students. *Harvard Educational Review* 57: 367–95.

Gartrell, N.; J. Herman; S. Olarte; *et al.* 1986. Psychiatric-patient sexual contact—results of a national survey: Prevalence, *American Journal of Psychiatry* 143: 1126–31.

Gasper, J., and D. Katkin. 1980. A rationale for the abolition of juvenile courts power to waive jurisdiction. *Pepperdine Law Review* 7: 937–51.

Gasser, R., and C. Taylor. 1976. Role adjustment of single-parent fathers with dependent children, *The Family Coordinator* 25: 397–401.

Gault, H. 1991. Regular education initiative: What psychiatrists need to know. Paper delivered in a symposium on Issues in Psychiatric School Consultation, Annual Congress of the American Academy of Child and Adolescent Psychiatry, San Francisco, October 1991.

Gebhard, P.; J. Gagnon; W. Pomeroy; and C. Christenson. 1965. *Sex offenders: An analysis of types*. New York: Harper & Row.

Gelinas, D. 1983. The persisting negative effects of incest, *Psychiatry* 46: 312–32.

Genn, H. 1987. *Hard bargaining: Out of court settlement in personal injury actions*. New York: Oxford University Press.

Gensheimer, L., and J. Mayer. 1987. Community-based intervention. In H. Quay, ed., *Handbook of juvenile delinquency*. New York: Wiley.

Gensheimer, L.; J. Mayer; R. Gottschalk; and W. Davidson. 1986. Diverting youth from the juvenile justice system: A meta-analysis of intervention efficacy. In S. Apter and A. Goldstein, eds., *Youth violence: Programs and prospects*. New York: Pergamon.

George, C., and M. Main. 1979. Social interactions of young abused children, *Child Development* 50: 306–18.

Giarretto, H. 1981. A comprehensive child sexual abuse treatment program. In P. Mrazek and C. Kempe, eds., *Sexually abused children and their families*. New York: Pergamon.

Gibbons, T. 1963. *Psychiatric studies of Borstal lads*. London: Oxford University Press.

Gil, D. 1970. *Violence against children*. Cambridge, MA: Harvard University Press.

Gislason, I., and J. Call. 1982. Dogbite in infancy: Trauma and personality development, *Journal of the American Academy of Child Psychiatry* 21: 203–7.

Glenn, N., and K. Kramer. 1987. The psychological well-being of adult children of divorce, *Journal of Marriage and the Family* 47: 905–12.

Gleser, G.; B. Green; and C. Winget. 1981. *Prolonged psychosocial effects of a disaster: A study of Buffalo Creek*. New York: Academic Press.

Glueck, S., and E. Glueck. 1956. *Physique and delinquency*. New York: Harper & Row.

Gold, E. 1986. Long-term effects of sexual victimization in childhood: An attributional approach, *Journal of Consulting and Clinical Psychology* 54: 471–75.

Gold, M. 1987. Social ecology. In H. Quay, ed., *Handbook of juvenile delinquency*. New York: Wiley.

Goldstein, A. 1967. *The insanity defense*. New Haven: Yale University Press.

Goldstein, J.; A. Freud; and A. Solnit. 1979. *Before the best interests of the child*. New York: Free Press.

———. 1973. *Beyond the best interests of the child*, New York: Free Press.

Gomes-Schwartz, B.; J. Horowitz; and M. Sauzier. 1985. Severity of emotional distress among sexually abused preschool, school-age and adolescent children, *Hospital and Community Psychiatry* 36: 503–8.

Goodman, G., and C. Aman. 1987. Children's use of anatomically detailed dolls to report an event. Paper presented at the annual convention of the Society for Research in Child Development, Baltimore.

Goodman, G.; C. Aman; and J. Hirschman. 1987. Child physical and sexual abuse: Children's testimony. In S. Seci, M. Toglia, and D. Ross, eds., *Children's eyewitness memory*. New York: Springer.

Goodman, G., and A. Clarke-Stewart. 1991. Suggestibility in children's testimony: Implications for sexual abuse investigations. In J. Doris, ed., *The suggestibility of children's recollections*. Washington: American Psychological Association.

Goodman, G.; J. Golding; and M. Haith. 1984. Jurors' reactions to child witnesses, *Journal of Social Issues* 40: 139–56.

Goodman, G., and V. Helgeson. 1988. Children as witnesses: What do they remember? In L. Walker, ed., *Handbook on sexual abuse of children: Assessment and treatment issues.* New York: Springer.

Goodman, G.; D. Hepps; and R. Reed. 1986. The child victim's testimony. In A. Haralambie, ed., *New issues for child advocates.* Tucson, AZ: Council of Attorneys for Children.

Goodman, G.; D. Jones; L. Estrada-Prado; E. Pyle; L. Port; T. England; R. Mason; and L. Rudy. 1987. Children's reactions to criminal court testimony. Paper presented at the Annual Meeting of the American Psychological Association, New York.

Goodman, G., and R. Reed. 1986. Age differences in eyewitness testimony, *Law and Human Behavior* 10: 317–32.

Goodman, G.; E. Taub; D. Jones; P. England; L. Port; L. Rudy; and L. Prado. 1992. Testifying in criminal court: Emotional effects on child sexual abuse victims, *Monographs of the Society for Research in Child Development* 57, no. 5: 1–162.

Goodwin, J. 1985. Post-traumatic symptoms in incest victims. In S. Eth and R. Pynoos, eds., *Post-traumatic stress disorder in children.* Washington: American Psychiatric Press.

Goodwin, J.; L. Cormier; and J. Owen. 1983. Grandfather–granddaughter incest: A trigenerational view, *Child Abuse and Neglect* 7: 163–70.

Goodwin, J.; T. McCarthy; and P. DiVasto. 1981. Prior incest in mothers of abused children, *Child Abuse and Neglect* 5: 87–95.

Gordon, A., and J. Jameson. 1979. Infant–mother attachment in patients with nonorganic failure-to-thrive syndrome, *Journal of the American Academy of Child Psychiatry* 18: 251–59.

Gordon, D. 1965. The unborn plaintiff, *Michigan Law Review* 63: 579–627.

Gordon, D., and J. Arbuthnot. 1987. Individual, group and family interventions. In H. Quay, ed., *Handbook of juvenile delinquency.* New York: Wiley.

Gordon, R. 1976a. Prevalence: The rare datum in delinquency measurement and its implications for the theory of delinquency. In M. Klein, ed., *The juvenile justice system.* Beverly Hills, CA: Sage.

Gordon, R.; J. Short; D. Cartwright; and F. Strodtvick. 1963. Values and gang delinquency: A study of street-corner groups, *American Journal of Sociology* 69: 109–28.

Gottschalk, R.; W. Davidson; L. Gensheimer; K. Leah; and J. Mayer. 1987. Community-based interventions. In H. Quay, ed., *Handbook of juvenile delinquency.* New York: Wiley.

Gould, C. 1988. Signs and symptoms of ritualistic abuse in children. Unpublished manuscript, 1661 Ventura Blvd., Suite 303, Encino, CA 91436.

Grady, M. 1988. Why are people negligent? Technology, nondurable precautions, and the medical malpractice explosion, *Northwestern University Law Review* 82: 293–334.

Graham, M. 1991. *Handbook of federal evidence.* 3d. ed. St. Paul: West.

Grapentine, W.; C. Picariello; B. Nurcombe; A. Scioli; and R. Seifer. 1990. Validating the diagnosis of borderline personality disorder in adolescence (study by Emma

Pendleton Bradley Hospital, East Providence, Rhode Island). Paper presented at Annual Meeting of American Academy of Child and Adolescent Psychiatry, Chicago.

Gray, E. 1993. *Unequal justice: The prosecution of child sexual abuse.* New York: Free Press.

Gray, O. 1980. The standard of care for children revisited, *Missouri Law Review* 45: 597–620.

Greaves, G. 1980. Multiple personality: 165 years after Mary Reynolds, *Journal of Nervous and Mental Diseases* 168: 577–96.

Green, A. 1988. Special issues in child sexual abuse. In D. Schetky and A. Green, eds., *Child sexual abuse: A handbook for health care and legal professionals.* New York: Brunner/Mazel.

———. 1985. Child abuse and neglect. In D. Sheffer, A. Ehrhardt, and L. Greenhill, eds., *The clinical guide to child psychiatry.* New York: Free Press.

———. 1983. Child abuse: Dimensions of psychological trauma in abused children, *Journal of the American Academy of Child Psychiatry* 22: 231–37.

———. 1976. A psychodynamic approach to the study and treatment of child abusing parents, *Journal of the American Academy of Child Psychiatry* 15: 414–29.

Green, A.; R. Gaines; and A. Sandgrand. 1974. Child abuse: A pathological syndrome of family interaction, *American Journal of Psychiatry* 131: 882–86.

Green, A.; V. Liang; R. Gaines; and S. Sultan. 1980. Psychopathological assessment of child-abusing, neglecting, and normal mothers, *Journal of Nervous and Mental Diseases* 168: 356–60.

Green, A., and D. Schetky. 1988. True and false allegations of child sexual abuse. In D. Schetky and A. Green, eds., *Child sexual abuse: A handbook for health care and legal professionals.* New York: Brunner/Mazel.

Green, M. 1992. Expert witness and sufficiency of evidence in toxic substances litigation: The legacy of agent orange and bendectin litigation, *Northwestern University Law Review* 86: 643–99.

Green, R. 1978. Sexual identity of 37 children raised by homosexual or transsexual parents, *American Journal of Psychiatry* 135: 692–97.

Greenberg, M.; M. Speltz; and M. DeKlyen. 1993. The role of attachment in the early development of behavior problems, *Development and Psychopathology* 5: 191–214.

Grief, J. 1979. Fathers, children, and joint custody, *American Journal of Orthopsychiatry* 49: 311–19.

Griffith, D. 1991. The best interests standard: A comparison of the state's parens patriae authority and judicial oversight in best interests determinations for children and incompetent patients, *Issues in Law and Medicine* 7: 283–338.

Griner, D. 1991. (Note) Paying the piper: Third party payor liability for medical treatment decision, *Georgia Law Review* 25: 861–922.

Grisso, T. 1986. *Evaluating competencies.* New York: Plenum.

———. 1983. Juvenile's consent in delinquency proceedings. In G. Melton, G. Koocher, and M. Sacks, eds., *Children's competence to consent.* New York: Plenum.

———. 1981. *Juvenile's waiver of rights: Legal and psychological competence.* New York: Plenum.

Grisso, T., and P. Appelbaum. 1992. Is it ethical to offer predictions of future violence? *Law and Human Behavior* 16: 621–33.

Grisso, T.; M. Miller; and B. Sales. 1987. Competency to stand trial in juvenile court, *International Journal of Law and Psychiatry* 10: 1–20.

Grisso, T., and L. Vierling. 1978. Minor's consent to treatment: A developmental prospective, *Professional Psychology* 9: 412–27.

Grob, G. 1991. *From asylum to community: Mental health policy in modern America.* Princeton, NJ: Princeton University Press.

———. 1973. *Mental institutions in America: Social policy to 1875.* New York: Free Press.

———. 1966. *The state and the mentally ill: A history of Worcester State Hospital.* Chapel Hill: University of North Carolina Press.

Groth, A. 1982. The incest offender. In S. Sgroi, ed., *Handbook of clinical intervention in child sexual abuse.* Lexington, MA: Lexington Books.

Groth, N., and A. Burgess. 1979. Sexual trauma in the life histories of rapists and child molesters, *Victimology* 4: 10–16.

Group for the Advancement of Psychiatry. 1980. *Divorce, child custody, and the family.* New York: Mental Health Materials Center.

Group for the Advancement of Psychiatry. 1974. *Misuse of psychiatry in the criminal courts: Competence to stand trial.* New York: Group for the Advancement of Psychiatry.

Gruenberg, E., and J. Archer. 1979. Abandonment of responsibility for the seriously mentally ill, *Milbank Memorial Fund Quarterly/Health and Society* 57: 485–506.

Gudjonsson, G. 1984. A new scale of interrogative suggestibility, *Personality and Individual Differences* 5: 303–14.

Guggenheim, M. 1984. The right to be represented but not heard: Reflections on legal representation for children. *New York University Law Review* 59: 76–155.

Guggenheim, P., and R. Garmise. 1985. The assessment of psychopathology in juvenile delinquency: The family court perspective. In R. Rosner and R. Harmon, eds., *Criminal court consultation: Critical issues in American psychiatry and the law.* Vol. 5. New York: Plenum.

Guidubaldi, J. 1988. Differences in children's divorce adjustment across grade level and gender. In S. Wolchik and P. Karoly, eds., *Children of divorce.* Lexington, MA: Lexington Books.

Guidubaldi, J., and J. Perry. 1984. Divorce, socioeconomic status and children's cognitive-social competence at school entry, *American Journal of Orthopsychiatry* 54: 459–68.

Gunther, G. 1991. *Constitutional law.* 12th ed. Westbury, NY: Foundation Press.

———. 1972. The Supreme Court, 1971 Term—Foreword: In search of evolving doctrine on a changing court: A model for a newer equal protection, *Harvard Law Review* 86: 1–48.

Gurry, F. 1984. *Breach of confidence.* Oxford: Clarendon Press.

Gutheil, T. 1985. *Rogers v. Commissioner*: Denouement of an important right-to-refuse-treatment case, *American Journal of Psychiatry* 142: 213–16.

Gutheil, T., and P. Appelbaum. 1982. *Clinical handbook of psychiatry and the law.* New York: McGraw-Hill.

Guyer, M. 1991. Civil liability issues in the forensic evaluation. Paper delivered in an Institute on Forensic Psychiatry, Annual Conference of the American Academy of Child and Adolescent Psychiatry, San Francisco, CA.

Guze, S. 1976. *Criminality and psychiatric disorders*. New York: Oxford University Press.

Hacker, A. 1983. *U.S.: A statistical portrait of the American people*. New York: Viking.

Hafemeister, T., and G. Melton. 1987. The impact of social science research on the judiciary. In G. Melton, ed., *Reforming the law: Impact of child development research*. New York: Guilford.

Hagan, J.; A. Gillis; and J. Chan. 1978. Explaining official delinquency, *Sociological Quarterly* 19: 386–98.

Hall, M. 1978. Lesbian families: Cultural and clinical issues, *Social Work* 23: 380–85.

Hall, M. A. 1991. The defensive effect of medical practice policies in malpractice litigation, *Law and Contemporary Problems* (Spring) 54: 119–45.

————. 1988. Institutional control of physician behavior: Legal barriers to health care cost containment, *University of Pennsylvania Law Review* 137: 431–536.

Halleck, S. 1980. *Law in the practice of psychiatry: A handbook for clinicians*. New York: Plenum.

Handel, W., and B. Sherwyn. 1982. Surrogate parenting, *Trial* 18: 56–60.

Hannaway, P. 1970. Failure to thrive: A study of 100 infants and children, *Clinical Pediatrics* 9: 96–99.

Hare, R. 1986. Twenty years of experience with the Cleckley psychopath. In W. Reid, D. Dorr, A. Walker, and J. Bonner, eds., *Unmasking the psychopath: Antisocial personality and related syndromes*. New York: Norton.

Harper, F.; F. James; and O. Gray. 1986. *The law of torts*. 2d ed. Boston: Little, Brown.

Harris, J. 1972. *Congress and the legislative process*. 2d ed. New York: McGraw-Hill.

————. 1982. Non-organic failure-to-thrive syndromes: Reactive attachment disorder of infancy and psychosocial dwarfism of early childhood. In P. Accardo, ed., *Failure to thrive in infancy and early childhood*. Baltimore: University Park Press.

Harvard Medical Practice Group. 1990. *Parents, doctors, and lawyers: Medical injury, malpractice litigation, and patient compensation in New York*. Cambridge, MA: Harvard Medical Practice Group.

Haugaard, J. 1987. The consequences of child sexual abuse: A college survey. Unpublished manuscript, Department of Psychology, University of Virginia, Charlottesville.

Haugaard, J., and N. Reppucci. 1988. *The sexual abuse of children: A comprehensive guide to current knowledge and intervention strategies*. San Francisco: Jossey-Bass.

Henn, F.; R. Bardwell; and R. Jenkins. 1980. Juvenile delinquents revisited, *Archives of General Psychiatry* 37: 1160–63.

Hentoff, N. 1988. How the press fails all the Lisa Steinbergs. *Village Voice*, January 26.

Herjanic, B., and W. Campbell. 1977. Differentiating psychiatrically disturbed children on the basis of a structured interview, *Journal of Abnormal Child Psychology* 5: 127–34.

Herman, J. 1981. *Father–daughter incest*. Cambridge, MA: Harvard University Press.

Hermann, D. 1986. Barriers to providing effective treatment: A critique of revisions in procedural, substantive, and dispositional criteria in involuntary commitment, *Vanderbilt Law Review* 39: 83ff.

Hermann, D., and H. Gagliano. 1989. AIDS, therapeutic confidentiality, and warning third parties, *Maryland Law Review* 48: 55–76.

Herr, S. 1991. Children without home: Rights to education and to family stability, *University of Miami Law Review* 45: 337–85.

Hess, A.; K. Hess; and H. Hard. 1977. Intellective characteristics of mothers of failure-to-thrive syndrome children, *Child Care, Health and Development* 3: 377–87.

Hetherington, M. 1989. Coping with family transitions, *Child Development* 60: 1–14.

———. *Stress and coping in children and families.* Pp. 7–33 in A. Doyle, D. Gold, and D. Moskowitz, eds., *Children in families under stress: New directions for child development.* San Francisco: Jossey-Bass.

———. 1979. Divorce, a child's perspective, *American Psychologist* 34: 851–58.

Hetherington, M., and W. Clingempeel. 1992. *Coping with marital transitions.* Chicago: University of Chicago Press, for Society for Research in Child Development. Two full issues of *Child Development* 57, nos. 2 and 3: 1–242.

Hetherington, E.; M. Cox; and R. Cox. 1981. Effects of divorce on parents and children. In M. Lamb, ed., *Nontraditional families.* Hillsdale, NJ: Earlbaum.

———. 1979a. The development of children in mother-headed families. In D. Reiss and H. Hoffman, eds., *The American family: Dying or developing?* New York: Plenum.

———. 1979b. Play and social interaction in children following divorce, *Journal of Social Issues* 35: 26–49.

———. 1978. The aftermath of divorce. In J. Stevens, Jr., and M. Mathews, eds., *Mother–child, father–child relationships.* Washington: National Association for the Education of Young Children.

———. 1976. Divorced fathers, *Family Coordinator* 25: 417–28.

Hetherington, M.; M. Stanley-Hagen; and E. Anderson. 1989. Marital transitions, *American Psychologist* 44: 303–12.

Hindelang, M.; T. Hirschi; and J. Weis. 1981. *Measuring delinquency.* Beverly Hills, CA: Sage.

———. 1979. Correlates of delinquency: The illusion of discrepancy between self-report and official measures, *American Sociological Review* 44: 995–1014.

Hinshaw, S.; B. Lakey; and E. Hart. 1993. Issues of taxonomy and comorbidity in the development of conduct disorder, *Development and Psychopathology* 5: 31–50.

Hirschi, T. 1969. *Causes of delinquency.* Berkeley: University of California Press.

Hodges, W.; R. Wechsler; and C. Ballantine. 1979. Divorce and the preschool child: Cumulative stress, *Journal of Divorce* 3: 55–67.

Hoeffer, B. 1981. Children's acquisition of sex-role behavior in lesbian mother families, *American Journal of Orthopsychiatry* 51: 536–44.

Hoge, S., and T. Grisso. 1992. Accuracy and expert testimony, *Bulletin of the American Academy of Psychiatry and the Law* 20: 67–76.

Holder, A. 1988. Constraints on experimentation: Protecting children to death, *Yale Law Review and Policy Review* 6: 137–56.

Hollar, S. 1989. The never-never land of mental health law: A review of the legal rights of youth committed by their parents to psychiatric facilities in California, *Berkeley Women's Law Journal* 4: 300–15.

Holmes, O. 1881. *The Common Law*. Boston: Little, Brown.

Horner, S. 1990. The Health Care Quality Improvement Act of 1986: Its history, provisions, application and implications, *American Journal of Law and Medicine* 16: 453.

Horner, T.; M. Guyer; and N. Kalter. 1993. Clinical expertise and the assessment of child sexual abuse, *Journal of the Academy of Child and Adolescent Psychiatry* 32: 925–31.

Horowitz, B., and I. Wolcock. 1981. Material deprivation, child maltreatment and agency interventions among poor families. In L. Pelton, ed., *The social context of child abuse and neglect*. New York: Human Sciences Press.

Horowitz, M. 1976. *Stress response syndromes*. New York: Jason Aronson.

Horowitz, R., and H. Davidson, 1984. *Legal rights of children*. Colorado Springs: Shepard's/McGraw-Hill.

Hoving, K.; N. Hamm; and P. Galvin. 1969. Social influence as a function of stimulus ambiguity at three age levels, *Developmental Psychology* 1: 631–36.

Howitt, D. 1993. *Child abuse errors: When good intentions go wrong*. New Brunswick, NJ: Rutgers University Press.

Huard, L. 1956. The law of adoption: Ancient and modern, *Vanderbilt Law Review* 9: 743–63.

Huber, P. 1991. *Galileo's revenge: Junk science in the court room*. New York: Basic Books.

Huefner, D. 1991. Judicial review of the special educational program requirements under the Education for All Handicapped Children Act: Where have we been and where should we be going? *Harvard Journal of Law and Public Policy* 14: 483–516.

Hutchens, D., and M. Kirkpatrick. 1985. Lesbian mothers/gay fathers. In D. Schetky and E. Benedek, eds., *Emerging issues in child psychology and the law*. New York: Brunner/Mazel.

Hyman, C. 1981, Families who injure their children. In H. Frude, ed., *Psychological approaches to child abuse*. Totowa, NJ: Rowman & Littlefield.

Hymans, A. 1992. Expert psychiatric evidence in sexual misconduct cases before state medical boards, *American Journal of Law and Medicine* 18: 171.

IJA–ABA Joint Commission. 1980. *Standards relating to interim status: The release, control, and detention of accused juvenile offenders between arrest and disposition*. Cambridge, MA: Ballinger.

Ilfeld, F.; H. Ilfeld; and J. Alexander. 1982. Does joint custody work? A first look at outcome data of relitigation, *American Journal of Psychiatry* 139: 62–66.

Irving, H.; M. Benjamin; and N. Trocme. 1984. Shared parenting: An empirical analysis utilizing a large data base. In J. Folberg, ed., *Joint custody and shared parenting*. New York: Guilford.

Isaac, R., and V. Armat. 1990. *Madness in the streets: How psychiatry and the law abandoned the mentally ill*. New York: Free Press.

Jackson, A.; N. Warner; R. Hornbein; N. Nelson; and E. Fortescue. 1980. Beyond the best interests of the child revisited: An approach to custody evaluations, *Journal of Divorce* 3: 207–22.

James, J., and J. Meyerding. 1977. Early sexual experience as a factor in prostitution, *Archives of Sexual Behavior* 7: 31–42.

Jameson, E., and S. King. 1989. The failure of the federal government to care for disabled children: A critical analysis of the Supplemental Security Income Program, *Columbia Human Rights Law Review* 20: 309–42.

Jampole, L., and K. Weber. 1987. An assessment of the behavior of sexually abused and nonsexually abused children with anatomically correct dolls, *Child Abuse and Neglect* 11: 187–92.

Jennings, W.; R. Kilkenny; and L. Kohlberg. 1983. Moral development theory and practice of youthful and adult offenders. In W. Laufer and J. Day, eds., *Personality, theory, moral development and criminal behavior*. Lexington, MA: Lexington Books.

Jensen, G., and J. Grabel. 1988. The erosion of purchased insurance, *Inquiry* 25: 328–43.

Johnson, A. 1990. *Out of Bedlam: The truth about deinstitutionalization*. New York: Basic Books.

Johnson, A., and S. Szurek. 1952. The genesis of antisocial acting-out in children and adults, *Psychoanalytic Quarterly* 21: 323–43.

Johnson, B., and H. Morse. 1968. Injured children and their parents, *Children* 15: 147–52.

Johnson, C.; L. Miranda; A. Sherman; and J. Weill. 1991. *Child poverty in America*. Washington, DC: Children's Defense Fund.

Johnston, J. 1989. *On the edge of evil: The rise of satanism in North America*. Dallas: Word Publishing.

Johnston, J., and L. Campbell. 1989. *Impasses of divorce*. New York: Free Press.

Jones, D., and M. McQuiston. 1985. *Interviewing the sexually abused child*. Denver: C. Henry Kempe National Center for the Prevention and Treatment of Child Abuse and Neglect.

Jones, J. 1992. *Bad blood: The Tuskegee syphilis experiment*. New and expanded ed. New York: Free Press.

Jones, N. 1991. Essential requirements of the Act: A short history and overview. *Milbank Quarterly* 69: 25–54.

Jorgenson, L.; S. Bisbing; and P. Sutherland. 1992. Therapist–patient sexual exploitation and insurance liability, *Tort and Insurance Law Journal* 27: 595–614.

Jurkovic, G., and N. Prentice. 1977. Relation of moral and cognitive development to dimensions of juvenile delinquency, *Journal of Abnormal Psychology* 86: 414–20.

Justice, B., and R. Justice. 1979. *The broken taboo*. New York: Human Sciences Press.

Kalter, N., and J. Rembar. 1981. The significance of a child's age at the time of parental divorce, *American Journal of Orthopsychiatry* 51: 85–100.

Kanovitz, J. 1992. Hypnotic memories and civil sexual abuse trials, *Vanderbilt Law Review* 45: 1185–1262.

Kaplow, L., and S. Shavell. 1989. Legal advice about information to present in litigation: Its effects and social desirability, *Harvard Law Review* 102: 565–615.

Katz, A., and L. Teitelbaum. 1978. PINS jurisdiction, the vagueness doctrine, and the rule of law, *Indiana Law Journal* 53: 1–34.

Katz, J. 1984. *Silent world of doctor and patient*. New York: Free Press.

Kaufman, I.; A. Peck; and C. Tagiuri. 1954. The family constellation in overt incestuous relations between father and daughter, *American Journal of Orthopsychiatry* 24: 266–79.

Kaye, D. 1982. The limits of the preponderance of the evidence standard: Justifiably naked statistical evidence and multiple causation, *American Bar Foundation Research Journal*, pp. 487–516.

Keeton, W., *et al.* 1984. *Prosser and Keeton on the Law of Torts*. 5th ed. St. Paul: West.

Kelly, J., and J. Wallerstein. 1976. The effects of parental divorce: Experiences of the child in later latency, *American Journal of Orthopsychiatry* 46: 256–69.

Kempe, H. 1973. A practical approach to the protection of the abused child and rehabilitation of the abusing parent, *Pediatrics* 51: 804–12.

Kempe, H.; F. Silverman; B. Steele; W. Proegemueller; and H. Selver. 1962. The battered child syndrome, *Journal of the American Medical Association* 181: 17–24.

Kempe, R., and H. Kempe. 1978. *Child abuse*. Cambridge, MA: Harvard University Press.

Kendall, P., and A. Finch. 1978. A cognitive-behavioral treatment of impulsivity: A group comparison study, *Journal of Consulting and Clinical Psychology* 46: 110–18.

Kiesler, C., and A. Sibulkin. 1987. *Mental hospitalization: Myths and facts about a national crisis*. Newbury Park, CA: Sage Publications.

King, J. H. 1986. *The law of medical malpractice*. 2d ed. St. Paul: West.

King, J. L. 1980. *A comparative analysis of juvenile codes 39–40*. Washington: Office of Juvenile Justice and Delinquency Prevention.

Kinsey, A.; W. Pomeroy; C. Martin; and P. Gebhard. 1953. *Sexual behavior in the human female*. Philadelphia: Saunders.

Kirkpatrick, M.; K. Smith; and R. Roy. 1981. Lesbian mothers and their children: A comparative study, *American Journal of Orthopsychiatry* 51: 545–51.

Klaff, R. 1982. The tender years doctrine: A defense, *California Law Review* 70: 335–72.

Klassen, D., and W. O'Connor. 1988. A prospective study of predictors of violence in adult male mental patients, *Law and Human Behavior* 12: 143–58.

Klein, M. 1976. Issues and realities in police diversion programs, *Crime and Delinquency* 22: 421–27.

Kluft, R. 1984. Multiple personality in childhood, *Psychiatric Clinics of North America* 7: 121–34.

Knapp, S. 1987. *Privileged communications in the mental health professions*. New York: Van Nostrand Reinhold.

Knight, B.; F. Osborn; and D. West. 1977. Early marriage and criminal tendency in males, *British Journal of Criminology* 17: 348–60.

Kohlberg, L. 1976. Moral stages and socialization: The cognitive-developmental approach. In T. Lickona, ed., *Moral development and behavior: Theory, research and social issues*. New York: Holt, Rinehart & Winston.

Kopf, K. 1970. Family variables and school adjustment of eighth grade father-absent boys, *Family Coordinator* 19: 145–50.

Koppitz, E. 1968. *Psychological evaluation of children's human figure drawings.* New York: Grune & Stratton.

Kotelchuk, M. 1980. Non-organic failure to thrive: The status of interactional and environmental etiologic theories, *Advances in Behavioral Pediatrics* 1: 29–51.

Kuhn, T. 1970. *The structure of scientific revolutions.* 2d ed. enl. Chicago: University of Chicago Press.

Kurdek, L.; D. Blisk; and A. Siesly. 1981. Correlates of children's long-term adjustment to their parents' divorce, *Developmental Psychology* 17: 565–79.

Lacey, M., and K. Haakonsson, eds. 1991. *A culture of rights.* Cambridge, Eng.: Woodrow Wilson Center, Cambridge University Press.

LaFave, W. 1965. *Arrest: The decision to take a suspect into custody.* Boston: Little, Brown.

LaFave, W., and A. Scott. 1986. *Criminal law*, 2nd ed. St. Paul, MN: West Publishing Co.

LaFond, J., and M. Durham. 1992. *Back to the asylum: The future of mental health law and policy in the United States.* New York: Oxford University Press.

Landes, W., and R. Posner. 1987. *The Economic Structure of Tort Law.* Cambridge: Harvard University Press.

Landsman, K., and M. Minow. 1978. Lawyering for the child: Principles of representation in custody and visitation disputes arising from divorce. *Yale Law Journal* 87: 1126–90.

Lange, J. 1928. *Crime as destiny.* London: Allen & Unwin (English translation, 1931).

Langelier, P., and B. Nurcombe. 1984. *Family evaluation in child custody disputes.* Unpublished manuscript, Department of Psychiatry, University of Vermont, Burlington.

Langevin, R.; L. Handy; H. Hook; D. Day; and A. Russon. 1983. Are incestuous fathers pedophilic and aggressive? In R. Langevin, ed., *Erotic preference, gender identity and aggression.* Hillsdale, NJ: Erlbaum.

Langsley, D.; M. Schwartz; and R. Fairbairn. 1968. Father–son incest. *Comprehensive Psychiatry* 9: 218–26.

Lanning, K., and A. Burgess. 1984. Child pornography and sex rings, *F.B.I. Law Enforcement Bulletin*, January, pp. 1–7.

Larrivee, B., and L. Cook. 1979. Mainstreaming: A study of the variables affecting teacher attitudes, *Journal of Special Education* 13: 315–24.

LaTessa, E.; L. Travis; and G. Wilson. 1984. Juvenile diversion: Factors related to decision-making and outcome. Pp. 145–68 in S. Decker, ed., *Juvenile justice policy: analyzing trends and outcome.* Beverly Hills, CA: Sage.

Latin, H. 1987. Good science, bad regulation, and toxic assessment, *Yale Journal on Regulation* 5: 89–148.

Lazare, A. 1973. Hidden conceptual models in clinical psychiatry, *New England Journal of Medicine* 288: 345–51.

Lerman, H. 1988. The psychoanalytic legacy: From whence we come. In L. Walker, ed., *Handbook on sexual abuse of children: Assessment and treatment issues.* New York: Springer.

Leventhal, J. 1981. Risk factors for child abuse: Methodologic standards in case-controlled studies, *Pediatrics* 68: 684–90.

Leventhal, J.; J. Hamilton; S. Rekedal; A. Tebano-Micci; and C. Eyster. 1989. Anatomically correct dolls used in interviews in young children suspected of having been sexually abused, *Pediatrics* 84: 900–906.

Levitin, T. 1979. Children of divorce: An introduction, *Journal of Social Issues* 35: 1–25.

Levitt, E. 1971. Research on psychotherapy with children. In A. Bergin and S. Garfield, eds., *Handbook of psychotherapy and behavior change*. New York: Wiley.

Levmore, S. 1986. Waiting for rescue: An essay on the evolution and incentive structure of the law of affirmative obligations, *Virginia Law Review* 72: 879–941.

Lewin, E. 1981. Lesbians and motherhood: Implications for child custody, *Human Organization* 40: 6–14.

Lewis, D. A.; S. Roger; and H. Rosenberg. 1991. *Worlds of the mentally ill: How de-institutionalization works in a city*. Carbondale: Southern Illinois University Press.

Lewis, D. O. 1980. Diagnostic evaluation of the delinquent child: Psychiatric, psychological, neurological and educational components. In D. Schetky and E. Benedek, eds., *Child psychiatry and the law*. New York: Brunner/Mazel.

Lewis, D. O., and D. Balla. 1976. *Delinquency and psychopathology*. New York: Grune & Stratton.

Lewis, D. O.; J. Pincus; S. Shanok; and G. Glaser. 1982. Psychomotor epilepsy and violence in an incarcerated adolescent population, *American Journal of Psychiatry* 139: 882–87.

Lewis, D. O.; S. Shanok; and D. Balla; 1979. Perinatal difficulties, head and face trauma, and child abuse in the medical histories of seriously disturbed delinquent children, *American Journal of Psychiatry* 136: 419–23.

Lewis, D. O.; S. Shanok; J. Pincus; and G. Glaser. 1979. Violent juvenile delinquents: Psychiatric, neurological, psychological, and abuse factors, *Journal of the American Academy of Child Psychiatry* 18: 307–19.

Lewis, K. 1980. Children of lesbians: Their point of view, *Social Work* 25: 198–203.

Lewis, M., and P. Sarrel. 1969. Some psychological aspects of seduction, incest, and rape in childhood, *Journal of the American Academy of Child Psychiatry* 8: 606–19.

Lidz, C.; A. Meisel; E. Zerubavel; M. Carter; R. Sestak; and L. Roth. 1984. *Informed consent: A study of decisionmaking in psychiatry*. New York: Guilford Press.

Lidz, C.; E. Mulvey; and J. Gardner. 1993. The accuracy of predictions of violence to others, *Journal of American Medical Association* 269: 1007.

Lieberman, K., and A. Derse. 1992. HIV-positive health care workers and the obligation to disclose: Do patients have a right to know? *Journal of Legal Medicine* 13: 333–56.

Lifshitz, M.; D. Berman; A. Galili; and D. Gilad. 1977. Bereaved children: The effects of mother's perception and social system organization under short-term adjustment, *Journal of the American Academy of Child Psychiatry* 16: 272–84.

Lindberg, M. 1991. An interactive approach to assessing the susceptibility and testimony of witnesses. Chapter 4 in J. Doris, ed., *The suggestibility of children's recollections*. Washington: American Psychological Association.

Lipkin, R. 1990. Free will: Responsibility and the promise of forensic psychiatry, *International Journal of Law and Psychiatry* 13: 331–59.

Lipsitt, P.; D. Lelos; and L. McGarry. 1971. Competency for trial: A screening instrument, *American Journal of Psychiatry* 128: 105–9.

Lipton, D.; R. Martinson; and J. Wilks. 1975. *The effectiveness of correctional treatment: A survey of treatment evaluation studies.* New York: Praeger.

Litwack, T. 1993. On the ethics of dangerousness assessments, *Law and Human Behavior* 17: 479–82.

Litwack, T., and L. Schlesinger. 1987. Assessing and predicting violence: Research, law and application. In I. Weiner and A. Hess, eds., *Handbook of forensic psychology.* New York: Wiley.

Loeber, R., and T. Dishion. 1983. Early predictors of male delinquency: A review, *Psychological Bulletin* 94: 68–99.

Loeber, R.; T. Dishion; and G. Patterson. 1984. Multiple gating: A multistage assessment procedure for identifying youths at risk for delinquency, *Journal of Research on Crime and Delinquency* 24: 7–32.

Loeber, R., and M. Stouthamer-Loeber. 1987. The prediction of delinquency. In H. Quay, ed., *Handbook of juvenile delinquency.* New York: Wiley.

———. 1986. Family factors as correlates and predictors of juvenile conduct problems and delinquency. In N. Morris and M. Tonry, eds., *Crime and justice: An annual review of research.* Vol. VII. Chicago: University of Chicago Press.

Loeber, R.; P. Wung; K. Keenan; B. Giroux; M. Stouthamer-Loeber; W. Van Kammen; and B. Mangham. 1993. Developmental pathways in disruptive behavior disorders, *Development and Psychopathology* 5: 103–34.

Loveless, C. 1989. Sexual abuse allegations in child custody cases, *Journal of the American Academy of Matrimonial Lawyers* 5: 47–61.

Low, P.; J. Jeffries; and R. Bonnie. 1986. *The trial of John W. Hinckley, Jr.: A case study in the insanity defense.* New York: Foundation Press.

Lowery, C. 1981. Child custody decisions in divorce proceedings: A survey of judges, *Professional Psychology* 12: 492–98.

Luepnitz, D. 1982. *Child custody: A study of families after divorce.* Lexington, MA: Lexington Books.

Lukianowicz, N. 1972. Incest, *British Journal of Psychiatry* 120: 301–13.

Lustig, N.; J. Dresser; S. Spellman; and T. Murray. 1966. Incest: A family group survival pattern, *Archives of General Psychiatry* 14: 31–40.

MacCarthy, D. 1974. Effects of emotional disturbance and deprivation (maternal rejection) on somatic growth. In J. Davis and J. Dobbing, eds., *Scientific foundations of pediatrics.* Philadelphia: Saunders.

Maccoby, E., and R. Mnookin. 1992. *Dividing the child: Social and legal dilemmas of custody.* Cambridge, MA: Harvard University Press.

MacFarlane, K., and S. Krebs. 1986. Techniques for interviewing and evidence gathering. In K. MacFarlane, ed., *Sexual abuse of young children.* New York: Guilford.

Machotka, P.; F. Pittman; and K. Flomenhaft. 1967. Incest as a family affair, *Family Process* 6: 98–116.

Mack, J. 1909. The juvenile court, *Harvard Law Review* 23: 104–22.

MacVicar, K. 1979. Psychotherapeutic issues in the treatment of sexually abused girls, *Journal of the American Academy of Child Psychiatry* 18: 342–53.

Magid, K., and C. McKelvey. 1987. *High risk: Children without a conscience.* Golden, CO: M&M Publishing.

Mandel, J.; M. Hotvedt; and R. Green. 1979. The lesbian parent: Comparison of heterosexual and homosexual mothers and children. Paper presented at the Annual Congress of the American Psychological Association, New York.

Manicas, P., and P. Secord. 1983. Implications for psychology of the new philosophy of science, *American Psychologist* 38: 399–413.

Marin, B.; D. Holmes; M. Guth; and P. Kovac. 1979. The potential of children as eyewitnesses: A comparison of adults and children on eyewitness tasks. *Law & Human Behavior* 3: 295–305.

Maron, A. 1975. Constitutional Problems of Diversion of Juvenile Delinquents, *Notre Dame Lawyer* 51: 22–47.

Marron, K. 1988. *Ritual abuse.* Toronto: Seal Books, McClelland–Bantam.

Martin, G. 1992. The delinquent and the juvenile court: Is there still a place for rehabilitation? *Connecticut Law Review* 25: 57–93.

Martin, H. 1981. The neuropsychodevelopmental aspects of child abuse and neglect. In N. Ellerstein, ed., *Child abuse and neglect: A medical reference.* New York: Wiley.

Martin, H.; E. Conway; P. Beezley; and H. Kempe. 1974. The development of abused children, part I: A review of the literature, *Advances in Pediatrics* 21: 25–44.

Martin, M.; M. Trebilcock; A. Lawson; and P. Lewis. 1993. Limits of freedom of contract: Commercialization of reproductive materials and services. Unpublished.

Martin, M., and J. Walters. 1982. Familial correlates of selected types of child abuse and neglect, *Journal of Marriage and the Family* 44: 267–76.

Martinson, R. 1974. What works? Questions and answers about prison reform, *Public Interest* 35: 22–54.

Marvasti, J. 1986. Incestuous mothers, *American Journal of Forensic Psychiatry* 7: 63–68.

Mason, M. 1991. A judicial dilemma: Expert witness testimony in child abuse cases, *Journal of Psychiatry and Law* 19: 185–219.

Maxwell, A. 1971. Multivariate statistical methods and classification problems, *British Journal of Psychiatry* 119: 121–27.

McBride, C. 1990. (Comment) Educational malpractice—Judicial recognition of a limited duty of educators toward individual students: A state law cause of action for educational negligence, *University of Illinois Law Review* 1990: 475–95.

McCann, J.; J. Voris; M. Simon; and R. Wells. 1990. Comparison of genital examination techniques in prepubertal girls, *Pediatrics* 85: 182–87.

———. 1989. Perianal findings in prepubertal children for nonabuse, *Child Abuse and Neglect* 13: 179–93.

McCarthy, L. 1986. Mother–child incest: Characteristics of the offender, *Child Welfare* 65: 447–58.

McCoid, A. 1959. The care required of medical practitioners, *Vanderbilt Law Review* 12: 549–632.

McCord, J. 1978. A thirty-year follow-up of treatment effects, *American Psychologist* 33: 284–89.

McCord, W., and J. McCord. 1964. *Psychopath: An essay on the criminal mind.* New York: Van Nostrand Reinhold.

McCormack, A.; M. Janus; and A. Burgess. 1986. Runaway youths and sexual victimization: Gender differences in an adolescent runaway population, *Child Abuse and Neglect* 10: 387–95.

McCormick, A. 1984. *McCormick on evidence*. E. Cleary, general editor. 3d ed. St. Paul: West Publishing.

McDermott, J. 1968. Parental divorce in early childhood, *American Journal of Psychiatry* 124: 1424–31.

McFadden, E. 1983. Placement of sibling groups, single parent adoption and transracial adoption: An analysis. In M. Hardin, ed., *Foster children in the courts*. Boston: Butterwork Legal Publishers.

McFarlane, A. 1987. Posttraumatic phenomena in a longitudinal study of children following a natural disaster, *Journal of the American Academy of Child and Adolescent Psychiatry* 26: 764–69.

McGarry, A.; W. Curran; P. Lipsitt; D. Lelos; R. Schwitzgebel; and A. Rosenberg. 1974. *Competency to stand trial and mental illness*. New York: Jason Aronson.

McGovern, K., and J. Peters. 1988. Guidelines for assessing sex offenders. In L. Walker, ed., *Handbook on sexual abuse of children: Assessment and treatment issues*. New York: Springer.

McIntyre, K. 1981. Role of mothers in father–daughter incest: A feminist analysis, *Social Work* 21: 462–66.

Meadow, R. 1982. Munchausen syndrome by proxy, *Archives of Diseases of Children* 57: 92–98.

———. 1977. Munchausen syndrome by proxy: The hinterland of child abuse, *Lancet* 2: 343–45.

Meadows, G. 1992. Wrongful death and the lost society of the unborn, *Journal of Legal Medicine* 13: 99–114.

Mechanic, D. 1975. Some social aspects of the medical malpractice dilemma, *Duke Law Journal*, pp. 1179–96.

Mednick, S. 1974. Electrodermal recovery and psychopathology. In S. Mednick, F. Schulsinger, J. Higgins, and B. Bell, eds., *Genetics, environment, and psychopathology*. Oxford: North-Holland.

Mednick, S.; W. Gabrielli; and B. Hutchings. 1984. Genetic influence in criminal convictions: Evidence from an adoption cohort, *Science* 224: 891–94.

Meisel, A. 1979. The exceptions to the informed consent doctrine: Striking a balance between competing values in medical decision making, *Wisconsin Review* 1979: 413–88.

Meiselman, K. 1978. *Incest: A psychological study of causes and effects with treatment recommendations*. San Francisco: Jossey-Bass.

Melton, G. 1981. Children's competency to testify, *Law and Human Behavior* 5: 73–85.

Melton, G.; J. Petrila; N. Poythress; and C. Slobogin. 1987. *Psychological evaluations for the courts: A handbook for mental health professionals and lawyers*. New York: Guilford.

Merton, R. 1957. *Social theory and social structure*. Glencoe, IL.: Free Press.

Miller, F. 1992. Denial of health care and informed consent in English and American law, *American Journal of Law and Medicine* 18: 37–71.

Miller, L. 1988. Neuropsychological perspectives on delinquency, *Behavioral Sciences and the Law* 6: 409–28.

Miller, W. 1958. Lower class culture as a generating milieu of gang delinquency, *Journal of Social Issues* 14: 5–19.

Mills, M.; B. Cummins; and J. Gracey. 1983. Legislative issues in mental health administration, *International Journal of Law and Psychiatry* 6: 39–55.

Minow, M. 1990. *Making all the difference: Inclusion, exclusion, and American law.* Ithaca, NY: Cornell University Press.

Mnookin, R. 1985. *In the interest of children: Advocacy, law reform and public policy.* New York: W. H. Freeman.

———. 1978. *Child, family, and state: Problems and materials on children and the law.* Boston: Little, Brown.

———. 1975. Child custody adjudication: Judicial functions in the face of indeterminacy, *Law and Contemporary Problems* 39 (Summer): 226–93.

Mnookin, R., and L. Kornhauser. 1979. Bargaining in the shadow of the law: The case of divorce, *Yale Law Journal* 88: 950–97.

Mnookin, R., and D. Weisberg. 1989. *Child, family and state: Problems and materials on children and the law.* Boston: Little, Brown.

Monahan, J. 1981. *The clinical prediction of violent behavior.* Rockville, MD: U.S. Department of Health and Human Services.

Moore, J. 1982. Project thrive: A supportive treatment approach to the parents of children with non-organic failure to thrive, *Child Welfare* 61: 389–99.

Moore, M. M. 1985. Parents' support obligations to their adult children. *Akron Law Review* 19: 183–96.

Moore, M. S. 1984. *Law and psychiatry: Rethinking the relationship.* Cambridge: Cambridge University Press.

Moore, P. 1986. *Useful information on suicide.* Washington: U.S. Department of Health and Human Services.

Moran, R. 1981. *Knowing right from wrong: The insanity defense of Daniel M'Naghten.* New York: Free Press.

Morreim, H. 1989. Stratified scarcity: Redefining the standard of care, *Law, Medicine and Health Care* 17: 356–67.

———. 1987. Cost containment and the standard of medical care, *California Law Review* 75: 1719–63.

Morris, N. 1982. *Madness and the criminal law.* Chicago: University of Chicago Press.

Morris, N.; R. Bonnie; and J. Finer. 1986. Debate: Should the insanity defense be abolished? *Journal of Law and Health*, pp. 113–40.

Morse, C.; O. Sahler; and S. Friedman. 1970. A three-year follow-up study of abused and neglected children, *American Journal of Diseases of Children* 120: 439–46.

Morse, H. 1967. The tort liability of a psychiatrist, *Syracuse Law Review* 18: 691–727.

Morse, S. 1978a. Crazy behavior, morals, and science: An analysis of mental health law, *Southern California Law Review* 51: 527–654.

———. 1978b. Law and mental health professionals: The limits of expertise, *Professional Psychology* 9: 389–99.

Moss, L., ed. 1985. 1984 comparison of AFDC payments and poverty income levels, *Clearinghouse Review* 18: 962–71.

Mossman, D. 1992. The psychiatrist and execution competency: Fording murky ethical waters, *Case Western Reserve Law Review* 43: 1–95.

Mosteller, R. 1992. Child abuse reporting laws and attorney client confidences, *Duke Law Journal* 42: 203–78.

Mountain, H.; M. Nicholson; C. Spencer; and L. Walker. 1984. *Incest: Colorado State Department of Social Services revitalization training*. Denver: Nicholson, Spencer & Associates.

Mowrer, O. 1950. *Learning theory and personality dynamics*. New York: Ronald.

Mrazek, P. 1981. Special problems in the treatment of child sexual abuse. In P. Mrazek and C. Kempe, eds., *Sexually abused children and their families*. Oxford and New York: Pergamon.

Mullin, E. 1990. (Note) At what age should they die? The United States Supreme Court decision with respect to juvenile offenders and the death penalty, *Thurgood Marshall Law Review* 16: 161–89.

Muram, D. 1989a. Child sexual abuse: Genital tract findings in prepubertal girls, I. The unaided medical examination, *American Journal of Obstetrics and Gynecology* 160: 328–33.

————. 1989b. Child sexual abuse: Relationship between sexual acts and genital findings, *Child Abuse and Neglect* 13: 211–16.

Muram, D., and S. Elias. 1989. Child sexual abuse: Genital tract findings in prepubertal girls, II. Comparison of colposcopic and unaided examinations, *American Journal of Obstetrics and Gynecology* 160: 333–35.

Murray, J., ed. 1983. *Status offenders: A sourcebook*. Boys Town, NB: Boys Town Center.

Myers, J. 1992. *Evidence in child abuse and neglect*. 2d ed. 2 vols. New York: John Wiley & Sons.

Nace, A. 1991. (Note) Market share liability: A current assessment of a decade-old doctrine, *Vanderbilt Law Review* 44: 395–439.

National Advisory Committee for Juvenile Justice and Delinquency Prevention. 1980. *The Standards for the Administration of Juvenile Justice*. Washington: U.S. Department of Justice.

National Center on Child Abuse and Neglect. 1988. *Study Findings: Study of National Incidence and Prevalence of Child Abuse and Neglect, 1988*. Washington: U.S. Department of Health and Human Services.

National Council of Juvenile and Family Court Judges. 1984. The juvenile court and serious offenders: Thirty-eight recommendations, *Juvenile and Family Court Journal*, p. 5.

Neal, D., and D. Kirp. 1985. The allure of legalization reconsidered: The case of special education, *Law and Contemporary Problems* 48: 63–87.

Neal, J. 1983. Children's understanding of their parents' divorces. In L. Kurdek, ed., *Children and divorce*. New Directions for Child Development series. San Francisco: Jossey-Bass.

Nejelski, P. 1976. Diversion: Unleashing the hounds of heaven? In M. Rosenheim, ed., *Pursuing justice for the child*. Chicago: University of Chicago Press.

Neubauer, P. 1960. The one-parent child and his oedipal development, *Psychoanalytic Study of the Child* 15: 286–309.

New York State Task Force on Life and the Law. 1992. *When others must choose: Deciding for patients without capacity*. New York City.

Newberger, E., and R. Bourne. 1978. The medicalization and legalization of child abuse, *American Journal of Orthopsychiatry* 48: 593–607.

Newberger, E.; R. Reed; J. Daniel; J. Hyde; and M. Kotelchuk. 1977. Pediatric social illness, *Pediatrics* 60: 178–85.

Newman, J.; C. Widon; and S. Nathan. 1985. Passive avoidance in syndromes of disinhibition: Psychopathy and extraversion, *Journal of Personality and Social Psychology* 48: 1316–27.

Nicholson, R., and W. Johnson. 1991. Prediction of competency to stand trial: Contribution of offense, clinical characteristics, and psycholegal ability, *International Journal of Law and Psychiatry* 14: 287–97.

Note. 1992. Physician-assisted suicide and the right to die with assistance, *Harvard Law Review* 105: 2021–40.

Note. 1985. Rethinking medical malpractice law in light of Medicare cost cutting, *Harvard Law Review* 98: 1004–22.

Nottingham, E., and R. Mattson. 1981. A validation study of the competency screening test, *Law and Human Behavior* 5: 329–35.

Nouryan, L., and M. Weisel. 1990. Education of Children with Disabilities. *Journal of Psychiatry and Law* 18: 405–21.

Nunan, S. 1980. Joint custody versus single custody effects on child development, *Dissertation Abstracts International* 41: 4680B–81B.

Nurcombe, B. 1989. Goal-directed treatment planning and the principles of brief hospitalization, *Journal of American Academy of Child and Adolescent Psychiatry* 28: 26–30.

———. 1986. The child as witness: Competency and credibility, *Journal of the American Academy of Child Psychiatry* 25: 473–80.

Nurcombe, B.; J. LaBarbera; M. Tramontana; W. Mitchell; and W. Begtrup. 1994. Dissociative hallucinosis. In F. Volkmar, ed., *Psychotic disorders in childhood and adolescence.* Washington, DC: American Psychiatric Press.

Nurcombe, B., and J. Unutzer. 1991. Ritual abuse of children: Clinical features and forensic evaluation, *American Journal of Child and Adolescent Psychiatry* 30: 272–76.

Oates, R., and J. Yu. 1971. Children with non-organic failure to thrive, *Medical Journal of Australia* 2: 199–203.

O'Boyle, R. 1984. Voluntary minor mental patients: A realistic balancing of the competing interests of parent, child, and state, *Southwestern Law Journal* 37: 1179–1202.

O'Callaghan, M., and D. Hull. 1978. Failure to thrive or failure to rear? *Archives of Diseases of Children* 53: 788–93.

Ogloff, J., ed. 1992. *Law and psychology: The broadening of the discipline.* Durham, NC: Carolina Academic Press.

Oleszek, W. 1989. *Congressional procedures and the policy process.* 3d ed. Washington, DC: CQ Press.

O'Neil, W. 1981. *Educational ideologies: Contemporary expressions of educational philosophy.* Santa Monica, CA: Goodyear.

Orfinger, M. 1989. Battered child syndrome: Evidence of prior acts in disguise, *Florida Law Review* 41: 345–67.

Ornstein, P. 1991. Commentary: Putting interviewing in context. Pp. 147–52 in J. Doris, ed., *The suggestibility of children's recollections.* Washington: American Psychological Association.

Orr, D., and M. Downes. 1985. Self-concept of adolescent sexual abuse victims, *Journal of Youth and Adolescence* 14: 401–10.

Orthner, D., and K. Lewis. 1979. Evidence of a single father competence in child-rearing, *Family Law Quarterly* 13: 27–47.

Pagelow, M. 1980. Heterosexual and lesbian single mothers: a comparison of problems, coping and solutions, *Journal of Homosexuality* 5: 189–204.

Palmer, T. 1974. The California youth authority treatment project, *Federal Probation* 38: 3–14.

Palombi, J. 1980. Competence and criminal responsibility. In D. Schetky and E. Benedek, eds., *Child psychiatry and the law*. New York: Brunner/Mazel.

Panella, D., and S. Henggeler. 1986. The peer relations of conduct disordered, anxiety-withdrawal disordered, and well adjusted black adolescents, *Journal of Abnormal Child Psychology* 14: 1–11.

Park, R.; E. Burgess; and R. McKenzie. 1925. *The city*. Chicago: University of Chicago Press.

Patterson, C. 1992. Children of lesbian and gay parents, *Child Development* 63: 1025–42.

Patterson, G. 1976. *Mothers: The unacknowledged victims*. Chicago: University of Chicago Press for the Society for Research in Child Development.

Patterson, G.; P. Chamberlain; and J. Reid. 1982. A comparative evaluation of a parent-training program, *Behavior Therapy* 13: 638–50.

Patton, W. 1990. The world where parallel lines converge: The privilege against self-incrimination in concurrent civil and criminal child abuse proceedings, *Georgia Law Review* 24: 473–524.

Payer, L. 1988. *Medicine and culture: Varieties of treatment in the United States, England, West Germany, and France*. New York: Holt.

Paykel, E. 1978. Contribution of life events to the causation of psychiatric illness, *Psychological Medicine* 8: 245–53.

Pearson, R. 1976. The role of custom in medical malpractice cases, *Indiana Law Journal* 51: 528–89.

Pearson, T., and M. Ring. 1983. Judicial decision-making in contested custody cases, *Journal of Family Law* 21: 703–24.

Perr, I. 1986. Sexual involvement with patients, *Psychiatric Times*, May, p. 6.

———. 1985. Psychiatric malpractice issues. In S. Rachlin ed., *Legal encroachment on psychiatric practice*. New Dimensions to Mental Health Services series, no. 25. San Francisco: Jossey-Bass.

Peters, D. 1991. The influence of stress and arousal on the child witness. Chapter 5 in J. Doris, ed., *The suggestibility of children's recollections*. Washington: American Psychological Association.

Pett, M. 1982. Correlates of children's social adjustment following divorce, *Journal of Divorce* 5 (Summer): 25–39.

Petti, T. 1980. The juvenile murderer. In D. Schetky and E. Benedek, eds., *Child psychiatry and the law*. New York: Brunner/Mazel.

Pfeuffer, D. 1990. (Note) *Chiles v. Chiles:* Divorce, Torts, and Scandal—Texas Style, *Baylor Law Review* 42:309–27.

Phear, W.; J. Beck; B. Hauser; S. Clark; and R. Whitney. 1984. An empirical analysis of custody agreements: Joint versus sole legal custody. In J. Folberg, ed., *Joint custody and shared parenting*. New York: Guilford.

Piaget, J. 1932. *The moral judgment of the child*. London: K. Paul, Trench, Trubner & Co.

Plummer, K. 1979. Misunderstanding labelling perspectives. In D. Downes and P. Rock, eds., *Deviant interpretations*. London: Robertson.

Pocock, J. 1975. *The Machiavellian moment: Florentine political thought and the Atlantic Republican tradition*. Princeton, NJ: Princeton University Press.

Pollitt, E.; A. Weisel; and C. Chan. 1975. Psychosocial development and behavior of mothers of failure-to-thrive children, *American Journal of Orthopsychiatry* 45: 525–37.

Pollock, L. 1983. *Forgotten children: Parent–child relations from 1500 to 1900*. New York: Cambridge University Press.

Pollock, V.; J. Briere; L. Schneider; J. Knop; S. Mednick; and D. Goodwin. 1990. Childhood antecedents of antisocial behavior: Parental alcoholism and physical abusiveness, *American Journal of Psychiatry* 147: 1290–93.

Pope, K. 1990. Therapist–patient sexual involvement: A review of the research, *Clinical Psychology Review* 10: 477–90.

Porter, F.; L. Blick; and S. Sgroi. 1982. Treatment of the sexually abused child. In S. Sgroi, ed., *Handbook of clinical intervention in child sexual abuse*. Lexington, MA: Lexington Books.

Posner, R. 1987. The Decline of Law as an Autonomous Discipline 1962–1987, *Harvard Law Review* 100: 761–80.

Potuto, J. 1987. *Stanley + Ferber*—The constitutional crime of at-home child pornography possession, *Kentucky Law Journal* 76: 15–80.

Poythress, N. 1980. Coping on the witness stand: Learned responses to "learned treatises." *Professional Psychology,* 11: 169–79.

Pritchard, J. 1837. *A treatise on insanity and other disorders affecting the mind*. New York: Arno Press.

Putnam, F. 1985. Dissociation as a response to extreme trauma. In R. Kluft, ed., *Childhood antecedents of multiple personality*. Washington: American Psychiatric Press.

Putnam, F.; J. Guroff; E. Silberman; and L. Barban. 1986. The clinical phenomenology of multiple personality disorder: 100 recent cases, *Journal of Clinical Psychiatry* 47: 285–93.

Pynoos, R., and S. Eth. 1984. The child as witness to homicide, *Journal of Social Issues* 40: 87–108.

Qual, S. 1986. A survey of medical malpractice tort reform, *William Mitchell Law Review* 12: 417–57.

Quay, H. 1987a. Institutional treatment. In H. Quay, ed., *Handbook of juvenile delinquency*. New York: Wiley.

———. 1987b. Intelligence. In H. Quay, ed., *Handbook of juvenile delinquency*. New York: Wiley.

———. 1987c. Patterns of delinquent behavior. In H. Quay, ed., *Handbook of juvenile delinquency*. New York: Wiley.

———. 1986a. Classification. In H. Quay and J. Werry, eds., *Psychopathological disorders of childhood*. 3d ed. New York: Wiley.

———. 1986b. Conduct disorders. In H. Quay, and J. Werry, eds., *Psychopathological disorders of childhood*. 3d ed. New York: Wiley.

Quay, H., and R. Levinson. 1967. The prediction of the institutional adjustment of four subgroups of delinquent boys. Unpublished report, Bureau of Prisons, United States Department of Justice.

Quay, H., and C. Love. 1977. The effect of a juvenile diversion program on rearrests, *Criminal Justice and Behavior* 4: 377–96.

Quill, T.; C. Cassel; and D. Meier. 1992. Care of the hopelessly ill: Proposed clinical criteria for physician assisted suicide, *New England Journal of Medicine* 327: 1380–84.

Quinn, K. 1988. Children and deception. In R. Rogers, ed., *Clinical assessment of malingering and deception*. New York: Guilford.

Quinsey, V.; T. Chaplin; and W. Carrigan. 1979. Sexual preferences among incestuous and nonincestuous child molesters, *Behavioral Therapy* 10: 562–65.

Rachels, J. 1986. *The end of life: The morality of euthanasia*. New York: Oxford University Press.

Rappaport, D., and J. Parry, eds., 1986. *The right to refuse antipsychotic medication*. Washington: ABA Committee on the Mentally Disabled.

Raskin, D., and P. Esplin. 1991. Assessment of children's statements of sexual abuse. Chapter 9 in J. Doris, ed., *The suggestibility of children's recollections*. Washington: American Psychological Association.

Raskin, D., and M. Steller. 1989. Assessing the credibility of allegations of child sexual abuse: Polygraph examinations and statement analysis. In H. Wegener, F. Losel, and J. Haisch, eds., *Criminal behavior and the justice system: Psychological perspectives*. New York: Springer.

Ratner, G. 1985. A new legal duty for urban public schools: Effective education in basic skills. *Texas Law Review* 63: 777–864.

Read, J.; J. MacDonald; J. Fordham; and W. Pierce. 1982. *Materials on legislation*. Mineola, NY: Foundation Press.

Reckless, W. 1961. *The crime problem*. New York: Appleton-Century-Crofts.

Reid, J. 1986. Social-interaction patterns in families of abused and nonabused children. In C. Zahn-Waxler, M. Cummings, and R. Iannotti, eds., *Altruism and integration: Social and biological origins*. New York: Cambridge University Press.

Reinhart, M. 1987. Sexually abused boys, *Child Abuse and Neglect* 11: 229–35.

Reisner, R. 1985. *Law and the mental health system*. St. Paul: West Publishing.

Renshaw, D. 1982. *Incest: Understanding and treatment*. Boston: Little, Brown.

Reppucci, D. 1984. The wisdom of Solomon: Issues in child custody determination. In Reppucci *et al.* 1984.

Reppucci, D., *et al.* 1984. *Children, mental health and the law*. Beverly Hills, CA: Sage Publications.

Reskin, L. 1985. Parents must support disabled adult children, *American Bar Association Journal* 71: 133.

Roberts, A. 1989. *Juvenile justice: Policies, programs, and services*. Homewood, IL: Dorsey Press.

Robertson, J. 1988. *Psychiatric malpractice: Liability of mental health professionals*. New York: Wiley Law Publications.

———. 1983. Procreative liberty and the control of conception, pregnancy, and childbirth, *Virginia Law Review* 69: 405–64.

Robey, A. 1965. Criteria for competency to stand trial: A checklist for psychiatrists, *American Journal of Psychiatry* 122: 616–23.

Robins, L., and P. O'Neal. 1953. Clinical features of hysteria in children, *The Nervous Child* 10: 246–71.

Robinson, G. 1986a. Rethinking the allocation of medical malpractice risks between patients and providers, *Law and Contemporary Problems* 49 (Spring): 173–99.
———. 1986b. The medical malpractice crisis of the 1970's: A retrospective. *Law and Contemporary Problems* 49: 5–35.

Robinson, G., and K. Abraham. 1992. Collective justice in tort law, *Virginia Law Review* 78: 1481–1519.

Robitscher, J. 1978. Informed consent for psychoanalysis, *Journal of Psychiatry and the Law* 6: 363–70.

Roesch, R., and S. Golding. 1980. *Competency to stand trial*. Urbana: University of Illinois Press.

Rogers, C., and T. Terry. 1984. Clinical intervention with boy victims of sexual abuse. In I. Stuart and J. Greer, eds., *Victims of sexual aggression: Treatment of children, women, and men*. New York: Van Nostrand Reinhold.

Rogers, D.; J. Tripp; A. Bentovim; A. Robinson; D. Berry; and R. Goulding. 1976. Non-accidental poisoning: An extended syndrome of childhood abuse, *British Medical Journal* 1: 793–96.

Rohman, L.; B. Sales; and M. Low. 1987. The best interests of the child in custody disputes. In L. Weithorn, ed., *Psychology and child custody determinations*. Lincoln: University of Nebraska Press.

Roman, M., and W. Haddad. 1978. *The disposable parent*. New York: Holt, Rinehart & Winston.

Romig, D. 1978. Diversion from the juvenile justice system. In D. Romig, ed., *Justice for our children*. Lexington, MA: Lexington Books.

Rosanoff, A.; L. Handy; and I. Plessey. 1934. Criminality and delinquency in twins, *Journal of Criminal Law and Criminology* 24: 923–34.

Rosen, P. 1972. *The Supreme Court and social sciences*. Urbana: University of Illinois Press.

Rosenberg, I. 1983. Juvenile status offender statutes: New perspectives on an old problem, *University of California at Davis Law Review* 16: 283–323.

Rosenhan, D. 1973. On being sane in insane places, *Science* 179: 250–58.

Rosenn, D.; L. Loeb; and M. Jura. 1980. Differentiation of organic from non-organic failure-to-thrive syndrome in infancy, *Pediatrics* 66: 698–704.

Ross, A. 1986. Ritual child abuse: Is it real? *San Francisco Examiner*, September 29.

Ross, L. Moral grounding for the participation of children as organ donors, *Journal of Law, Medicine and Ethics* 21(2): 251–57.

Rossi, P. 1989. *Down and out in America: The origins of homelessness*. Chicago: University of Chicago Press.

Roth, L.; A. Meisel; and C. Lidz. 1977. Tests of competency to consent to treatment, *American Journal of Psychiatry* 134: 279–84.

Rothberg, B. 1983. Joint custody: Parental problems and satisfactions, *Family Process* 22: 43–52.

Rothman, B. 1989. *Recreating motherhood*. New York: Norton.

Rothstein, L. 1990. *Special education law*. White Plains, NY: Langman.

Rotter, J. 1966. Generalized expectancies for internal versus external control of reinforcement, *Psychological Monographs, General and Applied 80*: whole number
609.

Ruch, L., and S. Chandler. 1982. The crisis impact of sexual assault on three victim
groups: Adult rape victims, child rape victims, and incest victims, *Journal of Social Service Research* 5: 83–100.

Runyan, D.; M. Everson; G. Edelsohn; W. Hunter; and M. Coulter. 1987. Impact of
legal intervention on sexually abused children. Paper presented at the National
Family Violence Research Symposium, Durham, New Hampshire.

Russell, D. 1988. The incidence and prevalence of intrafamilial and extrafamilial sexual abuse of female children. In L. Walker, ed., *Handbook on sexual abuse of children: Assessment and treatment issues*. New York: Springer.

————. 1986. *The secret trauma: Incest in the lives of girls and women*. New York:
Basic Books.

————. 1984. *Sexual exploitation, rape, child sexual abuse, and workplace harassment*. Beverly Hills, CA: Sage.

————. 1983. The incidence and prevalence of intrafamilial and extrafamilial sexual
abuse of female children, *Child Abuse and Neglect* 7: 133–46.

Rutter, M. 1983. Stress, coping and development: Some issues and some questions.
In N. Garmezy and M. Rutter, eds., *Stress, coping and development in children*.
New York: McGraw-Hill.

————. 1981. Stress, coping and development: Some issues and some questions,
Journal of Child Psychology and Psychiatry and Allied Disciplines 22: 323–56.

————. 1979. Protective factors in children's responses to stress and disadvantage.
In M. Kent and J. Rolf, eds., *Primary prevention of psychopathology: Social competence in children*. Hanover, NH: University Press of New England.

————. 1978. Family area and school influences in the genesis of conduct disorders.
In L. Hersov, M. Berger, and D. Schaffer, eds., *Aggression and antisocial behavior in childhood and adolescence*. Oxford: Pergamon.

————. 1971. Parent–child separation: Psychological effects on the children, *Journal of Child Psychology and Psychiatry* 12: 233–60.

————. 1966. *Children of sick parents: An environment and psychiatric study*. Institute of Psychiatry Maudsley Monographs no. 16. London: Oxford University
Press.

Rutter, M., and H. Giller. 1984. *Juvenile delinquency: Trends and perspectives*. New
York: Guilford Press.

Rutter, M.; B. Maughan; P. Mortimore; J. Ouston; and A. Smith. 1979. *Fifteen thousand hours: Secondary schools and their effects on children*. Cambridge, MA.:
Harvard University Press.

Rutter, M.; D. Quinton; and C. Liddle. 1983. Parenting in two generations: Looking
backwards and looking forwards. In N. Madge, ed., *Families at risk*. London:
Heinemann Educational Books.

Sacks, H., and H. Sacks. 1980. Status offenders: Emerging issues and new approaches.
In D. Schetky and E. Benedek, eds., *Child psychiatry and the law*. New York:
Brunner/Mazel.

Sacks, O. 1985. *The man who mistook his wife for a hat and other clinical tales*. New
York: Summit Books.

Saks, M., and P. Blanck. 1992. Justice improved: The unrecognized benefits of sampling an aggregation in the trial of mass torts, *Stanford Law Review* 44: 815–51.

Sarason, I., and V. Ganzer. 1973. Modeling and group discussion in the rehabilitation of juvenile delinquents, *Journal of Counseling Psychology* 20: 442–49.

Savitsky, J., and D. Karras. 1984. Rights of institutionalized patients. In R. Woody, ed., *The law and the practice of human services*. San Francisco: Jossey-Bass.

Scharfetter, C. 1980. *General psychopathology*. Trans. H. Marshall. Cambridge, Eng.: Cambridge University Press.

Schetky, D. 1988. The clinical evaluation of child sexual abuse. In Schetky and Green, 1988, see below.

Schetky, D., and E. Benedek. 1985. *Emerging issues in child psychiatry and the law*. New York: Brunner/Mazel.

Schetky, D., and A. Green. 1988. *Child sexual abuse: A handbook for health care and legal professionals*. New York: Brunner/Mazel.

Schetky, D., and L. Haller. 1983. Child psychiatry and the law: Parental kidnapping, *Journal of the American Academy of Child Psychiatry* 22: 279–85.

Schmidt, W. 1985. Critique of the American Psychiatric Association's Guidelines for State Legislation on Civil Commitment of the Mentally Ill. *New England Journal on Criminal and Civil Confinement*, 11: 11–43.

Schmidt, W., and R. Otto. 1988. A legal and behavioral science analysis of statutory guidelines for children's mental health and substance abuse services: The Florida case, *Journal of Psychiatry and Law* 16: 9–65.

Schmitt, B. 1987. The child with nonaccidental trauma. In R. Helfer and R. Kempe, eds., *The battered child*. Chicago: University of Chicago Press. 4th ed.

———. 1981. Child neglect. In N. Ellerstein, ed., *Child abuse and neglect: A medical reference*. New York: Wiley.

Schoener, G.; J. Milgrom; J. Gonsiorek; E. Luepker; and R. Conroe. 1989. *Psychotherapists' sexual involvement with clients: Intervention and prevention*. Minneapolis: Walk-in Counseling Center.

Schoepflin, F. 1989. (Comment) Speech activists in shopping centers: Must property rights give way to free expression? *Washington Law Review* 64: 133–54.

Schopp, R. 1991. *Automatism, insanity, and psychology of criminal responsibility: A philosophical inquiry*. Cambridge, Eng.: Cambridge University Press.

Schowalter, J. 1978. The minor's role in consent for mental health treatment, *Journal of the American Academy of Child Psychiatry* 17: 505–13.

Schuck, P., ed. 1991. *Tort law and the public interest*. New York: Norton.

Schuetze, S. 1989. The jurisdictional dilemma of child custody cases under the Parental Kidnapping Prevention Act, *Pepperdine Law Review* 16: 409–30.

Schulsinger, F. 1977. Psychopathy: Heredity and environment. In F. Mednick and K. Christiansen, eds., *Biosocial bases of criminal behavior*. New York: Gardner.

Schultz, L. 1973. The child sex victim: Social, psychological, and legal perspectives, *Child Welfare* 52: 147–57.

Schwartz, B. 1972. *Constitutional law: A textbook*. New York: Macmillan.

Schwartz, I. 1989. Hospitalization of adolescents for psychiatric substance abuse treatment, *Journal of Adolescent Health Care* 10: 473–78.

Schwartz, V. 1971. Civil liability for causing suicide: A synthesis of law and psychiatry, *Vanderbilt Law Review* 24: 217–56.

Scott, E. 1992. Pluralism, parental preference, and child custody, *California Law Review* 80: 615–72.

———. 1986. Sterilization of mentally retarded persons: Reproductive rights and family privacy, *Duke Law Journal*, pp. 806–65.

Sedney, M., and B. Brooks. 1984. Factors associated with a history of childhood sexual experience in a nonclinical female population, *Journal of the American Academy of Child Psychiatry* 23: 215–18.

Sellin, T. 1938. *Culture, conflict and crime*. New York: Social Science Research Council.

Senior, N.; T. Gladstone; and B. Nurcombe. 1982. Childsnatching: A case report, *Journal of the American Academy of Child Psychiatry* 21: 579–83.

Sepejak, D. R. Menzies; and C. Webster. 1983. Clinical predictions of dangerousness: Two-year follow-up of 408 pre-trial forensic cases, *Bulletin of the American Academy of Psychiatry and Law* 11: 171–81.

Serrato, V. 1988. Expert testimony in child sexual abuse prosecutions: A spectrum of uses, *Boston University Law Review* 68: 155–92.

Sgroi, S. 1982a. Family treatment of child sexual abuse, *Journal of Social Work and Human Sexuality* 1: 109–28.

———, ed. 1982b. *Handbook of clinical intervention in child sexual abuse*. Lexington, MA: Lexington Books.

Sgroi, S.; L. Blick; and F. Porter. 1982. A conceptual framework for child sexual abuse. In S. Sgroi, ed., *Handbook of clinical intervention in child sexual abuse*. Lexington: Lexington Books.

Sgroi, S.; F. Porter; and L. Blick. 1982. Validation of child sexual abuse. In S. Sgroi, ed., *Handbook of clinical intervention in child sexual abuse*. Lexington, MA: Lexington Books.

Shaheen, E.; D. Alexander; M. Truskowsky; and G. Barbero. 1968. Failure to thrive: A retrospective profile, *Clinical Pediatrics* 7: 255–61.

Shavell, S. 1987. *Economic analysis of accident law*. Cambridge, MA: Harvard University Press.

Shaw, C., and H. McKay. 1969. *Juvenile delinquency and urban areas*. Rev. ed. Chicago: University of Chicago Press.

Shaw, R.; J. Randolph; and B. Manard. 1977. Ethical issues in pediatric surgery: A national survey of pediatricians and pediatric surgeons, *Pediatrics* 60: 588–99.

Sheldon, W.; S. Stevens; and W. Tucker. 1940. *The varieties of human physique*. New York: Harper.

Shinn, M. 1978. Father absence and children's cognitive development, *Psychological Bulletin* 85: 295–324.

Short, J. 1963. Street corner groups and patterns of delinquency: A progress report, *American Catholic Sociological Review* 24: 13–32.

Sigler, J. 1968. *An introduction to the legal system*. Homewood, IL: Dorsey Press.

Silbert, M., and A. Pines. 1981. Sexual abuse as an antecedent to prostitution, *Child Abuse and Neglect* 5: 407–11.

Simet, D. 1982. Power, uncertainty and choice, *University of Western Ontario Law Review* 20: 141–61.

Simon, R. 1987. *Clinical psychiatry and the law*. Washington: American Psychiatric Press.

————. 1982. *Psychiatric inventions and malpractice: A primer for liability prevention.* Springfield, IL.: Charles C. Thomas.

Simon, R., and R. Sadoff. 1992. *Psychiatric malpractice: Cases and comments for clinicians.* Washington: American Psychiatric Press.

Sivan, A.; D. Schor; G. Koeppl; and L. Noble. 1988. Interaction of normal children with anatomical dolls, *Child Abuse and Neglect* 12: 295–304.

Skinner, B. 1971. *Beyond freedom and dignity.* New York: Knopf.

Skinner, L., and K. Berry, 1993. Anatomically detailed dolls and the evaluation of child sexual abuse allegations: Psychometric considerations. *Law and Human Behavior* 17(4): 399–421.

Skolnick, A. 1975. The limits of childhood: Conceptions of child development and social context, *Law and Contemporary Problems* 39 (Summer): 38–77.

Skrzypek, G. 1969. Effect of perceptual isolation and arousal on anxiety, complexity, preference, and novelty preference in psychopathic and neurotic delinquents, *Journal of Abnormal Psychology* 74: 321–29.

Sloan, F.; R. Bovbjerg; and P. Githens. 1991. *Insuring medical malpractice.* New York: Oxford University Press.

Sloan, F.; P. Githens; E. Clayton; D. Hickson; D. Gentile; and D. Partlett. 1993. *Suing for medical malpractice.* Chicago: University of Chicago Press.

Slovenko, R. 1991. Psychiatric expert testimony: Are the criticisms justified? *Medicine & Law,* 10: 1–29.

————. 1983. The insanity defense in the wake of the Hinckley trial, *Rutgers Law Journal* 14: 373–95.

————. 1973. *Psychiatry and law.* Boston: Little, Brown.

Smith, J. 1986. *Medical malpractice: Psychiatric care.* Colorado Springs: Shepard's/McGraw-Hill.

Smith, L. 1986. Adoption: The case for more options, *Utah Law Review* 1986: 495–557.

Smith, S. 1991. Mental health malpractice in the 1990s, *Houston Law Review* 28: 209–83.

Snyder, J., and G. Patterson. 1987. Family interaction and delinquent behavior. In H. Quay, ed., *Handbook of juvenile delinquency.* New York: Wiley.

Sorosky, A.; A. Baran; and R. Panner. 1984. *The adoption triangle—Sealed or opened records: How they affect adoptees, birth parents, and adoptive parents.* Garden City, NY: Anchor Press.

Spencer, C., and M. Nicholson. 1988. Incest investigation and treatment planning by child protective services. In L. Walker, ed., *Handbook on sexual abuse of children: Assessment and treatment issues.* New York: Springer.

Spiegel, D. 1984. Multiple personality as a post-traumatic stress disorder, *Psychiatric Clinics of North America* 7: 101–10.

Spielman, B. 1992. Patient decisions and psychiatric hospitals: Quandries of the Patient Self Determination Act, *Developments in Mental Health Law* 12: 1–3.

Spinetta, J., and D. Rigler. 1972. The child-abusing parent: A psychological review, *Psychological Bulletin* 77: 296–304.

Spivack, G., and N. Cianci. 1987. High risk early behavior pattern and later delinquency. In J. Burchard and S. Burchard, eds., *Prevention of delinquent behavior.* Newbury Park, CA: Sage.

Springer, C., and J. Wallerstein. 1983. Young adolescents' responses to their parents' divorces. In L. Kurdek, ed., *Children and divorce*. New Directions for Child Development series no. 19. San Francisco: Jossey-Bass.

Starr, P. 1982. *The social transformation of American medicine*. New York: Basic Books.

Starr, R.; K. Dietrich; J. Fischoff; S. Ceresnie; and D. Zweier. 1984. The contribution of handicapping conditions to child abuse, *Topics in Early Childhood Special Education* 4: 55–69.

Steele, B. 1970. Parental abuse of infants and small children. In J. Anthony and T. Benedek, eds., *Parenthood: Its psychology and psychopathology*. Boston: Little, Brown.

Steinfels, M., and P. Steinfels, eds. 1976. Treating the defective newborn: A survey of physicians' attitudes, *Hastings Center Report* 6 (April): 2.

Steinman, S. 1981. The experience of children in a joint-custody arrangement: A report of a study, *American Journal of Orthopsychiatry* 51: 403–14.

Steinman, S.; S. Zemmelman; and T. Knoblauch. 1985. A study of parents who sought joint custody following divorce: Who reaches agreement and sustains joint custody and who returns to court, *Journal of the American Academy of Child Psychiatry* 24: 554–62.

Steller, M. 1989. Recent developments in statement analysis. In J. Yuille, ed., *Credibility assessment*. Dordrecht, Netherlands: Kluwer.

Stevenson, K., and M. Maholick, compilers. 1987. *Child and adolescent psychiatry: Guidelines for treatment resources, quality assurance, peer review and reimbursement*. Washington, D.C.: Journal of the American Academy of Child and Adolescent Psychiatry.

Stone, A. 1987. Psychiatry and the Supreme Court. In *Law, Psychiatry, and Morality*. Washington: American Psychiatric Press.

———. 1984. The trial of John Hinckley. In *Law, Psychiatry and Morality*, Washington, D.C.: American Psychiatric Press.

———. 1976. The *Tarasoff* decision: Suing psychotherapists to safeguard society, *Harvard Law Review* 90: 358–78.

Stone, M. 1981. Borderline syndromes: A consideration of subtypes and an overview—Directions for research, *Psychiatric Clinics of North America* 4: 3–24.

Stouthamer-Loeber, M., and R. Loeber. 1988. The use of prediction data in understanding delinquency, *Behavioral Sciences and the Law* 6: 333–54.

Strang, R. 1990. "She was just seventeen . . . and the way she looked was way beyond [her years]": Child pornography and overbreadth, *Columbia Law Review* 90: 1779–1803.

Strasburg, S. 1984. Recent national trends in serious juvenile crime. In R. Mathias *et al.*, eds., *Violent juvenile offenders: An anthology*, pp. 8–27. Washington, DC: National Council on Crime and Delinquency.

Street, T. 1906. *The Foundations of Legal Liability*, Vol. I: Tort. Northport, NY: Edward Thompson Company.

Stringfield, N. 1977. The impact of family counseling in resocializing adolescent offenders within a positive peer treatment milieu, *Offender Rehabilitation* 1 (Summer): 349–60.

Stromberg, C., *et al.* 1988. *The psychologist's legal handbook.* Washington, DC: Council for the National Register of Health Service Providers in Psychology.

Stromberg, C., and A. Stone. 1984a. *Statute: A model state law on civil commitment of the mentally ill.* Washington, D.C.: American Psychiatric Press.

———. 1984b. A model state law on civil commitment of the mentally ill. *Harvard Journal on Legislation* 20: 275–396.

Sturkie, K. 1983. Structured group treatment for sexually abused children, *Health and Social Work* 8: 299–309.

Sugar, M. 1983. Sexual abuse of children and adolescents, *Adolescent Psychiatry* 11: 199–211.

Sullivan, C.; M. Grant; and J. Grant. 1957. The development of interpersonal maturity: Applications to delinquency, *Psychiatry* 20: 373–85.

Summit, R. 1983. The child sexual abuse accommodation syndrome, *Child Abuse and Neglect* 7: 177–93.

Summit, R., and J. Kryso. 1978. Sexual abuse of children: A clinical spectrum, *American Journal of Orthopsychiatry* 48: 237–51.

Sunderman, L. 1989. (Note) The institutionalized child's right of counsel: Satisfying due process requirements through the Protection and Advocacy for Mentally Ill Individuals Act, *Valparaiso University Law Review* 23: 629–63.

Szasz, T. 1961. *The myth of mental illness.* New York: Hoeber-Harper.

Talbott, J. 1981. *The chronically mentally-ill: Treatment, programs, systems.* New York: Human Sciences Press.

Taub, S. 1982. Tardive dyskinesia: Medical facts and legal fiction, *St. Louis University Law Journal* 30: 833–78.

Taubman, S. 1984. Incest in context, *Social Work* 29: 35–40.

Taylor, P. 1983. (Note) An "appropriate" education for the handicapped: *Board of Education v. Rowley, Howard Law Journal* 26: 1645–60.

ten Bensel, R. 1984. Reporting child abuse, *Juvenile and Family Court Journal* 35: 41–44.

Terr, L. 1988. What happens to early memories of trauma? A study of twenty children under age 5 at the time of documented traumatic events, *Journal of the American Academy of Child and Adolescent Psychiatry* 27: 96–104.

———. 1985. Children traumatized in small groups. In S. Eth and R. Pynoos, eds., *Post-traumatic stress disorder in children.* Washington: American Psychiatric Press.

———. 1983. Chowchilla revisited: The effects of psychic trauma four years after a school-bus kidnapping, *American Journal of Psychiatry* 140: 1543–50.

———. 1981a. Psychic trauma in children: Observations following the Chowchilla school-bus kidnapping, *American Journal of Psychiatry* 138: 14–19.

———. 1981b. Forbidden games: Posttraumatic child's play, *Journal of the American Academy of Child Psychiatry* 20: 741–60.

———. 1979. Children of Chowchilla, *Psychoanalytic Study of the Child* 34: 547–623.

Thrasher, F. 1927. *The gang.* Chicago: University of Chicago Press.

Tobias 1989. Interspousal tort immunity in America, *Georgia Law Review* 23: 359–478.

Todres. F.; D. Krane; M. Howell; and D. Shannon. 1977. Pediatricians' attitudes affecting decision making in defective newborns, *Pediatrics* 60: 197–201.

Togut, M.; J. Allen; and L. Lelchuk. 1969. A psychological exploration of the non-organic failure-to-thrive syndrome, *Developmental Medicine and Child Neurology* 11: 601–7.

Torrey, F. 1988. *Nowhere to go: The tragic odyssey of the homeless mentally ill.* New York: Harper & Row.

Trasler, G. 1987. Biogenetic factors. In H. Quay, ed., *Handbook of juvenile delinquency.* New York: Wiley.

Treffert, D. 1973. Dying with their rights on, *American Journal of Psychiatry* 130: 1041.

Trevisano, M. 1982. The effects of sole and joint custodial arrangements on the emotional functioning and behavorial adaptation of children of divorce, *Dissertation Abstracts International* 43: 537B–638B.

Tribe, L. 1989. Remarks: Revisiting the rule of law. *New York University Law Review* 64: 726–31.

———. 1971. Trial by mathematics: Precision and ritual in the legal process, *Harvard Law Review* 84: 1329–1393.

Trunnell, T. 1976. Johnnie and Suzie, don't cry: Mommy and Daddy aren't that way, *Bulletin of the American Academy of Child Psychiatry and the Law* 4: 120–26.

Tsai, M.; S. Feldman-Summers; and M. Edgar. 1979. Childhood molestation: Variables related to differential impacts on psychosexual functioning in adult women, *Journal of Abnormal Psychology* 88: 407–17.

Tsai, M., and N. Wagner. 1979. Incest and molestation: Problems of childhood sexuality, *Resident and Staff Physician* 25 (March): 129–36.

———. 1978. Therapy groups for women sexually molested as children, *Archives of Sexual Behavior* 7: 417–27.

Tufts New England Medical Center, Division of Child Psychiatry. 1984. *Sexually exploited children: Service and research project.* Washington: U.S. Department of Justice.

Undeutsch, U. 1982. Statement reality analysis. In A. Trankell, ed., *Reconstructing the past: The role of psychologists in criminal trials.* Stockholm: Norstedt Soners.

Updike, J. 1986. *Roger's version.* New York: Knopf.

Van Eerdewegh, M.; M. Bieri; R. Parrilla; and P. Clayton. 1982. The bereaved child, *British Journal of Psychiatry* 140: 23–29.

Veeder, V. 1909. Absolute privilege in defamation: Judicial proceedings, *Columbia Law Review* 9: 463–91.

Virkkunen, M. 1974. Incest offenses and alcoholism, *Medicine, Science and the Law* 14: 124–28.

Visher, C., and J. Roth. 1986. Participation in criminal careers. In A. Blumstein, J. Cohen, J. Roth, and C. Visher, Eds., *Criminal careers and "career criminals."* Vol. I. Washington: National Academy Press.

Vito, G., and D. Wilson. 1985. *The American juvenile justice system.* Beverly Hills, CA: Sage.

Voeltz, L.; I. Evans; K. Freedland; and S. Donello. 1982. Teacher decision-making in the selection of educational programming priorities for severely handicapped children, *Journal of Special Education,* 16: 179–98.

Wadlington, W. 1992–93. Contracts to bear a child: The mixed legislative signals, *Idaho Law Review* 29: 383.

————. 1984. The silent world of doctor and patient, *Yale Law Journal* 93: 1640–51.

————. 1973. Minors and health care: The age of consent, *Osgoode Hall Law Journal* 11: 115–25.

Wald, M. 1979. Children's rights: A framework for analysis. *University of California, Davis,* 12: 255–82.

Wald, P., and Friedman, P. 1976. Brief for *Amici Curiae* submitted to the U.S. Supreme Court in the case of *Kremens v. Bartley* (No. 75-1064).

Walker, L. 1988. New techniques for assessment and evaluation of child sexual abuse victims: Using anatomically "correct" dolls and videotape of procedures. In L. Walker, ed., *Handbook on sexual abuse of children: Assessment and treatment issues.* New York: Springer.

Walker, L., and M. Bolkovatz. 1988. Play therapy with children who have experienced sexual assault. In L. Walker, ed., *Handbook on sexual abuse of children: Assessment and treatment issues.* New York: Springer.

Wallerstein, J. 1983. Children of divorce: Stress and developmental tasks. In N. Garmezy and M. Rutter, eds., *Stress, coping, and development in children.* New York: McGraw-Hill.

Wallerstein, J. 1977. Responses of the preschool child to divorce: Those who cope. In M. McMillan and S. Henao, eds., *Child psychiatry: Treatment and research.* New York: Brunner/Mazel.

Wallerstein, J., and S. Blakeslee. 1989. *Second chances.* New York: Ticknor & Fields.

Wallerstein, J., and J. Kelly. 1980a. Effects of divorce on the visiting father–child relationship, *American Journal of Psychiatry* 137: 1534–39.

————. 1980b. *Surviving the breakup: How children and parents cope with divorce.* New York: Basic Books.

————. 1976. The effects of parental divorce: Experiences of the child in later latency, *American Journal of Orthopsychiatry* 46: 256–69.

————. 1975. The effects of parental divorce: Experiences of the pre-school child, *Journal of the American Academy of Child Psychiatry* 14: 600–616.

Warboys, W. 1988. The Supreme Court view of the child 1987–88. *4th National Conference on Children and the Law*, ABA National Legal Resource Center for Child Advocacy.

Warren, M. 1969. The case for differential treatment of delinquents, *Annals of the American Academy of Political Science* 381: 47–59.

Wassermann, G.; A. Green; and R. Allen. 1983. Going beyond abuse: Maladaptive patterns of interaction in abusing mother-infant pairs, *Journal of the American Academy of Child Psychiatry*, 22: 245–52.

Waters, E.; G. Posada; J. Crowell; and K. Lay. 1993. Is attachment theory ready to contribute to an understanding of disruptive behavior problems? *Development and Psychopathology* 5: 215–24.

Watson, A. 1980. Children, families, and court: Before the best interests of the child and *Parham v. J.R. Virginia Law Review* 66: 653–79.

Weiler, P. 1991. *Medical malpractice on trial.* Cambridge: Harvard University Press.

Weinberg, S. 1955. *Incest behavior.* New York: Citadel Press.

Weiner, B.; V. Simons; and J. Cavanaugh, Jr. 1985. The child custody dispute. in D. Schetky and E. Benedek, eds., *Emerging issues in child psychiatry and the law.* New York: Brunner/Mazel.

Weiner, I. 1982. Delinquent behavior. In I. Weiner, ed., *Child and Adolescent Psychopathology*. New York: Wiley.

Weisberg, K. 1985. *Children of the night: A study of adolescent prostitution*. Lexington, MA: Lexington Books.

Weiss, C. 1987. The diffusion of social science research to policy makers: An overview. In G. Melton, ed., *Reforming the law: Impact of child development research*. New York: Guilford.

Weiss, E., and F. Berg. 1982. Child victims of sexual assault: Impact of court procedures *Journal of the American Academy of Child Psychiatry* 21: 513–18.

Weithorn, L. 1988. Mental hospitalization of troublesome youth: An analysis of skyrocketing admission rates, *Stanford Law Review* 40: 773–838.

———. 1987. Psychological confrontation in divorce custody litigation: Ethical considerations. In L. Weighorn, ed., *Psychology and child custody determinations*. Lincoln: University of Nebraska Press.

———. 1984. Children's capacities in legal contexts. In D. Reppucci, L. Weithorn, E. Mulvey, and J. Monahan, eds., *Children, mental health, and the law*. Beverly Hills, CA: Sage.

———. 1982. Developmental factors and competence to make informed treatment decisions, *Child and Youth Services* 5: 85–100.

Weithorn, L., and S. Campbell. 1982. The competence of children and adolescents to make informed treatment decisions, *Child Development* 53: 1589–98.

Weithorn, L., and T. Grisso. 1987. Psychological evaluations in divorce custody: Problems, principles, and procedures. In L. Weithorn, ed., *Psychology and child custody determinations*. Lincoln: University of Nebraska Press.

Weitzman, L., and R. Dixon. 1979. Child custody awards: Legal standards and empirical patterns for child custody, support and visitation after divorce, *University of California at Davis Law Review* 12: 473–521.

Welch, D. 1989. Walking in their shoes: Paying respect to incompetent patients, *Vanderbilt Law Review* 42: 1617–40.

Welsh, O. 1982. The effects of custody arrangements on children of divorce, *Dissertation Abstracts International* 42: 4946B–5129B.

Wennberg, J. 1984. Dealing with medical practice variations: A proposal for action, *Health Affairs*, Summer.

Wennberg, J., and A. Grittelsohn. 1973. Small area variations in health care delivery, *Science* 182: 1102–8.

West, D., and D. Farrington. 1973. *Who becomes delinquent?* London: Heinemann.

West, R. 1988. Jurisprudence and gender, *University of Chicago Law Review* 55: 1–72.

Wexler, D. 1990. *Therapeutic jurisprudence: The law as a therapeutic agent*. Durham, NC: Carolina Academic Press.

White, P. 1992. Essays in the aftermath of Cruzan, *Journal of Medicine and Philosophy* 17: 563–681.

White, S.; G. Strom; G. Santilli; and B. Halprin. 1986. Interviewing young sexual abuse victims with anatomically correct dolls, *Child Abuse and Neglect* 10: 519–29.

Whitten, C. 1981. Growth failure. In N. Ellerstein, ed., *Child abuse and neglect: A medical reference*. New York: Wiley.

Whitten, C.; M. Pettit; and J. Fischoff. 1969. Evidence that growth failure from maternal deprivation is secondary to undereating, *Journal of the American Medical Association* 209: 1675–82.

Whyte, W. 1955. *Street corner society*. Chicago: University of Chicago Press.

Weiner, R. 1992. A psycholegal and empirical approach to the medical standard of care. In J. Ogloff, ed., *Law and Psychology: The broadening of the discipline*. Durham, NC: Carolina Academic Press.

Wigmore, J. 1985. *Evidence in trials at common law*. Boston: Little, Brown.

Will, D. 1983. Approaching the incestuous and sexually abusive family, *Journal of Adolescence* 6: 229–46.

Wilson, J., and R. Hernstein. 1985. *Crime and human nature*. New York: Simon & Schuster.

Wisdom, C. 1989. The cycle of violence, *Science* 244: 160–66.

Wise, T. 1978. (Note) Where the public peril begins: A survey of psychotherapists to determine the effects of *Tarasoff*, *Stanford Law Review* 31: 165–90.

Wisely, D.; F. Masur; and S. Morgan. 1983. Psychological aspects of severe burn injuries in children, *Health Psychology* 2: 45–72.

Wolchik, S.; S. Braver; and I. Sandler. 1985. Maternal versus joint custody: Children's post separation experiences and adjustment, *Journal of Clinical Child Psychology* 14: 5–10.

Wolchik, S., and P. Karoly, eds. 1988. *Children of divorce: Empirical perspectives on adjustment*. New York: Gardiner.

Wolf, S.; J. Conte; and M. Engel-Meinig. 1988. Assessment and treatment of sex offenders in a community setting. In L. Walker, ed., *Handbook on sexual abuse of children: Assessment and treatment issues*. New York: Springer.

Wolinsky, H. 1991. Public medicine showing concern over doctor–patient sexual relationship, *American College of Physicians Observer* 11: 17–19.

Woodruff, R.; D. Goodwin; and S. Guze. 1974. *Psychiatric diagnosis*. New York: Oxford University Press.

Woody, R. 1977. Behavioral science criteria in child custody determinations, *Journal of Marriage and Family Counseling* 32: 11–18.

Wortley, M. 1977. First aid to passengers: Good Samaritan statutes and contractual releases from liability, *Southwestern Law Journal* 31: 695–713.

Wyatt, G. 1985. The sexual abuse of Afro-American and white-American women in childhood, *Child Abuse and Neglect* 9: 507–19.

Wyer, M.; S. Gaylord; and E. Grove. 1987. The legal context of child custody evaluations. In L. Weithorn, ed., *Psychology and child custody determinations*. Lincoln: University of Nebraska Press.

Yochelson, S., and S. Samenow. 1977. *The criminal personality*, Vol. II: *The change process*. New York: Jason Aronson.

———. 1976. *The criminal personality*, Vol. I: *The profile for change*. New York: Jason Aronson.

Young, D. 1983. Two studies of children of divorce. In L. Kurdek, ed., *Children and divorce*. New Directions for Child Development series. San Francisco: Jossey-Bass.

Young, H. 1992. (Note) Assisted suicide and physician liability, *Review of Litigation* 11: 623–56.

Yun, J. 1983. A comprehensive approach to child hearsay statements in sex abuse cases, *Columbia Law Review* 83: 1745–66.

Zaragoza, M. 1991. Preschool children's susceptibility to memory impairment. Chapter 3 in J. Doris, ed., *The suggestibility of children's recollections*. Washington: American Psychological Association.

Zelizer, V. 1985. *Pricing the priceless child: The changing social value of children*. New York: Basic Books.

Zima, J. 1992. (Note) Assisted suicide: Society's response in a plea for relief or a simple solution to the cries of the needy? *Rutgers Law Journal* 23: 387–408.

Zipursky, B. 1990. *DeShaney* and the jurisprudence of compassion, *New York University Law Review* 65: 1101–47.

Zirkel, P. 1983. Building an appropriate education from *Board of Education v. Rowley*: Razing the door and raising the floor, *Maryland Law Review* 42: 466–95.

Ziskin, J., and D. Faust. 1988a. *Coping with psychiatric and psychological testimony*, Vol. I: *Basic information*. Marina del Rey, CA: Law and Psychology Press.

———. 1988b. *Coping with psychiatric and psychological testimony*, Vol. II: *Special topics*. Marina del Rey, CA: Law and Psychology Press.

———. 1988c. *Coping with psychiatric and psychological testimony*, Vol. III: *Practical guidelines, cross examination, and case illustrations*. Marina del Rey, CA: Law and Psychology Press.

Ziv, A., and R. Israeli. 1973. Effects of bombardment on the manifest anxiety level of children living in kibbutzin, *Journal of Consulting and Clinical Psychology* 40: 287–91.

TABLE OF CASES

A Minor Boy v. State, 537 P.2d 477 (Nev. 1975), 539n.16.

A.E. v. Independent School Dist. No. 25, 936 F.2d 472 (10th Cir. 1991), 507n.42.

In re A Minor, 595 N.W.2d 1052 (Ill. 1992), 539n.41.

Aasheim v. Humberger, 695 P.2d 824 (Mont. 1985), 533n.189.

Abille v. United States, 482 F. Supp. 703 (N.D. Cal. 1980), 253, 534n.200, 536n.243.

Abraham v. Zaslow, No. 245862 (Santa Clara County Sup. Ct. October 26, 1970), 242, 533n.172.

Abrahamson v. Hershman, 701 F.2d 223 (1st Cir. 1983), 509n.81.

Adams v. Johns-Manville Sales, 783 F.2d 589 (5th Cir. 1986), 523n.62.

Adams v. Murakami, 813 P.2d 1348 (Cal. 1991), 536n.248.

Addington v. Texas, 441 U.S. 418 (1979), 68, 498n.112, 505n.189, 543n.35.

In re "Agent Orange" Product Liability Litigation MDL No. 381, 597 F. Supp. 740 (E.D. N.Y. 1984), 524n.80.

Agostine v. School District of Philadelphia, 527 A.2d 193 (Pa. 1987), 503n.142.

Ake v. Oklahoma, 470 U.S. 68 (1985), 493n.18.

Aladdin's Castle v. City of Mesquite, 630 F.2d 1029 (5th Cir. 1980), *rev'd on other grounds* 455 U.S. 283 (1982), 54, 501n.84.

Alberto B. v. Rosa O., 423 N.Y.S.2d 111 (N.Y. Fam. Ct. 1979), 512n.84.

Alcock v. Chief Constable of the South Yorkshire Police, [1991] 4 A11 E.R. 907 (House of Lords, Engl.), 522n.51.

Amalgamated Food Employees v. Logan Valley Plaza, 391 U.S. 308 (1968), 501n.79.

American Booksellers v. Webb, 919 F.2d 1493 (11th Cir. 1990), *cert. denied*, 111 S.Ct. 2237, 55, 501n.93.

Anderson v. Minneapolis St. P. & S. St. M. R.R. Co., 179 N.W. 45 (Minn. 1920), 524n.79.

Anderson v. Sears, Roebuck & Company, 377 F. Supp. 136 (E.D. La. 1974), 524n.89.

Angela L. v. Pasadena Independent School Dist., 918 F.2d 1188 (5th Cir. 1990), 508n.59.

Anisodon v. Superior Court, 285 Cal. Rptr. 539 (1991), 523n.58.

Ankenbrandt v. Richards, 112 S.Ct. 2206 (1992), 521n.21.

Anna J. v. Mark C., 286 Cal. Rptr. 369 (Cal. App. 1991), 104.

In re Anthony S., 341 N.Y.S.2d 11 (Fam. Ct. Rich. 1973), 539n.24.

Arche v. U.S. Dep't of Army, 798 P.2d 477 (Kan. 1990), 523n.68.

Artist M. v. Johnson, 917 F.2d 980 (7th Cir. 1990), 500n.49.

Marriage of Ashling, 599 P.2d 475 (Or. Ct. App. 1979), 515n.152.

Association for Retarded Citizens v. Olson, 713 F.2d 1384 (8th Cir. 1990), 330, 544n.71.

Atlanta Obstetrics & Gynecology Group v. Abelson, 398 S.E.2d 557 (Ga. 1990), 523n.68.

Auge v. Auge, 334 N.W.2d 393 (Minn. 1983), 513n.101.

Application of Auster, 100 N.Y.S.2d 60 (Sup. Ct. 1950), 516n.12.

Austin v. McNamara, 731 F. Supp. 934 (Cal. D.C. 1990), 533n.178.

Babb v. Knox County School Sys., 965 F.2d 104 (6th Cir. 1992), 508n.54, 509n.92.

Babcock v. Tyler, 884 F.2d 497 (9th Cir. 1989), 500n.61.

In re Baby M, 537 A.2d 1227 (N.J. 1988), 104, 115, 512n.64, 513nn.110, 115, 515n.173.

In the Interest of Bachelor, 508 P.2d 862 (Kan. 1973), 101, 513n.85.

Bah v. Bah, 668 S.W.2d 663 (Tenn. Ct. App. 1983), 512n.43.

Bailey v. Meister Brau, Inc., 57 F.R.D. 11 (N.D. Ill. 1972), 546n.25.

Baker v. Nelson, 191 N.W.2d 185 (Minn. 1971), 511n.5.

Baker v. Owen, 395 F. Supp. 294 (M.D. N.C. 1975), 502n.110.

Baker v. United States, 343 F.2d 222 (8th Cir. 1965), 526n.7.

Baltimore City Department of Social Services v. Bouknight, 493 U.S. 549 (1990), 51, 500n.62

Barclay v. Campbell, 704 S.W.2d 8 (Tex. 1986), 529n.85.

Barefoot v. Estelle, 463 U.S. 880 (1983), 324, 543nn.42, 43, 45.

Barnes v. Commonwealth (1937) 37 S.R. (N.S.W.) 511, 537n.270.

Bartolone v. Jeckovich, 481 N.Y.S.2d 545 (Sup. Ct. 1984), 524n.85.

Barton v. Owen, 139 Cal. Rptr. 494 (Ct. App. 1977), 527n.34.

Barton-Malow Co., Inc. v. Wilburn, 547 N.E.2d 1123 (Ind. App. 1989), 525n.97.

Bates v. Denney, 563 So. 2d 298 (La. App. 1990), 535n.216.

Bates v. Wishart, 512 So. 2d 977 (Fla. App. 1987), 514n.128.

Beattie v. Board of Education of City of Antigo, 172 N.W. 153 (Wis. 1919), 73, 506nn.9, 11.

Beck v. Beck, 432 A.2d 63 (N.J. 1981), 512n.53, 513n.101.

Bee v. Greaves, 744 F.2d 1387 (10th Cir. 1984), 545n.100.

Estate of Behringer v. Medical Center at Princeton, 592 A.2d 1251 (N.J. Super. 1991), 528n.67, 531n.129.

Belcher v. Goins, 400 S.E.2d 830 (W.Va. 1990), 525n.101.

Bell v. New York City Health and Hospital, 456 N.Y.S.2d 787 (Sup. Ct. 1982), 534n.210, 535n.221.

Bellah v. Greenson, 146 Cal. Rptr. 535 (Cal. App. 1978), 240, 531n.142.

Bellotti v. Baird, 428 U.S. 132 (1976), 497n.74.

Bellotti v. Baird, 443 U.S. 622 (1979), 499n.33, 500n.38.

Berger v. Weber, 303 N.W.2d 424 (Mich. 1981), 524n.94.

Estate of Berthiaume v. Pratt, 365 A.2d 792 (Me. 1976), 533n.174.

Betesh v. United States, 400 F. Supp. 238 (D.D.C. 1974), 527n.24.

Bezio v. Patenaude, 410 N.E.2d 1207 (Mass. 1980), 514n.151.

Big Town Nursing Home, Inc. v. Newman, 461 S.W.2d 195 (Tex. Civ. App. 1970), 535n.234.

Bindrim v. Mitchell, 155 Cal. Rptr. 29 (Cal. App. 1979), 256, 536n.258.

Bivens v. Six Unknown Named Agents of Federal Bureau of Narcotics, 403 U.S. 388 (1971), 496n.53.

In re State in Interest of Black, 283 P.2d 887 (Utah 1955), 512n.80.

Blackburn v. Dorta, 348 So. 2d 287 (Fla. 1977), 525n.112.

Bloss v. Bloss, 711 P.2d 663 (Ariz. App. 1985), 513n.108.

Board of Education, Island Trees Union Free School District No. 26 v. Pico, 457 U.S. 853 (1982), 59, 502n.118.

Board of Education v. Diamond, 808 F.2d 987 (3d Cir. 1986), 78, 509n.87

Board of Education v. Rowley, 458 U.S. 176 (1982), 78, 79, 506n.10, 507n.42, 509nn.76, 79, 80.

Bob Jones University v. United States, 461 U.S. 574 (1983), 24, 497n.64

Bond v. District Court, 682 P.2d 33 (Colo. 1984), 498n.109.

Bond v. Yount, 734 P.2d 39 (Wash. App. 1987), 514n.137.

Bonner v. Moran, 126 F.2d 121 (D.C. Cir. 1941), 496n.44.

Borne v. Northwest Allen County School Corp., 532 N.E.2d 1196 (Ind. App. 1989), 516n.26.

Bornmann v. Great SW. Gen. Hosp., 453 F.2d 616 (5th Cir. 1971), 528n.48.

Bowers v. Hardwick, 478 U.S. 186 (1986), 544n.86.

Boyd v. Albert Einstein Medical Center, 547 A.2d 1229 (Pa. Super. Ct. 1988), 538n.288.

Brady v. Hopper, 570 F. Supp. 1333 (D. Co. 1983), 531n.139.

Bramlette v. Charter-Medical-Columbia, 393 S.E.2d 914 (S.C. 1990), 535n.217.

Brandenburg v. Ohio, 395 U.S. 444 (1969), 495n.25.

Brandon v. Board of Education of Guilderland Central School District, 487 F.Supp. 1219 (N.D. N.Y. 1980), 635 F.2d 971 (2d Cir. 1980), 502n.123.

Brandvain v. Ridgeview Instit., 372 S.E.2d 265 (Ga. App. 1988), 535n.214.

Bray v. Lee, 337 F. Supp. 934 (D. Mass. 1972), 503n.132.

Breed v. Jones, 421 U.S. 519 (1975), 276, 538n.9.

Brenneman v. Hildebrant, 119 S.W. 452 (Kan. Ct. App. 1909), 90, 511n.18.

Breunig v. American Family Ins. Co., 173 N.W.2d 619 (Wis. 1970), 521n.8.

Briney v. Williams, 242 N.E.2d 132 (Ind. App. 1968), 497n.97.

Matter of Brown, 439 F.2d 47 (3d Cir. 1971), 539n.43, 9, 17, 60, 73, 494n.36, 495n.16, 498n.125, 503n.131, 506n.14.

Brown v. Board of Education, 349 U.S. 294 (1955), 509n.186.505n.186.

Brown v. Wilson County School Bd., 747 F. Supp. 436 (M.D. Tenn. 1990), 509n.186.

Brumfield v. Brumfield, 74 S.E.2d 170 (Va. 1953), 505n.186.

Buchanan v. Warley, 245 U.S. 60 (1917), 496n.31.

Buchholtz v. Iowa Dept. of Public Instruction, 315 N.W.2d 789 (Iowa 1982), 509n.90.

Buck v. Bell, 274 U.S. 200 (1927), 72, 506n.7

Burke County Bd. of Educ. v. Denton, 895 F.2d 973 (4th Cir. 1990), 509n.88.

Burnette v. Wahl, 588 P.2d 1105 (Or. 1978), 49,500n.51.

Burr v. Ambach, 863 F.2d 1071 (2d Cir. 1988), 508n.54.

Marriage of Bush, 547 N.E.2d 590 (Ill. App. 1989), 512n.54.

Matter of C.E.R., 796 S.W.2d 423 (Mo. App. 1990), 514n.135.

In the Matter of C.P., 543 N.E.2d 410 (Ind. App. 1989), 120, 530n.111.

C.T.W. v. B.C.G., 809 S.W.2d 788 (Tex. Ct. App. 1991), 523n.75.

Caban v. Mohammed, 441 U.S. 380 (1979), 518n.80.

Cain v. Rijken, 717 P.2d 140 (Or. 1986), 238, 531n.127.

California v. Hodari, 111 S.Ct. 1547 1991), 59, 503n.130.

Canterbury v. Spence, 464 F.2d 772 (D.C. Cir. 1972), 494n.4, 528nn..53, 65, 68, 70, 529n. 73.

Carbone v. Warburton, 94 A.2d 680 (N.J. 1953), 527n.39.

Carey v. Piphus, 435 U.S. 247 (1978), 542n.21.

Carey v. Population Services International, 431 U.S. 678 (1977), 47, 65, 496n.40, 499nn.33, 38, 40, 502n.100, 504n.165.

Carlin Communications v. F.C.C., 749 F.2d 113 (2d Cir. 1984). ("Carlin I"), 501n.955

Carlin Communications v. F.C.C., 787 F.2d 846 (2d Cir. 1986). ("Carlin II"), 501n.96.

Carlin Communications v. F.C.C., 837 F.2d 546 (2d Cir. 1988) ("Carlin III"), 56, 501n.97.

Carter v. Carter, 144 A. 490 (Md. App. 1929), 511n.16

Casey v. Planned Parenthood, 112 S.Ct. 2791 (1992), 37, 498nn.121, 123, 504n.161.

Cassidy v. Daily Mirror, [1929] 2 K.B. 331 (CA), 536n.255.

Centeno v. City of New York, 358 N.E. 520 (N.Y. App. Div. 1976), 534n.199.

Chambon v. Celender, 780 F. Supp. 307 (W.D. Pa. 1992), 191, 521n.24.

Chandler v. McMinnville School District, 978F.2d524 (1992), 502n.115.

Chaplinsky v. New Hampshire, 315 U.S. 568 (1942), 495n.24.

Chapsky v. Wood, 26 Kan. 650 (1881), 42, 499n.12, 511n.32.

Chavin v. West Jefferson Health Center, 597 So. 2d 134 (La. App. 1992), 535n.224.

In re Cheryl H., 200 Cal. Rptr. 789 (Cal. App. 1984), 142, 497n.94, 517n.53.

Chester v. Municipality of Waverly, 62 C.L.R. 1 (Austl. 1939), 511n.21.

Chi., Ind. & L. Ry. Co. v. United States, 219 U.S. 486 (1911), 497n.62.

Chiles v. Chiles, 779 S.W.2d 127 (Tex. Ct. App. 1989), 521n.21.

Christian v. Randall, 516 P.2d 132 (Colo. App. 1973), 513n.105.

Christy v. Saliterman, 179 N.W.2d 288 (Minn. 1970), 527n.19.

Chrite v. United States, 564 F. Supp. 341 (E.D. Mich. 1983), 532n.151.

Cidis v. White, 336 N.Y.S.2d 362 (N.Y. D.C. 1972), 41, 498n.3.

Cipollone v. Liggett Group, 112 S.Ct. 2608 (1992), 497n.63.

In re Clark, 281 S.E.2d 47 (N.C. 1981), 516n.35.

Clements v. Swedish Hospital, 89 N.W.2d 162 (Minn. 1958), 535n.218.

Clevenger v. Oak Ridge School Board, 744 F.2d 514 (6th Cir. 1984), 509n.92.

Clites v. State of Iowa, 322 N.W.2d 917 (Iowa Ct. App. 1982), 247, 533nn.182, 187.

Cohen v. Cowles Media Company, 111 S.Ct. 2513 (1991), 521n.25, 529n.94.

Collins v. Howard, 156 F. Supp. 322 (S.D. Ga. 1957), 529n.90.

Commonwealth v. Carey, 554 N.E.2d 1199 (Mass. 1990), 59, 502n.128.

Commonwealth v. Evans, 603 A.2d 608 (Pa. Super. Ct. 1992), 517n.54.

Commonwealth v. Hubert, 430 A.2d 1160 (Pa. 1981), 543n.55.

Commonwealth v. Walzack, 360 A.2d 914 (Pa. 1976), 542n.120.

In re Conklin, 946 F.2d 306 (4th Cir. 1991), 507nn.42, 47, 509nn.85, 91.

Coolidge v. New Hampshire, 403 U.S. 443 (1971), 496nn.36,50.

Copithorne v. Framingham Union Hosp., 520 N.E.2d 139 (Mass. 1988), 536n.247.

Corgan v. Muehling, 574 N.E.2d 602 (Ill. 1991), 522n.47, 532n.162.

County of DuPage v. Harris, 231 N.E.2d 195 (Ill. App. 1967), 24, 497n.61.

Cowe v. Forum Group, Inc., 541 N.E.2d 962 (Ind. Ct. App. 1989), 523n.72.

Coy v. Iowa, 487 U.S. 1012 (1988), 143, 517n.55.

Crowley v. Spivey, 329 S.E.2d 774 (S.C. App. 1985), 524n.88.

Cruzan v. Director, Missouri Dept. of Health, 497 U.S. 261 (1990), 333, 493n.9, 534n.205, 545n.96.

Cunningham v. Beavers, 858 F.2d 269 (5th Cir. 1988), 502n.109.

Curlender v. Bio-Science Laboratories, 165 Cal. Rptr. 477 (Cal. App. 1980), 523n.71.

Curran v. Bosze, 566 N.E.2d 1319 (Ill. 1990), 503n.150.

Currie v. United States, 644 F. Supp. 1074 (M.D.N.C. 1986), 531n.135.

Custody of a Minor, 393 N.E.2d 836 (Mass. 1979), 66, 505n.179.

D'Angelis v. Zakuto, 556 A.2d 431 (Pa. 1989), 527n.35.

D.B. v. Tewksbury, 545 F. Supp. 896 (D. Or. 1982), 539n.27.

D.R. v. Middle Bucks Area Vocational Technical School, 972 F.2d 1364 (3d Cir. 1992), 502n.104, 503n.136.

Dallas v. Stanglin, 490 U.S. 19 (1989), 54, 501n.83.

Daniel R.R. v. State Board of Education, 874 F.2d 1036 (5th Cir. 1989), 80, 509n.81, 510n.107.

Daniels v. Williams, 474 U.S. 327 (1986), 542n.24.

Daubert v. Merrell Dow Pharmaceuticals, 113 S.Ct. 2786 (1993), 494n.28, 546n.9.

David M. v. Margaret M., 385 S.E.2d 912 (W.Va. 1989), 511n.35.

Davis v. Lhim, 335 N.W.2d 481 (Mich. App. 1983), 530.113.

Davis v. Monsanto, 627 F. Supp. 418 (S.D. W.Va. 1986), 530n.115.

Davis v. State, 569 So. 2d 1317 (Fla. App. 1990), 517n.43,546n.11.

Davis v. Tirrell, 443 N.Y.S.2d 136 (N.Y. Sup. Ct. 1981), 527n.29, 537n.272.

DeBurkarte v. Louvar, 393 N.W.2d 131 (Iowa 1986), 533n.189.

Dennis v. Allison, 698 S.W.2d 94 (Tex. 1985), 526n.14.

Department of Health & Rehabilitative Services v. Whaley, 574 So. 2d 100 (Fla. 1991), 536n.250.

DeRosa v. City of New York, 517 N.Y.S.2d 754 (N.Y. App. Div. 1987), 503n.142.

DeShaney v. Winnebago County Department of Social Services, 489 U.S. 189 (1989), 17, 50, 495n.15, 500n.58, 546n.119.

Ex parte Devine, 398 So. 2d 686 (Ala. 1981), 511n.25.

Dial Information Services v. Thornburgh, 938 F.2d 1535 (2d Cir. 1991), 56, 502n.99.

Dick v. Lewis, 506 F. Supp. 799 (D.N.D. 1980), aff'd, 636 F.2d 1168 (8th Cir. 1981), 528n.47.

In re Dickson, 469 N.W.2d 357 (Neb. 1991), 543n.48.

In re Marriage of Diehl, 582 N.E.2d 281 (Ill. App. Ct. 1991), 514n.146, 515n.155.

Dillon v. Legg, 441 P.2d 912 (Cal. 1968), 196, 522n.44.

DiStefano v. DiStefano, 401 N.Y.S.2d 636 (N.Y. App. Div. 1978), 512n.66, 514n.151.

Dobbs v. Smith, 514 So. 2d 871 (Ala. 1987), 534n.195.

Doctors Hospital v. Kovats, 494 P.2d 389 (Ariz. App. 1972), 526n.7.

In re Doe, 519 P.2d 133 (N.M. App. 1974), 539n.35.

Doe v. Austin, 848 F.2d 1386 (6th Cir. 1988), 543n.36.

Doe v. Board of Education of Montgomery County, 453 A.2d 814 (Md. App. 1982), 503n.142.

Doe v. Cowherd, 965 F.2d 109 (6th Cir. 1992), 540n.15.

Doe v. Irwin, 615 F.2d 1162 (6th Cir. 1980), 504n.166.

Doe v. Roe, 400 N.Y.S.2d 668 (N.Y. Sup. Ct. 1977), 235, 529nn.89, 96.

Doe v. Smith, 879 F.2d 1340 (6th Cir. 1989), 510n.95.

Doe v. Shenandoah County School Board, 737 F. Supp. 913 (W.D. Va. 1990), 502n.125.

Doe v. Taylor Independent School District, 975 F.2d 137 (5th Cir. 1992), 502n.103, 503n.137.

Doe v. Woodbridge Nursing Pavillion, Ill. Cook County Cir. (Jan. 15, 1992), 522n.48.

Dolan v. Von Zweck, 477 N.E.2d 200 (Mass. App. 1985), 537n.264.

Dominguez v. Kelly, 786 S.W.2d 749 (Tex. Ct. App. 1990), 137, 516n.30.

Donaldson v. O'Connor, 493 F.2d 507 (5th Cir. 1974), vacated on other grounds, 422 U.S. 563, (1975), 542nn.4, 20, 543nn.34, 55.

Donohue v. Copiague Union Free School District, 391 N.E.2d 1352 (1979), 503n.140.

Doremus v. Farrell, 407 F. Supp. 509 (D. Neb. 1975), 543n.37.

Dorsey v. Board of Regents, 449 N.Y.S.2d 337 (N.Y. App. Div. 1982), 532n.164.

Dowling v. Dowling, 679 P.2d 480 (Alaska 1984), 511n.11.

Downer v. Veilleux, 322 A.2d 82 (Me. 1974), 527nn.35, 36.

Drope v. Missouri, 420 U.S. 162 (1975), 309, 541n.100.

DuBois v. Decker, 29 N.E. 313 (N.Y. App. Div. 1891), 526n.11.

Duckworth v. Bennett, 181 A. 558 (Pa. 1935), 527n.35.

Dumas v. Cooney, 1 Cal. Rptr. 2d 584 (Ct. App. 1991), 528n.49.

Dun & Bradstreet v. Greenmoss Builders, 472 U.S. 749 (1985), 536n.257.

DuPont v. DuPont, 216 A.2d 674 (Del. 1966), 513n.100.

Durham v. United States, 214 F.2d 862 (D.C. Cir. 1954), 541n.116.

Dusky v. United States, 362 U.S. 402 (1960), 309, 541n.99.

Eggers v. Bullitt County School Dist., 854 F.2d 892 (6th Cir. 1988), 508n.58.

Eisel v. Board of Education of Montgomery County, 597 A.2d 447 (Md. 1991), 522n.41, 535n.231.

Eisenstadt v. Baird, 405 U.S. 438 (1972), 47, 500n.40.

Ely v. Casteel, 341 So. 2d 730 (Ala. Ct. Civ. App. 1977), 514n.128.

Adoption of Embick, 506 A.2d 455 (Pa. Super. 1986), 530n.108.

Emory University v. Porter, 120 S.E.2d 668 (Ga. App. 1961), 536n.254.

Employment Division, Oregon Department of Human Resources v. Smith, 494 U.S. 872 (1990), 496n.30.

Endresz v. Friedberg, 248 N.E.2d 901 (N.Y. Ct. App. 1969), 523n.65.

Engel v. Vitale, 370 U.S. 421 (1962), 502n.122.

Erie R. Co. v. Tompkins, 304 U.S. 64 (1938), 16, 495n.14.

Ervin v. American Guardian Life Assur., 545 A.2d 354 (Pa. Super. 1988), 527n.23.

Marriage of Estelle, 592 S.W.2d 277 (Mo. App. 1979), 512n.43.

Estelle v. Gamble, 429 U.S. 97 (1976), 496n.53.

Estelle v. Smith, 451 U.S. 454 (1981), 546n.13.

Eubanks v. Clarke, 434 F. Supp. 1022 (E.D. Pa. 1977), 543n.55.

Eugene D. v. Karman, 889 F.2d 701 (6th Cir. 1989), 500n.61.

Evans v. District No. 17, 841 F.2d 824 (8th Cir. 1988), 509n.88.

F v. R. (1983), 33 S.A. St.R. 189 (S. Ct. S.A.), 528n.63.

F.C.C. v. Pacifica Foundation, 438 U.S. 726 (1978), 55, 501n.94.

Faigenbaum v. Cohen (Mich. Wayne County Court 1982) 244, 533n.181.

Falcon v. Memorial Hospital, 462 N.W.2d 44 (Mich. 1990), 528n.50.

Farber v. Olkon, 254 P.2d 520 (Cal. 1953), 207, 525n.119.

Fare v. Michael C., 442 U.S. 707 (1979), 46, 312, 499nn.32, 35, 539n.21, 541n.109.

Farwell v. Un, 902 F.2d 282 (4th Cir. 1990), 535n.230.

Feldman v. Feldman, 358 N.Y.S.2d 507 (N.Y. App. Div. 1974), 512n.81.

Fernandez v. Baruch, 244 A.2d 109 (N.J. 1968), 534n.209.

Ferriter v. Daniel O'Connell's Sons, Inc., 413 N.E.2d 690 (Mass. 1980), 524n.94, 525n.97.

Field v. Haddonfield Bd. of Educ., 769 F. Supp. 1313 (D.N.J. 1991), 508n.60.

Figueiredo-Torres v. Nickel, 584 A.2d 69 (Md. 1991), 532n.157.

Finlay v. Finlay, 148 N.E. 624 (N.Y. Ct. App. 1925), 511n.32.

Fischer v. Metcalf, 543 So. 2d 785 (Fla. App. 1989), 516n.26.

Fisher v. Carrousel Motor Hotel, 424 S.W.2d 627 (Tex. 1967), 521n.10.

Fitzgerald v. Manning, 679 F.2d 341 (4th Cir. 1982), 528n.47.

Flaherty v. Smith, 274 N.W.2d 72 (Mich. App. 1978), 513n.100.

Fleisher v. City of Signal Hill, 829 F.2d 1491 (9th Cir. 1987), 57, 502n.102.

The Florida Star v. B.J.F., 491 U.S. 524 (1989), 521n.23, 539n.41.

Ford v. Aldi, Inc., 832 S.W.2d 1 (Mo. App. 1992), 522n.49.

Franklin v. Gwinnett County Public Schools, 112 S.Ct. 1028 (1992), 49, 500n.52, 503n.135.

Friedman v. State, 493 N.E.2d 893 (N.Y. Ct. App. 1986), 536n.251.

Frye v. United States, 293 F. 1013 (D.C. Cir. 1923), 344, 546n.8.

Fuller v. Preis, 322 N.E.2d 263 (N.Y. Ct. App. 1974), 534n.212.

Furey v. Thomas Jefferson University Hospital, 472 A.2d 1083 (Pa. Super. Ct. 1984) 527n.35.,

Furniss v. Fitchett [1958] N.Z.L.R. 396, 258, 537n.270.

Gaido v. Weiser, 558 A.2d 845 (N.J. 1989), 249, 534n.213.

Gallo v. Gallo, 440 A.2d 782 (Conn. 1981), 512n.67.

Gann v. Delaware State Hospital, 543 F. Supp. 268 (1982), 544n.72.

Garratt v. Dailey, 279 P.2d 1091 (Wash. 1955), 188, 521n.2.

Garza v. State, 828 S.W.2d 432 (Tex. Ct. App. 1992), 517n.46.

Gates v. Jensen, 595 P.2d 919 (Wash. 1979), 494n.7.

In re Gault, 387 U.S. 1 (1967), 17, 43, 45, 274, 275, 495n.18, 496nn.37, 39, 499nn.1117, 26, 31, 510n.144, 538nn.2, 6, 539n.37, 540n.48.

Gelbman v. Gelbman, 245 N.E.2d 192 (N.Y. Ct. App. 1969), 525n.104.

Gerardi v. Nuclear Utility Services, Inc., 566 N.Y.S.2d 1002 (Sup. Ct. 1991), 523n.63.

Gerstein v. Pugh, 420 U.S. 103 (1975), 539n.33.

Gertz v. Robert Welch, Inc., 418 U.S. 323 (1974), 256, 536n.256.

Gesicki v. Oswald, 336 F. Supp. 371 (S.D. N.Y. 1971)499n.20, 540n.46.

Ginsberg v. New York, 390 U.S. 629 (1968), 55, 496n.43, 501n.91.

Gluckstern v. Gluckstern, 151 N.E.2d 897 (N.Y. Ct. App. 1956), 513n.91.

Goings v. United States, 377 F.2d 753 (8th Cir. 1967), 546n.23.

Goldade v. State, 674 P.2d 721 (Wyo. 1983), 517n.43.

Goodrich v. Tinker, 437 S.W.2d 882 (Tex. Civ. App. 1969), 497n.88.

Goodwin v. Shapiro, 545 F. Supp. 826 (D.N.J. 1982), 544n.67.

Gordon v. Gordon, 577 P.2d 1271 (Okla. 1978), 511n.27.

Goss v. Lopez, 419 U.S. 565 (1975), 58, 496n.39, 502n.111.

Gotkin v. Miller, 514 F.2d 125 (2d Cir. 1975), 537n.273.

Gould v. Gould, 342 N.W.2d 426 (Wis. 1984), 513n.87.

In re Grady, 426 A.2d 467 (N.J. 1981), 503n.151.

Marriage of Grandinetti, 342 N.W.2d 876 (Iowa App. 1983), 513n.88.

Graves v. Wooden, 291 S.W.2d 665 (Mo. Ct. App. 1956), 100, 512n.79.

Grayman v. Hession, 446 N.Y.S.2d 505 (N.Y. App. Div. 1982), 513n.94.

Great Atlantic & Pacific Tea Co. v. Roch, 153 A. 22 (Md. App. 1931), 521n.18.

Greenberg v. McCabe, 453 F. Supp. 765 (E.D. Pa. 1978), 528n.46.

Greenman v. Yuba Power Products, 377 P.2d 897 (Cal. 1963), 525n.117.

Greenspan v. Slate, 97 A.2d 390 (N.J. 1953), 505n.175.

Greer v. Rome City School District, 950 F.2d 688 (11th Cir. 1991), 80, 507n.42, 510nn.107, 108, 109, 111.

Griffin v. Illinois, 351 U.S. 12 (1956), 539n.43.

Griffith v. Johnston, 899 F.2d 1427 (5th Cir. 1990), 518n.84.

Grimes v. Cavazos, 786 F. Supp. 1184 (S.D. N.Y. 1992), 503n.134.

Griswold v. Connecticut, 381 U.S. 479 (1965), 47, 500n.40, 511n.7.

Grosslight v. Superior Court, 140 Cal. Rptr. 278 (Cal. App. 1977), 498n.111.

Gundy v. Pauley, 619 S.W.2d 730 (Ky. Ct. App. 1981), 544n.80.

Hagerty v. L&L Marine Services, 788 F.2d 315 (5th Cir. 1986), 198, 523n.59.

Halderman v. Pennhurst State School and Hospital, 673 F.2d 647 (3d Cir. 1982), 544n.83.

Halderman v. Pennhurst State School and Hospital, 901 F.2d 311 (3d Cir. 1990) (Enforcement of settlement), 321, 543n.266.

Hall v. Hilbun, 466 So. 2d 856 (Miss. 1985), 527n.41.

Hall v. State, 415 S.E.2d 158 (Ga. 1991), 517n.49.

Hamling v. United States, 418 U.S. 87 (1974), 546n.5.

Hamman v. County of Maricopa, 775 P.2d 1122 (Ariz. 1989), 531nn.139, 140.

Hammer v. Rosen, 165 N.E.2d 756 (N.Y. Ct. App. 1960), 242, 533n.171.

Harbeson v. Parke-Davis, Inc., 656 P.2d 483 (Wash. 1983), 523n.68.

Hardy v. Brantley, 471 So. 2d 358 (Miss. 1958), 527n.40.

Harris v. Harris, 343 So. 2d 762 (Miss. 1977), 513n.92.

Harris v. Jones, 380 A.2d 611 (Md. 1977), 521nn.13, 15, 19.

Harris v. McRae, 448 U.S. 297 (1980), 504n.157.

Harris v. Vasquez, 943 F.2d 930 (9th Cir. 1990), 511n.205.

Harrison v. Harrison, 359 So. 2d 266 (La. App. 1978), 512n.82.

Hartke v. McKelway, 526 F. Supp. 97 (D.D.C. 1981), 523n.72.

Hartogs v. Employers Mutual Liability Insurance Co. of Wisconsin, 391 N.Y.S.2d 962 (Sup. Ct. 1977), 532n.166.

Haselhorst v. State, 485 N.W.2d 180 (Neb. 1992), 202, 518n.66,524n.87.

Hathaway v. Worcester City Hospital, 475 F.2d 701 (1st Cir. 1973), 511n.8.

Hawaii v. Kim, 645 P.2d. 1330 (Haw. 1982), 520n.165.

Hay v. Medical Center Hosp., 496 A.2d 939 (Vt. 1985), 524n.93, 525nn.97, 98, 99.

In re Guardianship of Hayes, 608 P.2d 635 (Wash. 1980), 503n.151.

Hazelwood School District v. Kuhlmeier, 484 U.S. 260 (1988), 58, 495n.23, 502n.113.

Heaven v. Pender, 11 Q.B.D. 503 (1883), 522n.34.

Hedlund v. Superior Court of Orange County, 669 P.2d 41 (Cal. 1983), 531nn.143, 144.

Heller v. Doe, 113 S.Ct. 2637 (1993), 543n.52.

Helling v. Carey, 519 P.2d 981 (Wash. 1974), 13, 494n.6, 527n.33.

Helling v. McKinney, 61 LW 4648 (1993), 544n.72.

Hellstrom v. Commonwealth, 825 S.W.2d 612 (Ky. 1992), 517n.54.

Helms v. Franciscus, 2 Bland. Ch 544 (Md. 1830), 91, 511n.22.

Hendershott v. People, 653 P.2d 385 (Colo. 1982), 542n.121.

Henning v. Thomas, 366 S.E.2d 109 (Va. 1988), 527n.32.

Hernandez v. Smith, 552 F.2d 142 (5th Cir. 1977), 536n.253.

Herskovits v. Group Health Cooperative, 664 P.2d 474 (Wash. 1983), 528n.51, 533n.189.

Hibpshman v. Prudhoe Bay Supply, Inc., 734 P.2d 991 (Alaska 1987), 524nn.93, 95, 96, 525nn.97, 102.

Hickman v. Taylor, 329 U.S. 495 (1947), 546n.16.

Hicks v. United States, 368 F.2d 626 (4th Cir. 1966), 527n.22.

Hidding v. Williams, 578 So. 2d 1192 (La. App. 1991), 528n.66.

Higgins v. Higgins, 629 S.W.2d 20 (Tenn. App. 1981), 515n.171.

Higgins v. State, 265 N.Y.S.2d 254 (Sup. Ct. 1965), 536n.245.

Holder v. United States, 150 U.S. 91 (1893), 546n.21.

Hodgson v. Minnesota, 853 F.2d 1452 (8th Cir. 1988), aff'd, 497 U.S. 417 (1990), 499n.27, 500n.38.

Hoffman v. Board of Education of the City of New York, 400 N.E.2d 317 (Ct. App. 1979), 61, 503n.141.

Homer v. Long, 599 A.2d 1193 (Md. Ct. Spec. App. 1992), 532n.157.

Honeycutt v. Wichita, 796 P.2d 549 (Kan. 1990), 498n.4, 525n.116.

Honig v. Doe, 484 U.S. 305 (1988), 75, 507nn.33, 35, 42.

Horne v. Patton, 287 So. 2d 824 (Ala. 1973), 529n.93.

Horst v. McLain, 466 S.W.2d 187 (Mo. Ct. App. 1971), 511n.20.

Horton v. Niagara Falls Memorial Medical Center, 380 N.Y.S.2d 116 (App. Div. 1976), 536n.254.

Howard v. Drapkin, 271 Cal. Rptr. 893 (Cal. App. 1990), 225, 516n.33, 527n.26, 537n.270, 546n.12.

Hudgens v. NLRB, 424 U.S. 507 (1976), 53, 501n.80.

Hughley v. McDermott, 530 A.2d 13 (Md. Spec. App. 1987), 537n.267.

Humphers v. First Interstate Bank of Oregon, 696 P.2d 527 (Or. 1985), 234, 529nn.91, 92.

Humphrey v. Cady, 405 U.S. 504 (1972), 543n.54.

Huntley v. State, 464 N.E.2d 467 (Ct. App. 1984), 534n.202.

Hurley v. Eddingfield, 59 N.E. 1058 (Ind. 1901), 526n.15.

Hurley v. United States, 923 F.2d 1091 (4th Cir. 1991), 528n.49.

Idaho v. Wright, 497 U.S. 805 (1990), 141, 498n.104, 517nn.43, 46, 47.

In re Infant Doe, No. GU 8204-004A (Cir. Ct. Monroe County, Ind. April 12, 1982), 66, 505n.181.

Inabnit v. Berkson, 245 Cal. Rptr. 525 (Cal. App. 1988), 530n.107.

Ingraham v. Wright, 430 U.S. 651 (1977), 23, 58, 497n.59, 502n.108, 503n.138.

Inmates of Boys' Training School v. Affleck, 346 F. Supp. 1354 (D. R.I. 1972), 545nn.116, 118, 546n.120.

International Society for Krishna Consciousness v. Lee, 112 S.Ct. 2701 (1992), 501n.77.

Irving Independent School Dist. v. Tatro, 468 U.S. 883 (1984), 80, 507n.42, 510n.95.

Isaacs v. Isaacs, 358 S.E.2d 833 (W.Va. 1987), 511n.29.

J.B. v. A.B., 242 S.E.2d 248 (W.Va. 1978), 511n.27.

J.L.P.(H.) v. D.J.P., 643 S.W.2d 865 (Mo. App. 1982), 512n.68, 514n.148.

J.O. v. Alton Community School District, 909 F.2d 267 (7th Cir. 1990), 503n.1356.

J.P. v. P.W., 772 S.W.2d 786 (Mo. App. 1989), 512n.70, 513n.106.

Matter of J.S. & C., 342 A.2d 90 (N.J. Super. 1974), 514n.148.

Jackson v. Indiana, 406 U.S. 715 (1972), 309, 541n.96.

Jackson v. Power, 743 P.2d 1376 (Alaska 1987), 537n.287.

Jacobson v. Jacobson, 314 N.W.2d 78 (N.D. 1981), 514n.149.

Jacobson v. United States, 112 S.Ct. 1535 (1992), 501n.90.

Jefferson County Bd. of Educ. v. Breen, 853 F.2d 853 (11th Cir. 1988), 508n.54.

Jensen v. Archbishop Bergan Mercy Hosp., 459 N.W.2d 178 (Neb. 1990), 527n.45.

In re Jessica B., 254 Cal. Rptr. 883 (Cal. App. 1989), 517n.61.

Johnson v. Calvert, 61 LW 2721 (1993), 513n.116.

Johnson v. Greer, 477 F.2d 101 (5th Cir. 1973), 251, 536nn.235, 241.

Johnson v. Horace Mann Mutual Ins. Co., 241 So. 2d 588 (La. App. 1970), 502n.110.

Johnson v. Johnson, 681 P.2d 78 (Okla. 1984), 514n.130.

Johnson v. Lundell, 361 N.W.2d 125 (Minn. App. 1985), 513n.102.

Johnson v. Misericordia Community Hospital, 301 N.W.2d 156 (Wis. 1981), 537n.286.

Johnson v. Ruark Obstetrics & Gynecology Assoc., 395 S.E.2d 85 (N.C. 1990), 522n.49.

Johnson v. State, 334 N.E.2d 590 (N.Y. App. 1975), 522n.55.

Johnson v. State, 447 P.2d 352 (Cal. 1968), 531n.136.

Johnson v. State, 439 A.2d 542 (Md. 1982), 542n.120.

Johnson v. United States, 409 F. Supp. 1283 (M.D. Fla. 1976), 535n.220.

Johnson v. University of Chicago Hospitals, 61 LW 2400 (7th Cir. 1992).

Johnson v. West Virginia University Hospitals, 413 S.E.2d 889 (W.Va. 1991), 198, 523n.61.

Johnson v. Zerbst, 304 U.S. 458 (1938), 332, 544n.90.

Johnston v. Ohls, 457 P.2d 194 (Wash. 1969), 498n.100, 517n.42.

Johnston v. Sibley, 558 S.W.2d 135 (Tex. Civ. App. 1977), 527n.23.

Ex rel. Jones, 567 So. 2d 664 (La. Ct. App. 1990), 518n.74.

Jones v. Clear Creek Independent School Dist.,, No. 89-2638 November 24, 1992, 495n.28, 502n.124.

Jones v. Gerhardstein, 416 N.W.2d 883 (Wis. 1987), 545n.95.

Jones v. Fisher, 166 N.W.2d 175 (Wis. 1969), 521n.27.

Joy v. Eastern Maine Medical Center, 529 A.2d 1364 (Me. 1987), 531n.125.

Joyce-Couch v. DeSilva, 602 N.E.2d 286 (Ohio Ct. App. 1991), 521n.27.

Juvenile Dept. of Lane County v. Gibson, 718 P.2d 759 (Or. App. 1986), 499n.37.

K.H. v. Morgan, 914 F.2d 846 (7th Cir. 1990), 495n.17.

K.J.B. v. C.M.B., 779 S.W.2d 36 (Mo. App. 1989), 512n.71.

Kaehler v. Kaehler, 18 N.W.2d 312 (Minn. 1945), 512n.56.

Kaimowitz v. Dept. of Mental Health, No. 73-19434-AW (Mich. Cir. Ct., Wayne County, July 10, 1973), 228, 528n.56.

Karl v. Oaks Minor Emergency Clinic, 826 S.W.2d 791 (Tex. Ct. App. 1992), 528n.49.

Kates v. State, 261 N.Y.S.2d 988 (N.Y. Claims 1965), 535n.215.

Katz v. Enzer, 504 N.E.2d 427 (Ohio App. 1985), 257, 537n.268.

Katz v. United States, 389 U.S. 347 (1967), 539n.14.

Kaufman v. Western Union, 224 F.2d 723 (5th Cir. 1955), 522n.55.

Kent v. United States, 383 U.S. 541 (1966), 43, 68, 274, 275, 496n.37, 499nn.17, 26, 505nn.187, 188, 538nn.3, 5, 539n.35.

Kent v. Whitaker, 364 P.2d 556 (Wash. 1961), 534n.214.

King v. Smith, 539 So. 2d 262 (Ala. 1989), 535n.223.

King v. Vancil, 341 N.E.2d 65 (Ill. App. Ct. 1975), 511n.25.

Kirk v. Michael Reese Hospital and Medical Center, 483 N.E.2d 906 (Ill. App. Ct. 1985), rev'd, 513 N.E.2d 387 (Ill. 1987), 531n.125.

Kirker v. Orange County, 519 So. 2d 682 (Fla. App. 1988), 521n.22.

Klein v. Reynolds, 291 N.E.2d 446 (Ohio 1972), 535n.219.

Knight v. District of Columbia, 877 F.2d 1025 (D.C. Cir. 1989), 509n.81.

Koch v. Gorrilla, 552 F.2d 1170 (6th Cir. 1977), 527n.35.

Kozup v. Georgetown University, 663 F. Supp. 1048 (D.D.C. 1987), 528n.63.

Krichinsky v. Knox County Schools, 963 F.2d 847 (6th Cir. 1992), 508n.60.

Krieg v. Massey, 781 P.2d 277 (Mont. 1989), 534n.212.

Kuhlmeier v. Hazelwood School District, 795 F.2d 1368 (8th Cir. 1986), 495n.23.

L. v. Matheson, 450 U.S. 398 (1981), 497n.74, 499, 33, 38.

L.L. v. Medical Protective Co., 362 N.W.2d 174 (Wis. App. 1984), 532nn.167, 170.

Lacey v. Laird, 139 N.E.2d 25 (Ohio 1956), 505n.183.

Lake v. Cameron, 364 F.2d 657 (D.C. Cir. 1966), 329, 544n.65.

Lambert v. California, 355 U.S. 225 (1957), 501n.70.

Landau v. Weiner, 105 Sol. J. 1008 (1961), 532n.162.

Landeros v. Flood, 551 P.2d 389 (Cal. 1976), 138, 236, 516nn.27, 34; 529n.102.

Lanes v. State, 767 S.W.2d 789 (Tex. Ct. App. 1989), 538n.13.

Lascari v. Board of Educ., 560 A.2d 1180 (N.J. 1989), 509n.81.

LaShawn A. v. Dixon, 762 F. Supp. 959 (D.D.C. 1991), 51, 500n.63.

LaShawn A. v. Kelly, 990 F.2d 1319 (D.C. Cir. 1993), 500nn.48, 50, 63.

Lassiter v. Department of Social Services, 452 U.S. 18 (1981), 148, 516n. 36, 518n.76.

Lavit v. Superior Court, 839 P.2d 1141 (Ariz. Ct. App. 1992), 537n.264.

Lawson v. Brown, 349 F. Supp. 203 (W.D. Va. 1972), 505n.186.

Layton v. Foster, 460 N.E.2d 1351 (1984), 514n.136.

Lee v. Weisman, 112 S.Ct. 2649 (1992), 18, 495n.28, 502n.124.

Lehmann v. Toys "R" Us, 132 N.J. 587, 626 A.2d 445 (1993), 536n.246.

Lehr v. Robinson, 463 U.S. 248 (1983), 518n.80.

Leland v. Oregon, 343 U.S. 790 (1952), 35, 498n.116.

Lemon v. Kurtzman, 403 U.S. 602 (1971), aff'd, 411 U.S. 192 (1973), 502n.121.

Lessard v. Schmidt, 349 F. Supp. 1078 (E.D. Wis. 1972), 322, 543n.33.

Lester H. v. Gilhool, 916 F.2d 865 (3d Cir. 1990), 508n.54.

In re Lifschutz, 467 P.2d 557 (Cal. 1970), 530n.104, 546n.14.

Limjoco v. Schenck, 486 N.W.2d 567 (Wis. Ct. App. 1992), 533n.176.

Linder v. Bidner, 270 N.Y.S.2d 427 (Sup. Ct. 1966), 522n.38.

Lipari v. Sears, Roebuck & Co., 497 F. Supp. 185 (D. Neb. 19531n.140.80), 531n.140.

Lloyd v. North Broward Hosp. Dist., 570 So. 2d 984 (Fl. Dist. Ct. App. 1990), 523n.70.

Lo Dico v. Caputi, 517 N.Y.S.2d 640 (N.Y. App. Div. 1987), 527n.23.

Lochner v. New York, 198 U.S. 45 (1905), 496n.33.

Logan v. District of Columbia, 447 F. Supp. 1328 (D.D.C. 1978), 529n.90.

Looper v. McManus, 581 P.2d 487 (Okla. Ct. App. 1978), 514n.132.

Lotspeich v. Chance Vought Aircraft, 369 S.W.2d 705 (Tex. Civ. App. 1963), 527n.23.

Louisiana v. Perry, 61 L.W. 2288 (1992), 541n.106, 545n.97.

Loving v. Virginia, 388 U.S. 1 (1967), 510n.3.

Lubbock Civil Liberties Union v. Lubbock Independent School District, 669 F.2d 1038 (5th Cir. 1982), 502n.124.

Lundell v. Lundell, 387 N.W.2d 654 (Minn. App. 1986), 513n.98.

Lundgren v. Fultz, 354 N.W.2d 25 (Minn. 1984), 239, 531n.141.

Lux v. Hansen, 886 F.2d 1064 (8th Cir. 1989), 500n.61.

Lynch v. Baxley, 386 F. Supp. 378 (M.D. Ala. 1974), 543n.47.

Lyons v. Grether, 239 S.E.2d 103 (Va. 1977), 526n.17.

M'Naghten's Case, 8 Eng. Rep. 718 (H.L. 1843), 313, 541n.112.

M.A.B. v. R.B., 510 N.Y.S.2d 960 (Sup. Ct. 1986), 515nn.147, 153.

M.E.D. v. J.P.M., 350 S.E.2d 215 (Va. App. 1986), 511n.33, 512n.69.

Adoption of M.J.C., 590 N.E.2d 1095 (Ind. Ct. App. 1992), 514n.131.

Ex rel. M.W., 796 P.2d 66 (Colo. Ct. App. 1990), 518n.75.

MacDonald v. Clinger, 446 N.Y.S.2d 801 (App. Div. 1982), 530n.112.

Mahnke v. Moore, 77 A.2d 923 (Md. 1951), 525n.105.

Mailliard v. Gonzalez, No. 50424 (N.D. Cal.1971), *vacated and remanded*, 416 U.S. 918 (1974), 540n.46.

Maldonado v. Josey, 61 L.W. 2199 (10th Cir. 1992), 503n.136.

Marlene F. v. Affiliated Psychiatric Medical Clinic, Inc., 770 P.2d 278 (Cal. 1989), 197, 523n.56.

Marsh v. Alabama, 326 U.S. 501 (1946), 501n.79.

Martens v. Martens, 167 A. 227 (N.J. 1933), 525n.106.

Martin v. Hunter's Lessee, 14 U.S. (1 Wheat.) 304 (1816), 497n.75.

Marvin v. Marvin, 557 P.2d 106 (Cal. 1976), 511n.6.

Maryland v. Craig, 497 U.S. 836 (1990), 143, 493n.11, 498n.120, 517n.56.

Mathews v. Eldridge, 424 U.S. 319 (1976), 542n.22.

Matta v. Board of Educ., 731 F. Supp. 253 (S.D. Ohio 1990), 509n.81.

Matts v. Homsi, 308 N.W.2d 284 (Mich. App. 1981), 533n.175.

Mauro v. Raymark Indus., 561 A.2d 257 (N.J. 1989), 523n.59.

In re Maxwell, 456 N.E.2d 1218 (Ohio App. 1982), 511n.35.

Mazza v. Huffaker, 300 S.E.2d 833 (N.C. Ct. App. 1983), 532n.158.

Mazza v. Medical Mutual Insur. Co. of North America, 319 S.E.2d 217 (N.C. 1984), 532n.167.

In the Matter of McCauley, 565 N.E.2d 411 (Mass. Sup. Jud. Ct. 1991), 505n.177.

McClain v. McClain, 716 P.2d 381 (Alaska 1986), 512n.52.

McCleskey v. Kemp, 481 U.S. 279 (1987), 4, 493n.6.

McDonald v. United States, 312 F.2d 847 (D.C. Cir. 1962), 314, 542n.117.

McDougald v. Garber, 536 N.E.2d 372 (N.Y. App. 1989), 524n.92.

McGuire v. Almy, 8 N.E.2d 760 (Mass. 1937), 521n.7.

McIntyre v. Balentine, 833 S.W.2d 52 (Tenn. 1992), 525n.110.

McIntyre v. McIntyre, 452 So. 2d 14 (Fla. App. 1984), 513n.109.

McKeiver v. Pennsylvania, 403 U.S. 528 (1971), 276, 538n.8, 539n.39.

McKellips v. St. Francis Hospital, 741 P.2d 467 (Okla. 1987), 533n.189.

McNamara v. Honeyman, 546 N.E.2d 139 (Mass. 1989), 534n.195.

Medina v. California, 112 S.Ct. 2572 (1992), 541n.98.

Meiers-Post v. Shafer, 427 N.W.2d 606 (Mich. App. 1988), 494n.10.

Meinze v. Holmes, 532 N.E.2d 170 (Ohio App. 1987), 527n.23.

Menendez v. Superior Court, 279 Cal. Rptr. 521 (App. 1991), 236, 530n.114.

Meyer v. Nebraska, 262 U.S. 390 (1923), 496n.43.

Michael M. v. Superior Court of Sonoma County, 450 U.S. 464 (1981), 56, 502n.101.

Mikel v. Abrams, 541 F. Supp. 591 (W.D. Mo. 1982), 529n.90.

Miley v. Landry, 582 So.2d 833 (La. 1991), 524n.85.

In re Miller, 585 N.E.2d 396 Ohio (1992), 542n.21.

Mills v. Board of Education, 348 F. Supp. 866 (D.D.C. 1972), 74, 506nn.20,27.

Miner v. Miner, 11 Ill. 43 (1849), 91, 511n.23.

Mink v. University of Chicago, 460 F. Supp. 713 (N.D. Ill. 1978), 228, 528n.57.

Miranda v. Arizona, 384 U.S. 436 (1966), 278, 312, 539n.18, 541n.108.

Mississippi University for Women v. Hogan, 458 U.S. 718 (1982), 503n.133.

Missouri v. Jenkins, 491 U.S. 274 (1989), 543n.28.

Mittwede v. Mittwede, 490 S.W.2d 534 (Tenn. App. 1969), 98, 512n.73.

Mochen v. State, 352 N.Y.S.2d 290 (App. Div. 1974), 534n.211.

In re Moe, 432 N.E.2d 712 (Mass. 1982), 503n.151.

Mohr v. Williams, 104 N.W. 12 (Minn. 1905), 521n.11.

Molien v. Kaiser Foundation Hospitals, 616 P.2d 813 (Cal. 1980), 522n.52.

Molko v. Holy Spirit Ass'n., 762 P.2d 46 (Cal. 1988), 536n.240.

Monahan v. Dorchester Counseling Center, Inc., 961 F.2d 987 (1st Cir. 1992), 526n.10.

Moore v. Regents of University of California, 793 P.2d 479 (Cal. 1990), 231, 262, 529n.86, 538nn.292, 293.

In re Moorenovich, 634 F. Supp. 634 (D. Me. 1986), 523n.63.

Morales v. Turman, 535 F.2d 864 (5th Cir. 1976), reversed by 430 U.S. 322 (1977) 496n.58, 499n.19, 543n.25, 545nn.109, 118.

Morby v. Rogers, 252 P.2d 231 (Utah 1953), 523n.77.

Moss v. Weaver, 525 F.2d 1258 (5th Cir. 1976), 539n.33.

Mueller v. Mueller, 221 N.W.2d 39 (S.D. 1974), 533n.185.

Mulder v. Parke Davis & Co., 181 N.W.2d 882 (Minn. 1970), 246, 533n.183.

Mullaney v. Wilbur, 421 U.S. 684 (1975), 498n.118.

Mullen v. McKnelly, 693 S.W.2d 837 (Mo. App. 1985), 527n.25.

Muller v. Oregon, 208 U.S. 412 (1908), 498n.125.

Murray v. McMurchy [1949] 2 D.L.R. 442 (B.C. Sup. Ct.), 521n.26, 528n,55.

Murray v. Ministry of Defence [1988], 2 A11 E.R. 521 (H.L.), 536n.239.

In re N., 112 Cal. Rptr. 89 (Ct. App. 1974), 539n.43.

Naidu v. Laird, 539 A.2d 1064 (Del. 1988), 535n.228.

Nally v. Grace Community Church of the Valley, 763 P.2d 948 (Cal. 1988), 522n.42.

Naprstek v. Norwich, 545 F.2d 815 (2d Cir. 1976), 53, 501n.75.

Natanson v. Kline, 350 P.2d 1093 (Kan. 1960), 529n.75.

In re Nearhoof, 359 S.E.2d 587 (W.Va. 1987), 514n.136.

Negron v. Ward, 458 F. Supp. 748 (S.D.N.Y. 1978), 544n.67.

Nelson v. Concrete Supply Co., 399 S.E.2d 783 (S.C. 1991), 525n.110.

Nelson v. Heyne, 355 F. Supp. 451 (N.D. Ind. 1972), *aff'd*, 491 F.2d 352 (7th Cir. 1974), 339, 533n.182, 545nn.114,118.

Nelson v. Moriarty, 484 F.2d 1034 (1st Cir. 1973), 501n.69.

New Jersey v. T.L.O., 469 U.S. 325 (1985), 59, 339, 496n.52, 502n.126, 545n.113.

New York State Ass'n. for Retarded Children, Inc. v. Carey, 706 F.2d 956 (2d Cir. 1983), 542n.27.

New York State Ass'n. for Retarded Children, Inc. v. Rockefeller, 357 F. Supp. 752 (E.D.N.Y. 1973), 542n.25, 544n.67.

New York v. Ferber, 458 U.S. 747 (1982), 51, 495n.26, 500n.66.

Newmark v. Williams, 588 A.2d 1108 (Del. 1991), 66, 505n.176.

Nieves v. New York, 458 N.Y.S.2d 548 (App. Div. 1983), 534n.197, 535n.225.

Noto v. St. Vincents Hospital, 537 N.Y.S.2d 446 (Sup. Ct. 1988), 532nn.161, 163.

Nova Univ., Inc. v. Wagner, 491 So. 2d 1116 (Fla. 1986), 531n.139.

Novak v. Rathnam, 505 N.E.2d 773 (Ill. App. 1987), 531n.138.

O'Brien v. Cunard Steamship Co., 28 N.E. 266 (Mass. 1891), 522n.31.

O'Gilvie v. International Playtex, 821 F.2d 1438 (10th Cir. 1987), 524n.86.

O'Neal v. Division of Family Services, 821 P.2d 1139 (Utah 1991), 494n.10, 515n.1.

O'Neill v. Montefiore Hospital, 202 N.Y.S.2d 436 (App. Div. 1960), 224, 526n.16.

Ochoa v. Superior Court, 703 P.2d 1 (Cal. 1985), 522n.51.

Ohio v. Akron Center for Reproductive Health, 497 U.S. 502 (1990), 497n.74.

Oliver v. United States, 466 U.S. 170 (1984), 496n.51.

Olsen v. Nebraska, 313 U.S. 236 (1941), 496n.34.

Olson v. Western Airlines, 191 Cal. Rptr. 502 (App. 1983), 527n.29.

Osborne v. Ohio, 525 N.E.2d 1363 (1988), 51, 501nn.67, 88.

Osherov v. Chestnut Lodge et al., Maryland Health Claims Arbitration #82-262 (1982), 226, 231, 527n.22, 528n.47.

In re Owen, 295 N.E.2d 455 (Ill. 1973), 545n.108.

Pacific Mut. Life Ins. Co. v. Haslip, 111 S.Ct. 1032 (1991), 521n.28.

Paddock v. Chacko, 522 So. 2d 410 (Fla. App. 1988), 535nn.220, 226.

Palmer v. Durso, 393 N.Y.S.2d 898 (Sup. Ct. 1977), 537n.274.

Palmore v. Sidoti, 466 U.S. 429 (1984), 101, 513n.86

Palsgraf v. Long Island Railroad, 162 N.E. 99 (N.Y. 1928), 522n.37.

Parham v. R., 442 U.S. 584 (1979), 5, 18, 21, 45, 68, 325, 493n.13, 495n.19, 496n.46, 499n.31, 505nn.187, 190, 536n.237, 543n.53.

Park v. Park, 610 P.2d 826 (Okla. App. 1980), 511n.28.

Parvi v. City of Kingston, 362 N.E.2d 960 (N.Y. 1977), 536n.238.

Passoulas v. Ramey, 450 So. 2d 822 (Fla. 1984), 523n.71.

Pate v. Robinson, 383 U.S. 375 (1966), 309, 541n.95.

Patrick v. Burget, 486 U.S. 94 (1988), 497n.68.

Patterson v. New York, 432 U.S. 197 (1977), 498n.117.

Pauscher v. Iowa Methodist Medical Center, 408 N.W.2d 355 (Iowa 1987), 528n.54, 529n.71.

Payton v. New York, 445 U.S. 573 (1980), 539n.15.

In re Custody of Pearce, 456 A.2d 597 (Pa. Super. 1983), 513n.96.

Peck v. Counselling Service of Addison County, 499 A.2d 422 (Vt. 1985), 531n.142.

Pena v. New York State Division for Youth, 419 F. Supp. 203 (S.D. N.Y. 1976), 339, 545n.115.

Pendleton v. Burkhalter, 432 S.W.2d 724 (Tex. Civ. App. 1968), 252, 536n.242.

Pennhurst State School and Hospital v. Halderman, 465 U.S. 89 (1984), 544nn.81, 83.

Pennsylvania Asso. for Retarded Citizens v. Pennsylvania, 343 F. Supp. 279 (E.D. Pa. 1972), 74, 505nn.1,1,3,5,12,20,21,22,24,25,26.

People v. Beckley, 456 N.W.2d 391 (Mich. 1990), 142, 517n.51.

People v. Caplan, 238 Cal. Rptr. 478 (Cal. App. 1987), 530n.109.

People v. Castro, 462 N.Y.S.2d 369 (Sup. Ct. 1983), 499n.36.

People v. Crews, 522 N.E.2d 1167 (Ill. 1988), 541n.115.

People v. Decina, 138 N.E.2d 799 (N.Y. 1956), 542n.122.

People v. Ewing, 140 Cal. Rptr. 299 (App. 1977), 516n.8.

People v. Fogarty, 466 N.Y.S.2d 91 (App. Div. 1982), 520n.166.

People v. Hernandez, 168 Cal. Rptr. 898 (Ct. App. 1980), 134, 516n.10.

People v. Higgins, 159 N.E.2d 179 (N.Y. 1959), 542n.123.

People v. Izzo, 282 N.W.2d 10 (Mich. App. 1979), 517n.52.

People ex rel. Wallace v. Labrenz, 104 N.E.2d 769 (Ill. 1952), 496n.45.

People v. Nelson, 561 N.E.2d 439 (Ill. 1990), 516n.9.

Peoples Bank of Bloomington v. Damera, 581 N.E.2d 426 (Ill. App. 1991), 525n.109.

Perreira v. State, 768 P.2d 1198 (Colo. 1989), 531n.140.

Peter W. v. San Francisco Unified School District, 131 Cal. Rptr. 854 (Ct. App. 1976), 503n.140.

Petersen v. Bruen, 792 P.2d 18, Nev. (1990), 515n.1.

Petersen v. State of Washington, 671 P.2d 230 (Wash. 1983), 531n.126.

Petriello v. Kalman, 576 A.2d 474 (Conn. 1990), 523n.60.

In re Phillip B., 156 Cal. Rptr. 48 (Ct. App. 1979), 503n.147.

Pierce v. Society of Sisters, 268 U.S. 510 (1925), 495n.23, 496n.43, 502n.105.

Pierce v. Yerkovich, 363 N.Y.S.2d 403 (Fam. Ct. 1974), 512n.75.

Pisel v. Stamford Hosp., 430 A.2d 1 (Conn. 1980), 528n.48.

Planned Parenthood Ass'n of the Atlanta Area, Inc. v. Miller, 934 F.2d 1462 (11th Cir. 1991), 504n.162.

Planned Parenthood of Central Missouri v. Danforth, 428 U.S. 52 (1976), 64, 496n.39, 499n.33, 500n.38, 504n.158.

Planned Parenthood of Southeastern Pennsylvania v. Casey, 112 S.Ct. 2791 (1992), 47, 64, 494n.2, 496nn.35, 41, 497n.74, 500n.39, 504nn.159, 164, 511n.9.

Planned Parenthood of Southern Nevada v. Clark County School District, 441 F.2d 817 (1991), 58, 502n.116.

Platt v. McDonnell Douglas, 554 F. Supp. 360 (E.D. Mich. 1983), 524n.90.

Plyler v. Doe, 457 U.S. 202 (1982), 57, 502n.107.

Polk v. Central Susquehanna Intermediate Unit 16, 853 F.2d 171 (3d Cir. 1988), 78, 507n.42, 509nn.85, 86.

In re Polovchak, 454 N.E.2d 258 (Ill. 1983), 513n.99.

Pope v. Illinois, 481 U.S. 497 (1987), 55, 501n.92.

Powell v. Texas, 392 U.S. 514 (1968), 501n.70.

Power v. Arlington Hospital, 800 F. Supp. 1384 (E.D. Va. 1992), 526n.18.

Prejean v. Blackburn, 743 F.2d 1091 (5th Cir. 1984), 23, 496n.56.

Prince v. Massachusetts, 321 U.S. 158 (1944), 42, 133, 136, 496n.43, 499n.13, 516nn.2, 14,

Procanik v. Cillo, 478 A.2d 755 (N.J. 1984), 523n.70.

Pruneyard Shopping Center v. Robins, 447 U.S. 74 (1980), 53, 501n.82.

Public Utilities Comm'n v. Pollak, 343 U.S. 451 (1952), 501n.81.

Pusey v. Pusey, 728 P.2d 117 (Utah 1986), 511n.25.

Quarles v. Sutherland, 389 S.W.2d 249 (Tenn. 1965), 529n.90.

Quilloin v. Walcott, 434 U.S. 246 (1978), 518n.80.

In Re R [1991], 4 A11 E.R. 177, 505n.183.

R.A.V. v. St. Paul, Minn., 112 S.Ct. 2538 (1992), 495n.25.

R.J.D. v. Vaughan Clinic, 572 So. 2d 1225 (Ala. 1990), 25, 536n.237.

Radford v. Matczuk, 164 A.2d 904 (Md. 1960), 512n.74.

Ravi v. Williams, 536 So. 2d 1374 (Ala. 1988), 525n.122.

Reaves v. Ortho Pharmaceutical Corporation, 765 F. Supp. 1287 (D.C. Mich. 1991), 524n.86.

Reed v. Reed, 404 U.S. 71 (1971), 496n.38.

Reighley v. International Playtex, Inc., 604 F. Supp. 1078 (D. Colo. 1985), 524nn.96, 97, 100, 102.

Rennie v. Klein, 462 F. Supp. 1131 (D.N.J. 1978), *vacated*, 458 U.S. 1119 (1982) 332, 545n.92.,

Reno v. Flores, 113 S.Ct. 1439 (1993), 539n.26.

Reynolds v. United States, 98 U.S. 145 (1879), 510n.4.

Ricci v. Okin, 781 F. Supp. 826 (D. Mass. 1992), 543n.27.

Richardson v. Richardson-Merrell, Inc., 857 F.2d 823 (D.C. Cir. 1988), 494n.28.

Richmond v. Arizona Department of Corrections, 61 L.W. 4013 (1992), 496n.57.

Riggins v. Nevada, 112 S.Ct. 1810 (1992), 311, 541nn.97, 105, 545n.98.

In re Riley, 301 S.E.2d 750 (N.C. Ct. App. 1983), 539n.20.

Ex rel. Riley, 653 F.2d 1153 (7th Cir. 1981), 499n.37.

Rivers v. Katz, 495 N.E.2d 337 (N.Y. 1986), 333, 545n.94.

Robbins v. Footer, 553 F.2d 123 (D.C. Cir. 1977), 527n.31.

Roberts v. Louisiana, 396 So. 2d 566 (La. App. 1981), 523n.74.

Robertson v. Sixpence Inns of America, Inc., 789 P.2d 1040 (Ariz. 1990), 525n.118.

Robinson v. Lindsay, 598 P.2d 392 (Wash. 1979), 523n.78.

Roe v. Federal Insurance Co., 587 N.E.2d 214 (Mass. 1992), 532n.167.

Roe v. Minister of Health, [1954] 2 Q.B. 66; [1954] 2 A11 E.R. 131 (C.A.), 527n.44.

Roe v. Wade, 410 U.S. 113 (1973), 37, 47, 64, 88, 494n.2, 498m.112.

In re Roger S, 569 P.2d 1286 (Cal. 1977), 327, 544n.61.

Rogers v. Commissioner of Department of Mental Health, 458 N.E.2d 308 (Mass. 1983), 333, 545n.92.

Rogers v. Horvath, 237 N.W.2d 595 (Mich. App. 1975), 527n.23.

Rogers v. Janzen, 711 F. Supp. 306 (E.D. La. 1989), 537n.263.

Rogers v. Okin, 821 F.2d 22 (1st Cir. 1987), 542nn.6, 18, 544n.87.

Rosenberg v. Helinsky, 616 A.2d 866 (Md. 1992), 537n.265.

Rosendorf v. Blackmon, 800 S.W.2d 377 (Tex. Ct. App. 1990), 514n.125.

Ross v. Ross, 400 A.2d 1233 (N.J. Super. Ct. 1979), 511n.11.

Rouse v. Cameron, 373 F.2d 451 (D.C. Cir. 1966), 330, 335, 544n.73.

Rowley v. Board of Education, 483 F. Supp. 528 (S.D. N.Y. 1979), *affirmed*, 632 F.2d 945 (2d Cir. 1980), 509nn.77, 86, 510n.95.

Roy v. Hartogs, 366 N.Y.S.2d 297 (Civ. Ct. 1975), 532n.159.

Rozycki v. Peley, 489 A.2d 1272 (N.J. Super. 1987), 524n.88.

Rubenstein v. Baron, 529 A.2d 1061 (N.J. Super. 1987), 516n.29.

Ruby v. Massey, 452 F. Supp. 361 (D. Conn. 1978), 503n.151.

Rudy v. Meshorer, 706 P.2d 1234 (Ariz. App. 1985), 534n.196.

Rufo v. Inmates of Suffolk County Jail, 112 S.Ct. 748 (1992), 543n.29, 544n.77.

S.L.H. v. D.B.H., 745 S.W.2d 848 (Mo. App. 1988), 514n.150.

Sable Communications of California v. F.C.C., 492 U.S. 115 (1989), 56, 501n.98.

St. Paul Fire & Marine Insurance Co. v. Mitchell, 296 S.E.2d 126 (Ga. App. 1982),532n.165.

Salgo v. Leland Stanford University, 317 P.2d 170 (Cal. App. 1957), 533n.184.

Salyer v. Patrick, 874 F.2d 374 (6th Cir. 1989), 500n.61.

In re Sampson, 317 N.Y.S.2d 641 (N.Y. Fam. Ct. 1970), 505n.178, 511n.10.

Samuels v. Southern Baptist Hospital, 594 So. 2d 571 (La. App. 1992), 254, 536n.246.

Sanborn v. Sanborn, 465 A.2d 888 (N.H. 1983), 513n.89.

Sanders v. Oklahoma, 811 P.2d 910 (Okla. Ct. App. 1991), 518n.73.

Santana v. Collazo, 533 F. Supp. 966 (DPR 1982), *aff'd in part and vacated and remanded in part*, 714 F.2d 1172 (1st Cir. 1983), 545nn.107, 116.

Santosky v. Kramer, 455 U.S. 745 (1982), 148, 149, 518n.77.

Sard v. Hardy, 379 A.2d 1014 (Md. 1977), 529n.74.

Savidge v. Fincannon, 836 F.2d 898 (5th Cir. 1988), 331, 544n.75.

Schall v. Martin, 467 U.S. 253 (1984), 276, 279, 324, 339, 539n.23, 543n.46, 545n.111.

Schrempf v. State, 487 N.E.2d 883 (N.Y. 1985), 526nn.7,8.

Schumm v. Schumm, 299 A.2d 423 (N.J. Super. 1973), 511n.11.

Schwarz v. Regents of University of California, 276 Cal. Rptr. 470 (Cal. App. 1990), 197, 523n.57

Scott v. Bradford, 606 P.2d 554 (Okla. 1979), 528nn.64, 69.

Scott v. Plante, 532 F.2d 939 (3d Cir. 1976), 544n.80.

Searcy v. Auerbach, 980 F.2d 609 (9th Cir. 1992), 536n.260.

Secretary of Public Welfare of Pennsylvania v. Institutionalized Juveniles, 442 U.S. 640 (1979), 327, 544n.60.

Seef v. Sutkus, 583 N.E.2d 510 (Ill. 1991), 523n.66.

In re Seiferth, 127 N.E.2d 820 (N.Y. 1955), 504n.173.

Sharman v. Evans, 138 C.L.R. 563 (1977) (Austl.), 524n.91.

Sharpe v. South Carolina Dept. of Mental Health, 354 S.E.2d 778 (S.C. App. 1987), 531n.135.

Shaw v. Glickman, 415 A.2d 625 (Md. App. 1980), 531n.135.

Shelley v. Kraemer, 334 U.S. 1 (1948), 496n.32.

Shelley v. Westbrooke, 37 Eng. Rep. 850 (1917), 90, 511n.17.

Shelton v. Tucker, 364 U.S. 479 (1960), 329, 544n.64.

Sherman v. Community Consolidated School Dist. 21 of Wheeling Township, No. 91-1684 (7th Cir November 20, 1992), 502n.112.

Shookoff v. Adams, 750 F. Supp. 288 (M.D. Tenn. 1990), 339, 545n.110.

Sibley v. Lutheran Hospital of Maryland, Inc., 709 F. Supp. 657 (D.C. Md. 1988), 536n.261, 537n.266.

Sidaway v. Bethlehem Royal Hospital [1985] A.C. 871 (H.L.), 528n.53.

Silberstein v. Cordie, 474 N.W.2d 850 (Minn. Ct. App. 1991), 522n.39.

Simonds v. Blue Cross-Blue Shield, 629 F. Supp. 369 (W.D. Mich. 1986), 537n.269.

Sindorf v. Jacron Sales Co., 341 A.2d 856 (Md. Spec. App. 1975), 536n.260.

Skar v. City of Lincoln, Nebraska, 599 F.2d 253 (8th Cir. 1979), 253, 536n.244.

Skyywalker Records, Inc. v. Navarro, 739 F. Supp. 578 (S.D. Fla. 1990), 495n.26.

Sloan v. Metropolitan Health Council of Indianapolis, 516 N.E.2d 1104 (Ind. App. 1987), 538n.288.

Slocum v. Food Fair Stores, 100 So. 2d 396 (Fla. 1958), 521n.16.

Small v. Howard, 128 Mass. 131 (1880), 527n.37.

Smith v. Daily Mail Pub. Co., 443 U.S. 97, (1979), 23, 281, 496n.55, 539n.40.

Smith v. Department of Insurance, 507 So. 2d 1080 (Fla. 1987), 538n.298.

Smith v. Organization of Foster Families for Equality and Reform, 431 U.S. 816 (1977), 145, 518n.65.

Smith v. Robinson, 468 U.S. 992 (1984), 508n.57.

Snow v. State, 469 N.Y.S.2d 959 (N.Y. App. Div. 1983), 503n.43.

In re Snyder, 532 P.2d 278 (Wash. 1975), 513n.99.

Society for Good Will to Retarded Citizens, Inc. v. Cuomo, 737 F.2d 1239 (2d Cir. 1984), 337, 544n.69, 545n.101.

Solloway v. Dept. of Professional Regulations, 421 So. 2d 573 (Fla. App. 1982), 532n.164.

South Carolina Medical Malpractice Liability Insur. v. Ferry, 354 S.E.2d 378 (S.C. 1987), 532n.169.

Southern Pacific Co. v. Jensen, 244 U.S. 205 (1917), 494n.8.

Speiser v. Randall, 357 U.S. 513 (1958), 498n.114.

Spencer v. Community Hospital of Evanston, 408 N.E.2d 981 (Ill. App. 1980), 533n.176.

Stafford v. Nipp, 502 So. 2d 702 (Ala. 1987), 533n.184.

Standlee v. St. Paul Fire & Marine Insur. Co., 693 P.2d 1101 (Idaho App. 1984), 532n.168.

Stanford v. Kentucky, 492 U.S. 361 (1989), 499n.25, 28.

Stanley v. Georgia, 394 U.S. 557 (1969), 54, 50nn.86, 89.

Stanley v. Illinois, 405 U.S. 645 (1972), 496n.43, 518n.80.

Stapley v. Stapley, 485 P.2d 1181 (Ariz. App. 1971), 513n.90.

Starnes v. Cayouette, 419 S.E.2d 669 (Va. 1992), 515n.1.

State Rubbish Collectors Ass'n v. Siliznoff, 240 P.2d 282 (Cal. 1952), 521n.14.

State v. Axford, 409 N.W.2d 893 (Minn. App. 1987), 497n.82.

State v. Bellotti, 383 N.W.2d 308 (Minn. App. 1986), 517n.41.

State v. Fan, 445 N.W.2d 243 (Minn. App. 1989), 501n.68.

State v. Fitzgerald, 694 P.2d 1117 (Wash. App. 1985), 520n.116.

State v. Fox, 480 N.W.2d 897 (Iowa Ct. App. 1991), 517n.54.

State v. Grover, 437 N.W.2d 60 (Minn. 1989), 516n.25.

State v. Hansen, 743 P.2d 157 (Or. 1987), 498n.110, 530n.110.

State v. Hill, 556 A.2d 1325 (N.J. Super. 1989), 516n.31.

State v. Jurgens, 424 N.W.2d 546 (Minn. App. 1988), 497n.78.

State v. Loebach, 310 N.W.2d 58 (Minn. 1981), 497n.93.

State v. Lucero, 647 P.2d 406 (N.M. 1982), 516n.11.

State v. Middleton, 657 P.2d 1215 (Or. 1983), 497n.91.

State v. Moran, 728 P.2d 248 (Ariz. 1986), 497n.92.

State v. Payton, 481 N.W.2d 325 (Iowa 1992), 517n.54.

State v. Perricone, 181 A.2d 751 (N.J. 1962), 504n.172.

State v. Propst, 161 S.E.2d 560 (N.C. 1968), 542n.125.

State v. R.H., 683 P.2d 269 (Alaska App. 1984), 137, 516n.32.

State v. S.H., 465 N.W.2d 238 (Wis. App. 1990), 529n.97.

State v. Tanner, 675 P.2d 539 (Utah 1983), 516n.9.

State v. Wagner, 508 N.W.2d 164 (Ohio App. 1986), 33, 498n.101

State v. Watts, 350 N.Y.S.2d 285 (N.Y. Fam. Ct. 1973), 511n.25.

State v. Whatley, 320 So. 2d 123 (La. 1975), 539n.19.

State v. White, 464 N.W.2d 585 (Minn. App. 1990), 501n.70.

State v. Zimmerman, 829 P.2d 861 (Idaho 1992), 517n.44.

State in Interest of T.L.O., 463 A.2d 934 (N.J. 1983), 496n.52.

Stenger v. Lehigh Valley Hospital Center, 609 A.2d 796 (Pa. 1992), 529n.98.

Stepakoff v. Kantar, 473 N.E.2d 1131 (Mass. 1985), 527n.32, 535n.227.

Matter of Stefanel Tyesha C., 556 N.Y.S.2d 280 (App. Div. 1990), 136, 516n.18.

In re Stephen W., 271 Cal. Rptr. 319 (Cal. App. 1990), 516n.17.

Sterling Drug v. Yarrow, 408 F.2d 978 (8th Cir. 1969), 524n.86.

Stevens v. People, 796 P.2d 946 (Colo. 1990), 546n.11.

Stevison v. Enid Health Systems, Inc., 920 F.2d 710 (10th Cir. 1990), 504n.154, 526n.18.

Stiver v. Parker, 975 F.2d 261 (6th Cir. 1992), 514n.122.

Stoneking v. Bradford Area School District, 882 F.2d 720 (3d Cir. 1989), 503n.136.

Strachan v. John F. Kennedy Memorial Hospital, 538 A.2d 346 (N.J. 1988), 822n.54.

Stricker v. Stricker, 474 So. 2d 1146 (Ala. Civ. Ct. App. 1985), 514n.134.

Strong v. Allen, 768 P.2d 369 (Okla. 1989), 498n.4.

Strunk v. Strunk, 445 S.W.2d 145 (Ky. 1969), 503n.151, 534n.207.

Sullivan v. O'Connor, 296 N.E.2d 183 (Mass. 1973), 526n.13.

Summers v. Tice, 199 P.2d 1 (Cal. 1948), 524n.81.

Surrogate Parenting v. Commonwealth, 704 S.W.2d 209 (Ky. 1986), 513n.116.

Suter v. Artist M, 112 S.Ct. 1360 (1992), 48, 500n.48.

Suttles v. Suttles, 748 S.W.2d 4217 (Tenn. 1988), 512n.72.

T.J. v. State, 538 So.2d 1320 (Fla. App. 1989), 59, 502n.127.

Tabor v. Doctors Memorial Hospital, 563 So. 2d 233 (La. 1990), 535n.232.

Talmage v. Smith, 59 N.W. 656 (Mich. 1894), 521n.6.

Tamsen v. Weber, 802 P.2d 1063 (Az. App. 1990), 531n.128, 532n.151.

Tarasoff v. Regents of University of Cal., 529 P.2d 553 (1974), aff'd in part, rev'd. in part, 551 P.2d 334 (1976), 238, 239, 240, 254, 263, 522n.40, 524n.88, 53nn.132, 133, 134.

Taylor v. Ledbetter, 818 F.2d 791 (11th Cir. 1987), 495n.17, 518n.64.

Taylor v. Vallelunga, 339 P.2d 910 (Cal. App. 1959), 521n.17.

Teeters v. Currey, 518 S.W.2d 512 (Tenn. 1974), 494n.10.

Texarkana Memorial Hospital v. Firth, 746 S.W.2d 494 (Tex. Ct. App. 1988), 534n.214.

Texas Dept. of Mental Health & Mental Retardation v. Petty, 817 S.W.2d 707 (Tx. Ct. App. 1991), 536n.236.

Theama v. City of Kenosha, 344 N.W.2d 513 (Wis. 1984), 525nn99, 100, 101.

Theodore R. v. Loretta J., 476 N.Y.S.2d 720 (N.Y. Fam. Ct. 1984), 514n.133.

Theriot v. Huval, 413 So. 2d 337 (La. App. 1982), 513n.103.

Thing v. LaChusa, 771 P.2d 814 (Cal. 1989), 522n.51.

Thomas v. Cincinnati Board of Education, 918 F.2d 618 (6th Cir. 1990), 506n.12, 507nn.33, 36, 42, 44, 49.

Thompson v. Carter, 518 So. 2d 609 (Miss. 1987), 533n.183.

Thompson v. County of Alameda, 614 P.2d 728 (Cal. 1980), 239, 531n.137.

Thompson v. Oklahoma, 487 U.S. 815 (1988), 499n.24.

Thompson v. Sun City Community Hosp., Inc., 688 P.2d 605 (Az. 1984), 533n.189.

Tibbs v. Commonwealth, 128 S.W. 871 (Ky. App. 1910), 542n.123.

Timothy W. v. Rochester, New Hampshire School District, 875 F.2d 954 (1st Cir. 1989), 509n.86.

Tinker v. Des Moines Independent Community School District, 393 U.S. 503 (1969), 18, 58, 495n.22, 502n.114.

Todd D. v. Andrews, 933 F.2d 1576 (11th Cir. 1991), 508n.54.

Tomfohr v. Mayo Foundation, 450 N.W.2d 121 (Minn. 1990), 534n.211.

Toogood v. Spyring, 1 C.M.&R. 181, 149 Eng. Rep. 1044 (1834), 536n.259.

Topel v. Long Island Jewish Medical Center, 431 N.E.2d 293 (N.Y. 1981), 534n.199.

Trower v. Jones, 520 N.E.2d 297 (Ill. 1988), 497n.83.

Truman v. Thomas, 611 P.2d 902 (Cal. 1980), 529n.82.

Tunkl v. Regents of the University of California, 383 P.2d 441 (Cal. 1963), 527n.30.

Ueland v. Pengo Hydra-Pull Corp., 691 P.2d 190 (Wash. 1984), 524n.93, 525nn.97, 98, 99, 102.

United States v. Azure, 801 F.2d 336 (8th Cir. 1986), 517n.52.

United States v. Brawner, 471 F.2d 969 (D.C. Cir. 1972), 315, 524n.199.

United States v. Brooks, 841 F.2d 268 (9th Cir. 1988), 501n.69.

United States v. Carolene Products Co., 304 U.S. 144 (1938), 496n.34.

United States v. Carroll Towing Co., 159 F.2d 169 (2d Cir. 1947), 523n.73.

United States v. Eichman, 496 U.S. 310 (1990), 495n.21.

United States v. Hinckley, 672 F.2d 115 (D.C. Cir. 1982), 541n.113.

United States v. Hudson and Goodwin, 11 U.S. (7 Cranch) 32 (1812), 495n.13.

United States v. Kantor, 677 F. Supp. 1421 (C.D. Cal. 1987), 20, 496n.42.

United States v. Lester, 749 F.2d 1288 (9th Cir. 1984), 546n.4.

United States v. Mendenhall, 446 U.S. 544 (1980), 59, 503n.129.

United States v. Nobles, 422 U.S. 225 (1975), 546n.16.

United States v. Pacelli, 521 F.2d 135 (2d Cir. 1975), 546n.5.

United States v. Persico, 832 F.2d 705 (2d Cir. 1987), 546n.10.

United States v. Pollack, 640 F.2d 1152 (10th Cir. 1981), 546n.22.

United States v. R.L.C., 112 S.Ct. 1329 (1992), 539n.42.

United States v. Salerno, 481 U.S. 739 (1987), 539n.26, 545n.112.

United States v. Smith, 111 S.Ct. 1180 (1991), 536n.252.

United States v. Smith, 578 F.2d 1227 (8th Cir. 1978), 546n.20.

United States v. Watson, 423 U.S. 411 (1976), 539n.15.

United States v. X-Citement Video Inc., 61 LW 2396 (9th Cir. 12/16/92), 501n.72.

Valerie J. v. Derry Cooperative School Dist., 771 F. Supp. 483 (D.N.H. 1991), 509n.83.

Matter of Vance A., 432 N.Y.S.2d 137 (N.Y. Fam. Ct. 1980), 144, 517n.62.

Vazquez v. Vazquez, 443 So. 2d 313 (Fla. App. 1983), 513n.93.

Vinchiarello v. Kathuria, 558 A.2d 262 (Conn. App. 1989), 534n.197, 535n.225.

Vineyard v. Kraft, 828 S.W.2d 248 (Tex. Ct. App. 1992), 516n.33, 527n.27, 537n.264.

Vitek v. Jones, 445 U.S. 480 (1980), 543n.38.

W. v. Louisiana, 437 F. Supp. 1209 (E.D. La. 1976), *aff'd* 622 F.2d 804 (5th Cir. 1980), 545nn.109, 117.

Re W (a minor) Child in Care: Medical Treatment [1992], 3 W.L.R. 758, 505n.83.

Waffen v. United States, Dept. of Health & Human Services, 799 F.2d 911 (4th Cir. 1986), 528n.49.

Walker v. Superior Court, 222 Cal. Rptr. 87 (Cal. App. 1986), 516n.16.

Wallace v. Jaffree, 472 U.S. 38 (1985), 18, 495n.27.

Walton v. Arizona, 110 S.Ct. 3047 (1990), 496n.57.

Washington v. Harper, 494 U.S. 210 (1990), 311, 333, 541n.106, 545n.97.

Washington v. United States, 390 F.2d 444 (D.C. Cir. 1967), 314, 542n.118.

Waters v. Barry, 711 F. Supp. 1125 (D.C. Cir. 1989), 53, 501n.76.

Watson v. City of Cambridge, 32 N.E. 864 (Mass. 1983), 73, 506n.8.

Weatherly v. State, 441 N.Y.S.2d 319 (Ct. Cl. 1981), 535n.222.

Weathers v. Pilkinton, 754 S.W.2d 75 (Tn. App. 1988), 534n.208, 535n.232.

Weil v. Seltzer, 873 F.2d 1453 (D.C. Cir. 1989), 527n.45.

Welsch v. Likins, 373 F. Supp. 487 (D. Minn. 1974), 544n.72.

West Virginia State Board of Education v. Barnette, 319 U.S. 624 (1943), 58, 495n.20, 502n.112.

Western Union Telegraph Co. v. Hill, 150 So. 709 (Ala. App. 1933), 521n.12.

Whalen v. Roe, 429 U.S. 589 (1977), 529n.99.

Whetham v. Bismarck Hospital, 197 N.W.2d 678 (N.D. 1972), 522n.43.

White v. Illinois, 112 S.Ct. 736 (1992), 141, 517nn.43, 44, 46, 58.

White v. Thompson, 569 So. 2d 1181 (Miss. 1990), 515n.152.

White v. United States, 780 F.2d 97 (D.C. Cir. 1986), 531n.145.

Whitesell v. Green, No. 38745 Honolulu Dist. Ct. (Nov. 19, 1973), 532n.161.

Wickline v. State, 239 Cal. Rptr. 810 (Cal. App. 1986), 261, 538n.289.

Wieter v. Settle, 193 F. Supp. 318 (W.D. Mo. 1961), 309, 541n.101.

Wilder v. Virginia Hospital Association, 496 U.S. 498 (1990), 48, 500n.44, 504n.155.

In re Marriage of Williams, 563 N.E.2d 1195 (Ill. App. 1990), 515n.152.

Williams v. Gering Public Schools, 463 N.W.2d 799 (Neb. 1990), 507n.42, 509n.81.

Williams v. Williams, 369 A.2d 669 (Del. 1976), 525n.104.

Williams v. Wilzack, 573 A.2d 809 (Md. App. 1990), 334, 496n.47, 545n.99.

Wilson v. Blue Cross of Southern California, 271 Cal. Rptr. 876 (Cal. App. 1990), 261, 538n.290.

Wilson v. Bodian, 519 N.Y.S.2d 126 (App. Div. 1987), 498n.102.

Wilson v. United States, 391 F.2d 460 (D.C. Cir. 1968), 311, 541n.103.

Windisch v. Weiman, 555 N.Y.S.2d 731 (App. Div. 1990), 527n.45.

In re Winship, 397 U.S. 358 (1970), 43, 276, 498n.115, 499n.18, 538n.7, 539n.38, 540n.48.

Winterstein v. Wilcom, 293 A.2d 821 (Md. Spec. Ct. App. 1972), 525n.114.

Wisconsin v. Yoder, 406 U.S. 205 (1972), 19, 57, 136, 496n.29, 502n.106, 516n.13.

Witmayer v. Witmayer, 467 A.2d 371 (Pa. Super. 1983), 513n.96.

Wojnarowicz v. Wojnarowicz, 137 A.2d 618 (N.J. Super. Ct. 1958), 513n.95.

Womack v. Eldridge, 210 S.E.2d 145 (Va. 1974), 498n.113, 522n.50.

Woods v. U.S., 720 F.2d 1451 (9th Cir. 1983), 533n.173.

Wrecsics v. Broughton, 426 A.2d 1155 (Pa. Super. 1981), 514n.129.

Wyatt v. Aderholt, 503 F.2d 1305 (5th Cir. 1974), 331, 544n.75.

Wyatt v. King, No. 3195-N (M.D. Ala. 1991), 543n.47.

Wyatt v. Stickney, 344 F. Supp. 387 (M.D. Ala. 1972), 321, 329, 330, 542nn.5, 25, 544nn.66, 74.

Ybarra v. Spangard, 154 P.2d 687 (Cal. 1944), 524n.83, 525n.120.

Young v. Huntsville Hospital, 595 So. 2d 1386 (Ala. 1992), 536n.249.

Youngberg v. Romeo, 457 U.S. 307 (1982), 330, 331, 332, 544nn.68,69,88, 545n.117.

Zbaraz v. Hartigan, 776 F. Supp. 375 (N.D. Ill. 1991), 504n.163.

Zinermon v. Burch, 494 U.S. 113 (1990), 542n.23.

Zobrest v. Catalina Foothills School Dist., 61 LW 4641 (1993), 509n.163.

Zoski v. Gaines, 260 N.W. 99 (Mich. 1935)504n.171.

INDEX

ABA juvenile justice standards, 340
Abandonment, child, 135
Abandonment, tort of, 225
Abuse, child; *see also* Abuse, physical; Abuse, sexual; Maltreatment, child; Neglect, child
civil and criminal proceedings compared, 138–39, 143–44
civil protection order, 139
confrontation, right to, by alleged abuser, 142–43
detention hearing, 139
disposition of case, 143–44
hearing on the merits, 139
legal definitions of, 133–34
malpractice and, 138
parental rights, criteria for terminating, 147–48
privilege, curtailment of, 137–38
prosecution of, 137, 139
protective custody, 139
reporting: immunity for, 136–38; penalty for failure to, 137; requirement, 134, 136–38
standard of proof in, 139
state reporting laws, 137–38
substantiation of, 135
teams, 338
videotape, use of, in abuse trials, 142–43
Abuse, emotional, definition, 135
Abuse, physical
characteristics of physically abused children, 151–52
characteristics of physically abusive parents, 150, 151, 152
failure to protect a child from, 134
injuries suggesting possibility of, 150–51
irrelevance of abuser's intent, 134
legal evaluation of, 134
mandated reporting of, 134, 136–38
outcome of, 152

psychopathology of, 151–52
statistics of, 150
Abuse, sexual; *see also* Abuse, child; Abuse, physical; Maltreatment, child; Neglect, child
alcoholism in fathers and, 161
borderline personality disorder after, 164–65
child sexual abuse accommodation syndrome, 163–64
coercive patriarchy, 162
consequences of, 157–59
depression after, 158, 159
deviant learning, theory of, 163
dimensions of, 154–55
dissociative disorder and, 165
evolution of intrafamilial, 157
factors affecting outcome of, 159–61
family dynamics in, 161–63
family systems pathology in, 162
father–son incest, 165
feminist theory of, 162–63
forensic evaluation, 167–85
grandfathers and, 166
legal definition of, 154
male victims of, 167
maternal psychopathology in, 161
mother–child incest, 165–66
multiple personality after, 159
paternal psychopathology in, 161
pedophilia in fathers, 161
pornography and, 166
posttraumatic psychopathology and, 164–65
posttraumatic stress disorder after, 157–58, 164–65
premature sexual stimulation, theory of, 163
prevalence of, 155–56
psychopathology of, 163–65
rape crisis trauma after, 157–58
recognition of, 156–57
ritual type, 166

[Abuse, sexual]
sexual dysfunction after, 159
sibling incest, 165
social transition theory of, 162
stepfathers and, 166
substance abuse after, 158
suicide after, 158–59
synonyms for, 154
traumagenic dynamics and, 164
victimization after, 159
Academic skills disorder, 217
Access, right to, 258
Actus reus, 312
Adjudicative process, 30–38; *see also* Evidence
Adjustment disorder, 212
Administrative Procedure Act, 24
Adoption
guidelines for selecting adoptive parents,
149
independent, 149
legal proceedings for, 149–50
"open," 148, 149
principles of, 148–49
records of, access to, 149
revocation of consent, 149
sequel to termination of parental rights,
148–49
unmarried fathers, rights of, 149
Adoption Assistance and Child Welfare Act
(AACWA), 48, 146, 150
Adult-Adolescent Parenting Inventory, 125,
179
Adversary system
definition, 1
description, 15–16
Adverse possession, 41
Advocacy, legal, 37–38
principles, 37–38
specialization within, 38
Affidavit, 37–38
Aid to Families with Dependent Children
(AFDC), 50, 63
Alimony. *See* Custody disputes
Amendment, First, 18–19, 51–52, 53, 54–56,
59, 281
and academic freedom, 18
and compulsory school attendance, 19
and "fighting words," 18
and school prayer, 18–19
and sexual exploitation, 18
Amendment, Fourth, 22, 59, 278
probable cause, 22
and school searches, 22
Amendment, Fifth, 20–21, 45–47, 51, 144

due process requirement, 20
and natural justice, 20
and *parens patriae,* 21
and parent–child–state triad, 21
and sexual exploitation of minors, 21
Amendment, Sixth, 22, 141, 142–43
and public access to juvenile court, 23, 281
Amendment, Eighth, 23, 43, 58, 320, 328
and death penalty for minors, 23
and right to bail for minors, 23
and school discipline, 23
Amendment, Thirteenth, 14
Amendment, Fourteenth, 14, 17, 18, 19–20, 22,
43, 57, 58, 60, 91, 133, 282, 320, 328
and discrimination on grounds of age, race,
and sex, 60, 73
due process requirement, 19–20
and juveniles, 20
liberty interest and, 19
Amenities of life, loss of, 203
American Law Institute, 17
Amicus curiae briefs, 10
Amnesia, and competency to stand trial, 311
Anti–Child Pornography Act, 51
Anxiety disorders, 213–14
Assault, 189
Attorney
defense, 30
state's, 30
Automatism, 315–16

Baby Doe regulations, 66–67
Bail Reform Act, 279
Battery, 187–88
Bereavement, uncomplicated, 212
"Best interests of the child" doctrine, 133; *see
also* Custody disputes
Bill of Rights, 17; *see also* Constitution; spe-
cific amendments
Bipolar disorder, 217
Borderline personality disorder, 164–65
Brief, legal, 38
Brief reactive psychosis, 215–17
"Bypass," judicial, 47, 64–65

Capacity, legal. *See* Competence
Capacity, parental, as criterion for termination
of parental rights, 146–47
Case plan, reunification, 146
Cause, proximate, 200–202
Certiorari, writ of, 27
Chance, lost, 248
Child Abuse Prevention and Treatment Act,
133, 137

Child Behavior Checklist, 125
  Parents' version (CBCL-P), 210, 211
  Teachers' version (CBCL-T), 211, 212
Child protection services, 138
Child support. *See* Custody disputes
Child Support Recovery Act, 89
Child witness
  anatomically explicit dolls, use of, 178
  competency of, 168–72
  content validity, 174–75
  contextual validity, 175–76
  credibility of, 172–76
  drawings, use of, 178
  effect of misinformation on, 170–71
  interview technique, 177–78
  suggestibility of, 170–72
  symptom validity, 176
Childhood, defined, 39–40
Civil commitment, 321–28; *see also* Psychiatric hospitalization
Civil Rights Act, 22, 48, 60, 224
Civil Rights of Institutionalized Persons Act
  (CRIPA), 321
Clinical work, purpose of, 2
Clinicians, compared with lawyers and scientists, 2
Communication Act, 55
Competence; *see also* Child witness; Forensic
  evaluation of juvenile offenders
  to consent to abortion, 64–65
  legal, age of, 40
  legal, and maturation, 44
  to refuse medical treatment, 67
  to stand trial, of juvenile offender, 308–12
Confidentiality, duty of, 234–35
Confrontation, right to, 142–43
Consent
  age of, defined, 40
  for sexual intercourse, 56
Consent, as defense against tort action, 193–94
Consent, informed, 340–50
Consent, of minors
  to health care, 62, 67, 68–69
  to research, 70–71
Consolidated Omnibus Budget Reconciliation
  Act (COBRA), 26, 224; *see also* Federal
  Emergency Care Act
Consortium, loss of, 203–4
Constitution, amendments to, 14
  federal, 14, 16; *see also* specific amendments
  state, 14, 16
Constitution, Bill of Rights provisions. *See*
  specific amendments

Contractual relationship, between clinician and
  patient, 224–25
Court, Clerk of the, 30
Courts
  appellate, 28
  district, 27
  federal, 27–28
  of first instance, 28
  functions of, 16
  of general jurisdiction, 28
  juvenile, 28
  of last resort, 28–29
  lawmaking by, 13–14
  and legislatures, 13–14
  of limited jurisdiction, 28
  probate, 28
  state, 28–30
  system of, 26–29
  traffic, 28
Credibility, of child witness, 172–76
Cross examination, of expert witness
  challenges to expert's ability, qualifications,
    or motives, 374–76
  challenges to expert's conclusions, 371–74
  disconcerting tactics during, 377–83
  "learned treatise" attack, 376–77
  methods of attack, 370–83
Custody
  alteration of: due to changed circumstances,
    102–3; due to relocation, 103
  alternating custody, 96
  cocustody, 96
  concurrent custody, 96
  coparenting, 96
  custodial parent, obligations of, 95
  joint custody, 96–97: research on, 96–97;
    types of statutes, 96
  joint managing conservators, 96
  least detrimental alternative, 98–99
  legal custody, 96
  parental preference, 99–100
  physical custody, 96
  "psychological parent," 99
  shared parenting, 96
  sole custody, 95, 97–98
  types of, 95–100
Custody, litigation of, 114–15
  answer, 114
  child support, 115
  complaint, 115
  decree nisi, 115
  depositions, 115
  determination of custody, 115
  discovery, 114

[Custody, litigation of]
  guardian *ad litem,* 115
  hearing on merits of case, 115
  interrogatories, 115
  judicial decision, 115
  legal proceedings, 114–15
  petitions, 114
  preliminary hearing, 115
  pretrial motions, 114
  visitation rights, 115
Custody disputes, 87–131
  alimony, 89
  annulment of marriage, 88
  "best interests of the child" doctrine, 91, 94,
    133
  child support, 88, 89, 115: failure to pay, 98
  custody proceedings, 89–90
  divorce: mediation, 89; "no-fault," 89; sta-
    tistics on, 87
  federal parent locator service, 107
  feminist legal theory and, 99–100
  grandparents' rights in, 106, 115
  guardianship proceedings, 89–90
  historical evolution of, 90
  homosexual parents, 107–9
  judges, factors significant to, 95
  judicial criteria in, 92
  kidnapping by parent to regain custody,
    106–7
  marriage: common law, 87–88; defined, 87;
    and privacy rights, 88; termination of,
    88–89
  maternal preference, 90–91, 94
  mental health evaluation in, 116–31
  mental instability of parents and, 95, 100–101
  moral character of parents and, 95, 100
  National Crime Information Center, 107
  parental competence and, 93
  parental obligations, 87–88
  paternal preference, 90
  preference of child, influence of, 102
  preference for primary caretaker, 93–94
  race, influence of, 101
  religion, influence of, 101
  sexual abuse, allegations of, 98, 105
  siblings, reluctance to separate, 102
  "substantial change of circumstances,"
    102–3
  surrogate parenting, 88, 103–5
  "tender years" doctrine, 90–91
  visitation: restrictions on, 98, 115; when
    parent incarcerated, 98
  visitation rights, failure to exercise, 98
"Customary Practice" rule, 13

Damages; *see also* Liability, civil
  compensatory, 187, 193, 202–3
  nominal, 187, 192
  punitive, 187, 192–93
Dangerousness of juvenile offender, 308
Defamation, 255–56
Deposition, 357–59; *see also* Witness, expert
  circumstances of, 358–59
  discovery and, 357–58
  need to check transcript after, 359
  preparation for, 356–57
  report preparation for, 356–57
  testifying at, 358–59
Determinism, in psychiatry and psychology, 3
Diminished capacity, 315
Diminished responsibility, 315
Discovery, 357–58
  pretrial, 36
Dissociative disorder, 165
Dissociative hallucinosis, 217
Divorce; *see also* Custody disputes
  child's gender, effect of, 112–13
  cross-sectional research on, 112–14
  developmental level, effect of, 112
  effect on children, 109–14
  environmental instability, effect of, 113
  impoverishment, effect of, 113
  interparental relations, effect of, 113
  longitudinal research on, 109–12
  parent–child relations, effect of, 113–14
  parental mental health, effect of, 113
Documents, 348
Due process, procedural, 320–21
Due process, substantive, 320–21
Duty of care, 194–99, 226–43
  breach of, 199–200
Duty to protect, 239–41
Duty to warn, 238–41

Education of All Handicapped Children Act
    (EAHCA), 75–81, 145; *see also* Rights of
    handicapped children, educational
  procedural requirements, 75–81
Education of the Handicapped Act, 61
"Eggshell skull" principle, 201, 217
Eighth Amendment. *See* Amendment, Eighth
Emancipation, common law doctrine of, 40
Enjoyment of life, loss of the, 193, 203
Evidence
  adjudicative process and, 30–38
  character testimony, 32
  child hearsay exception, 33
  circumstantial, 30–31
  clear and convincing, 35

credibility of, 343
demonstrative, 342
direct, 30
excited utterances, 33
Federal Rules of Evidence, 343, 344–45
hearsay rule, 32–33
material, 31
medical records, use of, 33
opinion rule, 32
physical, 342
prejudicial, 31
preponderance of the, 35
probative, 31
psychological profiles, 32
relevant, 31
reliability of, 343
rules of, 32–34, 342–43; *see also* Witness,
    expert
types of, 30–31
Examination
  cross, 343
  direct, 343
Expert, qualification of, 4
Expert evidence, admissibility of, 7–8
Expert witness. *See* Witness, expert

Family Support Act, 64
Federal Commission on Drunken Driving, 54
Federal Developmentally Disabled Assistance
    and Bill of Rights Act, 331
Federal Emergency Care Act, 63
Federal Employee Retirement Income Security
    Act (ERISA), 260
Federal Rules of Evidence, 343, 344–45
Fees, for forensic evaluation, 347–48
Fetus, not a person in law, 198
First Amendment. *See* Amendment, First
Food and Drug Act, 229
Forensic evaluation; *see also* Witness, expert
  cross-validation of, 350
  definition of consultant's role, 346
  definition of legal issues, 346
  determination of appropriateness of case,
      346–47
  documents, 348
  evaluation procedures vis-à-vis legal issues,
      350–51
  fee, 347–48
  informed consent, 349–50
  initial contact with referring agent, 345–48
  liability issues, 349
  pretrial conference, 355–56
  principles of, 349–51
  scheduling of case, 347

"skeletons in the closet," 347
  ultimate task of, 350–51
Forensic evaluation in child custody disputes;
    see also Custody disputes
  amicus curiae, preference for acting as, 116
  attorney, contact with, 124
  "best interests of the child" criteria, 119–20
  bias in, 117
  children's needs, 120–21: and parents' com-
      petence, 120
  circumstances of referral, 116
  convergent validity, 120
  criticism of validity of, 116–17
  discrepancies in information, 126
  ethical principles, 117–19
  forensic report, 128–31
  home visits, 127
  informed consent for, 118
  interviews, 125–26
  joint evaluation, 124
  joint interview of parents, 124–25, 127
  modes of clinical evaluation, 122–24
  of one parent only, 116
  other informants in, 126
  parental competence attributes, 122
  procedural principles, 119–20
  psychological testing, 125, 126
  referral, 116
  report preparation, 128–31
  schedule of contacts, 124–28
  solo assisted evaluation, 123
  solo evaluation, 123
  standardized assessments, 125
  team evaluation, 123
Forensic evaluation in child maltreatment
      cases, 167–85; *see also* Abuse, sexual
  alleged offender, 179
  anatomically explicit dolls, 178
  child competency, evaluation of, 168–72
  confabulation, 173
  credibility, 172–76
  delusion, 173
  drawings, use of with children, 178
  emotional contagion concerning, 173
  fabrication, 173
  gynecologic examination, 168
  indoctrination, 172–74
  interview technique, for children, 177–78
  memory, research into, 169–72
  misinformation, effect of, on child witness,
      170–71
  misinterpretation, 172–73
  nonoffending parent, 178–79
  pediatric examination, 168

[Forensic evaluation in child maltreatment cases]
preparation of child for court, 183–84
preparation of child to give testimony, 180–81
relationship between parents and child, 179
report for court, organization of, 184–85
suggestibility, research into, 170–72
treatment of parent, 183
treatment of sexually abused adolescents, 182–83
treatment of sexually abused children, 181–82
Forensic evaluation in civil liability cases; *see also* Liability, civil
academic skills disorder, 217
adjustment disorder, 212, 519
aggravation, evidence for, 218
anxiety disorders, 213–14
bereavement, uncomplicated, 212
bipolar disorder, 217
brief reactive psychosis, 215–17
causation, evidence for, 217–18
clinical questions to be addressed, 208–9
dissociative hallucinosis, 217
documents, review of, 208
impulse control disorder, 215
legal questions to be addressed, 207–8
malingering, 214
perpetuation, evidence for, 218
posttraumatic stress disorder, 212–13
precipitation, evidence for, 218
preexisting condition, evidence for, 217
procedures for, 209–11
prognosis, evidence for, 218
psychiatric disorder, types of, following trauma, 212–17
psychiatric disorder or impairment, evidence for, 211
psychological reports, 210–11
report preparation in, 219
somatoform disorder, 214–15
trauma, evidence for, 211
treatment recommendations, 219
Forensic evaluation in EAHCA hearings; *see also* Rights of handicapped children
circumstances of, 84–85
legal questions at stake in, 84
records involved, 82
"related services," recommendation for, 83
report, organization of, 85
"serious emotional disturbance," definition of, 85
"social maladjustment," definition of, 84

Forensic evaluation of juvenile offenders
amenability to treatment, 307
automatism, 315–16
circumstances of referral, 306
competence to stand trial, 307, 308–12: GAP criteria, 310; "McGarry test," 310
dangerousness, 308
diagnosis evaluation, 307
diminished capacity, 315
diminished responsibility, 315
disposition, recommended, 307–8
Dusky standards *re* competence, 309
interview technique, 316
legal issues at stake, 306–7
mental state at time of offense, 312–16
Miranda rights and, 312
mitigating factors, 315–16
psychotropic medication, to engender competency, 311–12
report preparation and organization, 317
sources of data, 316
waiver to adult court, 308
Foreseeability, reasonable, 195
Foster care, 144–45
authority of foster parents, 145
drift in, 133
as sequel to termination, 148
Fourteenth Amendment. *See* Amendment, Fourteenth
Fourth Amendment. *See* Amendment, Fourth
Free and Appropriate Education, legal definition of, 78
Freedom, individual, 4

Guardian *ad litem,* 137, 138, 140
confrontation, right to, 143
custody, protective, 138–39
function of, 42
hearing on the merits, 139
protection order, civil, 139

Habeas corpus, writ of, 30
Handicap, legal definition of, 77
Handicapped Children's Protection Act, 76–77
Health Care Quality Improvement Act, 26, 243
Health law, 10
Hearsay rule
exceptions to, 140–41
excited utterances and, 140–41
Hospitalization; *see also* Malpractice
dangerous patient, failure to control, 252–53
defamation, 255–56
false imprisonment, 251
fraudulent misrepresentation, 251

improper treatment, 255
loss of dignity, 252
malicious prosecution, 252
negligent diagnosis, 251, 252
negligent release, 253
patient, failure to protect, 253–54
records, improper release of, 255
substandard evaluation before, 251
third parties, failure to protect, 254
wrongful commitment, 251–52
wrongful injury, 254–55
Hypothetical questions, 345, 383–84

Illinois Juvenile Court Act, 273
Impulse control disorder, 215
Incest. *See* Abuse, sexual
Individual responsibility, in common law, 3
Individualized educational plan (IEP), 76
Individualized family service plan (IFSP),
  82–83, 84
Individuals with Disabilities Education Act
    (IDEA), 81
  procedural requirements, 81–83
Infancy, defined, 39–40
Information, communication of; *see also* Mal-
    practice
  defamation and, 255–56
  defenses available in liability suits, 257
  intentional infliction of emotional distress,
    256, 258
  malice and, 257
  noncommunication, liability for, 258
  privilege, absolute, 257
  records, right to access to, 258
  strict liability and, 256
Informed consent; *see also* Malpractice
  disclosure, 231
  and individual autonomy, 5
  in psychotherapy, 230–31
Insanity defense, 313–14; *see also* Forensic
    evaluation of juvenile offenders
  Durham test, 314
  "guilty but mentally ill," 314
  irresistible impulse standard, 313
  M'Naughten standard, 313
  model penal code standard, 313–14
Intent
  knowledge, 187
  purpose, 188–89
  transferred, 188
Intentional infliction of emotional distress,
    190–91, 256
  and civil liability, 196
Interrogatories, 36

Intoxication, as defense against juvenile delin-
    quency, 316

Judge
  function of, 29–30
  insulation of, 36
Judicial proceedings, 29–30
  administrative, 29, 30
  appeal, 28–29
  arraignment, 29
  civil, 30
  criminal, 29–30
  detention in, 29
  grand jury, 29
  indictment, 29
  initial hearings in, 29
  instruction of jury, 30
  juvenile, 30
  pleadings, 29
  prima facie hearing, 29
  sentencing, 30
  trial, 30
  types of, 29
  verdict, 30
Judicial reasoning, 36
  obiter dicta, 37
  and public policy, 37
  ratio decidendi, 37
  relevance of pleadings to, 36
  stare decisis, 37
Jurisprudence, positivist school of, 12
Jury
  deliberations, 362
  empaneling, 29
  grand, 29
  instructions to, 362
  selection, 361
  swearing, 361
  verdict, 30, 362
Juvenile delinquency
  age trends, 286
  behavioral variables predicting, 288–89
  biological research, 298–300
  blocked opportunity theory, 293–94
  brain dysfunction and, 299–300
  career length in, 284
  chromosomal abnormality and, 299
  class trends, 287
  clinical classification, 289–91; typologies,
    290–91
  community-based treatment, 304
  criminogenic social organization of the slum
    theory, 293
  culture conflict theory, 292–93

[Juvenile delinquency]
deficiency in behavioral inhibition and, 300
definition of, 283
developmental pathways, 291
differential justice theory, 294
empirical typologies, 289–90
environmental variables predicting, 288
epidemiology, 283–88
family interaction and social learning theory, 294–96
genetic factors, 298–99
historical trends, 286
incidence, 284
institutional treatment, reviewed, 303–4
labeling theory, 294
meta-analyses of treatment programs, 303–4
neuropsychological research, 297–98
prediction, 288–89
prevalence, 284
protective factors in, 300–302
psychoanalytic theories, 296–97
psychopathy, concept of, 296
psychosis and, 299
racial trends, 286–87
relative improvement over chance statistic, 288
sex trends, 286
social control theory, 294
social segregation theory, 291–92
sociological theories, 291–94
somatotype and, 299
sources of data, 285
treatment, 303–5
types of offense, 283
urbanization trends, 287–88
Juvenile Justice and Delinquency Prevention Act, 276–77, 279, 281–82, 340
Juvenile justice proceedings
adjudicatory hearing, 281
appeal, 282
apprehension, 277–78
dispositional hearing, 281–82
diversion, 278–79
hearing on the merits, 279
intake conference, 279
judicial detention hearing, 279
pretrial detention, 279: hearing, 279–80
probable cause hearing, 280
transfer to adult court, 280–81
Juvenile justice system
detention of suspects, 279
historical evolution, 273–76
Juvenile Justice and Delinquency Prevention Act, 277

juvenile justice standards, 277
legal proceedings, 277–82
press access to adjudicatory hearings, 281
reevaluation of, 274
rehabilitative goal, 273
status offenders, 282–83

Kidnapping by parent. *See* Custody disputes

Law
adversarial nature of, 15
case, 16
characteristics of the, 15–16
civil, 15
common, 13–14
constitutional, 17–23
inconsistency of, 12
nature and purposes of, 12–15
precedents, 13
private, definition of, 12
public, definition of, 12
purpose of, 1–2, 12–15
rule of, 14
sources of, 16–24
as theater, 16
Lawyers; *see also* Advocacy, legal
compared with clinicians and scientists, 2
Learned intermediary rule, 202
"Learned treatise" doctrine, 357
Least restrictive environment, 329–30
legal definition of, in education, 80–81
Legislation, 23–26
amendment of, 24
delegated, 24
omnibus bill, 26
process of, 24–26
repeal of, 24
role of Congress in, 24–26
role of president in, 26
Liability, civil
amenities of life, loss of, 203
appropriation, 191
assault, 189
battery, 187–88
breach of duty, 199–200
cancerophobia and, 198
causal connection, 195, 200–203
causation in fact, 200
causation, proximate, 200–202
consent, express or implied, 193–94
consortium, loss of, 203–4
court proceedings in, 206–7
damages: assessment of, 202–4; general, 203; special, 202–3; types of, 187, 192–93

duty of care, 194, 195–99
earning capacity, loss of, 193
"eggshell skull" principle, 201, 217
emotional distress, 196
enjoyment of life, loss of, 193, 203
fetus, not a person in law, 198
forensic evaluation of tort cases, 207–19
foreseeability, reasonable, 195
immunity, familial, 204
intent, 187–89
invasion of privacy, 191–92
learned intermediary rule, 202
loss or damage, 195
lost chance, 202
medical costs, 193
mental health clinician in, 187–88
mental suffering, 195–96
negligence, 194–206: comparative, 205;
    contributory, 204–5
objective standard, 202
pain and suffering, 193
privilege, 193
proof of case in, 206–7
public disclosure of private facts, 191
res ipsa loquitur, 206–7
risk, assumption of, 205
strict, 205–6
tort: definition of, 187; types of, 187
tort, intentional: and mental illness, 189;
    types of, 189–92
tort, outrageous, 191
tort action, defenses against, 193–94
tort suits between family members, 191
unreasonable intrusion, 191
wrongful birth and, 198
wrongful life and, 199
wrongful pregnancy and, 199
"zone of danger," 196
Limitation period, in damage claims, 14

Majority, age of, defined, 40
Malingering, 214
Malpractice; *see also* Hospitalization
    abandonment, 225
    abusive or outrageous treatment, 242–43
    causation, 247–48
    chance, lost, 248
    communication of information and, 256–58
    confidentiality, duty of, 234–35
    consultant, responsibility of, 225–26
    contractual relationship: initiation, 244; ter-
        mination, 225
    contraindicative conditions, failure to detect,
        246

diagnostic error prior to medication, 244–45
disclosure: circumstances justifying,
    235–37; elements of, in informed consent,
    231; exceptions to, 229–30
doctor–patient relationship, legal obliga-
    tions, 224
duty of care, 226–43
duty of protect, 238–41
duty to warn, 238–41
emancipated minor, and informed consent,
    230
endangered third parties and, 235–36,
    237–41, 253
fiduciary care, 231–32
guidelines to avoidance of, 264–65
hospitalization and. *See* Hospitalization
informed consent and, 228–32
legal reform and, 263–64
liability to third parties, 243
medication and, 244–48: failure to adminis-
    ter, 245; inappropriate choice of, 245; in-
    appropriate dosage or route, 246;
    inappropriate rationale for, 245
medication history, failure to obtain, 246
monitoring treatment, failure in, 247
new cost containment health structures and,
    259–63
opportunity, loss of, 227
patient rule, in informed consent, 228
Physicians' Desk Reference, use of, 244, 246
polypharmacy, 247
privacy, right of, 234–35
privilege: absolute, 257: therapeutic, 230
professional rule, in informed consent, 228
proximate cause, proof of, 227
sexual relations with patients and, 241–42
sovereign immunity, 254
standard of care: "locality" rule, 227; na-
    tional, 227
statistical profile of, 220–24
suicide and, 248–50; *see also* Suicide
suicide risk assessment, 267–71
success, lost chance of, 227
testimonial privilege and, 236
vicarious responsibility for suicide, 249–50
violence risk assessment, 266–67
wrongful death, 248–49
Maltreatment, child; *see also* Abuse, child;
    Abuse, emotional; Abuse, physical;
    Abuse, sexual; Neglect, child; Neglect,
    educational and medical
    "battered child" syndrome, 133
    "best interests of the child" and, 133
    child protection services, 138

[Maltreatment, child]
  ecological interpretation of, 132
  foster care drift, 133
  legal doctrines concerning, 132–33
  parens patriae and, 132–33
  permanency planning, 133
  reporting requirements for, 136–38
  serious risk of substantial harm and, 133
  statistics concerning, 133
Managed care
  duty of care under, 261
  potential liability risks under, 259–63
Marriage. *See* Custody disputes
Maternal and Health Care Block Grant Pro-
    grams (Title V), 63
Mature minor, competence of to accept health
    care, 67–68
McKinney Homeless Assistance Act, 62
Medicaid, 63
Medication. *See* Malpractice, medication and
Memory, research into, 169–72
Mens rea, 312
Mental Health and Developmental Disabilities
    Confidentiality Act, 258
Mental health expert, ethics of, 8–9
Mental health professions
  challenge to expertise of, 7–8
  disputes between, 6
  radical criticism of, 6
Mental illness, as myth, 6
Mental state at time of offense, 312–16
Michigan Child Custody Act, 92
Mitigating factors, 315–16
Millon Children's Multiaxial Inventory
    (MCMI), 179
Minnesota Multiphasic Personality Inventory
    (MMPI), 125, 179
Minor, "mature," unclear criteria for definition
    of, 44
Munchausen syndrome by proxy, 154

National Research Act, 229
Neglect, child; *see also* Neglect, educational
    and medical
  clinical definition, 153
  as criterion for termination of parental
    rights, 148
  legal definition, 134–35
  Munchausen syndrome by proxy and, 154
  neglect petition, applied to status offenders,
    135
  nonorganic failure to thrive: causation, 153;
    in infants and older children, 153; parental
    psychopathology, 153; recognition, 152

social background, 153–54
  willful abandonment, and termination of
    parental rights, 135
Neglect, educational and medical
  legal framework for, 135–36
  parental drug abuse during pregnancy and,
    136
  parental religious beliefs and, 136
  statutory exemptions from, 136
  types of, 135
Neglect, medical, 65–67
Negligence, 194–206
  comparative, 205
  contributory, 204–5
Nonorganic failure to thrive. *See* Neglect, child

Obiter dicta. See Precedent
Oklahoma Statutes, Title XXI, 136
Opportunity, loss of, 227
Outrage, 191

Parens patriae, 133, 320, 324
  Fifth Amendment and, 21
  historical importance of, 42–43
  in juvenile justice, 274
Parental Kidnapping Prevention Act (PKPA),
    107
Parenthood
  obligations of, 87–88
  surrogate, 88
Patient rule, in informed consent, 228, 229
Planning, permanent, 146–48; *see also* Abuse,
    child; Abuse, sexual; Maltreatment, child;
    Neglect, child
Police power, 320
  in regard to children's rights, 43
Pornography, 166
Posttraumatic stress disorder, 212–13; *see also*
    Abuse, sexual
Powers, separation of, 14
Precedent
  case, 36–37
  obiter dicta in, 37
  ratio decidendi of, 37
Pretrial conference, 355–56
President's Commission for the Study of Ethi-
    cal Problems in Medicare and Biomedical
    and Behavioral Research, 62, 70
Prima facie case, 188, 206, 207
Privacy
  invasion of, 191–92
  right of, 234, 258
Privilege, 34, 193
  absolute, 257

attorney–client, 34
child and, 34
confidentiality, 34
as defense against tort action, 193
doctor–patient, 34
testimonial, 236
therapeutic, 34, 230
waiver of, 34
Probability estimates, unsuitability for the
courts, 3
Probation officer, 30
Professional rule, in informed consent, 228,
232
Proof
in affirmative defenses, 35
beyond a reasonable doubt, 35
burden of, 34–36
clear and convincing evidence, 35
persuasion, burden of, 35
preponderance of evidence, 35
production, burden of, 35
standards of, 35
Protection of Children Against Sexual Exploitation Act, 51
Protection of human subjects, 229
Proximate cause, 227
Psychiatric hospitalization
American Psychiatric Association's criteria
for commitment, 324–25
American Psychiatric Association's recommendations *re* minors, 327
American Psychological Association's recommendations *re* minors, 327
civil commitment, standards for, 322–25
Civil Rights of Institutionalized Persons Act
(CRIPA), 321
dangerousness: difficulty of predicting, 324;
standard, 322–23
drug dependence and, 325
due process: procedural, 320; substantive,
320–21
history of, 318–20
Lanterman-Petris-Short Act, 322
legal principles concerning, 320–21
mental retardation and, 325
of minors, 325–28: abuses of, 337; *see also*
Rights of institutionalized children
parens patriae, 320
police power and, 320
recent pressure to relax commitment standards, 323
states' criteria for commitment, 324
Psychiatry, scientific status of, 6
Psychoanalysis, and culpability, 5

Psychological injury. *See* Liability, civil: mental suffering
Psychology, developmental, scientific status
of, 5

Qualification of expert witness, 363–65; *see also*
Witness, expert

Rape, statutory, 56–57
Rape crisis trauma. *See* Abuse, sexual
Ratio decidendi. *See* Precedent
"Reasonable minor," concept of, 55; *see also*
Rights of children, statutory
Records
of expert witness. *See* Forensic evaluation;
Witness, expert
improper release of, 255
organization of, 354
right of access to, 258
Refusal of medical treatment
by minors, 67
parental, 65–67
right to, 331–35
Regular educational initiative, 81
Rehabilitation Act, 67, 73
Report, forensic; *see also* Forensic evaluation;
Witness, expert
audience for, 353–54
format and organization, 351–54
guidelines for preparation, 351–54
organization, 184–85
style, 351–52
Res ipsa loquitur, 206–7
Research, legal. *See* Advocacy, legal
Rights of children, in common law, 40–71; *see
also* Juvenile justice system
abortion, 47, 64–65
adversary hearing prior to incarceration,
45
adverse possession and, 41
constitutional, 45–47: weighing values with
regard to, 45–47
contraception, 47, 67
contracts, 41
crimes, 41–42
foster children's, 145
fundamental, and the state's compelling interest, 45
historical evolution of, 42–44
illegitimacy, 41
inheritance, 41
juvenile justice, 43
nonfundamental, and the state's rational objective, 45

[Rights of children, in common law]
parens patriae and, 42–43
parental support, 49
police power and, 43
privacy, 64
procreative, 64–65
property, 41
torts, 41
voluntary admission to mental hospital, 46
waiver of *Miranda* rights, 46
Rights of children, educational, 57–62
compulsory attendance, 57
corporal punishment, 57–58
due process, 58
freedom of expression and, 58
handicapped children, 72–86
implied right of action, 61
per se negligence, 61
physical abuse, 60
racial discrimination, 60
suits for negligence, 60–62
school censorship, 59
school records, access to, 60
school's obligation to protect from violence
    or sexual molestation, 57
searches and seizures, 59
sexual harassment, 60
sexual segregation, 60
unregistered aliens, 57
Rights of children, health care, 62–70
abortion, 64–65
Baby Doe regulations, 66–67
clinical assessment of minors' competence
    to consent to, 68–70
under COBRA, 63
coercion, 69
competence to consent to abortion, 64; to
    voluntary hospitalization, 68
consent, of emancipated minors, 62
consent, parental, 62
contraception, 65
defective children, withholding of treatment
    from, 66–67
emergency care, 63
emotional freedom to consent to, 70
under Family Support Act of 1988, 64
inducement, 69
"judicial bypass," 47, 64
judicial review, 63
under Medicaid, 63–64
medical neglect, 65–66
medical treatment: mature minor's compe-
    tence to accept, 67–68; minor's refusal of,
    67

parental refusal of medical treatment, 65–67
privacy rights in, 65
substituted judgment, 62
under Title XIX of Social Security Act, 63
"undue burden" test, 64
undue persuasion, 69
Rights of children, as research subjects, 70–
    71
assent, 71
informed consent, 71
institutional review boards, 70
Rights of children, statutory, 47–49
access to health care, 50
Aid to Families with Dependent Children,
    50
alcohol, possession of, 54
assembly, freedom of, 53–54
child abuse, 50–51
child labor, regulation of, 50
child welfare legislation, 48–49
curfew laws, 53
dance halls, access to, 54
"dial-a-porn" services, access to, 55–56
driving, 52–53
to file suit for damages, 47–49
implied right of action, from statute, 48–49,
    61
marriage, 52
Medicaid, 50
pool halls, access to, 54
pornography, access to, 54–56
pornography industry, 51–52
prostitution, 52
sexual activity, 56–57
sexual exploitation, 51–52
shopping centers, access to, 53
tobacco, possession of, 54
videogame arcades, access to, 54
Rights of handicapped children, educational,
    72–86
administrative hearings, 76–77
amendments to Education for All Handi-
    capped Children Act, 81–83
attorneys' fees, 76–77
autistic children, 83
"behaviorally disordered," 85
brain-injured children, 83
"commensurate opportunity," 78
deaf and blind children, 83
developmentally delayed children, 83
due process hearings, 86
Education for All Handicapped Children Act
    (EAHCA), 75–81
evaluation committee, 75–76

"free and appropriate education," definition of, 78–79
"handicapped," definition of, 77
historical evolution, 72–75
individual educational plan (IEP), 76
individualized family service plan (IFSP), 82–83
Individuals with Disabilities Education Act (IDEA), 81–83
"least restrictive alternative," definition of, 80–81
"mainstreaming," 80–81
mental health consultant, role of, 84–86
mental health consultation reports, 85–86
parental involvement, 76
regular educational initiative, 81
"related services," definition of, 79–80
"satisfactory or meaningful progress," definition of, 79
"seriously emotionally disturbed," definition of, 77, 85
"social maladjustment," significance of, 84, 85
"stay put" provision, 77
"supportive service," definition of, 808
Rights of institutionalized children, 318–41
abuses of hospitalization, 336–37
age guidelines, 337–38
in correctional institutions, 339–40
external review of hospitalization, 338–39
Federal Developmentally Disabled Assistance and Bill of Rights Act, 331
incompetence to consent for treatment: best interests of the patient standard, 332–33; substituted judgment standard, 332–33
informed consent, 335–37
"least restrictive environment," 329–30
right to refuse treatment, 331–35
source of rights, 328–29
Standards for the Administration of Juvenile Justice (SAJJ), 335
treatment, right to, 330–31
voluntary admissions and, 335–37
Rights, parental
criteria for termination of, 147–48
residual, 144–45
Risk, assumption of, 205

Schizophrenia, 217; *see also* Forensic evaluation in civil liability cases
Science, purpose of, 2
Scientists, compared with lawyers and clinicians, 2

Sexual abuse accommodation syndrome, child, 163–64
Sexual contact, improper, 241–42; *see also* Malpractice
Social Security Act, 145
Somatoform disorder, 214–15
Sovereign immunity, 254
Standard of care, 227
Status offenders, 282–83
criticism of authority of family court, 282
due process, rights of, 283
legal proceedings for, 283
statutory descriptions of, 282
Strict liability, 256
Subpoena
ad testificandum, 354–55
definition of, 354–55
duces tecum, 354–55
response to, by expert, 355
types of, 354
Suggestibility, 170–72
Suicide
contributory negligence and, 248
foreseeability of, 248
and malpractice, 248–50
in outpatients, 250
risk-resource assessment, 267–72
statistics of, 248
vicarious responsibility for, 250
wrongful death and, 248–49
Supplemental Security Income Program (SSI), 50, 63
Supreme Court, United States
access to, 27
description of, 27
and social science, 9
Surrogate parenting. *See* Custody disputes
Success, lost chance of. *See* Malpractice

"Tender years" doctrine. *See* Custody disputes
Termination of parental rights; *see also* Abuse, child; Maltreatment, Child
criteria for, 147–48
legal proceedings for, 148
need for clear and convincing proof, 148
no automatic right to counsel, 148
Testimony, court, 360–88; *see also* Witness, expert
appropriate dress at, 360
conclusion of, 384
cross-examination, 370–83
direct examination, 368–69
hypothetical questions, 383–84
"invoking the rule on witnesses," 360

[Testimony, court]
jury selection, 361
order of events at trial, 361–62
preparation for, 360–61
qualification of witness, 363–65
re-cross examination, 384
redirect examination, 384
reference to notes during, 369–70
Tort; *see also* Liability, civil
defenses against tort action, 193–94
intentional, 187, 188–94
negligent, 187
outrageous, 191
strict liability, 187
tort law, 12–13
types of tort, 187
Treatment, right to, 330–31; *see also* Rights of
institutionalized children
Triad of rights
constitutional weighing of values with regard to, 45–47
parent-child-state, 43, 44–47
Trial; *see also* Testimony, court; Witness, expert
by battle, 15
case-in-chief, 361–62
closing arguments, 362
courtroom, description of, 362–63
jury, selection and swearing of, 361
jury deliberations, 362
jury instructions, 362
opening statements, 361
order of events at, 361–62
posthearing conviction proceedings, 362
preparation for, 356–57
rebuttal case, 362

"Undue burden" test, 157–58
Uniform Child Custody Jurisdiction Act
(UCCJA), 107
Uniform Marriage and Divorce Act (UMDA),
91, 102–3
Uniform Parentage Act, 41, 89
Uniform Putative and Unknown Fathers Act, 17
United Nations Draft Convention on the Rights
of the Child, 40
Utterances, excited, 140–41

Value identification, and constitutional adjudication, 18
Violence, risk-resource assessment of, 266–67

Waiver to adult court, for juvenile offenders,
308
Washington Involuntary Treatment Act,
323–24
Witness, child
competence of, 140
guardian *ad litem,* ethical dilemma of, 140
Witness, credibility of, 38
Witness, expert, 31–32, 342–88
in child abuse, 141–42
demeanor of, 365–68
distinguished from fact witness, 342,
344–45
Federal Rules of Evidence, 344
Frye test and, 344
guidelines for, 385–88
hearsay, 345
hypothetical questions, 345
liability issues, 349
permission to state opinion, 345
prohibited testimony: *re* child's veracity,
142; *re* defendant's fit with abuser profile,
142
qualification of, 344–45, 363–65
rationale for, 344
"reasonable certainty" standard, 345
subpoena. *See* Subpoena
testimony *re* characteristics of abused children, 141–42
Witness, fact, 343–44
Witness, lay, 31
Witnesses
cross-examination, 29, 30
direct examination, 29–30
Wrongful birth, 198
Wrongful death, 248
Wrongful life, 199
Wrongful pregnancy, 199

Zone of danger, 196